MAKING SENSE OF
International
Relations Theory

MAKING SENSE OF
International
Relations Theory

edited by
Jennifer Sterling-Folker

LYNNE
RIENNER
PUBLISHERS

BOULDER
LONDON

Published in the United States of America in 2006 by
Lynne Rienner Publishers, Inc.
1800 30th Street, Boulder, Colorado 80301
www.rienner.com

and in the United Kingdom by
Lynne Rienner Publishers, Inc.
3 Henrietta Street, Covent Garden, London WC2E 8LU

Library of Congress Cataloging-in-Publication Data
Making sense of international relations theory / Jennifer Sterling-Folker, editor.
   p. cm.
  Includes bibliographical references and indes.
  ISBN 978-1-58826-378-0 (hardcover : alk. paper)
  ISBN 978-1-58826-354-4 (pbk. : alk. paper)
  1. International relations—Philosophy. I. Sterling-Folker, Jennifer Anne, 1960–
II. Title.
  JZ1305.M32185   2005
  327.1'01—dc22

2005011005

British Cataloguing in Publication Data
A Cataloguing in Publication record for this book
is available from the British Library.

Printed and bound in the United States of America

  The paper used in this publication meets the requirements
∞ of the American National Standard for Permanence of
  Paper for Printed Library Materials Z39.48-1992.

5 4 3

*To the University of Connecticut undergraduates in
my course "Security and Human Rights in the Former Yugoslavia,"
Spring 2003*

Contents

Preface

As editor of this volume, I am responsible for the introductory chapter, the concluding chapter, the introductory material for each theoretical section, and all the miscellaneous formatting duties that any edited volume requires. I am also responsible for the volume's focus, structure, and the common vision that was imposed on all of its contributors. Thus, I take full responsibility for any errors, omissions, or criticisms the book might deserve.

At the same time, I cannot alone claim any praise or commendation the book might receive, as it has been a collective effort from its very inception. Credit for its best elements must belong equally to its editor, its publisher, its chapter authors, and the various students, both undergraduate and graduate, who have read and commented on its multiple drafts. I cannot even claim that the idea for this book was mine, since it was Lynne Rienner who first approached me with the concept.

What Lynne had in mind was a volume in which international relations (IR) scholars of different theoretical persuasions would analyze the same event or topic. Her goal was to produce a tangible example of what IR theories looked like in application and, simultaneously, in comparison with one another. In this way students and scholars of the international could immediately recognize the relevance of alternative perspectives and more easily identify differences between, say, a realist and a liberal analysis. Not only would such an exercise be enlightening in itself, it would also serve as an analytical guide to how IR theories might be applied to alternative international and current events.

When I first heard the idea I was intrigued, but it also seemed a daunting task to implement. What topic would be appropriate and fair to alternative, often diametrically opposed, theoretical perspectives? What theories should be represented in the volume, and how could we address or capture diversity within those theoretical perspectives? Who would be willing and able to write theoretically oriented chapters about an event or topic for which they might have no prior expertise? And who would ensure that the introductory material for each theoretical perspective was relatively fair and unbiased?

While the latter task fell to me as the volume's editor, as did tracking down the contributors for each theoretical section, Lynne and I worked collectively to shape the volume's content and structure in its initial conceptual stages. Together we discussed possible events and topics, such as genocide in Rwanda, globalization and protests at the World Trade Organization, US policy toward Cuba, and Eastern European adjustments after the Cold War. We settled on the initial topic of post–Cold War Yugoslavia, although this later evolved into a specific focus on Kosovo, thanks to serendipity at the 2002 annual meeting of the International Studies Association (ISA) in New Orleans and the suggestions of various contributors.

Determining the initial list of theoretical perspectives to be represented in the volume was also a joint effort, and even the title was a mutual decision reached after consideration of numerous alternatives. In our discussions, we often saw eye-to-eye, sometimes disagreed, and at other times learned from each other about the discipline and publishing for it. Because this edited volume has been a collaborative effort between publisher and editor, it is not stretching the truth to say that the book would not exist without Lynne's original vision and her support, advice, and patience throughout this process.

The volume was also shaped in its initial stages by numerous discussions with scholars in the discipline, some of whom later agreed to write chapters for it. Patrick Thaddeus Jackson served as an early sounding board for the project and its scope, and he was instrumental in pointing out that the provision of a traditional conclusion, which summarized all the chapters, would do justice to none of them. It was due to his input that the volume's conclusion is instead geared toward assisting the intrepid IR student in taking the first steps toward applying IR theory to a current event of their choice. Early on in the project I also benefited from e-mail correspondence and discussions with Andy Kydd about game theory and rational choice, Bob Denemark on world system theory, Karen Ruth Adams on realism, Francine D'Amico on feminism, and Rose Shinko about postmodernism. Yale Ferguson provided feedback early on in the project. All of these individuals deserve thanks, and some credit, for the final product.

The question of what theoretical perspectives to include in the volume was a particularly tricky one. Lynne had her own initial list, I had mine, and in asking other scholars for advice on this issue, it quickly became apparent that different categorizations and preferences abounded. Not only were there disagreements over which "isms" were most important and how to define them, but there were also difficulties in determining who was representative of these differing perspectives in the discipline. This was compounded by variations within most theoretical perspectives, so that a single application of a perspective often failed to do justice to it. This was a serious problem given that the book is meant to serve as a guide for students undertaking their own applications of IR theory. If, for example, there are multiple versions of constructivism that are often the subject of heated debate among established IR theorists, then offering students only one version has serious implications for both theorizing about constructivism and the student's ability to apply it.

Ultimately we decided to err on the side of greater diversity, but the result was a longer book, which even now I cannot claim is comprehensive. Final decisions regarding which perspectives and variants to include were determined by the need to balance, in a manageable book length, theoretical popularity with intraperspective diversity, and analytical fit with the chosen empirical subject matter. Thus, not all variants within a theoretical perspective are represented. There is, for example, no application of democratic peace theory, no example of offensive or defensive realism, and only one variant of the English School represented. Many of the authors discuss these and other missing variants in their chapters, as do I in my introductory chapters to each section. I also note representative disciplinary scholars of particular variants in the Further Reading sections, which, while not comprehensive, will at least point interested students and scholars in the appropriate direction.

Given the goals of the book, there are also important theoretical topics and questions within the discipline that are not directly addressed by it. While it covers a great deal of theoretical territory, there is still a great deal it leaves out that might have analytical bearings on the subject of Kosovo. These topics include general theories of conflict and war, the study of just war, the role of nuclear weapons and terrorism in the international system, the scientific study of war including the Correlates of War project, long-cycle theories of war, crisis decisionmaking and cybernetics, the use of simulation, the role of epistemic communities, two-level games analysis, bargaining theory, the role of environment and geography, and the clash of civilizations thesis, to name only a few. Some of these topics are pertinent to particular chapters and perspectives, however, and citations to relevant writings and debates may be found there.

Although there were conceptual difficulties in determining the perspectives and variants to be represented in the volume, these paled in comparison to the practical task of finding scholars who were both theoretically confident (and hence would self-identify with a particular perspective) and willing to write about the topic of Yugoslavia. In this regard, participation in the project was more demanding than for most edited volumes. With the exceptions of Sean Kay, Julie Mertus, and Tonny Knudsen, the contributors to this volume had not written about Kosovo before and are known instead for their commitment to a particular theoretical persuasion. Participation in the project required that they learn about a topic that, for many of them, was far removed from their particular empirical expertise and background. Before finding IR theorists who were willing and able to write particular applications for the volume, I contacted countless numbers of IR scholars in my search, many of whom provided me with advice or possible leads to follow, which I appreciate.

Those theorists who did agree to contribute chapters to the volume were directly involved in its planning stages. We coordinated a panel at the 2002 ISA annual meeting in New Orleans on which Patrick Thaddeus Jackson and Rose Shinko presented their initial chapters, with Yale Ferguson serving as discussant. We were joined by Brian Federking, whose work was later published in the *American Political Science Review,* and through sheer serendipity all three papers had focused on Kosovo. At a planning meeting held after the panel, and attended by Karen Ruth Adams, Annette Freyberg-Inan, Matt Hoffmann, Jeff Taliaferro, Patrick, Rose, Yale, and myself, the idea of focusing specifically on Kosovo crystallized. Another panel was coordinated for the 2003 ISA annual meeting in Portland on which Annette, Karen, and Jeff presented their chapters while Rose and I served as discussant and chair, respectively.

The feedback that the contributors provided me during those meetings and in countless e-mails was invaluable, as was their response and advice on my introductory material. The volume has been dependent upon its contributors and their willingness to plunge into a project that requested a great deal from them. They were subjected to numerous directions, suggestions, and revision comments, as I harangued them on everything from the proper formatting of sources to the evidence for their particular theoretical perspective. They were asked to revise their chapters three times on the basis of editor feedback, student feedback, and the advice of anonymous reviewers. Throughout all this, the contributors have been extremely responsive and patient. This has truly been a collective project.

Assisting me in the first and second revision stages for the chapters were my students, to whom I and the authors of the chapters owe a tremendous debt of gratitude. The first draft of the manuscript was read by the University of Connecticut undergraduates who took my "Security and Human Rights in the Former Yugoslavia" course during the spring 2003 semester. Their discussions, reactions, and advice served as the basis for the first round of revisions. I will always appreciate their willingness to read and seriously consider the material, and I have dedicated the book to them.

The second group of students to read a draft of the volume were the University of Connecticut graduate students in my "Proseminar in IR Theory" course during fall 2004. Their comments and discussions on the second draft were particularly helpful in writing and revising the introductory material to each chapter. They helped shape the final draft in a number of other important ways, and I thank them for acting as a test case.

A final note of thanks must go to Javier Morales-Ortiz, whose adminis-trative assistance made all drafts of this volume possible. It was Javier who researched websites, databases, and other materials for the contributors to rely on in their first drafts. It was Javier who made copies of pertinent arti-cles to send contributors and who organized my letters to them requesting revisions. And it was Javier who compiled, collated, and corrected the vol-ume's bibliography. I have appreciated all of his assistance and the great sense of humor he brings to even the most mundane tasks. He and numer-ous other individuals have made this volume possible and in the process, I hope, revealed what IR theory is, how it "works" in the discipline, what it can tell us about ourselves and the world around us, and why theorizing IR is a worthy philosophical undertaking in its own right.

—Jennifer Sterling-Folker

Acronyms

AMBO	Albanian-Macedonian-Bulgarian Oil Pipeline Corporation
CFSP	Common Foreign and Security Policy
CINCEUR	Commander in Chief of European Command
CSCE	Conference on Security and Cooperation in Europe
CSSCSE	Conference on Stability, Security, and Cooperation in Southeastern Europe
EBRD	European Bank for Reconstruction and Development
ECLA	Economic Commission on Latin America (UN)
EIB	European Investment Bank
EU	European Union
FRY	Federal Republic of Yugoslavia
GDP	gross domestic product
GNP	gross national product
GUUAM	Georgia, Ukraine, Uzbekistan, Azerbaijan, Moldova
ICTY	International Criminal Tribunal for the former Yugoslavia
IFI	international financial institution
IMF	International Monetary Fund
IO	international organization
IR	international relations
ISA	International Studies Association
JCS	Joint Chiefs of Staff
KDOM	Kosovo Diplomatic Observer Mission
KFOR	Kosovo Force
KLA	Kosovo Liberation Army
KPS	Kosovo Police Service
LDK	Democratic League of Kosovo
MNC	multinational corporation
NAC	North Atlantic Council
NATO	North Atlantic Treaty Organization
NGO	nongovernmental organization
NLI	neoliberal institutionalism
NSC	National Security Council

OAF	Operation Allied Force
ODF	Operation Deliberate Force
OSCE	Organization for Security and Cooperation in Europe
PKK	Kurdish Workers Party
SACEUR	Supreme Allied Commander in Europe
SECI	Southeast Europe Cooperation Initiative
SPSEE	Stability Pact for Southeastern Europe
UN	United Nations
UNCTAD	United Nations Conference on Trade and Development
UNHCR	United Nations High Commissioner for Refugees
UNMIK	United Nations Interim Administration Mission in Kosovo
UNPROFOR	United Nations Protection Force
UNSC	United Nations Security Council
WST	world system theory
WTO	World Trade Organization

chapter 1

Making Sense of International Relations Theory

Jennifer Sterling-Folker

This book is about making sense of international relations (IR) theory. It does so by making sense of a particular topic through the lens of IR theory. Rather than describe what IR theory is, then, the book demonstrates IR theory in tangible action and practice. By doing so, it reveals the core assumptions, differences, and similarities of various IR theoretical perspectives. This, in turn, provides an understanding of how IR theory can be applied to other historical and current events. By the time you have finished reading the book, you should be able to deduce what a variety of IR theoretical perspectives would have to say about any international or transnational topic or event. You will also understand why there are multiple and equally legitimate interpretations of and perspectives on the same topic or event. Thus, by allowing IR scholars of various theoretical stripes to make sense of one subject, this book is ultimately about making sense of IR theory.

The topic addressed by each theorist involves the events that transpired in Kosovo in 1998–1999. Most people know of Kosovo as a place in the former Yugoslavia where, during that period, there was escalating violence between the Kosovo Liberation Army (KLA), which was demanding independence from Serbia, and the Serbian police and military, which were randomly targeting the province's indigenous Albanian population in retaliation for KLA activities. In an effort to deter further violence, the North Atlantic Treaty Organization (NATO) issued a series of ultimatums to the Yugoslavian president, Slobodan Milosevic, demanding that the Serbs cease their harassment of the Kosovar Albanian population and withdraw military troops from the province. When the Serbs refused to comply, NATO initiated an air campaign known as Operation Allied Force (OAF) against Yugoslav targets in March 1999. The flood of ethnic Albanian

Yugoslavia, 1991

refugees from the province simultaneously reached crisis proportions, as the Serbian military attempted to ethnically cleanse the province of 90 percent of its inhabitants, and international relief agencies scrambled to provide for more than 800,000 displaced persons. In June 1999, Milosevic agreed to NATO's cease-fire terms, which involved Serbian military withdrawal and the imposition of a NATO peacekeeping force, known as Kosovo Force (KFOR), on the province. The status of Kosovo under NATO's terms was peculiar, as NATO insisted that Yugoslavia retain sovereign control over Kosovo, even as NATO forces occupied the province and a United Nations–mandated mission, known as the UN Interim Administration Mission in Kosovo (UNMIK), sought to rebuild it.

These are the elements that make Kosovo an event of interest to scholars of international relations.* It is an event that is ripe for multiple theoretical applications, since it involves a myriad of topics of interest to IR scholars, such as ethnic violence and war, identity politics, massive human rights violations, national sovereignty, cooperation among great powers, and international institutions, to name only a few of the more obvious. Because, as Sergei Medvedev and Peter van Ham have observed, "'Kosovo' symbolizes and exemplifies the relevance of many 'end'-debates and 'post'-debates within the academic literature," it also allows for diversity in focus and emphasis (2002: 2). It is for this reason that contributors to the volume were asked simply to write "about Kosovo," with no specific questions or puzzles assigned, so that what they chose to focus on would be a reflection of their theoretical perspective. And IR theorists, whose analytical perspectives are as divergent as those of game theorists and postmodernists, had something substantive to say about Kosovo. For most scholars it also appears to be a confinable event, with specific start and end dates as well as documents and memoirs now available for analysis that would not be accessible during the unfolding of a current event. Of course, as you will see, where one draws the boundaries of an event such as Kosovo, just how "confinable" it is, what aspects of it are puzzling, and what data are necessary to understand it, are all open to a great deal of interpretation and disagreement.

However, it is important to underscore that although Kosovo has some obvious pluses as a subject for comparative IR theoretical application, the subject of this book could just as easily have been another event or topic. Indeed, alternative events and topics, such as World Trade Organization (WTO) demonstrations and globalization, Afghanistan/Iraq and terrorism, Rwanda-Burundi and genocide, the UN system and international law, were

---

*A detailed overview of events in Kosovo is provided in the appendix to this book.

all discussed as possible subjects for the volume. As the empirical focus of this book, Kosovo is actually secondary to its primary purpose, which is to demonstrate how IR theory makes sense of the world. In this regard, IR theory is not about any one particular event or topic. It is instead about what goes on in international and transnational realms, and involves placing any particular event within these larger contexts. In other words, it is not, as Michael Doyle and G. John Ikenberry observe, "a recipe" or "a replacement for strategy" (1997a: 10). Rather it is about contextualizing specific events or topics, revealing how they are part of larger patterns (with regard to both IR events and how we as IR scholars tend to explain them), and exposing the underlying factors that produce either events such as Kosovo or our interpretations of them.

■ International Relations Theory: A Brief Overview

Before we proceed, it is important to address what IR theory is. Because the book provides introductory material for each theoretical section and examples of most of the major theoretical perspectives in IR at present, an overview of those perspectives will not be provided. Nor will a history of these perspectives and their disciplinary development in relation to each other be recounted, as excellent sources already exist on this subject (see Further Reading at the end of this chapter). Instead, we will deal here with the more fundamental questions of what is meant by IR theory and why it is useful for understanding what goes on in world politics. Not unexpectedly, different scholars provide different answers to these questions.

James Dougherty and Robert Pfaltzgraff define theory as "systematic reflection on phenomena, designed to explain them and to show how they are related to each other in a meaningful, intelligent pattern, instead of being merely random items in an incoherent universe" (1997: 15). Similarly, Paul Viotti and Mark Kauppi define theory "as a way of making the world or some part of it more intelligible or better understood," by going "beyond mere description of phenomenon observed and engag[ing] in causal explanation or prediction based on certain prior occurrences or conditions" (1999: 3). In both definitions there is a common assumption that there are patterns to international events and that IR theory is about revealing those patterns. This assumption is given expression in James Rosenau's oft-quoted advice to students of IR: "To think theoretically one must be predisposed to ask about every event, every situation, or every observed phenomenon, 'Of what is it an instance?'" As Rosenau goes on to observe, we often "have a hard time building up this habit," due to an inclination "to probe for the special meaning of an event, to explore it for what sets it apart from all other events, rather than to treat it as an instance of a larger pattern" (1999: 33). IR theorists are scholars who have broken this habit. While it is not the case that all IR theorists speak in terms of causality or prediction, all IR theorists do interpret particular events or subjects as instances of some larger pattern, phenomenon, or theoretical proposition and expression.

One way to think of IR theory is as a set of templates or prepackaged analytical structures for the multiple ways in which an event or activity that is international or transnational might be categorized, explained, or understood. These templates may be laid over the details of the event itself, allowing one to organize the details in such a way that the larger pattern is revealed and recognized within and through the event. Another useful analogy is to think of IR theory as a set of perspectives equivalent to the alternative lenses one might use on a 35mm camera. The subject may be an elephant in grasslands, but an alternative lens will reveal different aspects and details of the elephant and its surroundings so that, as Barry Buzan says, "looking through it makes some features stand out more strongly while pushing others into the background" (1996: 56).[1] The basic lens provides a shot of the elephant and its setting immediately to its front, back, and sides. A panoramic lens suddenly makes the elephant seem smaller in relation to its surroundings, which are now more expansive and more important to the image. A series of close-up lenses draw attention ever nearer to the elephant, enlarging it until its surroundings no longer seem relevant and details that had escaped attention before are noticeable. Tinted lenses of yellow, red, or blue highlight different shadows and features that had not seemed pertinent or particularly noteworthy with other lenses. And so on.

In much the same way, it is possible to see an IR topic or event from multiple perspectives and to view it as an instance of more than one pattern in world politics. Just as camera lenses are developed, produced, and prepackaged for use, so too are IR theoretical perspectives, many of which have rich analytical and interdisciplinary lineages. Each IR perspective consists of various assumptive building blocks, some of which are shared across perspectives but which are put together by each in specific ways in order to identity and highlight particular patterns in IR. Each perspective thereby illuminates slightly different elements of a given topic or event and hence patterns relevant to it, revealing aspects and details that were not obvious or particularly pertinent in other perspectives. The advantage of studying and understanding IR theory as an analytical domain distinct from any particular empirical event or topic is that it acquaints you with the multiple ways of seeing and understanding the various contexts for any particular event or topic, whether it is a historical, current, or future scenario. These contexts are the "bigger pictures" that, in the camera analogy, would involve an understanding of how 35mm cameras operate, the principles of photography (including color, lighting, and perspective), and the techniques of film development. While an amateur photographer does not need to know these things in order to take a picture, a professional photographer does.

It is important not to push the camera analogy too far, however, since one does not need to subscribe to a particular worldview, ideological perspective, or philosophical position in order to be a photographer or produce a zoom lens or use it in one's own photography. While the type of camera lens you use might depend on why you are taking the elephant's photo in the first place, whether you should use a zoom or panoramic lens to photograph it is usually not a matter of heated debate or the source of sharp divisions among your colleagues. IR theory, however, is premised on alternative philosophical, ideological, and normative commitments, many of which are antithetical to one another and hence diverge sharply over how to understand IR. These commitments undergird the assumptive building blocks and analytical frameworks of IR theory. They typically involve disagreements over the nature of being (referred to as ontology), how we know and acquire knowledge about being (referred to as epistemology), and what methods we should adopt in order to study being (referred to as methodology).

One of the most common ontological and epistemological divides you will encounter in the pages that follow is whether "a fact is a fact" and hence whether it can be objectively known and measured. A scholar's judgment on this question determines how he or she will conceptualize, study, and write about a subject such as Kosovo and what types of templates he or she will utilize in order to categorize it. Those scholars who insist that there is an objective state of being, an objective "reality," that is relatively obvious and can be accurately known and measured, are commonly referred to as positivists. For most positivists, the primary activity of an IR theorist is to test IR theoretical perspectives against one another. This is done by collecting data and by devising methods that would be the equivalent of an experiment in the hard sciences (no easy feat in a subject area that does not allow for controlled experiments in order to isolate causal variables). The goal of the IR theorist from a positivist's perspective is to weed out those theories and hypotheses that consistently fail to account for data, although one of the primary sources for diversity within particular theoretical perspectives is also theoretical revision in response to empirical anomalies. In undertaking such activity, the positivist hopes to produce more explanatory theories, which in an ideal world would make both prediction and better foreign policy making possible.

Positivists would tend to define the nature and purpose of IR theory in scientific terms as a result. Dougherty and Pfaltzgraff claim, for example, that theory is "a series of propositions or hypotheses that specify relations among variables in order to present explanations and make predictions about the phenomena," with its purpose "the discovery of laws that govern how people and collectivities . . . act under specific circumstances" (1997: 21–22). Similarly, Viotti and Kauppi state that, "'If *A,* then *B*' as hypothesis may be subject to empirical test—that is tested against real-world or factual data," so "the stage is set for making modest predictions about the nature and direction of change" (1999: 3). While positivists disagree among themselves over a variety of substantive theoretical issues, there is a shared consensus among them regarding the objective accessibility of reality and our ability to discover universal laws that are amenable to causal explanations and prediction. This consensus also provides the basis for common methodological and analytical tools, with the best known of these being levels of analysis.

Levels of analysis involves identifying where causal variables are located and categorizing them according to a micro-macro spectrum for the purposes of explanatory organization. Although there is variety in how many categorizing levels may be utilized, IR scholars have typically relied on three primary levels: the individual, the nation-state, and the system.[2] The individual level is the most micro, where causality is traced to the individuals who make foreign policy and the psychology of human decision-making. The nation-state level is a middle level and involves the examination of government structures, bureaucratic politics, interest groups, media influences, and other internal factors that might influence or account for a nation-state's foreign policy behavior. The systemic level is the most macro level, involving not only the examination of state-to-state relations but also environmental or structural factors, such as geography, relative power, or capitalist interdependence, that might influence or direct the behavior of all nation-states. Disagreements among positivists often involve which level of analysis, and particular factors therein, are responsible for and hence best explain a given outcome or event. Variants within a particular theoretical perspective often evolve as, in their quest to test and modify their theories against the empirical evidence, IR theorists pit levels of analysis against one another as if they were competing explanations (rather than useful heuristic, organizing tools).

Postpositivism, on the other hand, refers to IR scholars who are skeptical that "a fact is a fact" and that it can be objectively known and measured.[3] Postpositivists observe that all events are subject to interpretation, with the interpreter's own situation, context, and language often determining how an event is characterized and explained. Since neither language nor the act of communication is ever unproblematic or value-free, postpositivists challenge the notion that we could objectively know or access reality by relying on methods drawn from the hard sciences. Such methods are based on an erroneous conviction that, as Marysia Zalewski puts it, "what gets included and what gets excluded" in the theory and practice of IR is due to "'natural' or 'obvious' choices, determined by the 'real' world,

whereas they are instead *judgements*" about what should be taken seriously
and what can safely be ignored (1996: 34, emphasis original). Such judgments are never neutral or innocent. They are instead made by those who
hold relative power, both among nation-states and within the IR discipline
where positivism dominates. This means that certain equally important topics, perspectives, and choices are marginalized by the very theories and
methods to which positivist IR scholars subscribe. Zalewski notes, for
example, that war has been a central concern of IR theorists and policymakers, yet it is poverty, which receives very little attention among IR
scholars, that is the leading cause of death in the world today (1996: 351).

For most postpositivists, the primary activity of an IR theorist is to
reveal how policymakers and positivist IR theorists describe international
events, act upon those descriptions as if they were natural, and then justify
their actions and arguments in a self-fulfilling circle of codetermination.
Revelation is accomplished by examining the texts of policymakers and
fellow IR theorists, with the goal being to reveal not only the philosophical
commitments, biases, and commonly subscribed to social realities that
ground the activity of IR (in both its policymaking and theoretical forms),
but also what has been excluded or marginalized by such activity.
Postpositivists do this by providing alternative readings and interpretations
of how policymakers and theorists have characterized and justified events
and topics. Critics often disparage postpositivist methodology as mere
"interpretivism," which lacks any standard of judgment and could lead to
"a form of epistemological anarchy" in the discipline (Dougherty and
Pfaltzgraff 1997: 36).[4] Yet from a postpositivist perspective, such counterinterpretations, whether they are of a policymaker's speeches or of a fellow
theorist's articles, play an essential role in revealing the ideas that we take
for granted, that shape the way we see the world, that we rely upon to justify the actions we take, and that reproduce the world we take for granted.

Postpositivists would define the nature and purpose of IR theory very
differently in comparison to positivists as a result. Testing competing
hypotheses, developing causal explanations, and making predictions are
seen as the dominant and relatively destructive ways in which we have
come to interpret the world, impose meaning, and continually re-create particular patterns of knowledge and behavior in IR. According to Zalewski
while most positivists think of IR theory as merely a tool or critique, a postpositivist would define it as "everyday practice" in which "theorizing is a
way of life, a form of life, something we all do, every day, all the time,"
which means that "theorists are global actors and global actors are theorists" (1996: 346, 348). Similarly Steve Smith argues about IR that "what
we think about these events and possibilities, and what we think we can do
about them, depends in a fundamental sense on *how* we think about them.
In short, our thinking about the 'real' world, and hence our practices, is

directly related to our theories" (1996: 1, emphasis original). Although postpositivists eschew the notion that there are universal laws that are objectively discoverable with scientific methods, they do see patterns to the way positivists describe and theorize IR. Such patterns could derive from the values of eighteenth-century European Enlightenment (which promotes a faith in science) or the politics of identity within IR (which is dominated both in practice and in theory by men).

It might help to return briefly to the 35mm camera analogy in order to summarize the fundamental divide between positivists and postpositivists in the discipline of IR. If both were photographers, then positivists would be those who shared a dominant consensus that tinted lenses captured the reality, being, or essence of the elephant. The quarrel among them would be over which of the colors on the spectrum best revealed the true nature of the elephant. Much of their activity would be devoted to photographing the elephant with various shades of whichever color they preferred. Alternatively, postpositivists would be photographers who asked why positivists were so convinced that tinted lenses best captured the nature of the elephant in the first place. They would be concerned with revealing both this shared preference for tinted lenses and how it ignored and denigrated other types of lenses that would be equally legitimate for capturing an image of the elephant. Both types of photographers would be engaged in revealing larger patterns and in answering Rosenau's "of what is it an instance?" Yet positivist answers would involve a conviction that they were documenting the patterns of reality itself, while postpositivist answers would involve revealing, as a pattern in itself, the positivist's conviction that reality was being documented.

While this book does not disparage positivism, neither does it make an attempt to evaluate alternative theoretical perspectives according to their explanatory abilities. Instead it reflects a belief that all IR theoretical perspectives capture a reality of sorts, that there are multiple realities to and readings of IR, and that all of them are "true" in the sense that they give us some purchase on and understanding of IR events and topics. This does not mean that no standards have been applied and that what is presented here is "epistemological anarchy." Each chapter has been read by multiple groups, including IR scholars, undergraduates, and graduate students. The authors revised their chapters after each of these readings in order to address questions and misunderstandings, fix empirical mistakes or deductive errors, and refine incomplete or unclear readings. Those revisions were not undertaken in a competitive spirit, and so they do not involve arguing whose theoretical perspective is the "correct" perspective for understanding the events in Kosovo. This may be implicit in some of the positivist selections, but it was not a goal of the book or the individual chapters. Instead, each author attempted to address more fundamental questions, such as why you, the reader, should be acquainted with their particular theoretical perspective and what it will help you see or understand that you had not been aware of before reading it.

Of course, as the reader, you are free to make judgments regarding what you find most and least compelling. As you do so, keep in mind that one of the most important intellectual steps you can take as an analyst of IR events and topics is to recognize *your own* philosophical and ideological commitments, about which you may be entirely unaware. Because the book has been designed to present IR theories impartially, it can assist you in discovering these commitments. As you read, consider which perspectives you find most compelling or convincing, which you find most repellent or least convincing, and why you have these responses. Answering such questions and identifying what it is specifically about an approach that you find convincing or offending should help you to recognize your own normative commitments and ideological biases. Such recognition is the first step in gaining some distance from those commitments, which is necessary for fairly assessing alternatives you might otherwise initially dismiss or ignore. It is also necessary for seeing international events and topics other than Kosovo in these larger contexts and theoretical patterns.

Of what is Kosovo an instance then? In the pages that follow, you will find differing interpretations, explanations, and understandings of the same basic events, as IR scholars attempt to answer this question according to their particular theoretical perspectives.

■ Further Reading

Two of the better-known texts that provide detailed descriptions and discussions of the most popular IR theories are Dougherty and Pfaltzgraff 1997 and Viotti and Kauppi 1999, both of which have been revised and reprinted several times. The Viotti and Kauppi source contains textual examples from seminal scholars in particular theoretical perspectives, and includes a reprint of the "Thinking Theory Thoroughly" piece by Rosenau (which was subsequently developed into a 2000 book with Durfee). Another text that reprints seminal pieces for the purpose of juxtaposing alternative theories is Der Derian 1995a. Alternatively, Neumann and Wæver 1997 provides original essays that summarize and analyze the writings of particularly seminal thinkers in each of the major theoretical perspectives.

Doyle and Ikenberry 1997b is an edited collection on the subject of new thinking in IR and provides original essays from scholars of different theoretical perspectives, all of whom discuss the nature of change in IR. A special issue of *Foreign Policy* titled "Frontiers of Knowledge" (1998) has original essays that summarize research in each of the main IR theoretical perspectives. It also provides lists for further readings on particular perspectives (as do the theory introduction sections of this book). Other texts that provide overviews and extended discussions of IR theory include Baylis and Smith 2001, Booth and Smith 1995, Burchill et al. 2001, Ferguson and Mansbach 1988, Ferguson and Mansbach 1991, Groom and Light 1994, Holsti 1985, Morgan 1986, Thompson 1996, and Weber 2001.

A number of texts have overviews of disciplinary history and describe the ways in which theories developed in relation to one another. These include Alker and Biersteker 1984, Kahler 1997, Olson and Groom 1991, Rothstein 1991, Schmidt 1998, Wæver 1997, and Wæver 1996b. For works that compare US IR as a discipline to the study of IR in other countries (and the difference this makes for theorizing about IR), see Crawford and Jarvis 2000, Jørgensen and Knudsen 2006, Smith 2002, and Wæver 1998b.

On the subject of positivism and postpositivism in IR theory, a number of texts could be consulted, including Smith, Booth, and Zalewski 1996 (Smith's chapter in particular provides numerous citations on both subjects), Booth and Smith 1995, Hollis and Smith 1990, George 1988, George 1994, and *International Studies Quarterly*'s "Exchange on the Third Debate" (1989), which contains several articles devoted to the subject of the "third debate" (as it is sometimes called) by T. Biersteker (1989), K. Holsti (1989), and Y. Lapid (1989). Other citations on this subject are provided in the overview chapter on postmodernism and critical theory.

■ Notes

1. The subject of an elephant in this analogy is intentional, as it recalls the story of the blind men who each touch a different part of an elephant and believe they have sufficiently grasped its reality, though none can grasp the whole. The analogy was used earlier by Robert North (1969) in a plea for greater tolerance and research pluralism in the discipline. The lens metaphor has also been utilized elsewhere; in particular see V. Spike Peterson and Anne Runyan (1999: 1–3).

2. Extended discussions of the levels-of-analysis issue in IR theorizing can be found in Singer 1969, Waltz 1959, Waltz 1960, and Buzan 1995. Dougherty and Pfaltzgraff also provide a description of alternative levels of analysis beyond the standard three (1997: 26–33).

3. *Postpositivism* is an umbrella term for those theoretical perspectives that are skeptical of the positivist project in general. It should not be conflated with postmodernism, which is but one variant of this skepticism, and other postpositivist approaches represented in this book, such as critical theory and critical feminist theory. Dougherty and Pfaltzgraff use the term "postempiricist" for postpositivism (1997: 35), and the terms "rationalism" and "reflectivism" are sometimes used for positivism and postpositivism respectively, but the latter are more common in the literature (see Smith 1996).

4. Since this book seeks to impartially provide both positivist and postpositivist applications, it may give the misimpression that there is rapprochement between positivists and postpositivists within the discipline. In fact, however, the exchanges between scholars of these two perspectives are often heated and nasty. As Ole Wæver observes, "there is no such repressive tolerance" between them,

because "they rather see each other as harmful, at times almost 'evil,' definitely not as a legitimate parallel enterprise." This is because the postpositivists believe that "the mainstream is co-responsible for upholding a repressive order," while the post-positivists are viewed by the positivist mainstream as "subversive, anti-scientific, and generally a bad influence on students" (1997: 22).

chapter 2

Realist Approaches

2.1   *Jennifer Sterling-Folker*

Realism

Realism is typically described as the dominant theoretical perspective in the IR discipline. However, the vast majority of IR theorists are not realists, and realism's "main presence is in the form of the object of attack, that which most scholars feel a need to deal with and try to rout" (Wæver 1997: 26). Why does realism prompt such a reaction? The answer can be found in its pessimistic conviction that there are severe limitations on human reason and its ability to achieve the progressive, liberal goals that most of us take for granted as moral truths. Thus it questions the extent to which we can achieve goals such as human rights, economic parity, and lasting security on the basis of reasoned argument, common interests, and shared moral principle. Most people do not find it a particularly endearing theoretical proposition as a result, yet its insistence that relative power is essential to what *is* achievable in the world has resonated throughout the discipline. In fact, it is difficult to find an alternative theoretical perspective that denies that relative power plays some role in determining "who gets what" in world politics, and it is realism that has set the parameters of theoretical discourse in the discipline.[1]

There are a myriad of ways that power could be defined, with the simplest being the ability of actors to acquire the resources they need and want. But in IR the term *power* is generally utilized relationally, to indicate the ability of one group to influence and control either another group or outcomes and events that pertain to them (Baldwin 1979). What distinguishes the realist treatment of relative power from its use in other perspectives is the causal omnipotence it is assigned. All outcomes in realist analysis, whether they involve trade negotiations, human rights violations, or military intervention, are ultimately dependent on the relative power of the actors involved, with those having greater power determining outcomes

13

according to their own interests. Hence what the relatively powerful actors want will set the stage for all other actors, interests, and outcomes. Realist analysis tends to focus almost exclusively on powerful actors as a result, and some variants of realism concentrate on how polarity, or the number of great powers in a given period of time, produces particular behavioral patterns. The likelihood of warfare between the great powers might vary, for example, depending on whether there is bipolarity (two great powers) or multipolarity (three or more great powers), while a unipolar system (one great power) has its own unique patterns and outcomes.

According to realists, what allows "might makes right" to be an unfortunate but enduring feature of global politics is the absence of a higher authority to protect and dispense justice equitably. This absence or condition is called anarchy and, as with relative power, a number of alternative theoretical perspectives also utilize the concept to characterize the contexts or conditions within which global interactions occur, although there are important differences in how it is defined and hence its causal significance.[2] From a realist perspective, the combination of anarchy and relative power leads to a behavioral pattern called balance of power, in which power is sought by the relatively weak in order to counter the relatively strong. This can occur either in alliances with similarly weak states, which amounts to a pooling of power against a common threat (or source of frustration), or it can occur independently through the development and marshaling of resources internal to a group in order to increase their own power.

These two forms of balancing are not mutually exclusive and can occur simultaneously, but neither are guaranteed to provide security or effectively deter an ambitious opponent. Realism retains its skepticism even here, suggesting that while security measures can be taken in an anarchic environment, whether they are successful is another story. Power has dynamic, situational, relational, and perceptional properties that generate uncertainties and make its efficient accumulation and exercise difficult. These uncertainties lead to decisions and outcomes that realists argue are the inevitable consequences of anarchy. One such consequence is the security dilemma, in which nation-states arm themselves for defensive purposes and in so doing induce the same behavior in neighboring states, but then become mutually suspicious of one another's "real" intentions in arming (Herz 1950, 1976; Jervis 1978). The misperception of power can also lead to an unwarranted faith in one's alliances or free-riding on the balancing efforts of others, consequences that Thomas Christensen and Jack Snyder refer to as "chainganging" and "buckpassing" (1990). Because such outcomes were never intended by the participants involved, whose rational behavior in the pursuit of their interests instead combined in unanticipated ways, realists are apt to characterize the condition of IR as "the tragedy of power politics" (Mearsheimer 2001).

To support their theoretical propositions, realists often cite Thucydides, who in "The Melian Dialogue" recorded the Athenian's observation that "the standard of justice depends on the equality of power to compel and that in the fact the strong do what they have the power to do, and the weak accept what they have to accept" (quoted in Viotti and Kauppi 1999: 101). Realist scholars trace the theory's lineage back to seminal political thinkers in Western civilization, such as Thucydides, Niccolò Machiavelli, Thomas Hobbes, and Jean Jacques Rousseau. The extent to which any of these writers can be characterized as "realists" is the subject of dispute, but the desire to identify prior realist thinkers derives from the belief that the limitations on human reason and its ability to achieve progressive ends are timeless. As Kenneth Waltz has put this claim, "the enduring anarchic character of international politics accounts for the striking sameness in the quality of international life through the millennia" (1979: 66). According to realists, the relevance and dynamics of relative power are not due to any condition or attribute of the modern world, then, but can be recognized as a central feature of prior epochs as well.

Most scholars who describe realism provide a list of assumptions to which all realist scholars supposedly subscribe. Such lists typically include the centrality of the nation-state to global politics, the treatment of the nation-state as a unitary, rational actor, and the dominance of national security over all other IR issue areas. Such lists are ultimately misleading, however, since they suggest that there is consensus among realists. Alternatively, Barry Buzan observes that "beneath the apparently smooth surface of realism lies not a single linear theory handed down from ancient times, but an ever-changing discourse about the nature, application and effect of power in an ever-changing historical environment" (1996: 51). There are a variety of realisms as a result, including classical realism, neorealism (also referred to as structural realism), offensive realism, defensive realism, neoclassical realism, and security materialism. Of these, the two most seminal to disciplinary developments are classical realism and neorealism.

Classical realism tended to assume that a human lust for power was the motivation for conflict, and it combined theoretical determinism with policy prescription. Neorealism, associated with the work of Waltz (1979), rejects human nature as a source of conflict and attempts to create a purely structural version of realism that also conforms to scientific expectations. Other variants of realism, such as offensive realism, defensive realism, and neoclassical realism, build upon and depart from these two overarching realisms. Offensive realism assumes that nation-states want to maximize their aggregate power and will therefore be predisposed to expansionist policies. Defensive realism assumes that states want to maximize security and anticipate a wider range of possible policies and outcomes as a result. Neoclassical realism focuses on internal variables as intervening variables between the pressures of the international system and the nation-state's policymaking response. And security materialism focuses on the impact of geography, science, and technology on the quest for security.

One of the fundamental differences between some realist variants is their level of analysis, which is reflected in the two theoretical applications provided in this section. In Chapter 2.2, Karen Adams applies a neorealist perspective to Kosovo. She focuses on systemic-level attributes such as anarchy and polarity to explain Yugoslavia's disintegration and NATO's intervention in Kosovo. Alternatively, in Chapter 2.3, Jeffrey Taliaferro utilizes neoclassical realism. He focuses on the domestic and individual levels of analysis and argues that psychological factors explain why US decisionmakers were motivated to intervene despite the absence of clear national interests in Kosovo. These selections represent only a small sample of either the variants of realism or the ways in which each variant might be utilized to interpret an event such as Kosovo.[3]

It is true that most realists focus their analytical efforts on the behavior of the nation-state, because they assume that it has remained relatively more powerful than other types of transnational entities and forces, such as international organizations (IOs), multinational corporations (MNCs), or capitalist markets, religions, and cultures. Yet realists are clear that their propositions are supposed to apply to groups in general and that a dynamic of competitive, relative power can be found in the behavior of all types of groups throughout time (Gilpin 1981; Sterling-Folker 2002, chap. 3). Realism also has a relatively ambivalent relationship to rationality and reason, since on the one hand most of its variants are decidedly positivist, yet on the other hand rationality is being employed to uncover the universal truth that reason does not afford us greater control. Thus realism is, as Martin Griffiths and Terry O'Callaghan observe, "a codification of constraints on the use of reason to reform international relations" (2001: 197).[4]

It is this last element that standard lists of assumptions ascribed to realism most often miss. What unites the analytical variants of realism under a common umbrella is not a list of commonly shared positivist assumptions but the denial of basic, qualitative progress in IR. As Ole Wæver puts it, "This 'no' unites realists," and what distinguishes realists is that "they have found different ways to argue the *no* (human nature, structure, philosophy of history, pessimism of knowledge)" (1997: 10). Chapters 2.2 and 2.3 reflect both this unity and the different ways in which progress may be denied.

■ Further Reading

Hans Morgenthau is a founding figure in the development of realism as a theoretical perspective in the US IR discipline. His most famous work is *Politics Among Nations* (1985, 6th ed.), which is an example of classical realism. A striking example of realism's deep skepticism toward progress can be found in Morgenthau's earlier work *Scientific Man vs. Power Politics* (1946). Kenneth Waltz is another seminal figure in the disciplinary development of realism, and his work *Theory of International Politics* (1979) spawned neorealism. An earlier work by Waltz, *Man, the State, and War* (1959), provides an accessible account of the levels-of-analysis issue and justifications for the systemic perspective.

Other seminal realist works in the discipline include Carr 1939, Herz 1950, Herz 1976, Kissinger 1964, Gilpin 1981, Kennedy 1987, Walt 1987, Grieco 1990, Buzan, Jones, and Little 1993, Schweller 1998, Krasner 1999, and Mearsheimer 2001. The literature on polarity is vast, but a good sampling of the variety of arguments that have been made in relation to it can be found by comparing works such as Copeland 1996, Deutsch and Singer 1964, Layne 1993, Mastanduno 1997, Mearsheimer 1990, Schweller and Priess 1997, and Waltz 1964.

Examples of offensive realism include Mearsheimer 2001 and Zakaria 1998. Examples of defensive realism include Posen 1984, van Evera 1999, and Snyder 1991, although the latter might also be cited as an example of neoclassical realism. It varies in neoclassical realism, in which levels of analysis, and variables within it, are the focus of explanation; examples include Friedberg 1988, Schweller 1998, Sterling-Folker 2002, Taliaferro 2004, and Wohlforth 1993. Examples of security materialism may be found in Deudney 1993 and Deudney 2000. For discussions of these variants and overviews of realist theorizing in general, see Adams 2003–2004, Brooks 1997, Frankel 1996, Freyberg-Inan 2003, Glaser 2003, Jervis 1999, Rose 1998, Spirtas 1996, Taliaferro 2000–2001, and Walt 2002.

■ Notes

1. As Wæver subsequently observes, "realism is much talked about, much attacked, but not represented in the crowd," yet in the discipline "a position can be upheld even if it is hard to find a live incarnation of it because each position is partly defined by the other" (1997: 27–28). In other words, realism remains dominant not because most IR scholars subscribe to it, but because it allows IR scholars to define alternative theoretical perspectives in relationship to it.

2. Compare Grieco 1990 and Keohane 1984. See also Milner 1991 and Powell 1994.

3. For example, other neoclassical realists might focus on government institutions, interest groups, or economic cycles, with the common thread among them being their nonsystemic focus. Contrast, for example, Adams's and Taliaferro's chapters with Posen 2000, which mixes realism's structural and neoclassical aspects but focuses on Milosevic's political-military strategy instead.

4. And modern variants of realism, particularly neorealism, are unusual because, as Griffiths and O'Callaghan go on to observe, they are "epistemologically progressivist, even though [realists] are highly skeptical of progress as a political goal" (2001: 195). See also Kahler 1998 for an analysis of realism's ambiguous relationship to rationality.

Structural Realism: The Consequences of Great Power Politics

Because "the fates of all the states . . . in a system are affected much more by the acts and the interactions of the major ones than of the minor ones," structural realists tend to focus on the actions and interactions of great powers (Waltz 1979: 72–73, 161–176).[1] Yet structural realist theory can also illuminate the challenges less powerful states face. In fact, without considering the structure of the international political system, it is impossible to understand why weak states select the policies and undergo the experiences they do. Thus, to explain the 1998–1999 war in Kosovo, I examine the effects of international anarchy, polarity, relative capabilities, and the security dilemma on the Yugoslavian government's ability to maintain a monopoly of force over all of its territory, the US decision to intervene when the government was trying to reassert control over Kosovo, and the conduct, outcome, and consequences of the intervention.[2]

I argue that the ultimate causes of Yugoslavia's civil wars were anarchy, Yugoslavian weakness, unipolarity, and the security dilemma. Unipolarity was especially important. In the multipolar and bipolar eras, when Yugoslavia's independent, integral existence served the interests of the world's great powers, they helped create, re-create, and maintain it. But as bipolarity waned, the United States redefined its interests, inadvertently reducing the Yugoslavian government's power relative to its constituent republics and creating insecurity within the state. I also argue that anarchy and unipolarity affected the US decision to intervene in the Kosovo war and the conduct and outcome of the war. The United States faced neither an international sovereign to keep it from intervening nor a peer to make it think twice before doing so. Moreover, unrivaled power enabled it to dominate NATO decisionmaking and compel the Yugoslavian government to stop attacking Kosovar Albanians. Finally, I argue that Kosovo's current limbo makes it possible that the former Yugoslavia will once again be a stage upon which great power politics play out.

■ Systemic Sources of Yugoslavia's Civil Wars

Although "war begins in the minds and emotions of men, as all acts do" (Waltz 1959: 9), the permissive cause of war is international anarchy. Because there is no world government to prevent states from using force, states may pursue policies of war in their efforts to survive and pursue any other goals they may have (Waltz 1959: 232–233; Waltz 1979: 91). Moreover, even if states do not choose war, they may find themselves embroiled in one, either because other states attack them or because they stumble into the security dilemma.[3]

International anarchy is not only the permissive cause of international war; it is also the permissive cause of civil war. Because there is no international sovereign to protect states from domestic dissent or make them treat their inhabitants fairly, domestic actors may use force to resist governmental directives, and governments may use force to compel them to comply. When this occurs, the state's hierarchy is weakened, and domestic politics come to resemble international ones. Political outcomes no longer bear the imprint of law or authority. Instead, they reflect the relative capabilities of the participants. When the government is politically, economically, and militarily strong relative to domestic dissidents, it is likely to prevail.[4] When the government is weak, it may lose some of its territory through secession, or it may lose the monopoly of force over all of its territory through revolution, disintegration, or collapse (Adams 2000: 2–5). Because the stakes are so high—state death on the one hand and elimination of domestic dissent on the other—the actors in domestic political crises respond to and worry about others' capabilities. Thus, like international actors, they can become entangled in the security dilemma and end up fighting wars no one wants.[5]

Weak states should be more vulnerable to civil war than their stronger counterparts, for two reasons. First, weak states are likely to have been the targets of great power conquest and intervention in the past. Thus their international borders, as well as their domestic political and economic systems, may have been constructed primarily for the convenience of outsiders. When this is the case, groups within the state often have strong desires for secession, irredentism, or restitution—desires that the state, in its weakness, may lack the capability to head off or satisfy. Second, weak states are unlikely to have the capabilities to adapt to changing international and technological circumstances. Thus weak states that manage to satisfy their populations in one period may find it difficult to do so in another, especially if international or technological changes beyond their control— such as great power decline, changing international polarity, or military and economic revolutions—make great powers that once helped them less willing to do so (Adams 2002, 2003–2004).

Thus, in applying structural realist theory to understand the causes of Yugoslavia's civil wars, it is necessary to consider Yugoslavia's relative capabilities. It is also necessary to explore the possibility that historical great power interventions planted the seeds of domestic discontent and to examine the effects of systemic changes in bringing discontent to a boil.

Finally, it is necessary to consider the possibility that the wars arose from domestic security dilemmas.

In 1989, when one of Yugoslavia's constituent republics (Slovenia) first declared its independence,[6] Yugoslavia's economic and military capabilities were dwarfed by those of the strongest states in the international system. Moreover, only in terms of military personnel did its economic and military capabilities exceed the international average (and they were just 107 percent of average).[7] Thus Yugoslavia was weak relative to both the strongest states in the international system and the average state in the system. Given international anarchy, this weakness made Yugoslavia vulnerable to war.

Yugoslavia's weakness in 1989 was by no means new. For centuries, its history was a story of conquest and intervention by great powers. Although Serbia was the most powerful state on the Balkan peninsula at the beginning of the fourteenth century, it was no match for the Ottoman Empire, which conquered it in 1459 and occupied it for more than 400 years. After 1867, when Russia (which was competing with Austria-Hungary for influence in the Balkans) pressured the Ottomans to leave, Serbia gained its independence. But in 1914, it was conquered again—this time by Austria-Hungary, which feared growing Russian influence in the region and Serbian plans to unify with or conquer Slovenia, Croatia, and Bosnia (all part of the Austrian Empire) and Albania and Macedonia (which remained under Ottoman rule).[8] After World War I, Serbia came back to life as the Kingdom of Serbs, Croats, and Slovenes (renamed Yugoslavia in 1929), but it fell again during World War II, this time to Germany and Italy and their allies.[9] The country was liberated in 1944 only because the Allies opened an Eastern front in the Balkans and supported the efforts of Yugoslavian communist partisans led by Marshal Tito (Allcock 2000: 236–238).

Given Yugoslavia's history of conquest and rebirth at the hands of great powers, we should not be surprised if its domestic political history is punctuated by civil conflict. Moreover, we should expect its civil conflicts to have roots in and be strongly affected by great power politics. Yugoslavian history strongly supports these expectations. From the founding of the Kingdom of Serbs, Croats, and Slovenes in 1918 until the present day, Yugoslavians have disagreed with one another about what kind of state Yugoslavia should be. Moreover, many of these differences are the result of great power occupation and intervention. For example, the presence of ethnic Serbs in Croatia and Bosnia and of ethnic Albanians in Kosovo can be traced to the Ottoman conquest of Serbia in 1459, which pushed Serbs north into Austria and brought other groups (such as Albanians) into erstwhile Serb lands. Similarly, the introduction of Islam to Bosnia, Herzegovina, and Albania can be traced to the Ottoman policy of granting land and lower taxes to converts (*The New Encyclopaedia Britannica* 2002, vol. 14: 601). Likewise, the post–World War I creation of the Kingdom of Serbs, Croats, and Slovenes did not simply reflect the aspirations of these groups. Instead, the birth and borders of this state reflected the designs and desires of some of the most powerful states in the international political system: the United States, which espoused Woodrow Wilson's ideas about national self-determination; France, which sought a Balkan line of defense against Germany; and Italy, which wanted to expand its coastline (Jelavich and Jelavich 1977: 298–304). Yugoslavia's rebirth as a multinational state after World War II also reflected international considerations, especially the Allies' belief that such a state would most effectively limit German influence in the region (Allcock 2000: 236–238).

The combining and dividing of ethnic groups during centuries of great power intervention made ethnic differences important throughout the decades of Yugoslavian unity. Yet the salience of these differences and the violent or pacific nature of their resolution waxed and waned in response to international circumstances. When Serbia, with Russia's assistance, became independent of the Ottoman Empire, Albanians living in Serbia were pressured to emigrate. Most of them went to Kosovo, which (with Albania) remained under Ottoman control. As the empire weakened, the possibility of an independent, unified Albania arose but was lost as Bulgaria, Serbia, Greece, and Montenegro attacked the nascent Albanian state (which was even weaker than they) and divided it among themselves. From 1912 to 1915, Serbian and Montenegrin armies ruthlessly consolidated their control over Kosovo. In 1915, with Austria's conquest of Serbia, the tide turned and Albanians became Kosovo's privileged group—until Serbs returned with the Allies and began a new round of reprisals (Judah 2000: 11–20).

During the interwar years, the Yugoslavian government closed Albanian schools in Kosovo, encouraged Serbs and Montenegrins to move to the region and appropriate Albanian lands, and pressured Albanians to emigrate to Turkey (Judah 2000: 21–26). In the absence of effective domestic opposition, what was to prevent it from doing so? Unlike the Albanians, the Yugoslavian government had an army at its disposal. Moreover, in the 1920s there was neither a world government nor any great power interested in making the government treat Albanians differently.

During World War II, the situation changed again. Yugoslavia was divided among five Axis powers, and all Yugoslavians, but especially Serbs, were brutalized.[10] Thus, when the war was over, the challenge was to manage deeper divisions than had ever existed before. For decades, Tito's communist government did so very effectively. It devolved considerable authority to Yugoslavia's six constituent republics and later to Serbia's provinces. Moreover, it used Western-bloc aid and loans to fund a proportional distribution of government jobs and budget outlays (Crawford 1998: 207–222; Woodward 1995, chap. 2).

Yugoslavia's Cold War alliances had no effect on the systemic balance of power between the United States and the Soviet Union. But the 1948 expulsion of Yugoslavia from the Communist Information Bureau (Curtis 1990) left it without allies just as the United States was trying to encourage states to break with Moscow. Thus Yugoslavia received considerable US assistance, and this assistance kept it in business. US military aid helped Yugoslavia deter the Soviets from intervening in Yugoslavian politics as they had in East Germany, Hungary, and Czechoslovakia, and US financial assistance provided Yugoslavia's republics and territories with incentives to hang together.

External assistance fell off substantially after the late 1970s, when the oil shocks led the United States and its European allies to erect trade barriers and provide less capital. Combined with large international loans resulting from high oil prices and pressure from the US-dominated International Monetary Fund (IMF) to liberalize in exchange for further assistance, this threw Yugoslavia into economic crisis and the government became less able to satisfy its citizens (Woodward 1995: 47–57).[11] In the late 1980s the demise of the Soviet Union further weakened the state. Specifically, it released Yugoslavians from their fear of Soviet takeover (and hence their loyalty to the government), and it meant that the United States redefined its interests in the region. Instead of supporting the Yugoslavian government to maintain an international balance of power to its liking, as great powers had done throughout the multipolar and bipolar eras, the United States began to lend its voice to calls for the speedy democratization of the country (Allcock 2000: 242–244; Woodward 1995: 148–152). In doing so, it inadvertently contributed to the election of separatist governments in Slovenia and Croatia, as well as to the civil wars of the early 1990s in which the Yugoslavian army and Serbian leaders tried to stop their secession, seize parts of Croatia and Bosnia with substantial Serb populations, and retain control of the provinces of Kosovo and Vojvodina.

The inconstancy of international assistance in an anarchic world was not the only cause of Yugoslavia's civil wars. It was just a permissive cause. World leaders and Yugoslavian leaders could have made other decisions. But the space in which leaders could operate was very constrained. With the end of the Cold War, Western-bloc countries came under domestic pressure to cut their military and other Cold War–related spending. Moreover, with the decline of the Yugoslavian economy, which affected different parts of Yugoslavia differently, a domestic security dilemma was building. Slovenia benefited from falling commodity prices and IMF pressure to liberalize trade and halt subsidies to poorer regions and began to buy commodities abroad instead of from Serbia. Throughout the 1980s, it had full employment. In Serbia, by contrast, unemployment was 17–18 percent from 1981 to 1985; in Kosovo it was over 50 percent. Thus as Serbia lost its traditional markets and subsidies, it tried to recapture control of the federal budgets for Kosovo and Vojvodina, which had been devolved to them in the 1960s (Woodward 1995: 63–65). But these measures to increase Serbian security were contrary to the greater independence that Kosovar Albanians increasingly sought (Judah 2000: 38–40, 309). Moreover, as the situation between Serbia and Kosovo worsened and Eastern European borders frozen by the Cold War began to thaw, Yugoslavia's most advanced republics, Slovenia and Croatia, began to look west to Europe and ally with states that could help them adjust to the changing international economy (Judah 2000: 56–57; Woodward 1995: 72). By the late 1980s, both were talking about secession. Slovenia and Croatia did not intend to make Serbia insecure, but their moves toward independence nevertheless created insecurity in Serbia. As Serbs saw the economic, political, and military system crumble for lack of Slovenian and Croatian support, they became more responsive to Slobodan Milosevic's calls to create a Greater Serbia (Woodward 1995: 68–69, 74, 133).[12]

By mid-1992 the post–World War II Yugoslavian state had disintegrated with the secessions of Slovenia, Croatia, Macedonia, and Bosnia-Herzegovina. Moreover, due to the weakness of the new Yugoslavian state, comprising just Serbia and Montenegro, Milosevic effort to capture land in Croatia and Bosnia had failed. Thus the government's goal was simply to hang on to its remaining territory, including Kosovo and Vojvodina, with their energy-generating capabilities and mineral and agricultural wealth (Allcock 2000: 427; Woodward 1995: 29). For several years it looked like the government's capabilities relative to the Kosovar Albanians, who barely had the capability to wage a campaign of passive resistance, would enable it to do so. But when the Albanian economy and government collapsed in 1997, Kosovar Albanians suddenly had easy access to arms and a neighboring state from which to launch raids (Judah 2000: 61, 67, 126–134). By August 1998 the KLA controlled 40 percent of Kosovo and was attacking police, assassinating officials, and targeting government buildings and installations (Layne and Schwarz 1999). Thus the Yugoslavian government was at once fearful that it would be further dismembered and determined to see that this did not occur. In the absence of a world government to provide for its security and regulate its response to the Albanians' campaign for independence, the government had to help itself if it was going to survive. Moreover, it could do what it liked to undermine the secessionist movement. Thus the Yugoslavian government mounted a counterinsurgency war against the KLA until the United States and NATO launched the spring 1999 bombing campaign known as Operation Allied Force and compelled it to stop.

Thus structural realist theory illuminates a great deal about the causes of Yugoslavia's civil wars. It demonstrates that Yugoslavia's vulnerability to war arose from its weakness. It also calls attention to the role of historical great power interventions and recent international political changes in creating ethnic conflicts and bringing them to a boil. Finally, structural realist theory suggests that the wars arose out of two security dilemmas, one international and the other domestic. First, as the Soviet Union declined and unipolarity emerged, the United States redefined its security in terms of the spread of US political and economic values, but this inadvertently reduced the security of the Yugoslavian government it had long supported and created an opening for civil wars contrary to US security interests. Second, as Yugoslavians watched their state weaken, they took steps to provide for their own security. But the steps taken by each group increased the insecurity of the others. Because there was not a strong Yugoslavian government, another great power, or an international sovereign to mediate their differences, Yugoslavians fell to war.

■ Systemic Sources of US Intervention

International anarchy means that there is nothing to prevent states from intervening in the affairs of others. Weak states such as Yugoslavia are especially vulnerable to intervention, because, if either their stronger neighbors or the most powerful states in the system take an interest in directing their affairs, there is little such states can do to stop them. Great power intervention in the affairs of weak states is more likely in a unipolar system than in multipolar or bipolar ones, for the dominant state in a unipolar system faces no significant opposition from other states. Yet great power indifference to weak states is also most likely in a unipolar system, because the dominant state has no reason to worry that other great powers will manipulate situations to their advantage. Thus it is difficult to say whether great power intervention in weak states should occur most often in unipolar, multipolar, or bipolar eras. All we can say with certainty is that weak states should always be vulnerable to intervention, because anarchy means there is nothing to rule it out and great power "tempts one" to intervene, whether to balance the power of other states or simply "for the 'good' of other people" (Waltz 1979: 27).

Since the fall of the Soviet Union, the unbalanced power of the United States has left it free to follow its whims. Nowhere is this more clear than in the US position on Yugoslavia's civil wars, which has changed repeatedly.[13] During the Yugoslavian government's war with the Kosovar Albanians, unipolarity enabled the United States to switch from calling the KLA a "terrorist group" (US special envoy Robert Gelbard, quoted in Judah 2000: 138) to intervening on its behalf—all without fear of sparking a crisis among the major states in the system. Moreover, unipolarity allowed the intervention to be predicated on a motley collection of goals—

from President Bill Clinton's lofty aim of ensuring human rights (Clinton 1999c) to the less noble goal of maintaining US dominance by perpetuating and expanding NATO (Kurth 2001), preempting the formation of a European defense identity,[14] and warning "rogue states" that they should not challenge the international status quo (Chomsky 1999b: 6–8).

International anarchy and relative capabilities also played a role in the intervention. Anarchy's effects are obvious in the ability of the United States and other NATO countries to flout the NATO Charter, ignore their obligations as United Nations members to obtain a Security Council resolution authorizing war, and disregard international "norms" against intervening in the domestic conflicts of other states.[15] Moreover, in the absence of a world government, the United States and NATO were not obliged to intervene in similar ways in similar conflicts elsewhere in the world. Structural realist theory suggests that if states are treated differently, either they have different capabilities or a powerful state is being fickle (because it can be). Because Russia and China, which are far more powerful than Yugoslavia, and Turkey, which is a US ally, have not faced international opprobrium for similar human rights abuses in Chechnya, Tibet, and Kurdistan (Kurth 2001: 80–81), the effects of relative power and privileges of great power are clear.

■ The Conduct and Outcome of US and NATO Intervention in the War

When Operation Allied Force began, the United States, NATO, and the Yugoslavian government moved from "diplomacy backed by force" to "force backed by diplomacy" (US secretary of state Madeleine Albright, quoted in Clark 2001: 253). Specifically, the United States and its allies used force to compel the Yugoslavian government to accept the terms of the February 1999 Rambouillet Agreement, which guaranteed a NATO peacekeeping mission if the KLA abandoned its goal of independence from Yugoslavia. The Yugoslavian government used force to resist. Because the war that ensued was thus the continuation of international politics by other means (Clausewitz 1976: 87), anarchy and polarity affected both its conduct and its outcome.

US and NATO Strategy and Operations

Because the United States intervened in the Kosovo war with the assistance of its NATO allies and because all nineteen of NATO's member states participated in decisionmaking for OAF and fourteen contributed aircraft (Arkin 2001: 1, 21), the operation is widely regarded as "the most multilateral campaign ever" (Betts 2001: 126). Yet the dominant power of the United States was decisive. More than 80 percent of the weapons delivered by the alliance were of US origin (Arkin 2001: 21). Moreover, the strategy and operational guidance for the use of these weapons consistently reflected US priorities.

In their war with the Yugoslavian government, the United States and NATO adopted a compellent, air-war strategy (Art 1980: 7–10). Specifically, they bombed governmental installations and other targets in Serbia to convince the Serb-dominated Yugoslavian government to stop its counterinsurgency operation against the KLA and accept the Rambouillet Agreement. This strategy was adopted because the United States preferred it. In spite of support for a ground campaign among US Commander in Chief of European Command (CINCEUR) and Supreme Allied Commander in Europe (SACEUR) General Wesley Clark, British prime minister Tony Blair, and other NATO allies, the Clinton administration repeatedly ruled out the ground option (Clark 2001: 206, 269, 319, 330, 332, 450; Daalder and O'Hanlon 2000b: 162, 164).

US dependence on NATO in implementing this air-war strategy has been vastly overstated. The administration's decision to cloak the operation in NATO garb was a tactical choice driven by Clinton's need for domestic legitimacy and the convenience of using regional air bases. Moreover, as William Arkin explains, "US planning for what would become Operation Allied Force began prior to and proceeded separately from the planning effort within NATO. . . . [E]ven as the conflict began, separate NATO and 'US-only' tracks continued, with alliance members denied the details of US cruise-missile strikes and operations by B-2 and F-117 stealth aircraft" (2001: 3). Furthermore, it was up to the United States to decide whether operational details would be determined in the NATO track. As CINCEUR and SACEUR, US general Wesley Clark had two bosses: the United States and NATO. But as CINCEUR, Clark had a great deal of discretion about when to activate the NATO decisionmaking process, and he used this discretion to advance US interests.[16] When he did not do so to Washington's satisfaction, he was overruled and ultimately fired (Clark 2001: 227, 278, 288, 319, 411, 451).

Because NATO had no intelligence capabilities of its own, it relied almost exclusively on whatever intelligence the United States was willing to share. Thus 99 percent of target nominations originated in the United States (Clark 2001: 427). Moreover, it was the United States that initiated the process of target-by-target approval by civilian leaders (Clark 2001: 201–202, 224; Daalder and O'Hanlon 2000b: 163); preauthorized targets only if they "were projected to generate . . . small numbers of accidental casualties" (Clark 2001: 236, 317); ordered aircraft to fly above 15,000 feet to reduce the risk of allied casualties (Daalder and O'Hanlon 2000b: 161); nixed the use of Apache helicopters to diminish the Yugoslavian government's ability to attack Kosovar Albanians (Clark 2001: 227, 278,

288, 303, 319); and ordered the escalation of the bombing campaign in the final week of the war (Clark 2001: 352–353). Thus it was simply not the case that NATO members "all [had] a vote on everything" (US major-general Charles Wald, quoted in Cohen 2001: 51) or that NATO opted for "lowest common denominator tactics" (US retired admiral Leighton Smith, quoted in Daalder and O'Hanlon 2000b: 159). OAF was waged from Washington.

As a result, understanding the conduct of OAF requires an understanding of US decisionmaking. As always, factors at the individual and state levels of analysis—especially Clinton's aversion to casualties and the Pentagon's desire to stick with the preestablished two-major-theater war strategy instead of committing to the only operation the United States actually had under way (Clark 2001: 265, 306, 313, 421, 456)—were extremely important. But these factors were far more salient in the unipolar international political system than they would have been in a bipolar or multipolar system, for unipolarity meant that the conflict had virtually no chance of escalating into a confrontation that would directly threaten US security. Policymakers could afford to indulge the belief "that the campaign will last two nights and that after two nights, Mr. Milosevic would be compelled to come to the table" (a senior US general, quoted in Arkin 2001: 2), and the Pentagon could afford to conduct bureaucratic politics as usual. Had the threat to the United States been greater, the operation would have been conducted differently (Posen 1984: 233–235)—as demonstrated by the fact that the only time Clark obtained Washington's support for using the Apache helicopters was after Russia sent troops to occupy the Pristina airfield (Clark 2001: 392).

Yugoslavian Strategy and Operations

Just as the dominance of the United States strongly affected NATO's strategy and operations, the weakness of the Yugoslavian government left an indelible mark on its approach to the war. How could it be otherwise? Yugoslavia's gross national product (GNP) and defense budget were less than 1 percent of NATO's (Posen 2000: 49). Moreover, its recent civil wars and eight-year international isolation meant the military capabilities the government did have were degraded and outdated.

Given the great and growing disparity between Yugoslavian and NATO military forces, the Yugoslavian government's decision to fight the United States and NATO instead of yielding to their demands requires explanation. Here again, anarchy and polarity played vital roles. Anarchy meant that the Yugoslavian government was concerned with its survival (which was jeopardized by the Rambouillet Agreement)[17] and there was no one to stop it from doing whatever it took to survive. Moreover, because unipolarity made states uncomfortable with US power, Yugoslavia hoped to benefit from opposition to the US-led war effort within NATO and from Russia and China.

Because it was outgunned, Yugoslavia (like other weak states such as Finland, Switzerland, and Sweden) adopted a strategy of conventional deterrence.[18] Specifically, it attempted to demonstrate its ability to "make [NATO's] pain exceed its gain" so the allies would give up and go home. This strategy had three elements. First, to deter a ground invasion, Yugoslavia tried to eliminate the KLA from as much of Kosovo as possible and reinforce, hide, and harden its military capabilities in the province. Second, to strain the alliance's solidarity and tax its logistics, it tried to create a refugee crisis. Third, to weaken the allies' resolve, Yugoslavia called attention to collateral damage and international tensions caused by NATO attacks (Posen 2000: 50–54).

Operationally, the key to implementing this strategy was to deter the allies from flying below 15,000 feet by using Yugoslavian air defense capabilities often enough to frighten them but not so often that the allies could gather enough information to target Yugoslavian defenses. This would provide cover for Yugoslavia's counterinsurgency campaign against the KLA and expulsion of Kosovar Albanian civilians (Posen 2000: 54–58).

The War's Outcome

Despite the enormous gap between Yugoslavian and NATO capabilities, Yugoslavia held out for seventy-eight days, successfully played air-defense cat-and-mouse throughout the war, and obtained a far more favorable peace agreement than Rambouillet. Together, these aspects of the war's outcome confirm that, in an anarchic system, power—even unbalanced power in a unipolar era—does not equal control (Waltz 1979: 191–192).

Carl von Clausewitz's observation that "everything in war is simple, but the simplest thing is difficult" was not given much credence by the US policymakers who believed the Yugoslavian government would surrender in just two nights. But it should have been, for great power does not guarantee the weather. Neither does great power ensure effortless management of the "countless minor incidents—the kind you can never really foresee" (Clausewitz 1976: 119). Friction and the fog of war are part of the terrain in all wars and should have been expected to be especially troublesome in a multilateral effort. After all, although the United States continually overrode the objections of its allies,[19] it still had to deal with them. Moreover, although the unbalanced power of the United States meant that Russia, China, and other states were reluctant to come to the aid of the Yugoslavian government, because the US and NATO strategy was to attack targets "with little true military justification" (Arkin 2000: 48), there was nothing to stop the government from using the capabilities it had. Thus Yugoslavia employed and preserved its air-defense system for the duration of the war

(Posen 2000: 58–62). Given allied (especially US) concern with combat fatalities, this meant that NATO planes rarely flew below 15,000 feet. As a result, Yugoslavian troops were able to degrade the KLA's capabilities, push the KLA and hundreds of thousands of Kosovar Albanian civilians into Albania and Macedonia, and reinforce the government's military capabilities in Kosovo (Posen 2000: 62–66; Clark 2001: 251, 422). Yugoslavia successfully raised the costs NATO would have to bear to invade the country and, in doing so, contributed to US opposition to a ground war.

Yet Yugoslavia's success in creating a refugee crisis did not fracture the alliance. Because the crisis created an even larger problem for an already weak Europe, it enhanced European willingness to endure US unilateralism—at least in the short term. Moreover, despite several shocking incidents of collateral damage, as well as the accidental bombing of the Chinese embassy, Yugoslavia was never able to drive enough of a wedge among the NATO allies or between NATO and Russia or China to obtain significant assistance in the war. Russia did what it could with the capabilities it was willing to risk on a conflict that did not directly imperil the Russian homeland.[20] But none of this caused more than a few ruffled feathers in Washington (Clark 2001: 209, 212, 226). It did, however, demonstrate the limits of Russia's ability to oppose the United States and, as such, provided the impetus for Yugoslavia and Russia to try to end the war.

By mid-May 1999, it was clear that neither Russia nor China was able or willing to deter further NATO attacks and that Yugoslavia's success in deterring a ground war in Kosovo had no effect on the vulnerability of its industry and infrastructure. In fact, as the war dragged on, the United States and NATO struck more and more targets, including factories, bridges, government buildings, and electrical installations. Thus, in the end, the result foreshadowed by the power imbalance did unfold: the Yugoslavian government agreed to accept some of NATO's terms.

But Yugoslavia did not accept all of NATO's terms. In fact, with German and Russian help, it negotiated a deal that was far more lenient than Rambouillet. Whereas Rambouillet had called for the withdrawal of Yugoslavian military and police forces from Kosovo, a NATO military presence in Kosovo and throughout Yugoslavia, and, within three years, elections and other measures to determine whether Kosovo would secede from Yugoslavia ("Rambouillet Agreement" 1999), the peace agreement simply provided for the withdrawal of Yugoslavian military and police from Kosovo and the introduction of an international military presence in the province. The stipulations that the forces would be under NATO command, that they would have access to all of Yugoslavia's territory, and that there would be a firm process and timetable for determining Kosovo's final status were eliminated. Moreover, although the peace agreement provided for "substantial autonomy and meaningful self-administration for Kosovo," it also recognized the sovereignty and territorial integrity of Yugoslavia, provided for the demilitarization of the KLA, and gave the UN Security Council the primary responsibility for Kosovo's political administration, including determining its final status ("Peace Agreement" 1999).

This result reflected, at once, Yugoslavia's inability to shield itself from further attacks and NATO's inability to obtain the conditions set out in the Rambouillet Agreement without waging a ground war that its dominant member, the United States, saw as peripheral and possibly damaging to its interests. Once again, great power interest in Yugoslavia had waxed, then waned. But although the United States and its NATO allies obtained less from the war than they sought, their power still got them quite a bit. Their troops occupied the territory of another state, and the leader of that state was tried in a war-crimes tribunal set up by a state that refused to subject itself to the International Criminal Court.[21] Thus both the conduct and the outcome of the war illustrate that, in an anarchic system, "the strong do what they can and the weak suffer what they must" (Thucydides 1993: 290).

The Peacekeeping Operation

Today, anarchy's effects are evident in the allocation of peacekeeping sectors among members of NATO's KFOR, as well as in the performance of nonsectoral responsibilities such as providing economic assistance for reconstruction and responding to flare-ups in other sectors. The effects of anarchy are also evident in Russia's participation in the peacekeeping operation and in the lack of authority of the international organizations involved in the operation.

As the dominant state in the world, the United States has the greatest capability to take on peacekeeping and other "system management" responsibilities (Waltz 1979, chap. 9). But the United States also has the greatest capability to walk away from such responsibilities, for its exposure to problems is low. Besides, apart from US citizens, who can make it take on such responsibilities? Thus, although when KFOR peacekeeping sectors were allocated the United States could have chosen the "most sensitive" northern sector of Mitrovica, which borders Serbia, it chose the southeast sector, which "appeared to be the easiest."[22] Similarly, despite its military and economic dominance, in 2000 the United States contributed just 20 percent of the troops in Kosovo and 13 percent of the funds used to administer the territory (Daalder and O'Hanlon 2000b: 165–166). Moreover, although the United States sometimes comes to France's aid when violence erupts in Mitrovica, sometimes it does not (O'Neill 2002: 43; International Crisis Group 2002: 12).

The effects of anarchy are also apparent in Russia's role in the peacekeeping operation, which provides further evidence that power does not necessarily lead to control. In the international system, agreements hold when they are compatible with realities on the ground. On paper, NATO won the war. But because NATO troops did not invade Kosovo during the war, the fighting over the province was still up for grabs. As negotiations to end the war were drawing to a close, Russia threw a wrench in the long-laid peacekeeping plan by demanding control of the northern sector and sending 200 troops to secure the Pristina airfield, from which it planned to deploy troops north (Clark 2001: 369, 371–378). Russian weakness—specifically its inability to compel Hungary, Romania, and Bulgaria to allow it to use their airspace—left it unable to implement this plan. But Russia's position at the airfield and Clark's inability to convince Britain to respond to the Russian deployment with force meant that the United States and NATO agreed to put 750 Russian troops in charge of security and transport at the airfield and to allow 3,600 others to participate in operations in the French, German, and US sectors (Clark 2001: 390–402; Gall 1999; US Department of State 1999a).

Anarchy's imprint is also evident in the lack of authority of the various international organizations involved in the peacekeeping operation. Although, on paper, administrators on the civil side of the operation are appointed by the UN secretary-general, states have pressured Kofi Annan not to select his preferred candidates.[23] Similarly, although the commanders of the five sectors are supposedly subordinate to KFOR, they also report to their own national governments (O'Neill 2002: 43). Thus rules of engagement vary from sector to sector.[24]

■ Consequences of the War

One of the central insights of structural realist theory is that state actions in international anarchy often have unintended consequences (Waltz 1979: 64–65). Here again, the Kosovo war provides ample support for the theory. Although anarchy and unipolarity were the permissive causes of the war, the desire to stop human rights abuses, strengthen NATO, and preserve the international status quo were important immediate causes. Yet the effects of the war on Kosovo, NATO, and the international balance of power have been and are likely to continue to be contrary to these intentions.

Since the war, Kosovo has been "one of the most dangerous places on Earth" from the standpoint of individual security (Taylor 2002). As time passes, the situation is likely to become even worse, for three contradictory pressures are at work: the peace agreement stipulates that Kosovo is part of Yugoslavia; Kosovar Albanians still want to secede from Yugoslavia; and the province has been divided into five occupation zones commanded by states whose interests have a good chance of diverging. Thus the conflict continues to simmer as the KLA tries to drive Serbs from Kosovo and resists KFOR pressure to disarm, and as the Yugoslavian government reestablishes control of the northern part of the province. But if and when the UN Security Council takes action on Kosovo's final status, the KLA resumes its efforts to secede, the government makes a bid to retake the province, or the occupation forces are withdrawn, the conflict could come back to a boil.

Because there is no world government to enforce a resolution between Yugoslavian and Kosovar Albanian claims to Kosovo or compel the occupation forces to remain indefinitely and rationalize their administration of the province, Kosovo's best chance for peace probably lies in the consolidation of Yugoslavian authority over the area north of Mitrovica and the steady handing over of UN and KFOR authority to Kosovar Albanian authorities. Yet even this is no guarantee of peace, for once KFOR troops leave the province there will be nothing to stop Yugoslavia from reclaiming Kosovo, or Kosovar Albanians from claiming land north of Mitrovica, as well as parts of Macedonia and Albania. Besides, just as the creation and re-creation of Yugoslavia after World Wars I and II depended on great power politics, a measured and forward-thinking withdrawal of KFOR occupation forces depends on NATO cohesion and Russian and Chinese acquiescence, neither of which is assured.

Instead of strengthening NATO, the Kosovo war weakened it. US NATO allies came to view the alliance as a US appendage or rubber stamp, and the United States came to see it as an encumbrance.[25] Thus OAF is likely to be remembered as NATO's first and only war. Moreover, because the stability of the Balkans directly affects the political, economic, and social stability of several of the major European states and because European and US forces are already deployed in Kosovo and Bosnia, these former Yugoslavian territories could well be where European states come together to balance US power. Already, there is movement toward a unified European approach, as the French and British occupation sectors and the Italian and German sectors prepare to merge, while the US sector, where the United States has built a large base, continues to function independently (KFOR 2002; Finn 2002). But whether the United States and Europe become competitors in Kosovo depends on developments in the larger international political system.

Structural realist theory "predicts that balances disrupted will one day be restored," for "dominant powers take on too many tasks beyond their own borders" and "even if a dominant power behaves with moderation, restraint, and forbearance, weaker states will worry about its future behavior" (Waltz 2000: 27–28). Since the demise of the Soviet Union, there has been an imbalance rather than a balance of power. The war and peacekeeping operation in Kosovo starkly demonstrated US dominance. Despite Russian and Chinese opposition to violating Yugoslavia's sovereignty, the

United States led NATO to war. Despite allied opposition to the way the war was fought, the United States stuck to its high-altitude, air-war strategy. Despite fighting the war to end "instability in the Balkans so . . . bitter ethnic problems are resolved by the force of argument, not the force of arms" (Clinton 1999c), the United States negotiated a peace agreement likely to lead to further instability. Finally, despite having the greatest capability to manage the postwar situation in Kosovo, the United States has repeatedly passed the military and economic buck. Yet although the Kosovo war and peacekeeping operation have underscored US dominance, they have not called forth a new balance of power. Europe, Russia, and China would clearly like to balance US power, but they are not yet able to do so. In the anarchic international political system, capabilities, not intentions, are what transform the balance.

■ Conclusion

Neither Yugoslavia's disintegration nor US intervention in the Kosovo war was foreordained. Yugoslavia could have adopted policies more conducive to domestic harmony, and the United States could have been more mindful of Yugoslavia's dependence on US aid. But due to the structural constraints of international anarchy, polarity, relative capabilities, and the security dilemma, "patterns of behavior nevertheless emerge" (Waltz 1979: 92). The causes, conduct, and consequences of Yugoslavia's civil wars conform closely to structural realist expectations about these patterns. Yugoslavia, a weak state, experienced both civil and international war. Moreover, the United States, a state with unrivaled power, intervened in Yugoslavia's domestic problems and dominated international decisionmaking about how to respond to them. But US power did not lead to control. In fact, the more the United States exercised its power, the more other states sought to curtail its reach.

Given the scope and scale of US dominance, much could change in Kosovo before a new balance of power emerges. Depending on how "the spirit moves it" (Waltz 2000: 29), the United States could take over the whole peacekeeping operation, walk away altogether, hold its position in the southeastern sector while the European sectors are consolidated, or even lead the way to a lasting settlement. None of these possibilities can be ruled out. In an anarchic realm, dominant power gives its possessor "wide latitude in making foreign policy choices" (Waltz 2000: 29).

Already we have seen the range of action permitted by US power. Great powers have always blown hot and cold in the Balkans, but the United States has changed its position several times in the past two decades, from supporting the Yugoslavian government during the Cold War to intervening against it in 1999, then limiting US responsibilities as the peacekeeping operation got under way. In 2005, despite George W. Bush's 2000 campaign promise to get US forces out of the Balkans, the United States continued to occupy one-fifth of Kosovo.

As permanent members of the UN Security Council, the United States, Britain, France, Russia, and China can each veto changes to KFOR's authorization, as well as any measure resolving Kosovo's final status. More important, Britain, France, Germany, Italy, Russia, and the United States have troops on the ground. Thus, barring US domestic pressure to withdraw from Kosovo or negotiate a lasting settlement before new great powers rise, Kosovo could be among the places US power is first checked when a bipolar or multipolar system emerges. But even if the Kosovo conflict winds down or the United States is balanced on some other stage, international anarchy and Yugoslavia's relative weakness mean that whether Yugoslavia survives, dies, or is further dismembered will continue to hinge on the assistance and indifference of states far more powerful than itself.

■ Notes

1. For comments on earlier versions of this chapter, I thank Andrew Bacevich, Rachel Bzostek, Mark Gasiorowski, James Hardy, Michael Lipson, Susan Martin, Christopher Muste, Michael O'Hanlon, Karl Roider, Rosemary Shinko, Jennifer Sterling-Folker, and Kenneth Waltz. I also thank Lise Howard for bibliographic suggestions, and Rebekah Bowlin, Paula Duncan, Geoffrey Plauche, and Kathryn Weir for research assistance.

2. Contrary to those who call Yugoslavia "Serbia" after 1992, I follow the preferences of the state itself. Because Serbia and Montenegro called the new state they created in 1992 the Federal Republic of Yugoslavia (FRY) and, under pressure from the European Union (EU), renamed it Serbia and Montenegro in 2003 (Simpson 2003a, 2003b), I use those names for these periods. On the decision of the UN Security Council not to recognize the FRY as the successor government of the Socialist Federal Republic of Yugoslavia, see Woodward 1995: 251. On the difficulties of using diplomatic recognition as an indicator of a state's existence (or, in this case, its name), see Adams 2003.

3. The security dilemma arises when the actions that a state takes to secure itself backfire by inadvertently making other states less secure and thus more likely to do something that harms the state. On the international security dilemma, see Glaser 1997, Herz 1950, Jervis 1978, and Waltz 1979: 186–187.

4. On the importance of overall capabilities (not just military ones), see Waltz 1979: 131.

5. On the domestic security dilemma, see Kaufmann 1996, Posen 1993, Rose 2000, and Snyder and Jervis 1999.

6. On September 27, 1989, the Slovenian Republican Assembly declared that Slovenia was "an independent, sovereign, and autonomous state" with the right to self-determination and secession. Similar declarations were made in July 1990, June 1991, and September 1991 (Higham, Mercurio, and Ghezzi 1996: 66–68).

7. In 1989, Yugoslavia's gross national product (GNP) per capita was just 10 percent of Switzerland's (the richest state in the world on a per capita basis); its energy consumption (a good indicator of economic development) was just 2 percent

of that of the United States (the state that consumed the most energy); and its military spending was less than 1 percent of that of the United States (the state with the largest military budget). Moreover, its annual military budget and iron and steel consumption, which are good indicators of military capability, were 41 percent and 92 percent of the international average, respectively. Yugoslavia's economic capabilities were even lower. Its energy consumption was 84 percent of the international average; its total population and urban population were 74 percent and 59 percent of average; and its GNP per capita was 68 percent of average. Statistics on GNP per capita are derived from Cross-National Time-Series Data Archive 2001. Those on energy consumption, military expenditure, military personnel, iron and steel production, total population, and urban population are derived from Singer and Small 1999.

8. In 1913, Austria's population was seventeen times larger than Serbia's. Moreover, its army and military budget were eleven and thirty times larger, respectively (Singer and Small 1999). Thus Serbia's relative weakness was clearly an important source of its vulnerability to conquest.

9. In 1941, when Germany invaded Yugoslavia, Germany's population was more than five times larger than Yugoslavia's, and its military was more than forty-five times larger (Singer and Small 1999).

10. Germany occupied Serbia and established a fascist state in Croatia and most of Bosnia. Italy took Montenegro and (through Albania, which it had conquered in 1939) annexed Kosovo. Finally, Germany and Italy divided Slovenia, Hungary got Vojvodina, and Bulgaria absorbed Macedonia. "Of [the Serbs] living outside Serbia proper, one third were murdered by the Croatian *Ustashe,* one third were forced to convert to Catholicism, and one third were deported to Serbia. Irregular Serbian forces . . . retaliated in similarly brutal fashion, and after the war exacted their revenge on tens of thousands of Croatians" (Daalder 1996: 40). Moreover, Serbian and Montenegrin settlers in Kosovo were killed and expelled by Albanians avenging their treatment during the interwar years (Judah 2000: 26–27).

11. As S. Woodward explains, "all economic indicators were negative and worsening after 1982. By the end of 1984 the average income was approximately 70 percent of the official minimum for a family of four, and the population living below the poverty line increased from 17 to 25 percent" (1995: 52, 55). From 1979 to 1991, Yugoslavia's growth in gross domestic product fell from 15 to 5 percent.

12. When the new nationalist government in Croatia purged Serbs from public payrolls in 1990, Serbs feared a return to the anti-Serb violence of World War II (*The New Encyclopedia Britannica* 2002, vol. 14: 641).

13. In March 1991, President George H. W. Bush said that the United States would not "encourage or reward those who would break up Yugoslavia." Two months later, he cut off aid to the government, only to reinstate it after several weeks (Higham, Mercurio, and Ghezzi 1996: 67). Similarly, in June 1991, Secretary of State James Baker told Slovenia and Croatia the United States would not recognize them if they declared independence, but six months later the Bush administration did just that (Judah 2000: 76). Finally, after Senator Robert Dole criticized the Clinton administration's Bosnia policy during the 1994 congressional elections, arguing that the UN peacekeeping operation made the United States look weak, the administration moved from peacekeeping to aiding the Bosnians and Croats (Claiborne 1993).

14. The Bush administration's inaction in Bosnia in 1991–1992 may have reflected its hope that Europe's involvement there would tie up Germany's new-found relative power so that it would not try to build a European alternative to NATO (Higham, Mercurio, and Ghezzi 1996: 10; Woodward 1995: 153). If so, the

strategy met with early success, when efforts to activate the Conference on Security and Cooperation in Europe stalled due to the requirement that decisions be made by consensus and efforts to enforce European-brokered peace agreements floundered on the rocks of European military weakness (Daalder 1996: 59–60). But by December 1998 the EU had begun to adopt common foreign and security policies, and Britain and France had agreed to work toward a European military force that could act even when NATO and the United States preferred not to become involved (Whitney 1998). Thus the Clinton administration's attention to Kosovo can be seen as an attempt to head off increasingly active and focused European military efforts by demonstrating, as Madeleine Albright liked to put it, that the United States was "the indispensable nation."

15. The NATO Charter stipulates that NATO is a purely defensive alliance (*North Atlantic Treaty,* arts. 1, 3, 5–6). According to the UN Charter, which all UN members promise to uphold, regional organizations such as NATO can be used to enforce peace only with the authorization of the Security Council (*Charter of the United Nations,* art. 53). The United States and NATO did not approach the Security Council for a resolution authorizing Operation Allied Force because it was clear that Russia and China would veto such a resolution (Ibrahim 1998). On international norms against intervention, see Jackson and Zacher 1996: 24, Zacher 2001, and Wendt 1999: 279.

16. For example, toward the end of the war when Yugoslavia had promised to withdraw in exchange for a suspension of the bombing, Clark "decided that the way to do this was simply to stop dropping bombs, without formally requesting any measures from the political machinery at NATO. That way, if we needed to resume the strikes, there was no formal diplomatic permission required" (2001: 370).

17. The agreement would have provided for unrestricted movement and basing of NATO forces throughout Yugoslavia ("Rambouillet Agreement" 1999, app. B).

18. This discussion is based on inferences from Yugoslavia's Cold War strategy and actions in the Kosovo war (Posen 2000: 40–41), because despite speculation about "Operation Horseshoe," a Yugoslavian plan for expelling ethnic Albanians from Kosovo, Yugoslavia's actual strategy and operational plan remain unclear (Judah 2000: 240; Mertus 2001: 142).

19. For example, the United States denied Greek, Italian, and German requests for bombing pauses, ignored French and German concerns about collateral damage, and rejected British calls for a ground war (Clark 2001: 209, 330, 350–354).

20. Russia canceled US-Russian military contacts, suspended cooperation with NATO, threatened to pull its troops out of Bosnia, introduced a Security Council resolution calling the war a "flagrant violation of the UN Charter," and deployed an intelligence ship to the Mediterranean (Clark 2001: 197, 209, 212, 226).

21. In June 2002, in an effort to obtain an exemption for US forces from the jurisdiction of the International Criminal Court, the United States threatened to pull its forces out of Kosovo and vetoed a Security Council resolution renewing the mandate for peacekeeping and police forces in Bosnia. Several weeks later, it received a one-year exemption, which was renewed in 2003 (Schmemann 2002a, 2002b; Barringer 2003).

22. "That way," a senior military official told Clark, "we can withdraw early, and leave it to the Europeans" (Clark 2001: 163). France chose the northern sector.

23. In 2003 the United States rejected one of Annan's favorite candidates for the position of UN mission head because he opposed the US war against Iraq. Italy

rejected another candidate because he was on the outs with the Italian prime minister (Dempsey 2003; McGrath 2003).

24. The rules of engagement in the French sector have been especially contentious, for two reasons. First, unlike KFOR troops in other sectors, which were ordered to stop revenge attacks on Serbs by Kosovar Albanians, French troops were ordered "to let them pillage." Second, France has effectively partitioned its sector, establishing a checkpoint at the Ibar River in Mitrovica that prevents Kosovar Albanians from returning to their homes in the northern part of the northern sector and allows Serbia to reestablish control over that territory, which is the part of Kosovo that has the most mineral wealth and is closest to the Serbian border (O'Neill 2002: 44–46; International Crisis Group 2002: 3–4, 12–13). According to the International Crisis Group, "Belgrade's institutions . . . operate with full impunity" north of the Ibar River (2002: 3).

25. Just a month after the war ended, German foreign minister Joschka Fischer questioned US hopes to use NATO as an expeditionary force in the future (Dennis et al. 1999) and affirmed the quest for a common European foreign and security policy in which Germany would take "a leading role" ("Germany Comes Out of Its Post-War Shell" 1999). Two years later, after the terrorist attacks on the World Trade Center and Pentagon, NATO invoked the mutual defense clause in its founding treaty for the first time in history. But while Washington "obviously want[ed] the NATO stamp of approval in making Mr. bin Laden a target," it did not ask NATO to join the war on terrorism (Daley 2001: B6). Neither did it ask NATO to join the 2003 war against Iraq. Instead the United States asked individual NATO countries to participate (Gordon 2002).

Jeffrey W. Taliaferro

Neoclassical Realism: The Psychology of Great Power Intervention

Since June 1999 there have been debates over whether NATO's war in defense of Kosovo was a success or a failure.[1] However, two questions about this "strange little war" receive less attention. First, what drove President Bill Clinton and his advisers to initiate Operation Allied Force in March 1999? While US aircraft conducted approximately four-fifths of the 28,000 sorties against Serb police and paramilitary forces in Kosovo and Serbian government command and control facilities in Belgrade, the United States had few intrinsic security or economic interests in the Balkans after the collapse of the Soviet Union (Lambeth 2001, esp. chap. 5). The Federal Republic of Yugoslavia was a poor, weak country on the periphery of Europe. Arguably, the Kosovo conflict may have posed a potential threat to US "extrinsic" or secondary interests in Europe, given the province's proximity to key NATO allies and the possibility that massive refugee flows might destabilize the Balkans. However, even these concerns are open to dispute (see Mandelbaum 1999; and Layne 2000a).

Second, why did the administration persist in the bombing campaign, despite abundant evidence that doing so would produce outcomes on the ground that officials sought to avoid, namely ethnic violence, the large-scale displacement of Kosovar Albanians, and civilian causalities among Serbs and Kosovars? As Andrew Bacevich and Eliot Cohen note: "NATO's abject failure (or inability) to put an end to the displacement and massacre of large (if disputed) numbers of ethnic Albanian Kosovars made a mockery of the campaign's grand moral justifications, leaving the United States and its allies fending off accusations of gross miscalculation, callousness, or outright bad faith" (2001b: ix–xiv).

This chapter seeks to make the case for neoclassical realism, which posits that the relative distribution of material power shapes the parameters of states' foreign policy behavior. However, these systemic forces can only influence foreign policy through the medium of leaders' perceptions and calculations of relative power and prestige. I argue that the leaders' aversion to perceived losses—in terms of their state's relative power and prestige—drives great power intervention in peripheral regions. Officials initiate risky diplomatic and military intervention strategies to avoid such losses. Instead of cutting losses, leaders will often continue to invest blood and treasure in failing intervention strategies in tertiary regions.

Clinton and his advisers initiated the Kosovo war because they feared a further erosion of US credibility within NATO. With the collapse of the Soviet Union in 1991, the raison d'être of the North Atlantic alliance disappeared. The Clinton administration, like its immediate predecessor, sought to maintain US preponderance. Although the stated rationale for NATO's preservation and eastward expansion was to enlarge "the zone of democracy" in Eastern and Central Europe, there was clearly a realpolitik subtext: an expanded NATO would be the instrument through which the United States perpetuated its hegemonic role in Europe after the Cold War (Layne 2000b; Wohlforth 2002).

Nonetheless, by the late 1990s, the US commitment to European security suffered from a credibility dilemma. The violent disintegration of Yugoslavia emerged as the single greatest security issue in post–Cold War Europe. Yet there was a contradiction between the Clinton administration's insistence on US leadership in European security and repeated threats to use force against Serbia, on the one hand, and its perceived unwillingness to use ground forces or to sustain military casualties to end the Bosnian civil war and later the Kosovo crisis, on the other (Hodge 2001; Kay 2000; Mandelbaum 1999). The failure of the Rambouillet and Paris talks left officials little choice but to initiate air strikes against Serbia rather than suffer a further erosion of US credibility. When limited bombing not only failed to coerce Yugoslav president Slobodan Milosevic, but also created an opportunity for Serbian forces to kill, brutalize, or displace nearly 1 million Kosovars, officials escalated the bombing. Furthermore, they hinted that an invasion of Kosovo and Serbia itself was likely—an option that Clinton, Secretary of State Madeleine Albright, Secretary of Defense William Cohen, and Assistant to the President for National Security Affairs Samuel (Sandy) Berger publicly ruled out in March and April 1999 for fear that it would split the alliance.

As with the other theories in this volume, neoclassical realism illuminates certain aspects of the Kosovo war while leaving other aspects unexplained. This chapter will reveal that throughout the Kosovo crisis (January 1998 to June 1999), the Clinton administration was preoccupied with preserving US prestige—the reputation for having military power and a willingness to use it—even at the risk of disagreements with the NATO allies and later the continuation of a bombing strategy that was largely irrelevant to the stated aims of OAF. The next section briefly summarizes neoclassical realism with an emphasis on the role of elite perceptions of relative power and prestige. A discussion of the emergence of the US credibility gap with respect to the Balkans and NATO follows. The third section reviews the Clinton administration's initiation and conduct of the war. The conclusion discusses the broader implications of neoclassical realism for US grand strategy after the September 11, 2001, terrorist attacks on New York and Washington, D.C.

■ Neoclassical Realism and Foreign Policy

Neoclassical realism represents a fusion of two strands in realist thought: the structural realism (or neorealism) of Kenneth Waltz and Robert Gilpin and the classical realism of E. H. Carr, Hans Morgenthau, Arnold Wolfers, and others. "Like other [structural] realist theories, the neoclassical variant sees the [international] system as anarchic, emphasizes the importance of relative power, and highlights the importance of security and in the face of rival centers of power" (Walt 2002: 210). Consequently, all variants of realism tend to downplay the autonomous role of international institutions, domestic political institutions, and purely ideational variables in world politics.[2]

Neoclassical realism parts company with structural realism in two respects. First, the two variants of realism seek to explain different phenomena. In general, structural realism seeks to explain international political outcomes—phenomena resulting from the interaction of two or more actors in the international system. Neoclassical realism, on the other hand, seeks to explain why different states, or even the same state at different times, pursue particular strategies in the international arena. Neoclassical realist theories are theories of foreign policy.[3]

The second area where structural realism and neoclassical realism differ involves the mechanism through which systemic forces translate into political behavior. For structural realists, the causal path between systemic variables and political outcomes is direct and unproblematic. States, particularly the great powers, respond to systemic imperatives or face elimination at the hands of stronger states (Waltz 1979). Neoclassical realism, as Gideon Rose writes, holds that "there is no immediate or perfect transmission belt linking material capabilities to foreign policy behavior" (1998: 146–147).[4] Flesh-and-blood officials actually make foreign policy decisions and sometimes they misperceive the actual distribution of power or make erroneous estimates about power trends. Aaron Friedberg notes:

> Structural considerations provide a useful point from which to begin the analysis of international politics rather than a place at which to end it. Even if one acknowledges that structures exist and are important, there is still the question of how statesmen grasp their counters from the inside, so to speak, of whether, and if so how, are able to determine where they stand in terms of relative national power at any given point in history.[5] (1988: 8)

Elite perceptions of power are not the only factors that shape states' foreign policy. Perceptions of prestige—that is, a state's reputation for having power, especially military power—and status—that is, a state's recognized position within the international hierarchy—also play an important role in world politics. Classical realism recognized the importance of prestige and status rivalries. Thucydides, Niccolò Machiavelli, Thomas Hobbes, and Jean Jacques Rousseau identify security, self-interest, and honor as the three great motives for conflict at both the individual and the interstate level (see Markey 1999: 133–155). Building upon this tradition, Morgenthau writes, "whatever the ultimate objectives of a nation's foreign policy, its prestige—its reputation for power—is always an important and sometimes the decisive factor in determining the success or failure of its foreign policy" (1965: 95). Although subjective and entirely dependent on other states' assessments, prestige serves an instrumental function as a proxy for the use of military force. He further observes that

> in the struggle for existence and power [among states, as well as among individuals]—which is, as it were, the raw material of the social world—what others think about us is as important as what we actually are. The image in the mirror of our fellow's mind (that is, our prestige), rather than the original, of which the image in the mirror may be but the distorted reflection, determines what we are as members of society.[6] (1965: 73)

The prestige motivation for international conflict plays no role in the structural realism of Waltz (1979, 1986, 1996), which rejects the "reductionist" foreign policy theories of Morgenthau, Wolfers, and Carr in favor of a deductive, systemic framework for understanding continuity in international politics.[7] Neoclassical realists such as Randall Schweller (1999), Daniel Markey (1999), and William Wohlforth (2002) have sought to reincorporate the prestige motivation into realism.

Whereas classical realists and neoclassical realists such as Schweller, Wohlforth, and Markey see states' desire to *gain* prestige and status as an integral part of positional competition, I suggest that the *prospective loss* of relative prestige and status weighs more heavily in leaders' calculations than the desire to acquire additional prestige. Even among allies, the fear of losing relative prestige as well as objective fears of abandonment or entrapment can drive leaders to undertake diplomatic and military commitments that may not necessarily enhance their own state's security. Such considerations come into play even when there is a power disparity among the allies.[8]

How might leaders' aversion to perceived losses in relative material capabilities and prestige influence their propensity to intervene in the periphery—geographic areas where actual conflict (or likely conflict) cannot directly threaten the security of a great power's homeland? In particular, how does the above argument apply to the United States in the 1990s, where it enjoyed overwhelming preponderance in all underlying components of material power? (See Wohlforth 1999, 2002; Brooks and Wohlforth 2002.) Across different international systems, adverse developments in geographic areas previously deemed peripheral to a great power's security or prestige will suddenly take on tremendous importance in elite deliberations. When faced with perceived losses to their state's prestige, leaders are more likely to adhere to the so-called domino theory—a set of interconnected beliefs and assertions about the interdependence of commitments, the opportunistic nature of adversaries' actions, and the cumulative effect of conquests (Jervis 1996: 118–122; also Jervis 1991). Leaders' aversion to losses in their state's relative power or prestige leads to the adoption of risky intervention strategies in peripheral regions. This same tendency drives leaders' calculations about ongoing intervention strategies. Diplomatic and military interventions rarely involve a single once-and-for-all decision. On the contrary, once officials decide on a particular strategy, they will often have several opportunities to continue, modify, or terminate that strategy in response to negative feedback.

Neoclassical realism suggests that great powers are more concerned with preserving the relative power and prestige they already have than in augmenting those commodities. Three propositions flow from this theory. First, senior officials are more likely to initiate diplomatic and military strategies in the periphery to avoid perceived losses in relative power or prestige. Second, when faced with perceived losses to their states' relative power or prestige, these officials will gravitate toward the more risk-acceptant of available options. In other words, the preferred option will have more numerous and extremely divergent outcomes than the other available options. In selecting that option, decisionmakers perceive that negative outcomes are at least possible and are often highly probable. They will further recognize that their subjective probability estimates may be flawed or completely incorrect. Third, officials will likely continue and even escalate their commitment to risky, and often failing, intervention strategies in the periphery. Therefore, they are unlikely to reassess, scale down, or terminate ongoing strategies (Taliaferro 2004, chaps. 1–2). The following sections show how these neoclassical realist hypotheses illuminate different aspects of the Clinton administration's handling of the escalating Kosovo crisis in 1998 and the initiation and conduct of Operation Allied Force in 1999.

■ Post–Cold War US Grand Strategy and the Credibility Dilemma

In order to understand why the Clinton administration went to war in defense of the Kosovar Albanians in spring 1999, a neoclassical realist account would begin with a discussion of systemic imperatives and the overall goals of US grand strategy. With the collapse of the Soviet empire in Eastern and Central Europe in 1989, followed soon thereafter by the demise of the Soviet Union itself, the international system shifted from bipolarity to unipolarity. Moreover, the United States now enjoyed a commanding lead in all the elements of material power: economic, military, technological, and geographical (Wohlforth 1999). Yet there was no corresponding transformation in grand strategy. Instead, the George H. W. Bush and Clinton administrations continued the strategy of maintaining a preponderance of power through a deep security engagement in Europe, East Asia, and the Middle East first formulated by the Truman administration (Wohlforth 1999, 2002; Leffler 1993).

While there were post–Cold War changes in US force structure and military doctrine under Bush and Clinton (see Cohen 2001; and Kurth 2001), the main objectives of grand strategy remained unchanged. These were (1) to maintain US preponderance; (2) to prevent the reemergence of a multipolar international system within Europe; and (3) and to prevent the emergence of peer competitors, including the Peoples' Republic of China, Germany, a revanchist Russia, or a united European Union. NATO would serve as vehicle toward perpetuating the US role as a "European power." Consequently, the first Bush administration insisted that a reunified Germany be a full NATO member, as a means both to contain and control German ambitions in post–Cold War Europe and to marginalize Russia as a future player in European security (Layne 2000b; Zelikow and Rice 1995). It also reacted coldly to suggestions that a pan-European security institution, such as a Conference on Security and Cooperation in Europe (CSCE), or a multinational military/peacekeeping force under the auspices of the EU, might replace NATO (Art 1996, 1998–1999). In 1997 the Clinton administration not only extended NATO eastward to include Poland, Hungary, and the Czech Republic, but also expanded its mission into Europe's peripheries—the Caucasus, Central Asia, Ukraine, the Baltic States, and the Balkans. However, by assuming the role as Europe's stabilizer and insisting that a US-dominated NATO be at the center of the continent's security arrangements, the Clinton administration also inadvertently signaled its intention to prevent instability on the European periphery from threatening its core.

When Clinton assumed the presidency in January 1993, he inherited an escalating Bosnian war and growing calls from the EU for a more active US role in ending it. During the 1992 presidential campaign, Clinton strongly criticized Bush for not doing more to protect Bosnian Muslims, and in doing so raised expectations about possible US intervention (see Clymer 1992; and Fulwood 1992). Once in office, however, the new president was reluctant to intervene because of his inexperience in foreign policy, his discomfort with the military, and his ambitious domestic agenda (Daalder and O'Hanlon 2000a). In February 1993, Clinton's secretary of state, Warren Christopher, reiterated the previous administration's Christmas 1992 warning to Milosevic: "We remain prepared to respond against the Serbians in the event of conflict in Kosovo caused by Serb action" (Christopher 1993). However, the Bosnian war, not the simmering crisis in Kosovo, soon dominated the administration's foreign policy agenda.

Contradictions quickly emerged between the Clinton administration's insistence on the US role as a European power and its willingness to use military force in support of its stated political objectives. The resulting credibility dilemma would have implications for the Kosovo crisis in 1998–1999. The details of the Bosnian war and the Clinton national security team's rejection of the Vance-Owen Plan and support for the so-called lift and strike option despite British and French objections in 1993–1995 have been discussed elsewhere (see Daalder 1999). Suffice to say that after two years of hollow threats, during which an estimated 250,000 Bosnian Muslims died or disappeared, Clinton and his advisers concluded that a continuation of the war would further undermine the credibility of the US position as the European security guarantor. Again, neoclassical realism suggests that officials in Washington were not so much concerned about the credibility of NATO as an institution, but rather that alliance's preservation as a vehicle to perpetuate US hegemony in Europe. The president sent Richard Holbrooke, former assistant secretary of state for European affairs and former ambassador to Germany, to resolve the Bosnian war, backed by the threat of unilateral military action. This decision convinced NATO's North Atlantic Council (NAC) to authorize air strikes against Bosnian Serb targets in retaliation for the August 28, 1995, shelling of a Sarajevo market, which killed forty people. Operation Deliberate Force (ODF)—consisting of some 3,500 sorties launched between August 25 and September 14, 1995—coincided with counteroffensives by Bosnian Croat forces in the Krajina region and Bosnian Muslim forces around Sarajevo.

The resulting shift in the balance of forces in Bosnia, along with Milosevic's willingness to abandon his Bosnian Serb clients in order to secure the removal of UN sanctions, brought the Serbs to the bargaining table. Unfortunately, Clinton and his advisers inferred from the "success" of ODF that the mere threat of air strikes, or if necessary, several days of bombing, would be sufficient to ensure Serbia's compliance no matter what the issue at stake. At the same time, Milosevic inferred that the United States lacked the resolve to intervene decisively in another Balkan war. At best, the Clinton administration would respond in much the same way that it responded in Bosnia: frequent threats and deadlines for negotiations that it would reset once passed. At worst, the United States and its NATO allies would bomb for a few days and declare victory (Daalder and O'Hanlon 2000b: 94–95). When Holbrooke convened the Dayton peace conference, Kosovo was not on the agenda. "Bosnia was then the emergency, and it had to be stopped," he later recalled, adding, "otherwise there would have been a real risk that Bosnia would merge with Kosovo into a huge firestorm that would destabilize the whole region" (quoted in Sciolino and Bronner 1999: A1).

■ The Road to Rambouillet, January 1998–February 1999

Over the next several years, the gap widened between the Clinton administration's threats, on the one hand, and its willingness to carry out those threats, on the other. Furthermore, as Ivo Daalder and Michael O'Hanlon observe, the Clinton national security team preferred to use military force "in small, demonstrative doses, claiming that it had 'degraded' or 'damaged' an enemy's capabilities, declaring victory, and ending its combat operations regardless of the broader strategic implications of the outcome achieved" (2000b: 160). These two tendencies contributed to the escalation of the 1998 Kosovo crisis and eventually placed the administration in the position of having to wage war as a means to avert a further erosion of US prestige and credibility.

Throughout 1998, Secretary of State Madeleine Albright repeatedly threatened military force if Milosevic did not halt the crackdown on the KLA. On March 3 she declared: "We are not going to stand by and watch Serb authorities do in Kosovo what they can no longer get away with doing in Bosnia. The time to stop the killing is now, before it spreads. The way to do that is to take immediate action against the regime in Belgrade" (Albright 1998). During a March 8 meeting with UN Secretary-General Kofi Annan, Clinton said, "We do not want the Balkans to have more pictures like we've seen in the last few days, so reminiscent of what Bosnia endured" (Clinton 1998). Albright reminded the five-member Contact Group on March 9, "When the war in the former Yugoslavia began in 1991, the international community did not react with sufficient vigor and force. Each small act of aggression that we did not oppose led to larger acts of aggression that we could not oppose without great risk to ourselves. . . . This time, we must act with unity and resolve" (Isaacson 1999: 29).[9]

These statements suggest that officials had begun to see the Kosovo crisis as having broader implications for the US leadership role in NATO. However, as the crisis worsened over the next several months, they returned to a pattern of equivocation, repeated deadlines for negotiations, contradictory statements, and vague threats. While Albright and Robert Gelbard, special envoy to the Balkans, threatened air strikes, Sandy Berger, Clinton's national security adviser, worried about the consequences of making more empty threats or undertaking unilateral military action. Similarly, Secretary of Defense William Cohen recalled, "I was absolutely convinced that the United States could not afford to take any unilateral action, from a political viewpoint, and certainly we were not going to recommend to the president and to the Congress that we intervene unilaterally without NATO consensus and support" (PBS 2000).

■ Launching Operation Allied Force, March–April 1999

Neoclassical realism suggests that leaders of great powers are more likely to initiate military operations in peripheral regions as a means to avoid or halt a perceived loss in their state's relative power or prestige. In early 1999 the Clinton administration found itself in this predicament. For over a year, officials had repeatedly threatened to use force if Milosevic did not comply with US, Security Council, and Contact Group demands regarding Kosovo. A failure to act upon those threats would undermine US prestige within NATO, lead the allies to question the future of Washington's security commitment, and possibly set in motion an erosion of the hegemonic position of the United States in Europe. In a televised address to the American people on March 24, Clinton stated NATO's war aims:

> Our mission is clear: to demonstrate the seriousness of NATO's purpose so that the Serbian leaders understand the imperative of reversing course. To deter an even bloodier offensive against innocent civilians in Kosovo and, if necessary, to seriously damage the Serbian military's capacity to harm the people of Kosovo. In short, if President Milosevic will not make peace, we will limit his ability to make war. (Clinton 1999c)

Albright offered a similar rationale the following day: "First, we must be clear that there is one reason only that we have moved from diplomacy backed by the threat of force to the use of force backed by diplomacy. That reason is President Milosevic" (Albright 1999). Cohen described the air campaign's goal as demonstrating "the resolve of the part of NATO alliance" or "to make him [Milosevic] pay a substantial price" (quoted in Harris 1999: A20).

How then might neoclassical realism account for the Clinton administration's repeated invocation of NATO's credibility? It is worth noting that while Clinton, Albright, and others publicly justified the start of bombing in terms of the need to demonstrate NATO's resolve, the fact remains that the United States, not the alliance as a whole, had the leading diplomatic role in handling the Kosovo crisis up to that point (Daalder and O'Hanlon 2000b). The January 1999 Racak massacre, in which Serb forces killed forty-five Kosovars, violated an agreement that Milosevic had concluded with Holbrooke three months earlier (Crawford 2000–2001).

Furthermore, in any air campaign against Serbia, the United States would supply the majority of aircraft, and US Air Force and Navy personnel would fly most of the bombing missions. General Wesley Clark, concurrently NATO SACEUR and US CINCEUR, would command the entire operation. Most of Clark's subordinate commanders were US officers. For all of the congressional and public concern about burden sharing within the alliance, there was a gross disparity in capabilities between the United States and its closest allies. In short, from a strategic, operational, and tactical standpoint, the United States did not need allied help to wage war against Serbia. Cohen admitted as much in an interview after the Kosovo war: "If we were to carry out and act unilaterally, we would have a much more robust, aggressive, and decapitating campaign. . . . The difference here, of course, is that we are acting as an alliance" (PBS 2000).

As Daniel Byman and Matthew Waxman note, "the presence of international partners can expand the domestic coalition that supports the operation to include the partisans of the ally or alliance involved" (2002: 157). Recall that officials initiated the Kosovo war weeks after Clinton had survived an impeachment trial in the US Senate. The president's domestic standing, particularly with the Republican-led Congress, was at an all-time low. In spring 1999 the Clinton administration "could reasonably claim that the credibility of NATO was at stake in the operation, thereby helping to win the assent of opinion leaders who believed in preserving NATO as an important foreign policy goal even though they questioned the importance of saving Kosovo" (Byman and Waxman 2002: 157).

As neoclassical realism expects, when faced with perceived losses in US prestige at the hands of Milosevic in early 1999, the Clinton administration gravitated toward the riskier of two options, namely a phased air campaign against select Serb targets in Kosovo and Serbia proper. Admittedly, US-led air strikes were less risky that a full-scale invasion, in terms of both likely causalities and the cohesion of the alliance. However, ground operations in a "nonpermissive" environment were simply not under consideration in early 1999. General Klaus Naumann of Germany, the chairman of NATO's Military Committee, recalled that US officials tried to remove any consideration of using ground troops from the list of military options presented to the NAC in August 1998 (PBS 2000). The administration ruled out an invasion a month earlier and did not reconsider the decision until April 1999. As the Kosovo crisis escalated, the European allies signaled their opposition to the use of ground forces. Even British prime minister Tony Blair, the most hawkish of the NATO heads of government, told Clinton in January that "ground troops could not be used to fight a war [against Serbia]" (quoted in Sciolino and Bronner 1999: A12).

In January and February 1999, only two options remained under active consideration: continued negotiations brokered by the Contact Group and NATO or the initiation of an air campaign to coerce Milosevic's compliance. Neither option was risk-free. The first option, in effect, would require the administration and NATO to back down from the Contact Group's

January 29 ultimatum. This might have avoided US involvement in another Balkans war, but at the cost of a certain diminution in US prestige among the NATO allies.

The second option, the phased air campaign, was a gamble in several respects. First, the initiation of air strikes was a bluff. There was no consensus within the administration, let alone among the other NATO members, over what to do if hostilities extended beyond forty-eight hours. The war plan called for a "phased" air campaign, which implied the possibility of escalation should Belgrade not comply with the Contact Group's ultimatum. However, in order to achieve some semblance of consensus among the eighteen member states to back threats with military action, the administration postponed any decision regarding what escalation of OAF would actually entail. If Milosevic called the bluff, officials in Washington would face a choice between escalating the air campaign and reopening the contentious issue of ground operations in Kosovo.

Second, an air war was a risky option because there was a low chance that bombing—particularly bombing conducted at 15,000 feet—could achieve the policy aims Clinton announced on March 24, namely to *deter* Serb attacks on Kosovars. On the contrary, General Hugh Shelton, the chairman of the Joint Chiefs of Staff (JCS), had warned that, without an invasion threat, the air campaign would not deter the Serbs (Graham 1999). Third, there was a good chance that the bombing would lead the Serbs to escalate their crackdown on the Kosovars, code-named Operation Horseshoe. US intelligence officials warned that the air campaign would likely exacerbate the Kosovar refugee crisis and increase popular support for Milosevic among the Serbs (Kay 2000: 74; Whitney and Schmidt 1999).

■ Failure Is Not an Option, May–June 1999

The Clinton administration undertook a risky strategy in initiating OAF. As neoclassical realism expects, officials took additional risks in perpetuating and escalating the war, despite abundant evidence that their military strategies were not producing the desired political outcomes. The first two phases of the air war were largely irrelevant to the political objective set forth in the president's March 24 address. Instead, Serb forces accelerated their operations, and by late April nearly 1 million Kosovars had fled across the borders with Macedonia and Albania, while an additional 500,000 had become internal refugees (Daalder and O'Hanlon 2000b: 136; Arkin 2001: 26–27). As Barry Posen notes, "the weight of evidence suggests that NATO forces began the war over Kosovo without a well worked-out plan for employing air power to affect directly the ability of Serb forces to operate in Kosovo" (2000: 66).

The most divisive issues among the NATO allies concerned a possible ground invasion of Kosovo. Albright, who had been confident of a short war, concluded by early April that a victory over Serbia would require the introduction of ground forces. She failed, however, in her early attempts to persuade Cohen, Berger, and Clinton, who were inclined to simply escalate the bombing until Milosevic capitulated (Daalder and O'Hanlon 2000b: 137). Prime Minister Blair, who had warned against the deployment of ground forces in January, traveled to Washington on April 21, two days before the start of NATO's fiftieth anniversary summit (April 23–25), to make the case for an invasion to the administration. Clinton urged Blair to stop talking publicly about an invasion, because doing so had raised domestic problems for the other European allies and made the Russians unwilling to serve as mediator between Belgrade and NATO. In exchange, Clinton privately agreed to a compromise under which NATO Secretary-General Javier Solana could use his personal authority to ask Clark to reassess plans for a ground war prepared in summer 1998 (Daalder and O'Hanlon 2000b: 138–139). The NATO summit communiqué expressed the alliance's determination to win in Kosovo, but it contained no mention of a possible ground invasion, largely in deference to European opinion.

By mid-May, Clark developed preliminary plans for an attack on Kosovo from the south by 175,000 troops, of whom 100,000 would be Americans, mostly through a single road from Albania (Daalder and O'Hanlon 2000b: 157; Priest 1999: A1; Erlanger 1999b, sec. 1: 6). On May 18, Clinton pointedly said that "all options were on the table" with respect to Kosovo, and within days Clark had arrived in Washington to discuss war plans with the JCS. Clinton agreed in a May 23 telephone conversation with Blair to give Solana approval to formulate a detailed plan for ground operations. He also approved the deployment of up to 45,000 NATO troops (including 7,200 Americans) in Macedonia to serve as the core of either a NATO occupation force in Kosovo, if Milosevic capitulated, or the core of an invasion force, if he did not (Erlanger 1999b, sec. 1: 6).

On June 2, Berger convened a White House meeting of several foreign policy experts who had publicly advocated sending ground troops into Kosovo, including Jeane Kirkpatrick, a former ambassador to the United Nations in the Reagan administration; William Howard Taft IV, a former ambassador to NATO and a former deputy secretary of defense in the Reagan administration; General George Joulwan (retired), Clark's immediate predecessor as SACEUR; Robert Hunter, another former ambassador to NATO; and Ivo Daalder, a former member of the National Security Council (NSC) staff during the Bosnian war. Berger told the gathering that US policy proceeded from four facts: "First, we will win. . . . There is no alternative. Second, winning means what we said it means. Third, the air campaign is having a serious impact. Fourth, the president has said that he has not ruled out any options. Go back to 1: we will win" (quoted in Daalder and O'Hanlon 2000b: 158). The national security adviser then elaborated on the four points. Berger noted that failure to win "would do serious, if not irreparable harm, to the US, NATO, and European stability." Winning the war, on the other hand, meant Belgrade's acceptance of an international military force "with NATO at its core" to deploy in Kosovo so that all refugees could return home. According to Berger, the administration would win "in or outside NATO. . . . [A] consensus in NATO is valuable. But it is not a *sine qua non*. We want to move with NATO, but it can't prevent us from moving" (quoted in Erlanger 1999b, sec. 1: 6).

The fact that they did so and that the likelihood of a US-led ground attack increased in May and June is perfectly consistent with neoclassical realism: the administration escalated its commitment to risky (albeit ineffectual) bombing strategy and made preparations for a ground invasion as well. To admit that OAF had failed to achieve the aims Clinton set forth on March 24 would call the US leadership role in NATO, and thus its status as Europe's security guarantor, further into question. Ultimately, the Clinton administration prevailed in the interalliance debate over an invasion because of the tremendous power disparity between the United States and the other members of NATO. As Berger noted, the United States could and would act without the support of its allies in order to end the Kosovo war successfully.

■ Conclusion

Operation Allied Force ranks as one of the most lopsided military conflicts in modern history. The United States enjoys overwhelming preponderance in all categories of material power. Its defense budget for fiscal year 1999 ($454 billion) was fifteen times the size of Yugoslavia's entire gross domestic product ($19 billion). The United States has a population of 220 million people, compared to 10 million people in Serbia and Montenegro. While the US armed forces have the world's most advanced military technology and power projection capabilities, the Yugoslav army missed a generation of military technological modernization. Serbia has no military allies, a relatively basic military industry, and an economy crippled by a decade of UN sanctions and continual warfare (see Posen 2000: 49–50; and International Institute for Strategic Studies 1998).

Neoclassical realism highlights the importance of power distributions, as well as elite perceptions of relative power and prestige, in shaping foreign policy. The argument developed here is not limited to the Clinton administration's conduct of the 1999 Kosovo war. It has relevance in explaining international history and current policy issues. History abounds with cases in which states have pursued relatively risky interventions in peripheral areas because their leaders feared a loss of relative power and prestige. Examples include Athens's expedition to Sicily during the Peloponnesian War, Britain's involvement in the two Afghan wars in the nineteenth century, Japan's pursuit of economic autarky through empire in Southeast Asia in the 1940s, France's war against independence movements in Indochina and Algeria in the 1950s, the US interventions in the Korean War and later the Vietnam War, and the Soviet Union's invasion and occupation of Afghanistan in the 1980s (Taliaferro 2004). Furthermore, in each of these cases, leaders persisted in failing interventions despite mounting political, economic, and military costs. While the Kosovo war was illustrative of this dynamic, it was unusual in that the geopolitical stakes and the costs incurred by the United States were quite low.

Neoclassical realism is also useful in understanding how the George W. Bush administration responded to international challenges in the aftermath of the September 11, 2001, terrorist attacks. The administration found itself drawn into expanding the war on terrorism to Iraq and elsewhere, not because of any objective or immediate threat to US security, but rather to avert the possibility that so-called rogue states and terrorist organizations might acquire or use weapons of mass destruction in the future. Fear of potential relative power loss and challenges to US prestige appeared to drive the administration's strategy, at least in part.[10] The potential dangers for the United States are twofold. The first danger is entrapment in the periphery. Preventive war to remove rogue regimes entails the prolonged occupation and reconstruction of those countries. As the events of summer 2003 illustrated, the presence of large numbers of US troops in Iraq exacerbated popular anger, and postwar occupations of restive populations can quickly degenerate into guerrilla warfare. The second danger of a preventive war strategy involves US relations with second-tier great powers and regional states. While full-scale great power balancing against Washington is unlikely in the near future, other states can, have, and will continue to withhold cooperation in a number of areas.

■ Notes

1. Scholarly debates about the Kosovo war focus on the utility of air power as a coercive tool (Stigler 2002–2003; Byman and Waxman 2000; Byman, Waxman, and Larson 1999); the implications for the so-called revolution in military affairs (Cohen 2001; Kurth 2001; Vickers 2001); the growing capabilities gap between the United States and its European allies (Tonelson 2000: esp. 46–54; Parmentier 2000; Yost 2000; Peters et al. 2001); the balance between human rights and state sovereignty (Roberts 1999; Wheeler 2000; Booth 2001; Coll 2001); the factors that contributed to Milosevic's capitulation (Posen 2000; Hosmer 2000); and the effectiveness of NATO peacekeeping operations and postwar relations with Kosovo's Serb and Albanian populations (Daalder and O'Hanlon 2000b; Hodge 2001; O'Neill 2002).

2. This is an oversimplification of the diversity of views among self-identified realists on the role of international institutions, domestic politics, and ideas. For more detailed discussions of each, see Copeland 2000, Desch 1998, Desch 2003, Jervis 1999, Mearsheimer 1994–1995, Schweller and Priess 1997, Sterling-Folker 1997, and Sterling-Folker 2002.

3. There is actually a vigorous debate over whether neorealism (or structural realism) provides a theory of foreign policy. While Waltz claims that his balance-of-power theory only purports to explain broad systemic outcomes, he repeatedly uses that theory to make very specific (albeit probabilistic) inferences about US foreign policy (Waltz 1979, 1986, 1996, 2002). Other contributions to this debate include Elman 1996a, Elman 1996b, Zakaria 1998, Rose 1998, and Taliaferro 2000–2001. For an argument that challenges this distinction between theories of international politics and foreign policy, see Telhami 2002.

4. Rose cites Brown et al. 1995, Christensen 1996, Schweller 1998, Wohlforth 1993, and Zakaria 1998 as examples of neoclassical realism. Other works that explicitly adopt the neoclassical realist label or that are broadly consistent with neoclassical realism include Friedberg 1988, Markey 1999, Brooks and Wohlforth 2000–2001, Cha 2000, Cha 2002, Byman and Pollack 2001, Rynning and Gallois 2001, Byman and Waxman 2000, and Taliaferro 2004.

5. For other discussions of the relationship between neoclassical realism and structural realism (or neorealism), see Glaser 2003, Walt 2002, Rose 1998, and Brooks 1997. One can further divide structural realism into defensive realism and offensive realism. The offensive and defensive variants are competing in that they disagree over the prevalence of conflict actually caused by the international system. See Taliaferro 2000–2001, Walt 2002, and Glaser 2003. However, neither offensive realism nor defensive realism are necessarily inconsistent with neoclassical realism. Contrary to Rose (1998), I do not see defensive realism, offensive realism, and neoclassical realism as competing foreign policy theories.

6. Although they parted company with classical realism in many respects, proponents of power transition and hegemonic stability theories expanded upon this relationship between material power and status hierarchies (see Organski 1968: 106–111; Kugler and Lemke 2000: 130–140; DiCicco and Levy 1999; and Levy 1998).

7. In this respect, Gilpin (1981) parts company with Waltz (1979). Gilpin's hegemonic theory of war and change explicitly links the distribution of prestige among the great powers with the likelihood of major (or hegemonic) war. He writes, "an inconsistency may, and in time does, arise between the established hierarchy of prestige and the existing distribution of power among states. As a consequence the governance of the system begins to break down as perceptions catch up with the realities of power" (1981: 33). For Gilpin then, prestige, rather than material power, is the everyday currency of world politics.

8. Prospect theory, a psychological model of decisionmaking under conditions of risk and uncertainty, underpins this aspect of my theory. Briefly, prospect theory provides a descriptive and predictive explanation for why people are extremely sensitive to losses, why they value what they possess more than what they seek to acquire, and why they display different risk propensities when faced with prospective gains or losses (see Levy 1994a, 1994b, 1997, 2000; Jervis 1994; and Tversky and Kahneman 2000a, 2000b). Elsewhere, I discuss how prospect theory provides a firm behavioral foundation for neoclassical realism and defensive realism (Taliaferro 2001, 2004).

9. The Contact Group for the former Yugoslavia consists of the foreign min-

isters of the United States, the United Kingdom, France, Germany, Italy, and the Russian Federation.

10. An examination of the George W. Bush administration's complex motivations for going to war against Iraq in March 2003 (Operation Iraqi Freedom) is beyond the scope of this chapter and the volume as a whole. Rather, I am only addressing one of the leading public rationales for the war.

chapter 3

Liberal Approaches

Jennifer Sterling-Folker

Liberalism

If realism can be characterized as the dominant theory in the discipline, liberalism must certainly be identified as its primary theoretical competitor. To some extent the research programs of realists and liberals have converged over the years, particularly in their shared focus on the nation-state as the central actor in contemporary world politics. This focus was antithetical to earlier liberal IR literature, which was usually called "pluralism" due to its claims that a variety of nonstate, transnational actors and forces were gradually breaking down nation-state boundaries and transforming world politics in the process.[1] This claim has been moderated over time, so that today most liberal scholars work with a state-centric perspective instead. Yet the beliefs that inform contemporary liberal IR theory still remain exactly opposite those of realism. There are many variants of liberal IR theory, but "the first thesis" of all liberal theories is, according to Mark Zacher and Richard Matthews, "that international relations are gradually becoming transformed such that they promote greater human freedom by establishing conditions of peace, prosperity, and justice" (1995: 109). Thus, what all liberal variants share is a faith "in at least the possibility of cumulative progress" in human affairs (Keohane 1990: 174).

This faith sharply distinguishes liberal scholars not only from realist scholars but from many other theoretical perspectives in the discipline as well. It is derived directly from the writings of such European Enlightenment philosophers as John Locke, Jean Jacques Rousseau, and Immanuel Kant, and it reflects "a belief in the human capacity to reason, and with that reason, the possibility of uncovering untainted universal truth" (Enloe 1996: 187). Liberal IR scholars have relatively greater faith in the ability of human beings to obtain progressively better collective outcomes as a result. Although prior liberal IR theorizing has often been disparagingly characterized as mere "idealism" by its critics, such a label is both unfair and misleading. Liberal IR theorizing consists of a variety of distinct strands, all of which are sophisticated analytical statements about both the possibilities and the difficulties of achieving beneficial collective outcomes. It would be more accurate to describe liberalism as the exploration of what *prevents* progress from being achieved, with the underlying assumption being that progress could be realized if we could uncover the barriers to collective action and promote their resolutions.

There are several strands of contemporary liberal IR theory, focusing on different types of collective actions, barriers, and possibilities. One strand has its philosophical precursor in the work of Kant and is sometimes called republican liberalism or democratic peace research. It focuses on how the increasing number of democracies in the world might promote greater international peace and cooperation, because democracies appear to be pacifistic in their foreign relations with one another. Other strands focus on how a condition of interdependence in certain issue areas, such as capitalist markets, military technology, or the natural environment, could generate common interests that are only obtainable with international cooperation. Still other strands focus on the importance of education or knowledge to the shaping of values, interests, and priorities, or on the impact of international organizations and transnational interaction as facilitators for international cooperation. Despite these differences in focus, all of these strands share a set of common assumptions about contemporary world politics that make them more compatible than explanatory competitors.

First, liberal scholars assume that the possibilities of cooperation have increased over time due to the processes of industrialization and modernization. Many liberal IR scholars concur that realism is a relatively accurate way to describe world politics prior to the nineteenth century, and it may still be an appropriate way to examine some arenas of world politics (Goldgeier and McFaul 1992). They argue, however, that realism ignores or misunderstands the significant changes that have occurred in the daily conduct of global affairs. At the push of a button, human beings now have the ability to communicate, drop bombs, and move vast sums of money regardless of distance. While other theoretical perspectives interpret such developments as simply new and more efficient ways to compete for power or oppress people, liberal IR scholars argue that these changes can provide greater opportunities for cooperation in world politics. How this is possible is best reflected in the strand of liberalism that highlights interdependence, since this has spawned some of the more influential liberal research programs in the discipline.

Liberal interdependence scholars posit that processes of modernization have led to a condition of interdependence in particular issue areas of world politics, where nation-state behavior has reciprocal, unintended, and often negative effects. This condition sets the stage for common interests among nation-states. Capitalist economics and environmental degradation are two exemplary issue areas. The pace and scope of industrialization now threaten to deplete Earth's ozone layer. This is a problem that all nation-states are responsible for producing and that is creating reciprocal, negative effects on each of them. The problem does not recognize national boundaries or the relative power among nation-states, nor is it amenable to violent resolution or unilateral action. All nation-states have a common interest in finding a solution to the problem as a result, and it can only be resolved through cooperative efforts. Thus there is greater potential for cooperation in this particular issue area. Similarly, those nation-states whose capitalist markets are most advanced are also the most economically entwined, which means they can only maintain their levels of profit and gross national product through free trade with one another. These nation-states have a common interest in maintaining open markets, eschewing unilateral action, and cooperating with one another to this end. Hence global economics is an issue area in which there is a potential for cooperation, and it, along with other issue areas that are characterized by relatively higher levels of interdependence, is the primary focus of liberal IR scholarship.

This does not mean that liberals believe cooperation will automatically occur in these issue areas, however, because the second assumption that all liberal variants share is that significant barriers exist to the realization of cooperation. Robert Keohane notes, for example, that Romeo and Juliet clearly shared common interests, yet "actors may fail to cooperate even when their interests are entirely identical" (1984: 65). Even when common interests exist—in cleaning up the environment, preventing nuclear disasters, resolving a global financial crisis, or stopping a civil war—there are still significant barriers to achieving collective action. Actors may lack information about one another's true preferences, they may fear that others will cheat by taking advantage of their cooperation, they may wish to prevent others from free-riding off their cooperative efforts, or they may wish to avoid the transaction costs that a cooperative deal might entail. All of these factors might prevent cooperation from being achieved, even if all actors involved recognize that they have a common problem and that cooperation would be the best solution to that problem.

A third assumption that liberal IR variants share is the belief that information and communication can play an essential role in overcoming barriers to collective action. This is because improved knowledge and communications allow nation-state decisionmakers and other actors to realize that they have common interests that might not have existed in prior historical periods. Ongoing interaction and information sharing can also reveal true preferences, build trust in one another's intentions, and uncover concerns about cheating, free-riding, or transaction costs, which can then be addressed directly by negotiators and decisionmakers (Axelrod 1981; Oye 1986). Anything that promotes the ongoing exchange of information and communication among nation-state decisionmakers is of interest to liberal scholars as a result. Technological advances and relative power, in the form of a hegemonic state willing to facilitate economic interaction, are often cited as key underlying factors for increased interaction among nation-state decisionmakers and hence cooperation (Keohane and Nye 1998; Keohane 1984).

Many liberal scholars also argue that the necessary ongoing interaction between nation-states has been promoted by the development of international institutions. These may be formal institutions, such as the UN, the EU, and NATO, or they may be informal, consisting of "sets of implicit or explicit principles, norms, rules, and decision-making procedures around which actors' expectations converge in a given area of international relations" (Krasner 1983: 2). The latter are called "regimes" in the liberal literature, and the term is used to refer to all the cooperative elements in a given issue area. There is, for example, a regime of capitalist free trade that consists not simply of formal IOs, such as the WTO, but also of a myriad of international laws, practices, norms, and rules of behavior, all of which are informed by such principles as reciprocity and most-favored-nation clauses. Thus "regimes" is the umbrella term for all of the elements that assist cooperation in an issue area characterized by high levels of interdependence.

Although IOs or international regimes are not central to every variant of liberal IR theory, the integral role that institutions play in collective efforts is the fourth assumption shared by liberal IR scholars. As Keohane puts it, liberalism "seeks to understand how aggregations of individuals make collective decisions and how organizations composed of individuals interact" (1990: 174; see also 1989). In exploring this topic, there is a shared assumption among liberal IR scholars that the structure or design of collective institutions and organizations plays a large role in determining the extent to which cooperation can be achieved. The strand of liberal theorizing that focuses on the democratic peace, for example, understands the state "to be, at root, an institution designed to solve the problems of collective action rather than an institution which was central to the constitution of the collectivity itself, and to individual personality" (Brown 2000: 209). Democratic states may then be regarded as a particular type of institutional governing arrangement that, when compared to other types of arrangements, can more effectively resolve collective action problems on an international scale. How and why this particular type of institutional arrangement produces such an outcome has been the central focus of the democratic peace literature.

One of the best-known variants of liberal IR theory in the discipline is neoliberal institutionalism (NLI), sometimes called rational choice institutionalism, and the first theoretical application in this chapter is an example of it. NLI relies on the concepts of interdependence and regimes to explore how existing international institutions assist nation-states in obtaining collective ends. According to Robert Jervis (1999: 48), because NLI scholars "believe that there are many mutually beneficial arrangements that states forgo because of the fear that others will cheat or take advantage of them, they see important gains to be made through the more artful arrangement of policies." Thus in Chapter 3.2, Sean Kay examines the extent to which NATO's institutional attributes facilitated military cooperation over Kosovo, with an eye to making policy recommendations for how NATO's structure might be redesigned to assist such efforts more effectively (see also Kay 2000). NLI has led to a variety of related research programs that focus on particular aspects of its general propositions, including the study of the rational design of institutions (Koremenos, Lipson, and Snidal 2001) and principal-agent theory, which examines why nation-states delegate authority to IOs in the first place.

The second theoretical application in this chapter works within the general liberal framework, but represents an example of public goods analysis instead. Public goods produce a particular type of collective action problem, because actors who do not contribute to their provision cannot be excluded from enjoying them. The traditional example of a public good is the state's provision of a public park, which can be enjoyed even by those who do not pay their taxes. While public goods analysis is drawn from the study of economics, in IR it has often been applied to collective national security and alliances such as NATO, in which free-riding is argued to be a central problem of the cooperative effort (Olson 1965; Sandler 1977; Sandler and Forbes 1980). In Chapter 3.3, Mark Boyer and Michael Butler argue that security in Kosovo represented a public good for the members of NATO, and they explore how problems endemic to the provision of this sort of public good were finally resolved in favor of intervention.

Both selections are concerned with exploring the impediments to collective action, and yet both are also driven by the underlying rationale that, in revealing such barriers, it might also be possible to overcome them in the future. In so doing, they reflect the liberal belief "that mutualities of interests and noncoercive bargaining will become more prominent features of international life" (Zacher and Matthews 1995: 110). That said, few liberal scholars are comfortable with Francis Fukuyama's bold claim that, with the end of the Cold War, we have reached "the end of history" because liberalism's triumph reflects "the end point of mankind's ideological evolution and the universalization of Western liberal democracy as the final form of human government" (1989: 4). Zacher and Matthews point out that such teleological thinking may actually violate classical liberal theory, which "does not project the emergence of a particular historical end state in which humankind will realize perfect freedom" but argues instead that progress will be varied and can only be achieved through the antagonism of ideas (1995: 109; see also Richardson 2001a). While a faith that there can be progress in human affairs informs all liberal scholarship, ultimately liberalism in IR is not a philosophical statement about human perfectibility, but an analytical project concerned with exploring the possibilities of international peace and cooperation.

■ Further Reading

One of the most influential scholars in early liberal IR theorizing was David Mitrany, who argued for a functional approach to global problems in *A Working Peace System* (1943). Functionalism asserted that most global problems were largely technical and nonpolitical, and could be dealt with more effectively by functional experts rather than politicians. The approach later evolved into neofunctionalism, which was primarily associated with the study of integration in Europe and best reflected in the work of Ernst Haas (1958, 1964). Haas directly influenced the work of Robert Keohane and Joseph Nye, who are two of the more prominent scholars in contemporary liberal IR theorizing. Their transnational relations theory (1971; see also Risse-Kappen 1995a) was later supplanted by their complex interdependence and regimes argument, which is articulated in *Power and Interdependence* (Keohane and Nye 1977) and *After Hegemony* (Keohane 1984). It is based on these texts that the NLI approach and a number of other liberal research programs in the discipline evolved.

Succinct overviews of liberalism and its various strands, as well as examples of liberal descriptions of contemporary world politics, can be found in Doyle 1986, Held 1996, Fukuyama 1989, Jervis 1991–1992, Keohane 1990, Zacher 1992, and Zacher and Matthews 1995. Another good overview is the introductory chapter of Adler and Crawford 1991, which is a tribute to the impact of Haas's work on the discipline. The contemporary literature on the democratic peace is vast, but representative work includes Chan 1997, Doyle 1997, Maoz and Russett 1993, Risse-Kappen 1995b, Rummel 1979, and Russett 1993.

The study of interdependence and regimes in capitalist free trade has its philosophical precursors in the work of Adam Smith and David Ricardo, and it has been a subject of inquiry among liberal scholars since the late nineteenth century (Delaisi 1925; de Wilde 1991). More contemporary liberal work, besides the work of Keohane and Nye, includes Cooper 1968, Morse 1976, Rosecrance 1986, Rosenau 1976, and Rosenau 1980. Liberal scholarship has explored a variety of particular issue areas from a regimes perspective, including Young 1989, on environmental regimes; Zacher with

Sutton 1996, on communication regimes; Donnelly 1986, on human rights regimes; and Jervis 1983, Haftendorn, Keohane, and Wallander 1999, and Martin 1992, on security regimes.

Building on the NLI literature is rational design theory, which is best represented by a special issue of *International Organization* edited by Barbara Koremenos, Charles Lipson, and Duncan Snidal (2001), and can also been found in Martin and Simmons 1998, Wallander 2000, and Wallander and Keohane 1999. Principal-agent theory works from an NLI foundation as well, and some representative examples of it include Hug 2003, Nielson and Tierney 2003, Pollack 1997, and Thatcher and Sweet 2003. Overviews of the regimes literature in IR, and general defenses of it, are provided in Keohane and Martin 1995, Keohane 1998, Krasner 1983, Hasenclever, Mayer, and Rittberger 1997, and Rittberger 1993.

Examples of liberal IR works that focus on military technology, interdependence, and deterrence include Brodie 1946, Jervis 1989, Mueller 1989, and Nye 1987. Examples of liberal IR work that explore the role of education, knowledge, and ideas in IR cooperation are Adler and Crawford 1991, Goldstein and Keohane 1993, Haas 1990, Haas 1997, and Ray 1989. The best example of liberal work on communication flows and cultural patterns remains Deutsch et al. 1957. Seminal works in IR public goods analysis include Boyer 1993, Cornes and Sandler 1984, Olson 1965, Sandler 1977, Sandler 1992, and Sandler 1997.

■ Note

1. Liberalism and pluralism are not exactly the same thing, although the relationship between them is quite close. Classical liberalism is a political philosophy, best reflected in the work of Locke and Rousseau, that considers the individual to be the most important unit of analysis and argues that the state should play a minimal role in politics and economics. Pluralism, on the other hand, was a label drawn from the study of political science in general, and Richard Little notes that "it applies to a school of thought that defines politics in terms of the interaction among competing interest groups and largely deprives the state of any independent status" (1996: 68). Most IR authors who were grouped under the pluralist label did not actually use the term to describe themselves, but they did share a number of assumptions, including that nonstate actors were important entities in world politics, that the nation-state was not a unitary, rational actor, and that the agenda of international politics was more extensive than realists allowed (Viotti and Kauppi 1999: 199–200). These assumptions were certainly compatible with the tenets of liberalism, but they were not directly derived from it and developed instead within the confines of the IR discipline as a reaction to realist theorizing. The differences between pluralism and liberalism are relatively minimal, however, and today liberalism is the preferred umbrella term for IR scholars who work within this tradition.

3.2 Sean Kay

Neoliberalism: Institutions at War

This chapter examines the applicability of neoliberal institutional theory in times of international conflict. The role of NATO and the relationship between its institutional attributes and warfighting are applied to the case of its 1999 war in Kosovo. The evidence shows that neoliberal theory explains why the NATO allies went to war when they did and why they fought as they did. However, core neoliberal assumptions that information sharing, rules, and decisionmaking procedures can lower the transaction costs of cooperation are disproved. These results have serious implications for NATO and illustrate both the uses and the limitations of neoliberal theory.

■ Institutions and Security

Neoliberal theory posits that formal international institutions can make international cooperation easier to attain than in their absence. International institutions reflect the general, embedded framework of international principles, rules, norms, and decisionmaking procedures around which states seeking to maximize their interests will converge (Krasner 1983; Keohane 1989). Neoliberal theory looks to state behavior in formal international institutions as evidence that, in an interdependent world, states will seek efficiency in managing collective problems presented by international anarchy. International institutions also help states to both define acceptable international behavior and to provide for a means of punishing defectors from agreed community standards.

Traditionally, neoliberal institutional theory focused on issues such as economic and environmental cooperation, whereas security studies were dominated by the classical realist and neorealist schools of international relations. Security, after all, places high value on the risks from failure of cooperation in that a state's very survival might be at stake. However, with the end of the Cold War, some neoliberal scholars saw the adaptation of institutions such as NATO as evidence that institutions mattered in the security realm (Weber 1992; Duffield 1996; McCalla 1996; Wallander 2000). As Robert Keohane, Joseph Nye, and Stanley Hoffmann (1993: 2–3) have shown, some types of security institutions can aid the exercise of influence, constrain bargaining strategies, balance or replace other institutions, signal governments' intentions by providing others with information and making policies more predictable, specify obligations, and impact both the interests and preferences of states. Charles Kupchan (1994: 50–51) shows that institutions are relevant to security because they increase the level of information available to all parties by enhancing transparency, raising the costs of defection and defining what constitutes defection, increasing the likelihood of issue linkage, and advancing interstate socialization by promoting the concept of an international community. Also, institutions are seen as important mechanisms for lowering the costs of establishing international cooperation and creating more efficient outcomes (Keohane 1984; Wallander 2000).

It is important to note what neoliberal theory does not posit. Neoliberal scholars do not maintain that institutions matter in all cases. Moreover, the theory does not suggest that institutions act independent of the distribution of power among states. Also, neoliberal scholarship does not intrinsically assume that states pursuing policy guided by liberal assumptions of international politics will necessarily produce peaceful outcomes. As the leading neoliberal scholar, Keohane writes, "neoliberal approaches can backfire as policy prescriptions" (2002: 54). Neoliberal scholars concede that cooperation under international anarchy is difficult to achieve (Keohane 1984). However, the theory posits that multilateral cooperation will, under some conditions, be easier to accomplish than in the absence of formal international institutions.

This chapter uses two core components of neoliberal institutional theory to shed light on the effectiveness of NATO as an international institution as it performed during the Kosovo war. First, NATO's decision to launch an offensive war against Yugoslavia is assessed in terms of the content of the principles and norms that came to reflect NATO's institutional mandate by the late 1990s. Second, the relationship between information sharing, rules, and decisionmaking procedures within NATO are examined to test the ability of an institution to lower the transaction costs of international security provision. When security is at stake, it is crucial for neoliberal theory to be held to a very hard test. Neoliberal scholarship that focuses only on the adaptation of international institutions to a new security environment only tells half of a story. The relationship between institutions as an independent variable and the provision of security as a dependent variable must also be considered if students of international relations and policymakers are to have a sound understanding of how international institutions matter.

■ Principles and Norms: NATO Goes to War

Neoliberal theory assumes that states are interest-maximizing, rational actors. In that sense, the approach does not necessarily say much about the content of principles and norms—but rather presumes that states will define these as most befitting their common interests. However, as states converge on shared normative assumptions, institutions become important promoters of community values and also tools for channeling enforcement policies (Abbott and Snidal 1998). NATO's post–Cold War mission reflects a transition from collective defense organized to defend against an attack from the Soviet Union to a new mission of spreading Western values. NATO would be a tool for consolidating Western principles and norms in Central and Eastern Europe. Strategic benefits from sustaining NATO would also matter—including sustaining the transatlantic relationship, reassuring its neighbors about the rising power of united Germany, and hedging against any future Russian threat. However, the daily routine in NATO came to reflect the functional application of a new normative policy agenda establishing a particularistic set of principles and norms of international cooperation both among, and extending beyond, institutional membership.

The 1998–1999 Kosovo crisis was elevated to a top-tier security problem not because of the threat from the internal conflict, which had been and could be contained. Rather, the credibility of an institution—NATO—that the United States and its European allies cared about was being undermined. Instability and humanitarian crises in Kosovo directly threatened NATO's "New Strategic Concept," approved in the midst of the war at its April 1999 Washington summit. The institution's new mission was to "stand firm against those who violate human rights, wage war and conquer territory." NATO would "contribute to building a stronger and broader Euro-Atlantic community of democracies—a community where human rights and fundamental freedoms are upheld; where borders are increasingly open to people; ideas and commerce; where war becomes unthinkable."

Up to 1998, Kosovo had been managed by a bilateral deterrent threat from the United States, which warned Belgrade at Christmas 1992 that any military action taken by the Serbs against ethnic Albanians in Kosovo would be met with a forceful response. However, the need to attain international legitimacy for carrying out this threat converged with the need to rescue the credibility of NATO's new mission, and prompted Washington to shift its bilateral approach to the multilateral channels of NATO. Quickly, divergent policy priorities between Washington, which sought a credible threat of force against the Serbs, and the European allies, which hoped to delay implementing such a threat or first achieve United Nations approval, froze NATO into inaction. The decision to multilateralize its Kosovo policy via the formal institutional procedures of NATO best explains why there was no use of force in fall 1998. NATO would go through a symbolic exercise of releasing military activation orders. However, the internal divisions among the NATO members over the actual authorization of force prevented implementation. By March 1999, when diplomatic efforts to negotiate a settlement between Kosovar Albanians and Serbs had reached their limit, the European allies agreed to authorize war via NATO—a year after the crisis in Kosovo began. Even the most skeptical NATO allies, such as Greece, where 90 percent of its public opposed war, favored NATO's credibility over immediate interests.

Neoliberal theory provides an important, if not the best, explanation for why NATO went to war in Kosovo when it did. NATO served as a means to constrain the United States from acting in fall 1998, but when its members crossed a threshold of concern for the credibility of the institution, they agreed to launch a war in March 1999. This would be NATO's second major foray into the Balkans and it had now been through ten years of post–Cold War adaptation for this very kind of crisis. Its members thus had reason to believe that NATO's role in warfighting would be positive. Once at war, however, NATO's members could not agree on policies that would effectively align the institution with the principles and norms that it was intended to defend and promote.

When NATO went to war, it violated a basic principle of international law as codified in the United Nations. According to the UN Charter, which all NATO members are signatory to, only the Security Council can authorize the use of force for the kind of humanitarian campaign that NATO waged. By disregarding the UN Charter, NATO's members actually infringed on the core principles of their own institution. Article 1 of the North Atlantic Treaty states that the members must "refrain from the use of force in any manner inconsistent with the purposes of the United Nations." Article 7 of the NATO treaty requires its members to respect "the primary responsibility of the Security Council for the maintenance of international peace and security." NATO members rationalized, nevertheless, that they were acting in the spirit of the UN and its human rights dimensions by intervening against Serbia.

While NATO eventually did win the war, the means of the fighting raise questions about whether it was acting consistently with stated principles and norms. When NATO bombed, its members could only agree to do so above 15,000 feet, to protect allied pilots and aircraft. Scores of innocent civilians were accidentally killed by NATO bombs because of poor target identification—including a large convoy of misidentified Albanian refugees. NATO's bombing strategy eventually led it to target and bomb Serb civilian infrastructure, particularly electric power grids, which also damaged drinking water. Attacking civilian targets was necessary to pressure Slobodan Milosevic and his political allies in Belgrade. However, this action was a technical violation of the principles of the international law of war. NATO's tactics seemed to imply that the only way to protect innocent civilians was to make other innocent civilians feel pain. When the war ended and ethnic Albanians returned to Kosovo, about 100,000 ethnic Serbs were forced from their homes in reverse ethnic cleansing. Now, however, NATO troops were present on the ground and did not stop it.

In fighting for principles and norms, NATO was challenged by an internal irony created by its membership: Why was Serbia held to a higher moral standard than NATO's own member Turkey? Turkey consistently violates Kurdish human rights in its antiterrorist campaign against the Kurdish Workers Party (PKK). The US State Department reports of Turkey that, "as part of its fight against the PKK, the Government forcibly displaced non-combatants, failed to resolve extra-judicial killings, tortured civilians, and abridged freedom of expression" (US Department of State 1999b). Turkey had forcibly removed approximately 560,000 villagers from their homes and depopulated between 2,600 and 3,000 villages in the Kurdish southeastern region of the country. Between 1984 and 1999, some 23,638 PKK and 5,302 noncombatant civilians had been killed by Turkish security forces. NATO as an institution has done nothing to challenge its own member, even though by spring 1999 only 2,000 ethnic Albanians had been killed by Serb forces—less than 10 percent of the number of Kurds killed by Turkey.

These caveats do not negate neoliberal assumptions about international cooperation, but do indicate a high degree of competing national priorities, confusion, and inconsistency. However, the proposition that states will use a variety of means channeled through international institutions, including warfighting, to advance community standards of state behavior, is confirmed by the decision to wage war through a formalized multilateral institution. The degree of emphasis that its members placed on NATO as an institution together with the desire to sustain institutional credibility was the primary reason that war broke out when it did and in the manner that it did. NATO served as a mechanism through which small states could constrain larger ones and thus have an impact on international agenda setting that they would not otherwise have shared. Moreover, when the United States went to war, it was forced by the nature of the institution to choose a warfighting doctrine far removed from its strategic preferences. The presence of NATO raised a third-tier security problem into a first-order concern for the great powers. In return, the leading NATO members, especially the United States, gained a degree of international legitimacy for implementing their policy toward Kosovo.

■ Information Sharing, Transaction Costs, and Security

A second key test of neoliberal institutional theory and NATO's war in Kosovo is derived from the proposition that, as states coordinate multilateral policy, institutions will lower the transaction costs of cooperation in ways that would not be possible were there no institution available. Information sharing facilitated via institutional rules and decisionmaking procedures is seen as helping states better identify security challenges, overcome various obstacles to cooperation, and therefore produce efficiency gains in security management. Neoliberal theory often measures transaction costs in terms of the relative benefits of working through an international institution versus other alternatives. The assumption is that states can reap efficiency gains via institutional cooperation.

Information sharing as embodied in multinational planning and exercising is the lifeblood of NATO's institutional activity. NATO's "habit of consultation" emerged in the 1950s to ensure that conflicts that occur outside the NATO area do not negatively affect allied cohesion. Such information exchange in NATO does not come easy, as the sharing of information on security policy is often something that even the closest of allies are hesitant to do. Also, information flows within NATO can highlight differences among allies and thus reduce institutional cohesion. Nevertheless, over time, NATO members perceived important gains from information sharing and multinational military planning. The proximity of diplomats at NATO headquarters, working closely with the support of the international secretariat, helps the member states better identify challenges and seek collective solutions to problems. Moreover, this high degree of military transparency would lead to reassurance, for example, as occurred over the rearming of Germany in the mid-1950s and the unification of Germany in the 1990s (Kay 1999).

Regarding Kosovo, NATO planners and member state officials were not lacking for information about the potential for a major crisis on Kosovo. Analysts in and out of the organization had been warning since the early 1990s that instability stemming from Kosovo could prompt an uncontrollable conflict in the Balkans. Within NATO, information sharing over the nature of the threat was high—the international staff, and all allied governments, understood the nature of the problem presented by an unchecked civil war in Kosovo. Moreover, NATO officials had several years of direct experience in managing Balkans engagements in Bosnia-Herzegovina and elsewhere. Crucially, officials from the institution understood the causes of stability in the region. As NATO's SACEUR, General Wesley Clark, told Yugoslav leader Slobodan Milosevic in 1995 (during the Dayton peace negotiations over Bosnia): "Mr. President . . . NATO didn't even fight this war. You lost it to the Croats and Muslims" (Clark 2001: 67). NATO military experts understood that air power alone had not defeated the Serb forces in Bosnia in 1995, but rather a combination of air attacks and a major Croat-Muslim ground offensive. However, in 1998–1999 NATO's information channels failed to transmit this institutional knowledge into effective decisionmaking. Instead, the leaders of the NATO countries convinced themselves it was the limited application of air power that proved decisive in 1995 and that this would work again.

Neoliberal theory assumes that institutions will help member states to make decisions that economize the pursuit of particular objectives. Yet NATO military planners were not permitted to prepare for the possibility that the Serbs would not cooperate with NATO's demands once bombing commenced. When NATO began bombing, its members had only authorized several days' worth of targets. Soon after the war began, key allies pushed for a cease-fire and further negotiation. NATO went to war declaring that its mission was to deter further attacks on Kosovar Albanians. Yet Serbia responded to NATO's bombing with a rapid attack by 40,000 Serb forces against civilian ethnic Albanians called Operation Horseshoe. Such a response was predictable, and expert analysis shared among NATO members and in public had in fact predicted it. In early fall 1998, the US Central Intelligence Agency had begun warning of the Serb plans for Operation Horseshoe. On April 1, 1999, the *New York Times* reported that prior to the war, US intelligence officials warned that the air campaign was likely to exacerbate a refugee crisis and strengthen the Serb regime in Belgrade. On April 5, 1999, the *New York Times* reported that the US Joint Chiefs of Staff had warned that, without a ground threat, the air campaign would not deter further attacks on Kosovar Albanians. NATO leaders knew that the most serious threat of an expanded conflict was the risk of refugee strains collapsing Albania and Macedonia. However, just three days before the NATO bombing began, UN refugee services in Albania had a capacity to receive only 10,000 refugees. The total number to flee during the conflict was 863,000. Given that the greatest threat to regional stability was the possible collapse of Albania and Macedonia, and that NATO members had over a year to prepare for such an eventuality, this was a glaring planning failure.

Realizing that NATO's members held significantly diverging policy preferences, Serb leaders calibrated their policies to affect NATO's consensus. Through fall 1998, Milosevic was said to have adopted a doctrine of graduated ethnic cleansing in Kosovo, believing that "a village a day keeps NATO away." During the war, the Serbs gained "interior lines" of information within NATO. A French officer was convicted after the war of supplying the Serbs with classified NATO war plans. The presence of a persistent pro-Serb Yugoslav reporter at daily press briefings at NATO headquarters in Brussels served as a convenient information asset for Milosevic. Operationally, sensitive military communications were undermined by the high-tech capabilities of US jets, which were not shared by the other NATO members. Classified communications about targets and flight patterns were thus undertaken on less secure channels and picked up by Serb intelligence, which relayed the information on intended targets, which could then be quickly relocated. An information failure misidentified the Chinese embassy in Belgrade as a Serb military target—a building that Western diplomats had visited often—and NATO bombed it. US secretary of defense William Cohen concluded that, "clearly, faulty information led to a mistake in the initial targeting of this facility. In addition, the extensive process in place used to select and validate targets did not correct this original error." Cohen eventually determined that the accidental bombing was an "institutional error"—resulting from NATO's incoherent rush to find targets following the early failures of its war strategy (Lambeth 2001: 145).

The degree of NATO's inefficiency was so significant that, as the war commenced, it actually seemed that NATO might lose. Especially ironic for neoliberal theory, it was the presence of NATO's rules and decisionmaking procedures that increased the transaction costs of security provision. NATO's basic rule is that all decisions are taken by consensus. Nothing becomes NATO policy unless all of its members approve. Decisionmaking therefore centers on the negotiating process, wherein any member can exercise a veto over consensus building. This process is lengthy, complicated, and can involve considerable bargaining and trade-offs facilitated, as necessary, by the international staff in Brussels, though it is a fundamentally state-driven process. The benefit from NATO's rules and procedures comes from the political solidarity that is achieved when the institution's policies reflect the will of its members. Consequently, as an enforcer of community norms, NATO can provide a degree of legitimacy. However, NATO policy also reflects only the lowest common denominator of decisionmaking that all of its members can agree on. NATO would escalate a series of threats against Milosevic through fall 1998, but given the lack of consensus for action in NATO, the chairman of the Military Committee, General Klaus Naumann, asserted that Milosevic "rightly concluded that the NATO threat was a bluff" (Naumann 1999: 3). Russia, which was granted access to some NATO procedures in 1997 via a NATO-Russia founding act, was also able to use its leverage with specific NATO members to frustrate the consensus process. NATO's decisionmaking procedures created a circumstance in which nonmembers could wield influence over the members and thus raise the costs of increasing security in Kosovo.

Because the NATO decisionmakers believed the war would be over in a matter of days, they only approved an initial set of bombing targets to last three days. On May 24, 1999, the *Washington Post* reported that, prior to the air campaign, when Italian prime minister Massimo D'Alema asked President Bill Clinton what would happen if air strikes failed, Clinton had no answer. NATO's military leaders in Belgium had asked to update and widen the scope of planning both before and during the war, but these requests were rebuffed by the political leadership of the NATO members. Had SACEUR Wesley Clark insisted on considering the consequences of failure of the initial air campaign, there might not have been any authorization for a war at all. NATO did have three stages of intensity planned for the air campaign. However, there never was a "fourth level" if the first three failed. According to NATO's theater commander, Admiral James Ellis

(1999), the operational costs of the "short war syndrome" included a lack of coherent campaign planning, a lack of adequate component staffing, a race to find suitable targets, and negative impacts on the Joint Task Force activation, staff composition, facilities, command and control, and logistics and execution.

Throughout the war, maintaining institutional cohesion in light of Serb unwillingness to follow NATO's game plan became the immediate measure of success. NATO did succeed in that there were no member state defections from the agreed consensus for an air campaign. However, knowing the rules and procedures in NATO, Milosevic could gamble that he might survive by waiting out the air strikes, hope to divide NATO politically, and ethnically cleanse Kosovo in the process. Only the brutality of Serb atrocities carried out against ethnic Albanians prevented Milosevic from succeeding, as NATO's members remained united to halt the growing humanitarian catastrophe in Kosovo. However, NATO members could never agree on a warfighting strategy that would align objectives with tactics. Some decisions were taken but never implemented. NATO agreed to a naval blockade of Yugoslav ports but never carried it out. NATO deployed Apache attack helicopters but never agreed to use them. As Benjamin Lambeth demonstrates, NATO's strategy "gave Milosevic time to bolster his forces, disperse important military assets, hunker down for an eventual bombing campaign, and lay the final groundwork for the ethnic cleansing of Kosovo" (2001: 14).

As its leaders met to celebrate NATO's fiftieth anniversary in Washington, D.C., on April 23–24, 1999, the institution was suffering severely from the weight of its inability to defeat Milosevic. The measure of the summit's success was that the members remained united on the overall war goals. However, no serious decisions were taken to adjust strategy to win the war beyond continuing to do more of the same. NATO agreed not to quit—but remained deeply divided on how to win. This was an important outcome, however, because it undermined Milosevic's goal of waiting out the bombing with the hope that NATO would give up. Nonetheless, discussion of ground planning was left off the formal agenda and the United States even lobbied to have SACEUR Wesley Clark kept out of the summit meeting for fear he might push for a ground invasion of Serbia. Even on the issue of air power, the allies were severely divided, with Washington preferring to undertake strategic bombing at the center of Yugoslav gravity in Belgrade, while the Europeans preferred tactical bombing that would take the pressure off the Kosovar Albanians.

The neoliberal assumption that international institutions can lower the transaction costs of cooperation is wrong if the key test is whether NATO increased security during the war. Consequently, the application of this particular test of neoliberal theory via NATO illustrates the limits of the theory. According to Admiral Ellis, the institutional environment affected "every aspect of planning and execution." In particular, NATO's institutional attributes caused "incremental war" instead of decisive operation. Excessive collateral damage concerns created sanctuaries and opportunities for the adversary that were successfully exploited, and the difficulties of conducting out-of-area NATO operations were not anticipated. Ruling out a ground option also corrupted joint forces command, communications, and control continuity, removed effective campaign planning, challenged command and control, and resulted in a hasty last-minute ground-planning effort. The lack of the ground threat likely prolonged the air campaign unnecessarily, and NATO's only sequential plan was to do more of the same (Ellis 1999).

As NATO's war in Kosovo progressed, key decisions within the alliance were relegated to a "quad" of the four major NATO powers (the United States, Britain, France, and Germany, and occasionally Italy), which made operational choices on behalf of the institution—thus moving away from the institutional rules and procedures codified in NATO. Eventually, the lead NATO allies approved a variety of targets from a more advanced stage of NATO planning without the collective approval of the NATO consensus process. NATO's means of warfighting were highly inefficient and decreased security for the very people that it was trying to help. The key problem for neoliberal theory is that the causal factor of the increase in transaction costs was the presence of the rules and procedures of the institution. The way to lower the transaction costs of security provision was to skirt NATO's rules and procedures.

After three months of failure, NATO nearly had its first defection—that of its key member, the United States. As reported on November 22, 1999, by the *New York Times,* on June 2, 1999, US national security adviser Sandy Berger asserted that Milosevic would be defeated by any means necessary. According to Berger, victory would be won "in or outside NATO. . . . [A] consensus in NATO is valuable. But it is not a *sine qua non.* We want to move with NATO, but it can't prevent us from moving" (quoted in Erlanger 1999b, sec. 1: 6). The United States appeared ready to abandon NATO when on June 3, 1999, Milosevic capitulated. However, NATO's military strategy was not the decisive factor in his capitulation. After-action assessments within NATO showed that the air campaign had very little real impact on the Serb military—and it clearly had not deterred Serb atrocities against the Kosovar Albanian population. The war ended because Milosevic chose to end it. It was, of course, important to his decision that NATO apparently could not be divided over its basic commitment to continue. However, the most crucial factors—growing pressure for a ground invasion, enhanced by a resurgence of the Kosovo Liberation Army on the ground, combined with Russian diplomatic pressure—appeared to convince

Milosevic to quit. Whatever the primary reason for Milosevic's decision to end the war, none of the likely explanations had anything to do with actions promulgated by NATO as an institution beyond the initial decision to begin a limited air campaign.

■ Beyond Kosovo: Future Directions for Neoliberal Theory

This examination of the role of NATO as an institution at war illustrates both the utility and the limits of neoliberal theory. Core elements of neoliberalism explain why the United States went to war when it did, and the way it did, in Kosovo. The moral dilemma posed by Serb actions within Kosovo undermined the viability of the new mission of NATO—an international institution important to all of its members. Consequently, the United States shifted its unilateral policy toward Kosovo into a multilateral framework—both to gain legitimacy for action and to help rescue the credibility of NATO. However, the trade-off was that the rules and procedures in NATO created a condition in which the United States could not fight a war in the most effective way possible. A key challenge from neoliberal theory would be whether an alternative policy, absent the institution, would have been more effective. In this case the answer is yes, and this has been reflected by geopolitical trends since the Kosovo war.

During the Kosovo campaign, US leaders became increasingly frustrated with what they saw in NATO as a "war-by-committee." While Washington was itself a major constraint on effective allied action, the presence of nineteen countries, all with a say on various elements of war strategy, was too much to bear for US military planners. After the war, US secretary of defense Cohen proclaimed that, "if we were to carry out and act unilaterally, we would have a much more robust, aggressive, and decapitating type of campaign. . . . The difference here, of course, is that we're acting as an alliance" (PBS 2000). By 2000, NATO was no longer prioritized in US military planning. When the United States went to war in Afghanistan, NATO's political support was welcome, but its operational involvement was rejected. The legacy of the Kosovo war has been a rapid decline in the relevance of NATO for its most important member, the United States, and for some European allies now prioritizing the European Union. As one senior NATO official concluded, the fundamental lesson of Kosovo was that "we never want to do this again" (Clark 2001: 417).

A critical course correction for NATO, guided by neoliberal theory, would be to take NATO out of the warfighting business and instead prioritize postcrisis peace support operations. NATO has played a major role in peace support activity in Bosnia-Herzegovinia, Albania, Kosovo, and Afghanistan. By summer 2003, there was increasing discussion of having

NATO troops play a peace support role in the Middle East and Iraq. NATO might eventually serve to legitimize military intervention led by coalitions of the willing. However, once military action is authorized, NATO would best disengage during warfighting and then be reengaged in times of peace in conjunction with other complementary international institutions. Whether such responsibility sharing is politically sustainable is questionable. A situation such as the 2003 Iraq war, where the United States chose where and how to intervene in a crisis, only to call on its European allies to clean up the aftermath (as was also the case in Afghanistan), will not be sustainable unless the Europeans also have a say in the initial decisionmaking.

If it is accurate that the best role for institutions is to be engaged after a war to facilitate burden sharing, then it appears that NATO members have learned the wrong lessons of the Kosovo campaign. Many NATO officials concluded that the reason that the Europeans lacked influence with Washington was because they did not have the military capabilities to operate with the United States. Consequently, NATO agreed in fall 2002 to invest in a multilateral 20,000-person high-tech rapid deployment force. However, the real reason that Washington has skirted NATO is not for lack of capabilities, but rather because of the rules of the institution, which give the Europeans influence over Washington's policy preferences. A NATO rapid deployment force shifts investment away from the area where NATO can best play a role—postcrisis peace support operations—but also fails to recognize that if Europeans had more capabilities, this would only further drive the United States away from NATO because of the real influence such capabilities would give the European NATO members.

The evidence of the Kosovo war suggests that NATO's basic problem is not military but rather political and that the cause of NATO's inefficiency is its institutional attributes. At war, NATO's rules and procedures proved to be the independent factor that led to less, not more, provision of security. An obvious solution would be to reform NATO's rules and procedures—for example, by moving toward an exclusion clause for defecting members, weighted or majority voting, or a consensus-minus-one framework. However, the dilemma for NATO is that the very rules and procedures that need reforming prevent it from being reformed. What small state in NATO is going to give up its influence gained from the existing consensus processes? As the 2003 Iraq crisis showed, even tiny Belgium is willing to use NATO assets to block the will of the United States. Such activity illustrates how NATO matters as a tool of small states to constrain larger powers. However, it also shows the difficulty in making NATO work as an institution for security provision. NATO increasingly appears politically unmanageable, militarily dysfunctional, and strategically irrelevant to the new threats of the day, particularly international terrorism. The result is that the key scholarly question may not be NATO's adaptation, but rather what institutional form is best suited to replace NATO.

This case study of NATO's war in Kosovo illustrates a continuum of relevance for neoliberal institutional theory. The approach has a high value in explaining the reasons for NATO's war, but confronts limitations over the assumption that transaction costs will be lowered via institutionalized security management. The theory is especially challenged in that the analytical stress on institutional assets such as rules and procedures, which are supposed to lower transaction costs, had the completely opposite effect. This is especially problematic given that NATO's adaptation during the 1990s was seen by neoliberal scholars as strong evidence to support the assumptions behind the theory. However, as this chapter shows, institutional adaptation alone is insufficient when security is at stake—security outcomes must also be considered if the theory is to stand the test of hard cases. The case of NATO's war in Kosovo suggests that neoliberal theory would be stronger if more aggressively held up to hard cases, so that in future institutional design, operational weaknesses can be avoided. Multilateral institutions are crucial to managing the complex world that states now confront. Issues ranging from the environment to international terrorism demand multilateral cooperation. Neoliberal theory, rigorously tested against lessons learned from hard cases such as the Kosovo experience, can serve as an important guidepost for scholars and decisionmakers who must sort through the complexity of modern international relations. It is crucial, however, that institutions serve to provide clarity to international relations, and not, as was the case of NATO's role at war in Kosovo, make matters worse.

Mark A. Boyer & Michael J. Butler

Public Goods Liberalism: The Problems of Collective Action

Few people like to do "dirty work." Such a statement is a truism not only for people but also for states in the international arena, particularly when thinking about the messiest of international situations: military intervention for peacekeeping or humanitarian purposes in an ongoing conflict. Even when multinational consensus exists about the necessity for intervention, disagreements often arise over who will bear the brunt of its costs and thus pose significant problems for collective action. During the Cold War, peacekeeping efforts were constrained by the realities of great power politics, and thus relatively few peacekeeping operations were undertaken. In the post–Cold War era, however, the number of operations has increased dramatically worldwide, in turn raising the significant issues of who pays for such operations, who commits the needed resources to them, and who is in charge of decisionmaking.[1]

This chapter applies theoretical constructs derived from the theory of public goods in an attempt to explain why and when states are willing to take on "burdens" outside their borders whose costs, at least on the surface, appear to outweigh any direct benefits from involvement. We will discuss issues of leadership within collective action situations and the effects leadership has on the ability of a collective entity to provide the public goods of peace and security in a particular region at a particular time. Given the theoretical constructs employed in the chapter, much of the discussion centers on US policy toward intervention in Kosovo, as the United States was a central player in burden sharing and policymaking. This central role is further emphasized by the theoretical constructs we employ from a liberal internationalist, public goods perspective. We turn first to a brief discussion of public goods theory and the rationale it provides for liberal internationalist engagement. Subsequently, we apply lessons derived from the theory of public goods—particularly pertaining to the allocation of the costs of collective action—in examining the prevailing dynamics within NATO during the run-up to its military intervention in Kosovo.

■ A Primer in Public Goods Theory

Pure public goods, such as the desirable circumstances of global peace and security, are defined as "commodities" that are fully joint and nonexcludable. Pure public bads, such as pollution, exhibit similar characteristics. But in contrast to public goods, where the commodity is desirable, most international actors seek to decrease production and subsequent consumption of a public bad. *Jointness* means that consumption by one party does not reduce the amount available for consumption by another. For example, if I consume national security, it does not reduce the amount available for others in my country to consume. *Nonexcludability* refers to the fact that once a good or bad is made available to one party, no other party can be barred from consuming it. Even if I do not pay my taxes to the government, I can still consume national security, unless I am put in jail at some location outside the region defended by the national security apparatus. Purely private goods, such as an apple, and bads, such as cancer, cannot by jointly consumed and are exclusionary in terms of consumption.

Most of the goods—public or private—that are provided in international affairs lack "purity"; that is, they exhibit degrees of jointness as well as some excludability of consumption. For example, some "public" goods can be depleted or will deteriorate through overuse, similar to what happens to public parks as more and more people use the common areas. Likewise, some goods may be available only to members of a particular "club," such as an alliance, and nonmembers can be excluded from consuming the goods.[2]

In the context of humanitarian intervention, a public goods perspective focuses on the provision of three interdependent conditions—security, well-being, and justice—each of which can be viewed as a public good (Hamburg and Holl 1999: 367). Clearly, the security good for actors in the region, and throughout Europe more broadly, was central to NATO's intervention decision in Kosovo, even if the particular security considerations in question varied for different involved actors. Well-being for the citizens of Kosovo was the primary normative interest and the rhetorical vehicle for US policy in particular and for NATO's decisions more generally. Justice played a similar normative and rhetorical role throughout, increasing in prominence after the conflict had deescalated and issues of war crimes rose to the fore.[3] With each of these broad categories of intervention-related goods, there is an implicit set of assumptions that some commonality of values exists cross-nationally that helps to promote the pursuit of those goods when the need arises generally or more acutely during crises. Yet as we will see below, even the existence of such value commonality does not mean a priori that the goods will be provided efficiently or in sufficient quantities. Thus, it is necessary to consider how those values get translated into action in a world comprised of states.

Across diverse policy situations there is unlikely to be one single best strategy for promoting the provision of public goods or the reduction of public bads, just as there is unlikely to be one particular approach to conflict resolution that applies across all conflicts. What does exist, however, is a broad menu of potential strategies for the provision of public goods, where each possible strategy features policy options specific to that approach and generates incentives and disincentives for the actors who might contribute to the provision of the good in question.

Recent work sponsored by the United Nations Development Programme and the World Bank has focused attention on three particular strategies aimed at coping with the underprovision of public goods and the oversupply of public bads in our changing world community (Kaul, Grunberg, and Stern 1999; Kaul et al. 2003; World Bank 2001). These three approaches are labeled *best shot, weakest link,* and *summation.* We only discuss the best-shot approach in detail here, because of its direct relevance to the Kosovo case.[4]

Each approach to public goods provision poses substantially different collective action problems and different challenges for the policymakers who see an interest in pursuing the production of the public goods in question (Jayaraman and Kanbur 1999). Best-shot approaches depend on the willingness and ability of a single actor, or very few actors, to bear the lion's share of provision costs. Such an approach fits closely with what Mancur Olson (1965) called "privileged group" provision, where public goods can be provided by an individual actor or a small group if they so desire, because one or more of the privileged group value the public good highly enough to bear the costs of production themselves and also possess the resources to do so.

It also parallels Robert Keohane's argument (1984) that international regimes that provide public goods for the international system require the existence of a dominant player at the point of regime formation, even if they do not require that actor to continue its dominant role over the longer term. In Keohane's view, the hegemon inculcates norms and values in other actors over time that will maintain the collectively valued goods after the hegemon's decline. In the present context, this may mean that intervention in deadly conflicts requires the leadership of a major power willing and able to take on the burdens of peacekeeping and peacemaking in the region. Without the dominant power's leadership, smaller states will view the costs of intervention as too large and the benefits as too indirect for them to take action by themselves or even collectively without the "big guy" playing the major role. As we demonstrate below, much of the buildup to the eventual NATO intervention in Kosovo appears to follow the logic of a best-shot strategy.

■ Contemplating the Costs of Kosovo

Conventional wisdom tells us that alliances, such as NATO, are reluctant to get involved in "new security" problems in the absence of a direct threat to any member's territory or property (Lepgold 1998). Nonetheless, as the crisis endured, a fairly broad and durable consensus did emerge within NATO in favor of doing something about Kosovo. This consensus was motivated largely by the goal of protecting and propagating the liberal international human rights regime, and by a shared conviction among NATO's leading members that applying concerted pressure on Slobodan Milosevic would prove the best way to attain that goal.

As noted by the Independent International Commission on Kosovo (2000), Kosovo presented the West with two challenges: cultivating the *political will* to intervene and establishing the *readiness to expend resources*. This latter dimension has often been obscured by debates over the perceived justice or injustice of Operation Allied Force. These dual challenges also highlighted the changing nature of NATO's mission in the post–Cold War world, where "out-of-area" threats seemed more likely than the ones for which NATO was created.

Since operations such as humanitarian intervention were not among the "traditional functions" assumed by NATO, their status outside the direct purview of the alliance's Charter provided greater room for the exercise of political and legal discretion among member states. In addition, the binding commitments to collective security, such as those embodied in Article 5, were rendered largely irrelevant. With a new type of action on NATO's radar, and with the perceived absence of direct stakes for most of the actors, a heightened potential for discord existed. Further complicating these matters was the prevailing uncertainty over the scope and allocation of the short-term operational costs associated with deployment in a "new security" crisis such as Kosovo. Uncertainty also characterized the possible long-term costs of material contributions to postconflict peacebuilding in Kosovo and to a redefined NATO.

Given the introduction of this uncertainty into a decisionmaking environment where member states possessed a greater than normal degree of institutional freedom, it is not altogether surprising that NATO efforts during the year preceding intervention were fragmented and tentative with respect to the stated goal of halting the conflict. What resulted from this fragmentation was what Ivo Daalder and Michael O'Hanlon have termed a "least common denominator" approach throughout much of that year (2000b: 27).

Phase One: Shrinking from Force, March–July 1998

Prior to the summer offensive, consensus about the utility of force, even in the abstract as background noise to facilitate a diplomatic solution, was clearly lacking within NATO circles. As early as March 1998, hardcore liberal internationalists—the so-called Albright camp within the US foreign policy community, backed by Tony Blair's Foreign Office—favored the strategy of binding political efforts to a credible threat to use force (Daalder and O'Hanlon 2000b). Indeed, after the siege of Drenica, the US State Department boldly and unilaterally withdrew diplomatic concessions to Belgrade instituted after the Dayton Accords. This claiming of the "high ground" by Madeleine Albright was intended as a signal to those reluctant NATO allies also in the Contact Group (France and Italy in particular) that diplomatic overtures or economic sanctions alone were insufficient in the absence of a credible threat to use force (Daalder and O'Hanlon 2000b). Though backed by the Blair government—as typified by Robin Cook's singular assertion that "we do not accept that this is an internal matter" (quoted in Independent International Commission on Kosovo 2000: 138)— Albright was ultimately unsuccessful in convincing the overlapping members of NATO and the Contact Group to do much aside from reinstituting the arms embargo against Yugoslavia in spring 1998.

The period of hesitancy, between NATO's recognition of Kosovo as teetering on the brink of crisis in winter 1997–1998 and the increasing decisiveness about the need for action in the wake of the Serbs' July 1998 offensive, reflects the continuing legacy of what Olson (1965) described as group asymmetry, with the European allies reverting to the customary position of following the US lead. In this instance, however, US indecision prevented free-riding from occurring. Aside from Albright's immediate cadre, other top-ranking administration officials, such as National Security Adviser Sandy Berger and Secretary of Defense William Cohen, as well as the Pentagon more generally, were as hesitant to plunge headlong into intervention in Kosovo as the Europeans (Shattuck 2003). This combination of rhetorical posturing and deliberative delay by the United States not only restricted specification of a clear mandate for action, but also allowed discord to fester within the alliance over what role (if any) force would play in NATO's response.

While some policy analysts have cited this period of internal political discord as the basis for NATO's eventual "stumbling into war" without full preparation, firm conviction, or clear objectives (see Daalder and O'Hanlon 2000b; and Zenko 2001), such characterizations have too often been made without reference to the legacy of a half-century of collective action problems dogging NATO. Though the Clinton administration did revert to form in speaking loudly and carrying a small stick, NATO's leading lights in Europe possessed neither the capacity nor the wherewithal necessary to undertake a significant portion of any decisive action in Kosovo.[5] Facing these limits within the alliance, and given the US desire to garner allied support in order to diminish the likelihood of unilaterally bearing the costs of a Kosovo intervention, the administration elected to temper its tough rhetoric. On the whole, the United States seemingly preferred to stake out a firm public position, while allowing itself time to assess the stands of its

European allies and formulate an effective intra-alliance strategy. This was a wholly prudent position given the history of burden-sharing problems within the alliance. In many ways, this intra-NATO stalemate approximates the classic free-rider problem: the Europeans wait for the United States to provide collective good X; the United States wishes to provide X, but refrains from doing so out of concern that the Europeans will free-ride on US efforts to cope with a regional European problem; thus X is underprovided, if provided at all.

Employed until Milosevic's unintentional contribution to NATO cohesion in midsummer 1998, the politics of delay cultivated by the United States reflects more than a continuing reticence on the part of US decision-makers to deepen its already substantial economic, technological, and personnel commitments to NATO. The distinct avoidance of undertaking a decision-forcing action proved effective from a strategic perspective as well. While contributing to inaction and keeping discord in the alliance alive, the approach also kept a range of high- and low-cost options on the table, thereby preventing a scenario where defections among those states wavering in the face of the possibility of increased alliance burdens might occur. This calculation also paid off handsomely for the United States in the domestic arena, allowing the Clinton administration to appear simultaneously decisive, prudent, and hamstrung by European foot-dragging and indecision.[6] The prospects for long-term success associated with this decidedly shortsighted approach seem dubious at best, given the degree of uncertainty and significant information gaps among actors that it perpetuated; in any case, the point was rendered moot in practical terms by Milosevic's ratcheting up of the violence in Kosovo that summer.

Phase Two: Crisis Motivation for Collective Action, July–October 1998

In the words of the Independent International Commission on Kosovo, the decision to escalate the level of violence in July 1998 was Milosevic's "most crucial mistake," in that it galvanized European and international opinion and convinced NATO of the merits of direct action (2000: 89). Put simply, the generation of what the West perceived to be a humanitarian crisis provided the sense of urgency needed to propel the more reluctant allies toward undertaking collective action. Instrumental in this regard was the fact-finding mission by Julia Taft, US assistant secretary of state for population, refugees, and migration, conducted in the wake of the summer offensive and detailing an "eerie landscape" in the province teetering on the brink of genocide (Zenko 2001: 3).[7] The mission's subsequent report, featuring an October 15 deadline for Milosevic to cease and desist the violence, served as a powerful and highly public catalyst for what was slowly and torturously becoming the dominant strain of thinking among NATO powers—the need for decisive action structured around the threat and/or employment of military force.[8]

With the question of "whether" public goods would be provided more or less answered, the "how" and "how to pay" questions remained open and subject to debate. Indeed, the persistent factionalism driven by distrust and confusion over the allocation of NATO burdens was at least partially exacerbated by the looming specter of a more decisive operation and its attendant costs, demonstrating the degree to which the various facets of public goods dilemmas in the international sphere are overlapping concerns (Lepgold 1998). Even with an emerging consensus to "do something," what that "something" would be was complicated by what it would cost and how those costs would be distributed.

One prominent example of the burden-sharing problems that continued to plague the alliance was the US-led Kosovo Diplomatic Observer Mission (KDOM). Nominally designed to unify the disparate elements of Kosovar Albanians, the mission proved a disaster in practical terms, resulting in further escalation of violence against the civilian populace (DeCamp 2000). The significance of KDOM to the argument of this chapter, however, is that it reflected the first hint of willingness on the part of the United States to break from the politics of delay and assume its customary position within the alliance, as the underwriter of public goods provision. As much as any other single factor, the growing conviction among US decisionmakers that conditions on the ground had devolved to the point where appeals to the Serbs for restraint were pointless explains the genesis of KDOM (Weller 1999a). Returning to the language and logic of collective action, KDOM's ultimate significance from a liberal internationalist, public goods perspective is that it was the first major demonstration by the United States that it was willing to consider heading up a best-shot approach for provision. KDOM's ultimate impotence suggests this decision may have been premature.[9] It also shows that a demonstration of willingness to pay by the "great" is a necessary, but not sufficient, condition for the success of a best-shot approach.[10] Best-shot approaches also depend at least in part on agreement among the "small" over the content and course of action; this condition was still lacking at the onset of KDOM.

By late summer 1998, however, this critical element in the effective provision of public goods through a best-shot approach began to emerge. The tenor of the European-led diplomatic advances was changing, suggesting the possibility that NATO's internal stalemate might be on the verge of ending. These changes belied a shift in the view of the Europeans toward greater recognition of the utility of NATO assuming a more coercive posture toward Belgrade (Duke, Ehrhart, and Karadi 2000). One example of this recognition on the part of the Europeans was the adoption in September, at Germany's prompting, of UN Security Council (UNSC)

Resolution 1199. This resolution was by far the most strongly worded statement to date of the West's determination to act militarily through NATO in
order to provide security and well-being in Kosovo, even if the conditions
for military actions remained ambiguously defined.

Moreover, the passing of Resolution 1199 can be interpreted in at least
two ways. Either the resolution represented the culmination of US and
British efforts to convince their allies of the importance of a credible threat
in the form of air strikes and/or armed peacekeepers, or it suggested a continuation of European reluctance to take NATO down the path to war
absent the backing of the international community.[11] Regardless of one's
perspective on these interpretations, the wording and passage of UNSC
Resolution 1199 without question signaled that the internal political balance within NATO had tilted decisively toward accepting the use of force
as a blunt instrument pivotal to arrest a perceived humanitarian disaster. By
the time of the vote in favor of the activation order in October 1998, the
stances of several European states formerly opposed to the hawkish US
position had dramatically evolved. In the process, the political environment
in which NATO deliberations were situated shifted accordingly, allowing
the unfolding of a successful best-shot strategy. The previously identified
"necessary" condition—willingness on the part of the "great," in this case
the United States, to assume a disproportionate share of the costs of the collective action—had been complemented by the "sufficient" condition of
unanimity of purpose on the course and content of action among the
"small."

With this said, it is still necessary to understand what explains this
somewhat dramatic reversal of events within NATO's deliberative circles,
particularly as it focuses on the key Contact Group members that had previously opposed the US position. From a public goods standpoint, the key to
comprehending this change lies in recognizing it as the outcome of an evolutionary process rather than a stark reversal. The European member states
that had previously expressed reservations over the military option—
France, Italy, and Germany—had each identified significant private gains
that could be captured by ensuring the provision of security and well-being
in Kosovo. Though each of these states remained somewhat dubious
regarding the desirability of an outright air war over Kosovo, these concerns were outweighed by the potential direct private gains associated with
supporting action in Kosovo. The importance of these private gains as
spillovers resulting from the provision of public goods through NATO
action—the costs of which would be largely defrayed by the United
States—lends further credence to our understanding of how the best-shot
approach was ultimately adopted and implemented. Such considerations are
even more important when realizing that the costs of intervention would be
largely defrayed by the United States.

■ Rationales for Reversal

Rationale for French Support

France was the first of the three major European holdouts to reposition itself in favor of using force in Kosovo. This was due to failed previous attempts to forge a special diplomatic relationship with the Milosevic *regime* in general and Milosevic the *individual* in particular, so as to portray France as the guarantor of future Balkan stability (Ministère des Affaires Étrangères 1999). These attempts dated back to the Bosnian crisis, but transcended the particulars of that conflict and acknowledged Kosovo as a potential tinderbox. Nonetheless, French initiatives such as the Balladur Plan and the Royaumont Initiative proved ineffective in the face of Milosevic's determination once again to wield the blunt instrument of Serbian nationalism in Kosovo (Duke, Ehrhart, and Karadi 2000). Though these relatively idiosyncratic efforts on the part of the French were consistent with recent French interests in pursuing an independent foreign policy generally, and with France's unique role within NATO specifically, their failure and the comparative success the United States enjoyed at Dayton demonstrated to the French that, in dealing with Milosevic on Kosovo, the proverbial stick must be wedded to the carrot ("Interview with Hubert Védrine" 1999).

But while earlier attempts at diplomacy had failed the French, threats of force as championed by the United States and Britain seemed overly vague, lacked credibility, and were thus resisted until shortly after the summer offensive made that stance untenable. This public intransigence, however, stood in direct contrast to France's behind-the-scenes pragmatism. First, although France sought to guarantee that the Contact Group would remain an open forum for the expression of Russian concerns and alternatives during this period, the French position never wavered in its support for the five conditions that would eventually become the "Fischer peace plan," forming the basis of the rationale for NATO intervention (Ministère des Affaires Étrangères 1999). France persisted in this course even in the face of strong Russian opposition (Baranovsky 2000). At the same time, the Foreign Ministry and President Jacques Chirac himself embarked on an intensive public relations campaign to convince the French public of the justice of any potential war over Kosovo, basing this justification on the need for France to maintain and even increase its leadership role in providing peace and security in Europe, lest such responsibility be usurped by Germany, Britain, or the United States (Duke, Ehrhart, and Karadi 2000). Finally, when Germany made its eventual decision in September to seek out some form of UN Security Council authorization for action, France clearly communicated to the United States and Britain that it would not participate in any effort to obtain a UN mandate that might tie NATO's hands, thus effectively joining the Anglo-American coalition that would provide the impetus behind the eventual adoption of a best-shot approach.

France, though reluctant to back openly the early US promotion of a NATO response structured around military force, nonetheless remained willing to consider such overtures throughout the crisis, throwing its full weight behind a threat of forceful action when events in Kosovo devolved to the point where doing so became a safe, and indeed popular, choice. The reason for this ambivalence lies in the Chirac government's growing recognition of the direct private benefits that would accrue to France. Whether in supporting its own rhetorical claims to the mantle of the world's foremost champion of human rights, promoting its self-selected role of Balkan protector, or expanding the European project to which it had long ago hitched its cart, collective action served France's particular interests well.

The Europeanist dimension was especially compelling for France, since its interests in European security and foreign policy integration would clearly be served by going along with the United States and Britain on Kosovo. First, France had long advocated the construction of an autonomous European crisis management command within NATO and saw in Kosovo, if not the potential to employ such a command, the ready material to construct a rationale for one (Ministère de la Défense 2000). Second, France had also taken a primary role within the EU in championing an independent European foreign and defense policy, which it desperately sought to shape. In order to realize these independent policy initiatives, France would have to assume a considerable presence in any armed response to Kosovo, particularly in planning and leadership, if not in direct material contribution. Thus, France's relatively early if publicly muted openness to the Anglo-American position can be best understood by the risks associated with delay. Should the United States and Britain force the issue within NATO, or decide to pursue a military intervention outside the NATO framework, France could not afford to give the appearance of indecision, if it truly hoped to carve out a greater and more independent role on matters of European security.

Rationale for Italian Support

Italy assumed a two-track strategy similar to that of France. Despite its more direct stakes in providing the public goods of Kosovo security and well-being (Albania was, after all, just on the other side of the Adriatic), Italy, too, dithered publicly in the Contact Group meetings, though comparatively less so within NATO deliberations (Kostakos 2000). In part this public obstruction by the ruling left-center coalition was driven by a need to demonstrate foreign policy resolve in the face of US pressure, given ongoing challenges from domestic constituencies opposed to undue US influence on European matters (BBC News 1999c). At the same time, Italy quickly communicated to NATO its willingness to allow its airfields and planes to be used if air strikes came to fruition. This low-key yet significant move was emblematic of the political tightrope that former communist prime minister Massimo D'Alema navigated, in which NATO commitments would be quietly kept while his political power base, which was largely against the intervention, would be placated with public statements opposing the use of force. This impulse perhaps explains the government's steadfast commitment to sounding out Russian grievances as well.

A sufficient explanation for Italy's eventual support from a public goods perspective again requires contemplation of the private goods motives prompting a change in the Italian stance. First, Italy had long considered Albania a satellite state within its sphere of influence. This consideration was reaffirmed by Italy's leadership of the UN's multilateral protection force Operation Alba in 1997. Thus Italy did not wish to allow the unfolding of a scenario where the ethnic violence plaguing Kosovo might spill over to an already tenuous Albanian state. Second, and in some ways related, was the rising sentiment in both the Italian public and in Italy's foreign policy elite for expanding Italy's "place in the sun" through carving out a greater role for Italy as a southern counterweight to Franco-German dominance within the EU and as an alternative voice within NATO (LaPalombara 2001). With a security crisis in the southeastern corner of Europe, Italy's repeated claims that Europe's attentions must shift in a southerly direction were borne out. As in the case of France, Italian opportunism reared its head, and collective action and its attendant private gains trumped, in this case, the largely domestic gains of NATO stalemate. Following from this regional security concern, of course, was the possibility of massive refugee inflows to an Italy already struggling to assimilate refugees from the earlier Balkan crises and plagued by inflation, low rates of economic growth, and rising anti-immigration sentiment (BBC News 1999a). NATO's eventual articulation of this concern as a primary rationale for intervention seemingly bears Italy's stamp (Kostakos 2000).

Historical and material factors also played a crucial role in the eventual Italian decision to support a forceful response. Italy wields relatively less influence than France or Germany over NATO decisions, and was the weakest European state within the Contact Group. As a result, Italy faced comparatively greater risk of being on the "outside looking in," if in fact a decision to intervene with force reached a critical mass among member states. Having initially supported some type of action for practical as well as symbolic reasons, Italy was constrained by its relative lack of power within NATO (LaPalombara 2001). In a sense, Italy transformed this weakness into relative power. Not only could it free-ride and capture significant private gains in a best-shot approach, but it could (and did) also use the political cover provided by the best-shot provider (the United States) to deflect potential domestic opposition to its implicit support for decisive action.

Rationale for German Support

Germany proved the most intractable opponent for those interested in promoting NATO military intervention in Kosovo. Historical and cultural factors cannot be underestimated in driving this opposition. After all, as Simon Duke, Hans-Georg Ehrhart, and Matthias Karadi point out, German participation in any use of force in Kosovo would be the first since World War II, and would fly in the face of what Foreign Minister Joschka Fischer cited as one of the two driving principles of postwar German foreign policy—the doctrine of "no war again" (2000: 133). Yet in broad terms it was the second principle Fischer cited—"no Auschwitz again"—that explains Germany's willingness to remain a party to the NATO and Contact Group debates over whether and how to act.

These two goals came into direct conflict with each other as the situation in Kosovo worsened throughout 1998, as the gruesome possibility of massive war crimes and echoes of Holocaust-like forced migrations grew seemingly more likely by the day. Still, the weight of history rendered supporting an approach structured around military force exceedingly problematic for Germany. As a result, Germany was loath to contemplate backing or participating in a NATO-led military assault without an international mandate to do so (BBC News 1999b). Germany's decision to emphasize the necessity of UN backing and discussion of the issue in the Security Council by August and September 1998, however, represented a major shift in the German stance on the US-British position. Germany's commitment to opposing NATO involvement outright in Kosovo had waned and its attention had shifted to pro forma concerns pursued through other political vehicles such as the UN (Donfried 2000).

This recasting of the German position stems from the compelling nature of the potential private interests Germany could secure with a NATO action in Kosovo. First, on the domestic side of the political ledger, the Schroeder government, newly elected and lacking experience in foreign policy, could not afford a decrease in its governance credibility resulting from being on the losing side of the NATO debate. This is borne out in Gerhard Schroeder's campaign rhetoric, where his response to attacks from the right led to strident assurances that a red-green coalition would not lead to the diminution of Germany's commitment to its alliance obligations (Duke, Ehrhart, and Karadi 2000). Indeed, he had forcefully argued that under his chancellorship, Germany would increase its influence over European security as a "civilizing" agent, a position consistent with Germany's long-standing role as a "civilian power" (Maull 1999). Thus, public opposition to the Anglo-American position on the use of force was offset by internal recognition of the ultimate prudence of adhering to a status quo position within the alliance.

Similar to the French and Italian cases on the domestic front, the Schroeder government faced significant political pressure on immigration, particularly given the tightening of European immigration and asylum policies in the 1990s after years of openness (Rudolph 2003). These pressures, emanating mainly from the nationalist right and sustained by sluggish economic performance, were particularly intractable for left-center coalition governments such as Schroeder's (as well as D'Alema's in Italy). Facing the prospects of an increased number of Balkan refugees on top of the first wave in the early and mid-1990s, who had yet to be successfully integrated into domestic society, the German government recognized the private gains that could be captured by joining with any effort seeking to contain the crisis within Kosovo proper, or at least within the FRY.

Turning to Germany's role on the world stage, Kosovo offered a potential opportunity for a unified Germany to finally shed its confining historical legacy and assume a place within the pantheon of major military powers. For Defense Minister Rudolf Scharping and to a lesser extent Fischer, Germany's goal of permanent Security Council membership would be greatly served by involvement in Kosovo ("Interview with the German Foreign Minister Joscha Fischer" 1998). Perhaps as important from the German perspective, direct military contributions to a NATO action offered the potential for a left-leaning coalition to use its newfound leverage to pursue a sought-after redefinition and expansion of NATO's mission (Hyde-Price 2000). On top of this already significant chance at realizing German interests within the NATO framework, Germany envisioned the possibility that the Kosovo campaign could provide a significant window of opportunity for recasting Europe's security climate along more Eurocentric lines. This would in effect give greater substance to the EU's Common Foreign and Security Policy (CFSP), as well as to arguments favoring enlargement.[12] Portrayals to the German public by the Schroeder government of Kosovo as a war of European unification support this contention (Duke, Ehrhart, and Karadi 2000). The end result was a triumph for the "logic of appropriateness" that had long bound Germany's activities within the major institutions of the European security regime, particularly NATO (Brauner 2000). As this "logic" had benefited Germany in the past—namely in providing private goods such as protection from the Warsaw Pact—so too did it generate significant private goods in the case of Kosovo.

Confirmation of NATO's rapid transformation from a consensus on the *need* to act, to reaching something close to consensus on *how* to act, flowed directly from the adoption of the Security Council resolution. On October 13, 1998, NATO voted to authorize air strikes against both Serbian positions in Kosovo and against targets in Serbia proper should FRY security forces remain in the province. The institution of this "activation order" represented perhaps the fullest embodiment of the elevation of the utility of force within the decisionmaking calculus of the NATO allies. While undoubtedly a by-product of intensive internal lobbying by the United States, this decision confirms that any remaining holdouts within the NATO decisionmaking structure were willing to acquiesce in their opposition to imposing a credible threat, largely due to the private gains that could be captured through this acquiescence. Though the failed negotiations in Rambouillet and Paris in the spring of 1999 suggest that some NATO members still held out hope for a diplomatic solution, the idea that such an outcome could be secured in the absence of an overwhelming military threat to the Milosevic regime had been jettisoned.

■ The Impact of Private Goods on Collective Decisions

Even though the best-shot approach ultimately defined NATO's collective action in Kosovo, it is difficult to overestimate the impact that jointly produced private goods had on the overall public goods outcome. NATO involvement in Kosovo provides confirmation of this "joint product" thesis.[13] Security, well-being, and justice to Kosovo were each composed of a mixed, impure public character that provided the needed selective incentives or "side payments" to facilitate the actual production of the goods. Each of the key NATO member states were eventually willing to support the air campaign, though by greatly varying commitments, because each identified specific private gains that it alone could capture. Moreover, these privately consumable gains were not recognized earlier in the crisis and thus slowed decisionmaking on the eventual alliance course of action.

Of course, the identification and pursuit of selective private goods for NATO countries was hardly restricted to the European states. As the global hegemon, the United States certainly stood to benefit the most from the provision of the impure public goods of security and well-being in Kosovo, thus explaining its sudden policy reversal and willingness to accept a disproportionate burden-sharing arrangement (e.g., the United States flew over 60 percent of all sorties, and over 80 percent of all strike sorties [Independent International Commission on Kosovo 2000]). Some of the private gains accruing specifically to the United States were of a symbolic, normative character, such as projecting itself, as it had in Bosnia, as singularly possessing both the will and the resources to act to prevent humanitarian catastrophe. More generally, this case showed that the United States was willing to stand up to challenges to the liberal international order. Others were of a more directly material nature, such as the potential for market liberalization in the region after its stabilization and establishing an economic and political presence in Eastern Europe as a significant counter-weight to the EU. This reading is consistent with a US Institute of Peace report conclusion that the engagement of the United States in the Balkan region generally, and in Kosovo in particular, was prominent for the purposes of "delivering assistance and providing access to markets and institutions" and "offering market access in exchange for reform" (2002: 2).

■ Kosovo and Incremental Liberalism?

The impure public goods provided by NATO through its humanitarian intervention in Kosovo were obtained through a congruence of private gains to individual NATO allies and underlying values that created at least a rhetorical rationale for involvement and greater burden sharing. In short, private benefits in the short term lay the groundwork for future and more significant collective action that will ultimately lead to greater collective value achievement. While this conclusion might sound more like a state-based, realist argument about the rationale for public goods provision, we argue that it is more accurately evidence of the changing nature of the current international system. Liberal international values and structures are developing in incremental ways that will ultimately lead to greater levels of cooperation over the long term.

In addition, given the legacy of perceived collective action problems within NATO, the agreement within the alliance on the utility of applying force against a sovereign state for the first time in the alliance's history represents a truly remarkable and unprecedented development. NATO's member states had identified a dangerous challenge to the liberal international order in the return of ethnic cleansing to the Balkans. But even though this determination was made consensually rather early in the crisis, little operational commonality existed beyond that recognition for the first nine months that the West defined Kosovo in crisis terms. This was largely because of uncertainty over the extent and allocation of the costs to be incurred by intervening in Kosovo and resulted in the imposition of a series of incoherent and halting actions by the West despite agreement on the significant underlying stakes involved. Suddenly, in the fall of 1998, these burden-sharing problems were alleviated; indeed, the most costly option (short of deploying ground troops) was put squarely on NATO's agenda. As was the case with inaction, the source of NATO's newfound decisiveness can also be located within the realm of public goods theory, and specifically in the concept of joint production.

States are and will continue to be pushed toward greater internationalism in the long term through the need to defend national interests and provide national benefits in the short term. The urge to protect domestic interests and cultivate private goods outcomes is at one level an artifact of the globalized penetration of states that is increasingly occurring today. This is not to say that states currently hold liberal international values dearly to their core, but we argue that liberal values did convince the NATO actors of the singular importance of the Kosovo case. However, those underlying values did not compel them to act in a decisive way, while the pursuit of private goods payoffs did. Nonetheless, moving toward collective action in this rather roundabout way over the short term may have a precedent-setting character over the longer term, leading ultimately toward greater institutionalization of this new NATO role and purpose. As G. John Ikenberry (2000) argues, by intervening in Kosovo, the West (and particularly the United States, as the hegemon) enjoyed significant gains in preserving and even expanding NATO credibility as an instrument of liberal internationalism.

In sum, this is what should have been expected of NATO as an organization dominated by the United States. After all, in a post–Cold War framework, whereby liberal institutions and values reign supreme at least rhetorically, there is no compelling reason to assume that the interests of liberal states were or should be incongruent with the interests of the international order. This recognition leads to the conclusion made by Boutros Boutros-Ghali that "in the future, if peace enforcement is needed it should be conducted by countries with the will to do it" (quoted in Jentleson 1997: 64). He might have added that only through such provision will others see the need and follow suit over the longer term.

■ Notes

1. For a more detailed discussion of the evolving role of peacekeeping operations and who participates in and pays for them, see Bobrow and Boyer 1997, and Bobrow and Boyer 2005.

2. For much greater detail on public goods approaches and their theoretical nuances see Sandler 1997, Murdoch and Sandler 1982, and Cornes and Sandler 1984.

3. Though still worth mentioning in this context, the ascension of justice as a public good through the deployment of KFOR after the intervention places it outside the purview of this analysis.

4. The weakest-link approach is the flip side of best shot in that it focuses on eliminating the impact of the largest negative contributor to the provision outcome. Contributions, such as sending troops to conflict-torn areas to help suppress the negative producer, can help contain the weakest-link actor's negative inputs to the conflict process. The summation approach centers on the summed contribution of all involved actors. The potential for success of this approach is premised on the notion that the actions of a very few will not be decisive for achieving goals, but that the sum of the collective is substantial and effective in achieving policy goals.

5. The striking divergence in opinion within NATO's command structure over the utility of carrying out a threat exercise, Operation Determined Falcon, in June 1998 only served to confirm US skepticism. Much of NATO's European com-

mand contingent, led by the chairman of NATO's Military Committee, General Klaus Naumann, strongly opposed the exercise and deemed it a failure (Zenko 2001).

6. It also allowed the administration to recover from the less than successful threats of force against Saddam Hussein's regime in Iraq over the on-again, off-again UN weapons inspections.

7. The State Department's dispatch of Taft, given her title and position, hardly seems incidental, especially given the credence that a report issued by a high-ranking official specifically concerned with refugees and displacement would lend to Albright's public assertions that the situation was devolving toward genocide and therefore justified military intervention. The high-profile mission led by John Shattuck, a self-described "human rights hawk" (and at the time, assistant secretary of state for democracy, human rights, and labor), following closely on the heels of Taft's mission, can be thought of in a similar vein (Shattuck 2003).

8. This line of reasoning was further cemented, particularly for the more reticent NATO members, by Security Council blessing of unspecified "additional measures" should the Serbs refuse to comply in full with UNSC Resolution 1199 (September 23, 1998).

9. The roundly criticized ineffectiveness of the observer mission can be easily attributed to this persistence of disagreement within NATO over what should be the favored course of action and the role for force in that course of action ("As Prelude to Cease-Fire" 1998).

10. "Success" is used here in an economic sense, to refer to a situation in which the good is actually provided, not in a normative sense, as in the desirability of providing a good in this way.

11. A third, interesting, possibility has been suggested by Simon Duke, Hans-Georg Ehrhart, and Matthias Karadi (2000); namely, that the resolution was indicative of a "good cop/bad cop" dichotomy within NATO, wherein Germany and Italy (as "good cops") ran interference in an attempt to assuage Russia and gain international backing for the preferred strategy of the alliance's "bad cops" (the United States and Britain).

12. The reality of Germany's coming assumption of the EU presidency (on January 1, 1999) seemingly played a role here as well. Certainly the timing of the crisis, and the prospect that continuing delay and inaction might lead to the unfolding of a scenario in which a full-fledged humanitarian disaster in Europe occurred on Germany's "watch" (i.e., during its presidency), was not an outcome the German government wished to see realized.

13. Todd Sandler (1977) introduced joint products into the alliance public goods model.

chapter 4

Game Theory Approaches

4.1   *Jennifer Sterling-Folker*

Game Theory

Because game theory is most often seen as a supplementary approach to realist and liberal theorizing, it is appropriate to discuss it immediately following those perspectives. It differs from realism and liberalism in that it is concerned with the processes of nation-state decisionmaking, rather than with the totality of global politics. Some game theorists have hopes of developing the approach into a unified theory of the social sciences,[1] yet most would concede that, at least for now, it is best considered a useful heuristic tool for specific questions in the discipline. It has been utilized by both realists and liberals to explore conflict and cooperation, and it has been particularly useful in the study of deterrence and alliance formation.

Game theory is used in the study of decisionmaking to simplify and streamline our conceptualization of the decisionmaking process in different situations. It is derived from the larger category of rational choice theory, which has its origins in the study of economics and is interested in the rationality of decisionmaking. In this context, rationality does not refer to the "rationalism" of the Grotian tradition and the English School, which are discussed later; nor does it mean "good" or "correct" or "wise." As Michael Nicholson notes, "'rational choice' is an unfortunate term," because it "implies approval, at least in some people's minds," but "the rationality involved is instrumental rationality which means little more than consistent choice under a coherent set of beliefs," and "'goal-directed choice theories' would be a better term" (1996: 138). In this sense, then, rational choice theory is not about assessing the particular content of an actor's goals (or whether it is morally correct or smart to pursue them). It is instead interested in tracing *how* human beings reason in order to obtain the goals they prefer.

Rational choice approaches assume that when human beings make decisions, they have goals that they rank in order of preference. They further assume that human beings consider different methods for attaining these goals and weigh the costs and benefits of these methods. Thus rational choice is the study of how human beings attempt to maximize their preferences or interests, which is referred to by game theorists as a "utility function" and is meant to indicate not only the ordering of preferences but their intensity as well. Game theory, which is also sometimes referred to as formal modeling, starts with the assumption that actors behave so as to maximize their utility function, but it focuses specifically on strategic interactions where choice is interdependent and decisionmakers are interacting and responding to one another's choices. It is important to underscore this difference, since it is possible to adopt a rational choice assumption and not be a game theorist. Many realists and liberals are rational choicers in this sense, but game theory is a particular type of rational choice theorizing that studies the strategic interaction between two or more actors trying to maximize their utility functions.

Game theory is also "an abstract form of reasoning arising from a combination of mathematics and logic," which utilizes mathematics to specify "what would happen in a situation in which actors—each with strategies, goals, and preferred outcomes—engage in interaction in the form of a game" (Dougherty and Pfaltzgraff 1997: 503). The use of the term "game" is deliberate, since the point of game theory is to see how each decisionmaker will attempt to maximize gains and minimize losses in a situation of competition, uncertainty, and incomplete information. Thus it has been likened to studying the moves in a game of chess, in which each player has a rank ordering of preferences and is simultaneously trying to obtain their own preferences while counterplanning to deny the preferences of their opponent. The analogy to chess is useful for highlighting why and how game theorists are interested in examining alternative strategies and logically understanding an opponent's motivations and calculations, but the analogy should not be stretched too far. Chess is only one type of strategic situation to which game theory can be applied, and many strategic situations in IR involve bargaining over more or less payoff for each competitor rather than complete loss and capitulation.

Game theorists have developed a range of games for analyzing different strategic situations in IR, and these are traditionally divided into games that are either noncooperative, referred to as zero-sum games, or cooperative, referred to as variable-sum or positive-sum games. Both types involve conflicting goals and competition to some degree, but in zero-sum games the gain by one opponent automatically means the equivalent loss by the other. Examples of zero-sum games include chess, checkers, or blackjack. Alternatively, in variable-sum games both opponents can gain (or lose) from their interaction, but the gains (or losses) will be unequal and the strategic bargaining involves determining how much each player can gain (or lose) while still remaining in favor of the interaction.

Variable-sum games are particularly useful for examining coalition formation and bargaining, because they highlight the difficulty of finding a mutually satisfactory solution even when all actors have an interest in finding one. Games such as chicken, stag hunt, harmony, deadlock, and bully are variable-sum, but the most famous is the Prisoners' Dilemma, in which two fictitious prisoners are held incommunicado and given the option to remain silent and go to jail, or turn in their accomplice and go free, but only if the other prisoner remains silent. If both players behave rationally, both will refuse to cooperate and both will go to jail, which as Roger Hurwitz notes "was a puzzle and a surprise for game theorists . . . because the prisoner's rational choices do not produce a reasonable outcome," at least for the prisoners (1989: 116).

Which game a theorist chooses to apply will depend on the parameters of the strategic situation being examined. Beginning in the 1950s there was considerable interest in, and US government support for, the development of game theory research as a possible aid in Cold War strategic planning. This led to an early erroneous belief in the discipline that game theory and rational choice were only appropriate to realist theorizing, which was also interested in strategic military security issues. It became increasingly clear, however, that game theory was "applicable across a broad spectrum encompassing political, military, and economic issues that are often treated as fundamentally different from each other but nevertheless contain actors seeking goals reflected in strategies and anticipated payoffs or benefits" (Dougherty and Pfaltzgraff 1997: 504). While zero-sum games have been of most interest to realist scholars, liberal scholars have found variable-sum games to be useful for illuminating how cooperation can occur in a competitive, anarchic environment. Game theory has also been utilized in the study of public goods, collective action, and international political economy (Conybeare 1984).

Because game theory is relevant wherever strategic interaction takes place, it has been applied to topics as diverse as arms races, trade negotiations, crisis and conflict resolution, and the formation and maintenance of international organizations, security alliances, and international regimes. The topic of international conflict and war has also received considerable attention from game theorists, who have employed rationalist explanations and expected utility models to demonstrate that "war may occur when two states each estimate that the expected benefits of using force outweigh the expected costs" (Viotti and Kauppi 1999: 56). Another foreign policy topic to which game theory has frequently been applied is deterrence, which involves convincing an opponent, through a continuous process of signaling and feedback, that a particular action will elicit a damaging response that outweighs the benefits of taking that action. Chapter 4.2, by Stephen Quackenbush and Frank Zagare, is concerned with what is called perfect deterrence theory, and it utilizes game theory in order to examine the strategic interaction between Serbian violence in Kosovo and NATO's reliance on air strikes to try to end it. In doing so, the authors map out the choices and consequences that logically followed as the two sides interacted.

Game theory is most appropriate to situations involving two actors or sides, because games involving more than two actors, called *n*-person games, can be extremely complex to develop and analyze. This has led some critics to argue that, because it cannot yet capture the multiple actors or interests and interactions that occur simultaneously in the complicated world of IR, game theory does not tell us anything we did not already know. Critics also note that preferences are taken as givens in game theory analysis, so that the social institutions, norms, beliefs, and structures from which actor preferences derive are never examined. To be fair, however, game theory is meant to be an artificial rendering that is kept intentionally simple in order to analyze the strategic, interactive choice itself. Its adherents do not argue that game theory can tell us how or why decisionmakers form their preferences, nor do they claim that it accounts for how decisionmakers actually make decisions in the real world. Game theory is instead a heuristic device "based on mathematical-logical analysis and which purports to show what kind of strategy a rational player should play (when he or she presumes the opponent to be rational)" (Dougherty and Pfaltzgraff 1997: 510). As such game theory remains useful for the analysis of foreign policy decisionmaking, since strategic interaction remains an important element of international relations.

■ **Further Reading**

Early work that laid the groundwork for the study of rational choice and game theory in the discipline includes Thomas Schelling's *The Strategy of Conflict* (1960), Kenneth Boulding's *Conflict and Defense* (1962), Steven Brams's *Rational Politics* (1965), and William Riker's *The Theory of Political Coalitions* (1962). Examples of game theoretical work on negotiations and bargaining include Downs and Rocke 1990 and Snyder and Diesing 1977. Examples of game theoretical work that focus on conflict include Bueno de Mesquita 1981, Bueno de Mesquita and Lalman 1992, Fearon 1995, and Smith 1995. Seminal examples of game theoretical studies of deterrence are Kugler and Zagare 1987, Smith 1998, and Zagare 1990. A work that utilizes game theory to understand group conflict, and analyzes the breakup of Yugoslavia in this context, is Hardin 1995 (pp. 142–163 in particular).

Game theory that explores the role that reiterated interaction plays in cooperation includes Axelrod 1984, Axelrod 1981, Axelrod and Keohane 1986, Kydd 2000, and Taylor 1987. For game theory and political economy, see Carlson 2000 and Conybeare 1984. The literature on game theory in IR is vast, but a sampling of seminal pieces includes Brams 1985, Brams and Kilgour 1988, Breton et al. 1995, Howard 1971, Kydd 1997, Nicholson 1992, Olson and Zeckhauser 1966, Oye 1986, Powell 1991, Rapoport 1960, Rapoport and Chammah 1965, Smith 1999, Snidal 1991, Snidal 1986, and Snidal 1985. An introductory text on both game theory and the Prisoners' Dilemma is Poundstone 1992, and for a review of rational choice approaches in political science, see Lalman, Oppenheimer, and Swistak 1993. One of the most widely read critiques of rational choice and game theory is Green and Shapiro 1994.

■ Note

1. See Snidal 1986 or Brams and Kilgour 1988. J. Richardson notes that such a theory would "consist of testable propositions derived from specifying the interests of actors a priori, in accordance with certain simplifying assumptions," but that the complexities of numerous, heterogeneous, and interrelated actors in various contexts make interest specification impossible (2001b: 280).

4.2 *Stephen L. Quackenbush & Frank C. Zagare*

Game Theory: Modeling Interstate Conflict

Unlike many of the approaches used in this volume to examine NATO's conflict with Serbia over Kosovo, game theory is not a theory if, by "theory," one means a set of logically interrelated propositions or hypotheses. Game theory, though, could be considered a part of the more inclusive "rational choice" paradigm, but then so could classical and structural realism, neoliberal institutionalism, or any approach that posits purposeful or goal-directed behavior.

What then is game theory? For the purposes of this chapter, game theory is best thought of as a methodology for examining strategic behavior among interacting and interdependent units. If seen as a methodology rather than as a theory, it is clear that no definitive game theoretic interpretation of a sequence of real world events such as those that led up to the conflict in Kosovo could be developed. Nonetheless, a small set of critical assumptions and concepts would set any game theoretic treatment of Kosovo apart from that of other approaches illustrated in this volume.[1]

In game theory, the interacting units are called *players.* Who or what constitutes a player, however, is a determination left to the individual analyst. Normally, the identification of players depends on the analyst's purpose and the specific research questions addressed. One could, for example, conceive of the conflict in Kosovo as a two-person game between Serbia and the KLA, as a two-person game between the NATO alliance and Serbia, or as a three-person game among Serbia, NATO, and the KLA. An even more detailed analysis, however, that recognized important policy differences that separated the United States from France and Germany, might specify five (or more) players. In other words, both the number and identification of players are extra–game theoretic decisions that, in principle, should be driven by theoretical and/or empirical factors rather than by methodological considerations.

A realist who was also a game theorist would likely limit the specification of players to states. But players need not be so restricted. For example, one could employ game theory from within Graham Allison's (1971) organizational process model to focus on, say, the decisionmaking process within the US government. In this game, the players—such as the White House, the Departments of State and Defense, and other important bureaucratic departments and agencies—would be completely different *units* of analysis. But the analysis, nonetheless, could still be game theoretic.

Regardless of how they are specified, however, the players are assumed to make *choices* that, along with the choices of the other players, lead to specific *outcomes*. The specification of outcomes, like that of the players, is another important judgment call that an analyst must make. Thus a general analysis of the Kosovo conflict might simply specify "negotiation" as a possible outcome. By contrast, a more fine-grained study might distinguish between a negotiated outcome that favored the Kosovars and one that favored the Serbians.

In game theory, the players are assumed to evaluate (subjectively) the *utility* (or worth) of each possible outcome and to make choices that maximize their expected utility. Players who are expected utility maximizers are said to be instrumentally rational.[2] Instrumentally rational players, then, are those who *always* make choices they believe are consistent with their interests and objectives *as they define them*. In other words, instrumentally rational players are purposeful players.[3]

This is not to say, though, that the players evaluate the outcomes in the same way. In fact, many conflicts are traceable to disputes about the value of specific outcomes. For example, the KLA believed that by pressing its case against Serbia, an independent Kosovo would result. Serbian leader Slobodan Milosevic disagreed. Milosevic thought he could use force to stamp out the separatist movement in Kosovo and, in the process, consolidate his internal political standing.

To minimally specify a game, the players, the choices available to them, the consequences of their choices (i.e., the outcomes), and the players' utility for each outcome must be specified. James Morrow correctly observes that "the design of the game [is] the single most important decision in modeling" (1994: 57). Note, however, that these are decisions that must be made *before* the analytic tools of game theory can be used. This means that the explanatory power of any game theoretic analysis depends less on the methodology itself than on the theoretical sensitivity of the analyst. Nonetheless, as we hope to show, game theory provides a potentially useful methodological framework for analyzing international conflicts in general, and aspects of the conflict in Kosovo in particular.

■ Why Game Theory?

Why use game theory to examine real world interactions? Not all game theorists agree that game theory should be used for this purpose. Morrow asserts that "individual case studies are poor tests of rational choice models." He argues that "ex post reconstructions of historical events use information that the actors could not have at the time, subtly influencing us away from the strategic problems they faced [and] cannot explain the case precisely because the game cannot fail to fit the specified facts of the case" (1997: 29).[4] Although we agree with Harry Eckstein (1975) that "critical case studies" can and do serve important theoretical purposes, Morrow is undoubtedly correct in arguing that even a theoretically informed single case study, or what Robert Bates and colleagues (1998) call an "analytic narrative," would fall short of a *test* of a game theoretic model or, for that matter, any theoretical construct. The reason why is straightforward: one cannot generalize from an *n* of one, and the conflict in Kosovo is clearly a "one."

But this is not to say that ex post reconstructions of real world interactions that employ the formal apparatus of game theory are without theoretical merit. For one thing, such reconstructions can rely solely on information that was available to the actors at the time they made their decisions, as Bruce Bueno de Mesquita's analysis (1998) of the end of the Cold War demonstrates. For another, even if it is true that *some* game model can always be molded to fit the facts of almost any individual event, "closeness of fit" is not the only criterion by which explanatory models are judged. Like a historical description, a game theoretic explanation of an individual case can also be evaluated in terms of the plausibility of its assumptions about the motives of the players and other critical components of the model (i.e., the choices available to the players, the set of outcomes, and so on).[5]

■ For What Purpose?

In the literature of international relations, game theory is most commonly used to model *general* political processes such as those associated with crisis bargaining, alliance formation, and war. Here, however, we use it to model a single historical case. What analytic purpose could such a nonstandard application of game theory serve? We submit that there are several.

First, game theory could be used as a strictly *normative* tool to evaluate the efficacy of competing policy prescriptions. For example, Frank Zagare (1984) uses a game theoretic framework to analyze the 1973 crisis in the Middle East, finding that the decision of the Nixon administration to place US strategic forces on alert was not only justifiable, but also more efficacious than the less provocative approach of reassuring the Soviets of a US willingness to compromise.

Game theoretic models could also be employed *descriptively* to explain single cases that are intrinsically interesting or otherwise important (Bates et al. 2000: 700). Game theory is frequently utilized in this way. For example, Zagare's analysis (1979) of the 1954 Geneva Conference helps to reconcile the well-known but unexplained discrepancy between the public and private policy pronouncements of US decisionmakers both before and during the negotiations that ended the Franco-Vietminh war. Zagare (1982) uses the same game theoretic framework to eliminate competing, seemingly plausible, explanations of the Geneva Conference advanced by Ramesh Thakur (1982).[6]

A game theoretic analysis of a single historical case could also be thought of as an inductive step taken to facilitate the development of a general theory. If they are to be useful, formal models, game theoretic or otherwise, cannot be fashioned out of whole cloth. Game theory provides a useful framework for developing comparable case studies, which in turn could serve as a guide in the construction of more refined models or more powerful theories.

■ Perfect Deterrence Theory: A Game Theoretic Approach to Deterrence

To summarize briefly, a game theoretic study of a single case can serve a number of theoretical purposes: game theory can, inter alia, be used as a descriptive or as a normative device; it can also be employed as a (logical) standard by which competing explanations can be eliminated; and it could be utilized as a tool for theory construction. Beyond these purposes, however, well-developed game theoretic models can be used to shed theoretical light on individual events when an event is identified as an instance of the more general category that is part of the model's empirical domain (Rosenau and Durfee 2000: 3). This is the tack we take in the remainder of this chapter. More specifically, we consider the conflict in Kosovo as an instance of deterrence, and use a set of interrelated game models—called perfect deterrence theory (Zagare and Kilgour 2000)—to gain a deeper understanding of key aspects of the conflict.[7]

Perfect deterrence theory is a theoretical alternative to the standard formulation of deterrence, that is, to classical (or rational) deterrence theory. The two theories have widely divergent empirical expectations and policy implications. These critical differences can be traced to a slightly different axiomatic base. More specifically, classical deterrence theorists like Daniel Ellsberg (1959), Thomas Schelling (1960, 1966), and more recently, Robert Powell (1990) and Barry Nalebuff (1986), assume that conflict or war is always the worst possible outcome of any deterrence encounter. By contrast, in perfect deterrence theory, conflict may or may not be the lowest-ranked outcome of the players.

Given that classical deterrence theory was developed at the dawn of the nuclear age, the assumption that all other outcomes are superior to war is certainly understandable. But since this seemingly innocuous assumption leads to untenable logical and empirical conclusions, it is clearly not very useful. To see this, consider for now the *rudimentary asymmetric deter-*

rence game depicted in Figure 4.2.1. In this, the simplest deterrence situation that we can imagine, there are two players, State A and State B, and three outcomes, *status quo, A wins, and conflict.*

The rudimentary asymmetric deterrence game is a model of an asymmetric or one-sided deterrence situation: State B wishes to deter State A, but not the other way around. Thus, in the extensive-form game depicted in the figure, State A begins play at decision node 1 by deciding whether to *cooperate* (C) and accept the status quo, or to *defect* (D) and demand its alteration. If A chooses C, the game ends and the outcome is the *status quo.* But if State A defects, State B must decide at node 2 whether to concede (C) the issue—in which case the outcome is *A wins*—or deny (D) the demand and precipitate *conflict.* Let us accept, for the moment, two central assumptions of classical deterrence theory: that *conflict* is the worst possible outcome, and that the players are instrumentally rational. What then would instrumentally rational players do when presented with the choices in the rudimentary asymmetric deterrence game?

To answer this question, we examine the game tree of Figure 4.2.1 using a procedure know as *backwards induction.* Specifically, we work backwards up the game tree and determine first what an instrumentally rational State B would do at decision node 2, and then, using this information, specify the rational choice of State A at node 1. At node 2, State B is faced with a choice between conceding (i.e., choosing C), which brings about outcome *A wins,* and denying State A's demand (i.e., choosing D), which brings about *conflict.* But if *conflict* is assumed to be the worst possible outcome, an instrumentally rational State B can only choose to concede, since, by assumption, *A wins* is the more preferred outcome.

**Figure 4.2.1 Rudimentary
Asymmetric Deterrence Game**

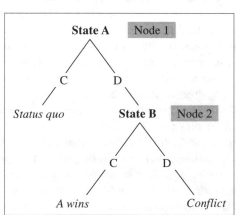

Given that an instrumentally rational State B will choose to concede at node 2, what should State A do at node 1? State A's choice is either to cooperate, in which case the outcome is the *status quo,* or to defect, in which case the outcome will be *A wins*—because an instrumentally rational State B will choose to concede at node 2. If State A has an incentive to upset the *status quo*—that is, if it needs to be deterred because it prefers *A wins* to the *status quo*—it will rationally choose D. In other words, given two of the core assumptions of classical deterrence theory, deterrence will rationally fail. When joined together, then, the two central assumptions of the standard version of deterrence theory are inconsistent with the possibility of deterrence success.

The inconsistency of these two core assumptions with the stability of the status quo poses a significant empirical problem for classical deterrence theory, namely explaining the stability of the strategic relationship of the superpowers during the Cold War. Recognizing the inconsistency, and attempting to eliminate it, classical deterrence theorists have responded by relaxing the rationality assumption. Schelling, for example, has suggested that a player (such as State B) feigns irrationality to convince another (such as State A) that it would in fact defect at node 2 and execute an irrational threat. Powell, by contrast, holds to the rationality assumption yet allows the threat to be executed, probabilistically, by a disinterested third player, called Nature, that has no stake in the game. Edward Rhodes (1989) abandons the rationality assumption altogether. All of which explains why Christopher Achen argues that "far from leaning too heavily on rational choice postulates, 'rational deterrence theory' necessarily assumes that nations are not always self-interestedly rational" (1987: 92).

Unlike classical deterrence theory, perfect deterrence theory assumes that the players are always rational. As well, it drops the assumption that *conflict* is always the worst possible outcome in a deterrence encounter, nuclear or otherwise. In perfect deterrence theory, then, the players may or may not prefer to execute a deterrent threat. It may be surprising to some readers that these two seemingly innocuous axioms lead to empirical expectations and policy prescriptions that are dramatically different than those of classical deterrence theory. But we now show how the implications of perfect deterrence theory provide insights into the Kosovo conflict that simply cannot be derived from the standard formulation of deterrence theory.

■ A Game Theoretic Analysis of the Conflict in Kosovo

The origins of the conflict in Kosovo are complex and ancient. They involve both ethnic rivalries and great power political machinations that date back centuries, the details of which need not concern us here. For our purposes, one need only go back to 1987 and the rise to power of Serbian president Slobodan Milosevic, who skillfully used unrest among the majority of ethnic Albanians in Kosovo for personal political advantage. Soon thereafter, Milosevic terminated Kosovo's autonomy (1989) and abolished its parliament (1990). Of course, Milosevic's repressive policies only made matters worse. In the mid-1990s, moderate Kosovars, such as Ibrahim Rugova, eventually lost influence to more radical elements, the most important of which was the KLA. Increasingly, the secessionist movement in Kosovo turned violent.

A major Serbian crackdown in March 1998 led to open conflict between Serbian military and police forces and the KLA. In short order, over 1,500 Kosovar Albanians were killed and more than 400,000 driven from their homes. The magnitude of the carnage, coupled with a fear that the conflict would spread, led to deeper NATO involvement. NATO's goals were clear: to resolve the conflict by deterring Serbia from continuing the conflict.[8]

Serbia, of course, was not so easily deterred. As John Vasquez notes, "one of the key theoretical questions is why such a small state would be willing to risk war with such a powerful state as the United States" (2002: 107). We address this question presently by bringing to bear the insights offered by perfect deterrence theory. In so doing, we place NATO's conflict with Serbia over Kosovo under what Carl Hempel calls a set of "covering" laws (1965: 345), and then use these laws to explain some of the particulars of that conflict.

To this end, consider first NATO's June 11, 1998, attempt to deter Serbia from further escalating the conflict. On that day, US defense secretary William Cohen directed General Wesley Clark, NATO's SACEUR, to demonstrate NATO's willingness to intervene in the ongoing conflict in Kosovo. Clark responded with a massive show of NATO air power along the Albanian and Macedonian borders. NATO's air exercise, however, failed to end Serbia's five-month counterinsurgency. Why did this specific attempt at deterrence fail? Micah Zenko's explanation is that NATO's threat lacked credibility:

> The threat failed because Yugoslav president Slobodan Milosevic recognized cracks in NATO's public display of unity. Before any actual bombing of Serbia could take place, France and Germany insisted that the alliance obtain the imprimatur of a UN Security Council resolution authorizing the employment of "all necessary means" to halt the killing in Kosovo. The United States disagreed, stating that NATO retained the right to act independently of the UN, while Great Britain was on the fence. The allies were aware that efforts to obtain UN support could be vetoed by Russia and China, both judging the violence in Kosovo to be an internal matter for Serbia. Milosevic recognized the operation as nothing more than symbolism, an exercise in public relations, not a rehearsal for war. (2001: 1)

One clear implication of Zenko's explanation is that had NATO's threat been credible, Serbian military operations in Kosovo would have been scaled back and the June 1998 attempt at deterrence would have succeeded. To accept this explanation, however, it must be the case that a credible threat is a sufficient condition for deterrence success. Since perfect deterrence theory reveals that credibility is neither a necessary nor a sufficient condition for deterrence success, Zenko's explanation must be qualified.

To demonstrate why, we must pause and formally define two terms central to any theory of deterrence: *threat credibility* and *threat capability*. We begin with credibility. In the traditional strategic literature, credible threats are oftentimes equated with threats that ought to be believed (e.g., Smoke 1987: 93). Since threats can be believed only when they are rational to carry out (Betts 1987: 12), only rational threats can be credible (Lebow 1981: 15).

The formal definition of credibility in perfect deterrence theory is consistent with the theoretical linkage between threats that are credible and threats that are both believable and rational: credible threats are precisely those that are consistent with rational choice, that is, with threats that the threatener *prefers* to execute.[9] Using the rudimentary asymmetric deterrence game of Figure 4.2.1, it is easy to show why Zenko's explanation of NATO's early attempt at deterrence might appear to be persuasive. We have already shown that the *status quo* is unstable, and deterrence is bound to fail, when State B prefers not to execute its deterrent threat. In terms of our definition, State B's preference for *A wins* over *conflict* renders its threat incredible—assuming, of course, that State A knows State B's preferences.[10]

But now assume that State B's threat is credible, that State B prefers *conflict* to *A wins* and that State A knows this. Consider now State B's node 2 choice in light of this assumption. At node 2, State B can either concede, in which case the outcome is *A wins,* or to deny, in which case the outcome is *conflict.* Given our new assumption about State B's preferences, it is clear that State B, if it is instrumentally rational, would choose to deny State A's demand.

Now consider State A's node 1 choice. If State A chooses to cooperate, the outcome will be the *status quo.* If State A chooses to defect, the outcome will be *conflict,* since State B is now assumed to prefer to execute its deterrent threat. Thus, when State B's threat is credible, the *status quo* is stable, and deterrence will succeed, *as long as State A prefers the status quo to conflict.* If deterrence success depends on both the credibility of State B's threat *and* State A's preferences, a credible threat cannot be a sufficient condition for deterrence to work. Thus, Zenko's explanation of NATO's failure to deter Serbia from continuing its offensive is inadequate. To be complete, Zenko's explanation would also have to speak minimally to Serbia's preference between the *status quo* and *conflict.*

In fact, in perfect deterrence theory, it is State A's preference between these two outcomes that establishes whether State B's deterrent threat is *capable*. Following Schelling (1966: 7), perfect deterrence theory defines a capable threat as a threat that hurts. Actions that hurt are those that leave a player worse off than if the action were not executed. Operationally, this means that one player's threat is capable only if the other, the threatened player, prefers the *status quo* to the outcome that results when and if the threat is carried out (i.e., *conflict*). In other words, a threat will lack capability whenever the threatened player prefers to act even when a deterrent threat is acted upon. Perfect deterrence theory demonstrates that a capable threat is a necessary condition for deterrence success. This means that deterrence will fail whenever the deterring state's threat lacks capability. It also means that in the absence of a capable threat, the credibility of the deterring state's threat is simply irrelevant. Hence the inadequacy of Zenko's explanation.

At this point the reader might feel as if we are simply picking academic nits. But the distinction between credible and capable threats is both theoretically and empirically significant. To see why, consider a March 1999 meeting between Serbian president Milosevic and US special envoy Richard Holbrooke. At this meeting, which was a last-ditch effort to avoid conflict, Holbrooke asked Milosevic, "Are you absolutely clear in your own mind what will happen when I get up and walk out of this palace?" Holbrooke reported that Milosevic replied, "You're going to bomb us" (McManus 1999: A1). To put this another way, Holbrooke's final threat failed to deter not because it lacked credibility. Indeed, President Milosevic knew that the threat would be carried out. Rather, the threat failed because it lacked capability; Serbia's president preferred to continue fighting in Kosovo regardless of whether or not the threat was carried out. Because the threatened action would not hurt enough, it was insufficient to deter the Serbian offensive.

In the rudimentary asymmetric deterrence game, capability and credibility are jointly necessary and sufficient for deterrence to succeed.[11] Thus it should not be surprising that many of the choices taken by NATO during the conflict were motivated by a desire to establish both (see Chapter 2.3).

■ Extended Deterrence and the Conflict in Kosovo

Although the rudimentary asymmetric deterrence game is useful for establishing the importance of credibility and capability (and distinguishing between them), more elaborate game models are necessary to examine the Kosovo conflict in greater detail. By March 1999 the situation in Kosovo was clearly one of extended deterrence. Extended deterrence occurs where one actor, the defender, attempts to deter a challenger from attacking a third party, the protégé. More specifically in this case, the United States (defender), by way of NATO, was attempting to deter Serbia (challenger) from engaging in ethnic cleansing in Kosovo (protégé).

To model situations such as these, Frank Zagare and D. Marc Kilgour (2000) have developed the *asymmetric escalation game*.[12] As in the rudimentary asymmetric deterrence game, the challenger begins play by choosing whether to cooperate (C) or defect (D). But as Figure 4.2.2 shows, the defender's response options in the asymmetric escalation game are more varied: at decision node 2, the defender can concede (C), it can respond in kind (D), or it can escalate (E). Depending on the defender's choice, the challenger can either escalate first (at node 3a) or counterescalate (at node 3b), or not. If the challenger escalates first, the defender has an opportunity, at node 4, to counterescalate. The outcomes associated with the various choices in the asymmetric escalation game are summarized in Figure 4.2.2.

Given this specification of the alternatives available to each side, the

Figure 4.2.2 Asymmetric Escalation Game

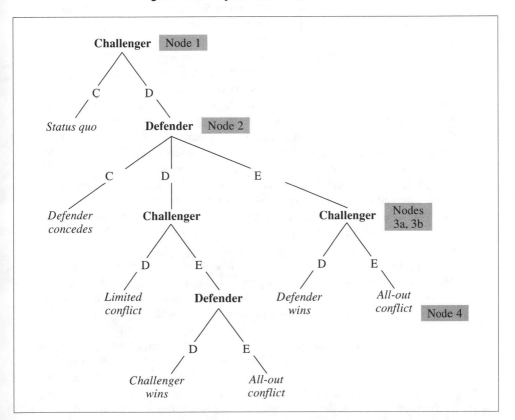

story of the Kosovo conflict can be told in terms of the asymmetric escalation game.[13] In March 1999, despite repeated warnings and threats from the United States and NATO, Serbia continued its campaign in Kosovo; in effect, this meant Serbia was choosing D at node 1. In response, NATO initiated the Operation Allied Force air campaign on March 24, thus also choosing D at node 2. Despite expectations that bombing would lead Serbia to back down quickly, Serbia instead did the opposite, escalating (E) the conflict at node 3a by launching Operation Horseshoe later in March. At this point, NATO decided not to counterescalate; hence ground forces were not deployed.

What led Serbia not only to stand firm in the face of NATO's clear intention to initiate an air campaign, but also to intensify its ethnic cleansing? Some argue that this question cannot be answered, that it is "impossible to know why Milosevic decided to escalate rather than hunker down, let alone capitulate in the manner many expected he would" (Daalder and O'Hanlon 2000b: 93). Through the lens of perfect deterrence theory, however, it is not difficult to explain the Serbian decision to escalate. But one must first recognize that the deterrence attempted by the United States and NATO in March relied on *two* threats: the threat to respond to Serbia's intransigence by an air campaign, and the threat to escalate to a ground war if necessary.

The meeting between Holbrooke and Milosevic on March 22 demonstrated that NATO's threat to bomb Serbia was indeed credible, as discussed above. However, NATO's escalatory threat was just as clearly not credible. And with good reason. As President Bill Clinton stated in his address to the nation on March 24, the United States and NATO did "not intend to put our troops in Kosovo to fight a war" (Clinton 1999c). Similar statements by Vice President Albert Gore, Secretary of Defense William Cohen, British prime minister Tony Blair, and others made it unmistakable that NATO's least-desired outcome was *all-out conflict.*

Given these preferences, one can solve the asymmetric escalation game using backwards induction to determine what outcome should be expected. Given Clinton's obvious signal that NATO would stick with an air campaign *even if Serbia escalated,* that is, that NATO would choose D at node 4, Serbia's node 3a choice is both predictable and easy to explain: after the bombing of Serbian positions, Milosevic decided to escalate because he preferred the outcome that would result if he escalated (i.e., *challenger wins*) to the outcome that would result if he did not escalate (i.e., *limited conflict*). From the Serbian point of view, then, escalation was an instrumentally rational choice.

The United States and NATO faced a more complicated decision at node 2. One thing, however, is incontrovertible: as we have seen, regardless of Serbia's response, a divided NATO was not interested in escalating. But what of the choice of D? In a situation of complete information where each player is fully informed of the other's preferences, NATO would have recognized that its choice of D at node 2 would lead eventually to *challenger wins*. This may have been less preferred than the *defender concedes* outcome that would have resulted if NATO had chosen to concede (C).[14] However, the United States did not expect Belgrade to escalate. Rather, the expectation in Washington was of a *limited conflict* that would, in short order, be resolved in NATO's favor. As Secretary of State Madeleine Albright stated on national television the night the bombing started, "I don't see this as a long-term operation. I think that this is something . . . that is achievable within a relatively short period of time."[15]

From this it can be inferred that the Clinton administration may have believed that the threat to bomb Belgrade was sufficiently capable and credible to deter Milosevic from fighting on. The belief, while erroneous, was not baseless. Many members of the Clinton administration were convinced that NATO's 1995 air campaign was responsible for Milosevic's capitulation that ended the war in Bosnia-Herzegovina.[16] Another logical possibility is that US decisionmakers did not have complete and accurate information about Serbian preferences, which is simply another way of saying that US intelligence was inadequate. In the end, the conflict did not remain limited as NATO's command had anticipated; rather, Operation Allied Force precipitated an acceleration of Serbia's campaign of ethnic cleansing and led, unexpectedly, to the outcome *challenger wins*.

How then did the situation change, leading Serbia to agree finally to withdraw all its forces from Kosovo and allow entry of an international security force on June 9? The strategic dynamic began to shift after President Clinton made it clear in a press conference on May 18, and a *New York Times* op-ed on May 23, that henceforth NATO would "not take any option off the table."[17] A series of meetings in Washington and in Europe were held in late May and early June to prepare for a possible ground war in Kosovo (Daalder and O'Hanlon 2000b). At about the same time, NATO built up its ground forces in Macedonia and Albania. Unlike the earlier situation, then, the United States and NATO had made sufficiently credible its threat to use ground forces to put a halt to the carnage in Kosovo.[18] Therefore, when it became obvious to Milosevic that Serbia would likely soon be faced with a choice between backing down and a ground war he could not expect to win, he backed down (Erlanger 1999b). In the end, US and NATO forces were able to prevail, but not until after first "losing the war" and then, in the words of Ivo Daalder and Michael O'Hanlon (2000b), "winning ugly."

■ Expectations for the Future

While to this point we have been concerned with explaining NATO's failure to deter Serbia in the spring of 1999, perfect deterrence theory can also be used to form expectations for the stability of future relations between

Serbia and NATO. The basic theoretical idea rests on the supposition that some deterrent relationships are inherently more stable than others. If correct, it follows that the specifics of any conflict settlement will condition and shape the future relationship of the combatants and have important consequences for the robustness of the peace (Senese and Quackenbush 2003).

Settlements of militarized interstate disputes fall into two broad categories: imposed and negotiated (Jones, Bremer, and Singer 1996). Winners of disputes that impose settlements are, in general, likely to be quite satisfied with the postsettlement status quo, while losers of those disputes (states that have settlements imposed on them) are likely to be dissatisfied with the new status quo. By contrast, both states in a jointly negotiated settlement are likely to be at once somewhat satisfied with the new status quo (they did, after all, agree to it), but also likely to be somewhat dissatisfied with it (they did not get everything that they wanted).

A state that is dissatisfied with the postsettlement state of affairs will have an incentive to challenge the status quo. To prevent an unwanted challenge, the threatened state will attempt to deter its dissatisfied former opponent from violating the terms of the settlement. Since each side is somewhat dissatisfied following negotiated settlements, mutual deterrence is required to maintain them. However, the maintenance of imposed settlements requires only unilateral (or one-sided) deterrence.

This distinction is important because, other factors aside, unilateral deterrence is easier to establish and maintain than mutual deterrence (Zagare and Kilgour 2000). In consequence, one would expect that imposed settlements to militarized interstate disputes will be more durable than negotiated settlements. Paul Senese and Stephen Quackenbush (2003) confirm this expectation empirically. In an analysis of 2,536 interstate conflict settlements, they find that imposed settlements last significantly longer than negotiated settlements. For example, the expected duration of an imposed settlement is nineteen years. Negotiated settlements, in contrast, are likely to persist for only nine years.

With this theory of recurrent conflict in mind, one can consider the settlement of the conflict in Kosovo.[19] The settlement reached through the Military Technical Agreement of June 9 (which called for the immediate cessation of hostilities and set timelines for the withdrawal of Yugoslav forces from Kosovo) and United Nations Resolution 1244 of June 10 (which welcomed the acceptance by the Federal Republic of Yugoslavia of the principles of a political solution to the Kosovo crisis, including an immediate end to violence and a rapid withdrawal of its military, police, and paramilitary forces) was clearly imposed.[20]

This settlement in large part instituted the provisions of the Rambouillet Accords—which Serbia had previously refused to sign, or even to seriously negotiate—including the deployment of an international security force (KFOR) to Kosovo to monitor adherence to the settlement. While there is likely to be lingering resentment among some Serbian leaders about these terms, the postconflict peace, and the unilateral deterrence relationship it rests on, are likely to persist, especially if the Federal Republic of Yugoslavia is reintegrated into Europe. This is not to say that a long-lasting peace is guaranteed. But there are both good theoretical reasons and compelling statistical evidence that suggest that the peace will likely endure for some time.[21]

■ Conclusion

Game theory is a powerful and versatile methodological tool that lends itself to political analysis in a variety of ways. It is particularly useful for constructing general theories of political interaction. It could also be used as a normative device to evaluate competing policy prescriptions, or as an empirical aid to structure in-depth case studies or even a series of comparable case studies. In this chapter, however, we have taken a less conventional approach. Specifically, we have identified the conflict in Kosovo as an instance of deterrence and then employed a set of interrelated game models, called perfect deterrence theory, to shed theoretical light on a number of aspects of the conflict. In other words, we have taken what we know about interstate conflicts in general in order to achieve a deeper understanding of a singular event.

For example, in perfect deterrence theory, a credible retaliatory threat is neither a necessary nor a sufficient condition for deterrence success. This means, inter alia, that the status quo may be contested, and deterrence may rationally fail, even when a defender's threat is in fact credible. Knowing this leads us to question Zenko's explanation (2001) that NATO's attempt to deter a Serbian escalation in June 1998 failed because NATO's threat was not credible. While Zenko may well be right that Serbian president Milosevic did not believe that NATO would use force if he did not deescalate the conflict in Kosovo, it is also likely that, in this instance, Milosevic's beliefs about NATO's intentions were simply beside the point. Indeed, there is considerable evidence that Milosevic intended to continue his Kosovo campaign regardless of whether NATO ordered air strikes. This means that NATO's early attempt at deterrence failed not because its threat was not credible but because it was not capable. In other words, the threat to bomb Serbia did not imply costs that were sufficiently hurtful to alter Serbian behavior.

As a general theory, perfect deterrence theory can also be used to identify the conditions associated with an array of extended deterrence outcomes, including acute crises, limited conflicts, and escalation spirals.

More specifically, crises occur whenever a defender's threat to respond in kind lacks capability or is insufficiently credible to deter aggression. When extended deterrence breaks down, the ensuing conflict is most likely to remain limited when a defender's escalatory threat is both capable and credible. Finally, crises are more likely to escalate when at least one of these two conditions is not satisfied.

The theoretical knowledge of extended deterrence outcomes provided by perfect deterrence theory helps us to provide an answer to what Daalder and O'Hanlon (2000b) claim is an "impossible" question, namely, why Serbia decided to escalate its campaign against the KLA. Using a generic asymmetric escalation game model as a guide, we argue that Serbia's decision to launch Operation Horseshoe was the rational course of action in light of the low credibility of NATO's escalatory threat. Why then did Serbia eventually back down? Clearly, NATO's escalatory threat to deploy ground forces had always been potent (i.e., capable). But when, in early June, it became patently obvious that an invasion was more than just a remote possibility, Serbia suddenly decided that it was in its interest to accede to the demands NATO laid out at Rambouillet. In an uncertain world, brandishing threats that are at once capable *and* credible is the surest path to peace—at least in the short run.

In perfect deterrence theory it is also the case that, other factors aside, deterrence is more likely to be successful, and will be easier to maintain, in unilateral or one-sided relationships than in relationships of mutual deterrence. Knowing this made it possible for us to make a prediction, based on explicit theoretical principles and buttressed by compelling statistical evidence (Senese and Quackenbush 2003), that the settlement imposed on Serbia will take hold.

In sum, our application of perfect deterrence theory to the conflict in Kosovo has enabled us to answer three important questions regarding that conflict. Two of our answers are not only different but are also more complete than answers provided by scholars who have not availed themselves of game theory's powerful analytic tools. We also note that because we have tried to make our discussion accessible to all readers, we have included little in the way of formal proof. Nonetheless, all of the conclusions reached here are grounded in strict logic developed elsewhere. We believe that it is the transparency and consistency of this logic, more than anything else, that makes our conclusions more compelling than the competing explanations we find inadequate.[22]

One criticism of formal theories in political science is that they have not been sufficiently tested and are thus often divorced from reality (Green and Shapiro 1994). Theories of international relations, formal or not, also need to be able to speak to specific real world issues. Recent strides have been made in bridging the divide between formal and empirical studies of deterrence on a large-sample basis (Quackenbush 2003). In our opinion, this chapter demonstrates that game theoretic models can also be used to gain insight into single cases that are intrinsically interesting, theoretically significant, or both.

■ Notes

1. Numerous textbooks provide an overview of the methodology. Among those we recommend are Dixit and Skeath 1999, Fudenberg and Tirole 1991, Gibbons 1992, Morrow 1994, Myerson 1991, Rasmusen 1994, and Zagare 1984.

2. For the distinction between instrumental and procedural rationality, see Zagare 1990. See also Quackenbush 2004.

3. Game theory is frequently criticized for assuming instrumental rationality. But the assumption is often implicit in the analyses of its critics and in what are taken to be antithetical conceptual frameworks. For example, in Chapter 6.2 in this volume, Rosemary Shinko argues that NATO's attempt to frame its intervention in Kosovo as a humanitarian act was *motivated* by a desire to disguise its underlying political character.

4. See also Elster 2000.

5. For a debate on this issue, see Elster 2000 and Bates et al. 2000. See also Ray 1995, chap. 4.

6. For a collection of similar applications, see Bates et al. 1998.

7. Because we are interested in deterrence, we focus on the relationship of Serbia and the NATO alliance. But this is not the only way to view the conflict in Kosovo. One could, for example, also interpret it as an instance of an ethnic conflict or as a civil war. In principle, game theory could be used to analyze those aspects of the conflict. But to do so, one would have to either use or, more likely, develop a general model appropriate to the specific interaction between the Serbians and the Kosovars.

8. Schelling (1966) would call NATO's objective "compellence," that is, a desire to stop an action already under way. For our purposes, the theoretical distinction between compellence and deterrence is not meaningful.

9. Credible threats are those that are consistent with Reinhard Selten's perfectness criterion (1975), that is, with instrumentally rational choices at every decision node of a game tree. Perfect deterrence theory's name comes from its association of credible threats with the perfectness criterion.

10. Technically, we are assuming a game of complete information. We make this simplifying assumption here for the sake of exposition. The general conclusions we reach, however, hold even when this assumption is relaxed. For a demonstration, see Zagare and Kilgour 2000.

11. This statement is not generally true. In some deterrence games, credibility is neither a necessary nor a sufficient condition for deterrence success. Capability, however, is always a necessary condition. For the details, see Zagare and Kilgour 2000.

12. The asymmetric escalation game is a general model. Because it is general, its application to any specific conflict is problematic. In other words, it is meant to apply to a class of events (i.e., situations of extended deterrence) rather than to any single event. We believe that it illustrates a general dynamic of the conflict in Kosovo. But the asymmetric escalation game would have to be modified substantially in order to explore more particular aspects of this or similar conflicts.

13. Our informal analysis of this game is meant to be suggestive. Hence we present only the broad outlines of the model. For a formal analysis that takes payoff parameters into account, see Zagare and Kilgour 2000.

14. However, Vasquez argues that "the United States backed itself into a corner in which the logic of coercive diplomacy made it necessary" to respond to Serbia's actions rather than concede (2002: 112; see also Judah 2000). Therefore the United States and NATO may have preferred to launch an air campaign rather than concede, regardless of what happened afterward.

15. Madeleine K. Albright, interview, PBS, *Newshour with Jim Lehrer,* March 24, 1999.

16. We are indebted to Jennifer Sterling-Folker for this observation.

17. "Remarks by the President and His Majesty Abdullah II, King of the Hashemite Kingdom of Jordan in Photo Opportunity," White House, Office of the Press Secretary, May 18, 1999.

18. Andrew Stigler (2002–2003) argues that the threat to introduce ground forces was not credible. But because he treats credibility as a dichotomous variable, Stigler overlooks the possibility that NATO's threat was *sufficiently* credible to force Serbia to surrender control of Kosovo. In our opinion, a more nuanced analysis is possible when credibility is measured on a continuum, as it is in perfect deterrence theory. For a discussion, see Zagare and Kilgour 2000, chap. 3.

19. Since our argument is supported empirically by an analysis of dyadic *inter*state disputes, we restrict our conclusions to the future relationship between NATO and Serbia. For an analysis of settlements to *intra*state conflicts, see Hartzell 1999.

20. The text of the military agreement is available online at http://www.nato.int/kfor/resources/documents/mta.htm, and the UN resolution text is available at http://www.un.org/docs/scres/1999/99sc1244.htm.

21. For a contrary view, see Efrid et al. 2000.

22. For the debate on the importance of logical consistency in theory construction, see Brown et al. 2000.

chapter 5

Constructivist Approaches

5.1 *Jennifer Sterling-Folker*
Constructivism

Although constructivism is a relatively new theoretical approach to the discipline of IR, it has quickly become one of its leading perspectives. While one can see disciplinary antecedents to it in liberal pluralism's integration literature of the 1950s and 1960s, IR scholars have borrowed very deliberately from other disciplines in order to develop the central tenets of constructivism. The study of literature and linguistics is particularly pertinent to its origins, as is the work of sociologists such as Emile Durkheim, Max Weber, and Anthony Giddens. However it was not until the late 1980s that constructivism was introduced into the discipline as a coherent theoretical package, and since then it has rapidly risen to disciplinary prominence. Ole Wæver has subsequently observed that from reading IR journals one gets the impression that 80 percent of the discipline is neorealist, but "if, then, one looks around an ISA [International Studies Association] conference at the actual participants, it will take hours to find anyone willing to be identified as a neo-realist, while a very high proportion of the young participants do constructivist or poststructuralist work" (1997: 26). Constructivism has gone on to occupy the space once reserved for Marxism in standard schematics of the three dominant theories of the discipline.

Why constructivism, or social constructivism as it is also called, became so popular so quickly is partly explained by current events. The end of the Cold War came as a shock to most IR theorists and posed considerable analytical problems for existing IR theories.[1] The failure of established theoretical perspectives to anticipate not simply the event itself, but also the speed with which it occurred, opened the door for new IR theoretical approaches to be considered. One advantage constructivism had was that the possibility of rapid, radical change was one of its central tenets. Radical change was feasible because, in the words of one influential constructivist, "anarchy is what states make of it" (Wendt 1992: 395). What Alexander Wendt meant by this was, contra to realism, a pregiven interest in survival is not induced simply by the condition of anarchy, and so power competition, security dilemmas, and war are not inevitable features of it. Constructivists argued instead that we create our own security dilemmas and competitions by interacting in particular ways with one another so that these outcomes appear to be inevitable. If the quality of interaction were to change, however, that is, if we were to perceive one another as potential friends rather than enemies, international outcomes could be very different.

The basis for such claims lies in the study of identity formation and how social interaction produces social identities. Constructivists observe that our identities and interests do not exist separately from the social situations to which they are appropriate, or, as Alice Ba and Matthew Hoffmann have put it, actor "interests and identities depend on the context in which they find themselves" (2003: 20). Identities and interests are *socially constructed* by the particular way in which we interact with one another, hence the name of the perspective itself, which was coined by Nicholas Onuf (1989). The collective knowledge and understandings that makes these identities possible is what constructivists call "intersubjective meanings." The process whereby intersubjective meanings and hence identities and interests are created involves a cycle of signaling, interpreting, and responding. We attempt to signal intent and meaning to one another through our words and actions, we interpret and ascribe meaning to those signaled words and actions, and we produce words and actions meant to signal responding intent and meaning.

This act of communicating, and the human dependence on both spoken and written language in order to do so, is an essential but not unproblematic feature of the process. It is problematic because, as has long been observed in the study of linguistics, language is subject to a "hermeneutic circle" in which "we cannot know the world independently of the language we use" to describe it (Adler 1997: 326). From the hermeneutic study of how we interpret or ascribe meaning with language, constructivists have derived an interest in how human beings collectively interpret and impose shared meanings on objects and actions, because in so doing, human beings collectively produce their own social realities. Money is a social reality, for example, and yet as a physical object it has no value except what we have collectively ascribed to it. According to Emanuel Adler, "social reality emerges from the attachment of meaning and functions to physical objects; collective understandings, such as norms, endow physical objects with purpose and therefore help constitute reality" (1997: 324).

Such collective understandings, and their accompanying social identities and interests, can become reified or embedded over time so that alternatives seem unimaginable. "Notions of what is right or wrong, feasible or infeasible, indeed possible or impossible, are all a part of an actor's social context," Ba and Hoffmann observe, "and it is these ideas that shape what actors want, who actors are, and how actors behave" (2003: 210). It seems natural to be handed a syllabus at the start of a course, for example, or to receive a grade for your work at the end, and for my efforts as a teacher to be monetarily compensated. These social practices are expected of today's teacher-student relationship, which produces an interest on your part in receiving a syllabus and a grade, and an interest on my part in being paid for my efforts. The specific interests and the specific relationship cannot be separated, but more to the point, we also share a common understanding of what the relationship entails, and we act in a particular way that reinforces our expectations. In so doing, we are reinforcing an established social institution that exists regardless of our participation in it, and that, as Patrick Thaddeus Jackson and Daniel Nexon have observed, must be "logically prior to the entities which make up the group" known as teachers/students (1999: 303).

Hence the social institution of teacher-student would remain even if we end our own participation in it, because the relationship is an embedded structure within our society. Many people participate in it, and there are so many cognitive and material social practices that support it that this identity relationship has a structured existence independent of its participating individuals. The relationship also entails specific expectations and behaviors that even individuals who are not themselves teachers or students will understand and support as natural nonetheless.[2] Parents pay tuition, stores sell notebooks and supplies, departments provide copy machines and classrooms, university administrations sign paychecks, and so on. You and I are participating in the social relationship of teacher-student as free and individual agents, and such a relationship is dependent upon individuals such as ourselves, who must all be interacting in a way that is relatively specific to this particular relationship. Yet rather perversely, we are also participating in a larger social structure over which we have little direct control, and by participating in it we are reinforcing it as an embedded social institution.

The idea that we are free agents who create our own social institutions, and yet are constrained by the social structures that our very free agency creates, is a basic philosophical conundrum. Constructivists refer to it as the problem of codetermination or the agent-structure debate, but they are certainly not the first to grapple with it. In fact it was Karl Marx who captured the essence of it best in observing that "people make history but not in conditions of their own choosing," and this is an observation that is central to other IR theoretical approaches, including postmodernism, critical theory, and many variants of feminist theory. But it was constructivism that was responsible for bringing it into the IR theoretical mainstream, and given its analytical interests and sources, constructivism has frequently been listed alongside other postpositivist approaches in the discipline as an example of reflectivism or interpretivism.[3] These are said to be in opposition to the rationalism or neo-utilitarianism of realism and liberalism, whose dominant variants subscribe to positivism, which in turn sanctions their shared assumption that interests and identities may be treated as pre-givens in an analysis (Katzenstein, Keohane, and Krasner 1998; Ruggie 1998; Wendt 1994).

In practice, however, most constructivist IR scholars subscribe to positivism as well, arguing that traditional scientific methodologies can be consistent with the interpretivist foundations of constructivism (Hopf 1998; Adler 1997; Dessler 1999; Checkel 1998). There are some differences between constructivists on this score, and it is possible to categorize constructivist variants according to their epistemological differences.[4] But in general, a great deal of constructivist analysis has not been as radical as one might initially think, because many constructivist scholars seek to occupy the middle ground between positivism and postpositivism (Adler 1997). What distinguishes constructivist analyses in the discipline is less the methodology or epistemology and more the topics or subjects that have been explored. In this regard, constructivism has legitimized certain subjects of inquiry that had either lain dormant in the discipline or had simply been ignored, such as collective identity formation and culture (see, e.g., Lapid and Kratochwil 1996).

The aggregate identity that has received the most attention in constructivist scholarship is the nation-state. Constructivists argue that interaction among nation-states can lead to the development of identities such as competitor and rival, or friend and ally, which can become entrenched over time and reinforced by continued interaction that appears to confirm the identity as true. Hence the nature of interaction between the United States and Soviet Union during the Cold War seemed to confirm as natural their identities as competing poles. While there is considerable disagreement within the discipline as to whether constructivism can actually explain how this relationship went from hostile to friendly almost overnight, the event does seem to confirm constructivism's overall point. Much of what we take as immutable structures in IR are actually embedded social relationships that are contingent to a large extent on how nation-states think about and interact with one another. If, as Adler puts it, "constructivism shows that even our most enduring institutions are based on collective understandings" (1997: 322), then it is also possible for those understandings to change and hence for so many of the IR structures we take for granted to change as well.

Constructivists have also been interested in exploring the role that ideas, norms, and culture play in promoting structural change. Some constructivists have concentrated on how the historical development of the nation-state represented a change in the constituent unit of the international system, thereby affecting shared collective understandings and subsequently reconstituting the international system in its own image. If today we take the Westphalian system and the sovereign nation-state as natural, it is only because we share collective understandings that it is so. As John Gerard Ruggie asserts, "constructivists also tend to believe, as a working hypothesis, that insofar as sovereignty is a matter of collective intentionality, in the final analysis, so, too, is its future" (1998: 21). Constructivists who focus on the contemporary international system tend to study the way in which norms serve as "collective expectations with 'regulative' effects on the proper behavior of actors with a given identity," or how culture represents "both evaluative standards (such as norms and values) and cognitive standards (such as rules and models) that define the social actors that exist in a system, how they operate, and how they relate to one another" (Katzenstein, Keohane, and Krasner 1998: 679–680). There is also an emphasis on studying "how *individual agents* socially construct these structures in the first place" (Adler 1997: 330, emphasis original), because some constructivists argue that social contexts, and hence identities and interests, may be consciously reshaped by particularly shrewd or conscientious individuals.

Because it focuses on interaction and the possibility of change, there is an obvious affinity between much of the constructivist norms or identity literature and liberal IR theory.[5] This affinity has been reinforced by the tendency among constructivist IR scholars to concentrate on the development of morally desirable norms and to prefer a systemic level of analysis, which effectively ignores how domestic actors internally and collectively constitute their nation-states. Yet analytically there is no reason why any of these propensities are inevitable to constructivism, and it is possible to do a form of realist constructivism that emphasizes the reification of embedded power structures rather than the prospects of their change.[6] It is also possible to explore the development of morally repugnant norms and identities or to conduct domestic-level analysis within a constructivist framework. In fact, Chapter 5.2 provides just such an analysis, as Matthew Hoffmann examines the collective identity of Yugoslavism that Joseph Tito promoted to hold the nation-state together, as well as the social process that led nationalist, ethnic identities to eventually overwhelm the larger collectivity of Yugoslavia itself.

A final constructivist topic of inquiry involves the study of narratives, rhetoric, speech acts, and signaling, since these are necessary to the interaction that produces identities and interests. If the social world is linguistically constructed and reproduced through the act of communication, then the words we use and the narratives that we invoke matter a great deal to the social reality that is created. By choosing particular narratives to justify our actions, we do not simply make sense of the world, as an epistemological positivist might assert, but actually make the world according to those narratives. These observations lie closer to the postpositivist end of the constructivist epistemological spectrum, as they are central to postmodernism, critical theory, and the English School as well, but here too one finds variety in how constructivists have utilized discourse analysis to examine narrative and rhetoric in IR. Some constructivists have focused on how speech acts invoke social rules that convey mutually recognizable validity claims in the international system (Onuf 1989; Frederking 2003). Others have attempted to document and reproduce the narratives that have been invoked to justify particular foreign policies and actions. Chapter 5.3 represents an example of the latter, as Patrick Thaddeus Jackson utilizes a relational constructivist perspective to examine the public debates and rhetoric invoked to legitimate NATO's bombing campaign in Kosovo.

Although the methodological differences between constructivists can appear stark, there remains a shared commitment to a transformational logic involving "the notion that actors' words, deeds, and interactions shape the kind of world in which they exist, and that the world shapes who actors are and what they want" (Ba and Hoffmann 2003: 15). As a result, constructivism has posed significant epistemological and ontological challenges to the discipline of IR, as established theories have sought to juxtapose, incorporate, or distance themselves from its central propositions. It has managed to galvanize and broaden IR theoretical debates in a relatively short time and in a way that other theoretical alternatives to realism and liberalism have not. As Wæver notes of the discipline, "with constructivism as a socially accepted alternative to mainstream rationalism and institutionalism, there is clearly a drift towards more philosophical and meta-theoretical debates" (1997: 25). And while constructivist scholarship has been faulted by its critics for simultaneously being too radical or not radical enough, it has also been able to integrate other IR theories within its ambit and apply its insights and propositions to a diverse range of topics within the discipline.

■ Further Reading

The antecedents to constructivism can usually be found in disciplines other than IR, although who in particular has been influential often varies according to particular constructivist scholars. Hence a list of antecedents might include such varied work as Bhaskar 1979, Berger and Luckman 1966, Durkheim 1965, Giddens 1979, Giddens 1984, Mead 1934, Searl 1995, Weber 1949, and Weber 1968. Although the work of Jacques Derrida, Michel Foucault, Jurgen Habermas, and Friedrich Nietzsche is also sometimes cited, these are more apropos to dedicated postpositivist approaches such as postmodernism, critical theory, and critical feminism.

The IR texts most responsible for introducing and promoting constructivism as a new approach in the discipline include Friedrich Kratochwil's *Rules, Norms, and Decisions* (1989), Nicholas Onuf's *World of Our Making* (1989), John Gerard Ruggie's *Constructing the World Polity* (1998), and Alexander Wendt's *Social Theory of International Politics* (1999; see also Wendt 1987, 1992, 1994). General reviews and discussions of constructivist works in IR can be found in Adler 1997, Dessler 1999, Checkel 1998, Hopf 1998, Palan 2000b, and Price and Reus-Smit 1998. For in-depth discussions of the problem of codetermination or the agent-structure debate, see Carlsnaes 1992, Dessler 1989, Friedman and Starr 1997, Hollis and Smith 1994, Wendt 1987, and Wight 1999.

Constructivist analysis that concentrates on historical and/or system transformation includes Johnston 1995, Hall 1998, Kratochwil and Ruggie 1986, Reus-Smit 1999, Spruyt 1994, Wendt 1999, and some of the essays reprinted in Ruggie 1998. Examples of contructivist analysis that focuses on the contemporary international system, and topics such as norms, culture, and identity, include Adler and Barnett 1998, Finnemore 1996, Finnemore and Sikkink 1998, Goff and Dunn 2004, Klotz 1995, Katzenstein 1996, Kratochwil 1989, Lapid and Kratochwil 1996, and Risse, Ropp, and Sikkink 1999.

Discourse analysis in constructivism can be found in two general forms, those that focus on speech acts (what Brian Frederking calls "rules-based" constructivism) and those that focus on narrative recovery or re-creation. For examples of the former, see Crawford 2002, Frederking 2003, Onuf 1989, Kubalkova, Onuf, and Kowert 1998, and Risse 2000. Examples of constructivist analysis that concentrate on recovering alternative narratives and narrative strategies can be found in Doty 1996, Hopf 2002, Fierke 2000, Jackson and Nexon 1999, Jackson and Nexon 2002, Mattern 2001, Milliken 2002, Neumann 1999, "Images and Narratives in World Politics" 2001 (a special issue of *Millennium*), Weldes 1999, and Wilmer 2002. Many of these narrative examples lie closer to the postpositivist end of constructivism's epistemological spectrum and, for this reason, might be cited as examples of postmodern or poststructuralist works instead.

■ Notes

1. Realist scholars had assumed either that bipolarity would continue indefinitely or that its collapse would involve a violent confrontation between the two poles. Alternatively, while liberal scholars had anticipated peaceful change, they had assumed it would occur gradually and had focused their analytical efforts not on East-West relations but on cooperation between the major industrials, who were essentially the alliance partners of one of the poles. Bipolarity was considered an embedded structure that would be nearly impossible to change, and realists were certain it would be difficult to change peacefully. Yet within the span of months, the

relationship between the United States and the Soviet Union shifted from outright hostility to cordial and cooperative.

2. Or as Adler puts it, "this knowledge persists beyond the lives of individual social actors, embedded in social routines and practices as they are reproduced by interpreters who participate in their production and workings. Intersubjective meanings have structural attributes that do not merely constrain or empower actors. They also define their social reality" (1997: 327).

3. Robert Keohane suggests the term "reflective" because such approaches "emphasize the importance of human reflection for the nature of institutions and ultimately for the character of world politics" (1988: 384). Alternatively the term "interpretivism" is sometimes used because such approaches posit that "in the social and interpreted world in which (as they see it) we live, only ideas matter and can be studied" (Adler 1997: 321).

4. See, for example, Ruggie 1998: 35–36, which provides such a typology by dividing constructivism into neoclassical, postmodernist, and naturalistic variants based on epistemological differences, or Hopf 1998, which categorizes constructivists according to a conventional–critical theory dichotomy. The differences epistemology can make to constructivist analysis can be illustrated by comparing texts such as Finnemore 1996 to Onuf 1989, or Keck and Sikkink 1998 to Weldes 1999 and Neumann 1999. For further discussion of epistemological issues in constructivism, see Delanty 1997.

5. As a result, it is common for constructivism to be described as a variant of liberalism. Mark Zacher and Richard Matthews (1995: 135–136) cite the work of Wendt and Ruggie as examples of "institutional liberalism" in their overview of liberal IR theory. Similarly, Paul Viotti and Mark Kauppi (1999: 217) include a discussion of constructivism in their review of the regimes literature. This normative affinity might partially account for "the emergence of a middle ground where neo-institutionalists from the rationalist side meet constructivists arriving from the reflectivist side" (Wæver 1996b: 168). See also Sterling-Folker 2000.

6. The possibility of creating a realist constructivist variant has been analyzed in Copeland 2000, Sterling-Folker 2001b, Barkin 2003, and "Realist Constructivism" 2004 (an *International Studies Review* symposium).

Matthew J. Hoffmann

Social (De)Construction: The Failure of a Multinational State

> The stability of the communist political order in Yugoslavia rests in large part on the party's ability to maintain social and political peace among the nationalities. (Burg and Berbaum 1989: 535)

In classrooms and lectures, James Rosenau is fond of asking his audience, "How do states make it from Friday to Monday?" in order to focus them on crucial questions of legitimacy, authority, and the processes that connect people (micro level) with their collectivities (macro level).[1] Of course, he is forcing his audience to consider what most citizens (and IR scholars) take for granted—the continuation of the state as a dominant political form, and the continued existence of particular states in the international system. Further, this question immediately invokes a state that literally did not make it from Friday to Monday—the Soviet Union—making his point all the more clear. Yugoslavia is another case of a state that did not make it from Friday to Monday, although in Yugoslavia, Friday to Monday is metaphorical, and the dissolution of the state was far less peaceful than the disappearance of the Soviet Union.

In this chapter, I examine the breakup of Yugoslavia with a social constructivist lens. Many factors, including economic crisis, predatory elites, nationalism, communism, and more, have been blamed for the violent evaporation of Yugoslavia, and indeed these have all played a role. However, I argue that it is crucial to understand the micro-macro processes between people (elites and the general population alike) and their collectivities, and how these relationships formed the context within which the other factors contributed to the rending apart of Yugoslavia. Social constructivism provides a framework for understanding these processes.

At its core, social constructivism helps us to understand how ideas and norms shape politics (as well as how politics shapes ideas and norms).[2] In the case of Yugoslavia, it is crucial to understand how the idea of a united nation of Southern Slavs (Yugoslavism) competed with, and eventually lost to, the idea of particularistic nationalisms. Collective identity is socially constructed in the interplay of elites, populations, and state institutions. By tracing this process of ideational competition over the foundation of the Yugoslav state, we can begin to understand how Yugoslavia was socially (de)constructed into separate nations in the minds of citizens and elites, before it was violently dismembered into separate nations by those same people.

The province of Kosovo takes center stage in this analysis for two reasons. First, as noted by Laslo Sekelj, "in the most drastic way, Kosovo revealed the lack of social integration within Yugoslav society and state alike" (1992: 193). Second, Kosovo was at the heart of the crisis in the late 1980s that led to the rise of Slobodan Milosevic—the crisis that would finally end the state of Yugoslavia. James Ron claims that Kosovo's importance "stems from its early role in triggering the ugly process of Yugoslav disintegration. Serbia's diaspora anxieties and resentment toward Yugoslav federalism began in its ethnic Albanian province, and it was while grappling with Kosovo's ethnic tensions that Slobodan Milosevic became a nationalist" (2001: 103).

In this chapter I will first briefly discuss my particular view of social constructivism. I then turn to a discussion of the slow process of the demise of Yugoslavia in two sections. The first examines the entrepreneurial role played by Joseph Tito and how Yugoslavism manifested in post–World War II Yugoslavia, as well as the obstacles that this idea faced in the 1960s and 1970s. The second section traces the ultimate demise of the idea of Yugoslavism in the 1980s and the rise of virulent nationalisms exemplified by the entrepreneurship of Milosevic. I conclude with some brief thoughts on the general applicability of this approach to world politics.

■ Social Constructivism and the Norm (Idea) Life Cycle

With their focus on the mutual constitution of agents and structures, constructivists have been at the forefront of trying to understand micro-macro relationships. Many constructivists focus on social norms when exploring such relationships, and they have attempted to explain how social norms emerge and diffuse in a population (whether the population is made up of individuals, states, or other actors/agents). Martha Finnemore and Karen Sikkink (1998) put forward a norm life cycle to explain the emergence of norms. While they restrict their analysis to norms, the general dynamic that they identify is applicable beyond norms to more generic ideas. We can use the norm life cycle dynamics to understand the emergence of and competition between ideas of collective identity like Yugoslavism and particularistic nationalities.

The norm life cycle is composed of three linked stages: emergence, cascade, and internalization (Finnemore and Sikkink 1998: 896–901). Finnemore and Sikkink begin by positing a catalytic role for norm entrepreneurs in fostering norm emergence. Norm entrepreneurs are actors (individuals in Finnemore and Sikkink's treatment, though organizations and states could play this role as well) that advocate different ideas about appropriate behavior from organizational platforms that give their ideas credence. Norm entrepreneurs work to persuade other actors to alter their behavior and beliefs in accordance with the norm entrepreneur's ideas about how actors should behave and think. How the entrepreneurs convince actors to change their ideas and actions is currently a matter for debate among constructivists (see, e.g., Checkel 1998; and Risse, Ropp, and Sikkink 1999), though such processes as coercion, persuasion, and socialization are all likely relevant.

When a "critical mass" of actors accepts the new ideas as appropriate, Finnemore and Sikkink (1998: 901) posit that a norm has emerged. After norm emergence, there is a rapid diffusion of the norm—a norm cascade. In the cascade stage, the norm acceptance rate rapidly increases, which Finnemore and Sikkink (1998: 902) describe as a contagion. Multiple agents, outside the critical mass, now begin to accept the appropriateness of the behavior called for by the new norm. The final stage in the cycle is internalization, when the norm becomes taken for granted, and conformance with its dictates is no longer (or at least rarely) questioned (Finnemore and Sikkink 1998: 904).

We can tell this same story with the idea of collective identity replacing the notion of a norm. We are justified in doing so because most scholars agree that collective identity is not an inherent or organic aspect of a person or a population. Andrew Wachtel, following Benedict Anderson's classic *Imagined Communities* (1983), argues that people belong to a nation, "not because of any objective identifying criteria such as common language, history, or cultural heritage (although in many particular cases such criteria can be and are adduced) but because they think they do" (1998: 2). It is quite simple to adapt the norm life cycle to our purposes for this chapter. Consider that entrepreneurs present ideas about collective identity, attempting to influence the process whereby people (elites and otherwise) identify with a collectivity. Sometimes entrepreneurs invent the collectivity itself (the United States was invented by the "Founding Fathers," for instance). Because, "national identity is never a finished product; it is always in the process of being constructed and reconstructed" (Doty 1996: 123), there is room for entrepreneurs to shape the process.

Similar to the norms process, a new national identity does not spring forth from the void instantaneously. Instead, the entrepreneur has to convince people to accept this new vision of the world—the new vision of collective identity. As Paul Kowert claims, "individuals are continually confronted with the problem of locating themselves, and others, in a web of social categories that periodically confront them as salient" (1998: 106). Entrepreneurs provide suggestions (or sometimes even demands) for how individuals should locate themselves. However, as with norms, we cannot say that a collective identity has emerged until a critical mass of individuals accept the entrepreneur's suggestion for locating themselves.

Once a critical mass has accepted the new identity, there are positive feedback effects to the new identity. Very simply, positive feedback means that the more people that accept a new identity, the more likely that others will accept it as well. This is the cascade that Finnemore and Sikkink discuss and it has been discussed in relation to the Yugoslav identity. As Steven Burg and Michael Berbaum argue, "in effect, the combination of higher education and interethnic contact induced individuals to declare Yugoslav identity in 1971, and the presence of these 'Yugoslavs' increased the rate at which others decided to do the same" (1989: 549). The final stage is internalization, where, in the case of collective identity, individuals do not question their allegiance or identification with a collectivity. Their collective identity becomes ingrained or taken for granted—naturalized.

The task for this chapter is thus to trace the idea life cycle with competing ideas of collective identity—Yugoslavism and particular nationalisms. To foreshadow, what is evident in the historical record of Yugoslavia is that the most recent suggestion of the Yugoslav idea, presented by Tito after World War II, was introduced through coercion. It was imposed, but did not reach critical mass and it was not fully internalized by the people who resided within the borders of Yugoslavia. This made both the Yugoslav idea and the Yugoslav state vulnerable to competing notions of collective identity—specifically, previously constituted nationalist ideas—and the result was the dissolution of the Yugoslav state. For as Roxanne Doty argues, "When it is no longer clear who makes up the nation, a state's internal sovereignty and the existence of the state itself is threatened" (1996: 122).

■ Tito and the Failure to Reach Critical Mass, 1945–1980

The idea life cycle provides a framework useful in sketching the contours of the story of the disintegration of Yugoslavia. With this framework we can trace how intersubjective understandings about Yugoslavism evolved over time and how the interplay between people (agents) and the state/national identity (structure) evolved.

Yugoslavism

The abstract idea of uniting Southern Slavs into a unified identity is not new and dates to the mid–nineteenth century (Pavkovic 1997; Wachtel 1998). In addition, some would claim that the Yugoslav identity has as long a history as the national identities that some current observers (mainly in the popular media) have categorized as ancient or even primordial. Andrew Wachtel argues that "many citizens of the Habsburg and Ottoman empires or the kingdoms of Serbia and Montenegro considered themselves members of a Yugoslav nation well before a Yugoslav state came into existence" (1998: 2). Throughout the nineteenth and twentieth centuries, the Yugoslav idea competed with "particularistic nationalisms" like Croatian, Serbian, Slovenian, and Bosnian among others (Wachtel 1998: 2). Yugoslavism certainly existed as a *potential* collective identity, and was no less "natural" than the particularistic nationalisms.

Hence, though the story of this chapter begins in 1945, it is crucial to remember that the idea life cycle process extends back 100 years prior to this analysis. This telling cuts into a process with significant history, as by 1945 the first Yugoslav state had already emerged (1918) and disintegrated and the Yugoslav identity had undergone at least two ideological transformations (Wachtel 1998: 1).[3]

The Entrepreneur: Joseph Tito

The most recent attempt to forge a Yugoslav identity began with the founding of the Yugoslav state in the aftermath of World War II. Tito, the leader of the communist Partisan resistance during the war, was the entrepreneur who put forth a new idea or conception of national identity—a socialist version of the Yugoslav idea. As per Finnemore and Sikkink's framework, Tito worked from a very powerful organizational platform. The communist party that he led emerged as the strongest political force after the war, eventually taking over and setting up modern Yugoslavia as a communist, totalitarian state.

From this platform Tito was able to articulate and disseminate his notion of the collective identity of the Southern Slavs. His (and the communist party's) ideas about the Yugoslav identity were forged in the war and were a reaction to the last instantiation of the Yugoslav identity from the interwar period. That version of the Yugoslav identity, institutionalized in a monarchical government, "failed to develop a grassroots appeal. . . . It also failed to provide the mass of Yugoslav citizens with a national identity replacing that of Serb, Croat, or Slovene varieties," and was instead too associated with Serbian hegemony (Pavkovic 1997: 23, 62).

Given this history and the interethnic conflict endemic to the Balkans during World War II, Tito and the communist Partisans projected a vision "of equality and harmony of all nations" (Pavkovic 1997: 39). Furthermore, "the communist recipe for national reconciliation after the war was quite simple: national unity has been forged through the Partisan struggle of national liberation in which all the nations and nationalities of Yugoslavia equally participated and in which all the forces of national hatred and conflict were defeated" (Pavkovic 1997: 44). This position on collective identity worked synergistically with the emerging power of the communist party to solidify Tito's organizational platform.

The Attempt to Reach Critical Mass

From 1945 through the 1950s, the new Yugoslav state actively advocated for this new manifestation of the Yugoslav identity. Through socialization, persuasion, and coercion, Tito's government attempted to convince individuals within the elite and general population to accept this new conception of the world and to identify with a Yugoslav nationality (see Hodson, Sekulic, and Massey 1994; and Sekulic, Massey, and Hodson 1994). He put forth a new socialist version of the unified Yugoslav identity that competed with extant national identities.[4]

As with any nation-building project, there are numerous tools available to those in power for socializing a population into a collective identity. Yugoslavia was no exception, as the Tito-led government employed economic, political, and cultural devices to try to achieve a critical mass of acceptance of the Yugoslav identity. Again, the critical mass is crucial, because collective identity is an intersubjective phenomenon—it is only "real" when people exhibit the identity. Thus the Yugoslav identity, crucial for stability in the Yugoslav state, only becomes "real" when the people of Yugoslavia accept it and act accordingly (self-identify as Yugoslav, support the Yugoslav state, use a common language, etc.). The policies that the state utilized to foster this identity included relatively benign socialization techniques such as education, linguistic policy, and support for certain literary/artistic initiatives, as well as more coercive policies designed to suppress national affiliations (see, e.g., Wachtel 1998: 5, 132–134; Pavkovic 1997: 50–51; and Stojanovic 1997: 76).

However, even given the apparatus of a totalitarian state (or perhaps because of it—see Stojanovic 1997 and Sekelj 1992), the process of building a new collective identity was no small task and it faced many obstacles. Competing ideas of collective identity, economic crisis, and political institutions worked against generating a critical mass or cascade around the Yugoslav idea.[5] The Yugoslav identity never garnered more that 6 percent of the population in census records and while self-identification as Yugoslav initially increased over time—1.3 percent in 1971 to 5.4 percent in 1981 (Sekulic, Massey, and Hodson 1994: 85)—it fell through the 1980s, down to 3 percent by 1991 (Hayden 1996: 798).[6] The people of Yugoslavia located themselves as Croats, Serbs, Slovenes, and so forth, more than as Yugoslavs. Further, this problem was most acute in Kosovo, where those self-identifying as Yugoslav only composed 0.5 percent of the population in 1961. This number plummeted to 0.1 percent by the time of the 1981 census (Sekulic, Massey, and Hodson 1994: 85).

This is an appropriate time to remark that an individual's political identity is not singular. The discussion in this chapter simplifies the process to a question of either Yugoslavism or particularistic nationalism, when in reality individuals can have multiple identities and express them situationally. The crucial point is that accepting and expressing the Yugoslav identity is at least "diffuse support" for the state of Yugoslavia (see Burg and Berbaum 1989), whereas expressing nationalist identities *could* and indeed did come to threaten the state. It is entirely possible that many people would feel and identify themselves as both Yugoslav and a particularistic nationality— many felt that they were Yugoslav citizens, but identified with a particular national group. What became important as Yugoslavia and the Yugoslav idea faced a series of challenges was to what degree would people identify *primarily* with Yugoslavism. Unfortunately, though many people held Yugoslavism as *an* identity, too few held it as their primary identity. Without the support of state apparatus, which eroded quickly through the 1950s and 1960s, this underlying weakness would soon make Yugoslavism vulnerable to entrepreneurs espousing particularistic nationalisms.

The Yugoslav idea had a difficult time reaching critical mass because the Yugoslav state failed to solve the national question. Competing collective identities representing particular nationalities made it difficult for the Yugoslav identity to gain acceptance. Post–World War II Yugoslavia was built on a compromise between national politics and the overarching Yugoslav state. Tito set up an "unstable dialectic" (Wachtel 1998: 134) based on his guiding principle of Yugoslavism, whereby "Yugoslavia would be unified, solid" but respect cultural and national differences (Djilas 1991: 37, quoted in Wachtel 1998: 132–133). The communists undertook "strategic nationalism" and attempted to "recreate Yugoslavia after the war, but without insisting on a highly centralized Yugoslav nation-state reminiscent of the Serbian-dominated state of the interwar period" (Sekulic, Massey, and Hodson 1994: 86). Yugoslavia was a federal state, with semiautonomous republics and the overarching institution of the federal, communist government and party. Given the constraints of history, the communist party failed to strongly promote Yugoslavism, and instead legitimated "national identifications" (Hodson, Sekulic, and Massey 1994: 1542).

Federalism did not serve to answer all of the national questions. Symptomatic and crucial among these questions was Kosovo. In Kosovo, the Yugoslav idea was not accepted by those of Albanian ethnicity—a majority of the population in the region.[7] Aleksandar Pavkovic argues that "it is doubtful that the federal structure which confined the Albanian population to the status of a national minority and [Kosovo] to a sub-federal unit (province) has ever won wide acceptance among Kosovo Albanians or their educated elites" (1997: 50). Already in 1945–1946, the Kosovar Albanians undertook mass uprisings to oppose this incorporation into the Yugoslav federal structure. This was a foreshadowing of things to come in 1968 and again in 1981. Hence, at the very least, the Yugoslav idea was not accepted in Kosovo—those identified as ethnic Albanians did not accept and act in a way as to instantiate the Yugoslav idea.

Another challenge to the Yugoslav idea and state was economic. Yugoslavia experienced uneven economic development and economic crises that facilitated national, rather than Yugoslav allegiances. Very quickly after World War II, the republics within Yugoslavia experienced vastly different economic trajectories, in terms of both productivity and income (see Sekulic, Massey, and Hodson 1994; and Sekelj 1992). Thus, republic-level communist parties began to take an interest in their "constituent" populations, which opened the door for economic nationalism and made it difficult for the state-level communist party to function as a driver of the Yugoslav idea (Sekulic, Massey, and Hodson 1994: 87–88). Sekelj argues that the "modernization" crisis of the 1950s and 1960s meant that "instead of Yugoslavism came nationalism, and instead of egalitarianism came the stress on national economies" (1992: 6).

Both the failure to deal adequately with the national question and the impact of uneven economic development were symptoms of a larger problem that stemmed from the attempt to balance national and Yugoslav institutions and identities. While the Yugoslav state through the 1950s attempted to build Yugoslav institutions and identity, by the 1960s it was clear that power was devolving to the republican level and "from the mid-1960s forward, the national principle became deeply institutionalized" (Hodson, Sekulic, and Massey 1994: 1540). This trend accelerated into the 1970s. The communist party (Tito) and the Yugoslav military became the only centralizing forces. The state itself became more of a confederation of autonomous polities than a centralized federal entity. Without support, the Yugoslav idea, which was weak vis-à-vis the other national identities to begin with, could not reach critical mass and no cascade occurred—the primary identity of most Yugoslavs remained based in particularistic nationalisms.

According to Pavkovic, by the 1960s "those who declared themselves as Yugoslavs only, found that they were ineligible for any elective Party or government positions" (1997: 64). The power structure of the entire state of Yugoslavia became more and more geared toward republic-level institutions and parties. Tito remained the ultimate authority, and the Yugoslav state did retain control of the media and army (Sekulic, Massey, and Hodson 1994: 87), but there was no longer any active support of the Yugoslav idea. Again, Kosovo provides the quintessential example. As power devolved to republican-level parties, the party in Kosovo became much more inwardly focused. The power structure facilitated the growth of an Albanian-centered Kosovo communist party, in addition to calls for full republican status for Kosovo (Pavkovic 1997: 65–68).

By 1974, a new Yugoslav constitution officially replaced the federal system with a confederation of republics. This new constitution reflected the reality of republican power bases as opposed to a national, Yugoslav power base (Pavkovic 1997: 69–70; Sekelj 1992: 6–8; Sekulic, Massey, and Hodson 1994: 87–88). "In the constitution of 1974 the communist national elites and their leaders in each republic and province received constitutional guarantees of full control over their respective republics and provinces" (Pavkovic 1997: 73).

The Demise of the Yugoslav Idea: Precursor to State Failure

What is evident to this point is an abbreviated norm life cycle. There was an entrepreneur, and there were early attempts to bolster the Yugoslav idea, made by the Yugoslav state. However, given competing entrepreneurs (multiple national elites had competing ideas about collective identity) and the obstacles mentioned above, there was a failure to reach critical mass and no cascade of change or internalization. In constructivist terms, people (agents) failed to act in a way that instantiated the intersubjective Yugoslav collective identity (structure). The 1960s and 1970s made the Yugoslav idea vulnerable to competing ideas. Indeed, some would claim that the 1974 constitution signaled the loss of the competition to particularistic nationalist ideas. According to Randy Hodson, Dusko Sekulic, and Garth Massey, "Yugoslavian state policies . . . set the stage for the mobilization of groups around nationality. . . . In the absence of other forms of political cohesion, nationalism appears to be the most readily available unifying doctrine" (1994: 1555). After Tito's death, competing ideas and entrepreneurs would gain the upper hand, a critical mass of individuals would coalesce around nationalist ideas promoted by entrepreneurs, and Yugoslavism would disintegrate in a cascade of nationalism and violence. It was in this period that Kosovo would play the key role in the Yugoslav disintegration.

■ Milosevic, Kosovo, and the Tragic Triumph of Nationalism, 1980–1989

Though in hindsight it is possible to see the beginnings of the end for the Yugoslav idea and the state of Yugoslavia in the 1960s and 1970s, it was not necessarily apparent at the time. Indeed, in the early 1980s (and even through the 1980s) social scientists were remarking on the growth of Yugoslav identification and its implications for the stability of the Yugoslav state (Hayden 1996: 789–790; Burg and Berbaum 1989: 535–536; Sekulic, Massey, and Hudson 1994). In addition, though difficult to conceive today, "it is clear that that national identity was not a primary focus of most people's concerns in the early 1980s" (Hayden 1996: 789). There was a dearth of overt identification as Yugoslav, but through intermingling and modernization people were beginning to see themselves differently (Hayden 1996; Hodson, Sekulic, and Massey 1994; Burg and Berbaum 1989).

However, Yugoslavism was vulnerable because of a lack of state support and the emergence of entrepreneurs using nationalist ideas to pursue a variety of agendas. Yugoslavism would soon display its weakness in a renewed competition with particularistic nationalisms—a competition that began in Kosovo almost immediately upon Tito's death in 1980. With the death of Tito, Yugoslavism no longer had an active entrepreneur (even in name only) advancing Yugoslav identity. In fact, advocating for the Yugoslav idea became extremely unpopular among party officials. Power within Yugoslavia had devolved to the republics and provinces and this facilitated the emergence of vocal and powerful entrepreneurs promoting particularistic nationalisms. The "Kosovo crisis" in the 1980s would engender violent debate over the nature of Southern Slavs' collective identity, and a new, powerful entrepreneur emerged in the late 1980s, Milosevic, who promoted a particularly virulent nationalism. The 1980s saw the final defeat for Yugoslavism and eventually the final death knell for Yugoslavia.

The Kosovo Demonstrations of 1980–1981: New Entrepreneurs and the Nationalist Challenge to Yugoslavism

The first post-Tito signs of trouble for the Yugoslav idea (and therefore the Yugoslav state) arose in Kosovo in 1980–1981. Student demonstrations, ironically begun over the quality of soup in the cafeterias, turned into riots demanding republican status for the region of Kosovo (Malcolm 1998; Mertus 1999a). These riots had many underlying causes, including economic crisis (Lee 1983: 67–68), but the overall objective of the riots and demonstrations was political—Kosovar Albanians demanded republican status within Yugoslavia (see Lee 1983; Mertus 1999a; Malcolm 1998; and Pipa 1989). What this clearly demonstrates is the lack of internalization of the Yugoslav idea in Kosovo, and further that the Kosovar Albanians were undertaking action that instantiated a different collective identity— Albanian nationalism. Again, collective identity is an intersubjective phenomenon and thus only real when people act as if it is real. In Kosovo in 1980–1981 the Albanian population stopped acting as if the Yugoslav idea was real and acted instead as if the Albanian collective identity was real.[8]

This display of Albanian identity did not arise from nowhere. Similar demonstrations in 1968 led to reforms that strengthened Albanian identity, setting the stage for the 1980–1981 disturbances. In fact, in 1969, Kosovo was permitted to use the Albanian flag, and Albanian-language universities were opened (Malcolm 1998: 325; Pipa 1989: 162). In addition, the devolution of political power to republican-level party elites (and province-level party elites in the case of Kosovo) also encouraged collective identification at the national, rather than Yugoslav level. What we see in 1980–1981 in Kosovo is the result of a history of people locating themselves as Albanian, and acting in a way to reinforce that collective identity. At the same time these actions further weakened the Yugoslav idea. As Pavkovic argues, "with hindsight, one could argue that the riots [of 1980–1981] signaled the failure of the 1974 constitutional arrangements to satisfy the growing demands of the newly emergent communist elites and their constituencies, as in the case of the Kosovo Albanians, for political autonomy and control over 'their' territory" (1997: 79).

The Serbian Reaction and New Entrepreneurs

The story of Kosovo in the 1980s is not a straightforward tale of a people (Albanians) who deny the Yugoslav idea and support and strive for self-determination as Albanians. Instead, as Julie Mertus proposes, "Kosovo exemplifies a society in which the identities of the two competing groups [Serbs and Albanians] have long been tied to Truths about the other. . . . The case of Kosovo illustrates what happens when political leaders exploit the most demeaning Truths about the other in order to create intense feelings of insecurity and victimization" (1999a: 4). In Kosovo, both Serbs and Albanians came to identify strongly with their national and religious groups, rather than with the Yugoslav idea.[9] While the two visions of collective identification were in competition from 1945 through Tito's death, in the 1980s the competition was won by particular nationalisms.

Nationalism in Kosovo begot nationalism in Serbia, due in no small part to Serbia's historical ties to the region and the Serbian foundational myths associated with Kosovo (see Mertus 1999a; and Malcolm 1998). The riots in Kosovo in 1980–1981 catalyzed the emergence of entrepreneurs who promoted a particular nationalism.[10] According to Mertus the riots changed the discourse in Yugoslavia, especially among the Serbian party elite. The riots elevated the position of and power of Serbian politicians and policies that were "hard" on Kosovo, and they led to a context where "Serbian politicians began exploiting the Kosovo issues to their gain. Nationalists were encouraged to speak more openly" (1999a: 44–45).

Serbian elites as nationalist entrepreneurs began to portray the Kosovo issue as one of victimization of Serbs in Kosovo and a larger problem with Yugoslavia as whole (Mertus 1999a: 99; Gagnon 1994–1995: 148). This set of entrepreneurial suggestions (to identify with a Serbian, rather than Yugoslav idea) was powerful. Indeed, the Albanian nationalism in Kosovo set off reactions that "led to a fundamental realignment of politics in Serbia and the growth of a dangerous, defensive, populist, and officially sanctioned nationalism" (Denitch 1994: 116, quoted in Mertus 1999a: 7).

In Kosovo and then Serbia, where the Yugoslav idea was never even close to reaching critical mass, entrepreneurs advocating a nationalist means of collective identification found willing ears. These suggestions fit with a population in Kosovo convinced that it was being oppressed (Kosovar Albanians) and that desired economic development and political autonomy. They also fit with a population of Serbs (in Serbia and Kosovo) that "were beginning to think that there was no Yugoslav interest defending their rights" (Mertus 1999a: 99).[11] Nationalism fit with a general population suffering through economic crisis and reminded of recent past atrocities. Nationalism fit with elites already in a system defined by national power centers. Nationalism fit and it would soon cascade and signal the end of Yugoslavia.

Kosovo 1987 and Milosevic: The Cascade of Nationalism

The nationalist idea for collective identification grew to critical mass through the 1980s. Mertus (1999a) describes a series of incidents that fueled the nationalist fire in Kosovo for both the Albanians and the Serbs. Further economic crisis and the political institutions that concentrated power at the republican level enabled nationalist entrepreneurs to successfully persuade, coerce, and socialize people into a particular notion of collective identity. Eventually the continuing Kosovo crisis in the mid-1980s facilitated the rise of the most infamous entrepreneur, Milosevic, and the final cascade and internalization of particularistic nationalism.

Throughout the early and mid-1980s, nationalist fervor in Serbia proper and among Serbian Kosovars grew and Kosovo, especially the Albanian population, became the foil for Serbian nationalism. Albanian "atrocities" against the Serbian people were condemned (see Mertus 1999a; and Malcolm 1998). The autonomy of Kosovo was decried (Mertus 1999a: 137–138). By the mid-1980s, it was the Serbian population in Kosovo that was full of unrest and protest, claiming victimhood and the need for protection against Albanian aggression. This second Kosovo crisis was the Serbian nationalist reaction to the original Albanian calls for a republic. Crucially, the Serbs in Kosovo were not crying out for Yugoslavia to save them, but rather they turned to their Serbian identity and Serbian elites.

It was in reaction to the Kosovo crisis that Slobodan Milosevic, to this point a relatively minor figure in the Serbian communist party, began to use nationalist, inflammatory language (Mertus 1999a: 140–141). As the head of the communist party in Belgrade, Milosevic oversaw "the start of a nationalist campaign . . . which sought to defend the 'national dignity of Serbia'" (Gagnon 1994–1995: 147). Milosevic was rapidly becoming a nationalist (see Sekelj 1992: 221; Pavkovic 1997: 102; Gagnon 1994–1995; and Wilmer 2002: 160), and in 1987 the Yugoslav president sent Milosevic to Kosovo to meet with a group of protesting Serbs. During an orchestrated fight between police and the protesters, Milosevic uttered what would become a rallying cry of Serbian nationalism: "No one should dare to beat you" (Malcolm 1998: 341).

Milosevic used the Kosovo crisis to vault into power by acting as a Serbian national entrepreneur. His nationalist stance "triggered open conflict between two factions within Serbia's leadership" and "while not interested in the Kosovo problem before 1987, Milosevic exploited it in the intra-party conflict" (Vljevic 2002: 774). The conflict facilitated Milosevic's rise to power. As Sekelj notes, "Slobodan Milosevic skillfully won the support of the majority of the discontented Serbian population, and channeled their energies in favor of the Community Party by means of Serbian nationalism, establishing himself as the indisputable national leader" (1992: 221–222). Mass rallies of Serbians demonstrating over the Kosovo problem ensued throughout 1987 and 1988 and helped Milosevic solidify his power base. The Kosovo issue also facilitated purges in the Serbian and Kosovo communist parties (see Mertus 1999a: 155).

The success of Milosevic's initial entrepreneurship was aided by numerous factors: the above-mentioned fit of his rhetoric with the Serbian population, economic crisis, the Serbian foundational stories associated with the Battle of Kosovo, and the alleged Albanian-perpetrated atrocities. However, his control of the media played a crucial role in moving from a critical mass to a cascade of nationalism that engulfed the entire country (see Sekelj 1992: 198; Wilmer 2002: 48; and Pavkovic 1997: 103). "Journalists who were allied with Milosevic . . . undertook a media campaign to demonize ethnic Albanians" (Gagnon 1994–1995: 147–148) and the nationalist sentiments engendered surged throughout Yugoslavia (in Serbian populations and beyond). Milosevic was able to obtain significant control over the media "and used it to persuade hundreds of thousands of citizens that their security depended on a successful and harsh military retaliation against 'other' ethnic groups" (Harvey 2000: 62). Nationalism had won over Yugoslavism. As Robert Hayden notes, "the politics of nationalism in the late 1980s and early 1990s thus turned territories populated by concentrations of the various national groups into states in which members of the majority nation were sovereign. The presumption of the politics was that the various Yugoslav peoples could not live together and that therefore their common state had to be divided" (1996: 788).

The End of Yugoslavism
Of course the story of Kosovo goes on beyond 1988. The late 1980s and 1990s saw the crisis in Kosovo and throughout Yugoslavia turn violent, and it eventually drew the UN and NATO into the conflict. Kosovo's autonomy was stripped in the late 1980s by a resurgent Serbia under Milosevic, and the "Serbian nationalism initially mobilized over Kosovo began to threaten other federal units" (Mertus 1999a: 8–9). Nationalism had swept away Yugoslavism throughout Yugoslavia. An idea of collective identification along particular national lines would thus destroy the state of Yugoslavia. For as Hayden argues, "thus extreme nationalism in the former Yugoslavia has not been only a matter of imagining allegedly 'primordial' communities, but rather of making existing, heterogeneous ones unimaginable" (1996: 783).

Without a foundation built on support for the Yugoslav idea, Yugoslavia was not strong enough to weather this storm. No one identified with the state, and the state, beset by crises, fell in a maelstrom of violence and tragedy.

■ Conclusion

Why did Yugoslavia fail to make it from Friday to Monday? The variables that "caused" Yugoslavia to break apart are relatively straightforward. The economy suffered greatly at key moments. Political institutions engendered centrifugal forces that devolved power and authority to the republics. Elites used nationalism as a way to maintain and expand their power bases. Yet all of these "facts" do not *explain* the fall of Yugoslavia. Explaining the fall of Yugoslavia entails specifying the mechanisms through which these factors could lead to the breakup of the state. This mechanism must link people (micro level) and their collectivities (macro level) and explain how micro-level actions interact and evolve with macro-level outcomes.

Social constructivism provides a framework with the necessary mechanisms. The norm life cycle, adapted to explore collective identities, gives structure to our examination of the fall of Yugoslavia. We can thus trace how the Yugoslav idea was suggested to the people of Yugoslavia and how entrepreneurs (Tito and the communist party in the 1950s) attempted to persuade (or coerce) the people of Yugoslavia to accept it. We can trace the failure of the Yugoslav idea to reach critical mass. Not enough people in Yugoslavia acted in accordance with this worldview—not enough people identified with the Yugoslav identity. We can trace the renewed suggestions of particular nationalist ideas by entrepreneurs in the 1970s and 1980s. At first nationalist ideas competed with Yugoslavism, but eventually they overcame them entirely. Unlike the Yugoslav idea, the particular nationalist ideas did reach critical mass and they cascaded in the late 1980s.

The social constructivist framework helps us to order the facts of the Yugoslav breakup and understand how micro-level actors and macro-level collectivities are related. The social deconstruction of Yugoslavism and the social construction of virulent nationalism were the processes that removed the underlying foundation for the state of Yugoslavia. Once the foundations were removed, Yugoslavia itself could not stand.

Beyond Yugoslavia: Applying the Norm (Idea) Life Cycle

The idea life cycle structured an explanation for the dissolution of Yugoslavia, but the details of this particular case may obscure the general applicability of the approach. Thus in concluding, let me suggest areas where the idea life cycle may prove useful. First, social constructivism and the idea life cycle are valuable approaches to cases of identity change like the failure of Yugoslavism. The approach can be applied to explore how people or political actors come to see themselves as similar (the social construction of an integrated group) or different (the social [de]construction of fragmenting groups). While Yugoslavia was obviously a case of the latter, there are multiple cases for each type of identity change:

Construction of Integrated Groups	Construction of Fragmenting Groups
• Indigenous rights movement	• Quebec issue in Canada
• "Melting pot" in the United States	• Ethnic conflict
• German unification in 1800s	• Breakup of the Soviet Union

In each of these cases, we can use the idea life cycle to trace how different identities emerge and change over time.

Beyond the social construction of identity, this approach can be used to explore the general role of norms and ideas in politics. Ideas about identity are a subset of a large set of ideas about what is appropriate in politics. How do political actors decide what actions to undertake? According to social constructivists, ideas and norms constitute the answer to this question (see Ba and Hoffmann 2003; Adler 1997; and Finnemore and Sikkink 1998). Ideas put boundaries on what actors see as appropriate behavior and even possible behaviors (Yee 1996). Thus the idea life cycle can be used to explore a number of issues:

- The US-led invasion of Iraq in 2003: the idea life cycle can be used to explain how such an action came to be seen as possible and appropriate by exploring ideas and norms of sovereignty, security, and the use of military power.
- Nuclear proliferation: how it came to be that a certain set of states are allowed to have nuclear weapons and others are not, as well as how this might be changing (see Price and Tannenwald 1996).
- The intervention in Kosovo: the idea life cycle can help to explain the aftermath of the Kosovo crises discussed in this chapter, and how the NATO intervention in Kosovo came to seen as possible and appropriate.

The social constructivist approach and the idea life cycle provide us with insight into how norms and ideas shape politics. They help us to understand the dynamic interaction of people and their collectivities. The hope is that they can help us to understand politics in such a way that tragedies like Yugoslavia can be averted.

■ Notes

1. For an exposition on this subject, see J. Rosenau 1990.

2. Constructivism has many variants. See Adler 1997 for a useful typology.

3. It is crucial to remember that collective identities are not static. What it means to be a Yugoslav can change. Further, this dynamism applies to particularistic nationalisms as well—what it means to be a Croat can change over time too.

4. To be very clear, entrepreneurship is not necessarily (or even very often) altruistic in nature. Some entrepreneurs advocate ideas for moral reasons (see Nadelmann 1990; and Finnemore and Sikkink 1998). Others advocate policies. Still others advocate ideas in order to achieve or maintain power. Clearly, most entrepreneurs have multiple motives. While it is certainly plausible that Tito "cared" about the Yugoslav idea and thought it would be best for the people of the Balkans, he also advocated Yugoslavism as a way to achieve and maintain power for the communist party. Constructivism does not tend to focus enough on questions of power, but a motivation of power for entrepreneurship is not antithetical to constructivist analysis.

5. These three obstacles may not, and almost certainly do not, encompass the entire set of variables that hindered the Yugoslav idea from reaching a critical mass of acceptance.

6. These numbers may be misleading on their face—the setup of the census actually worked against Yugoslav identification, making it equivalent with no nationality (Hodson, Sekulic, and Massey 1994: 1542–1543). However, this is part of the crucial point—without strong state support (discussed in detail later in the chapter), the Yugoslav identity was vulnerable.

7. In addition to composing a different ethnic group, the Kosovar Albanians also practiced a different religion than the dominant Slavic groups. The Albanians tend to be Muslim, while the Serbs tend to be Orthodox Christians. Religion can be a powerful aspect of political identity. However, in the case of Yugoslavia, according to Hodson, Sekulic, and Massey, "there are religious differences to be sure, but there is little evidence that religious differences per se provide a sufficient basis for differing national claims" (1994: 1541). Therefore in this chapter I will restrict my discussion to national identities (Albanian, Serbian).

8. This is a vast simplification for analytical purposes. Throughout the 1960s and 1970s, people within Kosovo, and indeed throughout the rest of Yugoslavia, acted in ways that would instantiate both the Yugoslav identity and particularistic national identities. However, in 1980–1981 we see the beginning of breakpoint change where the Yugoslav identity is no longer exhibited, losing the competition entirely to nationalist collective identities.

9. There was also grassroots organizing among the Serbian population in Kosovo, though it was generally in opposition to alleged Albanian abuses (see Vljevic 2002; and Dragnich 1989).

10. Finnemore and Sikkink (1998) argue that entrepreneurs are not somehow outside a social context. Instead, their "suggestions" are conditioned by their social context. Nationalist entrepreneurs emerged in the early 1980s in a context characterized by weak Yugoslavism and growing Albanian nationalism.

11. The fit of an entrepreneur's suggestion with predispositions in a target population are a key determinant of successful entrepreneurship, according to Finnemore and Sikkink (1998).

Patrick Thaddeus Jackson

Relational Constructivism: A War of Words

On April 14, 1999, a NATO pilot over Kosovo dropped a bomb on a convoy of Albanian refugees being escorted by Serbian military vehicles. Yugoslavian officials reported sixty-four dead, and Serbian president Milan Milutinovic used the opportunity to condemn the "massacre perpetrated today by the criminal NATO airforce against innocent civilians" (Auerswald and Auerswald 2000: 862).[1] NATO spokesman Jamie Shea countered at a press conference with the argument that "we can reduce the risk of accidents but we cannot eliminate them altogether," and followed this with an indictment of the Serbian regime's policy that had placed the refugees in harm's way:

> Why weren't the people in their homes, at their jobs, going about their normal lives? Why were they en route to the border? Because they had been forced from their homes and because they were on their way to joining the 580,000 Kosovar Albanians that have already been expelled from Kosovo. . . . Why was a NATO pilot 15,000 feet up in the air yesterday afternoon over Kosovo? Because along with about 1,000 other NATO pilots, he was risking his life every day to stop human suffering in Kosovo. (Auerswald and Auerswald 2000: 860)

This exchange brings into sharp relief a crucial issue often overlooked in realist and liberal analyses of world politics: the issue of *legitimation*. Social actors do not carry out their actions in a vacuum, and in particular do not carry out their actions in silence; rather, they provide reasons for why they did what they did or why they should do one thing rather than another. And these reasons are contestable, in that one set of legitimating reasons—NATO is bombing to "stop human suffering," and the bombing of the refugee convoy was an "accident"—can be opposed by a very different characterization of the "same" events, such as the characterization of the bombing campaign as "criminal." The war in Kosovo was certainly an exchange of weapons fire and casualties, but—like every war in human history—it was also an exchange of rhetorical efforts to characterize the situation in particular ways and thus render certain courses of action acceptable while ruling others unacceptable.

Indeed, the NATO bombing campaign itself was at least in part a product of a legitimation struggle, as the United States and its European allies pressed for a negotiated resolution to the conflict in Kosovo and the Yugoslavian regime refused to submit to their demands. The planes and bombs directed at Serbian targets in early 1999 were a continuation of that legitimation struggle, a struggle waged both against Yugoslavian character-izations of appropriate action and against alternative ways of understanding the duties and interests of the NATO allies when faced with the Kosovo conflict. The particular *rhetorical commonplaces* deployed in the course of debates about possible courses of action made the NATO bombing cam-paign in Kosovo possible in the first place, shaping the subsequent actions taken in NATO's name in important ways. Although never a war as a matter of international law, the military campaign in Kosovo was most certainly a war of words—words with deadly, and sometimes tragic, consequences.

■ Constructivism: A Relational Perspective

The constructivist approach that I will adopt in this chapter is a *relational* approach, concentrating on an ongoing process of social transaction rather than on the "norms" (Finnemore and Sikkink 1998) or "rules" (Onuf 1998) preferred as sites of analysis by other constructivists. The key mechanism producing outcomes in my relational constructivist account is legitimation, rather than the mechanisms of "internalization" and "social learning" (Adler 1997; Checkel 2001) preferred by other constructivists. While there are ways of accounting for the NATO bombing campaign from all of these constructivist perspectives, the relational perspective's emphasis on ongo-ing contestation and rhetorical struggle illuminates key features of the events in question in a particularly compelling way. I will briefly expand on the conceptual equipment utilized by a relational constructivist approach before developing my empirical account.[2]

The Agent-Structure Problem

Although there were constructivists in IR (even if they went by other names) before Alexander Wendt's seminal 1987 article on the agent-struc-ture problem, it is undeniable that the constructivist perspective received a conceptual shot in the arm from Wendt's discussion of this "central prob-lem in social and political theory" (Green 2002: 8). Wendt points out that the agent-structure problem derives from two "truisms about social life": people and their organizations act in purposeful ways, affecting outcomes through their actions; and society is made up of "social relationships, which structure the interactions between these purposeful actors" (1987: 337–338). The "problem" here is that it is difficult to do justice to both sides of this relationship at the same time; in practice, analysts tend to priv-ilege either agents or structures in their explanations of events and out-comes.

The agent-structure problem is a *theoretical* problem: How should we deal with this curious doubleness of social arrangements? Where most IR theorists privilege structures, with realists pointing to international anarchy and liberal rationalists pointing to the distribution of material interests,[3] constructivists seek to incorporate both agents and structures into their accounts. There are at least three ways of doing this: temporal-sequentially, so that agents establish a structure and then that structure affects their future decisions; "bracketing," so that agentic and structural dimensions of a situation are isolated conceptually although they run together in practice; and relationally, so that both agents *and* structures are understood to emerge from social networks and social relations more generally.

The relational approach garners a number of significant advantages over the other two constructivist options.[4] For example, the temporal-sequential solution to the agent-structure problem requires something to get the ball rolling, so to speak: some event or procedure that either frees agents from their previous structural constraints so that they can innovate, or freezes the innovative actions of agents into a newly solid context for social action. At the extreme, this kind of argument becomes quite dependent on various "magic moments" destabilizing or replacing previously stable social arrangements. Whether these moments are called "exogenous shocks" (Spruyt 1994) or "tipping points" (Finnemore and Sikkink 1998) or something else, they are not so much explanations of social change as descriptions of it. In addition, many constructivists rely on mechanisms like "socialization" or "internalization" to link agents and structures together (Adler and Barnett 1998: 41–45; Schimmelfennig 1998–1999: 211–213); but the use of these mechanisms creates the paradox that socialized agents cease to exercise effective agency, as they are now acting on the dictates of the norms that they have internalized (Tilly 1998). Relational constructivism, by focusing on the dynamics of the social environment surrounding actors, avoids these problems.[5]

The Relational Solution

"Solving" the agent-structure problem in a relational way is not like, for example, solving a crossword puzzle; instead, the relational solution begins by challenging the very terms in which the problem was originally posed. Most constructivist approaches begin from the position that social action is rather unproblematically carried out by "agents," individuals and organizations that are relatively stable at the moment of action; if NATO is going to make up its collective mind about whether or not to bomb Serbia, it does so *before* the particular bombings in question. Individual agents, then, are "primitive" units of analysis for most constructivists (and most IR theorists, as a matter of fact)—they, and their intentional activities, are the basic building blocks of an explanation.[6] This position logically leads to the stance that preserving agency means preserving the autonomy of those essential, primitive agents, whether by showing them making choices from a menu of structurally provided options or by illustrating that their choices produced that menu at some earlier point in time.

It is precisely this emphasis on agent autonomy, however, that leads to problems in other constructivist approaches. Instead of beginning with essential agents operating in a social context, relational constructivists begin with patterns of social transaction out of which both agents *and* structures congeal.[7] Instead of starting with an unproblematic entity called "NATO" and trying to explain why it did what it did, relational constructivism starts with the practical activities that continually produce and reproduce the actor called "NATO" and examines how these activities give rise to the observed social actions carried out in its name (Dessler 1989: 462). In particular, activities devoted to *legitimation* command the attention of relational constructivists, since these activities—including giving public reasons for a course of action, criticizing other options, attributing blame and responsibility, and disputing other efforts to do these things—are among the clearest moments at which actors are produced in practice.

Consider, for example, a sovereign territorial state, ordinarily considered to be the paradigmatic actor in IR. What does it really *mean* to say that some state "acts"? There are certain people authorized to speak on behalf of any given state in particular contexts, like ambassadors, governmental officials, and bureaucrats; when they speak and act "in the name of" the state, it is clear that they are only, as it were, conduits for or bearers of the authority of the state itself. Action, from a relational perspective, is a matter of social attribution, as certain activities are encoded or characterized as the doings of some social actor. This social attribution simultaneously produces the actor in question as legitimately able to perform the action in question, and legitimates the action inasmuch as the actor performs it. Out of the general flow of events, legitimation processes isolate certain activities (the collection of income taxes, for example, or the requirement to register with the government as a nonresident alien) and render them acceptable by characterizing them as the activities of "the state"; in so doing, they reproduce the state itself. It is in these boundary demarcations that "the state" has its most tangible existence and its most concrete presence in the daily lives of those under its authority.

What is true of the state is true of *any* social actor: it is less the determinate origin of any given social action and more a product of the processes of legitimation that produce and sustain it in particular concrete settings. "NATO," "Serbia," and even "Milosevic" are not simply and unproblematically the doers of the deeds in question; instead, their authority and responsibility have to be continually negotiated and sustained in practice. Thinking of social actors in this way allows us to grasp the stakes of the legitimation struggles—in this case, the "wars of words" accompanying and surrounding the use of military force in the Balkans—waged by politicians and other officials. Different actors have different rights and responsibilities, and can legitimately perform a different range of actions; "states" can get away with things that "firms" or "ethnic groups" cannot, much as a police officer with a warrant is empowered to enter a home and remove objects from it in a way that a burglar is not.

Hence NATO spokesman Jamie Shea's aforementioned argument that the NATO pilot who had (mistakenly)[8] bombed the convoy of refugees "was risking his life every day to stop human suffering in Kosovo" gains a different *status*. Instead of a statement that should be evaluated empirically in terms of whether or not the pilot in question was actually doing this, it becomes instead a statement that participates in an ongoing process of legitimation directed at the bombings in general and this operation in particular. In so doing, the statement does not advance completely novel arguments; rather it draws on various general rhetorical commonplaces already present in the social environment surrounding the specific incident (Kratochwil 1989: 40–42; Shotter 1993: 65–69). Specific articulations in the course of a public debate take these more general notions already in circulation and link them to particular policies, legitimating them and attributing them as actions to some particular actor.

Shea's particular statement deploys two commonplaces: the notion that military operations are "risky," uncertain, and unpredictable, and the notion that "human suffering" is the real target of the bombing. The risks associated with bombing are justified by the stakes involved, a stance that accounts for any civilian deaths as "errors," as "regrettable things" that are not sufficient reasons for "changing our mission," as President Bill Clinton told reporters that same day (Auerswald and Auerswald 2000: 858). Whether or not it is *true* that modern mechanized warfare must inevitably produce accidental civilian casualties is beside the point, as is the question of whether "human suffering" justifies military action according to some abstract ethical argument. What matters is that these are the commonplaces invoked, and that the pairing of these commonplaces affords certain kinds of action (NATO military operations on behalf of humanitarian goals) while ruling others (standing back and doing nothing, or withdrawing because of the civilian deaths) out of bounds. What makes this deployment "work" is precisely that it deploys extant commonplaces, so that the audience toward which the statement is directed will recognize the argument as sensible, and that it handles possible counterarguments in a relatively explicit fashion. Both of these components of a legitimation process are important aspects of a relational constructivist account.

Relational constructivism thus fulfills the mandate to preserve agency in two ways. First, rhetorical commonplaces stand in need of further specification in order to exercise their effects, and there are multiple commonplaces available in any given situation. Both the combinations of commonplaces deployed, and the specific interpretations of those commonplaces advanced by various speakers, are radically contingent in a way that more traditional notions of social structure are not. This contingency preserves human agency, as there is no way to predict in advance what a particular speaker will do in a situation, but whatever the speaker *does* do has consequential effects. This is the very definition of agency.[9]

■ Constructing the Bombing Campaign

What a relational constructivist approach has to say about Kosovo, and in particular about the NATO bombing campaign that took place between March 24 and June 10, 1999, depends on the application of these theoretical considerations to the concrete material generated by a number of organizations and individual persons during this period of time. Schematically, a relational constructivist analysis proceeds in three steps:

First, identify a course of action to be explained, and the locations at which public debates about this course of action were carried out. Some public debates take place in relatively well developed debating forums, such as legislatures and parliaments, but these are not the only sites of interest to this mode of analysis. Most organizations of interest to IR scholars have dedicated individuals or offices for providing reasons to the public via the news media, and the press releases and press conferences in which these individuals and offices engage also constitute good sources of data. Public speeches by authorized officials, websites,[10] and virtually any similar occasion for deploying commonplaces in public can also be tapped. For the Kosovo conflict, Philip Auerswald and David Auerswald (2000) have assembled a "diplomatic history through documents" that provides a reasonably comprehensive collection of the major public statements from officials and organizations involved both in carrying out the bombing campaign and in contesting its meaning and justification.[11] In what follows, I will rely almost exclusively on this collection.[12]

Second, map the rhetorical commonplaces deployed in the course of arguments about courses of action to be pursued. The point here is to develop something of a "rhetorical topography," a catalog of commonplaces used in practice during the relevant debates by the different parties, and to determine which commonplaces figure into patterns of justification as relatively central.[13] Special attention needs to be paid to social attributions of responsibility, in which action X performed by actor Y is justified by reason Z; such attributions simultaneously legitimate the action and bound the actor, and as such are particularly noteworthy. Commonplaces shared by the parties to a debate, but deployed in different ways by each of them, are especially important, as are commonplaces unique to one party that figure centrally in efforts to rebut criticisms.

Third, explain, historically, how the relevant commonplaces came to be available to interlocutors at a specific point in time, and trace their concrete deployment. This does not need to be done for every commonplace, but only for those commonplaces revealed to be important by the topographical sketch of commonplaces. This historical account sets the map in motion, as it were, illustrating how the deployment of commonplaces during a specific set of debates is able to produce a concrete outcome, both by rendering a specific course of action acceptable to the relevant audience and by rendering alternative proposals unacceptable. In what follows, I will briefly recount the results of implementing this procedure for the debates surrounding the 1999 NATO bombing campaign.

"We Are Upholding Our Values, Protecting Our Interests, and Advancing the Cause of Peace"

One of the most striking things that emerges from even a causal glance at the public pronouncements trying to legitimate the bombing campaign is the centrality of notions of value and identity to those pronouncements.[14] NATO Secretary-General Javier Solana's initial statement about the bombing advanced the claim that "we must stop the violence and bring an end to the humanitarian catastrophe now taking place in Kosovo. We have *a moral duty* to do so" (Auerswald and Auerswald 2000: 719, emphasis added). Eschewing the more conventional realist justifications of military action in terms of threats to territorial integrity or physical security, the leaders of NATO countries immediately joined in this justificatory strategy, with French president Jacques Chirac arguing that the bombing was justified as "a matter of peace on our continent . . . a matter of human rights on our continent" and German chancellor Gerhard Schroeder going so far as to claim that "we are not waging war . . . we are defending our common fundamental values of peace, democracy and human rights" (Auerswald and Auerswald 2000: 723–724). According to supporters of the bombing campaign, the issues involved were ethical, not material.

Opposed to this pattern of justification was an argument based on the traditional commonplace making reference to an autonomous national community: "sovereignty." Russian president Boris Yeltsin drew on this commonplace in order to characterize "the NATO military action against sovereign Yugoslavia" as "nothing other than an open aggression," and sent a message of support to Yugoslav president Slobodan Milosevic; Milosevic, for his part, publicly expressed gratitude for "the strong support of Russia to the efforts of Yugoslavia to protect its sovereignty and territorial integrity" (Auerswald and Auerswald 2000: 725–727). Qin Huasun, Chinese ambassador to the UN, elaborated:

> The question of Kosovo, being an internal matter of the FRY [Federal
> Republic of Yugoslavia], should be solved by the parties concerned in the
> FRY among themselves. Settlement of the Kosovo issue should be based
> on the respect for sovereignty and territorial integrity of the FRY. . . . We
> oppose interference in the internal affairs of other States under whatever
> pretext or in whatever form. (Auerswald and Auerswald 2000: 727)

This sovereignty-based objection to the bombing campaign was the center-
piece of a proposal brought before the UN Security Council on March 26,
two days after the bombing had begun. The draft resolution characterized
the NATO bombings as "a flagrant violation of the United Nations Charter"
and accused NATO of violating the principle of sovereignty in multiple
ways (Auerswald and Auerswald 2000: 750–751). Although the resolution
was defeated by a vote of twelve to three, with only Russia, China, and
Namibia voting in favor, this characterization of the bombing as "a threat to
international peace and security"—in the language of the UN Charter—certainly constituted a serious challenge to the arguments advanced by the proponents of bombing.

Advocates of the campaign needed to find some way to respond.[15] In
fact, there were *two* arguments to which they responded: the argument
about Yugoslavia's sovereignty and the "domestic" character of the
Kosovo problem, and the argument from within each of the participating
states that events in the Balkans were of no concern to them. These latter
arguments, although most often implicit, were serious enough concerns
that they were often explicitly articulated and addressed by proponents of
the bombing campaign, as when German officials arrayed themselves
against the notion of a *Sonderweg* (separate path) for the reunified
Germany, and US officials spoke out against a traditional US separatism.
The rebuttal to all of these objections was a two-pronged rhetorical strategy, part of which involved "nesting" the countries involved within broader
communities of reference such as "the West" and "civilization," and the
other part of which involved attributing the actions perpetrated in Kosovo
not to the sovereign state of Yugoslavia, but to a single individual:
Slobodan Milosevic, who was characterized as standing beyond the limits
of human civilization. This creative deployment of rhetorical resources
made the bombing campaign possible.

Nesting: Bombing in the Name of Civilized Humanity

What is particularly noteworthy about the deployments supporting the
bombing is that they explicitly undertook to reconfigure the "national interest" of supporting countries in terms stretching well beyond the gains and
losses to each individual participant. Schroeder suggested that "all Alliance
partners" stood to gain from this military operation to affirm and enforce
their common values, as "we cannot allow these values to be trampled on

just one hour by air away from here," while Chirac made reference to "Europe—which we are part of too" as the community that stood to benefit. Clinton was even more explicit in a televised address on the first evening of the bombing:

> Ending this tragedy is a moral imperative. It is also important to America's national interest. . . . Kosovo is a small place, but it sits on a major fault line between Europe, Asia and the Middle East, at the meeting place of Islam and both the Western and Orthodox branches of Christianity. To the south are our allies, Greece and Turkey; the north, our new democratic allies in Central Europe. (Auerswald and Auerswald 2000: 732)

Clinton's argument was that these alliances, and the broader religious and civilizational issues involved, justified US involvement. "Do our interests in Kosovo justify the dangers to our Armed Forces?" he asked rhetorically. The answer provides an opportunity to define "the national interest" in a way that would make many realists flinch:

> I am convinced that the dangers of acting are far outweighed by the dangers of not acting—dangers to defenseless people and to our national interests. . . . America has a responsibility to stand with our allies when they are trying to save innocent lives and preserve peace, freedom, and stability in Europe. That is what we are doing in Kosovo. (Auerswald and Auerswald 2000: 732)

That "the national interest" (and its closely related concept "national security") is a somewhat malleable category should come as no surprise to IR scholars who remember Arnold Wolfers's classic argument that such "political formulas . . . while appearing to offer guidance and a basis for broad consensus . . . may be permitting everyone to label whatever policy he favors with an attractive and possibly deceptive name" ([1952] 1962: 147). Indeed, subsequent scholarship—much of it in a relational constructivist style—has illustrated the dynamics of how "the national interest" has been constructed in a variety of circumstances (e.g., Ringmar 1996; Weldes 1999). But what is most interesting about the constructions characteristic of the supporters of the NATO bombings is precisely the fact that they seem to have very little to do with even the barest outlines of the traditional concept. Wolfers suggested that the concept of the national interest did "promote demands that are ascribed to the nation rather than to individuals, subnational groups, or mankind as a whole" ([1952] 1962: 147), even if the precise character of those demands was quite open-ended. To the contrary, the deployments surrounding the NATO bombing seem to reference quite different communities, most notably "Western civilization" and "humanity," and to interpret the national interest in terms of these communities.

Conceptually, these communities are broader than the sovereign territorial state in a number of ways: they encompass a larger geographical area, precede the sovereign territorial state historically, and in general operate at a more fundamental level than the collectivities over which national governments exercise authority. In a way, sovereign territorial states are "nested" (Ferguson and Mansbach 1996: 50–51) within them, almost as if the territorial borders of the state were surrounded by successive concentric circles of community membership: states belong to a civilization, which in turn belongs to humanity as a whole. Secretary of State Madeleine Albright made this concentric nesting fairly explicit in a press conference held some months before the bombings began, and shortly after the UN Security Council had passed a resolution (1199) calling for an immediate cease-fire in Kosovo. Albright interpreted this resolution as embodying "the long-standing political, humanitarian and military demands of the international community," and hence setting the framework for any subsequent action in the region; "the international community," with its commitment to "humanitarian" goals, serves as the broadest possible human community, encompassing all of the subordinate actors. Moving to the next ring inward, Albright argued that "it's time for the [NATO] alliance . . . to take the difficult but necessary decision to authorize military force if Milosevic fails to comply." Why was this necessary? "One of the keys to good diplomacy is knowing when diplomacy has reached its limits; and we are rapidly reaching that point now. We are not going to stop this conflict by constantly evaluating the situation and simply waiting to see what happens" (Auerswald and Auerswald 2000: 284–285).

"Humanity" as a community, organized into "the international community," can only do so much; diplomacy has set the goals, but can't proceed further down the path of implementation. "We must be prepared to take action because we know that if we are not there, there is nothing to stop them from going back to business as usual," Albright argued. But why should NATO take on this enforcement role in the name of humanity? Because "NATO is our institution of choice when it comes to preserving peace and defending Western values on the continent. It must be prepared to act when a threat of this nature exists on Europe's doorstep" (Auerswald and Auerswald 2000: 284–285). The logic here is striking: NATO is, in effect, the local enforcement arm of "humanity" as organized into "the international community." It is this complex nested commitment that justified the initial NATO order for air strikes if Yugoslavia did not implement Resolution 1199, and also supported the continuation of this threat of force in case the Yugoslav government stopped complying (Auerswald and Auerswald 2000: 307–308). It is this publicly declared position that provided the immediate context for the bombing campaign that began a few months later.

How Nesting Works

Nested community arguments are particularly powerful rhetorical common-places for several reasons. For one thing, they function as something of a rhetorical trump card when deployed against arguments referencing only a subordinate community, connoting as they do a concern with broader inter-ests and values. "Western civilization" has prominently played this role in a number of foreign policy debates, including those that led to the initial for-mation of NATO in 1949. In that case, the notion of a "Western civiliza-tion," which had to be protected through the combined efforts of all of its members, effectively overcame resistance based on more parochial notions of US identity (Jackson 2003). The ongoing prominence of this common-place can be seen in Albright's linkage of NATO with the preservation of "Western values." Its effects can be seen in US senator Joseph Biden's comment that "the United States is a European power . . . tied to the conti-nent through a web of trade, investment, human contacts, and culture to a degree unequaled by relations with any other part of the world" (Auerswald and Auerswald 2000: xiii). NATO speaks for this transatlantic community, serving as its organizational instantiation. This traditional commonplace provided Biden with rhetorical ammunition during a March 1999 Senate debate over a resolution authorizing military air operations against Yugoslavia: "NATO already acted. NATO got together and debated this issue. And NATO members all voted unanimously to use airpower if in fact one side or the other did not—did not—agree" (Auerswald and Auerswald 2000: 681).

This NATO mandate justifies a commitment of US forces to the planned operation, as the broader community can make demands of its sub-ordinate members in much the same way as "the nation" can make demands of its citizens (Anderson 1991: 9–11). Indeed, failing to go along with these demands can call a state's commitment to the larger community into question, a scenario often invoked by advocates of the bombing cam-paign against their domestic opponents. In a speech on the eve of the bomb-ings, Clinton declared:

> We asked them [the people of Kosovo] to accept peace on terms that were less than perfect and they said, yes. We said if they would do it, we would stick by them—not "we," the United States, "we" 19 countries in NATO. We cannot run away from that commitment now. . . . You've got to decide, my fellow Americans, if you agree with me that in the 21st century, that America, as the world's superpower, ought to be standing up against eth-nic cleansing if we have the means to do it and we have allies who will help us do it in their neighborhood. (Auerswald and Auerswald 2000: 699)

Clinton's argument blends a commitment to the West as NATO with a commitment to the world and humanity as standing against ethnic cleansing.[16] When combined with the aforementioned characterization of Kosovo as sitting on a "major fault line . . . at the meeting place of Islam and both the Western and Orthodox branches of Christianity," the argument has the effect of making Kosovo into a legitimate concern of the United States, shifting the effective boundaries from the territorial borders of the United States to the civilizational fault line traditionally thought to run through the Balkans. Biden drew on this characterization during the Senate debates, claiming that the historical importance of Kovoso stemmed from the 1389 battle between Ottoman forces and Serbian knights, in which the knights "saved Christianity and the rest of Europe" (Auerswald and Auerswald 2000: 683). The nesting logic is clear here as well: Kosovo is at the border of the civilizational community to which the United States belongs, and refusing to do something about the situation is tantamount to betraying that civilizational community.

Other officials, particularly in Germany, leaned more heavily on "the West" per se in their efforts to outflank domestic opposition. In a speech before the German Bundestag (Parliament), Schroeder reiterated arguments about NATO being "a community of values . . . human rights, freedom and democracy," but then argued that Germany in particular had to be sure to stand up for these values:

> Against the background of our German history, we may not leave any doubt about our reliability, determination and steadfastness. Germany's integration into the western community of states is a part of our national interest [*Staatsräson*].[17] We do not want a separate path [*Sonderweg*] for Germany. . . . We cannot withdraw from our responsibilities. (Schroeder 1999)

Schroeder's use of the word *Sonderweg* is significant here, as this term denotes a traditional argument that Germany has to go its own way, avoiding binding alliances with any other state, in order to work out its own unique destiny. Generally thought to have been discredited by the experience of World War II, the term lingered throughout the postwar period as a charge that Konrad Adenauer used to delegitimate the foreign policy positions advanced by his Social Democratic rivals; where Adenauer pressed for a firm alliance with "the West," others preferred to keep some distance from the United States and other NATO members in the hopes of achieving German reunification promptly (Schwarz 1966: 512–518). Schroeder—himself a Social Democrat—used this argument to recast the issue as a test of the commitment of a state to the broader cultural community, placing opponents of the bombing campaign in roughly the same position as those advocating neutrality during the Cold War.[18]

Nesting strategies engender commitment issues that can be used to combat opposition from within one's own subordinate polity, by characterizing inaction as a form of betrayal. The "necessity" often invoked by defenders of the bombing is the necessity of not backing out of that commitment. These commitment problems *only* exist inasmuch as the commonplace of membership in the broader community is deployed, as the nesting strategy is the condition of possibility for the argument about displaying commitment to that superordinate community.[19]

"Humanity" Versus Sovereignty

But this nesting strategy also manifests other abilities. As long as all interlocutors assent to membership in a single broader community, such a strategy can be used to deflect criticism "upward," as it were, and shift the discussion from a controversy about ends to a controversy about means. At the same time, principles and values attributed to the broader community can be used to undermine and delegitimate subordinate polities thought to be in violation of those principles and values. Both of these strategies feature prominently in the international debate over the NATO bombing campaign.

It is important to keep in mind that the NATO bombing campaign did not begin in a vacuum, but was preceded by several UN Security Council resolutions. Defenders of the bombing campaign spared no opportunity to point this out and to link NATO actions to these resolutions, even though on strictly legal grounds this linkage was quite tenuous (Behnke 2002: 135). But the importance of these repeated linkages is not their legal value, but their practical political effect, which was to shift the discussion to one about humanity's responsibility in the face of ethnic cleansing. The objection most prominently leveled against the campaign was that the Security Council had not adequately authorized it, *not* that inaction was appropriate or that events in Kosovo were not a legitimate object of concern for the international community. For example, in his initial statement on the bombing, Yeltsin criticized the campaign as "a NATO attempt to enter the 21st century as the policeman to the world" (Auerswald and Auerswald 2000: 725). This locution suggests that the problem is that NATO has assumed authority that it cannot legitimately assume—that it is masquerading as a law enforcement officer when it is not one; and this in turn implies that there *are* "real" policemen whose authority is being usurped.

Thus, another effect of the nesting strategy pursued by the bombing campaign's defenders is to change the question to: Who speaks for humanity? The most obvious candidate, the United Nations (and the UN Security Council in particular) was the focus of the earliest efforts to oppose the NATO actions. Unequivocal UN condemnation would have made it quite difficult for NATO officials to sustain their claim to merely be executing policies determined at a level higher than their own. But the Security Council, as we have seen, declined to issue such a condemnation, which left open the possibility for NATO officials to continue deploying the commonplace of "humanity" as a way of legitimating their actions.

UN Secretary-General Kofi Annan also remained decidedly ambiguous in his public statements on the bombing campaign, frequently coupling reservations about the use of force with a condemnation of the actions of Yugoslav authorities in Kosovo. On April 9, Annan—without explicitly approving of the bombing campaign—articulated five conditions for Yugoslavia to fulfill before NATO stopped bombing (Auerswald and Auerswald 2000: 808). Although the organized expression of the human community had not clearly voiced *approval* of military action, the UN now seemed to *accept* the bombing campaign as a way of furthering the previous demands of the international community. Unless they wanted to deny that "humanity" had a legitimate interest in Kosovo, opponents of the NATO actions could only work to pressure the Yugoslavian government to meet those conditions.

The linking of the commonplace of "humanity" to the bombing by a global institution was also accomplished more directly when the International Criminal Tribunal for the former Yugoslavia (ICTY) indicted Milosevic for war crimes in May 1999. Such explicit condemnation of Milosevic further diminished the rhetorical possibilities open to opponents, as defending Milosevic would now look uncomfortably like defending an international war criminal.[20] Advocates of military action repeatedly used this argument to delegitimate claims that the Kosovo problem was a "domestic" issue taking place within a sovereign state. Sovereignty, in their formulation, is subject to the more fundamental values and principles of human civilization, and someone standing in violation of these values and principles cannot help but be a legitimate target for the action of "humanity."[21]

According to this logic, Milosevic made himself a legitimate target of enforcement by violating appropriate standards of conduct. Clinton's public reaction to the indictment is illustrative, as he argued that the indictment "will make clear to the Serbian people who is responsible for this conflict and who is prolonging it" (Auerswald and Auerswald 2000: 1040). Albright drew the rhetorical conclusion:

> We believe that the indictment actually shows the validity of our campaign, which is that we are trying to deal with the heinous crimes that Milosevic has committed in Kosovo. We had said all along that the behavior of the Serb authorities and Milosevic himself in Kosovo was unacceptable in terms of how we deal with situations like that at the end of the 20th century. . . . Therefore, NATO—representing the international community, the West, the democratic values for which we stand and human rights—is doing the right thing in following up on an air campaign. (Auerswald and Auerswald 2000: 1041)

■ Conclusion

What light does a relational constructivist perspective shed on the NATO bombing of Kosovo? In this chapter, I have tried to illustrate precisely what such a perspective provides: a more nuanced appreciation of the public rhetoric surrounding military and diplomatic actions, a focus on strategies of public legitimation and their importance to social action, and an account of precisely who the actors in world politics are at any given point in time. By not foreclosing the question of actorhood in advance, a relational constructivist approach enables analysts to focus on how questions of authority and legitimacy are negotiated in practice. This also provides a way to account for courses of action without having to resort to speculation about individual motives: actions are caused by the specific configuration of rhetorical resources brought to bear at a given point in time. It is the analysis of these configurations, and of the specific histories of the commonplaces constituting each of them, that relational constructivism advocates.

■ Notes

1. Thanks to Chandra Dunn for research assistance.

2. Constructivists tend to be more self-conscious of their philosophical and conceptual equipment than other theory scholars, perhaps in part because that equipment differs from the "common sense" of much of the rest of society and calls the status of that common sense into question. But from a constructivist perspective, "facts" are produced largely by the way that analysts view their data, making these conceptual elaborations quite central to the constructivist enterprise.

3. There is a lot of confusion about this point in contemporary IR theory. Just because the mechanisms cited by liberal rationalists take place within states (often within individual human beings), this does *not* make their account an "agentic" one, particularly when they derive an actor's preferences from that actor's location in some economic structure.

4. For much more detailed arguments to this effect, see Jackson and Nexon 2002.

5. In the Giddensian approach, concrete social situations are always analyzed *twice,* once from the perspective of agents, and again from the structural perspective. But while this avoids the problems of temporal-sequentialism by theoretical and methodological fiat, it only preserves agency in a highly abstract and technical sense. Treating important aspects of the social environment as "chronically reproduced" makes change in that environment difficult to explain, and treating social action as "strategic" (Giddens 1979: 80) makes any stable patterns in that action equally difficult to explain—particularly when analysts choose to focus on only one of the two perspectives that Giddens recommends. Relational constructivism avoids these problems.

6. In fact, this point of view—a kind of "reductionism" focusing on individual agents, and often on individual *human beings* as the only "real" agents—is quite dominant in the ordinary lives of most people living in late modern industrial and postindustrial societies. The reasons are complex, but have a lot to do with the philosophical legacy of the European Enlightenment, particularly thinkers like Thomas Hobbes and John Locke and their utilitarian successors, for whom individ-

ual human beings simply *were* the basic building blocks of society. Reductionism of this sort is probably better thought of as a historical artifact. Michel Foucault's work on these issues (1972a, 1978) is quite suggestive.

7. It is this focus on networks of transaction, on *relations* between and among entities rather than on the putatively dispositional qualities of those entities, that gives "relational" approaches their name (Emirbayer 1997; Jackson and Nexon 1999).

8. It was only a "mistake" from a perspective that regards the bombings themselves as justified.

9. Technically, this is *a* definition of agency, emphasizing contingency and creativity rather than a more Kantian notion involving the capacity of an actor to make a rational choice unencumbered by external conditions. But equating agency and rational action creates some tricky theoretical problems, similar to those characterizing the "internalization" school of constructivism.

10. See Behnke 2002 for an analysis of NATO's website during the Kosovo bombing campaign.

11. Naturally this documentary collection does not contain *every* such contestation, but concentrates on those advanced in the name of some social actor directly implicated in the public debates that led to specific courses of action. Critiques of the bombing campaign that were simply ignored by the officials giving the orders, while useful as normative critiques, play no causal role in the processes under investigation here, and can be safely left aside for the moment.

12. In so doing, I am tacitly accepting that the Kosovo conflict was a "diplomatic" event—that is, a conflict among public authorities such as states and interstate alliances and international organizations. This is not the only narrative of the conflict that could be constructed, and perhaps it should not be the narrative that we unquestioningly prefer, but this is how the conflict was constructed by the actors socially responsible for the bombing campaign. Analyzing how this construction came to pass requires, at the very least, focusing attention on the kinds of social boundaries produced and reproduced in practice, and not simply dismissing those boundaries as normatively illegitimate and therefore unworthy of serious analytical attention.

13. Note that this topography is less representational than ideal-typical; different analysts will undoubtedly generate different topographies, as texts can be gathered up and organized in many different ways according to the values and interests of the researcher. But this does not detract from the value of the procedure, as a careful delineation of commonplaces and reconstruction of rhetorical positions in a debate has value even to those analysts operating with a very different set of values and interests (Weber 1949).

14. The title of this section comes from Clinton's speech at the outset of the bombing campaign (Auerswald and Auerswald 2000: 730).

15. Albright listed "ensuring that the necessity for military action is understood around the world" as the first of the diplomatic goals that the NATO allies needed to pursue (Auerswald and Auerswald 2000: 738). So this "need" was not so much a reflection of some kind of structural requirement as it was a task valued by the people involved.

16. The temporal aspect of this argument, with "the West" standing on the side of the present and the rational, peaceful future while "the Balkans," mired in history, continues to display brutal communal violence, has often been noted (van Ham 2002: 40). But most commentators noting this rhetorical deployment cannot refrain from expressing snide cynicism about the locution, as though there were something

particularly egregious about this particular social boundary-demarcation. As I have argued, the transcendental or philosophical validity of a commonplace should not be considered relevant to an explanation of its causal impact, and criticizing Western (and US) pretensions in claiming to speak on behalf of humanity's future seems to me a different endeavor than analyzing patterns of justification.

17. *Staatsräson* is more literally translated "reason of state." But Schroeder is also taking advantage of a linguistic parallel here: the "Western community of states" (*westliche Staatengemeinschaft*) uses the same root word: *Staat*. In effect, Schroeder is linking the core identity of the Federal Republic with the West, even at the level of particular word choice.

18. Others in Schroeder's cabinet—most notably Joschka Fischer, the foreign minister—also used language like this to justify Germany's involvement in the bombing (Zehfuss 2002: 115).

19. A nesting strategy also makes possible the argument that supporting a policy can *signal* that one should be considered a full member of the relevant superordinate community; this may help explain the staunch support for the US-led invasion of Iraq by newly admitted NATO countries.

20. The indictment of Milosevic was also easily incorporated into a strategy of making Milosevic personally responsible for events in Kosovo, a strategy that had been pursued for many months prior to the onset of hostilities (Auerswald and Auerswald 2000: 288).

21. John Locke articulated the basic logic of the claim several centuries ago: "The crime which consists in violating the law, and varying from the right rule of reason, whereby a man so far becomes degenerate, and declares himself to quit the principles of human nature, and to be a noxious creature," makes a person subject to retribution by all of humanity (Locke 1988: 8–10).

chapter 6

Postmodern and Critical Theory Approaches

6.1 *Jennifer Sterling-Folker*

Postmodernism and Critical Theory

Although postmodernism and critical theory will be discussed together, it is important to underscore that they are different theoretical perspectives. Postmodernism is derived from the study of literature, and critical theorists find its abandonment of the Enlightenment project objectionable. Alternatively, critical theory is a form of neo- or Western Marxist analysis, and postmodern scholars criticize it for continuing to participate in that same Enlightenment project. Hence the two schools of thought can be antagonists. Yet as Pauline Rosenau has observed, "the relationship between the two is far from simple" (1990: 104). Each is a dedicated post-positivist approach, and the term "critical theory" is sometimes used to indicate all theoretical perspectives that share this dedication.[1] Many scholars who work in either tradition have sought to build analytical bridges between them, because they share a set of philosophical precursors, including Friedrich Nietzsche, Martin Heidegger, Edmund Husserl, and Ludwig Wittgenstein. Thus there are good reasons for discussing them together, although their particular origins and goals of analysis are different.

Postmodernism is sometimes referred to as poststructuralism, and it derives from the French study of literature and language.[2] Some of the more seminal authors to its development include Jacques Derrida, Michel Foucault, Jean-François Lyotard, Roland Barthes, and Jean Baudrillard. It is not a theory in the positivist sense of providing causal explanations for social phenomenon. Rather it is a critique meant to reveal the disjunctures of Enlightenment modernity, which, postmodern scholars contend, imposes meaning on social activity and in so doing establishes hierarchies of power that are accepted as natural. Postmodernism seeks to upset what is taken for granted and reveal how discourse imposes meaning and hence a value structure that is both socially constructed and historically arbitrary. Alternatively, critical theory developed out of what is called the Frankfurt School, which was established prior to World War II by a group of German scholars who sought to salvage Marxist thought from its orthodox, political manifestations. Heavily influenced by the work of Nietzsche, the first generation of critical theorists included Max Horkheimer, Theodor Adorno, Herbert Marcuse, and Walter Benjamin. Best known among the second generation of scholars is Jurgen Habermas. From a critical theory perspective, it is Marxism, not liberalism, that is the true heir of Enlightenment thought. Critical theory shares with postmodernism a skepticism of the liberal claim to a universal and morally accurate value structure. It seeks to recover Marxism's emancipatory elements, by focusing on culture, philosophy, and language, rather than on political economy, as the potential sites for overcoming social domination and oppression.

Neither theoretical perspective was developed in the US discipline of IR, nor were they particularly pertinent to its early development, and both have been more influential to the European study of IR.[3] When these perspectives were introduced into the US discipline in the 1980s, they generated what is often referred to as the "third debate" (Lapid 1989), thus differentiating it from two prior periods of theoretical disagreement that galvanized the discipline.[4] What distinguished the third debate was that it struck at "the very core of what constitutes the international relations field and require[d] its thorough and complete reconstruction" (P. Rosenau 1990: 83). Proponents of these perspectives sought not only a change in the US discipline's preferred methodology or positivist epistemology, but also a change in the very ontology of the discipline, grounded as it is in a faith in our ability to accurately know a true social reality with positivism. As one postmodern IR scholar has put it, "rationalists cling to the faith that there is an objective reality out there that is waiting for the right method to come along and in the name of scientific progress make use of, make sense of, give order to it" (Der Derian 1997: 57). Alternatively, postpositivist approaches such as postmodernism and critical theory challenge this notion of objectivity and hence the premises upon which the US discipline of IR rests.

The philosophical antecedents of both perspectives may be traced to the study of language and linguistics, and from these both derive the idea that social reality is created through discourse. That is, how we discursively represent something also determines how we act toward it and hence what it will be. While we first encountered the "hermeneutic circle" when discussing constructivism, in postpositivist approaches it assumes greater significance. Not only can we not know the world absent the words we use to describe it, but we are also confronted with the essential dilemma that, "whenever people try to establish a certain reading of a text or expression, they allege other readings as the ground for their reading" (Adler 1997: 321–322). This means that we can never arrive at the one "true" reading of a text, only multiple, layered interpretations of it, so that the text itself (and its particular author) becomes less important than how it has been interpreted and meaning assigned to it. To put this another way, "all meaning systems are open-ended systems of signs referring to signs referring to signs. No concept can therefore have an ultimate, unequivocal meaning" (Wæver 1996b: 171). This makes the role or intentions of the author or speaker relatively unimportant, and in literary postmodernism the author is completely effaced from analysis.

Yet meaning-making is not an individual or random activity according to postpositivist approaches. It precedes from society and culture, and it reflects linguistic structures, "meta-narratives," or systems of discursive practice and knowledge-production that individuals are embedded within and that create and reproduce the world through them. Both perspectives see this as an act of subjugation, in that meaning is *imposed* on the individual by these meta-narratives rather than vice versa, and in fact, meaning-making reflects power at a very fundamental level. Meaning is always assigned through an oppositional arrangement in which some symbols, ideas, and values are elevated and others are subordinated. Truth itself then becomes a function of this discursive oppositional arrangement. We take for granted certain ideas and activities as naturally good or bad, when such judgments are actually products of specific knowledge-producing systems and hence specific historical circumstances.

One juxtaposition that has been most relevant in the study of IR is that of "self and other" (Doty 1996; Neumann 1999), which refers to the idea that we cannot know who we are unless we consider who we are not. This has obvious relevance to a Westphalian world, which is divided into territorial, political units with specific populations distinct from one another. In making such distinctions, say to speak of differences between Americans and Mexicans, we also engage in value judgments about what is or is not proper and in so doing produce and reify a world in which exclusion on the basis of those value judgments seems natural. To refer, for example, to "'Latin America' is not just to refer to [or represent] an area on the globe; it is to help reproduce an institutionalized form of dominance, one in which the minority, Hispanic part of populations in the region control the original indigenous groups" (Shapiro 1989: 15). Hence the social reality that is created by the imposition of meaning involves subjugation and social injustices that are uncritically and continually reproduced as if they were inevitable.

What postmodernism and critical theory share, then, is an interest in "how discourse is related to the construction and subjugation of humankind" (Gregory 1989: xxi). They seek to interrogate representations, asking why it is important to represent things in a certain way, so that embedded knowledge and value structures may be revealed and critiqued. Both are interested in what people say, how they describe the world, and how they justify what they do in it, because the verbal and written descriptions and justifications are as important to understanding the world as the deeds that follow. Both are interested in revealing these embedded value structures in order to oppose them, because revelation exposes the extent to which individual identity has been imposed, the extent to which "others" have been defined and excluded politically and economically by such imposition, and the extent to which violence against these "others" is sanctioned on the basis of identity difference. By pulling apart meaning-making, both argue that it is possible to reveal the knowledge-producing power structures underneath. Hence they both endeavor "to highlight the existence of counter-hegemonic or countervailing tendencies which are invariably present within all social and political structures" (Linklater 1996: 283). They do so by unpacking or pulling apart the meanings embedded or implicitly assumed in texts, whether these texts are public statements by policymakers or the writings of other IR scholars.

While many of the ideas about meaning-making and identity serve as the foundation for IR constructivism as well, ultimately constructivism seeks to close off the hermeneutic circle by arguing that since we do create a social reality, it is logically possible to use scientific methodology to understand and explain it. Neither postmodernism nor critical theory view this epistemological middle ground as morally viable, because, they argue, scientific methodology has been harnessed by the liberal Enlightenment project, which is not a value-free discursive structure. It is on the subject of science that the link between postmodernism, critical theory, and postpositivism becomes clear. Postpositivists argue that, like all knowledge-producing structures, liberalism excludes, marginalizes, and licenses violence and oppression against particular others. It has assisted a process in which scientific and technological advances have not emancipated human beings from the vicissitudes of nature, but rather controlled them for the sake of capitalism in particular. Hence liberalism has assisted a process of disciplining or repressing the individual, and any epistemology that assists it is morally implicated as well, protestations of objectivity to the contrary. In fact, those very protestations mark positivism as "logocentric," which means "mistakenly claiming legitimacy by reference to external, universally truthful propositions" (P. Rosenau 1990: 86), which cannot exist if social reality is a social and historical construction.

From a postpositivist perspective, positivism involves philosophical ignorance about the construction of social reality, one's role in that construction, and the extent to which liberalism is a historical meta-narrative that relies on power and domination, even as it is posing as morally superior universal truth. It reflects a failure "to understand that intellectual projects have important moral implications for the national and international distribution of wealth and power" (Linklater 1996: 281), or as Robert Cox has succinctly put it, "all theory is *for* someone and *for* some purpose" (1981: 128, emphasis original). Rather than discovering social reality, then, positivism merely succeeds in reproducing it, because it "champions a particular value orientation—instrumental rationality" (Leonard 1990: 34)—which serves the meta-narrative of liberalism and reifies its particular forms of subjugation, while providing no means of recognizing or opposing it. It is for this reason that postmodernism and critical theory have a contentious relationship with dominant or mainstream IR theoretical perspectives, all of which implicitly subscribe to positivism as the most appropriate means of understanding IR.

One topic that postpositivist scholars have tended to focus on and problematize in particular is the discipline's treatment of sovereignty as simply "the enunciation of a territorially based conception of community that demands the loyalty of its citizens" and having, therefore, "a natural essence to its existence" (Dunne 2001: 86). Tim Dunne notes that from a postpositivist perspective, sovereignty is "the founding moment of politics itself," because it "represents the fault-line between community and anarchy" (2001: 86–87). It is therefore "what makes Westphalian international politics possible" (see also Wæver 1996b: 167–169). Not surprisingly, then, in Chapter 6.2 Rosemary Shinko focuses on the concept of sovereignty in her postmodern contribution to this section, seeking to read Kosovo as an instance in which powerful nation-states sought to reaffirm their sovereign boundaries against anarchic possibilities.[5] According to Andrew Linklater, critical theorists are also interested in unpacking the concept and practice of sovereignty, because sovereignty "restricts the capacity of outsiders to participate in discourse to consider issues which concern them," while critical theory "envisages the use of unconstrained discourses to determine the moral significance of national boundaries and to examine the possibility of post-sovereign forms of political life" (1996: 294, 280).

It is here, however, that obvious differences between postmodernism and critical theory begin to emerge. While both are interested in discursive practices, postmodernism is skeptical of *all* meta-narratives, arguing that if truth is embedded in discursive structures then it is not "out there" waiting to be discovered. Postmodernism is concerned with revealing these structures in order to reveal the power and subjugation that supports them, but it is largely resigned to the "postmodern condition" in which truth is revealed to be a social construction (P. Rosenau 1990: 104). That is, if we cannot know right or wrong absent our own social creations, or as David Dessler puts it, "causally independent of the mind" (1999: 124), then all truth systems become equal and none can claim to be better. Conversely, critical theorists retain a belief in and commitment to Enlightenment ideals as a "true" discursive structure that liberalism has mischanneled or co-opted. The point of revealing the dominant liberal meta-narrative is in order to replace it with a discursive structure that does finally obtain the Enlightenment ideals of human emancipation. Hence critical theorists are interested in the discursive practices of policymakers not only to reveal discursive structures, but because they also want policymakers to live up to their own liberal rhetoric and actually achieve the Enlightenment's universal moral code.

Because critical theorists believe in a particular meta-narrative in a way that postmodernists do not, the latter are as inclined to critique the former as they are realists, liberals, and constructivists. The points of postmodern and critical theory analysis are quite different as a result. A postmodern perspective suggests that all meta-narratives require the disciplining of the individual and the subjugation of the other. Hence the desire to replace one meta-narrative with another on the grounds of morality is a sham, since it is essentially the replacement of one system of oppression with another. Because the discursive construction of social reality makes human emancipation an impossibility, the unpacking of the meta-narrative *is* the point of analysis for a postmodern scholar. In other words, postmodernism does not seek to replace the meta-narrative it is examining or to construct an alternative to it. In fact, given that we can never know reality or describe it accurately, postmodernism assumes that there are an infinite number of ways to interpret the same text or event and that all of them are of equal interest or value. The point of postmodernism is instead to challenge existing meta-narratives by utilizing alternative methodologies, and in so doing, "it accepts inconsistency and contradiction, feeling no need to reconcile oppositions or to choose between them" (P. Rosenau 1990: 86).

This can make postmodern IR analysis appear strange to the positivist, who would expect analysis to identify potential causal variables, chart possible causal linkages, present factual evidence, and provide conclusions about which variables proved most explanatory. Postmodern IR eschews this entire process, seeking instead to shake the reader's expectations, to appear strange in order to expose complacencies, and to focus on the discontinuities of discursive structures in order to reveal forced marginalizations. The postmodern IR scholar also focuses on what the positivist would consider trivial or unrelated to IR, such as the spy novel, football, defense manuals, *Star Trek,* and popular culture.[6] In an approach that views everything as a text and all texts as interconnected,[7] such topics allow us to see linkages that are unexamined (metaphors of war used in sports, for example), to turn meaning upside-down, and "reread" what we take for granted (why do we equate war with sport?).

Given that all universal truth claims are questioned in postmodernism, one of the standard accusations leveled against the approach is that it promotes moral relativism and a form of ethical resignation or despair. Many IR postmodernists counter that the opposite is true, and that it can instead produce greater forms of tolerance for identity difference. Because it is an "attempt to understand—without resort of external authorities or transcendental values—why one moral or political system attains a higher status and exercises more influence than another at a particular historical moment" (Der Derian 1997: 58), it can reveal how other theoretical perspectives in the discipline naturalize rather than oppose violence, poverty, and subjugation in world politics. In this regard, it is interesting to note that it is postpositivists, rather than positivists, who have been more interested in the explicit exploration of ethics in IR (Connolly 1989; Brown 1992; Der Derian 1997).

Critical theory shares these ethical concerns, but it differs from postmodernism in its desire to substitute or reconstruct what is believed to be the "true" Enlightenment meta-narrative. Critical theory seeks to achieve universal emancipation, which, it argues, could have been realized if not for liberalism's alliance with capitalism and science, which has effectively squandered and deflected this possibility. The result is that, although critical theory seeks to deconstruct the liberal meta-narrative in order to replace it, its "emphasis on the existence of foundations for making judgements between knowledge claims" demonstrates that theoretically it is "a direct descendant of the Kantian enlightenment project" (Smith 1996: 28). It also shares with constructivism a belief in the possibilities of fundamental change in IR, and it takes seriously the notion that IR theorists can play a significant role in promoting such change. As Richard Wyn Jones notes, its "willingness to face up to reality simultaneously includes a commitment to its transformation and a belief that such a transformation is feasible. Following Marx, critical theorists seek to understand the world in order to change it" (1999: 22). This means that unlike postmodernism, critical theory is meant to have practical, political intent.

However, as Stephen Leonard has observed, "forging a link between social theory and political practice is . . . no mean task" (1990: 3). How, for example, does one move from the same ontological position as that of postmodernism to one in which the Enlightenment project may be treated as a foundational narrative? How can this project and its goal of human emancipation be realized in actual political practice? And how can we, as IR scholars, recognize and promote the actions and policies necessary to achieve this goal? Different answers to these questions have produced different variants of critical theory. One of the better-known variants is based on the work of Habermas, and Chapter 6.3, by Marc Lynch, is an example of what can be called the "linguistic turn" in critical theory. What distinguishes this variant is its focus on communication acts as a possible site for foundational knowledge-claims and the practical achievement of emancipation. Habermas has argued that truth and ethics are inherent to language, and that we can, in principle at least, produce situations of "ideal speech acts" that depend on ethical consensus among participants. In such situations it would not be power, social identities, or cultural distortions that determined collective outcomes, but rather the rationally more convincing argument that would prevail.

The critical theory variant proposed by Habermas entails what is called universal pragmatics or discourse ethics, in which "participants aim to be guided by nothing other than the force of the better argument and agree that norms cannot be valid unless they command the consent of everyone who stands to be affected by them" (Linklater 1996: 286). Because consensual communication is a crucial element of the Habermasian variant, *how* nation-states reach collective decisions is just as important as the goals they collectively pursue. When goals appear to be ethically desirable but have not been consensually derived, the critical theorist is confronted with a moral dilemma, and Lynch's chapter explores this dilemma in the context of intervention in Kosovo. The need to overcome or dismantle nation-state sovereignty is also crucial to the application of discourse ethics in IR, because as a "bounded moral and political community," the nation-state excludes others and inhibits the kind of unconstrained communications needed for the achievement of ideal speech acts (Linklater 1996: 287). The result is that, although the Habermasian variant of critical theory focuses on different processes, it tends to "reflect a general left-liberal sensibility" (Wyn Jones 1999: 64), and it shares with liberal pluralism an explicit desire to move beyond the nation-state.

The variant proposed by Habermas entirely abandons economics as the potential site for change and emancipation. Other variants of critical theory have continued to focus on modes of production and class in providing alternative answers for how to link theory and practice within a neo-Marxian framework. One of those variants is called historical materialism and it, along with world system theory, is discussed in the next theoretical section. The difference this alternative focus can make for critical theory analysis is striking. While the Habermasian variant focuses on communication and discourse, the historical materialism variant focuses on "the effects of the globalization of relations of production and the linkages of elites in core and periphery on the distribution of the world's wealth" (Linklater 1996: 287). In seeking to identify and promote the potential sites for change, the Habermasian variant focuses on unrestrained communications, while the historical materialism variant encourages counterhegemonic political and social movements. Yet ultimately these different variants may be united under the same critical theory umbrella, because they share the same theoretical and practical goal. That goal is, according to Linklater, "to identify the sources of potentially far-reaching change so that human subjects can grasp the possibility of alternative paths of historical development which can be explored through collective political action" (1996: 283–284).

That goal is also why critical theory and postmodernism must be kept distinct, despite their many attributes in common. Postmodernism eschews the very goal of critical theory and is particularly skeptical of Habermas's notion of unconstrained communications. From a postmodern perspective, all conversation is a power struggle to impose meaning, and it is not possible to move beyond this to a place untainted by power. In order to circumvent the power struggle in their own writings, postmodernists seek alternative methodologies and presentation styles. Although they too seek to unpack meaning, the methodology of critical theory is not nearly as radical as postmodernism given its different goals. Yet despite these differences, the practitioners of these approaches in IR have tended to ally themselves in order to highlight their differences with the rest of the discipline. Their introduction into the discipline during the 1980s was by no means a congenial affair, involving a "post-structuralist guerrilla war against the 'system'" (Wæver 1996b: 169), accompanied by equally vehement positivist reactions, so that "not so long ago mental flak jackets were de rigueur if one so much as uttered the 'P-word' among IR scholars" (Der Derian 1997: 57). This overt hostility has modified over time, in part because constructivism's combination of postpositivist insights with the discipline's preferred epistemology has made the former more acceptable to the theoretical mainstream. It is probably the case, then, that postpositivist approaches such as postmodernism and critical theory are already having a significant but implicit impact on IR theorists in the making.

■ Further Reading

Richard Ashley is one of the best-known postmodern IR scholars (see 1984, 1987, 1996), particularly for his early postmodern critiques of Kenneth Waltz's theory of neorealism. Two other postmodern scholars whose work has been particularly seminal are R. B. J. Walker (1987, 1988a, 1993) and James Der Derian (1987, 1989, 1992, 1997). Der Derian's edited volume *International Theory: Critical Investigations* (1995a), juxtaposes well-known articles in IR (by both positivists and postpositivists) that collectively demonstrate the concerns of postmodernism and the English School (discussed later in this volume). Other examples of postmodern IR scholarship include Alker 1996, Campbell 1992, Campbell 1993, Connolly 1991, Falk

1988, George 1994, Klein 1994, Luke 1998, Luke 1993, and Shapiro 1987. Some feminist scholars, such as V. Spike Peterson, Christine Sylvester, or Cynthia Weber, work with a postmodern or critical perspective, but are discussed in the overview chapter on feminism instead. Other IR scholars whose writings might be characterized as postmodern, such as Roxanne Doty, Janice Bially Mattern, Iver Neumann, Jutta Weldes, and Franke Wilmer, are cited in the overview chapter on constructivism. In both cases, their placement in other sections is not definitive and might vary according to the different criteria of other authors.

Edited volumes of postmodern IR include, Der Derian and Shapiro 1989, Beer and Hariman 1996, and Shapiro and Alker 1996. There is also a special "dissident" issue of *International Studies Quarterly* (Ashley and Walker 1990a, 1990b), and a special issue of *Millennium* titled "Images and Narratives in World Politics" (2001). For background on postmodernism as it relates to the social sciences and IR specifically, see P. Rosenau 1990 and P. Rosenau 1992, as well as Hollinger 1994. The postmodern literature on sovereignty is considerable, but particularly seminal pieces include Ashley 1988, Bartelson 1995, Biersteker and Weber 1996, Campbell 1992, Edkins 1999, Inayatullah and Blaney 2003, Walker 1993, Walker and Mendlovitz 1990, and Weber 1995.

Among IR scholars who subscribe to a Habermasian critical theory, Linklater's work is among the best-known (1990, 1992, 1996, 1998). Other examples of this particular variant of critical theory include Baynes 1994, Hoffman 1987, Hoffmann 1991, Lynch 1999, Lynch 2000, Neufeld 1995, Payne 2001, Payne and Samhat 2004, and Wyn Jones 1999. Scholars who subscribe to critical theory's historical materialism variant, such as Robert Cox, Stephen Gill, or Craig Murphy, are discussed in Chapter 7.1. Wyn Jones 2001, an edited volume titled *Critical Theory and World Politics,* brings practitioners of both variants together. For background on the Frankfurt School and critical theory in general, see Bronner 1994, Held 1980, and Wiggershaus 1994.

On the relationship between postmodernism and critical theory, consult George and Campbell 1990 and Kellner 1989. The epistemological issues that these postpositivist approaches raise for the discipline have been considered in a number of special IR journal issues, such as *Millennium*'s "Philosophical Traditions in International Relations" (1988); *International Studies Quarterly*'s "Exchange on the Third Debate" (1989), which contains Yosef Lapid's "third debate" article and accompanying articles by Kal Holsti (1989), Thomas Biersteker (1989), and Jim George (1989); and the *International Studies Review* forum "Are Dialogue and Synthesis Possible in International Relations?" (Hellmann 2003). A variety of other sources explore this topic, such as Alker 1996, Alker and Biersteker 1984, Booth and Smith 1995, Crawford and Jarvis 2000, George 1988, Hollis and Smith

1990, Sjolander and Cox 1994, Smith 2002, and Smith, Booth, and Zalewski 1996.

■ Notes

1. This can obviously generate some confusion, and Tim Dunne notes that "many authors in the field draw a distinction between Critical Theory descended from the Frankfurt School, and critical theories referring to a range of anti- or post-positivist theories, such as feminism and postmodernism" (2001: 73). Since I am already using the term "postpositivism" for the latter purpose, critical theory will not be capitalized here, although its usage is meant to indicate the Frankfurt School perspective to which Dunne refers.

2. The two terms are often used interchangeably because, despite differences between postmodernism and poststructuralism, the differences are not significant enough to distinguish them. Both developed in the context of French structuralism, which "is a theory of signs, post-structuralism a critique of the sign; structuralism investigates how social phenomena can be explained by stable and pervasive meaning systems, post-structuralism shows how all meaning systems are precarious, self-defeating and only strive for closure without ever succeeding" (Wæver 1996b: 171). See Callinicos 1985 and George and Campbell 1990 on this issue.

3. Texts that examine the study of IR in US and non-US contexts include Crawford 2000, Crawford and Jarvis 2000, Wæver 1998b, and Smith 2002.

4. In overviews of disciplinary history, the first debate is usually identified as occurring in the 1920s and 1930s between idealism and realism, with the latter emerging as victorious. The second debate occurred in the 1950s and 1960s, involving methodological disagreements over whether to study IR as history or a behavioral science, with the latter emerging as victorious. However, scholars disagree over how to date these debates, what exactly their substance involved, or what their outcomes were; see, for example, Wæver 1997, Wæver 1996b, and Kahler 1997.

5. In fact, Kosovo is of particular interest to postmodern scholars, because it involves how we understand and reproduce both war and sovereignty simultaneously. See, for example, Ham and Medvedev 2002 and Wachtel 1997.

6. See the various contributions in Der Derian and Shapiro 1989, "Image and Narrative in World Politics" 2001, and Weldes 2003. The extent to which modern technology mediates representation is another subject of ongoing inquiry for postmodernists, since the mass media cannot simply "report the news" as if it were out there to be objectively discovered, but rely on discursive practices to convey meaning and create the "news" instead. Similarly the use of modern technology in war has become a substitute rather than facilitator for the activity, so that the blips on a computer screen now determine what victory means for combatants on the battlefield. From a postmodern perspective this has produced a crisis of representation, in which "the realities of world politics increasingly are generated, mediated, even simulated by successive technical means of reproduction, further distancing them from some original and ultimately mythical meaning" (Der Derian 1997: 57; see also Deibert 1997).

7. As Pauline Rosenau puts it, "post-modernism is text-centered and, in the extreme, all the world is a text: a life experience, a political rally, an election, negotiating a treaty, a personal relationship, a vacation, buying a car, seeking a job—all are texts. Even speech is assigned the status of text" (1990: 88).

Rosemary E. Shinko

Postmodernism: A Genealogy of Humanitarian Intervention

What is the postmodern difference? What does a view through a postmodern lens reveal? From what vantage point does a postmodern analysis begin? Postmodernism in international relations is distinguished by a variety of rather eclectic approaches. Postmodern scholarly writings have touched on subjects as diverse as discourse analysis, international democratic practices, identity, and globalization, to name just a few. Thus postmodernism is more aptly described as a collection of various strains of critique that cumulatively could be referred to as an approach, but not a theory. As a matter of fact, postmodernists vehemently resist the closure that the term "theory" implies. The postmodern vantage point is one of critique. Its aim is to unsettle, to jar, to challenge, and to subject our most fundamental beliefs and principles to intense critical scrutiny.

Postmodernism is not a theory of international relations precisely because its focus is one of resistance. It resists attempts to bound or close off various avenues of critical thought. By definition a theory not only attempts to stabilize and regularize patterns of explanation of current political events, but more important it strives for some type of predictive capability and generalizable applicability. Postmodernists focus instead on the "uniqueness" and "singularity" of each event by drawing attention to chance and the contingency of events.

Postmodern thought intersects both realism and liberalism while ultimately positioning itself as a practice of critical inquiry, which seeks to transcend the inherent limitations of both approaches. Realists and postmodernists speak in terms of power. Realists speak in terms of a state's influence, capability, or control, whereas postmodernists draw upon the Foucaultian insight that power is not merely a force that can be exercised or controlled, but that power is somehow productive. Postmodern thought also breaks with realism over its emphasis on "state" power. Much of postmodernity's efforts are directed toward deconstructing the role of the state in international relations and eroding the boundary between domestic and international politics (Bartelson 1995; Weber 1995). Perhaps the most fundamental point of departure between realism and postmodernism is realism's stress on continuity and the attempt to discover structural patterns of behavior in the conduct of international relations. According to postmodernism, there are no patterns of continuity lying out there waiting to be discovered, there are only patterns that we try to impose on events by attaching certain meanings to those events. Imposing structures of continuity on the world's events, according to postmodernism, undermines politics and short-circuits the exercise of individual freedom.

Thus postmodernism shares liberalism's attentiveness to the role of the individual, with one important caveat—that the individual should assume an ever more prominent role over and above the role of the state. Postmodernists criticize liberalism's acceptance of the state's role and their underlying acquiescence in the structural components of the state system. Pluralism and politics are the two strains of thought shared by postmodernists and liberals. Postmodern thought extols the virtues of agonistic politics, a politics where the free play of difference flourishes and where individuals actively engage in the process of political decisionmaking (Connolly 1991). Postmodernists envision a self-reflective individual involved in the process of self-creation who can resist the limitations of state power by transgressing the boundaries that hold the state's power in place (Ashley and Walker 1990a). The hallmark of agonistic politics is pluralism, contestation, and the courage to meet power with power. Postmodernists are realists in that they acknowledge the Machiavellian play of power in international politics and yet are liberal enough to reassert the significance of the role of the individual in resisting the inexorable pressures of the state (Walker 1988b).

This is the abstract trajectory of postmodern thought. But what does the practical application of postmodern critique entail? How does one engage in postmodern critique? What questions would a postmodernist raise? How are postmodern arguments structured? In short, what is a postmodern analysis and, in terms of this particular chapter, how would the events in Kosovo appear if viewed through a postmodern lens? The NATO-led military air campaign against Kosovo and its accompanying rationale, humanitarian intervention, presents us with intriguing possibilities for a postmodern analysis. The question posed here is an extremely familiar one; however, the response will be characteristically postmodern—that is, provocatively unfamiliar. The question this chapter seeks to address is: What compelled NATO, with the United States at its helm, to embark upon a seventy-eight-day bombing campaign against another sovereign nation without UN Security Council authorization?

What counts as a provocatively unfamiliar response to the question posed above? It is the refusal to attempt to resolve the paradoxical dilemma when we find ourselves confronted with what appears to be dichotomous pairs of ideas or events—that is, force and humanitarian intervention. Postmodernism revels in exploiting paradoxes. The typical realist response to the above question would characteristically focus on the issues of force, self-help, and national security, while liberal responses would be inclined

to draw attention to the emergence of humanitarian principles of intervention, cooperation, or other key aspects of interdependence. Each attempts to
resolve the paradoxical nature of the event by privileging one aspect over
the other. A postmodern approach attempts to draw our attention to the
ways in which force and humanitarian intervention are inextricably intertwined and how they literally coproduce one another. The postmodern
agenda entails investigating this paradoxical connection in order to demonstrate how one cannot stand without the other.

What trajectories of postmodern thought guide such an investigation?
This analysis will rely upon the postmodern insights raised by Friedrich
Nietzsche's technique of genealogy, Michel Foucault's critique of the disciplinary effects of power, Sigmund Freud's insights regarding the dissolution of civilization, and Jacques Derrida's method of deconstruction. What
emerges from the overlay of these postmodern strains of thought is the
issue of originary violence. This is perhaps one of the most crucial postmodern insights—that *all* structures of rule and morality are held in place
by violence.

The postmodern approach employed within this study of the humanitarian intervention in Kosovo seeks to encourage a critical dialogue about
the power to impose meaning and interpretation on international events, the
disciplinary power exercised by governments over their own populations,
the imposition of particular value systems, and the nature of politics occurring within the realm of international relations. A genealogical analysis is
one way to raise these issues and to explore the paradoxical conjunction of
the moral attribute "humanitarian" with the military action of "intervention." The following analysis will reveal how the logic of "humanitarian
intervention" exposes the operation of a will to truth.

Nietzsche introduced the theory that "in all events a *will to power* is
operating" (1967: 78). The relationship between will to power and truth is
characterized by Nietzsche as a process that involves "spontaneous, aggressive, expansive, form-giving forces that give new interpretations and directions" (1967: 79).

> Whatever exists, having somehow come into being, is again and again
> reinterpreted to new ends, taken over, transformed, and redirected by
> some power superior to it; all events in the organic world are a subduing,
> a becoming master, and all subduing and becoming master involves a
> fresh interpretation, an adaptation through which any previous "meaning"
> and "purpose" are necessarily obscured or even obliterated. (1967: 77)

Life is a series of subduings and resistances by competing wills exercising
power in order to impose their meanings and interpretations on the world's
events. Life consists of a "continuous sign-chain of ever new interpretations and adaptations" (1967: 77). The will to power is the will to impose

meaning, a meaning emplaced and undergirded by power, and to conjoin that meaning with "the true" and "the good."

Genealogy focuses on the present in order to identify that which is problematic in what otherwise might be considered the normal or natural course of events (Bartelson 1995). It is important to "investigate the multiple ways in which claims to the truth are connected with various value-judgments" (Geuss 2001: 328). Genealogy attempts to reveal the contingency of events and that the things that we value were constructed piecemeal in episodic fashion via a struggle between competing wills (Behler 1996). Genealogy begins from the perspective that events are never unmediated. Such an approach seeks to reveal the point at which form and meaning are imposed on events by contesting wills. The contest is exposed for what it is, a will to power and truth.

It is Foucault who expands upon this conjunction of truth, power, and knowledge. He focuses on the productive dimensions of power and draws our attention to power's positive role as a creative, constitutive force. Power is inextricably intertwined with truth (Bartelson 1995). "Truth is already power. . . . 'Truth' is linked in a circular relation with systems of power which produce and sustain it, and to effects of power which it induces and which extend it" (Foucault 1972b: 133). Truths are productions of power. The only truths are those that our power produces and seeks to maintain. Postmodernism regards truth as a political question because it emerges out of the contest between competing wills to power. Truth is a political battleground and postmodernism forces us to confront the contingent nature of our truths. Thus we must grapple with the question of the "value" that our truths hold for us.

Next we need to consider the Freudian insight that civilization is always threatened with its own dissolution from within. Aggressive impulses of neighbor against neighbor threaten to shatter the delicate unity that civilization so assiduously tries to maintain. "Instinctual passions are stronger than reasonable interests" (Freud 1961: 59). Ultimately the injunction to "Love thy neighbor as thy self" must be upheld by the state through its exclusive control over the exercise of violence. "[Civilization] hopes to prevent the crudest excesses of brutal violence by itself assuming the right to use violence against criminals" (Freud 1961: 59). What is intriguing about Freud's remarks is the opening they provide for us to expose the threat of force that underlies the veneer of "uncoerced" compromise. Force is the mechanism that holds compromise in place, not the rationality of the better argument.

Let's circle back and pick up the elements of deconstruction. Deconstruction can be characterized as a "genealogy of violence" that attempts to expose the instances of violence that lie buried at the heart of our institutional arrangements (Durst 2000: 676). It attempts to reveal "how every social order rests on a forgetting of the exclusionary practices through which one set of meanings has been institutionalized and various other possibilities—other possible forms of meaning—have been marginalized" (Shapiro 1989: 15). The deconstructive aim is to question the very structure of discourse in order to determine if that discourse is "complicit and apologetic for a system of power and authority or challenging to it" (Shapiro 1989: 15). Furthermore, deconstruction questions the hierarchical ranking or privileging of terms that emerge within a particular discourse. Deconstruction strives to expose as illusory the dichotomy between such terms, by questioning the truth claims or values that underlie the hierarchical ranking of those terms. Ultimately, if violence is the underlying common term sustaining humanitarian intervention, as well as other military forms of intervention, then the difference between the two terms collapses. We are left confronting the specter of violence that underwrites all of our systems of authority and morality.

Genealogy demands we pay particular attention to the ways in which power and morality converge in an attempt to secure the "truth" of humanitarian intervention in Kosovo. It is not physical or military power that we aim to problematize. We wish to draw attention to the power to serialize or narrate the sequence of events in order to establish a certain set of actions as "true" and to conjoin those actions with the precept "moral." Genealogy brings into focus the power that underlies the connection between particular events and specific values. This enables us to question what "value" the value of humanitarian intervention holds for us.

First consider the nexus of sovereignty issues relevant to Kosovo. Events in Kosovo did not command the attention of Western liberal governments until sustained and escalating acts of violence erupted between the Kosovar Albanians, driven by the actions of the KLA, and the Serbian police and security forces within Kosovo. This eruption of violence was influenced by the perceived need to establish and claim a basis of sovereignty. The recognition of sovereignty confers the mantle of legitimacy and establishes the authority to wield "authorized" violence in the name of the people. The meaning of sovereignty is anything but a settled matter. The meanings and values attached to sovereignty can be viewed as a competition among various "wills to power" attempting to impose meaning and attach moral value to this conceptual construct.

Conceptually sovereignty represents the presumption of a final locus of legitimate political authority and control (Hinsley 1966). It indicates the location of a source of final decisionmaking authority that is authorized to act on behalf of the larger political community or organization. Ultimately, sovereignty encompasses the authorized use of "violence" in the name of the people. Employing the term "sovereignty" denotes the authorized, legitimate exercise of political power, and as John Locke indicates, "political power [is] the right of making laws with penalties of death" (Locke 1980: 8). Along similar lines, Rousseau locates sovereignty in the hands of the body politic, unmediated by representatives. When the group exercises their authorized and legitimate authority on behalf of the group, they are aware of the realization that "whoever refuses to obey the general will shall be constrained to do so by the whole body, [in short] he shall be forced to be free" (Rousseau 1968: 64). In its external manifestation, sovereignty "means that [a state] decides for itself how it will cope with its internal and external problems, including whether or not to seek assistance from others and in doing so to limit its freedom by making commitments to them" (Waltz 1979: 96). Consider the nexus of sovereignty issues that emerged in conjunction with the events in Kosovo. Look for the various "wills" competing to impose the "truth" of sovereignty. Notice how "power" is implicit in this contest. Ask yourself, what violence rests at the heart of these conceptions of sovereignty?

Kofi Annan, speaking on behalf of the United Nations, represents one such will. The secretary-general unequivocally characterized the events in Kosovo as a "human rights tragedy." Kosovo presented the international community with the dilemma of intervention in the affairs of a recognized sovereign state without Security Council authorization, coupled with the stark tragedy of allowing "gross systematic violations of human rights, with grave humanitarian consequences, [to] continue unchecked" (Annan 1999: 49–50). Annan attempted to draw attention to the intersect between individual sovereignty (human rights) and state sovereignty. He sought to secure the UN's role in representing the common interest of the international community in situations involving armed force against a sovereign nation. "Humanitarian action must be universal if it is to be legitimate" (Annan 1999). He advanced a conception of conditional state sovereignty linked to a state's respect for and protection of its citizens' individual rights. The UN Charter "aims to protect individual human beings, not to protect those who abuse them" (Annan 1999).

Serbian leadership represented another will. "The Yugoslav breakup triggered a series of civil wars in which the Serbian leadership believed that legitimate Serbian interests were at stake" (Hagen 1999: 59). During Slobodan Milosevic's visit to the province of Kosovo in April 1987, he announced, "Yugoslavia and Serbia are not going to give up Kosovo" (Judah 2000: 53). The operative "truth," according to Milosevic, was that Yugoslavia was sovereign and as such could legitimately wield violence in order to ensure that Kosovo remained in Yugoslavia. Serbian leaders viewed their "efforts to retain and re-Serbianize Kosovo [as] entirely legitimate" (Hagen 1999: 61).

The Albanian community's desire for greater autonomy and expansion of their civil rights in Kosovo met with rebuke and the revocation of the province's autonomy, the imposition of direct control from Belgrade, and the Milosevic-inspired course of action to "re-Serbianize the public sphere" (Hagen 1999: 58). In a bid for sovereign independence, the Kosovar Albanians created the Republic of Kosova, elected a president, Ibrahim Rugova, and set up an assembly. In essence they created a shadow government, which attempted to simulate the effects of sovereignty. They created their own schools, health care network, legal system, and police force, and collected their own taxes. They wanted sovereign independence, not autonomy within Yugoslavia. What's interesting about the nonviolent, passive resistance tack taken by Rugova was his conviction that in order "for Kosovo to gain western support for independence, it must behave like a 'civilized' and nonviolent society" (Ron 2001: 108). The point was to try to convince the West to confer sovereign recognition on the province of Kosovo due to its commitment to Western democratic principles.

The KLA emerged on the scene in 1996 and gradually increased its visibility through a series of provocative, violent acts throughout 1997–1998 aimed at Serbian police and state officials. Sovereignty would not be conferred on the basis of "good" behavior, or through simulation. Kosovo would require a violent wrenching from its entrenched position within Yugoslavia. "The KLA is uncompromising in its quest for an independent Kosovo now and a Greater Albania later" (Hedges 1999: 24). Did the KLA play the NATO card in order to advance its own aims? Two countervailing pressures were at work in Kosovo. The KLA attempted to keep the pressure on Serbian officials through violent, guerrilla war tactics, while Serbia engaged in a ruthless suppression of any and all threats to its authority. "Without military intervention the KLA could not hope to challenge FRY supremacy in Kosovo on its own" (Independent International Commission on Kosovo 2000: 149). Internationalization of the conflict would enable the KLA to involve NATO in dislodging Serbia from Kosovo, thus opening up the possibility for sovereign independence. Unfortunately, NATO's involvement also had a countervailing movement, which enabled Serbia to pursue an extremely aggressive campaign of ethnic cleansing on the ground in Kosovo under the cover of NATO air strikes.

The Western nations had never made any secret of their opposition to Kosovo's secession from Yugoslavia. Western governments attempted to force successive Albanian administrations to stop advocating independence for Kosovo. Financial aid for Albania was premised on such a change in attitude and policy toward Kosovo. The existing sovereign borders of Yugoslavia had to be respected. The argument against independence for Kosovo rested on the US and European view that "Kosovo did not have the right to independence because of its provincial status" (Judah 2000: 76).

Thus the outlines of a political struggle over the meaning of sovereignty were clearly drawn. There was a very real contest among these various international actors to establish the "moral truth" of sovereignty and to confirm the legitimacy of certain political actions. But what accounts for the fact that after seventy-eight days of NATO air strikes, Serbia was militarily punished, but rewarded with the right to maintain the province of Kosovo within the territorial boundaries of Yugoslavia (Mandelbaum 1999: 5)? And further, why didn't UN Resolution 1244 include any provisions for protecting minority rights and promoting a multiethnic Kosovo (O'Neill 2002: 31)? The use of military force was justified on the basis of humanitarian principles in order to stop gross violations of human rights, genocide, and ethnic cleansing. Yet why was Kosovo consigned to remain within Yugoslavia absent institutional mandates or political mechanisms emplaced to address fundamental issues of multiethnicity?

Genealogy drives us to grapple with the question of the "value" that certain truths hold for us. In this instance we must ask what value sovereignty held for those NATO members complicit in the use of force against the sovereign state of Yugoslavia. What other values are bound up with the concept of sovereignty that nations would employ violence in order to secure their truth? What if we shift our gaze from what is obvious to what lies hidden in the margins? International relations tends to focus on external power relations among states, but what if we turn that assumption over and "read" international relations from the inside out by focusing on the disciplinary and productive aspects of power? What if we try to uncover the violent practices states use in order to secure and maintain their own foundational truths?

The boundary between sovereignty and intervention is precisely the point at which we can observe the disciplinary effects of power. Can the actions of the states that participated in the NATO bombing campaign be read as indicative of an attempt to reconfirm the validity of a particular set of Western political practices *in the minds of their own citizens*? It is Foucault (1995) who asserts that disciplinary tactics are employed by states in order to transform the singular into the multiple, the one into the many. Disciplinary techniques thus rest at the very heart of the creation of a unified state. Politics itself has become one such disciplinary tactic, whose aim is to achieve internal peace and order within the nation, as well as within the individual. Politics is not about a social contract, fundamental rights, or the operation of a general will. Instead it is a technique of discipline that relies upon a series of permanent coercions in order to train individuals to be docile (Foucault 1995: 168–169). This Foucaultian insight is crucial because it enables us to work from the margins and to deconstruct the humanitarian intervention discourses employed by the most powerful NATO members as they sought to impose meaning on the events in Kosovo.

Events in Kosovo were defined by the West as a "humanitarian tragedy" and as a result Kosovo became an object of study viewed through this particular prism. Thus Kosovo became an event about which we could create a body of knowledge. Knowledge is inextricably intertwined with power because ultimately it is power that holds knowledge in place. In the competition among the various "wills to power" attempting to impose meaning on the events in Kosovo, the leading NATO nations took a very active role in attempting to impose their meaning on the events in Kosovo. Foucault concludes that power produces knowledge and that those who become subjects of that knowledge learn to observe, analyze, and understand themselves in accordance with this established body of knowledge. What body of knowledge is established within the discourses of humanitarian intervention? What if we view the exercise of power by states as intertwined with how they attempt to establish a body of knowledge about international events and then ask ourselves how this intersection of power and knowledge enables those very same states to ensure the creation of disciplined, docile citizens? Perhaps Kosovo can be read in order to reveal the disciplinary effects associated with the use of external force, a force undergirded by the attempt to attach moral goodness and truth to its use.

The following statements are a sampling of the various humanitarian discourses that emerged in conjunction with the NATO bombing campaign. The focus here is on understanding how the use of force and morality were conjoined. All of the following statements fit neatly alongside Rousseau's dictate of "forcing them to be free."

The secretary-general of NATO, Javier Solana, stated that the objective of air strikes was "to prevent more human suffering and more repression." He concluded with the closing comment, "We have a moral duty to do so" (Solana 1999). The European Council, comprising the heads of state of the fifteen EU members plus the president of the European Commission, delivered a similar message: "The common objective [is] to stop a humanitarian catastrophe in Kosovo. . . . Europe cannot tolerate a humanitarian catastrophe in its midst. . . . [We] are under a moral obligation. . . . [W]e have a duty" (European Council 1999). Which states are entitled to use violence? Which states are presumed to bear this moral obligation? On what does such an obligation ultimately rest?

The leaders of the United States, Britain, and France all addressed their nations in similar terms and reiterated the same themes. Notice how interchangeable and closely synchronized their comments are. What stands out is the discursive imposition of one message: "We act to protect thousands of innocent people in Kosovo . . . to diffuse a powder keg at the heart of Europe . . . we are upholding our values. Ending this tragedy is a moral imperative. We need a Europe . . . that shares our values . . . the men and women of our Armed Forces are undertaking this mission for the sake of our values" (Clinton 1999c). What is especially significant here is the reiteration of a moral imperative to employ force in order to impose a particular value structure. Even more telling is the way in which the moral goodness and truth of those values is ultimately confirmed by the willingness of American young men and women to sacrifice their lives in order to promote those very same values.

"Britain stands ready with our NATO allies to take military action . . . to avert what would otherwise be a humanitarian disaster in Kosovo. We cannot contemplate, on the doorstep of the EU, a disintegration into chaos and disorder. . . . [T]o walk away now would . . . be a breach of faith" (Blair 1999b). "The aim of the military strikes . . . is crystal clear . . . it is to curb Milosevic's ability to wage war on an innocent civilian population. 250,000 of them are homeless, 2,000 killed since last spring. These are our fellow human beings. We are doing what is right for Britain, for Europe. That is simply the right thing to do" (Blair 1999a). "I feel very strongly that, as President Clinton has said, this is a battle over the values of civilization" (Blair 1999d). Once again, Tony Blair's comments draw attention to the fear of disintegration, the duty to use force in order to hold values in place, and the simple reiteration of "right."

In response to a question about whether or not it was going too far to call the NATO action a war, the French minister of foreign affairs, Hubert M. Vedrine, responded that "what is being undertaken is more of an international coercion operation." In conclusion, Vedrine did not equivocate: "We are being forced to use . . . coercive means. But the objective is still the same, it is to impose, in some way or other, an acceptable coexistence between the Kosovars and Serbs" (Vedrine 1999). Vedrine shifts the focus a bit and presents the argument that NATO is forced to use violence in order to *impose* a political settlement.

President Jacques Chirac's comments reveal what was at stake by his use of the phrase "the duty of solidarity": "At the moment when French pilots are carrying out an action which France has decided on in full sovereignty . . . I would like the whole nation to demonstrate its solidarity. These are universal values of our republican tradition that we are defending" (Chirac 1999). What emerges from Chirac's comments is nothing less than a reminder of French citizens' duty to support their forces coupled with a reconfirmation of the universal applicability of French values.

Within days of one another these leaders all strove to ascribe a particular meaning to the events in Kosovo. Kosovo became known as the place where Western values were threatened, where force had to be used to impose consensus and compromise, and where the moral obligation to intervene militarily rested with NATO. How does this portrayal of Kosovo as a site of humanitarian intervention relate to the disciplinary effects of power of the NATO nations over their own populations?

What if the external manifestations of violence by Western, liberal governments in the conduct of their international relations is not merely emblematic of the violent nature of "out there," of the conduct of international relations, but is endemic to the political practices of liberal democratic government itself? Stripping away the veneer that underlies humanitarian claims in order to justify the raw exercise of violent force reveals the problematic core that rests at the heart of liberal governments. The political community needs to be constantly and consistently reminded of the moral lesson of state sovereignty. If and when the political community itself or segments within it reject those formerly authorized to exercise violence on behalf of the community, violence must be wielded in order to maintain the "truth" of the reigning political ideology. Not only must violence be wielded, but it is also the moral obligation of those in power (i.e., the state) to do so.

This is not just about the disciplining of the Kosovar Albanians and the Serbs by the United States and its NATO allies. This is about how that very same disciplinary power is refracted back on the citizens of those Western governments in order to confirm the moral truth and superiority of their political ideology. James Der Derian raises the issue that haunts the postmodern turn in international relations, namely "the tradition's failure to assure a day of peace for international relations" (1988: 191). Thus we must interrogate the entire meaning of the exercise of violence, refusing to begin only at the water's edge of international relations. What violence and cruelty rests at the heart of the establishment of liberal morality and the liberal moral order? Who authorizes the violent use of force in order to impose and sustain a particular set of values? Who authorizes the sacrifice of individual lives in order to achieve some greater, future political objective?

The United States has moved in fits and starts toward becoming a fully integrated multiethnic society. Part of its national mythology still relies on the analogy of the "melting pot" to extol the virtues of diversity. France, Great Britain, and Germany all have growing immigrant populations and assimilation itself has emerged as a potentially divisive issue. Each has experienced ethnic tensions and incidents of reactionary violence against immigrants (Almond and Powell 1996). Ultimately, no nation is immune from ethnic tensions. Western states must constantly reiterate the truth and moral goodness of their particular version of diversity, while controlling the nature and character of the assimilation process. These states extol difference and diversity while moving toward solidarity and unanimity by attempting to close off debate over the most political of all issues, the debate over fundamental values. The internal force that compels people to agree, to compromise, must remain hidden in order to maintain the belief that compromise is uncoerced and free. Yet the lesson must somehow be inscribed deep within the individual's soul that the moral duty and legitimate use of violence rests with those states that subscribe to a particular set of Western values. Thus we can understand the pressing need to conjoin "humanitarian" with "intervention" in order to produce the "truth" of intervention coupled with the "moral goodness" of its aims.

The events in Kosovo are composed of a double movement. The first encompasses the humanitarian justifications for the use of force against a sovereign nation, while the second involves the disciplinary power of external violence on the internal "souls" of their own citizens. What is compelling about this sequencing of events is that its message is refracted back on and directed internally toward the citizens of the NATO nations themselves. Humanitarian justifications establish the conviction that the West is doing this for the benefit of the citizens of Kosovo in order to avert a humanitarian tragedy. The constant reiteration of the humanitarian mantra and its conjunction with the "truth" attempts to write the lesson deep within the souls of their own citizens that chaos, death, and destruction await those who challenge the fundamental values of the sovereign Western state. Nothing but force holds the "truth" of those values in place. This is precisely the excess meaning that threatens to spill over from the events in Kosovo. If people refuse to compromise, they must be compelled by force, that is, through the exercise of violence that the state claims as its exclusive right. The Western states were not concerned with ethnic diversity in Kosovo as evidenced by UN Resolution 1244, nor were they interested in self-determination for Kosovo. They were interested in reiterating and validating their own legitimacy and power in order to discipline politics within their own states.

What drew together nineteen nations, with varying political agendas and interests, in order to sustain seventy-eight days of bombing? They recognized the specter of dissolution that haunts all civilizations. They feared that their own nations could implode under similar circumstances. Thus they needed to convince their own citizens of the "justness" of the use of force, characterized as humanitarian intervention in order to reiterate their state's own sovereign value. Without Western states imbued with Western value structures, chaos and disintegration would reign. The discourses of humanitarian intervention all focused on the same key terms: universality, solidarity, duty, and right. They all held up as exemplary their own citizens' willingness to die in defense of their values. In this instance, the use of force is ultimately good, ultimately moral, because it sustains a particular version of the state that sustains the movement toward a uniform Western value structure.

The reason that the humanitarian version of the events in Kosovo emerged as the dominant interpretation lies in the connection established between "truth" and "moral imperative" throughout the entire process of meaning-making. When "the truth" and "the good" are conjoined, the dominant interpretation enjoys an unquestioned advantage in its ability to resist counterwills seeking to impose new counterinterpretations. However, in order to maintain the original conjunction of truth and goodness, meaning-making must continuously strive to reaffirm and sustain the established interpretation. The leading NATO nations have continued to impose their will on the meaning of unfolding events.

The "truth" of the results is merely an extension of the same process of trying to impose meaning on a particular sequence of events. It did not take long after the cessation of the allied bombing campaign for the claims of vindication and success to emerge. "In Kosovo we did the right thing. We did it the right way. We have achieved a victory for a safer world, for our democratic values and for a stronger America. The result will be security and dignity for the people of Kosovo" (Clinton 1999a). Ambassador Robert Hunter greatly exceeded Clinton's highly optimistic reading of the events, with his comment that "NATO ultimately succeeded for a reason embedded in the Washington Treaty: the worth and power of basic democratic values" (Hunter 2000).

In order to secure the morality of the actions in Kosovo, "truth" must continue to be produced, without which power can't be exercised. "The real test for the moral issues that legitimized the intervention in the Kosovo crisis will be the EU's ability to sustain a long-term commitment to help establish a European future for the Balkans" (Independent International Commission on Kosovo 2000: 257). What is illustrative in the above comment is the admission that the moral legitimacy of intervention can only be justified by the results. However, results themselves are also productions of truth.

Resolution 1244 calls for a commitment to "the sovereignty and territorial integrity of the Federal Republic of Yugoslavia" in addition to the provision "for substantial autonomy and meaningful self-administration for Kosovo." This political accommodation between Kosovar Albanians and Serbs is to be guaranteed by an international civilian administration supported by an international military presence. The Organization for Security and Cooperation in Europe (OSCE) is responsible for spearheading the democratization of the province of Kosovo and establishing the basis for democratic institutions. Economic growth and development is under the province of the EU and its Regional Stability Pact. The UN special representative of the secretary-general is empowered with "all legislative and executive authority, including the administration of the judiciary" (Independent International Commission on Kosovo 2000: 114). The powers exercised by these civilian and international administrators is extensive indeed, so extensive in fact that one cannot help but notice the level of force and compulsion necessary to convince Kosovo citizens of the "truth" and "value" of the UN/EU mission.

Chris Patten spoke before the Macedonian parliament in order to restate the EU's reason for intervening in Kosovo and to sketch out the nature of the ties that would serve to bind Macedonia ever closer to the EU. Two aspects of his speech are noteworthy in terms of our focus on Kosovo and the will to truth. One is the fact that Patten said, "You recognized that we could not continue to see our values—your values—violated in Kosovo, and that we had to make a stand." The key phrase of course is "our values are your values." The second aspect relates to how the stabilization agreement will ensure that "our values are your values." The agreement will "provide for close political dialogue between the EU and your country, it will commit you to approximate the legislation of your country to that of the European Community and it will include co-operation in a wide range of other areas such as justice and home affairs" (Patten 2000). The presumptive values, which underlie the stability agreement, are presented not only as "the truth," but also as the unquestioned foundation upon which integration into the European Community ultimately rests. Patten graciously offered to assist the Macedonians with the task of "approximating your legislation to that of the European Union." One can only ask: What then becomes of politics in the former Republic of Macedonia? Isn't politics the process whereby fundamental values are debated and discussed?

The conflict in Kosovo was/is political, but not for the reasons most apparent to realists or liberals. Why would the Italian, French, and German governments risk the political fallout from their own constituencies over intervention in Kosovo? Why would Britain push so strenuously for the introduction of ground troops in Kosovo? And why would the United States spearhead an effort that it initially gave scant regard? Perhaps the new internationalism touted by Tony Blair will provide some insight. According to Blair, "We [meaning Western democracies] are all coping with the same issues: achieving prosperity . . . social stability . . . and a role for government." The most telling line in Blair's speech comes with the admission that politics is over: "The political debates of the 20th Century—the massive ideological battleground between left and right—are over" (Blair 1999a). Western truths and the value of those truths will now prevail, unquestioned and unexamined. This is precisely the point at which postmodern critique emerges in order to challenge us to resist the imposition of such an ideological closure. Postmodernism compels us to reopen the debate and to question the validity of those values, which have sedimented into place. This chapter is but one small swath through the vast terrain of postmodern thought and international politics. The challenge now rests with you to read the postmodern texts anew and open up new vantage points of critique. If postmodernism holds out any hope, it is the possibility to think things other than they are (Foucault 1984).

Marc Lynch

Critical Theory: Dialogue, Legitimacy, and Justifications for War

Critical theory welcomes challenges to state sovereignty in the name of human rights as an essential step toward creating a more just world order, a norms-based international society taking individuals rather than states as primary. While innately skeptical of the moral posturing of powerful actors, and deeply troubled by the resort to violence, critical theory could under certain conditions welcome even military means. If all attempts at reason have failed, and the force is employed by internally democratic states that can justify their actions before a critical international public, then military intervention could potentially become a progressive force. States have no absolute right to be sheltered from the gaze of international public scrutiny and the enforcement of global norms (Linklater 1998). Against either the timeless interests of realism or the legalistic rigor of international law, critical theory locates legitimacy within an emerging international public sphere of world citizens, which offers dramatically new opportunities for the emancipatory potential of human reason. Such a critical theory is distinctively relevant to the intervention in Kosovo. NATO publicly justified its intervention not by state security or self-interest, but in terms of universal morality, the obligation to protect the innocent, and the aspiration toward the consolidation of progressive international norms. No analysis of the Kosovo campaign can be complete without taking into account these unusual and highly contestable legitimacy claims. A critical theory inspired by Jurgen Habermas is the most appropriate theory for evaluating such legitimacy claims—and the failure to command international consensus or to establish widely accepted new international norms.

While a bewildering range of theoretical perspectives claim the mantle of critical theory, the strand associated with Habermas is most relevant to making sense of the Kosovo campaign (Devetak 2001; Linklater 1996; Price and Reus-Smit 1998). Habermas himself publicly supported the Kosovo intervention, seeing in the multilateral power of the democratic nations of NATO the instrument for the progressive transformation of the world. Habermas saw the Kosovo intervention as holding genuine potential for "the transformation of the 'law of nations' into a law of world-citizens" (2000: 307). While not blind to the potential dangers of a war, Habermas argued that against these risks must be set the vision of a new normative environment grounded in compulsory respect for human rights, backed by the restrained use of force subject to democratic and multilateral control. Habermas's support for a potentially transformative war goes hand in hand with his theoretically grounded rejection of the realist acceptance of the world as it is, an anarchic world of self-interest and strategic action (Matustik 2002: 186–189). The aspiration for normative change means that, despite all skepticism and fear, "confronted with crimes against humanity, the international community must be able to act" (Habermas 2002: 15).

Such critical theorists remained troubled by the absence of a United Nations mandate for the intervention, however, since this seemed to undermine rather than to build the institutions of international order. The Independent International Commission on Kosovo, convened to grapple with these troubling contradictions, concluded that "the NATO military intervention was illegal but legitimate" (2000: 4). This distinction, while useful, places great weight on some theory of how the "legitimacy" of an illegal action might be established. The commission suggested a series of commonsensical standards, most familiar from just war theory: exceptional circumstances, right intention, last resort, proportional means, reasonable prospects of improving the situation, and right authority. Rather than a checklist, critical theory would judge potential interventions in terms of their contribution to the establishment of progressively transformative norms. Doing so requires careful attention to the process of legitimation, and particularly the extent to which the intervention was justified through public argument and debate. Such public argumentation is more than a procedural issue for critical theorists. No actor, no matter how powerful or well intentioned, and no scholar working from a series of guidelines, no matter how well constructed, can unilaterally establish legitimacy. Legitimacy can only be achieved by reaching consensus through open public argument among all affected actors under conditions roughly free of considerations of power and self-interest. Just war theory, or the commission's standards, *could* be applied in a critical theoretic way, if understood not simply as a checklist or a set of guidelines but as "a framework for debate and dialogue about the right causes and conduct of war" (Crawford 2003: 7).

Habermas's conception of legitimacy rests upon a core distinction between "strategic" and "communicative" action (1996, 2000). Strategic action occurs when an actor attempts to manipulate another, whether through threats, incentives, or rhetoric. Communicative action, by contrast, occurs when actors set aside their self-interest, their relative power, and even their identities in order to seek truth—or at least consensus about the right course of action. For Habermas, strategic action can produce an agreement, a temporary convergence of interests and power, but this will not command any normative weight. Such normative legitimacy can only be achieved through communicative action, in which all affected actors are able to effectively speak and be heard. By this standard, the unilateral definition of norms and standards inherently represents an act of power, a monologue to which others might or might not accede but to which they are not invited to contribute. Any unilateral claim to legitimacy—even by "good" actors—therefore must be viewed with great suspicion. Since legitimacy can only be achieved through an open dialogue among all affected actors, no single actor can alone define its terms. An actor that arrogates unto itself the power to dictate the terms of morality might convince itself of its own righteousness, or effectively win support among the like-minded or domestic audiences, but will not likely convince others. Using moral rhetoric to more effectively manipulate others, then, is just another form of strategic action, despite its outwardly communicative form.

Critical theory insists that legitimacy is only possible where actors enter into an open-ended dialogue in which the outcome is neither predetermined nor restricted in terms of whose interests are open to debate. The process of consensus formation matters, not because of a fetishization of process or of particular institutions, but because certain procedural rules are the only guarantee against powerful actors appropriating claims to "legitimacy" that they have not earned through rational argument. The campaign's legitimacy could only be secured through the open give and take of political argument in the public sphere (Habermas 1996; Bohman 1996; Lynch 2000). It is on those grounds, critical theory contends, that the Kosovo campaign could have succeeded, but in practice failed. Public arguments about Kosovo quickly deteriorated into harsh suspicion and mutual accusations, denying NATO any genuine international consensus. The failure of the Kosovo campaign lay in NATO's monologic rather than dialogic approach, and in its inability to muster genuine international consensus before acting. Rather than win wide support for its interpretation, NATO sidestepped the UN and simply asserted its superior moral authority. Habermas later admitted that contrary to his transformational hopes, NATO nations "did not appeal to 'principles' of a future cosmopolitan order but were satisfied to enforce their demand for international recognition of what they perceived to be the universalistic force of their own national 'values'" (2002: 15).

Because of the failure to win a communicative consensus in the international public sphere, the Kosovo campaign failed to live up to its system-transforming potential. This legitimation burden mattered even more because the war was fought in the name of establishing or defending norms—truly a war unlike other wars. Despite the powerful normative aspirations that accompanied the Kosovo campaign, it failed to establish any lasting new norms of humanitarian intervention. Indeed, for the most part the war has been largely forgotten, despite all the inspiring hopes and apocalyptic warnings surrounding it. The Kosovo precedent rarely surfaced during the long, bitter arguments about the invasion of Iraq, for example, despite obvious symmetries. The failure to bring about any decisive change derived in large part from the shortcomings of the intervention's procedural and substantive legitimation.

Critical theory cannot simply dismiss a multilateral humanitarian war waged to protect innocent civilians from the ravages of ethnic genocide. Nor can it ignore the progressive rhetoric that accompanied the intervention. At the same time, a genuinely critical theory cannot set aside its skepticism of the motivations of great powers or ignore the manifest disjuncture between inspirational rhetoric and developments on the ground. This chapter discusses how critical theory applies to the Kosovo campaign in terms of legitimation and international organizations, the conduct of the war, and the internal processes inside of Kosovo. It notes key points about which critical theorists disagree, rather vehemently, among themselves, and explores the significance of those disagreements. Finally, it briefly considers how the lessons of the Kosovo campaign as understood by Habermasian critical theory might apply to the arguments over war with Iraq.

■ Legality and Legitimacy

Kofi Annan argued that it "is essential that the international community reach consensus—not only on the principle that massive and systematic violations of human rights must be checked, wherever they take place, but also on ways of deciding what action is necessary, and when, and by whom" (1999). If this was its challenge, then the international community failed: it failed to produce a normative consensus about humanitarian intervention, and it failed to establish a precedent for future action. The failure to produce consensus went even deeper, extending to the most basic interpretive levels: it "provoked extremely divergent interpretations of what was truly at stake, the prudence of what was undertaken, and the bearing of law and morality" (Falk 1999: 847). What Habermas saw as the chance to establish stronger international norms, Russian diplomat Sergey Lavrov saw as "undermining the UN Charter and other norms of international law . . . to establish de-facto the primacy of force and unilateral diktat in the world" (Buckley 2000: 728). The challenge for critical theory is to explain how such deeply rooted suspicions and presumptions of hypocrisy might be overcome through public argument. A Security Council resolution that established a clear mandate and specific objectives, with the formal authority of the United Nations behind it, might have gone some way toward reconciling these divergent views. But without also reconciling these fundamentally divergent understandings of the meaning of the intervention, even a formal resolution would have failed to cross the threshold of progressive norm formation.

The formal illegality of the Kosovo campaign is not in serious doubt. The intervention violated international law and norms governing military intervention, and it could not be reconciled with Article 2(4) of the UN Charter (Glennon 2001). Only the Security Council can authorize military intervention, or express a collective mandate of the international community. Because of the near-certainty of Russian and Chinese vetoes, however, NATO chose to ignore the UN and to claim authorization on the basis of an appeal to universal international norms. The NATO decision to act outside of the UN left it without any recognizable formal international legitimacy.

Law and legitimacy are not necessarily identical, however, as critical theory has long argued. Laws passed through insufficiently communicative channels could easily represent an institutionalized injustice, systematic oppression that must be unmasked and exposed. International law governing intervention arguably represented such an illegitimate law, to the extent that it protected grotesquely oppressive regimes from international scrutiny or accountability. Under such conditions, critical theory—unlike more conventional multilateralists or liberals—would not defer to international law or the authority of formal institutions. NATO claims a legitimate right to act on the basis of universal humanitarian norms that need no higher authorization and therefore could not simply be dismissed out of hand. Action through formal institutions that reinforced rather than undermined international law would be preferable, since "moral norms appealing to our better judgment may not be enforced in the same fashion as established legal norms" (Habermas 2000: 310). But formal legality is ultimately subordinate to the demands of legitimacy.

Some critical advocates of humanitarian intervention therefore celebrated, rather than apologized for, the avoidance of a UN mandate. As Chris Brown summarized the argument, "the unwillingness of the UN to act was a sign that something was wrong with that body, but that in the absence of UN approval, action could still be legitimate" (2000). Why, they asked, should a UN dominated by nondemocratic states be allowed to check the moral impulses of democracies? Why should Russia, actively engaged in a brutally repressive war in Chechnya, or China, responsible for great atrocities in Tibet, be allowed to pass judgment on Western efforts to prevent ethnic genocide? Why allow the encrusted realist practice of states to interfere with a move to a more assertive enforcement of humanitarian norms? Indeed, Neta Crawford goes so far as to deny that a nondemocracy can be considered "communicatively competent" to engage in international public argument (2002: 423–425).

For all of its failings, the Security Council is the recognized "right authority" in international law, and provides a decision rule by which to determine whether or not an intervention enjoys formal legitimacy. If the UN is abandoned, no clear, universally accepted replacement exists. The claim that "a coalition of like-minded or 'enlightened' states excluding the blocking Permanent Members can still wield sufficient moral authority" offers no similarly universal formal legitimacy (Independent International Commission on Kosovo 2000: 173). The weakness of existing international organizations, combined with seemingly irreconcilable divisions in international public spheres, left the Kosovo campaign facing a profound legitimation crisis. NATO's decision to avoid the United Nations pointed out starkly the limitations of the currently existing world order. Whatever the claims to a higher morality, the absence of a UN resolution clearly mattered. Even UN Secretary-General Kofi Annan was of two minds about the tension between the primacy of the Security Council and the imperative of humanitarian intervention:

> Unless the Security Council is restored to its preeminent position as the sole source of legitimacy on the use of force, we are on a dangerous path to anarchy. But equally important, unless the Security Council can unite around the aim of confronting massive human rights violations and crimes against humanity on the scale of Kosovo, then we will betray the very ideals that inspired the founding of the United Nations. (Buckley 2000: 222)

But once the formal procedures of the Council are set aside, some other method of legitimation must be offered. Is this moral authority self-arrogated by great powers? Does it lie in some reading of international norms by jurists or by politicians? Critical theory argues that such a role must be filled by public argument within an emerging international public sphere (Lynch 2000; Bohman 1996). As Danilo Zolo puts it, "as politics and communications became increasingly globalized, the universalizing of humanitarian motivations is an effective rhetorical instrument; it allows one to set 'world public opinion' and 'universal ethics' against the deviant law-unto-itself of a single state or political regime" (2002: 39). Under conditions of globalization, legitimation within the nation-state can no longer alone establish the foundations for meaningful action. Neither, apparently, could the UN or other existing formal international institutions. The intervention's putative legitimacy came from the net positive effect of the intervention—whatever the procedural violations, whatever the mixed motivations, the outcome vindicated the intervention. But such claims remained highly debatable, and hotly contested. It is those contestations—or their absence—that define legitimacy from a critical theorist's perspective.

Unfortunately for the hopes of such legitimation through the public sphere, international dialogue over Kosovo degenerated quickly into "cantankerous exchanges in which fervent supporters of intervention on human rights grounds, opposed by anxious defenders of state sovereignty, dug themselves deeper and deeper into opposing trenches" (Evans and Sahnoun

2002: 101). Many in the human rights, development, and humanitarian nongovernmental sector not only endorsed but also actively pushed for the NATO intervention. Much of the Western media accepted and reproduced the official NATO narrative of ethnic cleansing and humanitarian response. Looking beyond the NATO member states complicates the verdict, however. Much of international public opinion viewed the NATO intervention with great concern, worrying at its seemingly arbitrary quality, its avoidance of the UN, and its rejection of long-cherished norms of state sovereignty. Rather than bring together a consensus on the morality of intervention, the Kosovo campaign deeply divided the international public sphere. This argument grew more and more heated, less and less communicative, until the end of the war put an end to an unresolved controversy. The failure to resolve this argument in either the formal institutions of the UN or the informal sites of the international public sphere doomed the attempt to translate the war into a legitimate norm of humanitarian intervention.

The move to replace legality based on the sovereign equality of states with a conception of legitimacy that equates international norms with the preferences of "enlightened" states seems to embody a monological, strategic conception of legitimacy (Zolo 2002: 2–3). Some critical theorists have argued that such liberal states are the only ones possessing a public sphere free enough to engage in serious political debate. If Western publics vigorously debated the legitimacy of the intervention, could this substitute for the absent wider international public consensus? Against the critical theorists who do take this position, I would have to say no. Discourse ethics requires the participation of all affected actors in dialogue, which means that nondemocracies cannot be shut out of the debate. Only the emergence of sites of communicative action in the international system, international public spheres, would allow for a dialogic morality that moves beyond the universalizing aspirations of powerful states. The acceptance by these critical theorists of NATO's claim to a higher moral standing, to the universal applicability of human rights and the appropriateness of war as a method to achieve them, and their inattention to the clear weakening of the United Nations both contradicted and undermined precisely their own carefully developed arguments for a transformative international practice. NATO's universalist claims seem to be the kind that critical theory was meant to unmask. More generally, a consensus that excludes the countries likely to be the targets of future interventions is not likely to be the foundation for a widely accepted international norm.

■ The Exposure of Hypocrisy

In Vaclav Havel's oft-quoted summation, "no person of sound judgment can deny one thing: this is probably the first war ever fought that is not being fought in the name of interests but in the name of certain principles and values" (Buckley 2000: 244). Javier Solana, NATO's secretary-general, argues that NATO acted "first and foremost . . . to stop the humanitarian tragedy." For Solana, "to stand idly by while a brutal campaign of forced deportation, torture and murder is going on in the heart of Europe would have meant declaring moral bankruptcy" (Buckley 2000: 218). Such moral rhetoric offered an irresistible target to its critics. Earnest assertions that the intervention in Kosovo was a uniquely moral war, one fought for reasons of virtue rather than reasons of self-interest, set a standard against which state behavior could rather easily be found wanting. Many self-proclaimed critical theorists fiercely rejected Habermas's arguments as an apologetic for the military power of the United States. For these critical critics, US hypocrisy, unilateralism, double standards, and imperial pretensions outweighed any conceivable good that might come from the NATO campaign. They furiously denounced Habermas's "aggressive, enthusiastic, and even contemptuous" support of an "unjustified, unjust, imperial intervention" (Marsh 2002: x). A reflexive skepticism of US moral claims based upon easily observed double standards shapes this kind of critique. How can NATO claims to be concerned with normative values be taken seriously, asks Noam Chomsky (2000b), when the same nations eager to act in Kosovo ignore similar or worse atrocities in East Timor? How can NATO claim a moral high ground against ethnic cleansing when one of its own members, Turkey, is guilty of crimes against its Kurdish population comparable to Serb atrocities in Kosovo? What is more, NATO's intervention in Kosovo seemed to be the wrong war, half a decade too late. The argument for an intervention in Bosnia from 1992 to 1995 was considerably stronger than the argument in 1999 for intervening in Kosovo, and yet state interests, domestic politics, UN weakness, and a general failure of international leadership prevented one.

As Jeffrey Isaac (2002) points out, simply exposing hypocrisy tells us little about how to craft a more moral foreign policy in a complex world of difficult choices. An embrace of radical skepticism cripples the very hope for progressive change so central to critical theory's transformative practice. A genuinely critical theory needs to be actively engaged. But critical theorists have good reasons to remain wary of aligning themselves with power, even if that power is exercised in the name of their own aspirations: "the issue of double standards cannot be resolved by giving reluctant support to the actions of the most powerful states when their particular interests and international law happen to coincide . . . critical theory cannot be a partner to the double standards of geopolitics" (Nakarada 2000: 71).

Such attacks raise important questions about the central purpose of critical theory. Even sympathetic critics saw Habermas as hopelessly naive or overly optimistic, and wondered what remained of his "critical" theory.

Rather than offer justifications for US military power, they argued, critical theory's role should be to "point out egregious instances of injustice and to marshal moral argument against obvious wrongs" (Nakarada 2000: 65). For Edward Said, "the first duty is to demystify the debased language and images used to justify American practices and hypocrisy" (1999). But should not the first duty be to protect the innocent? Or to create new normative standards of behavior by which US hypocrisy and double standards might be judged in a politically potent way? If critical theory depends upon exposing injustice and demanding a more moral practice, then what is the value of preemptively criticizing practices justified in progressive terms as presumptively amoral or of ridiculing tentative moves to embrace such norms?

Critical theory cannot afford radical skepticism, since this cripples any hope of progressive change. Problematizing universalizing claims made on behalf of self-interested actors does not mean that such claims must always, inevitably, be rejected in the name of a weary cynicism or a reflexive mistrust of US power. Indeed, such an automatic rejection of moral principle can only lead to the endless reproduction of a realist world, which critical theorists hope to change. If the United States is condemned when it does use its great power to prevent great atrocities from taking place, how can it then be condemned for a failure to act in Rwanda or Bosnia? Should the failure of the United States to save Rwandans prevent it from saving Kosovars? Even if the Kosovo campaign was the wrong war, too late, might it not still leave the world better off than had it not been fought? Given the reality that only the United States had the military and political capacity to act, David Rieff caustically noted, "those who fear American power are—this is absolutely certain—condemning other people to death" (1999: 9). Habermas could reasonably ask whether, whatever one's qualms about US power, a world in which ethnic cleansing or genocide passed without response would really be a better one. A critique of the Kosovo war that remains trapped between the manifest hypocrisy of NATO's moral claims and the manifest imperative to act to stop ethnic cleansing threatens political—and critical—paralysis. A theory committed to human emancipation and public reason must do better.

But simply endorsing transparently self-serving moral claims by states would equally cut against the spirit of critical theory. A genuinely critical theory must, in the words of Slajov Zizek (1999), "reject the double blackmail" of either excessively corrosive cynicism or enlistment in the service of covering for power. Richard Falk strikes such a balance, tentatively concluding that "genocidal behavior cannot be shielded by claims of sovereignty, but neither can these claims be overridden by unauthorized uses of force delivered in an excessive and inappropriate manner" (1999: 848). Rather than conclude with the exposure of hypocrisy and the condemnation of power, as if that alone were sufficient, a genuinely critical theory must generate an effective political practice. As Radmila Nakarada laments, "exposing the inconsistencies . . . has no preventive or transformative capacity. The forces of power have proven to be immune to such exposure" (2000: 68).

Critical theory can draw on constructivist international relations theory for such an effectively critical, transformative practice, by using the force of public exposure to bind states to their moral rhetoric, even if they employed it for nakedly strategic reasons (Price and Reus-Smit 1998; Risse, Ropp, and Sikkink 1999). Critical theory's attention to publicity directs attention toward the justificatory strategies employed by the intervening powers and invites detailed comparison between rhetoric and practice. If—and only if—a public sphere exists that can make compelling demands upon states to redeem their rhetoric, then even hypocritical moralizing can be leveraged into progressive change (Lynch 2000). Where such a public sphere exists, critical theory suggests that normatively oriented critics can work to force great powers to live up to their strategically chosen rhetoric. Holding the powerful to their public commitments, rather than dismissing them as insincere or hypocrites, opens up possibilities for the weak to exercise power over the strong by shaming them with their own words.

The unfolding of the Kosovo campaign at least partially supports this critical theory reading of the relationship between rhetoric and practice. Remarkably few persuasive "real" reasons seemed to lurk behind NATO's progressive rhetoric. There are no real natural resources to be exploited in Kosovo. It is not a particularly important place to position military bases. The demonstration effect of NATO power hardly seemed necessary, given the absence of any challengers to NATO's might. As Habermas responded to his critics, "the case at hand shows that universalist justifications do not by necessity always function as a veil for the particularity of unconfessed interests. The results of the hermeneutics of suspicion are quite meager" (2000: 322). Such meager findings could strengthen confidence in the stated reasons, if those reasons were defended in open public argument and were matched by deeds.

While the normative justifications might be little more than post facto constructions for a war chosen for other reasons, actors were forced to act as if they believed them. As Rieff describes it, "the fact that while the NATO powers are often willing to intervene they have also shown themselves almost never willing to take casualties suggests that this commitment is as much about having fallen into a rhetorical trap as about being guided by a new moralizing principle" (1999: 2). NATO's protestations of morality and overt repudiation of self-interest tied its hands in its conduct both during and after the war. NATO forces remain committed to governing Kosovo in order to live up to its humanitarian rhetoric. The ongoing

UN presence in Kosovo suggests that the need to live up to even hypocritical normative claims can powerfully shape state practice. Rather than "bomb and run," the United States felt bound to endorse a sustained presence in the province, to protect and to reconstruct the shattered region. Without the global scrutiny and the precedent of its own mobilizing rhetoric, would NATO have bothered with Kosovo once the crisis had passed? In order to maintain public support for a confusing war, NATO promised repeatedly to return the refugees to their homes and rebuild their shattered lives. It was this public promise, more than any directly evident interests, that tied its hands after the Serb withdrawal (Independent International Commission on Kosovo 2000: 89). And Slobodon Milosevic did eventually fall under the weight of popular dissatisfaction and was brought before the Hague tribunal to stand trial for his crimes against humanity. Harnessing state power to universalizable human interests represents exactly the kind of practice demanded by a critical theory, one that can make hypocrisies progressive by contributing to the establishment of new norms of humanitarianism.

■ NATO Military Conduct

The positive impact of international publicity noted above cannot mask the very real problems with the intervention from a critical theory perspective. Besides the failure to establish any meaningful new international norms, NATO's campaign, while careful by modern standards, still left gaping holes between the public rhetoric and the realities on the ground. As the bombing of Serbia accelerated and the international order teetered on the brink of collapse, the transformative hopes advanced by critical theorists seemed increasingly empty, alarmingly abstract, and failingly inadequate to grapple with troubling realities. The moral rhetoric seemed off-key after the United States failed to act on behalf of Bosnia during three long years of far worse ethnic cleansing, and its willingness to deal pragmatically with Milosevic at Dayton. The specific challenges of Kosovo even further complicated the moral equation. The KLA's tactics and strategies rendered the moral equation in Kosovo far less clear-cut than in Bosnia. NATO's preference for Serbia's demand for Kosovo to remain part of its sovereign territory, over the Kosovar desire for an independent state, left an odd tension between the intervention and its putative allies. The mismatch between NATO's moral rhetoric and the human costs of a campaign fought from the air generated significant doubts even among those who generally sympathized with the objective of putting an end to the poisonous ethnic politics of the former Yugoslavia. The NATO bombing campaign, for all the coalition's careful deliberations over targeting, did enormous and predictable damage to the Serb civilian population. US rejection of any ground campaign emboldened the Serb army in its campaign of ethnic cleansing and expulsion following the initiation of bombing.

More than most wars, Kosovo was fought in, and fought over, the international public sphere. The unprecedented care taken in the selection of military targets to avoid galvanizing public opinion, the consistent articulation of a moral justification for the intervention, the careful attention to maintaining both coalition and public consensus—all of these mattered as much to the course of the war as did any "real" events on the ground. NATO justified the war in terms of the defense, consolidation, and extension of international humanitarian norms. The demand for coalition consensus shaped even the most operational, strategic decisions. And coalition consensus in turn depended in large part upon satisfying the concerns of member governments that televised civilian casualties—or much worse, NATO military casualties—could turn public opinion against the war.

Because of the importance of public opinion to the intervention, NATO followed some of the most rigorous and multilateral rules of engagement in the history of modern warfare (Clark 2001). With every target vetted at a high level, and with all NATO members allowed an ongoing voice, the bombing campaign would seem to respond to at least some of the aspirations of a collective, multilateral conception of common security. Bombing campaigns have their own iron logic, however (Clark 2001; Daalder and O'Hanlon 2000b). What begins as a surgical, coercive operation regularly escalates as it fails to achieve its goals, the bombers run out of immediate military targets, and the bombers demand that more and more pain be inflicted. What is more, the careful attention to targeting decisions distracted attention from the fateful decision to not deploy ground troops and to not place NATO pilots at any risk whatsoever. These seemingly pragmatic decisions, prioritizing the lives of NATO personnel over the lives of the Kosovars being defended or the Serb civilians being encouraged to overthrow Milosevic, carried implicit moral decisions. As William Buckley put it, alliance unity "was purchased by shifting the risks to the civilian populations in an air campaign of combatant immunity" (2000: 237). As a result, "the Kosovo war was also a near disaster, for reasons that go to the heart of its moral justification: legitimate political concerns led the NATO allies to wage war in a way that endangered the very people the war was supposed to defend" (Luban 2002: 79). Such distinctions in the value of lives can scarcely be justified on the universalist terrain demanded by critical theory, which fundamentally rejects "differences among human beings [that] do not have the moral relevance that they have been assumed to possess" (Wyn Jones 2001: 27).

As the bombing campaign escalated to become quite disproportionate, the moral equation grew even more strained. The very claims to represent a new, more humanitarian style of warfare became a standard against which the war itself could and should be judged. As Edward Said put it, "if one wants to intervene to alleviate suffering or injustice . . . then one must make sure first that by doing so the situation will not be made worse" (1999). The bombing campaign made things worse, rather than better, at least in the short term, and critics charged that NATO should have anticipated this outcome. The major expulsion of Kosovar refugees followed, rather than preceded, the bombing campaign, for example. Only the images of these refugees fully justified the war, with most Western audiences failing to appreciate the sequence of events. The Serb campaign of ethnic cleansing, while perhaps not automatic, should have been—and there is considerable evidence that it was—anticipated by NATO. Similarly, the bombing campaign against the Serbs, which began as relatively carefully calibrated, rapidly escalated, causing great harm to Serb civilians in little position to influence the Milosevic government. Critical theorists can hardly feel sanguine about abetting such suffering.

■ The Potential for Dialogue

Andrew Linklater proposes that "critical theory judges social arrangements by their capacity to embrace open dialogue with all others" (1996: 280). Violence tends to foreclose dialogue and to harden group identities, which makes it the instrument of choice for extremists determined to prevent negotiated peace agreements. The hypernationalism of both official Serb discourse and the KLA violates any conception of individual human emancipation, virtually locking out any opportunity for the exercise of public reason. NATO's failure to confront this hypernationalism and violence on both sides, rather than only on the Serb side, represents a major shortcoming of the campaign for critical theory. In supporting the military intervention, "Habermas fails to imagine possible communicative and nonviolent alternatives to both genocide and the NATO bombing," alternatives implicit in his own theories (Matustik 2002: 189). David Held's judgment on the war in Afghanistan seems equally appropriate with regard to Kosovo: "the longer the bombing goes on, and the longer the forces of the US and its allies have to remain in place to secure foreign lands, the less optimistic one can be. An alternative approach is one which counters the strategy of 'fear and hate.' What is needed . . . is a movement for global, not American, justice and legitimacy, aimed at establishing and extending the rule of law in place of war and at fostering understanding between communities in place of terror" (2000).

   Indeed, critical theorists might argue that NATO's political and military strategies directly undermined, rather than advanced, the potential for dialogue and coexistence. As the United States attempted to increase pressure on Milosevic, its escalating threats and then bombing campaign helped to at least temporarily unite Serb opinion behind Milosevic after years of widespread protests and dissent. In particular, the incentives provided by US diplomacy encouraged the KLA in its campaign of violence and undercut the political appeal of more moderate Kosovars. The KLA had an explicit strategy of provoking violence in order to bring about a NATO intervention. As such, NATO's response to the KLA's preference for violence over dialogue directly undermined its own avowed commitment to multiethnic coexistence. The US intervention rested on a deeply problematic definition of the identity and interests of the relevant actors. US political goals more closely approximated the Serb than the KLA position: more acceptable internal conditions within a Kosovo that remained an integral part of Serbia, while firmly rejecting any moves toward Kosovar independence. The KLA, rejecting any Serb presence in Kosovo, advanced an ethnic exclusivist claim that rejected all formulations of coexistence or cooperation—a position deeply at odds with the universalist aspirations of critical theory. Without minimizing either Serb extremism or Milosevic's personal responsibility, it seems unlikely that the violence in the province would have escalated to the point it did without the violent provocations of the KLA. Pretending that the KLA shared its preferences, and that it authentically represented Kosovars, caught NATO in a political fiction that deeply confused the issue.

The decision to rely on the KLA and to employ a threat-based negotiating strategy was particularly unfortunate, because it undermined other, less exclusivist, alternatives, such as the nonviolent strategy developed by Ibrahim Rugova (Judah 2000). US officials insisted on a black-and-white rhetoric in which, as Jamie Rubin put it, "in order to move towards military action, it must be clear that the Serbs were responsible"—in other words, the construction of the political situation followed from a decision for war, rather than the reality of such a situation forcing the war (Independent International Commission 2000: 153). US negotiation strategy epitomized monologic, strategic action—presenting a solution with little regard for the expressed preferences or arguments of the most affected actors. Unwilling to compromise or to consider alternatives, and locked into a particular construction of the identity and interests of the actors, Madeleine Albright behaved exactly according to Habermas's "strategic" orientation. That KFOR peacekeepers were unable to prevent widespread acts of revenge by Albanians against Serbs, or the forced exodus of a substantial portion of the Serb population of the province, after the Serb withdrawal and the establishment of the UN protectorate in Kosovo made something of a mockery of the NATO argument that it had fought the war for the principle of ethnic coexistence.

■ Beyond Kosovo

A war waged by a unipolar power under conditions of systemic flux carries particularly potent burdens of legitimation. The uniquely dominant position of the United States in the late 1990s gave special force to this tension. How the United States chose to act had ramifications far beyond the immediate crisis at hand. Aware of the anxiety provoked by US power, the Clinton administration adopted a humanitarian rhetoric and a multilateralist practice to reassure others that its interventions were not predatory. The United States disappointed critical theorists by proving deeply reluctant to push for any general norm of humanitarian intervention. Afraid that such a norm would place unmanageable demands on the United States for interventions around the world—and against its strategic interests—the Clinton administration emphasized repeatedly the uniqueness of the Kosovo case. While undoubtedly prudent, this careful delimitation of the intervention's meaning powerfully undermined its transformative potential, and hence critical theory's reasons for supporting it. Despite these US efforts to not establish a norm, its refusal to work within the Security Council framework nevertheless generated great fears around the world about the precedent being set for future interventions.

For all its shortcomings, the UN Security Council placed some check on the ability of great powers to intervene at will. The potential for abuse in the "coalition of the willing" can be seen in the US-British campaign against Iraq, which similarly sidestepped a UN unwilling to mandate an intervention. It is striking that Kosovo was so rarely invoked in the campaign to build support for war against Iraq. After all, the humanitarian rhetoric of the George W. Bush administration to "liberate the Iraqi people" seems to be cut from the same cloth as the moral justifications for Clinton's intervention in Kosovo. The Bush administration made a similar argument on Iraq—that it would lead a coalition of like-minded nations against Iraq even if the Security Council refused to authorize a war. In part, the absence of the Kosovo precedent simply followed from the Bush administration's deep aversion to anything associated with its predecessor. Beyond that, however, the ambiguous outcome of the legitimation efforts in Kosovo left no clearly resolved norm upon which to draw. References to Kosovo appeared more after the war than before it, as the Bush administration attempted to shift attention from a deteriorating case based on weapons of mass destruction to the humanitarian claim of liberating Iraqis from tyranny. These post facto justifications are very different from highlighting such concerns before the war in an effort to build consensus. The primacy of the strategic arguments for war over the preceding year created a profound skepticism about the moral case, which seemed a quintessential case of rhetorical manipulation.

Habermas (2000), Falk (2003), and most other critical theorists who granted the Kosovo war some legitimacy despite its illegality therefore rejected the legitimacy of the Iraq campaign. The Bush administration's claims to a right of preemptive war and its unilateralist approach to almost all international institutions clearly undercut any idea of its contributing to building a more progressive international order. As in Kosovo, the overwhelming weight of international public opinion opposed the war. As in Kosovo, the Security Council would not authorize military action. US leaders again constructed a rhetorical case for war based upon universal moral claims that failed to convince a skeptical world. The pronounced strategic orientation in the US arguments for war, including a penchant for exaggerated rhetoric and the open use of threats and inducements to win support for its position, along with its refusal to take seriously any competing viewpoints or to consider alternatives to war, left little room for open communicative exchange. Beyond the specifics of this case, the failure to win any international consensus again suggests the difficulties inherent in a legitimation process severed from any procedural or substantive mandate.

chapter 7

Historical Materialism and World System Theory Approaches

7.1 *Jennifer Sterling-Folker*
Historical Materialism and World System Theory

As with critical theory, historical materialism and world system theory are neo-Marxian perspectives. "Historical materialism" is a term drawn directly from the work of Karl Marx and Friedrich Engels, although some of this approach's IR adherents refer to it as "transhistorical materialism" instead.[1] Within the discipline it is considered a variant of critical theory, and it shares with Habermasian critical theory the same epistemological commitments, as well as the same emancipatory goals. Yet historical materialism differs dramatically from that branch of critical theory because it retains the Marxist emphasis on capitalist economics. Because this is also central to world system theory, it is more common in IR for historical materialism and world system theory to be discussed together under a generic "Marxist" label.[2]

Prior to the end of the Cold War, Marxist IR variants were usually characterized as the third major theoretical perspective in the US discipline, along with realism and liberalism. Yet Marxist thought was relatively underdeveloped in the early discipline of US IR, and it was primarily sociologists committed to interdisciplinary work who introduced world system theory into the discipline in the 1970s. Historical materialism appeared in the following decade and its primary contributors were non-Americans. Because historical materialism has a slightly shorter comparative history within the discipline, it is sometimes given short shrift in disciplinary discussions of neo-Marxist IR, which tend to assume that world system theory is its only representative. Certainly it is the case that the two perspectives rely on and utilize a common set of assumptions and concepts so that their analyses may be complementary, as the two chapters in this section demonstrate. Yet important differences remain, and it is more appropriate to consider historical materialism and world system theory to be broadly similar but ultimately alternative neo-Marxist explanations.

What the two perspectives share is a set of assumptions drawn from Marxist thought that emphasize economic change as the driving force of world politics. One of the most fundamental concepts in this regard is the "mode of production," that is, *how* human labor is controlled in order to produce what is needed for survival (Wallerstein 1979: 136, 155). This "determines the nature of social and political relations within political entities and among them," so that "when a new mode of production develops, new classes arise, and a new class becomes dominant" (Zacher and Matthews 1995: 108). Alternative modes of production existed throughout history, but a number of factors beginning in the fifteenth century allowed the capitalist mode to gradually displace all others. Both historical materialism and world system theory utilize the concept of a world capitalist system in referring to the contemporary global dominance of capitalism, and both argue that IR can only be sufficiently understood within the context of this system. Capitalism has produced notable aspects of world politics today, such as ongoing economic disparities among nation-states and the willingness of the economically advantaged to resort to violence, or exploitation by other means, in order to maintain those advantages.

As a mode of production capitalism involves three basic elements: market exchanges, the political and social elevation of those with capital to invest in various market ventures, and the political and social subordination of those who labor to produce the goods in those ventures. The capitalist mode of production concurrently produces an ideology that justifies itself as appropriate and beneficial to all involved, even as it primarily serves the interests of the dominant, capitalist class. This ruling ideology or social consciousness is supported by and replicated in a host of political, legal, religious, moral, philosophical, and cultural institutions and social practices. These institutions and practices constitute what the historical materialist literature refers to as a "historic bloc," and the goal of revealing this bloc as a historically situated social construct, rather than a universal immutable truth, is one that historical materialism shares with critical theory and postmodernism. In contrast to some other IR theories, then, the sovereign nation-state is not the central unit of analysis in either of these perspectives, and as Paul Viotti and Mark Kauppi note, it becomes significant only "from the role it plays in actively aiding or hindering the capitalist accumulation process" (1999: 344).

While historical materialism and world system theory retain the Marxist assumption that capitalism leads inevitably to exploitation and class struggle, they have also developed modified views of class structure that are more appropriate to the study of IR. Although indebted to the writings of Marx and Engels for many of their core concepts, it was later writers in the Marxist tradition, such as John Hobson, Rosa Luxembourg, Rudolf Hilferding, and Vladimir Lenin, who considered how capitalism promoted "imperialism" in IR as a form of transnational exploitation. Imperialism is endemic to the capitalist world system, these authors argued, because capitalist societies regularly face the dilemma of overproduction of capital by the capitalist class and underconsumption of goods by the lower classes (who cannot afford to purchase them). This dilemma induces capitalist societies to seek markets abroad to reinvest surplus capital and promote the buying of surplus goods, yet the terms of interaction are never equitable. While resorting to outright conquest remains an option for capitalist societies, the nature of exploitation has become more subtle, involving transnational alliances among capitalist classes and a reliance on institutions, such as the IMF and the World Bank, to enforce the interests of wealthy capitalist societies around the globe (Gill 1998, 1995). These institutions are referred to as international financial institutions (IFIs), and they figure prominently in Chapter 7.3, in Annette Freyberg-Inan's world system analysis of Yugoslavia's economic decline, which exacerbated existing interethnic tensions and laid the foundation for separatist movements throughout Yugoslavia.

Imperialism can also lead to international rivalry and conflict among capitalist societies, as they compete with one another for dominance in alternative markets and regions. This ongoing impetus for balance-of-power politics prevents the development of a unified world state or the return to world empires. Imperialist rivalry is the theme of Chapter 7.2, in which Alan Cafruny argues that Kosovo must be understood in the context of US-European rivalry over the shape of the post–Cold War global capitalist order. Because the concept of imperialism remains fundamental to both historical materialism and world system theory, these perspectives are interested in relations between wealthy capitalist societies and the rest of the globe. Within the discipline their analytical predecessor is dependency theory, which originated in the 1960s to explain why Latin America and other regions had not developed as anticipated.[3] For all of these theories, the explanation for the continued poverty of so many of the world's nation-states lies not in processes and choices purely internal to nation-states and their societies, but in the position they occupy within the world capitalist economy. They also concur that world politics is driven by capitalist economic forces, and that "economic exploitation is an integral part of the capitalist system and is required to keep it functioning" (Viotti and Kauppi 1999: 349).

While alternative terms such as "North" and "South" or "first world" and "third world" have been used in IR to indicate the division between rich and poor societies, world system theory has developed a set of terms that is frequently used by scholars of both perspectives. The capitalist world system is said to consist of core, peripheral, and semiperipheral areas that differ according to their modes of labor control and what they specialize in producing. The core areas are the most advanced economically, and hence they are the most prosperous and powerful. The peripheral areas provide unskilled labor and raw materials to the core and are the poorest and weakest. The semiperipheral areas occupy a middle ground between the two, and have a combination of economic, political, and social attributes from both of the other areas. This international division of labor derives from the ceaseless accumulation of capital and essentially divides and conquers class interests and structures both within and across nation-states. The original Marxist formulation of a common interest within relatively separate classes, as well as the inevitability of conflict between these classes and the potential for revolution among the working class specifically, have been considerably modified by these perspectives as a result.[4]

Yet both historical materialism and world system theory retain a belief in the possibility of radical change and the eventual demise of the capitalist world order. Marx and Engels had argued that the mode of production that dominates in each period of history, and that hierarchically arranges its relevant classes, also carries the seeds of its own demise. Classes are always arranged dialectically, so that contradictions and tensions are inherent to their relationship, and from their inevitable clash new economic orders emerge. It is a matter of time, therefore, before the capitalist mode of production and the world economy it has spawned will be replaced. Historical materialists and world system theorists subscribe to this general view of the future, yet each has made considerable analytical modifications to it so that the possibilities of change within and of the world capitalist system are more open-ended, varied in content, and less deterministic. It is also at this juncture that clear differences begin to emerge between these two perspectives, since historical materialists subscribe to critical theory's goal of emancipatory practice in a way that world system theorists do not.

As a variant of critical theory, historical materialism is concerned with uncovering historically situated truth claims in order to reveal their embedded power and promote emancipation from them. Unlike Habermasian critical theory, however, it is not a direct analytical descendant of the Frankfurt School. In fact, in his overview of these two variants, Richard Wyn Jones observes that Antonio Gramsci, the Italian Marxist, is just as important a writer to the development of critical theory as are Max Horkheimer and Theodor Adorno, yet "they do not, on the whole, influence the same scholars" (2001: 5). Gramsci is not a central figure to Habermasian critical theorists, but his work *is* fundamental to historical materialists, who are sometimes referred to as "neo-Gramscian." It was Gramsci who developed the concept of a historic bloc with a hegemonic grip over social consciousness and identity. Building on his work, historical materialists investigate how global capitalism constitutes a material and ideational hegemony, which is sometimes described as a form of "disciplinary neoliberalism" or "global governance."[5] This hegemony relies on a complex interrelationship between identity, legitimating ideology, society, and the state, and it effectively obscures capitalism's inherently exploitative character. Because the state and society co-constitute one another within the capitalist world economy, historical materialists never study them separately and consider the separation of levels of analysis subscribed to by other IR theories to be a serious analytical flaw.

From Gramsci, historical materialists also take notions of volition, that is, the possibility of removing the "historic bloc," which serves as the primary obstacle to equitable social change by encouraging competing ideologies and social movements. It is for this reason that many historical materialists are interested in the idea of an emerging global civil society, and their discussions of social practices and intersubjective meanings can sound quite constructivist. As Andrew Linklater notes about historical materialism, it "emphasizes the revolt of the Third World states and political movements against the effects of the globalization of relations of production," and it focuses on "counter-hegemonic states and social movements and their ability to pool their political resources to transform the world economy" (1996: 287).

This emphasis on the active encouragement of contemporary social and political change is one of the ways in which historical materialism differs from world system theory, which remains, at heart, a structural theory about the historical development of the contemporary world order.[6] The analytical emphasis of world system theory is not on the praxis of contemporary change, or on the third world specifically, but on the changes to or within the structure of the world capitalist system itself. In other words, world system theorists are interested in studying structural changes such as a nation-state's movement from the category of semiperipheral to core, or the political and social effects of capitalist cycles of growth and contraction. It is for this reason that historical materialists claim that world system theory has a "system-maintenance bias" (Cox 1996: 87) and, despite sharing many analytical premises, are critical of it.

Certainly world system theory has always been committed to understanding world politics as a system, and so it shares with historical materialism the conviction that the standard levels of analysis, and categories such as politics, economics, and culture, are indivisible.[7] Thus the study of political structures and institutions, ethnicity and race, religion and culture, and even the formation and structure of households are examined within the context of the capitalist world economy. But world system theory does not trace its origins to Gramsci specifically or critical theory in general, and so it does not share historical materialism's goals of praxis, its analytical focus, or its epistemological preferences. It developed in the discipline of sociology as a reaction to modernization theory, which claimed that the South's inability to develop was due to its traditional cultures and that it would need to follow a similar development path as that of the North (see Rostow 1962). World system theory instead posited that it was the capitalist division of the world that accounted for the South's economic, political, and social plight. The development of world system theory is particularly indebted to the work of sociologist Immanuel Wallerstein, and many world system theorists continue to straddle the interdisciplinary line between sociology and IR.

The result is that world system theorists are not postpositivists and do not share historical materialism's epistemology, which Robert Cox describes as "dialectical in its explanation of change, and hermeneutic insofar as it inquires into purposes and meanings" (Cox with Sinclair 1996: 514). World system theorists remain committed to a positivist epistemology and methodologies, and they argue that the social sciences might serve as a vehicle for systemic change if interdisciplinary barriers can be overcome in order to understand the world system in its historical totality. Their emphasis on deep historical context is yet another way in which their scholarship is different from historical materialism, which, like other neo-Marxist perspectives, tends to focus on the contemporary world order.

World system theorists argue that it is only possible to understand the world system's current structure by tracing its historical evolution since the transition from feudalism to capitalism in the sixteenth century. Some world system theorists have pushed historical analysis back even further, so that the global economy of the thirteenth and fourteenth centuries is examined in order to understand Europe's subsequent rise to the core (Abu-Lughod 1989; Frank 1998). Even more far-reaching are claims that the world system perspective can be applied to precapitalist worlds (Chase-Dunn and Hall 1991, 1997) and to the start of regional trading, over 5,000 years ago (Frank and Gills 1993). Thus a central hallmark of world system theory is its emphasis on historical analysis in order to comprehend both the contemporary and the future international system. It is for this reason that it may be characterized as "a global spatiotemporal perspective" (Dougherty and Pfaltzgraff 1997: 246).

This emphasis on historical analysis has also produced variants within world system theory that are not neo-Marxist in origin. Evolutionary world politics, for example, is a variant that assumes world systemic changes are the product of evolutionary processes, such as selection and learning, that are not, its proponents argue, biologically determined. These processes produce long cycles in global politics, which are sometimes referred to as Kondratieff cycles or waves, after Nikolai Kondratieff, the scholar who first identified them. These cycles account for the regular patterns of war-making, trading, institution building, and coalition forming that we see in multiple regions throughout history. This evolutionary variant of world system theory was developed in the US IR discipline by George Modelski and William Thompson, and it emphasizes politics rather than economics as the prime motivating force for the system. Yet its analytical focus and goals are so similar to other world system variants that, as a means of capturing these divergent strands under the same rubric, it may be more appropriate to refer to world system theory as world system *history* instead (Denemark 1999; Frank 1991).

Because both historical materialism and world system theory demand that social reality be understood as a totality, the scope and comprehensiveness of their analyses is both daunting and impressive. They are the only IR theoretical perspectives that, given their assumptive frameworks, consistently and simultaneously examine the relationship between *all* nation-states in the international system. In so doing, they expand the discipline's vision of its own subject matter and provide a historical, systemic context for understanding global social problems that other perspectives either completely ignore or discuss only as they relate to the powerful core nation-states. In a discipline that tends to derive its theoretical insights from contemporary trends and so encounters serious analytical difficulties when those trends change or disappear, world system theory underscores the need for a long-term theoretical perspective. Both of these theories also prompt us to consider the extent to which the discipline of IR and its modes of thought are components of the capitalist "historic bloc," and by refusing to confront this complicity we participate in the ongoing production of global inequity.

■ Further Reading

The central figure in the development of critical theory's historical materialism variant is Robert Cox, who first described his approach in the widely reprinted essay "Social Forces, States, and World Orders" (1981), and subsequently expanded his arguments in the book *Power, Production, and World Order* (1987). Two other important works by Cox include an edited volume (1997) and a collection of his essays (1996) edited by one of his students, Timothy Sinclair. Other seminal historical materialist texts include Cafruny 1990, Galtung 1971, Gill 1988, Gill 1990a, Gill 1995, Gill 1998, Harrod 1987, Murphy 1994, Murphy 1990, van der Pijl 1984, van der Pijl 1998, Rupert 1995, and Sinclair 1994. Edited volumes devoted to historical materialism include Mittleman 1997, Murphy and Tooze 1991, Overbeek 1993, Palan 2000a, Palan and Gills 1994, and Rupert and Smith 2002.

For works that explore the influence of Gramsci on IR theorizing and the development of historical materialism, see Cox 1983, Germain and Kenny 1998, Gill 1993, Holub 1992, Murphy 1998, Rupert 1998, and Tooze 1990. The work of scholars who subscribe to the Habermasian variant of critical theory, such as Andrew Linklater and M. Hoffman, are discussed in the overview chapter on postmodernism and critical theory. Wyn Jones 2001, an edited volume titled *Critical Theory and World Politics,* brings practitioners of both variants together.

The central figure in the development of world system theory is Immanuel Wallerstein (1974, 1980, 2004). There are several collections that reproduce his most seminal essays, and the most widely read of these is *The Capitalist World Economy* (1979; see also 1991). A collection of essays about Wallerstein's work and influence on the discipline can be found in two special issues of *Journal of World Systems Research,* both edited by Giovanni Arrighi and Walter Goldfrank (2000a, 2000b). Another influential scholar in world system theory is Christopher Chase-Dunn (1981, 1982, 1989), who, within Wallerstein's categories of international division, differentiated state interests and policy strategies depending on variance in production advantages.

Other notable works of system theorists include Abu-Lughod 1989, Arrighi 1994, Arrighi and Silver 1999, Baran 1967, Braudel 1979, Burch and Denemark 1997, Chase-Dunn and Hall 1991, Chase-Dunn and Hall 1997, Chirot and Hall 1982, Denemark 1999, Frank 1998, and Frank 1991. There are numerous collections of world system theory, including Boswell and Wallerstein 1989, Chase-Dunn 1995, Frank and Gills 1993, Hollist and Rosenau 1981, Hopkins and Wallerstein 1996, Hopkins and Wallerstein 1982, Hopkins and Wallerstein 1980, and Schaeffer and Wallerstein 1989. A useful introduction to the perspective is Shannon 1989, and for an interesting analysis of the place of household structures in the world capitalist system, see Smith and Wallerstein 1992.

Evolutionary world theory can be found in the works of George Modelski (1996, 1987a, 1978) and William Thompson (2001, 1988, 1983), and together they have coauthored a number of important pieces in this perspective (1999, 1996, 1988). An early exchange between William Thompson, Christopher Chase-Dunn, and Joan Sokolovsky (1983) in

International Studies Quarterly underscores the differences between these two variants of world system theory. Other works on Kondratieff long cycles include the original formulation, Kondratieff 1984, as well as Freeman 1983, Goldstein 1991, Goldstein 1988, Kleinknecht, Mandel, and Wallerstein 1992, Rasler 1989, Rasler and Thompson 1994, and an edited volume on the subject, Modelski 1987b. Modelski has also maintained a home page on evolutionary world politics (http://faculty.washington.edu/ modelski), which provides essays, bibliographies, and links to other pertinent websites on the subject.

Representative works of dependency theory include Amin 1974, Amin 1977, Cardoso and Faletto 1979, Cohen 1973, Evans 1979, Frank 1969, Frank 1970, and Prebisch 1963. A special issue of *International Organization* devoted to dependency theory was edited by James Caporaso (1978). More recently, Robert Packenham (1992) provided an overview of the development of dependency theory.

■ Notes

1. Robert Cox refers to the approach as "historical dialectic" (Cox with Sinclair 1996: ix), and it is sometimes called "Coxian historicism." In linking the approach to Marxism and critical theory, Richard Wyn Jones notes that Horkheimer first named critical theory "interdisciplinary materialism" (1999: 14).

2. See, for example, Doyle 1997, Gilpin 1987, and Richardson 2001b.

3. Dependency theory was developed by Latin American scholars and was originally associated with the United Nations Conference on Trade and Development (UNCTAD) and its Economic Commission on Latin America (ECLA). Writers for ECLA and UNCTAD argued that Latin America was unable to develop due to its unfavorable terms of trade with capitalist societies. Dependency theorists also argued, along analytical lines developed by Lenin, that transnational alliances between capitalist and bourgeoisie classes in European and Latin American societies effectively exploited the workers of the latter.

4. Craig Murphy (1990) argues, for example, that there is a class alliance between the "Atlantic" or "trilateral" ruling class in the core, the "organization bourgeoisie" ruling class in the third world, and some of the subordinate classes in the core, which collectively subordinate all the other classes. See also Gill 1990a, Gill 1990b, and van der Pijl 1984.

5. The first term is drawn from Stephen Gill's theory of globalization (1998, 1995), which argues that various global market forces and agents discipline states and societies into neoliberal ideology and structures. The second term is used by multiple theoretical perspectives and hence has multiple meanings (see, for example, Hoffmann and Ba 2005), but in historical materialism it is used to indicate the hegemony of capitalist norms and discourse. As Timothy Sinclair notes, it means "to become hegemonic in the Gramscian sense of combining coercive power with a measure of consensus" (1999: 158). It is not a benign concept in the historical materialist context.

6. It is sometimes referred to simply as "structuralism." Baylis and Smith (2001), for example, claim that Marxist theory is also known as "structuralism" or

world system theory, so that all three are equated with one another. Viotti and Kauppi (1999: 356), on the other hand, refer to world system theory as "globalism" and historical materalism as "neostructuralism."

7. These ideas are drawn directly from Marx, who argued that politics and economics were interrelated, not separate domains, and that society had to be studied in its totality. As Viotti and Kauppi put it, "globalists argue that to explain behavior at any and all levels of analysis—the individual, bureaucratic, societal, and between states or between societies—one must first understand the overall structure of the global system within which such behavior takes place. As with realists, globalists believe that the starting point of analysis should be the international system. To a large extent, the behavior of individual actors is explained by a system that provides constraints and opportunities" (1999: 341).

Alan W. Cafruny

Historical Materialism: Imperialist Rivalry and the Global Capitalist Order

In this chapter I argue that the US-led seventy-eight-day bombing campaign against Serbia in the spring of 1999 was a decisive moment within a more general struggle between the United States and Europe over the shape of the post–Cold War global capitalist order. As a result of this campaign the United States realized a set of interlocking objectives, including the incorporation of a recalcitrant semiperipheral region within the neoliberal and Atlanticist international division of labor (see especially Chapter 7.3 this volume); the consolidation of US economic and military power on the European continent; and the extension of US influence in Central Asia and the Caucasus, an arena of increasingly fierce competition among states and multinational corporations over access to oil and gas deposits and transportation routes.

Historical materialism throws a spotlight on imperialist rivalry as the central factor of world politics. It does not, however, assert that the war in Kosovo—or indeed the phenomenon of war in general—can be explained reductively in terms of economic interests, narrowly conceived. The decision to drive Serbian forces from Kosovo and establish a de facto NATO protectorate expressed a complex set of mutually reinforcing political, ideological, and economic interests and objectives. A realist perspective, for example, might point to the geopolitical significance of the Albanian diaspora (Gompert 1996) or the salience of NATO's credibility after Serbia's refusal to capitulate at Rambouillet. Moreover, by the fall of 1998, humanitarian considerations clearly influenced the actions of US and European leaders, who had been harshly criticized for their unwillingness to prevent genocide in Rwanda and Bosnia (Bell 2000; Mayall 2000). However, I argue in this chapter that geopolitical and ideological factors are proximate causes that do not, in themselves, provide a comprehensive and satisfactory explanation for the war in Kosovo. Such an explanation must show how the breakup of Yugoslavia and subsequent great power interventions were linked to the structural crisis of world capitalism and the intensification of US-European rivalry following the collapse of the Soviet Union.

The first part of this chapter provides an overview of the most plausible and enduring assumptions of the historical materialist tradition as they have been used in the study of IR. The use of concepts deriving from the

Marxist tradition involves a timely and ironic resurrection. During the 1960s and 1970s Marxist and dependency theories became part of the "paradigm debate" in the study of IR (e.g., Gilpin 1975), but in the 1980s they were cast out of the temple. Yet the dramatic increase in international inequality, poverty, and dependency over the past two decades has spawned a growing global protest movement, and conservative and liberal commentators now routinely refer to US imperialism and celebrate its alleged merits (Boot 2003; Ignatieff 2003). As Fred Halliday has observed, "The study of globalization, and indeed of contemporary world politics, is first and foremost the study of contemporary capitalism. Indeed, paraphrasing Horkheimer, one may say, those who do not want to talk about capitalism, should not talk about international relations, or globalization" (2002: 77).

The second part of this chapter reviews the course of great power diplomacy toward Yugoslavia and its successor states within the context of the more general conflict between the United States and Europe over the reorganization of the global capitalist order. At the outset of the crisis the Bush administration was preoccupied with the breakup of the Soviet Union and German reunification and pursued a cautious and conciliatory strategy toward Europe. More generally, US foreign policy operated within a context of the post-Vietnam fear of military engagement and casualties, a consideration whose significance was magnified by the relative unimportance of Croatia and Bosnia (as opposed to Kosovo and Albania) to either the European powers or the United States. Consequently, the United States encouraged the European powers to play the lead role when the Yugoslav federation collapsed. However, by 1994 the Clinton administration had begun to abandon the cautious realism of the George H. W. Bush administration in favor of a more aggressive strategy of Atlanticism designed to consolidate US military power on the European continent and to extend the sphere of neoliberalism. A key aspect of this strategy was the decision to deploy air power against the Bosnian Serbs, culminating in the signing of a peace agreement at Dayton in 1995 that represented a clear triumph for US diplomacy.

As the third part of this chapter shows, Kosovo represented a crucial interest for the United States because of its potential to destabilize a region that served as a gateway to oil and pipeline routes linking Western Europe to the Black Sea and the Caspian basin. The defeat of Serbia thus not only preserved NATO and strengthened Atlanticist political forces in Western Europe, but also helped to consolidate US power in a region that has become increasingly significant during the past decade. As I conclude, the war in Kosovo, and more recently the war in Iraq, indicate clearly the increasing tendency in the post–Cold War era to use cosmopolitan and human rights rhetoric as a rationalization for imperialism and war.

■ The State, Imperialism, and Transatlantic Rivalry

The historical materialist concept of imperialism derives from the logic of capital accumulation and the functions the capitalist state acquires as capital pushes beyond the boundaries of its own nation-state. Mainstream approaches to the study of IR view the capitalist state either as a neutral actor that is connected to society in theoretically unspecified ways (liberalism and constructivism) or as an autonomous entity that acts independently of social forces (realism). Despite their many differences, these approaches are similar insofar as they adopt a more or less open-ended view of the possibilities of state action, which is assumed to result variously from public opinion, the preferences of interest groups or factions, shared norms and values, or the imperatives of a given geopolitical configuration. In all mainstream analyses "imperialism" refers to policies of military and political domination that are unconnected to capitalism or economic motives.

Historical materialism, by contrast, proposes an organic connection between the state and the capitalist class that sharply circumscribes the "limits of the possible" in domestic and foreign policy. On one hand, most top government officials and politicians are drawn from elite social and cultural networks and develop a special sympathy for the problems of "big business" (Miliband 1969). These networks are especially well defined and exclusive in the area of foreign policy (Domhoff 1970). On the other hand, elected officials are also "structurally" linked to capital by virtue of the need to establish economic and political conditions favorable to capital accumulation as well as their dependence on the approval of an essentially corporate media for electoral success (O'Connor 1973; Poulantzas 1975). The need to promote acquiescence and stability in domestic politics and (to a much lesser extent) in the international sphere through granting concessions to subordinate classes and countries gives the state an outward appearance of neutrality, but the special bias toward capital and the need to promote capitalist accumulation is a distinctive and permanent feature.

The capitalist state is inevitably drawn into the international sphere— and consequently imperialist rivalry—as a result of the concentration and centralization of capital and the consequent need to promote capital accumulation on a global scale. In the domestic arena the state stands apart (to at least some extent) from the struggles among individual capitals. In foreign economic policy, however, it cannot remain aloof. It is compelled to perform an even more challenging and potentially far more dangerous set of tasks. As Hannes Lacher writes:

> Internationally, individual states can use their political power to structure international competition in ways which benefit "their" capitals to the detriment of the capitals of other states. They can use their borders and currencies to mediate the competition between the multitude of individual capitals. Thus, the world market is not simply a system of individual capi-

tals competing with each other economically, but is a system in which states are parties in the competition for world market shares rather than guarantors of the market as such. (2002: 161)

The classic phase of imperialism resulted from intensified great power rivalry in the wake of British decline in the late nineteenth and early twentieth centuries, and focused on the control of raw materials and resources and access to markets and cheap labor. As capitalism evolved, the leading imperialist powers became more actively involved in securing the social and political conditions for the reproduction of the labor force and the maintenance of market discipline (Magdoff 1969).

The concept of "hegemony" refers to the systemic supervisory function that leading states have undertaken during certain historical periods. Because there is no "higher authority," imperialist rivalry has been a more or less permanent feature of the world capitalist system since its inception (Wood 2002). Rivalry, however, can be moderated either through the actions of a hegemonic power willing and able to maintain global order (Block 1977) or, more controversially, as a result of the emergence of a "transnational capitalist class" that would reduce the coercive aspects of intraregional or perhaps even international conflict (Gill 1990b; Robinson 2002; van der Pijl 1998).

Hegemonic leadership involves political-military supervision and stabilization, but also the establishment and reproduction of various regulatory programs or "concepts of control" that arise at the national level and are generalized throughout the international order (van der Pijl 1984). During the Bretton Woods period, for example, the United States pursued a project of embedded liberalism, implementing domestic and foreign economic policies that reproduced Keynesian macroeconomic policies and in which market forces were constrained in order to maintain full employment, regulated labor markets, and a relatively high degree of social stability throughout the core regions of North America, Western Europe, and Japan (Ruggie 1983). The United States made significant concessions to allies, especially in the area of trade policy, in order to secure coherence and consent, and thereby to minimize US-European rivalry (Cafruny 1990). As a result of the breakdown of the Bretton Woods system, the United States (and Britain) systematically began to dismantle the framework of embedded liberalism. The transition to disciplinary neoliberalism (Gill 1995) involved the deregulation of financial, trading, and labor markets and provoked greater transatlantic economic and political rivalry.

■ The Crisis of Atlanticism and the Neoliberal Offensive

US hegemony after World War II was based not only on economic and monetary power, but also on geopolitical supremacy. Especially within the context of the Cold War, Europe's political-military weakness undermined efforts to establish regional autonomy and a more equal transatlantic balance of power. The failure of the European Defense Community in 1954 made it clear that Western European security policies would be developed within a national framework and organized by NATO under US tutelage. With the exception of Britain, Western European states limited their defense spending in exchange for US occupation of the western half of a militarized continent. Geopolitical weakness also diminished the ability of European states individually or collectively to challenge US leadership of the world economy or, with the exception of sub-Saharan Africa, to retain primacy in former colonies. The US threat to withdraw troops from Europe helped to enforce European adherence to the dollar/gold standard during the 1960s, and defeated French attempts to break the Anglo-American control of international oil markets during the 1970s.

The contrast between the EU's strong bargaining position in international trade and its relative geopolitical weakness has led observers to describe it as a nascent European "civilian power." Yet this concept is misleading because it makes an artificial distinction between economic and political power. The Bretton Woods system was both economic imperium and an expression of US political-military supremacy. The privileged position of the dollar made it possible to finance the construction of a military colossus while defense expenditure and research and development generated massive economic benefits and served as a powerful Keynesian stimulant. By contrast, the EU has been unable to develop mutually reinforcing structures of economic and political power. If the euro were to challenge the primacy of the dollar and the neoliberal system it underpinned, Europe would need to build a polity that is both economically and politically independent of the United States.

When the European continent became indivisible as a result of the collapse of the Soviet Union, it appeared that the basic contours of such a polity were forming. The Maastricht Treaty codified ambitious plans for a common foreign and security policy (CFSP). As a European constitutional process began to unfold, many observers discerned the outlines of an emergent system of multilevel governance, the formation of an embryonic European transnational class, and even the "birth of a polity" (Hooghe and Marks 1997, 1999; van Apeldoorn 2002). A unified Europe was assumed to be a necessary (but not sufficient) condition for the defense of a distinctive European social market against neoliberalism, and a more humanitarian foreign policy based on principles of international law and multilateralism. Throughout the 1990s, moreover, the institutions of the CFSP gradually emerged, including the appointment of a high representative for the CFSP, the expansion of the Western European Union, and a rapid reaction force. These developments were accompanied not only by monetary unification, but also by the emergence of an embryonic European defense industry. The breakup of Yugoslavia thus coincided with the negotiations at Maastricht over the shape of the new European order. It served as a test case for the viability of an autonomous regional project that challenged US military and economic primacy on the European continent.

Neoliberalism and the Breakup of Yugoslavia

The breakup of Yugoslavia was directly precipitated by the global debt crisis. Throughout Eastern and Southeastern Europe the implementation of structural adjustment under the tutelage of the IMF had by the late 1980s dramatically exposed hitherto state-led economies to the full force of liberalization and market discipline. After 1989 most Eastern European countries withstood the shock of rapid transitions from state socialism to market-based systems, involving massive dislocation and impoverishment, without imploding, although Czechoslovakia managed a "velvet divorce." In Yugoslavia, however, existing ethnic and republican divisions in the context of mass unemployment produced an explosive mixture.

One of the legacies of the Cold War was Yugoslavia's engagement in the postwar global capitalist world on relatively favorable terms. But the devolution of economic decisionmaking to individual republics in the context of uneven development reinforced the tendency toward ethnic nationalism, which was greatly exacerbated by the twin crises of mass unemployment and rapid urbanization (Denitch 1994; Woodward 1995; Nairn 1998). Confronted with an external debt exceeding $22 billion, the closure of export markets in Western Europe, and the return of hundreds of thousands of "guest workers" from Germany, individual republics began to pursue their own methods for dealing with the crisis. The victory of Anton Marcovic in the 1989 federal elections offered Yugoslavs a final chance to preserve the federation. However, support for federation dissipated as a result of the ravages of shock therapy (Woodward 1995). Mass unemployment precipitated general strikes and encouraged republican leaders to pursue various strategies of integration into Western Europe, as in Slovenia, or ethnoreligious fascism, as in Serbia and to a lesser extent Croatia. Marcovic's initial popularity showed clearly that there was as late as 1990 strong residual support for unity. Indeed, had the West chosen an alternative to shock therapy the integrity of the federation might have been preserved.

European and US strategies toward Yugoslavia were thus formulated within the context of the intensifying transatlantic economic and political conflicts that accompanied the end of the Cold War. Attempts to establish a rival economic and political bloc, originating especially among segments of French and German capital, also provoked intra-European tensions, pitting those class fractions, parties, and states that favored the preservation of Atlanticism and adaptation to neoliberalism against those that advocated European autonomy and social markets. These tensions would arise in relation to regional and international economic policies, but they would also be clearly expressed with reference to competing national and EU policies toward Bosnia and Kosovo.

As centrifugal forces developed in 1990 and 1991, both the EU and the United States proclaimed their support for a federal Yugoslavia, but this initial support was primarily tactical: a means to support structural adjustment and loan repayment. As a result neither side seriously considered Slovenian or Croatian proposals for transforming an increasingly Serbian-dominated state into a democratic federation. In June 1991, US secretary of state James Baker's meeting with Slobodan Milosevic in Belgrade left Serbian generals with the impression that "the United States had no intention of stopping them by force" if they took military action against Slovenia and Croatia (Zimmerman 1996: 137). When Serbian units of the Yugolav People's Army attacked the provisional Slovenian militia, Jacques Poos, president of the European Council, asserted that "this is the hour of Europe. It is not the hour of the Americans" (*Financial Times,* July 1, 1991, p. 2). Nevertheless, with respect to the western Balkans in particular, neither the United States nor Europe appeared to have substantial real interests at stake. Europe's interest was primarily symbolic: to demonstrate Europe's new independence. US interests would be formulated with reference to the broader political and economic objectives and the maintenance of US power on the European continent.

Despite its nascent project of a common foreign and security policy, the EU quickly fragmented along traditional spheres of influence and patronage. A process of mediation and international recognition set out by the European Commission was rendered moot by savage fighting between Serb and Croatian forces in the fall and winter of 1991 as Serbs seized control of 30 percent of Croatia. Germany's strong support for recognition of Croatia and Slovenia antagonized France and Britain, both of which maintained long-standing political and economic ties to Serbia, antipathy to Islam, and favored a de facto Serbo-Croatian partition (Crawford 1996; Cafruny 1998; Libal 1997). Although at Germany's insistence the EU acquiesced to recognition of Croatia and Slovenia and a cease-fire was accomplished, no outside power was willing to give guarantees to Bosnia.[1] Unwilling to send ground troops but fearful of mass exodus of refugees, France and Britain provided humanitarian support and ineffectual "safe havens" under UN auspices. Through a succession of plans amounting to de facto partition and Serbo-Croat carve-up, EU-led UN negotiators sought to defuse the crisis while imposing an arms embargo that greatly handicapped Bosnian government forces.

The Road to Dayton: From Cautious
Realism to Atlanticist Consolidation

In keeping with the cautious realism and sphere-of-influence diplomacy that was its hallmark, the George H. W. Bush administration did not at the outset link the western Balkans to broader economic and political objectives. Preoccupied with the demise of the Soviet Union and German reunification, and fearful of military casualties, it consequently considered the region to be within the EU's sphere. As a result, policy toward Yugoslavia was essentially reactive and improvisational, with two notable and revealing exceptions. First, at the end of 1992 Bush delivered a strong warning to Milosevic that further moves in Kosovo would trigger US military intervention, a warning that was repeated by Bill Clinton in 1993. Second, in June 1993 Clinton sent 500 troops to Macedonia to serve as a "trip wire" to guarantee against a Serb invasion (Caplan 1998). These warnings and policies, which were especially clear and unambiguous given the usual torrents of empty rhetoric, sharply defined the US interest in establishing a bridgehead in the Albanian diaspora and preventing conflict from spilling over to Turkey, Greece, Albania, Macedonia, Bulgaria, or Hungary.

Preoccupied with the economy but also averse to military casualties in the wake of the debacle in Somalia, the Clinton administration was also slow to link the war in Bosnia to broader objectives. Several factors, including the tenacity of Bosnian government forces and the threat of wider instability, precipitated US intervention. However, the crucial context for intervention was the administration's abandonment in 1994 of the sphere-of-influence policy and the beginning of a forward strategy of Atlanticism (van der Pijl 2001) designed to expand and consolidate US military power and to preclude the development of an alternative model of European capitalism (see also Gowan 2000; and Achcar 2000). This strategy reflected the neoliberal activism of an administration whose center of gravity was in Wall Street investment banking and services, and that was strongly committed to fostering rapid economic growth, global free trade, and an expansion of the field of opportunities for US capital through an activist IMF and WTO. The new strategy also demanded that the evolving institutions of the EU should develop within the framework of US hegemony; it included more open resistance to a common European defense and the military and economic integration of Eastern Europe and Russia within the frameworks of Atlanticism and neoliberalism. NATO was to become the "central security pillar of Europe" (Holbrooke 1995), and Central and Eastern European states were to be incorporated within the US military industrial complex.[2]

The successful US military intervention in Bosnia after three years of European paralysis thus served to establish a role for the United States as arbiter of political Europe, as symbolized by the signing of the peace agreement at Dayton. The forging of a Croat-Bosnian alliance during the summer of 1994 and the subsequent air strikes against Bosnian Serb forces had a powerful demonstration effect, indicating to the EU in general—and to France in particular—that an independent European defense was not a realistic alternative to US hegemony and that NATO could act "out of area" under US leadership.

■ The Political Economy of War in Kosovo

Since the breakup of Yugoslavia all US administrations have recognized that the United States has direct geopolitical and economic interests in Kosovo. David Gompert, special assistant for national security affairs under George H. W. Bush, summarized the geopolitical dimension of US policy in the following terms:

> The chief American strategic concern during the Bush administration and later under Clinton was to keep the Yugoslav conflict from spreading southward, where its flames could leap into the Atlantic Alliance. Therefore, while the Bush administration was not convinced of the need to intervene in Bosnia, it took a markedly different attitude toward Kosovo. Washington feared that a Serbian assault against the Kosovar Albanians would consume the entire southern Balkan region in a conflagration that would pit one NATO ally against another. Hostilities in Kosovo would probably spill into Albania proper. This in turn could incite the large Albanian minority in Macedonia and lead to a Serbian or Greek intervention there. Bulgaria and Turkey would then feel pressure to act in order to prevent Greek control of Macedonia. Whereas the Bosnian war could be contained, conflict in Kosovo could not. (Gompert 1996: 136–137)

However, US policymakers and Anglo-American oil companies also recognized the strategic importance of Kosovo for the transit of oil and gas from Central Asia and the Caucasus to Western Europe. By the early 1990s it had become clear that both the United States and Europe were becoming increasingly dependent on Middle Eastern oil, and that diversification of supply was necessary to ensure continued dominance of international oil markets (Baghat 2002; Gokay 2002). Since that time the vast undeveloped energy reserves of the Caspian Sea basin have generated fierce international competition, and the United States has sought to destroy the Russian monopoly over both production and transportation of Caspian oil and gas to Western Europe. Western companies have invested $18 billion in Azerbaijan and Kazakhstan since the mid-1990s, and strong efforts have been made to detach these key former Soviet republics from Russia (Banerjee 2002). In the aftermath of Dayton the states along the Danube, including Bulgaria and Serbia, sought to establish the region as a transportation corridor for Russian and Central Asian gas and oil.

US multinationals have been discouraged for political reasons from building pipelines through Iran, despite their commercial viability, and supported alternative routes, some of which are commercially unprofitable and opposed by the oil companies. At various times the US government has both promoted and discouraged plans to build pipelines to the heavily trafficked Bosporus (Karayianni 2001). While geographically distant from Central Asia, Kosovo and Macedonia straddle or lie adjacent to an alternative route from the Caspian Sea to Western Europe, known as Corridor VIII, which has been designated by the EU as a strategic transportation route.

In September 2000 the Albanian-Macedonian-Bulgarian Oil Pipeline Corporation (AMBO), an Anglo-American firm based in New York, signed memoranda of understanding with the three countries for exclusive rights to a project for a 900-kilometer pipeline from Burgas (Bulgaria) to Vlore (Albania). The projected pipeline runs adjacent to the Presevo Valley and Camp Bondsteel, built in 1999 as part of a $330 million contract by Halliburton and the largest US military base in Southeastern Europe with permanent housing for 7,000 troops (Trofimov 2003). The project, which originated in 1996 but faces numerous difficulties owing to the difficult terrain, has been supported by the US government as a means of circumventing an alternative Burgas-Alexandroupolis route financed by Greek and Russian interests.

According to a report by the US Trade and Development Agency, which provided funds for a feasibility study, the project will "provide a consistent source of crude oil to American refineries . . . provide American companies with a key role in developing the East-West corridor, advance the privatization aspirations of the US government in the region [and] facilitate rapid integration of the Balkans with Western Europe" (quoted in Monbiot 2001). In 1998, former US energy secretary Bill Richardson linked the extraction and transportation of Caspian oil to US foreign policy goals in the region: "This is about America's energy security. It's also about preventing strategic inroads by those who don't share our values. . . . We've made a substantial political investment in the Caspian, and it's very important to us that both the pipeline map and the politics come out right" (quoted in Monbiot 2001).

The Abandonment of Neutrality

The decision at Dayton to ignore the plight of Kosovo was a reflection of the reluctance of the United States to undertake military intervention in the face of Serbian resistance. Recognizing the potential for broader regional destabilization, the EU and the United States relied on Slobodan Milosevic and the corrupt Berisha government in Albania to guarantee the peace (Clark 2000). At Dayton, the United States urged Milosevic to use restraint in Kosovo, hoping that the province would remain quiet. Ibrahim Rugova's pacifist opposition organized shadow institutions designed to accommodate Albanian participation in public life without provoking Serbs into open conflict. Yet within weeks of the Dayton Agreement the Kosovar Albanians began to mobilize behind the KLA as Rugova's nonviolent strategy lost credibility. By the fall of 1998 the United States began to tilt toward the KLA.

The interim agreement that the United States presented to the Serbs and KLA at Rambouillet in January 1999 expressed the clear shift in US strategy. Although it rejected the KLA's demand for self-determination, Serbia was compelled to allow a far-reaching autonomy for the Kosovar Albanians including self-governing institutions, a withdrawal of most security forces, and the acceptance of a force under NATO command that would enjoy freedom of action throughout the Federal Republic, including Serbia. Belgrade's refusal to sign the agreement precipitated NATO air strikes, despite strong opposition from Russia and the concomitant absence of a UN mandate, and significant resistance from France and other EU countries.

The argument that Rambouillet was designed to establish a pretext for the bombing by giving the Serbs an ultimatum they could not accept is therefore consistent with the overall trend of US diplomacy, which appears by late 1998 to have become predicated on the necessity of at least some level of military involvement subsequent to the abandonment of neutrality. Although the interim agreement contained provisions that were unacceptable to the Serbs, Milosevic did not attempt to negotiate changes in the text while continuing to amass troops in Kosovo and escalate attacks on the KLA as well as civilians.[3] Both Milosevic and the United States made significant miscalculations. Based on past experience Milosevic probably believed that the bombing would be light and of short duration and hoped for Russian support. The United States clearly also anticipated that a short campaign would compel capitulation or compromise. Once the war began, however, the United States recognized that the failure to defeat Serbia would endanger "NATO credibility," which by now was indistinguishable from its broader objectives in Europe and Eurasia.

Kosovo and the
Consolidation of US Hegemony in Europe

While US military intervention in Bosnia signaled a basic shift in US strategy with respect to Europe, the war with Serbia served to consolidate an even more fundamental transformation in the nature of the transatlantic relationship. The overwhelming dominance of the US military served as a powerful demonstration to Europe that the United States was henceforth the arbiter of all geopolitical developments on the continent. The war also established a precedent for NATO action outside the UN Security Council, weakening the ability of France, and by implication the EU, to limit US unilateralism. Serbia's capitulation served to restore NATO's credibility and paved the way for the further enlargement of 2002. More generally, the war facilitated the extension of US power into Eastern Europe and Central Asia. At NATO's fiftieth anniversary, GUUAM (Georgia, Ukraine, Uzbekistan, Azerbaijan, and Moldova) was established under Anglo-American-Turkish sponsorship. During the war Azerbaijan, Hungary, and Ukraine closed their air space to Russia, which was forced into a defensive position despite its brief occupation of Pristina airport. Between 1999 and 2002 the United States consolidated its relationship with Azerbaijan and Kazakhstan, and Russia has since opened up its oil holdings in the Black Sea to Western companies. Since 1999 the United States has gradually withdrawn forces from the Balkan region in favor of EU/UN administration, including in Macedonia. But the continuing presence of bases and troops—including the construction of Camp Bondsteel in Kosovo—underscores the structural military and economic power of the United States. The United States played a key role in orchestrating the 2000 elections in Serbia, the subsequent resignation of Milosevic, and his surrender to the International War Crimes Tribunal in The Hague, and continues to be the central arbiter with respect to Serbia. Reconstruction aid has been predicated on massive and debilitating economic reforms, including the privatization of public enterprises and sales of utilities and productive capacity to Western companies (Lebor 2002).

The war also served to fragment the EU and to confirm that European and Eurasian politics would assume a "hub and spoke" system of organization centered on Washington. The UK adopted its customary support for the United States. The debate over the war opened up deep divisions within the German Green Party, eventually leading to the abandonment of pacifism and support for the war effort. In both France and Germany the war served to isolate and marginalize critics of NATO intervention. Hence the "third way" initiatives of Tony Blair and Gerhard Schroeder had their counterpart in the Atlanticist vision of foreign policy that emerged in 1998–1999 and was reinforced as a result of the war. The resignation of German finance minister Oskar Lafontaine illustrated the close connection between geopolitics and economics. Lafontaine was compelled to resign from the government and his position as chairman of the Social Democratic Party just twelve days before the attack. Lafontaine had been a vocal critic of the war and of Atlanticism, and he had been the architect of an alternative Franco-German strategy against neoliberalism (Lafontaine 2000; van der Pijl 2001; Ryner 2003). With his resignation the *Financial Times* wrote that the "battle for European capitalism has begun in earnest" and that "the struggle between the Anglo-American model" of stock market capitalism and "stakeholder capitalism" based on corporatism had begun (quoted in van der Pijl 2001: 303).

■ Imperialism and Cosmopolitanism in the Twenty-First Century

Historical materialism offers an interpretation of the war in Kosovo that differs in significant ways from mainstream approaches. Against realism, historical materialism contends that the use of power in international relations cannot be explained comprehensively if it is considered in isolation from broader social and economic forces. The Kosovo war was fought in part for reasons of regional stability and the viability of NATO, but these factors can only be understood comprehensively within the context of the post–Cold War imperialist rivalry that is both political and economic in content. Or as Justin Rosenberg proposes:

> While the Realist is busy watching the statesmen playing the hands dealt them by the balance of power, those same international struggles are mediating a wholesale transformation of the form and conditions of social power in the world. One has only to consider the last hundred years and the relationship between imperial rivalries, the globalizing of a transnational capitalist economy and the emergence of a world state system: it ought to be obvious that something more has been afoot internationally than can be captured in the maxims of Thucydides. (1994: 20)

Indeed, European critics of US hegemony have been acutely aware of the close relationship between US military power and neoliberalism. As Charles Pasqua writes:

> The good will that [the United States] shows for the process of European monetary integration is the counterpart to the strategic advantage that it expects from the now generalized acceptance in Europe of the preeminence of NATO in the matter of European defense . . . the *European model* which is appearing before our eyes is a whole—monetarist, federal, Atlanticist—and it is impossible to accept one part of it without being forced to accept the other, nor to reject one part without renouncing the other. (2001: 210)

Historical materialism also provides a critique of constructivist approaches that emphasize the independent role of ideas in foreign policy. To be sure, doctrines of humanitarian intervention played a key role in great power intervention in the former Yugoslavia. Yet despite the rhetoric there is little evidence that the primary cause of intervention was concern for human rights. With respect to Bosnia, the arms embargo and provision of humanitarian assistance were designed not to protect the population but rather to avoid military intervention despite the fact that these policies favored the Serbs (and to a lesser extent the Croats) against the Bosnian government. Because a succession of "peace plans" rewarded ethnic cleansing, they encouraged Serb and Croat war crimes. Military intervention arrived after three years of war that witnessed more than 200,000 civilian casualties in Bosnia alone.[4]

Appeals to humanitarian concerns played an even stronger role in the justification for war in Kosovo. President Clinton declared that the war was being fought for "liberty and self-government" and that "we know our values are the right ones" (Clinton: 1999b). Vaclav Havel proclaimed that Kosovo was "probably the first war that has not been waged in the name of 'national interests' but rather in the name of principles and values" (Havel 1999: 31). And Prime Minister Blair stated that Kosovo was the site of "the worst case of ethnic cleansing and racial genocide since the second world war" (Cockrell 2000: 20). Yet with respect to the case for external military intervention there were morally and politically relevant differences in the nature and levels of violence in Bosnia and Kosovo. Although Serb (and Croat) actions in Bosnia clearly corresponded to the definition of genocide, the situation in Kosovo was very different. In Bosnia, a society that had achieved a high level of assimilation, the project of Serbianization necessitated ethnoreligious fascism and genocide. In Kosovo, by contrast, ethnic Albanians and Serbs were already living separately in an essentially colonial situation. The campaign of repression against ethnic Albanians, while at times undeniably violent and massive, was not strictly speaking genocidal and was often provoked or instigated by the KLA. Moreover, the failure of the United States to deploy ground troops or to plan for a refugee crisis also highlights the hypocrisy of the humanitarian rationale for war. To the extent that US policymakers believed their own rhetoric, their adherence to it was highly selective. The combination of humanitarian appeals and the desire to avoid casualties led inevitably to escalating violence against civilians as NATO air forces refused to bomb from less than 15,000 feet. As Howard Clark has observed, "NATO embarked on a campaign not to protect Kosovo, but rather to defeat and punish Serbia" (2000: 183).

In his classic study of the interwar period, E. H. Carr observed that universalistic and messianic projects have often served to advance great power imperialism (1939, esp. chaps. 2–3). Whereas during the colonial era such projects were presented in terms of the "white man's burden" or "civilizing mission," in the twentieth and twenty-first centuries they have been articulated within the context of liberal democratic theory. The essential similarity is the underlying political-economic and imperial *rationale*. As Kees van der Pijl writes:

> The Wilsonian impulse in American foreign policy among other things has served to express and project the build-up of strong, expansionary forces in the American economy. Combining a free trade and payments orientation with a full mobilization of the domestic labor force, the resulting offensive posture of the American state under those circumstances

articulated the need to pry open foreign markets and spheres of influence; with the definition of grand objectives, phrased preferably in terms of transcendent universalist goals such as freedom, democracy, or human rights. (2001: 277)

In the United States these universalistic and expansionary projects have tended to originate within the Democratic Party. Thus in place of the cautious diplomacy of the George H. W. Bush administration, by 1994 the Clinton administration had begun to aggressively pursue what Peter Gowan has recently termed a "neoliberal cosmopolitanism," which

seeks to overcome the limits of national sovereignty by constructing a global order that will govern important political as well as economic aspects of both the internal and external behavior of states. This is not a conception advocating any world government empowered to decide the great issues of the day. Rather, it proposes a set of disciplinary regimes—characteristically dubbed, in the oleaginous jargon of the period, "global governance"—reaching deep into the economic, social, and political life of the states subject to it, while safeguarding international flows of finance and trade. (2001: 79–80)

During his 2000 presidential campaign George W. Bush explicitly rejected Wilsonian goals in favor of a traditional and containment-based republicanism more characteristic of his father's administration. Republican critics called Kosovo "Clinton's war" while Bush advocated "humility" and promised to reduce US military forces in Bosnia and Kosovo. Since September 11, 2001, however, the ascendance of neoconservatives in the Bush administration has given rise to the Republican variant of neoliberal cosmopolitanism. The war in Kosovo foreshadowed the far more ambitious imperial offensive in Iraq in the spring of 2003. At the outset the Bush administration sought to justify a war fought for oil and strategic control of the Middle East in terms of security and disarmament. When this justification proved unconvincing it claimed to be fighting for democracy and human rights.

To emphasize the relationship between imperialism and the new discourse of human rights—aptly termed the "new military humanism" (Chomsky 1999b)—is not to imply that humanitarian intervention should be opposed either as a matter of general principle or on the grounds of an inevitable "selectivity" (Damrosch 2000). Rather, as D. Chandler proposes, "A real debate over the pros and cons of the 'new imperialism' essential to building an anti-war movement in the present climate has to tackle the elitist framework of great power domination as it is articulated in the 21st century language of human rights and cosmopolitan duties, rather than in the 19th century language of race and empire" (2002: 1). There is a pressing need to criticize and transcend the moral and political limitations of contemporary international legal and moral discourse as it is articulated and practiced by all of the great powers, but especially by the United States.

■ Notes

1. Germany's subsequent policy does not support the contention of German revanchism or a US-German division of Southeastern Europe. After the recognition of Croatia in December 1991, Germany did not undertake new diplomatic initiatives. It failed to support Croatian membership in the EU, and its foreign direct investment there has been negligible. Recognition antedated Serbia's attack on Croatia by several months and expressed domestic political concerns in ways that resemble Chancellor Gerhard Schroeder's opposition to war in Iraq in 2002–2003. The recognition crisis did indicate that Franco-German cooperation over monetary union could not be extended to a more comprehensive vision of a united Europe. See Cafruny 2003 and Libal 1997.

2. The US Committee on NATO, the leading lobby for the expansion of NATO in Central and Eastern Europe, was founded in 1994 by Lockheed Martin vice president Bruce Jackson. Lockheed Martin's $3.5 billion contract with Poland for the F-16 fighter, signed at the end of 2002, cemented close US-Polish relations and served as a template for further US defense industry involvement in "the new Europe" (*The Guardian,* December 27, 2002).

3. Appendix B of the "implementation" chapter of the Rambouillet Agreement states that "NATO personnel shall enjoy, together with their vehicles, vessels, aircraft, and equipment, free and unrestricted passage and unimpeded access throughout the FRY, including associated airspace and territorial waters." The argument that Rambouillet was an ultimatum is advanced by, inter alia, Noam Chomsky (Ali 2001) and Henry Kissinger, who wrote in *Newsweek* that "Rambouillet was not a negotiation—as is often claimed—but an ultimatum. This marked an astounding departure for an administration that had entered office proclaiming its devotion to the UN Charter and multilateral procedures" (quoted in Achcar 2000: 82).

4. The Clinton administration emphasized humanitarian concerns when it favored intervention in the former Yugoslavia, and "ancient hatreds" when it did not. In May 1993, for example, Secretary of State Warren Christopher declared that "this is at heart a European problem" and that Bosnia had become "a morass of ancient hatreds, a war between all, against all, with all parties guilty of atrocities" (*The Times,* London, May 20, 1993, p. 3). During the bombing campaign against Serbia in May 1999, Clinton apologized for having adopted this view: "There are those who say [ethnic conflicts] are the inevitable result of centuries-old animosities. . . . I have been guilty of saying that, and now I regret it" (*New York Times,* May 14, 1999, p. 7). As ambassador at the UN and secretary of state, Madeleine Albright was a leading advocate of humanitarian intervention in Bosnia and Kosovo. Yet she played a profoundly deceptive and cynical role in blocking UN intervention during the genocide of 1994 (Organization of African Unity 2000).

Annette Freyberg-Inan

World System Theory: A Bird's-Eye View of the World Capitalist Order

While other theories of world politics tend to look primarily at the capabilities, the interests, or the identities of the actors involved in a conflict in order to explain how it came about and evolved, world system theory (WST) looks at the bigger picture. With a focus on economic relationships of asymmetric interdependence and exploitation, it takes a bird's-eye view of the positions that the actors involved hold in the world capitalist system. Their positions in this system depend on and affect their capabilities, interests, and identities, but the focus here is not on the explanatory power of the internal characteristics of the actors. It is on the nature of the system as a whole and of the relationships that compose it. Their relative positions within the system shape the interests of actors and their opportunities for realizing those interests. Core powers, such as the United States or the European Union, are in a position to profit from their relationships with semiperipheral states such as the former Yugoslavia. They are also in a position to defend and expand their privileged positions. By comparison, underprivileged actors such as the FRY and Kosovo are doomed to remain the victims of pervasive structural violence inherent in the relationships of asymmetric interdependence that make up the world capitalist system and that are cultivated by an increasingly transnational capitalist core (Galtung 1969).

For the people of Yugoslavia, the transition from the temporary success of the Tito era's mixed economy model, through a massive economic crisis triggered by world economic fluctuations, to complete dependency on outside money lenders combined with domestic chaos, brought a level of insecurity and an experience of relative deprivation that was evidently too much for this multiethnic polity to bear. Clearly, Yugoslavia's and Kosovo's positions in and relationships with the agents of global capitalism are not sufficient explanations for the tragic course of Yugoslavia's recent history. This chapter will make the case, however, that they are necessary parts of the explanation. Core power economic interests not only encouraged the breakup of Yugoslavia, including the breaking away of Kosovo, but also motivated NATO's interventionism in the case of Kosovo and the former Yugoslav republics' current treatment at the hands of ostensibly benevolent foreign powers.

This world system analysis will raise three main points concerning the

Kosovo conflict.[1] First, Yugoslavia's position in the world capitalist economy, and particularly its relationship with international financial institutions—movers and shapers of the current world economic order—contributed significantly to the breakup of the federation. The conflict between Serbia and Kosovo, while it has deeper historical roots (Lee 1983), was fueled by this general trend of disintegration, which encouraged secessionist tendencies among the Albanians while simultaneously inciting Serb nationalism. At the same time, preexisting interethnic tensions were increased by the experience of exacerbated economic hardship, which resulted in large part from Yugoslavia's dependence in international markets and on the IFIs and the conditions they imposed. This chapter will link Kosovo's fate to Yugoslavia's position in the world economy, its relationships of asymmetric interdependence with the protagonists of the world capitalist order, and its tragic disintegration.

Second, Western policy toward the FRY as well as its successor states has always been strongly motivated by considerations of economic ideology and interest. Western support for the unraveling of the FRY up to and including intervention in the Kosovo conflict has brought concrete economic benefits to the Western actors involved. This chapter will show how core powers have stood to benefit from allowing Yugoslavia to fall apart and from intervening selectively to control the process. Kosovo provided the stage for a war fought largely to demonstrate and expand US hegemony in the world's current political-economic order.

Third, the democratic autonomy of Serbia, Montenegro, and Kosovo since the war has been severely restricted by the economic and political conditions in the region, which have resulted from core power interventionism in the form of sanctions, war, and other measures of control. Alongside other parts of the former Yugoslavia, they are kept in a position of dependence on outside money lending and rebuilt as semiperiphery to the benefit of Western entrepreneurs, speculators, and crusaders for the capitalist ideology. Western core power intervention has, in this case as in so many others, clearly served to protect and strengthen exploitative relationships of asymmetric interdependence.[2]

According to WST, of what is Kosovo an instance? The people who died in Serbia, Montenegro, and Kosovo as a result of ethnic strife and NATO intervention were ultimately the victims of the socioeconomic insecurity on which capitalism is in general predicated. The integration of former Yugoslavia into the world economy (via the intervention of the IFIs and the implementation of liberal economic policies) served to widen already problematic disparities within the country. The sudden demise of the support structure provided by the socialist state (which was here as elsewhere made a condition for "support" from the agents of international capitalism) further contributed to the climate of growing socioeconomic insecurity in the country. After a time of relative comfort and security provided by the communist party organizations in the individual republics and provinces, the peoples of Yugoslavia were sent scrambling for survival in a climate of political chaos.

Kosovo is a particularly tragic instance of this dynamic at work, because Kosovo had the least to gain economically from the unraveling of the FRY, having always been a net recipient of transfer payments from other regions. However, during the 1980s, first the continued denial of republic status, then the revocation of autonomy, and all along the increasing repression faced at the hands of dominant Serbia began to outweigh, in practical as well as psychological terms, the importance of any benefits to be gained from continued cooperation with(in) Serbia. As perceived levels of threat emanating from their Serb neighbors increased, Kosovar Albanian secessionism was strengthened. Thus a potentially workable system of multiethnic coexistence based on socioeconomic solidarity within a socialist federation gave way to the dog-eat-dog dynamics of a capitalism unleashed from domestic political control under the worst possible conditions. In the final analysis, the tragic fate of Kosovo is an instance of civil strife caused by the disparities and insecurities promoted by the neoliberal model. It is also an instance of the lengths to which the promoters of this model will go to disallow its questioning, first callously contributing to Yugoslavia's dissolution, then causing enormous civilian suffering in a blotchy (and bloody) attempt to manage it for their own benefits.

■ The Causes of Yugoslavia's Political-Economic Collapse

The fracturing of Yugoslavia was not the result of the much invoked "ancient" ethnic hatreds alone, but depended on more tangible causes, among them a deep economic crisis (Udovicki and Ridgeway 2000). The plight of Yugoslavia was significantly affected by the population's experience of relative deprivation, as the country went from a period of, for its part of the world, extraordinary well-being, to a period of great misery and disorientation, deftly exploited by unscrupulous populist politicians. From the point of view of WST, it is particularly significant that the deep economic crisis that triggered the disintegration was in large part caused by Yugoslavia's dependent position in the global economy, its reliance on the IFIs, and the latter's intervention, through the conditionality associated with their loans, in the republic's economic and social policies.[3]

While, officially, the IMF, World Bank, and European Bank for Reconstruction and Development (EBRD) assume no authority to exert political influence on the countries to which they loan, it is in fact clear that IFI lending has always been politically motivated and that the involvement

of these institutions has significantly affected the political as well as economic courses of development of their debtor countries (Raffer 1993). It is
of course commonsensical to expect that "injections of large sums of
money into a society inevitably affect the balance of power within it"
(Boyce and Pastor 1998: 43), and in Yugoslavia as elsewhere the IFIs have
worked to steer such effects for the benefit of the core powers and world
order they represent. But how did it come to pass that IFIs could gain such
a hold over Yugoslavia?

After Joseph Tito's break with the Soviet Union in 1948, Yugoslavia
found itself struggling on its own to recover from World War II and survive
a series of bad harvests at the beginning of the 1950s. Then the West and
especially the United States (directly but also through the IMF and World
Bank) began to reward the country for its independence and to cultivate it
"as a virus which could infect the *corpus communisti* body" (Gow 1997,
quoted in Pesakovic 2002: 3). The intention was to keep Yugoslavia afloat
as an independent but successful state within the Eastern bloc and thus an
attractive example for dissidence.[4] Thus, between 1950 and 1980
Yugoslavia received large amounts of money through different aid programs as well as loans from individual countries, private institutions, and
the IFIs.[5] This inflow of money contributed significantly to the industrialization and modernization of the Yugoslav economy during much of the
Cold War.

Initially, Yugoslavia's trade-dependent "third way" model of economic
organization seemed to function rather well. However, the country's
import-intensive development strategy and increasing dependence in international trade and money markets were unsustainable. Beginning in the
mid-1970s, global conditions became increasingly unfavorable and the true
implications of the country's dependent position became apparent. From
the point of view of WST, it is important that key dates in the country's
decline correspond closely to external stimuli, suggesting that this decline
was indeed "related to events in the *global* economy, more than anything
that was occurring internally" (Gibbs 2002: 18). The Yugoslav recession
was triggered in part by the rapid increase of oil prices in 1973–1974 and
the ensuing global debt crisis of the late 1970s and early 1980s (whose
peak coincided eerily with the death of Tito) and in part by the end of the
Cold War and the country's resulting loss of strategic importance.

Heavily dependent as it was on energy imports, Yugoslavia's import
bill increased dramatically at the same time as its export markets, especially
in Western Europe, contracted.[6] Many citizens who had temporarily worked
in Western Europe repatriated, contributing to rising unemployment and
reducing the inflow of foreign currency. Thus Yugoslavia was brought to its
knees by the twin shocks of drastically deteriorating terms of trade and the
increasing inability to finance imports vital for production. To correct the

burgeoning trade deficit, industrialized and trade-dependent Yugoslavia sought to increase income from exports and improve its terms of trade by moving more strongly into higher-end manufacturing. This strategy, however, required even more imports of petroleum, technology, and capital. Thus Yugoslavia began to borrow heavily on international money markets, its foreign debt increasing from $2 billion to $20 billion during the 1970s. By the end of the decade, however, international conditions had not improved, a second major oil price hike (in 1979) had further increased the trade deficit, and Yugoslavia stood before default, with foreign debt representing over a quarter of its national income and debt servicing taking up some 20 percent of its export revenue (Beams 1999; Gibbs 2002).

Due to insufficient controls, money received from private lenders during the 1970s had in some cases been "misplaced" or channeled into the creation of money-trap projects. An appreciation of the dollar (the currency in which most of its loans were denominated), increases in interest rates, and the declining prices of primary commodities (which still constituted an important part of Yugoslav exports) contributed to the country's inability to continue servicing its burgeoning debt (Pesakovic 2002). A major earthquake in 1979 and a series of bad harvests seemed cosmic confirmations of the end of Yugoslavia's good luck. The conclusion of an IMF standby agreement and a World Bank structural adjustment loan were presented as the only solution.

In the context of the world debt crisis, however, attracting new loans had become more costly. The money granted by IFIs was increasingly tied to strict austerity policy guidelines. In fact, this period witnessed the birth of "strict conditionality," which increased the influence of IFIs on domestic economic and social policy in debtor countries worldwide. A range of studies have in the meantime demonstrated the destructive effects of the drastic implementation of the policies that constitute the "Washington consensus."[7] For Yugoslavia, the imposition of strict IFI conditionality would have particularly damaging consequences, for three main reasons. First, Yugoslav citizens were at the time largely not accustomed to true economic hardship. Second, economic contraction occurred in parallel with the devolution of political power to the republics and provinces. Third, interethnic solidarity and a pan-Yugoslavian sense of identity had not grown as envisioned by Tito and communist party doctrine. Thus there was neither sufficient political nor cultural support for maintaining interethnic solidarity in times of crisis.

FRY "adjustment" to open market dynamics was premised on restoring macroeconomic stability by accepting an ostensibly temporary decrease in living standards. It began in 1979, intensified throughout the 1980s, and culminated in the county's breakup in 1991. Far from solving the debt crisis, adjustment loans had Yugoslav debt, by 1988, at still over $20 billion—

with roughly $1,000 per capita, the highest debt in Europe. At this point Yugoslavia requested a three-year moratorium with Western banks and a reduction of debt servicing from 40 to 25 percent of foreign exchange earnings. After this request was denied the country found itself concluding new agreements with the IMF and World Bank, which had foreign debt still standing at $16.5 billion by 1990, after over a decade of "adjustment" and on the eve of civil war (Gibbs 2002).

Throughout the 1980s the associated austerity programs sent shockwaves through the entire country and could not fail to have serious political repercussions. By 1989, 60 percent of Yugoslav workers lived below or at the minimum level of income guaranteed by the state, and the standard of living had fallen by 40 percent since 1982, to the level of the mid-1960s (Curtis 1990).[8] As David Dyker has observed, quite apart from interest payments on its foreign loans, the rate of debt repayment ensured that Yugoslavia was in fact "exporting capital to the developed West," participating in the "perverse transfer of resources" from semiperiphery to core that is characteristic of the world capitalist system (1990: 169). Kosovo was left with the thankless role of the last and weakest link in this chain. Even massive transfer payment receipts over many years had not been able to counteract the factors that conspired to keep this province the worst off in the FRY—peripheral within the semiperiphery. Here, "austerity" was already the order of the day, and the reduction of transfer payments from other increasingly hard-pressed parts of the FRY under conditions of devolution could not help but stimulate a pervasive sense of insecurity and defensive resentment among a traditionally victimized population.

Shock therapy, launched full-force in January 1990, had much the same effects in Yugoslavia as elsewhere. Wage freezes (to combat inflation) and the liberalization of prices, which initially led to a galloping inflation of 2,500 percent, resulted in a decline of real wages by 41 percent during the first six months of 1990 (World Bank 1991). Trade liberalization led to a significant increase in imports, further depressing the domestic economy. At the same time, illustrating the paradoxical nature of neoliberal "adjustment" techniques, consumer goods were forcibly removed from domestic consumption and shifted into exports to prop up the trade balance. As under tight budgetary constraints, state revenues were channeled toward financing external debt. Nowhere near enough money was left to stimulate domestic investment and production, support domestic demand, or compensate the losers of adjustment.

The people's standard of living continued to deteriorate substantially in the early 1990s as production declined heavily and the domestic economy contracted further. Privatization, an IFI condition, contributed strongly to unemployment, primarily in the banking sector, the public sector, and heavy industry. By the end of 1990 a full two-thirds of the industrial work force was either laid off or deemed redundant (World Bank 1991). These were not merely economic problems. Ernest Stern, then senior official at the World Bank, admitted at the time: "We fail to give weight in our thinking to the fact that structural adjustment means a major redistribution of economic power and hence of political power in many of the countries undergoing this process" (1991: 4). In Yugoslavia, this redistribution would ultimately lead to the collapse of the entire polity. Susan Woodward provides vitally important insight on this point:

> The system had been structured around substantive and participatory rights that depended on budgetary expenditures and public ownership, not the procedural rights of market-oriented democracies. Instead, the insistence that welfare should be provided either through free-market forces or by lower-level governments made average citizens more dependent on their local and republican governments and on nurturing informal networks of loyalty and support than on organizing around collective economic interests and Yugoslav-wide solutions. (1995: 383)

The progressive empowerment of particularistic elites occurred with particular ease in Kosovo, where informal networks are vital for ensuring a minimum level of predictability and order in an environment characterized by the brutal insecurity of everyday struggle for survival. Informal networks in Kosovo generally did not cross ethnic lines, and thus their strengthening, and the corresponding decline of centralized Yugoslav governance with its integrative agenda, only served to deepen existing ethnic cleavages. As shown by Michele Lee (1983) and Dusko Sekulic, Garth Massey, and Randy Hodson (1994), conditions in Kosovo were especially conducive for economic rivalries to turn into open ethnic conflict. The area was also less modernized (and less urbanized), and the political culture nonparticipatory. All in all, efforts by the centralized party leadership under Tito to merge Yugoslavia's ethnicities by establishing working-class solidarity through self-management had remained nothing but pipe dreams.[9] World system theory shares in the frequently expressed critique of the Washington consensus as promoted by the IFIs. The prescription of tight monetary and fiscal policy, price liberalization, and liberalization of international trade and foreign investment has brought increased inequality and widespread hardship to many developing countries around the world. As the end of the Cold War removed its strategic importance for the West, no foreign goodwill was left to cushion Yugoslavia from the disastrous social effects of such a development strategy. Economic restructuring thus effectively destroyed the basis for political stability and peaceful democratization across the country.

British member of Parliament Harry Barnes has been one of the most explicit critics of the Western complicity in this tragedy. He writes, "The former Yugoslavia was destroyed economically and politically. It was destroyed economically because of the requirements [of the IFIs] that debts should be repaid to international banks at all costs. Its government was obliged by the terms of the IMF and others to cut social expenditure to meet their requirements" (1999: 1). In the resulting climate of inequality, widespread misery, and insecurity, conflict was likely to erupt along any fault-line that could be conveniently exploited by ruthless power players. In this way, "intervention by the IMF and the western financial community . . . helped to create the socio-economic conditions under which nationalist demagogues . . . were able to flourish" (Gibbs 2002: 3).[10] Kosovo was a place where interethnic grievances were already real and explicable. Sparks therefore did not take long to fly here. All across the country, nationalistic sentiment became expressed in populist rhetoric that increasingly disregarded the communist vision of a peacefully united multiethnic federation. It combined with outside support for secessionism, which was motivated more by greed for the economic benefits to be reaped from the exploitation of a fractured Yugoslavia than by ideals of ethnic self-determination, to trigger a tragic multifront civil war.

During the 1980s the core powers had supported increased Yugoslav centralism (which fed Serb nationalism as well as resentment among other ethnicities) as a way to improve their chances of collecting Yugoslavia's debt (Lee 1983). Once the disintegrative effects of this shortsighted strategy could no longer be controlled, they switched to steering disintegration, with no less disastrous consequences. It is clear that in Yugoslavia, as elsewhere, wherever the representatives of the world capitalist order put their weight behind the systemic transformation of multiethnic societies, they cannot "divorce themselves from the phenomenon of ethno-national mobilization and the possibility that it might turn violent" (Reinicke 1996: 311). It is a serious indictment of the promoters of Yugoslavia's destructive transformation to observe how unwilling they have been to assume at least a partial responsibility for its consequences.

■ Managing the Semiperiphery: A Lesson in Guided Collapse

Socialist Yugoslavia suffered from larger economic discrepancies among its republics than any other socialist country (Flakierski 1989; Gibbs 2002). In 1988, for example, Slovenia's per capita gross social product was eight times that of Kosovo (Botev 1994). Vojvodina and Croatia were next, still above average in terms of a range of economic indicators, while Serbia fell at or slightly below the national average. Macedonia, Montenegro, and Bosnia were well below the national average, with Kosovo trailing always farthest behind (Baletic and Marendic 1992; Bookman 2002; Prifti 1984).

These discrepancies paralleled variation in living standards and were not reduced by extensive regional subsidy programs. Most of Yugoslavia's impressive industrial development had taken place in the north of the country, in Croatia and Slovenia, while the south, as a domestic periphery, primarily supplied raw materials. As the relative prices of raw materials fell during the 1970s and 1980s, economic inequality between the republics increased further. Relative deprivation constituted a constant source of grievance for the less developed regions, such as Kosovo, while many in the better-off regions resented having to support their poorer neighbors.

Under the competitive conditions of crisis, regional inequalities intensified further. A 1989 public opinion survey that showed alarmingly high levels of ethnic and religious intolerance throughout the country also demonstrated that intolerance was greatest at the extremes of economic inequality, in the richest as well as the poorest regions (Hodson, Sekulic, and Massey 1994). Kosovo showed the highest levels of intolerance, and Kosovar Albanians, the poorest sector of the population in the country, were the least tolerant of all. Before Serbia's revocation of Kosovo's de jure autonomy status in 1989, secessionism still appeared irrational, since Kosovo already essentially possessed the status of a republic within the federation. After the revocation, however, and as repression again intensified, secessionism became a rational response—but one that was unacceptable to Serb Kosovars and leaders (Kostovicova 1997). The ground was thus prepared for economic shock to trigger interethnic violence.

Rising intolerance between ethnic and religious groups combined with an increased alienation between all Yugoslavia's republics and provinces. The central government, delegitimized by the collapse of "communist" governments all around as well as the continuing economic crisis, was progressively weakened. Democratization efforts failed as popular grievances could not be or were not successfully expressed through democratic means. A case in point is the Kosovar Albanians' boycott of the December 1990 elections in Serbia to protest Serb repression. Moreover, the advent of populist mass politics, exemplified by the racist demagogues Slobodan Milosevic and Franjo Tudjman, served to lift remaining "taboos against displays of ethnic hatred" (Gibbs 2002: 21). It was within this climate that the movement to break up Yugoslavia was initiated by the two richest republics, Slovenia and Croatia, which had obvious economic interests in secession. They were supported in their endeavor by foreign capitalist interests, notably Germany, which, after neoliberal parties had come to power in both republics with the 1990 elections, expected that an independent Slovenia and Croatia would move more quickly than an intact Yugoslavia to provide willing markets and attractive investment opportunities.

The dissolution of Yugoslavia would be determined by three interlinked sets of interests of international capital: first, the insistence on debt repayment (which ensured continuing interference with domestic social and economic policy); second, the crusade for the hegemony of neoliberalism; third, the actual "opening" of markets (to maximize opportunities for exploitation). David Gibbs holds that, as late as mid-1990, "debt relief was still a realistic alternative to war" (2002: 36). Even the populations in Slovenia and Croatia appeared undecided about possible secession. However, by June and despite shock therapy, inflation increased once more and the initial promising popularity of Yugoslav prime minister Markovic suffered accordingly. On June 25 and June 26, Slovenia and Croatia declared their independence, and the Yugoslav National Army intervened to prevent the secessions. A decade of bloodshed had begun.

As Gibbs has estimated, "forgiving Yugoslavia's debt would surely have been less costly than the various efforts at military intervention during the period 1991–99" (2002: 39). Perhaps this could not have been foreseen in 1990 (although some strategic foresight may be demanded from all meddlers). What is clear is that "the structural adjustment programs that were imposed upon Yugoslavia beginning in 1979 were not inevitable. They were the result of choices made by western officials to pursue debt repayment and to disregard the social and political consequences of these policies" (Gibbs 2002: 39). During Yugoslavia's time of economic struggle, during a period when civil war and the collapse of a federalist experiment were still avoidable, "the western financial community, led by the IMF, clearly opted for the imposition of austerity measures, in order to ensure at least some measure of repayment" (Gibbs 2002: 16). In addition, the crisis was exploited as a welcome opportunity to bring Yugoslav policies in line with the Washington consensus. Jerome Levinson has pointed out that to

> the US Treasury staff . . . the debt crisis afforded an unparalleled opportunity to achieve, in debtor countries, the structural reforms favored by the Reagan Administration. The core of these reforms was a commitment on the part of the debtor countries to reduce the role of the public sector as a vehicle for economic and social development and rely more on market forces and private enterprise, domestic and foreign. (quoted in Henwood 1993)

Clearly the "foreign enterprise" envisioned was none other than US-based interests looking for cheap labor, pliable governments, and elastic markets. Thus, International Finance Corporation official William Ryrie called the global debt crisis a "blessing in disguise," as it allowed international organizations like the World Bank and IMF to push forward the liberalization of the world economy by taking advantage of the disorientation, disappointment, and lack of alternatives of the debtor countries (quoted in Gibbs 2002: 17). While "adjustment" is of course typically presented by its adherents as a set of obvious technical solutions to problems of poverty and underdevelopment, its political objective has been and still is the marginalization and replacement of alternative systems that grant more control of their economic fates to states and, in varying degrees, to their citizens. Thus Jude Wanniski has asked whether austerity measures might not have been forced onto Yugoslavia "at the instigation of the [US] foreign policy establishment, which did not like the fact that Yugoslavia was making a success of market socialism" (1999). Such suspicions are confirmed by Gibbs, who in a comparison of the Western response to the two racist demagogues Milosevic and Tudjman finds that "the principal reason for the hostility towards Milosevic was [that] he advanced views and to some extent specific politics that were anticapitalist, and he was widely perceived as a constraint on the full incorporation of Yugoslavia into the capitalist west" (Gibbs 2002: 27). In comparison, the equally authoritarian and intolerant Tudjman was "presented as a fine example of the type of democratic and free market liberal that the west favored" (Gibbs 2002: 30).

Practically razed to the ground, politically weakened by division and the legacies of their violent recent histories, and without any apparent policy alternatives, Yugoslavia's successor states have been (with the exception of Slovenia) readied to join the global economy at just the level of disadvantage fit for a semiperiphery. As postcommunist states, they have had some bargaining power inasmuch as they possessed geostrategic importance, harbored natural resources (especially oil), represented sizable future markets for manufactured goods from core countries, and constituted a source of cheap and relatively well educated labor fit for use in modern manufacturing and the electronics industry (provided they promised the requisite legal and political stability as well). However, their designated role in the global economy has clearly been semiperipheral: home to a mass of docile cheap laborers with just enough means to ensure a positive balance of trade to core trading partners. For this reason, increasing socioeconomic disparity within these countries was tolerated if not encouraged, while domestic elites were granted extensive leeway in ensuring domestic tranquility. The Balkans have a better-educated and better-trained work force than former colonies in Asia, Africa, or Latin America—more fit for the demands of modern industry. Still, during its so-called transition the region has taken over the role previously ascribed to colonized territory, fulfilling essentially the same purpose of providing cheap labor, whose comparatively meager income would be spent in good part on imports from the wealthier countries (Adamovich 2002).

Kosovo not only fits within this general picture of the three sets of interlinking core power economic interests in the region,[11] but it also possesses particular strategic importance, which crucially influenced US policy during the conflict. It stars as a corridor in Western pipeline dreams:

vital territory for routing oil and gas from Central Asia and the Caucasus to Western Europe (and from there to the wider world). The NATO intervention in the conflict between Serbia and the Albanians of Kosovo cannot be understood unless it is placed within the context of the web of economic interests that have guided the development and foreign policies of core powers and the competition between them in the region.

■ The Legacies of Core Power Strategy

The unraveling of the former Yugoslavia involved four republics becoming sovereign states and two parts of a loose confederation, while one formerly autonomous province became an international protectorate. What has this meant for the economies of the newborn entities? Unsurprisingly, given the lucrative potential of the newly accessible semiperipheral territories, all manner of core-country sponsors and donors have made themselves available to the postcommunist world, at times even before having been invited. And just as in the case of colonial relations, "most of the foreign aid funding, except for the humanitarian aid in kind . . . is finding its harbor closing the circle back in the country of origin" (Adamovich 2002: 5). At this point it is worth remembering that, according to WST, the constant flow of wealth from periphery and semiperiphery to core is the central dynamic of global capitalism. Even where core powers are providing aid or debt relief, such measures are tactical, in the longer term serving core interests, for example by preventing the disappearance of markets. Where aid involves the contracting of private firms or consultancy, the money granted usually finds its way back to companies or consultancy firms in the donor countries. Kosovo is no exception to this pattern.

All across former Yugoslavia, "well-paid missionaries of the free enterprise ideology" (Adamovich 2002: 12) have begun to colonize their new playing field, both independently and in the context of the various regional stabilization and development initiatives, such as the Southeast Europe Cooperation Initiative (SECI), the Conference on Stability, Security, and Cooperation in Southeastern Europe (CSSCSE), or the Stability Pact for Southeastern Europe (SPSEE), which is the main international instrument driving efforts to develop postwar Kosovo.[12] The SPSEE foresees vital roles for the IFIs and a close coordination of the World Bank and the European Commission in its promotion and coordination. But such initiatives not only encourage a continued dependence on international lending, they also help institutionalize the results of the core powers' ingenious strategy of "divide and conquer" in the region. Politically divided and in many cases implacably hostile toward one another, the former Yugoslav republics (and province of Kosovo) have no means of establishing solidarity to tackle common problems or organizing effectively to protect their common interests. At the same time, material necessity conspires with bribes and threats from the representatives of the world capitalist order to drive them toward establishing a common market. Membership in a free trade area facilitates their parallel incorporation into the regional and world capitalist economy and maximizes the ease with which their markets can be conquered and foreign investments made profitable. Exploitation is thus facilitated, and resistance hobbled.

As shown by Milica Bookman, regional disparities within the former Yugoslavia have not lessened since 1991 despite uneven exposure to destruction through war of physical and human capital, an uneven influx of capital from outside, and internal measures of redistribution of resources. "The largest per capita transfusion of assistance Europe has even experienced" has done nothing to reduce these gaps (2002: 31). Instead, here as everywhere, structural adjustment has only served to entrench and widen existing inequalities. The ranking of former republics and provinces essentially remains the same. Only Serbia has fallen from its previously average position.

The post-Milosevic government inherited "an economy in shambles" (Bookman 2002: 26). Serbia's economy in 2002 was a third of its size in 1989, with 20 percent of the contraction directly attributable to the NATO war (Bookman 2002). Unemployment is estimated at close to 50 percent. Average wages amount to some $45 per month. Inflation is at 50 percent, and the country still faces a crippling foreign debt. Corruption and institutional chaos abound. According to some estimates, 70 percent of all economic activity takes place beyond regulation and taxation (Bookman 2002). Among the causes for this misery are the disruption of interrepublic trade, the loss of resources through war on the breakaway republics, the effects of the sanctions, a massive influx of refugees, the destruction caused by NATO bombings, as well as mismanagement and failed reforms. Moreover, Serbia has lost a large portion of its skilled and educated workers to emigration.[13] As a result of all these factors, a country that is rich in natural resources and that has been highly industrialized—a former center for communication, transport, and energy—faces extraordinary economic challenges. Budgetary constraints imposed by IFI conditionality have led to cuts in social spending. Unsurprisingly, the population expresses strong dissatisfaction with the current situation and governments have to operate in a legitimacy crisis.[14]

Kosovo continues to lag far behind the other regions of former Yugoslavia. It is poor in resources, with little productive capacity and an economy that relies mostly on agriculture, small-scale trade, and extractive industries (Bookman 2002; Prifti 1984). Since Kosovo became a UN protectorate, the UN has taken an active role in its economic affairs, developing a fiscal and supporting legal system and introducing the German mark (now the euro) as legal tender. These obvious signs of policy independence from Serbia have clashed with Kosovo's official status as part of the FRY, a clash made even more sensitive by a host of unresolved issues relating to Serbian property and business interests in the former province. Production is minimal and the economy is based almost entirely on trade, much of it illegal. Local demand is unable to sustain a service sector and so it caters to the abnormal presence of foreigners in the country. It is quite clear that the core powers that intervened in the Kosovo conflict had no interest in creating a new polity that could autonomously sustain and develop itself. Instead, they intervened to manage relations within and with a semiperipheral region in which they had vital interests and in which order, access, and adherence to the dominant economic ideology thus had to be ensured.

Throughout the former Yugoslavia Western intervention has served to protect and strengthen exploitative relationships of asymmetric interdependence. What is left of Yugoslavia has been made "safe" to provide access to foreign and transnational capitalist interests. The hegemony of neoliberalism is further consolidated at the expense of more egalitarian forms of economic development as well as with more participatory forms of democracy. This has affected the evolution of civil society as indicated by extremely high levels of political apathy in the region.[15] Where did the "substantive and participatory rights" go, which Woodward (1995: 383) identified in the FRY and which existed during the federation's most promising times not only in theory? In Serbia and Montenegro, political apathy combines with the supposed *Sachzwang* (pressure of facts) of the neoliberal agenda to lead to the de facto disenfranchisement of the ordinary citizen. In Kosovo, we are told, political culture cannot (yet) support full self-governance.

What then do their newfound liberty and democracy in a protectorate mean for the people in Kosovo? The majority of Serbs who once lived there have fled. Interethnic and, increasingly, also political violence remain serious problems (O'Neill 2002). The Albanian population is in large part dissatisfied with their current situation, continuing to call for complete independence from Serbia and increasingly resentful of the intervening powers (O'Neill 2002; Qirezi 2002). Instead of being autonomous, Kosovo is completely dependent on foreign money as well as governance. Movement toward self-rule is slow and fraught with problems, its apparent lack of success embarrassing those who have defended the supposed humanistic objectives of the intervention (O'Neill 2002). It seems clear that, as argued by Howard Clark (2000), Kosovar Albanians should have pursued a strategy of economic self-empowerment during the 1990s, rather than relying almost exclusively on outside help. At the time, such a strategy could have helped build morale as well as allow for more effective resistance against repression. Its payoffs now would be an improved foundation for self-steered development. Instead, Kosovo has been steered into continuing dependence and domination.

■ Conclusion

Applying the perspective of WST to the fate of Yugoslavia and Kosovo reveals a coherent ideology and a consistent set of interests that have motivated and guided the dissolution of Yugoslavia, defined the role of Western as well as domestic actors in this process, and provided a normative context in which the suffering of human beings and the autonomy of human communities meant very little. Instead, strategic calculations of diminishing resistance to a hegemonic political and economic ideology and of ensuring stability and access for the sake of their (military and) economic interests outweighed humanitarian considerations in the strategic thinking of the Western powers. The obvious benefits reaped by core interests through managing the political fracturing of this semiperipheral region newly open to exploitation suggest, cynically, that things have gone as planned for the dominant agents of the world capitalist order.

WST draws our attention to the effects of global structural inequity and its military correlate—the use of force by privileged nations and regions to maintain their positions vis-à-vis those who would threaten their hegemony and to create an environment of maximum efficiency for exploitation. As Alejandro Bendana (1996) has pointed out, in the absence of the mythical invisible hand that would have people everywhere benefiting from global capitalism, there are those who require a visible fist in order to obstruct the vision and reduce the options of those who do not. The violent dissolution of Yugoslavia and the Western military intervention in Kosovo cannot be properly explained or judged without recognizing the logic of global capitalism and getting beyond the self-justificatory rhetoric of its dominant ideologies.

Where will core powers next intervene to uphold the current world economic order? WST tells us what to be on the lookout for. We can expect a reaction from the governments of the privileged if a nation or region seeks to adjust the balance in its relationships of interdependence with more privileged partners. Such nations or regions could do so by attempting to assert more control over vital resources (such as oil), by protecting vulnerable sectors of their economy from potentially destructive competition (for example, by erecting barriers to trade), by shielding vulnerable sectors of their society or culture (for example, by reducing the influx of foreign investment and influence), or by seeking to improve their terms of trade through organizing with others in similar positions. In these instances, we can expect a reaction from core governments, where leaders depend on overfeeding their voters through the continued exploitation of less fortunate human beings abroad and at home.

The lessons of core power strategy in the process of dissolution of Yugoslavia are clear. Access to semiperipheral markets, labor, and resources, and conditions under which all three can be exploited with maximum ease and profit, will be ensured, if necessary by force and with little regard for human suffering. It is likely that, as you are reading these words, these dynamics are playing out elsewhere in the world. What are the strategic economic considerations driving contemporary military interventions? Who is defending their privileged access to what, where, and against whom? World system theory teaches us to ask these vital questions, so that we will not be taken for fools by the rhetoric of those with a vested interest in fooling us. It also teaches us that, while global capitalist relations of exploitation remain in place, the structural violence inherent in this system will continue to provoke violent conflict, bringing continued inequity, deprivation, and unimaginable suffering to human beings and communities around the globe.

■ Notes

1. A fourth point, that NATO intervention was undertaken for economic self-interests and not humanitarian reasons, is not elaborated here, since it is covered in the chapters on historical materialism and critical theory. It is important to keep in mind, however, that it is consistent with WST. See, for example, Chomsky 1999a, Chomsky 1999b, Frank 1999a, Frank 1999b, Frank 1999c, Frank 1999d, Wallerstein 1999a, Wallerstein 1999b, Gibbs 2002, O'Neill 2002, Beams 1999, and Lieven 2001.

2. Core power efforts to keep Balkan nations weakened by division date at least as far back as British refusal to support the idea of a Balkan Federation in the early 1940s. See Lee 1983.

3. See Gibbs 2002, Pesakovic 2002, Pesakovic 2003, Chossudovsky 1997, Woodward 1995, Beams 1999, Wanniski 1999, and Barratt Brown 1993.

4. See Gow 1997 and Stremlau and Sagasti 1998.

5. From 1961 to 1990 the country signed ten standby agreements with the IMF, amounting to $3.5 billion in the period 1979–1990. By late 1991 Yugoslavia was the sixth largest user of IMF funds in the world. The World Bank lent, in the period from 1949 to 1991, a total of over $6 billion distributed through ninety loans. The European Investment Bank (EIB), between 1976 and the beginning of UN sanctions, granted twenty-one loans totaling over ECU760 million, out of which 50 percent were disbursed (Pesakovic 2002).

6. Not receiving subsidized oil from the Soviet Union, Yugoslavia had to buy at world market prices.

7. See, for example, Danaher 2002, Vreeland 2003, and Peet 2003.

8. As reported by Leonard Cohen (1995: 31), average annual growth rates were 8.8 percent, 6 percent, and 6.1 percent for GDP; 7.7 percent, 5 percent, and 5.1 percent for GDP per capita; 4.8 percent, 4.3 percent, and 2.7 percent for labor productivity in the public sector; and 6.3 percent, 6.1 percent, and 2.7 percent for real personal income during the periods 1956–1964, 1965–1972, and 1973–1979. During the period 1980–1984, for reasons explained in the text, average annual growth rates dropped to 0.4 percent for GDP, –0.3 percent for GDP per capita, –2

percent for labor productivity in the public sector, and –2 percent for real personal income.

9. The failure of this project and the evolution of regional rivalries in Yugoslavia until 1993 are well described in Sekulic, Massey, and Hodson 1994. On the communist party's vision of nationality building through worker empowerment, see also Kardelj 1960.

10. Jude Wanniski puts it more succinctly: "It was the International Monetary Fund that tore the Yugoslav Federation to pieces" (1999). See also Pesakovic 2002.

11. On the postwar economic evolution of the former Yugoslavia and Kosovo, which confirms the arguments made here, see Gligorov 1999, Gligorov and Sundstrom 1999, and Holzner 2003.

12. The SPSEE, which operates under the auspices of the OSCE, emerged by way of a master plan agreed upon by the core powers to reconstruct the region in parallel with and dependent on its incorporation into the capitalist regional and world economy. Instrumental in its conception had been the EU, the United States, the IMF, the World Bank, the EBRD, the EIB.

13. Gordana Pesakovic (2001), for example, suggests that 67 percent of all registered workers in research and development left the country between 1990 and 1993. The refugees who have entered and remained in Serbia, by comparison, are poorly educated.

14. According to an October 2001 poll, only 12.3 percent of the Serbian population are satisfied, 27 percent are undecided, and almost 60 percent are dissatisfied with their situation (reported in Pesakovic 2002). Vojvodina has shared Serbia's fate over the past decade, as has Montenegro, although its president, Milo Djukanovic, attempted to chart an independent course by means of the introduction of the German mark (now the euro), but Montenegro was a poor region even before the breakup, possessing few resources and little infrastructure. It received transfer payments from its sister provinces and continued to stay afloat through Western support received during the reign of Milosevic. Today it remains strongly dependent on capital inflows and supportive terms of trade (Bookman 2002).

15. For example, Serbian 2002 presidential elections failed repeatedly due to insufficient voter turnout.

chapter 8

Feminist Approaches

Jennifer Sterling-Folker

Feminism

Feminist IR theory draws upon a variety of literatures and perspectives from multiple fields of study so that it has always been an interdisciplinary undertaking. Yet as with other approaches that have postpositivist leanings, IR feminism was met with skepticism and resistance in the US IR discipline when its scholarship began to flourish in the early 1980s. The first IR journal issue devoted to the topic of women and IR was *Millennium*'s 1988 special issue, and in 1990 a section on feminist theory and gender studies was launched in the ISA. The burgeoning interest in and literature on feminist IR theory can be attributed to a community of feminist IR scholars—such as Cynthia Enloe, V. Spike Peterson, Christine Sylvester, and J. Ann Tickner—who read and commented on one another's work, and who collectively considered the parameters and substance of feminist IR theorizing. As Birgit Locher and Elisabeth Prügl observe, these scholars developed "a set of programmatic writings" that influenced the development of feminist IR theory and "still provide an important point of reference" for feminist IR scholars today (2001: 115).

Not all feminist IR theory is postpositivist, but there is, as Tickner argues "a strong resonance for a variety of reasons including a commitment to epistemological pluralism as well as to certain ontological sensitivities" (1997: 619). The introduction of feminist and postmodernist theoretical perspectives occurred at roughly the same time in the US discipline, and together they laid the groundwork for the more epistemologically moderate constructivism. Yet Locher and Prügl point out that for feminists the question of "who knows" is central, and that "whereas epistemology is thus a secondary matter for most IR constructivists, it continues to be a central topic of feminist debates" (2001: 120). There is confusion on this score, however, since some of the early feminist IR literature was positivist and involved the empirical study of women in global political leadership positions, or lack thereof. This work was labeled "liberal feminism," because it was driven by the central question "Where are the women?" and it tended to assume that the political and economic marginalization of women could be overcome simply by increasing their involvement in existing political processes.

The early liberal emphasis on "add women and stir" (Kinsella 2003; Zalewski 2003) has contributed to a number of misconceptions in the discipline about feminist IR scholarship. There is, for example, a misperception that feminist theorizing is simply data collection about the status of women in world politics and that all feminist theories subscribe to the goal of increasing representation in order to end discrimination. It is also frequently assumed that all feminist IR theorists believe a world ruled by women would be a more peaceful place given that caregiving comes "naturally" to women (see Fukuyama 1998). Building on these first two fallacies is a third, which assumes that feminist IR theory elevates "women's issues" at the expense of more important IR subject matter, such as wars, trade negotiations, international organizations, and terrorism. Studying IR from a feminist perspective is believed to be a trivializing activity in this regard, because it supposedly does not address more important IR topics and diverts our attention from them instead. Feminist work that relies on the narratives of average women who are not directly involved in political and economic decisionmaking is particularly subject to this criticism.

Most fallacies are born out of ignorance and these are no exception. IR feminism is a multifaceted theoretical enterprise involving numerous variants that grapple with ontological, epistemological, and methodological issues as they relate to women and gender. While some feminist scholars believe that women are innately more peaceful than their male counterparts, a vast majority of feminist IR theorists do not. There has been substantial debate within feminist IR theorizing over this very issue, yet as Helen Kinsella notes, "the impulse to categorize this range of feminist theorizing to a simple substantive claim that there is an essential subject (woman) and a primary goal (ending oppression) reduces a productive cacophonous counterpoint to a single note" (2003: 294). In fact, a great deal of feminist scholarship documents the greater extent to which women have participated in or supported and sustained, rather than opposed, war-making.[1] Most IR feminists would concur with Jean Bethke Elshtain that while, "historically and currently, feminism has driven towards utopianism in many of its most widely known incarnations . . . this, as 'peace politics,' winds up empty as explanatory theory and naïve as politics" (1995: 358). Hence IR feminist theorizing cannot be characterized as the simple and speculative equation between women's participation in IR and the end of warfare.

It has also been feminist IR scholars themselves who have been at the forefront of problematizing the assumption that biology determines gender differences. To address this issue, feminist scholarship posits a distinction between sex and gender: "Whereas biological sex identity is determined by reference to genetic and anatomical characteristics, socially learned gender is an acquired identity gained through performing prescribed gender roles" (Peterson and Runyan 1999: 5). While there might be universal biological sex identities, the same cannot be said for gender roles. Even a cursory glance at historical and contemporary global cultures reveals stark comparative differences in expectations of appropriate gender behavior and underscores the fact that notions of femininity and masculinity are culturally constructed and variable, not timeless and immutable. The causal dividing line between sex and gender has been the source of considerable discussion, debate, and exploration in the feminist IR literature, and there is increasing evidence that many of the biological sex differences we take for granted are actually up for cultural grabs.[2] Yet most IR feminists do not deny that biology makes a difference; instead they concur with V. Spike Peterson and Anne Runyan that, "although biology is ostensibly the basis for establishing gender models, it plays an ambiguous and often purely symbolic role in our actual use of gendered concepts" (1999: 30).

Gendered concepts are instead created and sustained as collective projects. As Peterson and Runyan note, "we *learn,* through culturally specific socialization, what characteristics are associated with masculinity and femininity and how to assume the identities of men and women" (1999: 7, emphasis original). Hence gender imparts different social meanings to men and women and proscribes different parameters for what it means to be male/masculine or female/feminine in a given culture. It is gender identity, not sex identity, that is the primary focus of IR feminist literature. As with postmodernism and critical theory, many IR feminists are interested in exploring the extent to which our identities are shaped and informed by social truths that are historically constructed. They share the postpositivist commitment to questioning what we take for granted and to problematizing what is given as truth or knowledge.

Given that gender roles are socially constructed, feminist IR scholars have been among the first to question whether it is appropriate to assume we know what women are (referred to as "essentializing women") and can posit that there are universal feminine characteristics such as caregiver or nurturer (Elam and Wiegman 1995). This has also led feminist scholars to question whether men aren't also essentialized. After all, if "there is nothing natural, inherent or biologically inevitable about the attributes, activities and behaviors that come to be defined as either masculine or feminine" (Zalewski 1995: 341), then to what extent are both women *and* men socially constructed by the cultures to which they are born? The feminist literature argues that the concept of gender indicates an interdependent relationship between male/masculine and female/feminine, in which attributes of each are always oppositionally defined in relation to the other. Hence feminist IR scholarship is not simply about women, it is about the interdependence of masculine and feminine as socially constructed categories that shape how we know and experience the world. In this context it is more appropriate to characterize IR feminism as the study of gender (rather than women) and the differences that gender makes to world politics.

The differences it makes are enormous, according to feminist scholars, because gender is a powerful meta-narrative that establishes oppositional hierarchies in which some ideas are privileged, others marginalized, and social inequalities are produced on that basis. Many IR feminists concur with postmodernists, then, that there is a tendency in scientific Western thought to create hierarchical either-or oppositions that are treated as natural or given (Peterson and Runyan 1999: 39–40). Despite dramatic cultural differences in gender roles, the relational characteristics of masculine and feminine are always hierarchical, with the masculine characteristics more highly prized, valued, and privileged. Tickner notes that "in the West, certain characteristics, such as power, autonomy, rationality, and public are generally perceived as masculine, while their opposites, weakness, dependence, emotion, and private are stereotypically associated with femininity" (1996: 455). Similarly, Peterson and Runyan observe that "constructions of masculinity (agency, control, aggression) are not independent of, but rely upon, contrasting constructions of femininity (dependence, vulnerability, passivity)" (1999: 9).

These oppositional characteristics are not simply abstract talking points; they are the foundation for justifying who gets what and why in world politics. The elevation of what is masculine and the denigration of what is feminine translates into political, economic, and social structures and processes that produce and reify severe gender inequalities on a global scale. It is no accident, then, that two out of three women on the planet live in poverty or that there is a thriving global sex industry involving the forced prostitution of girls and women from almost every region (Zalewski 1995). Nor is it accidental that in developing countries women do more of the work and family care, and yet they receive less adequate health care, education, nutrition, and compensation than do men (Tickner 1996). Nor is it accidental that in core societies, and in comparison to men, women still receive a third less pay for equal work and effort (Tickner 1997). The construction of gender differences is the construction of a normative, material hierarchy that is the very essence of global politics and power. By deconstructing gender as the socially constructed meaning of masculinity and femininity, feminist IR scholars argue that they are revealing the power undergirding unequal political, economic, and social global arrangements.

The notion that feminist IR theory is not addressing the "real" subject matter of IR is greeted with considerable consternation by IR feminists as a result. Feminist scholars have countered the disciplinary charge of trivialization with two arguments. First, any list of subjects deemed most relevant to the study of IR must take categories as given and therefore "completely misses the politics and power of conceptual definition and the relationship of concepts to understanding. Categories and concepts are not neutral" (Kinsella 2003: 296). Categories are instead value judgments that reflect specific interests and hierarchies of power, and to insist upon consensus regarding them is "a coercive strategy to relegate the interests of the less powerful to the margins" (Zalewski 1996: 350). Hence the very claim that the subject matter of IR involves studying things like interstate relations, national security, economic power, and IOs is itself problematic from a feminist perspective.

The second point feminist IR scholars have made about the standard subject matter of IR is that it tends to ignore the essential role that women play in all of its activities. Neither war nor trade would be possible without the participation of women, but because the discipline insists that women are "the 'background' that is never important enough to warrant being spotlighted—we in fact are unaware of what the background actually is and what relationships it actually has to the main story" (Peterson and Runyan 1999: 41). Women, both as physical presences and as categories of femininity, have been essential to IR undertakings such as waging war and the globalization of capitalism. Enloe's work (1993, 1990) demonstrates, for example, that

> women are always *inside* international relations through their work in the practice of its politics—as diplomats' wives and secretaries, as assemblers of commodities for export, as tourists bringing foreign exchange to the nearly empty tills of third world countries and dirty laundry for poor handmaids to wash, as consolers of soldiers based far from home, and wearers of khaki—if we choose to see them there. (Sylvester 1991–1992: 33, emphasis original)

Similarly, Elshtain's work (1994, 1992) on the politics of identity and war documents the extent to which war-making relies on civic identities for and sacrifices of both men and women. By failing to examine the everyday politics of IR, feminist scholars charge that the discipline has failed to appreciate how much IR relies on the subjugated role of women in order to operate.

Alternatively, feminist IR scholars argue that we should examine world politics through gender-sensitive lenses, because while other socially constructed categories, such as race, ethnicity, class, and nation, are also important, ultimately "gender structurally organizes not just sexual practices but virtually all aspects of social life in all cultures" (Peterson and

Runyan 1999: 31). Given what they describe as the discipline's gender bias, however, feminist scholars are not particularly optimistic that the discipline can or will change. Jan Jindy Pettman argues that IR is, "a male-dominated and masculinist discipline," because "particular understandings of masculinity infuse the discipline" that are "constructed out of the experiences and fears of (elite) men in or near the centers of global power" (2001: 255). Hence the title of Tickner's 1997 *International Studies Quarterly* article, "You Just Don't Understand: Troubled Engagements Between Feminists and IR Theorists," captures what feminist believe is the true relationship between IR feminism and the rest of the discipline.[3]

The difficulties that feminist IR scholars have encountered may also be attributed to the epistemological and ontological skepticism that all postpositivist perspectives have encountered in the discipline. Feminist scholarship may be at a dual disadvantage, however, if feminist scholars are correct that positivism is itself a gendered concept that relies on notions of rationality, objectivity, and truth that are masculine. Hence the discipline may discount gender analysis because it would "contaminate the fundamental and ostensibly neutral binaries of fact-value, problem solving–critical theory, and brute-social so beloved by international relations scholars and upon which claims are staked and careers are made" (Kinsella 2003: 297).

Such assertions have not gone unchallenged within the feminist literature itself, however, and it is important to underscore that not all feminist IR scholars are postpositivists.[4] There are a number of feminist theoretical variants that draw upon and reshape familiar analytical perspectives in IR, such as liberalism, postmodernism, critical theory, and neo-Marxist perspectives in general. Yet it can also be difficult to categorize IR feminist scholars because, despite important analytical disagreements, their practitioners have frequently experimented with the alternative ideas, methodologies, and epistemologies proposed by other variants. The result is that while some variants might be distinguished according to their substantive focus, they cannot easily be categorized according to epistemological commitments.

Postcolonial feminism, for example, focuses on the extent to which women of color are oppressed by the ideologies and practices of racism, colonialism, and capitalist imperialism. It draws upon Marxist feminism, which focuses on class inequalities, as well as from socialist feminism, which focuses on the interaction of patriarchy and capitalism, and it has relied upon both positivist and postpositivist epistemologies.[5] Even the development of what is considered an epistemology exclusive to feminism, standpoint feminism, cannot be assigned to any particular feminist IR variant. This epistemology seeks to illuminate the everyday experiences of the marginalized, on the assumption that "the perspective or standpoint of the outsider or the excluded, is likely to produce more objective knowledge than that of dominant groups whose ways of thinking fit all too closely with dominant institutions and conceptual schemes" (Tickner 1996: 456). By relying on narrative techniques and genealogies, standpointers situate knowledge, reveal its gendered construction, and link everyday gendering to global politics.

Standpoint narratives have been relied upon by postmodern feminism, which is "critical not just of gender dichotomies and categories but also of the concept of gender itself" because it "still contains within it traces of biological determinism and 'essentialism'" (Peterson and Runyan 1999: 175).[6] Standpoint narratives have also been utilized by liberal feminism, which is most often associated with positivism and has been criticized for taking gendered categories as givens and for emphasizing the goal of equal access to male-dominated spheres of influence. Yet most feminists also credit liberal feminism with having opened the door to radical feminist approaches because, as Peterson notes, "in many unanticipated ways, 'adding women' exposes the constructed nature of 'to what?' and disrupts many of the previously unquestioned foundations of Western discourse and its knowledge claims" (1992a: 10).

Liberal feminist IR scholars have also been willing to consider alternative analytical positions, and they "engage post-positivist insights when they link women's exclusion from political power to the undervaluing of women's responsibilities in the home and recognize that simply 'adding women' to formal power structures is insufficient for transforming male-defined structures" (Peterson and Runyan 1999: 28). This is precisely the point of Chapter 8.2, in which Julie Mertus continues to ask, "Where are the women?" but complements this question with standpoint narratives and a consideration of how gender roles have been defined by the IOs responsible for reconstructing Kosovo. Alternatively, in Chapter 8.3, Francine D'Amico draws upon a variety of postpositivist approaches, including postmodernism and critical theory, and blends a neo-Marxist focus on class with postcolonial feminism's emphasis on race and color. D'Amico does so in order to deconstruct the standard narratives of Kosovo and reveal their gendered assumptions and hierarchies.

While diversity is one of the hallmarks of feminist scholarship, common threads do run through the feminist IR literature. What unites all these feminisms into a common IR perspective is that they all investigate the extent to which the role of women and gender in political, economic, and social processes has been ignored within the discipline of IR. All of them question the extent to which the disregard for women and gender is licensed by claims to neutrality, objectivity, and value-free assessments of the world and how it functions. And all of them are committed to uncovering two myths about gender: "one is that divisions and differences assigned by gender are either 'god-given' or 'natural' and therefore out of the realm of political analysis; the other is that gender has nothing to do with international processes and events" (Zalewski 1995: 341). In revealing these assumptions as myths, the shared goal of feminist IR is to transform our ways of knowing and understanding the very subject to which we are committed as a discipline.

■ Further Reading

Unlike many other IR theoretical perspectives, there is no single, dominant scholar to whom the development of feminist IR theory can be credited. Instead a variety of scholars have been equally important in advancing the arguments of feminist scholarship in IR. Enloe is best known for her feminist standpoint argument in *The Morning After: Sexual Politics at the End of the Cold War* (1993) and *Bananas, Beaches, and Bases: Making Feminist Sense of International Politics* (1990). Other well-known IR feminist scholarship includes Elshtain's *Women and War* (1994; see also 1981); Sylvester's *Feminist Theory and International Relations in a Postmodern Era* (1994); and Tickner's *Gender in International Relations* (1992).

An accessible textbook on the subject is Peterson and Runyan's *Global Gender Issues* (1999). Zalewski has written a number of pertinent essays, with her "Well, What Is a Feminist Perspective on Bosnia?" (1995; see also 1996) being particularly appropos to this book. Other important feminist works include Moghadam 1993, Pettman 1996, and Stearns 1998. Seminal edited volumes of feminist scholarship include Beckman and D'Amico 1994, Cooke and Wollacott 1993, Grant and Newland 1991, Peterson 1992a, Turpin and Lorentzen 1996, and Zalewski and Parpart 1998. Also consult the special issues of *Millennium* devoted to the topic, such as "Women in IR" 1988 and "Gendering the International" 1998.

Examples of critical theory feminism, which apply a neo-Gramscian perspective to world politics, include Stienstra 1994 and Whitworth 1994. Liberal and empiricist feminism can be found in Kardam 1991, Karl 1995, Randall 1987, Schwartz-Shea and Burrington 1990, and Stiehm 1989. Two works that argue that feminism and peace should be equated are Ruddick 1989 and Brock-Utne 1985.

Postcolonial feminist works include Alexander and Mohanty 1997, Grewal and Kaplan 1994, Mohanty 1988, and Mohanty 1991. An example of the intersection between gender and development issues in IR, which Sylvester (1991–1992) points out has been inspired by world system theory, may be found in Smith et al. 1988. Other examples of standpoint feminism, besides the work of Enloe, include Hartsock 1983 (which introduced the term), Pateman 1988, and Mies 1986. Many of these works could be categorized in other ways, since the Mies source, for example, employs a socialist feminist framework, while the Hartsock source is a form of feminist historical materialism.

While I have concentrated on describing IR feminism in this introductory section, there is a vast body of interdisciplinary feminist literature upon which it relies. Two helpful overviews of and introductions to this literature are Tong 1998 and Lorber 1998. Finally, on the relationship between feminist theory, positivism, and postpostivism, consult Haraway 1989, Harding 1991, Harding 1986, and Peterson 1992b.

■ Notes

1. A sampling of this literature includes Berkin and Lovett 1980, Elshtain 1995, Elshtain 1994, MacDonald, Holden, and Ardener 1988, Tetreault 1994, and West 1987.

2. Joshua Goldstein has found, for example, that "culture directly influences the expression of genes and hence the biology of our bodies," and that "no universal biological essence of 'sex' exists, but rather a complex system of potentials that are activated by various internal and external influences" (2001: 2). Both Goldstein (2001) and Enloe (1993) have also noted the tremendous effort that is required to create the supposedly "natural" masculine military persona.

3. See also the follow-up forum to Tickner's piece, which included responses by Keohane, Marchand, and Tickner, in "Dialogue" 1998.

4. See, for example, Caprioli 2003, Carpenter 2002, and "Gender and International Relations" 2003.

5. The difference between Marxist and socialist feminism is that the latter "foreground[s] economic forces, revealing how capitalism and patriarchal gender relations interact to disadvantage women in the workplace and the home" (Peterson and Runyan 1999: 28). Radical feminism argues for autonomy from and rejection of male-defined norms and institutions, and it has in turn been influential in the development of postmodern feminism. Peterson and Runyan note that radical feminists might be further divided into "cultural feminists" and "ecofeminists," but what they share is the belief that "the politics of sexuality is paramount." They argue that a fundamental source of women's oppression is male domination of women's bodies and that "radical feminists have no interest in being equal to men, if being equal means becoming like or the same as male oppressors" (1999: 169–170). In addition to the feminist variants already discussed, one should add psychoanalytic feminism, which emphasizes the gendering role of the unconscious (see Gilligan 1982), and feminist empiricism, which is less a theoretical approach and involves collection of data on the status of women.

6. Sylvester also points out, however, that third world women have challenged the assumption that Western feminists will understand their standpoint or that the standpoints of particular women are representative of all women. "Whose standpoint, they implicitly ask, finds its way into feminist standpoint; whose tools of science reinforce Western-subject-centered otherness; and whose deconstructions are required to displace it?" (1991–1992: 35). Sylvester notes elsewhere that, while postmodern feminism does draw upon everydayness, "it understands experience, however, as mobile, indeterminate, hyphenated, homeless" (1996: 271).

Julie Mertus

Liberal Feminism: Local Narratives in a Gendered Context

Marysia Zalewski (1996) has observed the multiple usages of theory in the field of international relations: as a tool, as a critique, and as everyday experience. One intellectual tradition that exemplifies these three usages, but that has been marginalized in international politics, is liberal feminism. As this book demonstrates, there are many ways to analyze international relations problems. Studies based on liberal feminism uncover the subjectivity of traditional approaches to international relations by "searching for silences" and imagining the addition of "unheard voices." Feminist methods "emphasize conversations and dialogue rather than the production of a single, triumphant truth" (Charlesworth 1999b: 379). This approach has particular resonance as applied to Kosovo, an area where local voices have been eclipsed by international interests and truths remain contested (see Mertus 1999a).

To the field of international relations, liberal feminist critique contributes both a methodology and a deep normative critique. "While the crux of the term feminist is method," Katharine Bartlett explains, "there is a critical aspect of feminist method that is substantive in nature. Feminist method works from a hypothesis which, in its simplest terms, boils down to something like this: the circumstances of women are unjust in significant respects and ought to be improved" (1999: 34). The approach to IR "as it should be" must be responsive to women, reflect their experiences, and seek to transform their lives in a manner that recognizes individual agency and corrects disproportionate power imbalances (Slaughter and Ratner 1999: 416). The liberal feminist does draw on the traditional themes of liberal theory, stressing the importance of individual rights, the rule of law, and other supportive institutional mechanisms. But it is the combination of feminist methodology and normative critique that makes liberal feminism so useful in analysis and problem solving.

This chapter reads like no other in this book because, unlike other chapters, it employs feminist methodology. Feminist methodology includes personal experience as a theoretical starting point, narrative, contextual reasoning, and multiperspectivity (Schneider 1986). The application of feminist methodology distinguishes this chapter in four ways. First, even before I outline the theory, I begin with a note on my own personal experiences in Kosovo and throughout the text I value other narratives. Second, although I remain interested in the exercise of power at the "top" of the international arena, I understand world events by listening to local narratives and drawing lessons from "below." Thus, instead of focusing on such "big" actors and structures at the top—like NATO, the United States, the Yugoslav army—I look at the "little" actors and structures at the bottom—village women leaders, grassroots anticonscription organizations, and shoestring humanitarian efforts. Third, unlike other contributors to this book, I am interested not only in applying my assigned theory to the abstract issue of Kosovo, but also in how specific local actors use or resist the theory. Finally, because I am self-reflective and aware of the contested local contexts, I know that it is not enough to present liberal feminism absent a critique. Accordingly, this chapter also challenges traditional notions of liberal feminism and exposes shortcomings in its application to Kosovo.

■ The Starting Point for Feminist Methodology: Personal Narrative

It was the winter of 1994. With the master plans for genocidal conflict being promulgated just blocks away from our Belgrade flat, and with the gates of the decaying city opening only to admit despair and eject hope, I sat around a kitchen table with a group of women who tried to imagine the dawn of a just world.[1] "There would be no borders!" exclaimed one. "No police checkpoints!" another woman chimed in. It became a free-for-all. "No fighting militaries!" "No militaries at all!" "No, maybe just one military!" "No wars, no militaries!" "No passports!" "No green cards!" "Rights for women!" "Rights for gypsies!" "Rights for all minorities!" "Rights for everyone!" "No need for rights, equality for all!" The women around the kitchen table were of all ages and backgrounds—doctors, lawyers, journalists, psychologists, human rights investigators, and antiwar activists. We shared some common experiences, enough so that we had a familiar language and way of understanding, yet disagreed with each other on just about everything except for the need for more diverse participation in the international and local politics running our lives. The issue of Kosovo was a divisive one, but even the most nationalist among us vowed to work for peace. The electricity flickered off and on, and the grocery shelves were bare, but we were still filled with hope. "If only there were more women running things . . ." more than one activist was heard to say, fully aware of the power of women to inflict harm, but somehow convinced that the addition of our voices could make a difference.

It was the summer of 1998. The war in Bosnia had been over for nearly three years, but the low-intensity conflict that had been going on for a decade in Kosovo was now beginning to roar. Over 75,000 people had been displaced from their homes as Serbian forces flooded Kosovo and battles erupted between Serbs and Albanians. This time I was sitting around a kitchen table in Pristina, the dusty capital of Kosovo. The heady "can do" feeling of the women's activism that had, as in Belgrade, once infused Pristina, had long since dissipated. The doctor, nurse, journalist, student, and school teacher sitting around the table were as busy as ever, "doing something" to resist what they experienced as Serbian occupation, but their activities had become increasingly defensive—and grim. Instead of providing family planning education for girls and young women, they were counseling war-traumatized children and gathering emergency supplies for families trapped in the front lines. They were angry at their Serbian friends, who had not called or e-mailed—not even the ones who had come to visit when relations between Belgrade and Pristina women's groups thawed after the World Conference on Women in Beijing and the signing of the Dayton peace accord in 1995. "Maybe they are afraid," I suggested. "What do they know about fear?" the journalist snarled and the women erupted in agreement. "They don't care really." "They only care about themselves." "Everyone is first part of their nation and then a woman." With no hope left, the women turned to talking about what they would do when "the war begins." "I will send my sons out, but I will stay," one woman vowed. And that is exactly what she would do, becoming one of many women who was raped in the war of 1999.

As I look back on those and many other kitchen table sessions, I recognize that these groups of women sat far outside state structures, while powerful decisionmakers carried on, oblivious to their existence. Nonetheless, I came to understand that the "kitchen tablers" are central to understanding the larger issue of political and social conflict in Kosovo. By using the modes of governance that are part of transnational civil society, it is the kitchen tablers who try to shape the way people think about social-change issues. Kitchen tablers use the language of human rights treaties and seek the support of liberal state institutions, but in so doing shape the understanding of the words to fit their local lived realities. Thus, not only do kitchen tablers have access to liberal discourse as a tool to advance their claims, but to some extent also they *are* the discourse. The kitchen tablers, inundated with the demands of outsiders pressing a liberal agenda (from yesterday's warmongers to today's peacebuilders), have at their disposal various liberal feminist techniques, and their choice as to how to proceed shapes local and international understandings of liberal feminism. The insight I gained from the kitchen tablers informs the following outline of liberal feminism as well as its application.

■ The Theory and Its Applications

The theory and politics of liberal feminism are shaped by a conception of human nature, individual agency, and rationality identified with liberal political theory (Donnelly 1999: 81). Also known as bourgeois feminism, the theory "is grounded in the claims of the classical liberal philosophy developed by Locke, Rousseau, Bentham and Mill for equal rights, individualism, liberty and justice" (Andermahr, Lovell, and Wolkowitz 1997: 123). The notion of *progress* is important for liberals; liberals share a faith in the progressive unfolding of humankind's ability to reason and a belief that disputes can and should be resolved by recourse to rational argument. They urge that international relations can and should be regulated through fair application of universal laws. Beyond this, however, liberals disagree with one another on many key issues, including whether human nature is essentially benign and cooperative or sinful and competitive; the proper relationship between state and society; whether and when a state can intervene in another to promote international norms; the proper weighing of the shared values of community against liberal tolerance; and the role of capitalist markets and free trade in securing justice and peace (Smith 1993).

The diversity of liberal thinking has accommodated many feminists with different informing ideologies and agendas, but with a belief that women's equality with men may be promoted through a system of legally enforceable individual rights (Vincent 1986: 152). Here lies the radical potential of liberalism for women advancing their claims under a rights framework. Women are empowered as capable subjects of the law (and not mere objects), and states (and in some cases other duty bearers) are burdened with the duty to recognize and respond appropriately to their demands.

The idea of individual rights necessitates recognition of the agency and identity of the individual that may exist apart from the community (Donnelly 1999: 81). Nonetheless, the liberal recognition of individual worth does not negate the importance of communal life. Individuals are not free-floating entities; they exist and gain meaning through social relationships and communal responsibilities and duties (Brown 1999). Identification and enforcement of the individual rights of women depends greatly on community (Cahill 1980: 284). Thus a liberal feminist agenda may very well incorporate a communal orientation along with recognition of the rights of individuals within communities.

Three feminist approaches to international relations problems that have relevance to the case study at hand can be identified (see table 8.2.1). While the first approach is most commonly identified with liberal feminism, both the second and third approaches have been used by liberal feminists who blend the liberal emphasis on individual rights and institution building with more structural critiques of women's subordination.

Where are the women? That is the question most associated with liberal feminism. This first approach, characteristic of "equality" feminists,

Table 8.2.1   Feminist Approaches to International Relations Problems

Problem	Explanation	Solution	Long-Term Result
Women invisible (unless same as men)	Men run world; men run IR; women's role not valued	Add women	See women; value women
Way of "being in" world distorted (in a manner that obscures gender power): who counts, what counts, how the game is played	"Male lens"	Use of descriptive gender lens/"gender perspective"	Transform ontology; expose constructed nature of difference; expose gender power
Way of "knowing" world distorted (constitutive concepts incomplete): state, sovereignty, security, development, power/authority	Process of acquiring knowledge; political; informed by ideology	Add gender as a tool of analysis; reorient top-down approach; link to other analyses of domination/ subordination	Transform epistemology; expose political nature of methodologies; generate demands for change

looks for the ways in which women are "invisible" in international relations analysis, unless, that is, they are "like men" and play male roles (e.g., Margaret Thatcher or Madeleine Albright). The explanation for this problem has been articulated variously as (1) "men run the world," thus there simply are few women in the kinds of positions that matter in international relations; (2) there are women who should be made visible, but men run the field of international relations and they will not or cannot see women; or (3) women have been there in the international relations landscape all along, but their role has been undervalued and thus overlooked. In the case of Kosovo, this would mean not only identifying women occupying positions of power traditionally reserved for men—for example, noting Edita Tahiri's influential role in Ibrahim Rugova's government[2]—but also valuing women wholly apart from men, and recognizing as important actors in international politics the women that others overlook—the village school teacher, the urban female doctor (see, e.g., Enloe 2000).

A liberal feminist examining the landscape of a transitional society like Kosovo would note the absence of women in positions of power and stress the consequences of the failure of local and international actors to take into account women's differing interests, skills, and expectations (see Mertus 2000b). The most simplistic IR policy prescription furthered by liberal feminism has been characterized as "add women and stir," the notion that inclusion of females satisfies feminist demands for equality. In other words, all we need is more women everywhere, but particularly in decisionmaking positions in the space identified as public.

The second feminist approach moves beyond "adding women" and finds that the orienting assumptions of international policy analysts—their very way of being in the world—is distorted in a manner that privileges men. Zalewski has observed that the issues deemed important and relevant in international relations, assumptions about who and what counts and how the game is played, reflect the interests of the powerful (i.e., the masculine) while the less powerful (i.e., the feminine) are pushed to the margins (1995: 350). The explanation for this problem of ontology is the use of a male or masculine lens that accepts differences as natural and overlooks the deeply embedded impact of patriarchy. "That there are these differences [between men and women] is undeniable," Zalewski urges, "but what really matters, in terms of effects on people's lives, is how these differences are interpreted and acted upon" (1995: 344). The use of a gender perspective thus "can be used to challenge dominant assumptions about what is significant or insignificant, or what are central or marginal concerns" in Kosovo (Stearns 1998: 5). For example, a gender-sensitive ontological status would encourage analysis of the impact of state-condoned "public" violence on violence within Kosovar families and, conversely, the influence of identities and values fostered in family life on the existence of "public" violence. Furthermore, attention to women as the leading cultural transmitters within Kosovo would help us to understand how individual and collective identities and sociocultural meaning systems that support violent conflict are (re)produced and resisted (Peterson 2000: 18).

The third feminist approach finds that the dominant approach to understanding international problems is distorted by an epistemological orientation that relies on a set of inadequate claims about the world. The typical top-down analysis focuses on states, sovereignty, security, power, and conflict and overlooks individuals, social movements, cooperation, and human relations. At the same time, the significance of these constructs in relationship to women's subordination is obscured. The explanation for the shortcomings, J. Ann Tickner has asserted, is that "knowledge constructed in terms of binary distinctions such as rational/emotional, objective/subjective, global/local, and public/private, where the first term is often associated with masculinity, the second with femininity, automatically devalue certain types of knowledge" (2001: 133). The mere adoption of a gender perspective will not correct the epistemological bias. The political nature of the construction of knowledge must be interrogated and challenged. The goal of this more radical gender analysis in Kosovo would be to transform epistemological orientations and in so doing uncover *and challenge* sites of power (Scott 1991) and domination and expose *and challenge* the apolitical nature of methodological assumptions (Hirschmann 1992). Beyond mere description, a gender analysis for Kosovo would "generate demands for change, for satisfaction of women's needs" (Cockburn 2001: 15).

Each of these three approaches, outlined in Table 8.2.1, holds some utility both for our understanding of Kosovo and for Kosovars' self-understanding. How would a liberal feminist begin to apply these approaches? Quite likely he or she would look at specific narratives from the field and, in so doing, ask such questions as: Where are the women? How does conflict impact men and women differently? What are the skills, interests, and expectations that the men and women bring to addressing this conflict?[3]

■ Two Narratives

Flora, June 1998

In one of the walled gardens in Pristina, the provincial capital of Kosovo, Flora sits patiently on a stone bench fiddling with a picture book.[4] The five-year-old's left leg is propped up with a large pillow; two wooden bars prevent her from moving her knee. A piece of a grenade has been in her knee for over a month. Her doctor cautioned that movement may cause the metal to sever her nerve permanently. Flora, along with some 100,000 ethnic Albanians, was driven out of her home in the spring of 1998 by Serbian forces in Kosovo. The local hospital would not treat her, but a private surgeon offered to do what he could for free. It was not enough. The shrapnel remains. The best he could recommend was another surgeon in Macedonia, but the road to Macedonia is blocked by fighting militia. Her face pale with pain, Flora waits for someone to tell her what will come next.

The girl's thirty-one-year-old mother, Hedije, and fifty-five-year-old grandmother, Hajrije, take care of the other children in a small basement room: the newborn who arrived after the family had fled their home in Decan and who sits in a corner swaddled in borrowed blankets, and the vivacious two-and-a-half-year-old girl who keeps the entire family awake with her nightmares. Hajrije apologizes for the children's old clothes: "We had everything before," she says. "I had bought the baby such beautiful new things and we left them all behind." They had left in the night in their slippers when Serbs began shelling their home. "We had three stores on the main street," the woman sighs, "and now they are completely gone." When asked about the young men in the family, she says they have gone back to look after the livestock, but everyone knows they stayed to fight. No one has heard from them in over two months.

Hedije's eyes are red from tears and exhaustion. She was nine months pregnant when she fled on foot from Decan to the village of Ismiq. It was there that five Serbian policemen gave her a ride to the hospital in Peja (Pec) to give birth. While she was in the delivery room, another group of police beat up her husband in the waiting room, accusing him of lying about his wife's pregnancy. Within minutes of giving birth, with the placenta still attached, Hedije was wheeled into the hospital waiting room to prove to the police that she had indeed been pregnant; only then did the police stop beating her husband.

The next day, she returned to the village, and it was there that she heard Flora's piercing scream that "just would not stop." Hedije is apologetic: "I didn't know she was hit, I thought she was only afraid. But then I saw the blood." Hedije made a makeshift tourniquet to stop the bleeding and waited for some neighbors to bring a doctor. Flora had her first surgery on the floor of a house in Iqmiq. Hedije is apologetic again: "We thought it was done. We didn't know why she still had pain. We didn't know there was more inside her knee and that it could move to her nerve." The family used a horse cart to move the children to Pristina, with the women walking alongside it.

Hedije is quick to point out that they are among the lucky ones because they have a safe place to live now, with a nice host family. While many displaced Kosovar Albanians live with relatives, even more, like this family, are dependent on others for shelter. Pristina is the family's third place of refuge in three months. They had to leave the first two places because of Serb shelling; both of those villages, previously 100 percent ethnic Albanian, are now uninhabitable and controlled by Serbs. They had first stayed in Pristina in the apartment of Hedije's sister, a student at the private (and officially illegal) Kosovar Albanian university. But that was a tiny apartment across the street from the police station in the city center and Hedije spent all her time trying to hush the children. She was afraid to open the windows, lest the neighbors hear their cries. When she sought medical care at the Center for the Protection of Women and Children, a Kosovar Albanian nongovernmental humanitarian organization, they suggested a room with a host family. The host family itself depends upon aid from the Kosovar Albanian solidarity fund to get by from month to month, so it could offer little except space and moral support.

Marta, March 1999

Marta stands less than four and a half feet tall and looks more like a child than a woman in her late thirties. She flashes a smile and has a kind word for everyone we meet on the street; everyone greets her with overwhelming respect. It takes us a long time to reach the cafe where Marta can relax and remember:

The first day the NATO planes began to bomb was on the 24th of March, a Wednesday. Our villages were surrounded with military and Serbian police. On Thursday, the houses began to burn [in the village Krusha e Vogel]. We who were on the other side of the River Drini saw what was happening. There was smoke and flames, rising and spreading.

That same morning a family came down our road on a tractor. They were from that village on fire. They did not have the words to explain how they escaped. All they could say is a policeman came and told them to go across the river and get out of the village. They were shaken and scared. I took them into my family's home and I was scared about what was happening.

On Friday morning, the houses were still burning. From the front door of my mother's house I could see a lot of people leaving the village and heading toward the river. People in my village were scared to do anything. I told my mother that I must go help. She pled with me to stay, but I insisted. My brother got our tractor and went with me.

When we got down to the river, we saw that they were all women and children—some very small children, some babies. They were crying, shouting. At the moment we got closer, everyone began to scream, "please help us, please help us." They told us that for two days and two nights, forces had surrounded their village. During this time, the people didn't have food, didn't have water, and their houses were burning. The police separated the women and children from their men. They threw them out of their homes. The police directed the women to take their children and go drown them and themselves in the river.

At that moment I was no longer afraid. I knew what we had to do. The people all wanted to get on the tractor at the same time. So I said, "Do not be afraid, we can take you all." I stayed on the far side of the river bank and helped women and children to get onto my brother's tractor. He drove them to the other side. Eventually, some other people from our village came with tractors and began to help. And, back and forth and back and forth like this . . . we brought over about 500 of them. The river was deep, strong and very cold. We were afraid the whole time that someone would fall in or that the water would rise too high and swallow the tractors.

After about an hour and a half, almost everyone was at the other side. There was one very old woman walking with two younger women and three children. They weren't yet at the river. I went to get them. At that moment, police started to lob grenades over us. I told them to keep moving and somehow we got them over the river.[5]

Marta learned later that Serbian police and paramilitary had attempted to murder all 120 of the men in the village. Some were tied and burned alive in their houses; others were shot execution-style in mass pits. Two men escaped the massacre by feigning death while the other bodies were piled on top of them. After the military left, they crawled from underneath their dead friends and ran to Marta's village. Less than two days later, the entire village fled across the mountains into Albania.

When the NATO bombing ended, the women from Krusha e Vogel returned as soon as they could. They discovered a ghost town. All of their

Serb neighbors had fled. While every Serbian house remained standing, Albanian homes had been razed to the ground. Picking through the scarred landscape, the women found the charred remains of many of their men. In a rage, the women set fire to the Serbian homes, burning them to the ground. The next thing they did was to make makeshift homes for themselves and learn how to perform the farming tasks normally undertaken by men. With the help of a local women's group that was founded during the war and funded by Western European donors, the women learned how to drive and became proficient in running their own farms.

Although a handful of men have returned and a few boys have matured to manhood, the village remains populated largely by women and children. Although life is hard, by all accounts the women are doing extremely well. In contrast to the prewar times, women have enhanced decisionmaking authority in village life. Among their successful business ventures, they grow grapes, which are shipped to Slovenia and bottled under a Slovenian label. They also run a driving school in nearby Prizren, operate a small library, and staff a women's center that, among other purposes, serves—in the words of one teenager—"as a place just to be and to be sad." Although the education level of girls remains low compared with that of boys, more girls are enrolled in school for longer periods of time than prior to the war. Moreover, contact with visiting journalists and humanitarian assistance workers has created greater awareness among women as to the larger legal, social, and political issues affecting their lives.

■ Analysis

Approach 1: Where Are the Women?

The first question the liberal feminist following the traditional framework would ask is: Where are the women in Kosovo narratives? By looking closely at these stories we can see the roles they play as mothers, nurses, victims, saviors, revenge arsonists, and war survivors. For each role we can identify the specific needs, interests, and skills that flow from occupying that position. This helps us to understand the women not as victims, but rather as complex actors with agency to make decisions regarding their own lives.

Identifying where women are in the narratives underscores where they are not. Women are certainly not at the negotiating table. Women were not included in the decision to begin the violence in the first place, nor were they involved in the decisions as to when and how to make peace. Would the addition of women have exerted any significant impact upon the outcome of the negotiations? Opinions vary on whether women negotiate differently from men and the consequences of any such differences. There can be no definitive response regarding the impact of including women in decisionmaking on the initiation and cessation of violence. We can see from the above individual narratives that women are not necessarily pure and peace-loving. They are both subjected to violence and, as witnessed in the revenge house burnings in Marta's narrative, capable of committing violence.

Liberal feminists, however, would emphasize a question of gender equity and stress its impact on democracy. Strengthening equal participation of women and men is the right thing to do on a moral level, because we value equality. But also, more equal participation is instrumentally desirable, as participation strengthens democracy. Moreover, because women experience conflict differently from men, they bring different skills, interests, and needs to conflict analysis and problem solving; excluding women is not in the interests of anyone. The women of Kosovo, like women in most parts of the world, have primary responsibility for taking care of children and elders and thus they are the best ones to consult on these issues. But also, liberal feminists remind us, it is women who have staffed the majority of human rights and humanitarian nongovernmental organizations (NGOs) (although the chief leader in these NGOs is most often male). The inclusion of women would offer a wider range of expertise and thus would invite deeper analysis of priorities and strategies for reconstruction.

What is the impact of conflict on these women's lives? This traditional liberal feminist approach would look largely at the individual level for evidence of impact. Among the issues this approach would identify from the narratives are personal violence, including rape and other forms of sexual violence; sexual and reproductive health issues and needs, including prenatal and new baby care; trauma from witnessing or participating in violence; and psychosocial impacts such as loss of identity and degrading of self-esteem flowing from changes in roles and relationships within family and community (el-Bushra 2000: 77). The international and domestic nongovernmental and governmental organizations in Kosovo have in fact embarked on a myriad of projects addressing these issues. For each step of the reform process, feminists have wondered where the women are and have pushed for the inclusion of more women in decisionmaking positions in both international and domestic institutions (Kvinna Till Kvinna 2001).

The liberal feminist approach, however, has never been allowed to reach its potential, as implementation has been flawed. Instead of including women on an equal basis with men in the peacebuilding project, the international community has ghettoized Kosovar women into "women's projects," spanning from women's microcredit enterprises, to postagreement trauma counseling, to women's health care projects, to women political leadership training.[6] An audit of these projects conducted by Rachel

Wareham and Diana Quick (2001) found them severely underfunded and often misdirected. In education, for example, UNMIK has focused on rebuilding damaged schools, but given little priority to girls' attendance. Women and girls have also almost exclusively been offered gender-stereo-typed training such as hairdressing and sewing, rather than training in wider skills proposed by themselves or by local women's NGOs, such as women's publishing presses or architecture firms (Abdela 2000). The liber-al feminist goal of enhancing women's political participation has also failed to achieve its objectives in Kosovo. Ironically, women have fared better in obtaining representation in purely local institutions than in international or mixed international/local institutions (Kvinna Till Kvinna 2001).

The promise of the liberal approach of "adding women" to positions of authority in the public sector rests in the "spillover effect." This is the idea that the positive inclusion of women in the public sector will impact cultur-al attitudes and thus influence the treatment of women in the private sphere. With local women virtually excluded from sites of power in the Kosovo reconstruction project, the spillover effect has been largely negative. The lesson the international community provides to the general public is that exclusion of women is an acceptable norm. The one area, however, where the spillover effect seems to be working is in the inclusion of women in the local police force.

As of 2001 roughly 19 percent of the local police were female (Kvinna Till Kvinna, 2001). When I interviewed Kosovar men in the summer of 2000 about the new policy, they responded with such comments as: "Can you believe she pulled me over [for speeding] and I had to stop!" "I used to never respect a police officer, but now look at them, they are so profession-al!" and "Police used to work with machine guns here, now they use their minds." While skeptical of the ability of women to work as police in crowd control and other dangerous situations, Kosovar men believed they could bring "dignity" and "professionalism" to policing (Kvinna Till Kvinna 2001). These answers support the theory that adding women (in this case to policing) can prove more radical than first appearances suggest; adding women may influence individual consciousness and eventually bring about cultural change. The problem then may rest in the implementation of liberal feminist ideas, but not in the ideas themselves.

Approach 2: What Are the Roots of Oppression?

This approach goes beyond adding women and tries to rethink the assump-tions informing who wins and who loses. Instead of adding women and cre-ating "special" programs for them, this approach demands that international organizations adopt a gender perspective to address the socially constructed roles of men and women and thus expose the very root of exploitation and domination of women and challenge the institutions that perpetuate inequality (see Mertus 2000b: 15). Instead of just meeting the individual needs of the women in the narratives (such as the need to be free from violence and to have shelter and basic medical care), this approach would require thinking about *why* those needs exist in the first place. Who wins and who loses as long as those needs continue to arise? How do seemingly neutral norms and behaviors exclude or disadvantage women?

A gender perspective would invite examination of a broader set of issues, as it would recognize that conflict impacts not only women's individual needs, but also hierarchical social relations within the household. In times of violent conflict, women's reproductive role may be expanded, as women are literally expected to replenish the nation, the quality of marital relationships may deteriorate, and forced marriage and prostitution may become more common (el-Bushra 2000: 77). This approach also encourages recognition of the continuities between wartime and peacetime. All violence against women or men—in war or peacetime—can be understood as gendered phenomena within the context of patriarchal social relations (Kelly 2000). And all violence against women or men—in war or peacetime—can be "situated analytically within a 'sexual violence' approach" (Jacobs, Jacobson, and Marchbank 2000: 4). In the case of the narratives, we thus would want to inquire about the existence of violence in both war and peacetime and to try to understand the gender differences that have an impact on power relations within society.

Adopting a gender perspective, feminist activists in Kosovo have pressed for greater attention to violence within the family, to forced prostitution and the trafficking in women (and the role of internationals), and in general to increased consideration for the roles women play within family life (Kvinna Till Kvinna 2001; Mertus 1999b). These projects have met with some degree of success in attracting donor dollars[7] and, like the introduction of women into policing, may play a long-term role in transforming social attitudes toward women. However, family and criminal law reforms have been hampered by larger structural problems. In particular, the delay in establishing a functioning legal system has effectively allowed some existing laws to remain in force, or allowed customary law, which treats women very poorly, to take precedence over statutory law (Wareham and Quick 2001).

In practice, while the adoption of a gender perspective has been conducive to a better identification of the issues and description of the problem, it has rarely led to transformative institutional and programmatic change on gender issues in international and domestic institutions. A study of the reconstruction in Kosovo conducted by Chris Corrin in 2000 aptly illustrates the continued failure of humanitarian organizations to address gender concerns fully and consistently and to integrate local and international women in decisionmaking positions in program formation, adoption, and implementation. The main problem is that processes of gender main-streaming have not been "two-way (i.e., happening within international and local structures) and transparent" (Corrin 2000). While some organizations have examined their own management practices, most of the changes have been focused on overseas activities. And despite well-honed gender policy statements at headquarters and the pronounced desire for programmatic changes, overseas activities continue to approach gender unevenly and largely without the valuing of local expertise.

Approach 3:
How Does the Way We Know the World Limit Us?

To push a more normatively driven gender analysis that values local knowledge and generates demands for change, local and international feminists have also utilized a third feminist approach, challenging epistemological orientations. For example, they ask such questions as: What is violence? What is security? What is war? Who has the authority to define these terms? They criticize reliance on the state as *the* unit of analysis and of the realist notion of power as *control over* others, and suggest the centrality of other transstate and substate actors and invoke the concept of power as *cooperation*. The way in which the women in our narratives worked together for the common good illustrates the cooperative exercise of power.

Kosovo feminists, while welcoming the liberal rights agenda and supporting the creation of international tribunals to prosecute war crimes, have questioned overreliance on rights and the efficacy of the delivery of justice through adversarial proceedings. Instead of these state-focused measures, some feminists have argued for more of a focus below the state: the empowerment of individual women and communities of survivors, the encouragement of cross-communal dialogue, cooperative memory projects, and grassroots truth-finding mechanisms (Mertus 2004). Other feminists have sought to move beyond the state: in networking with other individuals and organizations outside their own state borders, local feminists have influenced human rights fact-finding, advocacy, and negotiation, and impacted delivery of economic assistance.[8]

In moving away from the state, Kosovar feminists have broken from liberal feminism and have joined those who assert that women stand to benefit as state borders break down and sovereignty becomes more fragmented and textured over time. These theorists expose the ways in which the maintenance and expansion of the territorially bounded state relies in large part on the silencing and suppression of women (see Peterson 1992a, 1992b). Iris Marion Young explains this sentiment: "Founded by men, the modern state and its public realm of citizenship paraded as universal values and norms which were derived from specifically masculine experience: militaristic norms of honor and homoerotic camaraderie; respectful competition and bargaining among independent agents; discourse framed in unemotional tones of dispassionate reason" (1990: 120).

One insight from critics of liberal feminism is that states are patriarchal institutions not only because they exclude women from decisionmaking, but also because they are based on the concentration of power in an elite and the legitimization of a monopoly on the use of force to maintain that control (Charlesworth, Chinkin, and Wright 1991: 622; see also Charlesworth and Chinkin 2000). Even if state institutions do not overtly discriminate against women, they effectively exclude or inhibit women's participation by adopting a male worldview as the standard by which behavior is judged (Tickner 1992: 64). International institutions are viewed as "functional extensions of states" that are similarly based on male norms (Tickner 1992: 64), and thus Kosovar feminists view these institutions with skepticism as well. The movement away from the inviolable state to a more permeable and fluid entity thus opens new opportunities for the dismantling of the institutionalized subordination of women in international law, international institutions, and their processes (Knop 1993).

By focusing both below and above the state, Kosovar feminists have affected a shift in the loci for formation of rights or duties, decisionmaking, and law enforcement from a space controlled exclusively by the state to one influenced by other entities. This change is not without its drawbacks. The shift in power from the state to transsovereign private and corporate sectors could become another way to exclude women's participation in decisionmaking. V. Spike Peterson and Anne Runyan (1999: 104) worry that women have little influence over the international governmental organizations that control their lives. The increased devaluation of the public sector at the state level greatly reduces the political space for women to gain power and use it to promote equality. The goal, Peterson and Runyan have suggested, should be maintaining and reimagining state boundaries, not dismantling them altogether. Organizing to address the gender issues facing displaced men and women thus entails working with states, not against them, and strengthening state responsibilities and capacities, not weakening them (see, e.g., Romany 1994).

As if taking a page from Peterson and Runyan, feminists in Kosovo have chosen a pragmatic political strategy that draws on their experiences and skills and essentially utilizes all three of the feminist approaches described in this chapter. Even as they have demanded the addition of women into the liberal reform agenda, they have challenged the male lens that dominates the reform landscape and pushed for radical social and cultural transformation to end the subjugation of women. The result is a liberal focus on individual rights and democratic institutions, but with a distinctly critical Kosovar flavor. As Igballa Rugova wrote in a memo on behalf of the Kosova Women's Network to the heads of UNMIK and the OSCE mission in Kosovo: "We are doing it our way, because we know how to make it happen."[9]

■ Conclusion

Liberal feminism offers both a method and substance for analyzing international relations problems. As Bartlett has pointed out, if feminism is viewed in terms of method, policy analysts are feminist so long as they ask the right kinds of questions to the right kinds of people. This entails valuing the lived experiences of the little guys. As substance, however, liberal feminism refers to the answers feminists get. "Within this view, analysis of conflict and the proposals that follow are feminist only if they conform to whatever substantive criteria are attached to the term," explains Bartlett (1999: 32). For the liberal feminist, this means advancement of women's rights through rights-protecting institutions and other endeavors to advance women's equitable share of power in relation to men.

■ Notes

1. A longer version of this story appears in Mertus 2000a.

2. Edita Tahiri was long the most influential woman in the dominant Kosovar political party.

3. Looking at specific narratives from the field is beneficial because it not only provides background for applying the three feminist approaches discussed here, but also provides an example of how to apply a narrative feminist methodology to this and other conflicts: listen to the local narrative. The drawback is that it may be viewed as space consuming, and it might lead a reader to believe that these two cases represent the totality of women's experiences in Kosovo and the limits of liberal feminists' interest in Kosovo. Rather, women's experiences in Kosovo are extremely varied and liberal feminists are interested in all aspects of the Kosovo scenario.

4. This information is based on my field research in Kosovo in May–June 1998, which was funded by the Women's Commission for Refugee Women and Children. It appeared as an internal report for the commission in July 1988.

5. Author interview with anonymous, Krusha e Vogel, Kosovo, August 2001. "Marta" is not her real name.

6. See, for example, "Terms of Reference: Office of Gender Affairs, United Nations Interim Administration in Kosovo," November 3, 2000 (on file with author); and STAR Network, http://www.worldlearning.org/star.

7. See, for example, OSCE-sponsored programs addressing domestic violence, available online at http://www.osce.org/kosovo/features/in_focus/safe_house.php3.

8. Author e-mail correspondence with Rachel Wareham, October 2001; author interview with Igballa Rugova, Pristina, Kosovo, August 2001; author interview with Serdie Ahmeti, Colby College, Maine, November 2001.

9. Author interview with Igballa Rugova, Pristina, Kosovo, August 2001.

Critical Feminism: Deconstructing Gender, Nationalism, and War

Feminist scholars of international relations ask different kinds of questions than do realists, who see powerful states competing in an anarchic international system, or pluralists/liberal internationalists, who focus on states, international organizations, and nonstate group actors cooperating in an evolving international community. Feminist inquiry requires that we begin our analysis of international relations by focusing on living, breathing, in-the-flesh people: Who are the people who "do" international relations? A critical feminist perspective argues that traditional theoretical approaches to the study of IR respond to this question in ways that are deeply gendered. For realists, the people who "people" IR are statesmen and soldiers, that is, political leaders of powerful states and the armies they command; for pluralists/liberal internationalists, leaders and soldiers are joined by diplomats from intergovernmental organizations and managers from multinational corporations. Most of the people who occupy these positions of power worldwide are male: this vision of international relations might be represented by a "Men at Work" highway sign.

Liberal feminist approaches to the study of IR shift our focus to "Women at Work" in these power positions. Critical feminist perspectives shift our attention even further to "Gender at Work," that is, to consider how gender shapes the kinds of decisions made by those who occupy these power positions and the effects of their choices. A critical feminist perspective on Kosovo asks: How are the causes, conduct, and consequences of this conflict gendered? Critical perspectives also ask how other "dimensions of difference," like race/ethnicity, shape power relations and decisions and thus affect people's lives.

The study of international relations is essentially the study of power. Traditional or mainstream IR analysts define power narrowly as the relative military might of states or as a combination of military and economic capacity. These traditional approaches are content to consider who has power and how they use it. Critical perspectives broaden the definition of power to include both international and interpersonal power, and they explore how power is acquired or lost. They ask how the structures of power came to be and who benefits or is hurt by them. To do this, critical theorists use a variety of analytic techniques or tools, including deconstruction and discourse analysis. They ask: Whose fight is it? Whose law is it? Who is a "citizen"? What kind of language—literally, what choice of words—do we use to talk about power? Nationalism? Intervention? Why these words and not others? What implicit meanings or significance do these terms have? What images do they invoke? Critical feminist analysis uses the tools of critical theory to focus our attention on gender as an organizing principle for the distribution of power in international relations.[1]

Critical feminist perspectives developed from critiques of the liberal feminist approach to international relations. As Julie Mertus points out in Chapter 8.2, a liberal feminist approach tends to focus on women only, seeing gender merely as a descriptor, that is, as an attribute of individuals like height, weight, or political party identification. Liberal feminism sees women as atomistic, autonomous individuals. To get us to look past the traditional "Men at Work" in IR sign, Cynthia Enloe asks us to begin by considering the question "Where are the women?" (1990: 7), which appears to be a liberal feminist question. However, Enloe observes that power "infuses all international relationships" and that ignoring women "on the landscape of international politics perpetuates the notion that certain power relations are merely a matter of taste and culture," while "paying serious attention to women can expose how much power it takes to maintain the international political system in its present form" (1990: 2–3). Looking for women in international relations uncovers a gendered dimension of power that we did not previously see. Liberal feminists advocate paying attention to women in or adding women to existing structures of power; critical feminists reveal the conceptual foundations of those power structures and advocate their demolition.

Critical feminist perspectives expand the conceptualization of gender by asking, "Which women?" From this perspective, international relations is a series of intersecting power hierarchies constructed and maintained to advantage, privilege, or benefit those at the top of each hierarchy and to disadvantage, subordinate, or harm those at the bottom. We call these hierarchies "dimensions of difference." Gender is just one of the perceived differences among people that society says "makes a difference," that is, that determines who gets valued or devalued, who gets valorized or victimized. Yet there are multiple dimensions of difference in every society, and people can occupy positions of privilege on one dimension, such as gender, and yet be disadvantaged on another dimension, such as race/ethnicity. For example, gender and ethnicity combined in Kosovo to give Serbian men political power and to exclude Albanian men from that power; gender and ethnicity also combined to protect some women from sexual assault by men from their own ethnic group but to make other women targets because of their different ethnic identity. A critical feminist perspective allows us to grasp the diversity of both women's and men's lived experiences and to view the entire power matrix in and across societies rather than just one dimension, that is, gender.

In considering the conflict in Kosovo through a critical feminist lens, we ask: How are concepts of gender and other dimensions of difference mobilized to frame our understandings of Kosovo? How have these concepts constructed community identities and policy strategies? What images of Kosovar women and men are portrayed in the narratives produced by the media and by policymakers? Which women and men do we see and hear? What are their experiences? Whose stories and voices are unheard? How are these images used to support a particular agenda for responding to the conflict and for reconstructing Kosovar society? Understanding how gender and other dimensions of difference shaped the situation in Kosovo can help us to examine how the "lessons" learned in Kosovo may be (mis)applied to other contemporary conflicts and make us more cautious in our evaluation of "scripts" for intervention in places like Afghanistan and Iraq.

■ Where Are the Women . . . and Men?
Media Images of the Kosovo Conflict

When we ask Enloe's question "Where are the women" in the story of Kosovo, we find that what is most conspicuous is their relative absence from positions of power. None of the political or military leaders of the parties in the conflict were women. Few of the diplomats, negotiators, soldiers, insurgents, or peacekeepers were women, and the few women professionals who do appear in the narrative are often in gender-traditional roles. The story of Kosovo has a cast of thousands, yet only a handful of women are visible in the official narrative, mainly in gendered roles of victim, witness, or refugee: women are symbols of suffering, family, and community.

The starting point for liberal feminist inquiry is individual women, so liberal feminist analysts begin by looking for women among the decision-makers in the Kosovo conflict. But women policymakers and high-ranking diplomats are few and far between in the story of Kosovo: the most prominent women in the media accounts were US secretary of state Madeleine Albright and chief prosecutor for the ICTY Carla del Ponte. Critical feminist analysis reads these few women as "tokens," appointed to give the process an *appearance* of gender inclusiveness but who, by their very visibility, only highlight the relative absence of women at every policy decision level. A critical feminist perspective also observes that the participation of a few elite women in some far-removed aspect of the policy process provides little representation for Kosovar and Serbian women living (and dying) in the conflict zone. Their voices were heard neither in the

Kosovar, Serbian, and NATO strategy rooms nor in the UN Security Council.

Critical feminist analysis notes that other women in international leadership positions in the story of Kosovo are in gender-traditional "caretaker" roles, that is, people responsible for or engaged in relief or refugee work, such as Margaret O'Keefe, director of UN refugee operations in Kosovo in Belgrade; Julia Taft, US assistant secretary of state for refugees in Washington, D.C.; and Morgan Harris, a representative of the UN Refugee Commission Office (Perlez 1998d). Their participation in these positions is seen by policymakers and portrayed by the media as normal or "natural" rather than exceptional, reflecting an essentialized vision of what it means to be a "woman" working in international relations. Relief work and refugee assistance are "homemaking" on a global scale. This is not to say that this work is not vitally necessary, only to observe that our ideas about gender "assign" certain tasks to women (caring) and other tasks to men (soldiering), such that we do not see the gendered pattern until the tasks are reversed, namely "woman soldier" versus "male nurse." This is the power of gender: it makes what are really decisions about "who does what" seem natural and inevitable, so that few people question the rationale behind or the consequences of these assignments.

In examining media reports about the conflict in Kosovo, what is most noticeable is not women leaders in prominent political or decisionmaking roles but rather women in the conflict zone in three categories: victim, witness, and refugee. Women are made visible as victims in the recurrent phrase "women, children, and the elderly"—that is, they are among society's vulnerable, unarmed civilians: they are the objects of action rather than actors or agents in their own right (Perlez 1998d). Contrast these portrayals with those of men, who appear as independent actors as soldiers or terrorists/insurgents, depending upon the political sympathies of the individual journalist or particular media outlet. In this gendered conceptualization of conflict, men kill and are killed because they have some measure of power to fight; women are either evacuated or killed because they are powerless. Women's casualties in war evoke an emotive response, while the deaths of men are taken for granted, given, expected. We read of men's sacrifice versus women's slaughter. In the media coverage on Kosovo, images of women as victims were pervasive: women are pregnant, mutilated, voiceless bodies, atrocity stories, illustrations of the human face and cost of war (see, e.g., Perlez 1998e). Their vulnerability to rape, a tactic employed extensively by the Serb forces, required that they be given safe passage from the conflict zone; their defenseless slaughter required that someone come to their rescue. As Charli Carpenter (2003: 661–694) notes, this gendered conceptualization of "fighter" versus "victim/refugee" led in the

Bosnian civil war to mass executions by the Serb army of thousands of men
and boys of "military age" (from sixteen to sixty) who were disarmed by
the UN embargo and refused evacuation from Serb-besieged towns and villages by the UN Protection Force (UNPROFOR).

One intriguing aspect of the media imaging of Kosovar women as victims of Serb military attacks and sexual aggression is that the violence they
experience in their own homes, families, and communities, in domestic violence and sexual assault by members of their own ethnic community, merits
no coverage. This "background" intracommunity violence is taken as
given, as a norm, something perhaps to be regretted but surely to be expected. So the media focus is not gendered violence per se but ethnicized gender violence. Although UNMIK has kept crime statistics, the data for
2000–2001 are not reported by gender. However, the data do indicate that
murders, robberies, and arsons declined in the immediate postwar period,
while sexual assault reports increased and peaked between March and
September in both 2000 and 2001.[2] Inattention to gendered crime patterns
(perpetrators and victims) makes law and order and recovery issues difficult to address.

Other media reports depict Albanian American volunteers who are off
to join the KLA as praised and cheered by mothers, sisters, daughters.
Some of the volunteers belong to the National Guard, others are veterans of
Yugoslav or US armed forces. With one noted exception, all of the soldiers-
to-be are men. That exception is Sanije Bruncaj, nineteen, a student at
Mercy College who "was toughened up for combat" playing football at her
Yonkers high school, according to the interviewer (Dobnik 1999). A critical
feminist lens notes that Sanije Bruncaj is an exception to the gendered rule
that men fight, women witness; her gender-nontraditional sports participation confirms not only this exceptionality, but also the gendered norm
itself.

A critical feminist perspective helps us understand that when mainstream Western media and NATO decisionmakers depict women in Kosovo
primarily as victims, witnesses, and refugees, this has several negative consequences. First, it obscures women's active participation in the conflict.
Instead, women's bodies are seen as part of the field of battle. Second, this
enables women's "relief" from wartime violence and displacement as rape
victims or refugees but disables women's agency, such that their claims to
political voice and place in both the conflict resolution process and the
postconflict recovery and reconstruction are delegitimized. That is, if
women have not been an active part of the fight but merely "background,"
they have no say in how the fighting should end or what should come after.
A common example of this gendered delegitimation in the reporting on
Kosovo reveals women's vicarious nationality and conceptualization of a
gender power hierarchy: "a Serb and his wife" (Erlanger 1999a). Third, this

obscures the gendered dynamics of the "humanitarian" practices of refugee evacuation and relief services.

■ Who Are "We"? Ethnicized/ Gendered Nationalism and Autonomy

This section explores the construction of identity in the former Yugoslavia, in particular the ethnicized and gendered patterns of nationalism in the territory of Kosovo and the subsequent quest by Kosovar Albanians for full autonomy from Belgrade. "Identity is a means of self-definition and a reflection of cultural values, norms, and orientations, but identity is also a product of adaptive and protective mechanisms in response to contextual and situational factors" (Duffy 2000: 234). Ethnicity can have different meanings assigned to it by different societies. In some societies, ethnicity is a difference that makes no difference in our social status, standing, opportunities; it is simply an identity we embrace, a heritage we celebrate, a set of shared social beliefs and practices, a cultural affiliation. In the former Yugoslavia, ethnicity is a place we get put, a categorization that carries tremendous significance regarding social status, rewards, opportunities: critical perspectives call this "racialized ethnicity." In the context of Kosovo, Serb ethnicity was scripted as dominant and Albanian ethnicity was racialized as subordinate. The Serb government's revocation of Kosovo's limited regional autonomy in 1989 exacerbated this subordination and symbolically feminized the Kosovar Albanian community. To overcome this feminization, Kosovar Albanian nationalists embraced a militarized masculinity to reassert their ethnic identity (Enloe 2000: 150–151).

Sule Toktas observes the gendered dimension of nationalism and national identity and the gendered roles of women in national state-making processes. She argues that ethnonational projects in the former Yugoslavia represent "a revival and celebration of the traditional gender codes" (2002: 31). Nationalism enforces unity and obscures hierarchies within a community:

> "Who are 'we'?" "We" are citizens with a shared ethnic identity. This is also defined by the converse: "'We' are not 'them.'" The twin models of ethnic nationality or citizenship are gendered. There is a military or martial citizenship for men and a care-taking or maternal citizenship for women. We are either a citizen-soldier [or] a mother/wife-of-soldier. The military is "the guardian of national identity" and military service "is constitutive of masculinity." (Toktas 2002: 38–40)

Conversely, "women's identity became closely associated with national, cultural, and family survival" (Duffy 2000: 221).

How was gendered nationalism constructed in Kosovo? From 1974 to

1989, Kosovo was designated a semiautonomous province of the FRY with some degree of local governance. In 1989 the Belgrade government under Slobodan Milosevic abolished this measure of autonomy. The initial Kosovar Albanian response was guided by Ibrahim Rugova, a university professor and a leader of the Democratic League of Kosovo (LDK) who promoted a campaign of "passive" (that is, nonviolent) resistance or noncooperation, modeled after that of Mohandas Gandhi in the 1940s in the struggle for Indian independence from Britain. Rugova reasoned that because ethnic Albanians were the numerical majority in Kosovo (some 2 million of the province's inhabitants), their resistance campaign would convince the government to reinstate at least the previous measure of autonomy to the region. Using funds solicited from Kosovar Albanians in diaspora as well as a local tax, the LDK set up a "parallel" system of schools and medical clinics and avoided encounters with Serb-dominated state organs, the police, and the courts. This was the main Kosovar Albanian strategy from 1989 to 1995 (O'Neill 2002: 21–22).

Why did Serbs revoke the limited Kosovar Albanian autonomy, and why did Kosovar Albanians then insist on the use of military force to obtain complete autonomy? Part of the answer can be found in the gendered dynamics of the power relationship between the Kosovar Albanians, the Yugoslav government in Belgrade, and the US government in Washington, D.C. When Serb leaders (under duress) and US diplomats met in Dayton, Ohio, in 1995 to negotiate a settlement of the war in Bosnia, the US representatives pressed their agenda for Bosnian sovereignty. Kosovar Albanians were not invited to attend the conference, and the question of Kosovar autonomy was not on the agenda. Neglect of the Kosovo question in the Dayton peace accord led many Kosovar Albanians to criticize the "passive resistance" strategy of Rugova and the LDK. This exclusion made many Kosovar Albanians feel powerless, subordinate, "feminized." The lesson many took from this marginalization was that only military action would be taken seriously, whether by the Serb authorities in Belgrade, by the international community in New York, or by US leaders in Washington.

When the tactic of noncompliance was discredited, Kosovar Albanian militancy led by the KLA was met with increasingly violent repression by the government in Belgrade, including, ultimately, a campaign of systematic rape of Kosovar Albanian women to punish the resistance. This policy response only intensified the Kosovar Albanian commitment to military means to achieve full autonomy. For Kosovar men to be "real men," that is, protectors of women in their community, the rapes of "their" women had to be avenged, the rapists punished. The possibility of peaceful settlement of the question of Kosovo's political status was foreclosed by the gendered interpretation of policy options.

According to William O'Neill, the "disappointment of Dayton" was accompanied by an increase in arms shipments from Albania, and the KLA began attacking Serb targets in Kosovo, including police stations. O'Neill cites a Human Rights Watch report stating that in a retaliatory raid by Serb police on March 5, 1998, "fifty-eight people died, including eighteen women and ten children" (2002: 23). The phrasing here is oft-repeated in subsequent media reports on the conflict: attention is drawn to the presence and number of women and children among the casualties (Erlanger 1999a). Why remark upon these deaths in particular? Because gender marks these as "innocent victims," that is, incapable of defending themselves. The point here is not that they are not "innocent," but rather that their gender status translates into a particular position as object of violence rather than as subject or agent of violence. The possibility that any of these women were combatants or otherwise complicit in the conflict as, for example, collaborators or couriers, is precluded by the gendered phrasing. The obverse of this is, of course, that the male victims were somehow less than innocent; men were automatically held responsible or accountable for the violence of conflict in ways women were not. This gendered frame is reflected in O'Neill's language here: "Rugova's strategy to gain Kosovo's independence by passive resistance had been overtaken by events. Now the men with guns would decide Kosovo's future" (2002: 23).

Were there no women with guns? On March 8, 2000, in an observance to mark what the United Nations has designated as International Women's Day, at a ceremony in Belgrade, one Yugoslav official estimated that 10 percent of the Serb armed forces were women, but another countered that less than 1 percent of combatants (that is, "real" soldiers) were women. Another praised the contribution of women to the Yugoslav army's morale and efficiency, and a message from the pro–Serb government Patriotic Alliance of Yugoslavia read in part: "As mothers, wives, daughters, sisters, and beloved girls, the women of Yugoslavia will fight for the freedom of the fatherland." That is, their contribution was made in fulfilling traditional gender roles. While the official ceremony proceeded, the peace group Women in Black held a vigil for victims of the war; their members were denounced by Serb government supporters as feminists who "propagate homosexuality." Across Kosovo on March 8, Kosovar Albanian women staged silent marches to protest the detention in Serbia of 1,300 people since 1998 as suspected terrorists; one participant said, "We demand the release of our fathers and brothers because our mothers have cried enough tears for their children and husbands" (Fletcher 2000). Thus, women may witness, mourn, and protest in their gendered roles as wife, sister, daughter; however, this apparently excludes them from making demands for peace on their own behalf or from taking up arms in their own defense.

■ Scripting the Conflict: Kosovo as Victim, Serbia as Villain, the United States/NATO as Hero

How is our understanding of Kosovo gendered? Gender is deployed to depict women primarily as innocent victims of mass rape, Serbia as rapist, and the United States/NATO as hero/rescuer. Consider the rationale offered for NATO intervention. In a televised address to the American public on March 24, 1999, US president Bill Clinton made his case for military intervention by depicting Kosovars as innocent, defenseless victims of dictator Milosevic's reign of terror. Clinton is trying to provide an answer to the question, "Of what is Kosovo an example?":

> We act to protect thousands of innocent people in Kosovo from a mounting military offensive. . . . We've seen innocent people taken from their homes, forced to kneel in the dirt and sprayed with bullets; Kosovar men dragged from their families, fathers and sons lined up and shot in cold blood. This is not a war in the traditional sense. It is an attack by tanks and artillery on a largely defenseless people whose leaders have already agreed to peace. Ending this tragedy is a moral imperative. . . .
>
> Our mission is clear: to demonstrate the seriousness of NATO's purpose so that the Serbian leaders understand the imperative of reversing course; to deter an even bloodier offensive against innocent civilians in Kosovo; and, if necessary, to seriously damage the Serbian military's capacity to harm the people of Kosovo. In short, if President Milosevic will not make peace, we will limit his ability to make war. (quoted in Murphy 1999: 630)

Clinton also expressed concern for Kosovar refugees (read "women and children," since Kosovar men were rounded up and shot). So Clinton has tried to persuade us to "read" Kosovo as a rescue. Imagery of women's suffering is used to justify military intervention by casting it as humanitarian.

This gendered interpretation of what constitutes "humanitarian" intervention is reflected in a symposium of jurists and legal scholars debating the legality of US/NATO air strikes. Louis Henkin found the intervention lawful and just: lawful because the escalating violence threatened regional stability and hence international peace and security, which the UN Security Council recognized after the fact, and just because of the obvious "need to halt horrendous crimes against humanity, massive expulsions and war crimes" (1999: 824–825). Henkin, like President Clinton, casts Kosovo as victim, Serbia as villain, and the United States/NATO as hero/rescuer/first responder. Jon Charney offers a different interpretation, contending that humanitarian grounds for intervention are "designed to mask other political objectives" and that NATO's air campaign was actually an unauthorized and unlawful "'anticipatory humanitarian intervention' based on past actions of the FRY regime and future risks" (1999: 841). From this perspective, the United States is the "bully on the beach" using physical force against a weaker opponent simply because it could.

In her essay "Kosovo: A 'Good' or 'Bad' War?" Christine Chinkin brings a critical IR perspective to bear in observing the racial-ethnic selectivity of humanitarian intervention. In essence, she asks, "Whose rights does the international community think are worth protecting?" and argues that current practice suggests a distinction has been made between European and African peoples: "Military intervention on behalf of the victims of human rights abuses has not occurred in, inter alia, Sudan, Afghanistan, or Ethiopia" and was "woefully inadequate and delayed in Rwanda" (1999: 847). This critique addresses the race/color/nationality dimension of difference. She further observes that continued use of gendered dichotomous constructions such as "combatant/civilian" obscured the complexity of the consequences of the conflict in ways that would inhibit postconflict recovery (1999: 846).

In some accounts of Kosovo, gender was explicitly deployed to marshal support for military intervention by appealing to a militarized version of masculinity. During the NATO air campaign, columnist/author Andrew Marr scolded the British government for balking at sending ground troops to Kosovo, arguing that war ennobles and toughens men. He declaims: "We have been feminised and . . . NATO has done that feminizing" because the Cold War distanced Britain from the battlefield. "The idea that our people should go (to Kosovo) and die in large numbers appalls us. Killing our enemies appalls us, too." Marr continues: "If we wish to be world policemen, then we have to rethink our general queasiness about violence. We have to return, at times, to places and risks that the NATO umbrella taught us to forget." He concludes: "We have become unrealistic, under the nuclear umbrella, about how things are. Like the Serbs, we are undignified prisoners of history, but soft and flabby in our case, rather than racist and paranoid." This last reference invokes impotence, the loss of masculinity in a failure to perform. In short, Marr argues that war makes males/boys into "real" men (Marr 1999).

Responding to Marr's gendered call to arms, Charlotte Raven observes that Blair's decision to deploy ground troops has been interpreted by Marr and other armchair generals as "a positive sign of NATO's masculinity." She defends "queasiness" about British war casualties not as cowardice but as evidence of humanity; she notes that initial queasiness about Serb atrocities brought NATO to the point of action in the first place (Raven 1999).

How does a critical feminist lens "read"/interpret this narrative? First, we must note that the means chosen to defend those "innocent victims" and to avenge the widows/mothers who wept and mourned for their menfolk—NATO airstrikes on Belgrade—created massive casualties on the Serbian side. But the US administration asserted that the air campaign "aimed narrowly": Serbian civilians were not the target of the attacks but were merely "collateral damage" from approximately twenty weapons straying from their intended targets—witness the accidental bombing of the Chinese embassy in Belgrade (Murphy 1999: 633).[3] Second, Serbian citizens, presumably, were not "innocent" victims. They were tainted because they either failed to challenge or actively approved of and supported Milosevic's campaign of terror in Kosovo. This made them guilty by association. Third, the Clinton administration blamed Serbian civilian casualties on Milosevic's failure to agree to peace on US terms at Rambouillet. Milosevic's recalcitrance brought the promised consequences. Here hegemonic US masculinity rebukes insubordinate Serbian masculinity: "show 'em who's boss," and Clinton knocks out Milosevic. Finally, the US government sought to preclude the use of force by Kosovar Albanians as well. They would not be allowed to fight their own battles but rather would be constrained in a dependent or subordinate position to US military hegemony.

■ Kosovo's Gendered Consequences

One consequence of the war in the former Yugoslavia has been that mass systematic rape has been identified as a war crime under international law. This would seem a vast improvement from a liberal feminist perspective, because the law now "sees" women, until we stop to consider the critical feminist question, "Whose law is it?" Hilary Charlesworth critiques the construction of rape only as a war crime against a community rather than also as a gender crime against a woman/women as a part of that community. Charlesworth finds defining mass rape as a war crime problematic because it is based on a gendered interpretation of rape as "a stain on a woman's honor" and as a weapon to humiliate the men in the community or ethnic group. This interpretation reinforces the notion of women as men's property: the rape victim is damaged goods for which proper restitution must be made. Further, under the new law, the understanding of rape as a tool of ethnic cleansing to produce children of ethnic identities different than their mothers focuses on the child and the group, not the physical violence done to the woman who was raped. She is merely a cultural object or body "on which and through which war can be waged" (1999a: 387).

Charlesworth points out that testifying before international criminal tribunals such as the ICTY may further traumatize women who have survived rape, yet little international funding has been directed to victim support and recovery. Moreover, she argues, the focus on rape in war with woman-as-victim obscures other gendered effects of war, such as the differential effect of food and medical shortages caused by sanctions on poor women and girls and differential access to relief supplies when international aid workers seek out men as heads of household (1999a: 388). Charlesworth concludes that international human rights law's focus on individual acts of violence against women "may obscure the structural relations of power and domination that make them possible and the continuity between the ways women are treated in 'peacetime' and in times of 'conflict': rape in armed conflict is made possible by the prevalence of rape in times of peace" (1999a: 390–391).

Another consequence of the conflict in Kosovo and subsequent international intervention has been an increase in the trafficking of women beginning in July 1999 to provide sexual services for 45,000 NATO KFOR troops as well as UNMIK and NGO personnel. Observers note that little effort was made and few resources were expended to assist women trafficked against their will who wanted to return to their country of origin, or to provide medical assistance to sex workers in brothels. Roma Bhattacharjea, who was in charge of women's affairs for UNMIK, confirmed that trafficking was not a top priority given other problems during the occupation. If we ask, "Which women were trafficked?" we find that women from Eastern Europe, especially Russia, Ukraine, Moldova, and Bulgaria, were preferred by peacekeepers. Prohibitions against patronizing sex workers in the community of deployment developed after Cambodia meant that Kosovar women were displaced by the Eastern European women and excluded from one of the few lucrative postconflict employments ("NATO Forces Spur Prostitution" 2000).

A third consequence of the conflict has been the exclusion of local women from decisionmaking based on gendered and ethnicized interpretations of women's "place" in Kosovar society, or their inclusion in particular places based on the same assumptions. In her "gender audit" gathering information about women's position in society of postconflict Kosovo, analyst Chris Corrin found women working to rebuild their communities in such groups as Motrat Qiriazi in Kosovo, the Centre for Women War Vicitms in Zagreb, and the Centre for Legal Assistance for Women and Medica in Zagreb (2001: 78–98). However, she also found that the assumptions of "internationals" about the "traditionalism" of ethnic Albanian/Muslim communities disadvantaged Kosovar women and their organizations. For example, UNMIK officials assumed women heads of households would be unable to drive tractors, so they hired men to plow; however, many of the women wished to learn to drive tractors for themselves. Here, intersecting conceptions of gender and ethnicity kept women from making their own choices (Corrin 2001: 81). Had UNMIK officials included representatives of the Rural Women's Network in planning reconstruction in the countryside, this faulty assumption could have been avoided (Corrin 2001: 82).

As Julie Mertus notes in Chapter 8.2, liberal feminists are pleased that women in Kosovo are being recruited for and included in the civilian police force: the Kosovo Police Service (KPS).[4] Yet a critical feminist perspective observes in NATO's website reports that in the tenth class of KPS, "19% of cadets are female, and almost 14% belong to ethnic minorities," as though the categories of gender and ethnicity are mutually exclusive, so we don't know "which women" are participating, or in what capacities.[5] This focus on the percentage of women police officers now on duty and in training with the KPS obscures the reasons for their inclusion and their relative absence from all other parts of the criminal justice system, namely as judges, prosecutors, and attorneys (O'Neill 2002: 112–113). Part of the reason women are being recruited to these police positions is simply a lack of *man*power, not a commitment to gender equality. Part of the reason also has to do with gendered assumptions about who is more likely to engage in violence or to succumb to corruption or to ethnic partisanship. In other communities, women have been recruited to police work to give the force a "kinder, gentler" public image.

Finally, gendered assumptions and expectations present additional challenges for conflict resolution and postconflict reconstruction. While there is an opportunity for women to move from victim to survivor, to reclaim their agency, and to participate actively in both the conflict resolution and recovery processes, there are conflicting pressures for a return to the home and traditional gender tasks (Duffy 2000: 227). Further, as Kosovo grapples with questions of identity, there is a tendency to answer the question "Who are 'we'?" with an either/or dichotomy: Serb/Orthodox or Albanian/Muslim. Of course, these boundaries have been blurred by the multiethnic children born of the rape campaign, but they remain the markers for identity in postconflict Kosovo. Yet efforts to attend to ethnic diversity in the postconflict representation scheme obscure the general lack of gender diversity in power positions throughout Kosovo today. The paucity of women's political representation in postconflict governments is criticized by ZEST in Serbia (Duffy 2000: 216).[6]

Unlike traditional perspectives on international relations that accept the current world order as a given, critical feminist perspectives seek to understand how the current world order developed and to recognize who benefits or is hurt by the present array of power relations, from the international to the interpersonal. International relations is not about reified "states" but about people enmeshed in multiple intersecting power hierarchies. As in the game of Jenga, if we seek to dismantle the intricate tower of these intersecting hierarchies, we must not only attend to the gender dimension, which would remove some of the blocks but still leave the power structure standing, but also address other dimensions of difference, such as race/ethnicity and class/caste, to deconstruct the foundational rationale that any kind of difference "makes a difference" in our life chances and opportunities. Liberal feminism's political project is to gain access for women to existing power structures with a focus on "Women at Work" in international relations. Critical feminism seeks to identify the origins and consequences of those power structures and to work to replace them with a "People at Work" highway sign.

■ Notes

1. In order to avoid confusion, it should be noted that the term "critical theory" is not being used in this context to indicate the Critical Theory of the Frankfurt School exclusively or specifically. It is being used in its broader sense to indicate a postpositivist commitment in general.

2. See http://www.unmikonline.org/civpol/statistics.htm.

3. The US government later apologized for bombing the Chinese embassy on May 7, 1999, and made restitution (Murphy 2000).

4. See http://www.osce.org/kosovo/police.

5. See http://www.nato.into/docu/facts/2000/kosovo-ff.htm.

6. ZEST was formed in fall 1990 as a women's party (the Z stood for "women," E for "ethics," S for "solidarity," and T for "tolerance"). ZEST had three principles of activity: (1) "For democracy and against all forms and aspects of discrimination and authoritarian power and authority in society," (2) "For peace, tolerance and co-operation among nations and peoples," (3) "For quality of life as a crucial aim of development." Its aim was to improve the lives of women, and they organized public discussions about housewives, women artists, and work. As militarism grew they lobbied the parliaments of the republics to negotiate a peace (see Mladjenovic and Hughes 1999).

chapter 9

Biopolitical Approaches

Jennifer Sterling-Folker

Biopolitics

While both biopolitical and feminist IR theorizing are concerned with the dividing line between the biology of the sexes and the social construction of gender, ultimately biopolitics puts its emphasis on the biological rather than the socially constructed end of the equation.[1] There is no single, unified biopolitical perspective, nor is there necessarily agreement over whether works that could be charaterized as biopolitical should even be given such a label. What links the approaches discussed here under a common analytical umbrella is a shared interest in exploring the role that human biology, psychology, cognition, perceptions, and emotions might play in IR. What differentiates biopolitical approaches from feminist IR theorizing, then, is that biopolitical scholarship generalizes behavioral attributes across the human species and argues that these attributes have relevance to IR outcomes and events.

The development of and interest in biopolitics within the US discipline (and social science in general) has been uneven. Some of the earliest disciplinary work on the causes of international war and violence were biopolitical in nature. Classical realists tended to assume that a human lust for power accounted for warfare, while others claimed that it was the innate aggression of the human species. For example, Konrad Lorenz (1967) argued that aggression was an instinct or urge developed to ensure survival of the individual and the species by warding off competitors. Other work on human aggression included "frustration-aggression theory," which argued that externally produced frustration triggered violent responses, and the study of socialization, displacement, and projection, all of which attempted to develop the analytical link between individual and group aggression.[2] However, as tempting as it is to trace the cause of international conflict to innate human nature and behavior, such "first-image" or "microcosmic" explanations of warfare were problematic from the start.

One obvious problem is that there is no single reading of human evolutionary history or what it has bequeathed to us. Many psychologists and sociologists contest the notion that there is an innate human tendency to aggression, arguing instead that aggression is largely learned and culturally specific. Many evolutionary biologists argue that cooperation, altruism, and nurturing were also important to species survival (see, for example, Silverberg and Gray 1992), and these attributes could be just as pertinent to behavioral patterns in IR. How, then, can we rely on human nature to make explanatory claims about IR, when the substance of human biology is contested and its implications for group behavior and interaction are unclear?

This problem is compounded by what should now be a familiar observation: the reality of human existence is largely socially constructed so that the dividing line between instinct and learned behavior is ambiguous. While numerous postpositivist IR perspectives have raised this point, it is not considered a radical observation in the biological sciences. Even evolutionary biologists concur that the dividing line between instinct and learned behavior is ambiguous, which suggests that when we derive explanations for IR behaviors and patterns from human nature assumptions, we are engaging in a normative, not objective, exercise.

The second problem with tracing international war to the human attribute of aggression involves the analytical difficulties of moving from the individual's to the nation-state's choices and behavior. As James Dougherty and Robert Pfaltzgraff observe, "it is impossible to describe the causes of war purely in terms of individual psychology, as if it were the case of psychic tensions within individuals mounting to the breaking point and then spilling over into large-scale conflict," because "in the case of war, those who make the momentous decision to lead a state into war do not themselves do the fighting on the battlefield," and "conversely, those who actually engage in the battle are likely to have had little or nothing to do with the actual decision to fight" (1997: 263). Wars can be waged with little enthusiasm, or they can be averted even when hostility is widespread, because there are complex social, political, and economic mechanisms that must translate human emotions, psychic tension, and aggression into warfare. Since human attributes alone cannot produce wars in the absence of such mechanisms (and may be necessary but ultimately insufficient as causes), explanatory emphasis in IR has tended to focus on the mechanisms rather than the biology. The relationship between biological propensities and the socially constructed mechanisms necessary for them to be translated into collective behavior is one that Vincent Falger and Johan van der Dennen explore in Chapter 9.2. They argue that rampant ethnic violence and rape in Kosovo had its origins in the behavioral propensities of both the human species *and* Serbian military policies.

Unfortunately, the difficulties of doing biopolitical analysis have led most social scientists to simply ignore the role of biology in their explanations for social phenomena.[3] This is problematic since, with the exception of feminism, all other IR theoretical perspectives make implicit assumptions about human nature and biology that serve as the unexamined foundations for their assumptions about IR. Robert Crawford has observed, for example, that emotions are "implicit and ubiquitous, but under theorized" in the discipline (2000: 116). And Daniel Deudney notes that, "even when aspects of human biological nature (particularly emotions and appetites) have been a factor in Western political theory, human nature is typically considered in isolation from its ecological and geophysical contexts" (1996: 129). Thus even when they adopt a systemic level of analysis, realists still tend to assume that human beings are highly aggressive or fearful, and liberal IR theorists that humans are highly rational and cooperative.[4] This then makes an enormous difference to how each analyzes IR events, although their microfoundations are rarely acknowledged or critically examined. This is regrettable, since biopolitical analyses that explicitly grapple with the relationship between biology, psychology, and social construction have important insights to contribute to the study of IR.

As noted in Chapter 8.1, there is a growing body of literature that examines the relationship between the biology of sex difference, the social construction of gender difference, human aggression, and warfare. There is also a considerable literature devoted to examining the psychological, cognitive, and perceptual elements of IR, and IR scholars have borrowed numerous theories from the study of psychology. These include theories of cognitive dissonance and consistency (which argue that individuals reduce inconsistencies between their values and behavior), attributional error theory (which amounts to a double standard in assessing one's own behavior and that of others), social identity theory (which argues that individual identity develops within groups), and "intolerance of ambiguity" theory (in which humans reduce everything to simple schemas of opposition).[5] In fact, the neoclassical realist contribution to this volume (Chapter 2.3) could also be classified as biopolitical, since it borrows psychology's "prospect theory" in order to explain the Clinton administration's motivation for intervention in Kosovo.

Thus for some scholars, such as Falger and van der Dennen, biopolitics means a commitment to "the validity of neo-Darwinian evolutionary theory" for understanding political behavior (Somit and Peterson 1998: 566). They would argue that "without an understanding of the evolutionary and genetic aspects of behavior, we cannot fully comprehend the inner principles by which human life is organized" (Dougherty and Pfaltzgraff 1997:

263). Hence the evolutionary past of the human species has produced behavioral repertoires or propensities that have relevance for IR today and for patterns as varied as international violence, warfare, cooperation, and altruism. For other scholars, biopolitics is not an overt commitment to neo-Darwinian evolutionary theory, but rather a willingness to openly explore the relevance of human psychology, cognition, perceptions, and emotions to IR phenomena. It would be more accurate, then, to characterize biopolitics as the acknowledged inclusion of biologically derived tendencies and propensities in IR analysis. Biopolitics is a relatively broad analytical umbrella as a result, because it usually contains IR scholarship that might alternatively be categorized according to many of the theoretical perspectives already discussed in this volume.

■ Further Reading

Overviews of biopolitical work in the social sciences include Albert Somit and Steven Peterson's *Neo-Darwinism and the Social and Behavioral Sciences* (2001) and Thomas Wiegele's *Biology and the Social Sciences* (1982). Examples of work in political science and IR that is explicitly biopolitical include Corning 1971, Shaw and Wong 1989, Shaw and Wong 1987 (see also Goldstein's and Kitcher's reaction pieces in the 1987 source), Falger 2001a, Falger 2001b, Falger 2001c, Falger 1997, Falger 1994, Fukuyama 1998, Fukuyama 1997, Hopple and Falkowski 1982, Masters 1983, Reynolds, Falger, and Vine 1987, Somit and Peterson 2001, Somit and Peterson 1999, Somit and Peterson 1998, Thayer 2000, and Wiegele 1979. For a biopolitical approach that examines the relationship between macro social behaviors (such as war and trade) and equations of mathematical biology, see Epstein 1994, Epstein 1992, and Epstein with Axtell 1996. Examples of work in the field of sociobiology include Barash 1977, Gregaroy et al. 1978, Fetzer 1985, and Wilson 1975.

A sampling of work on the role of emotions or ingroup/outgroup biases includes Crawford 2000, Druckman 1994, Hinde 1993, Kowert 1998, Mercer 1999, Mercer 1996, Mercer 1995, Petersen 2002, and Sterling-Folker 2001b. The most widely cited work on the role of perception is Robert Jervis's *Perception and Misperception in International Politics* (1976). Other work on perception and psychological factors in IR includes Cottam 1986, Deudney 1996, Goldstein 2001, Hermann and Kegley 1995, Jervis, Lebow, and Stein 1985, Larson 1985, Levy 1983, Vertzberger 1990, and Wiegele et al. 1985.

The seminal work on the phenomenon of "groupthink" remains Janis 1972, but see also Hart, Stern, and Sundelius 1997. For an interesting work that seeks to combine the study of bureaucratic politics and biopolitics, see White and Losco 1986. And for works that examine the cognitive-rational debate in decisionmaking, see Geva and Mintz 1997 and Hermann and Fischerkeller 1995. Additional citations that might be appropriate can be found in the overview chapter on feminism.

■ Notes

1. This is also what distinguishes a biopolitical argument from the evolutionary world system approach of George Modelski and William Thompson (discussed in Chapter 7.1).

2. James Dougherty and Robert Pfaltzgraff (1997, chap. 7) provide a comprehensive overview of these and other biopolitical theories. Consult Waltz 1959 for a review of other "first-image" explanations for international conflict.

3. The exception to this is sociobiology, which is a relatively new and controversial field that attempts to combine the study of animal behavior with sociology. Its founder, Edward O. Wilson, argued that there are some basic patterns of aggressive behavior that various species have adapted in order to ensure their survival. Sociobiologists study the genetic roots of social behavior in a variety of species including humans and seek "to bridge the gap between the genetic inheritance of individuals on the one hand and social processes and institutions on the other" (Dougherty and Pfaltzgraff 1997: 264).

4. For works that explore implicit human nature assumptions in IR theorizing, see Falger 1997, Freyberg-Inan 2003, Spirtas 1996, Sterling-Folker 2001a, and Sterling-Folker 2001b.

5. See Dougherty and Pfaltzgraff 1997: 279–282, 487–500, for overviews and citations for many of these theories.

Vincent S. E. Falger & Johan M. G. van der Dennen

Biopolitics: Evolutionary History and Modern Conflict

War is almost always seen as an exclusively human activity, and once "invented" as a social institution some 5,000 years ago in Mesopotamia, it spread by diffusion, or perhaps was invented independently in different regions of the world (e.g., Harris 1975; Cioffi-Revilla 1996; Keeley 1996). This picture has become challenged by the discovery of male coalitional aggression and "lethal male raiding" in free-ranging chimpanzees and battle-type intergroup violence in social carnivores and a great number of primates (Goodall 1986; Wrangham 1999). Instead, an evolutionary view, in which interactions including warfare make sense only if they serve reproduction on which natural selection works, makes room for a truly natural historic continuity (Meyer 1981; Low 1993; van der Dennen 1995).[1] Evolutionists—scientists who apply the insight that all organisms are the outcomes of a long-term descent under selective forces—distinguish between the so-called *ultimate* dimension of causality and the *proximate* dimension. Ultimate explanations give answers to fundamental questions like "Why has warfare (or, the behavioral propensity for warfare) evolved in the first place?" and "Why has warfare evolved only in so few species?" Answers to these questions help to provide foundations under or contexts for proximate questions like "What are the motives or conditions that led to this particular war?" Ultimate and proximate causative factors are complementary rather than mutually exclusive, and they do not imply consciousness of the effects of behavior by the actor(s). It will be clear that the preceding chapters all deal with proximate causation and explanations of the Kosovo conflict, and as such they are necessary and informative, and yet insufficient to see it as one example of the amazing recurrence of warfare in human history.

The evolutionary (or Darwinian or selectionist) paradigm proceeds from the repeatedly empirically confirmed assumption that all organisms, including humans, have evolved; that all living organisms descended from other organisms that successfully mated and reproduced in past environments; and that—ultimately—all organisms have come in one uninterrupted chain from the first simple multiplying cells, and are thus phylogenetically related to one another. In the end, all organisms are the products of the former successful reproductive strategies of their genes. This reductionistic theory applies not only to the physical dimension of organisms like bones and organs, but also to their behavioral repertoires, up to and including what we want to call politics (e.g., Rubin 2002). As long as living organisms adapt to the environment in which they live and reproduce differentially, selection promotes the best-adapted copies of any species. Human evolution (that is, the natural history of the species *Homo sapiens sapiens*) is no exception; on the contrary, our species has been so successful in terms of numbers that it seems to have gained dominance over its own environment. Even though this implies an increasing behavioral flexibility (for example, we do not have natural enemies anymore, and meanwhile we have cultural institutions that in principle allow eternal peaceful coexistence), the inheritance of human and even primate behavioral repertoires is far from lost. In fact, warfare is a good illustration of an ancient repertoire surviving (and thus changing) hundreds and thousands of generations of cultural adaptations.

In general, two types of warfare in animals and mankind have been distinguished: raiding (lethal male raiding, or ambush or dawn surprise attack), and battle (the confrontation of two opposing lines or phalanxes). In so-called primitive societies, raiding is the most bloody and lethal form of warfare, due to small but rapidly accumulating casualties, and occasional near-genocidal routing.[2] Anthropologist-primatologist Richard Wrangham explained lethal male raiding with his "imbalance of power" hypothesis, and he suggested the distinct possibility that the chimpanzee-hominid common ancestor already had this raiding pattern in its behavioral repertoire. Even if this is unproven, it certainly makes sense evolutionarily, in which case this raiding capability is at least 6 million years old. The "imbalance of power" hypothesis suggests that coalitional killing is the expression of a drive for dominance over neighbors. Two conditions are proposed to be both necessary and sufficient to account for coalitional killing of neighbors. First, a state of intergroup hostility, and second, sufficient imbalances of power between parties such that one party can attack the other with impunity. Under these conditions, it is suggested, selection favors the tendency to hunt and kill rivals when the costs are sufficiently low. Given the chimpanzee evidence, Joseph Manson and Richard Wrangham (1991) proposed that such an imbalance-of-power mechanism must have been an important factor favoring the evolution of lethal male violence in humans also—even before the evolution of weapons.

Battle-type warfare occurs in many primate species and some other group-territorial mammals, such as social carnivores. Battles result mainly from chance encounters by primate groups, failed raids or surprise attacks and chance encounters in "primitive" peoples, and among standing armies in historical and contemporary warfare in which armies are too big to operate undetected. In social carnivores and "female-bonded" primate species, female participation in these more noisy than bloody battles commonly

exceeds male participation. Tournament-like "ritualized" combat is generally found among "advanced" tribal societies with fairly dense populations
(e.g., New Guinea), and is supposed to test the (numerical) strength of the
opponent while leaving room for a more peaceful solution of the conflict by
mediators—but the ritual battle can easily develop into a rout and a massacre if a substantial imbalance of power is detected by one of the parties
involved (Wright 1942; Divale 1973; Durham 1976; Otterbein 1999).

The contention that war must have existed before humankind evolved
as we know it today is based on the proven evolutionary continuity between
nonhuman and human primates, and on the multimale coalition argument.
As soon as a species has solved the problem of coordinated cooperative
action by more than two (in most cases male) individuals, it is capable of
warfare because this kind of "selfish cooperation" (Corning 1983) is an
excellent instrument for escalated and violent intercoalition and intergroup
contest competition. "Cooperation-for-conflict has probably always been
the key to human survival," as Robert Bigelow puts it (1969: 217). Until
now, at least two brainy species have accomplished this: us and the common chimpanzee (*Pan troglodytes*). Additionally, some ethnocentric xenophobia between groups would be selectively favored in a potentially hostile
and violently competitive environment, exacerbated by the sharp decreas-
ing genetic kinship at the groups' boundaries (Sumner 1906; Wilson 1978;
Reynolds, Falger, and Vine 1987; Shaw and Wong 1989; Thienpont and
Cliquet 1999; Vanhanen 1999).

The answer to the question of why *males* are the warriors in raiding-
type warfare is an important and old one for understanding the evolutionary
roots of the phenomenon (Darwin 1871; Tiger 1972; Trivers 1985;
Wrangham and Peterson 1996; Sanderson 2001). Raiding evolved as a
high-risk/high-gain male coalitional reproductive strategy (van der Dennen
1995). To understand this claim, we must lead you to the essence of evolutionary theory. Reproductive success is the only criterion that counts in
evolution. Male and female organisms have evolved different strategies for
the optimalization of their reproductive success, because what for one sex
is a highway to genetic immortality is for the other sex a one-way ticket to
genetic oblivion (paraphrasing Symons 1979). For male organisms, females
are generally the limiting resource. For human males, women are the highly
strategic "good" (always short in supply) that can convert the other
resources controlled by the males into offspring (Melotti 1990).
Accordingly, among chimpanzees (a species in which the males stay in the
group in which they are born, in contrast to females), the ultimate benefit of
lethal male raiding is hypothesized to be increased access by raiding males
to reproductively valuable females, via either incorporation of neighboring
females or encroachment on the territory of neighboring groups and elimination of numerically weaker males.

Wrangham argued that selection favors the tendency to hunt and kill rivals when the costs are sufficiently low. This goes for chimpanzees and humans, and in particular the combination of male-male cooperation, "proto-ethnocentrism," group territoriality, and female transfer has been pointed at in the literature as the starting condition for lethal intergroup violence (Alexander 1979; Wrangham and Peterson 1996). Richard Wrangham and Dale Peterson note that the underlying (evolutionary) psychology of "male bonding" is no different for chimpanzee raiding parties, human urban gangs, prestate warrior societies, and contemporary armies. The clear conclusion is drawn by anthropologist Bobby Low: "Through evolutionary history, men have been able to gain reproductively by warring behavior; women have almost never been able to do so" (1993: 19). Evolutionary psychologists John Tooby and Leda Cosmides (1988) have formulated this important insight somewhat differently, but the message is the same: (1) men, but not women, have evolved psychological mechanisms designed for coalitional warfare, and (2) sexual access to women will be the primary benefit that men gain from joining male coalitions.

However, since reproductive success is an individual criterion, not a group phenomenon, we also have to address the rationale for groups to compete *as groups*. In cases of intergroup contest competition, several strategies can be pictured. Merging of the groups is one strategy (but this decreases inclusive fitness of the individuals belonging to the group). Violent conflict between individuals of the two groups is another possibility (but then it is hardly intergroup in character). Scramble competition is a third one, and violent *group* conflict or warfare is the most practiced strategy. The war-prone group would be most successful if other groups practiced any of the other strategies. The warmongers' genes will be represented relatively more in the next generation (ultimate or evolutionary consequence). Indeed, the only possible competitive strategy for survival in competition with a group practicing warfare is warfare itself, either defensive or offensive. Humans thus became quintessentially first-strike creatures. Unlike other animal species, they were able to kill adult conspecifics (members of the same species) by surprise when their adversaries were unarmed and vulnerable—and even from a distance by throwing projectiles (Pitt 1978; Baer and McEachron 1982; McEachron and Baer 1982; Gat 2000).

Among many hunting-gathering peoples, a man's quality as a warrior and his hunting prowess are directly related to the number of wives he can obtain (Chagnon 1990; Low 2000). Van der Dennen's investigation (1995) of the evolutionary origins of intergroup conflict in social carnivores and primates identified the capability to form polyadic coalitions (that is, selfish and opportunistic cooperation with more than one conspecific) as the necessary precondition, which in turn required (1) sociality (intergroup conflict will occur only in long-lived social species); (2) Machiavellian (opportunistic or strategic) intelligence; and (3) proto-ethnocentrism. Proto-ethnocentrism is supposed to imply some kind of group identity or the ability to recognize ingroup versus outgroup members, to discriminate between these categories, and to preferentially treat ingroup members to positive reciprocal (altruistic) interactions such as protection, nepotism, and sharing of resources. On this basis, sociocultural change leads to stages in sociopolitical complexity, at least in the human case.

Sexually reproducing organisms transmit the physical and behavioral properties of their offspring via genetic recombination, to be developed in the environment the organism happens to find itself. Adaptation to this environment—that is, to survive and reproduce again—is for many species more preprogrammed and for some species less so, since these have evolved into environments that are partially influenced or even shaped by previous generations. Culture—the nongenetic component of behavioral and environmental properties that influences the development of every individual substantially, be it a human, chimpanzee, or other animal—builds on the basis of the biological preconditions. Although technology has made behavioral options available that seem to oppose evolutionary logic (one can easily think of examples in the reproductive area of human life), it still is more productive to view culture not as the reversal or denial of nature, but its complement. This also goes for macrosocial developments like social evolution.

The well-known stages or levels of sociopolitical development—egalitarian society, rank society, stratified society, and state-level society (more or less equivalent with the band, tribe, chiefdom, and state stages) (Sahlins and Service 1960; Fried 1967; Lenski and Lenski 1970)—may incorporate a growing proportion of cultural conditioning, but this doesn't mean that the evolutionary heritage of humankind has become irrelevant or obsolete. We are still a sexually reproducing, social species with a behavioral repertoire, the origins of which date back hundreds of millennia. This cannot but have influenced individual human behavior in the successive stages of sociopolitical development.

■ Contemporary War

The development of chiefdoms and states changed the character of warfare. Whereas the main proximate causes and motives for war and feuding among band-level and tribal societies were revenge, women, scarce resources and territory, status, prestige and glory, and supernatural motives such as headhunting (Gat 2000), the proximate causes of war among chiefdoms and (city) states were mainly economic (booty, plunder) and political (conquest, empire). Evolutionarily (ultimate causation), only the effects count, not the motives. As Thucydides and many others have made clear in their histories, "Conquerors have usually been very generous with their genes. Also, they have frequently killed off or enslaved the males of their vanquished opponents and pre-empted the women" (Corning 1983: 372).

Although there is no general agreement among researchers about the role played by war in the creation of more complex societies, there would probably be agreement that the development of historical war was the transformation of armed men into manned arms, while the reproductive rewards have become increasingly "unhooked" from the warring behavior as described above (Low 2000). The historical development of warfare is not simply a matter of technology, but it is certainly one of social organization. Discipline and coordination in battle provide the watershed between warrior and soldier. The psychology of the warrior gave way in Western history when warfare changed from guerrilla-like raids and ambushes to massive battle. Men began to fight in an organized and purposive manner.

Rape in war, mass rape included, gradually developed from a victorious soldier's reward (as part of the legitimate booty and spoils of war), to an instrument of institutionalized intimidation and terror, to a weapon of war. Documented history is full of accounts of mass rapes in war, the main short-term point being to humiliate enemy males by despoiling their valued property and to signal defeat for the men who failed in their roles as protectors by the degradation and molestation of the vanquished women (Goldstein 2001; Stiglmayer 1994).

Meanwhile, in evolutionary terms war has become an increasingly maladaptive and cost/benefit suboptimal solution to political problems. This does not contradict an evolutionary perspective of war, but it does indicate that the formerly functional behavioral repertoire associated with organized intergroup violence is active in a changed social "environment." Wars of the future will probably be waged for scarce resources (in particular clean water, oil, and "security") and "ethnic nationalism" (secessionist, irredentist, and ethnonational wars are, and probably will remain, mainly *intra*national), but not without mobilizing a complex of evolved human behavioral propensities partly dating back to prehuman times. Without acknowledging this heritage, we do not and cannot understand the deepest, ultimate motives and causes of war upon which every unique historical example is necessarily built. We are not arguing that we should accept war as inevitable because it is "natural," but we do draw some reductionistic evolutionary conclusions that underlie our discussion of the Kosovo war.

First, waging war is an almost exclusively male activity, at both the political and the practical level, irrespective of the stage of social complexity or historical period of any case. Second, the coalitional or group character is essential for understanding the phenomenon of war. The definition of ingroup and outgroup may have a more factual (kinship, similarity) or imaginary (ethnic, racial, religious, political) basis, but it will always be present, as will a good-evil categorization of the groups involved. Dehumanization of the opponent group(s) flows from this and is common throughout history.

A third conclusion is that, under influence of modern tactics, weapons, and political ideology, warfare has changed in a number of respects but not totally. Since interstate or international wars have become increasingly costly to wage, warfare has become rarer. However *intra*state wars have become more numerous and these are no less subject to the first and second points relating to evolutionarily relevant male intergroup behavior. And finally, women (and their dependent children), though noncombatants, are potential or actual victims in some phase of any war because of their sex. The history of warfare usually focuses on its political and military aspects (almost exclusively male of course), whereas concentration on the impact of war on women points to the relevance of evolutionary analysis.[3]

■ The Case of Kosovo

Whatever moment we take in the Kosovo conflict since 1998, *the main antagonists are overwhelmingly male*. This is so absolutely self-evident— as in all other cases of war—that it does not draw attention in any of the "schools" of international relations theory, with the partial exception of feminist perspectives (see the section on feminism in this book). However, the male character of war in general, and by implication of the Kosovo war, is one of the deep structural causative factors, trespassing the time- and culture-bound, short-term proximate historical context of the conflict. Since its male character is self-evident, we do not need to add substance to what can best be seen as an axiom: *war is a male business, using evolved psychological mechanisms of male coalitions*. Stating its self-evidence, however, is not the same as reducing its importance as a causal factor. William O'Neill adds that most at risk in Kosovo were young men of fighting age, with the observation of the Kosovo Verification Mission that "the pattern of violence against Albanian women differed in important respects from the attacks against men" (2002: 25). That the perpetrators of this violence were males is nowhere stated explicitly, but it is safe to assume it until other evidence emerges. This is, however, not to deny the supposedly very significant *indirect* influence of women, such as Slobodan Milosevic's wife, Mira Markovic (e.g., Djukic 2001).

The *coalitional dimension of warfare* also draws attention to the ingroup/outgroup differentiation, which is no less characteristic of all instances of warfare. The Kosovo conflict may not be reducible to one instance of "us" against "them," but as has been demonstrated in the historically descriptive elements in various chapters of this book, to many instances with variations according to time and circumstances. The great historical conscience of the people in the Balkans is an articulated form of a "sense of belonging," be it in ethnic, religious, or political terms. All authors on Kosovo point to the mythical character of any of the local historical narratives, which form the bases of ideologically constructed identities. As long as these different identities were overarched by more powerful "federal" constructions, as in Joseph Tito's time and previously under the Turkish sultanate, these separate identities did not contribute to open intergroup conflicts—these were effectively suppressed.

Although the Kosovo conflict grew violent only after the policy of expressly nonviolent "parallelism" created a small group of dissatisfied people who aimed at political independence for Kosovo, the history of marginalization and degradation of the formerly quite autonomous Kosovar Albanian region is itself an illustration of the ingroup/outgroup differentiation. Violence was not the main causative factor of the conflict. However, the Serbia-instigated inferiorization of the non-Serbian population of Kosovo made violence more and more likely. The growing political and economic domination by the Serbs was to counteract the demographic imbalance, as seen in Belgrade, but it could not be accomplished without using the differentiation mechanism.

The fact that not *all* Serbs in Kosovo wanted to behave as they were ideologically supposed to was personally courageous and risky at the same time. Nor did *all* Kosovar Albanians wish to forget that they had been friends or partners with the Serbs under Tito (O'Neill 2002: 13–19). We do not need to dig deeply into history to see when and how Milosevic's nationalism became the most efficient instrument for the mobilization of support from subgroups who expected to gain in this coalition of superiority. The first armed resistance of the early KLA was, in this perspective, a welcome excuse for the Serbs to begin the practice of ethnic cleansing in Kosovo, as it had been applied in Bosnia-Herzegovina before. The KLA, in its turn, grew from a collection of small, often squabbling groups into a coalition that was soon a main political factor. The suggestion in the literature that the KLA needed Serbian counterviolence is a Machiavellian explanation of the reinforcing group identification mechanism that fits easily onto group behavioral propensities of evolutionary age. The good-evil dichotomy accentuates the structural process accordingly.

Modern warfare has changed since ancient and premodern raiding practices occurred exclusively. However, this change should not be overestimated. In the Kosovo case, Serbian troops, police, and irregular groups used a variety of tactics against their Kosovar Albanian enemies, which included raiding tactics, as we will see later. At the other extreme lies the hypermodern air warfare of NATO, which successfully prevented victims on "our" side. Air war is a "clean" job, stripped from any personal dimension, and the enemy is only a target in terms of geographic coordinates, preferably to be exterminated by "smart" weapons. Dehumanization of the enemy in this perspective has to be taken literally: the opponents are not human but anonymous points of resistance to be cleared. Fighting an air war today is hardly more risky than the endless routine of exercise. For those on the ground it is quite different, though. Since the Serbians could not kill their NATO enemies, they took revenge on the Kosovar population, thereby reinforcing the raiding character of this intrastate war. The air war did not *cause* the ethnic cleansing of Kosovo, but it is safe to suggest that it speeded up the process substantially.[4]

What clearly had not changed in the Kosovo case, under the influence of modern technology, was the use of that age-old ingroup/outgroup mechanism. As in the war against Bosnia-Herzegovina, Serbian nationalist propaganda systematically marginalized, downgraded, and dehumanized the Kosovar Albanian population according to this classical "us against them" dichotomization, so well-known in all cultures and times. The media used may have been modern, but the message was not. By using basic group antagonism potential, the Serbian government illustrated the relevance today of the human behavioral repertoire, which is relatively easy to mobilize because of its evolutionary roots.[5] In the next paragraphs we will focus on the same roots when discussing rape as a weapon of warfare in the Kosovo case.

Because of their sex, women have been traditionally potential or actual victims in all wars (Seifert 1994). In many premodern cultures, war ended (temporarily) with the capture of women and small children, after the males were killed. In his famous "Melian Dialogue," Thucydides reports vividly how the ancient Athenians present the independent Melians with a classic dilemma: submission of Melos to militarily superior Athens, or face death of all male Melians and the enslavement of all women and children (Thucydides 1954). Women as a prey of war is a theme that has countless variations, and the practice of Serbian soldiers, policemen, and their accomplices in Bosnia-Herzegovina and Kosovo fits the theme perfectly. In both wars, rape was used as a weapon of "ethnic cleansing."

Although this weapon was used even more frequently in Bosnia-Herzegovina, it was no less systematically used in Kosovo. The remainder of this section is based on a thoroughly researched and documented Kosovo case by Human Rights Watch (Vandenberg 2000), but the war in Bosnia-Herzegovina has also been well documented (e.g., Stiglmayer 1994; Grandits et al. 1999). At first sight (from a short-term or proximate perspective), all this has much more to do with political dominance and power than with the evolutionarily relevant, ultimate effect of reproduction. From a biopolitical perspective, however, it is important to understand that the physical struggle of one group for dominance over another always has *rela-*

tive reproductive consequences. That is, even if rape is followed by killing the women, the enemy is deprived of reproductive capacity, while the sexual satisfaction of the raping soldiers is a motivation to go on with the fight and next time a conception after rape may result in a child. Neither perpetrators, political leaders, nor women victims need to be conscious of this ultimate *mechanism* to be effective, but it helps to explain the ease with which the mechanism is employed. In quite another political situation—Palestinians versus Israelis—we see that differential reproductive success has become a very significant factor in the local conflict, be it completely outside anyone's control.

Human Rights Watch researcher and reporter Martina E. Vandenberg (2000) summarizes ninety-six well-documented and "recognized" cases of rape of women in Kosovo between March and June 1999, although she repeatedly argues that this must be only the tip of an iceberg, as tradition in Kosovo makes it very, very difficult for women to admit publicly that they have been raped. The sanction of being declared unfit for marriage—and therefore unfit for any prospect of social acceptance and economic subsistence—is heavier than suppressing physical and emotional damage following the experience of rape. However, the ninety-six cases show enough communality to conclude the following patterns. Depending on the situation (homes attacked, in flight, or temporarily detained), males were isolated from the women or were not present at all (except young boys and old-aged). In most cases it was gang rape (two or more perpetrators). In most cases raping was done by the irregular paramilitary groups consisting of skinheads, long-haired, bearded, scarf-wearing, or masked males, often with long knives apart from their guns. In the cases where Serbian troops or policemen were involved, officers sometimes gave permission (not orders), looked on, but did nothing to stop the raping.

Frequently the rape was performed in front of family members or in adjoining rooms where the screaming of the victims was loud and clearly heard. Some women were taken one by one, in other cases several women were selected at once. Several cases of rape-threat were averted by women who gave all the money they had with them, but in other cases they were raped nevertheless. Old-aged women were usually left alone, except in one case where three of them were taken separately and shot dead afterward. There is a description of a fourteen-year-old girl who was ordered to be left alone because a woman of twenty years old was "available," but other very young girls were raped as well. Women having their period were rejected or abused in other ways. In one reported case a seven-months-pregnant woman described how she was raped several times, beaten, and threatened with the cutting out of her unborn ("enemy") child. Repeatedly we read in these descriptions that the perpetrators enjoyed what they were doing: they humiliated their victims by requiring them to strip naked and to let them serve as if they were slaves, by acting verbally aggressive (biting is also reported repeatedly), and by laughing at the verbal and physical resistance the victims exhibited. Most women were sent back to their groups after having been abused, but quite a number were killed afterward. The report concludes that rapes were not rare and isolated acts committed by individual members of the forces, but rather were used deliberately as an instrument to terrorize the civilian population, extort money from families, and push people to flee their homes.

Rape furthered the goal of forcing ethnic Albanians from Kosovo. It is clear that what happened to women in Bosnia-Herzegovina cast a shadow of terror in the Kosovo war, and the threat of rape and actual rape was very much a part of the assault on Kosovo. Vandenberg also analyzed the Serbian propaganda against Albanian women in Kosovo, and the following quotation points directly at the biopolitical dimension of this war:

> Official state propaganda in Yugoslavia in the decade preceding the war served to dehumanize and stereotype Kosovar Albanian women. Serbian propaganda contrasted Serbian women, viewed as "cultured, strong, and worthy of motherhood," with Albanian women, portrayed as "indiscriminately fecund." According to Ahmeti, "During the late 1980s there was tremendous propaganda against Albanian women—we were portrayed as open-legged, stupid, uneducated women ready to have sex." This attack on Albanian women in the state-controlled media fed Serbian nationalist hysteria, encouraging conflicts and abuses. Combined with official propaganda denouncing Kosovar Albanian men as "terrorists," the images portrayed in the media manipulated the fears of the ethnic Serbian population.
>
> The nationalist propaganda also exploited fears of Albanian population growth. Serbian media "pump[ed] out portraits of Albanian women as baby makers, calling their offspring 'biological bombs,' labelling Albanian family life primitive and backward." Some young women victims of rape expressed fear that they could not expect to marry following the attack. One purpose that rape in the war may have served was discouraging women from reproducing in the future. (Vandenberg 2000, chap. 3)

In several cases the role of officers is described in sufficient detail to conclude that they encouraged the assaults on women, sometimes in their presence.[6] Whether or not there is enough legal proof to qualify raping in Kosovo as an officially Serb-instigated policy, it is undeniable that it was more than local and temporarily irregular behavior by individuals only. This legal question, however, doesn't change the character of sexual abuse in conditions of war. But besides the many recorded and unreported cases of male abuse of sexual differentiation, which repeats an age-old practice of war in general (itself rooted in human evolutionary history), there are two consequences of rape as a weapon of war in Kosovo that are particularly interesting from the perspective of IR.

The first is the reconfirmation of the seriousness of rape as a weapon of war. Vandenberg notes that "the international response to reports of rape reflected the long-overdue acknowledgement of the use of rape as a weapon of war. ICTY Prosecutor Carla Del Ponte has stated that she intends to investigate, and when appropriate, indict, and prosecute perpetrators who committed crimes of sexual violence in Kosovo as part of her 'normalization' policy of prosecution of sexual violation of humanitarian law" (2000, chap. 4). This attention had been raised by the many reports of rape in the war in Bosnia-Herzegovina preceding the Kosovo war, and coincides with the same theme in cases brought before the International Criminal Tribunal for Rwanda. Until then, rape in war conditions had always been dealt with (by men) as an isolated individual excess of troops, and not as a war crime. This change of focus is important, although Vandenberg noticed the exclusion of evidence of rape or other forms of sexual violence in the forensic medical protocol for experts performing autopsies in the field in Kosovo. Del Ponte's "normalization" policy would be complete with the standard inclusion of such examination in the forensic medical protocol to be used in Kosovo and elsewhere in the world. It would underscore verbal testimonies of women who, despite shame and cultural taboos, want to testify at the ICTY in The Hague, and it may set a standard for the future.

The second point about the international political impact of rape in Kosovo is controversial but undeniable:

> Soon after the bombing campaign began, NATO leaders repeated unconfirmed reports in press conferences, referring to "systematic rape" early in the conflict before such determination could reasonably be made. The propaganda war waged by NATO spokesmen during the conflict included inflated rhetoric about rape, some based on sketchy allegations that remain unsubstantiated. This opportunistic use of rape allegations was criticized by human rights experts and members of the press. As a party to the conflict, NATO used premature and unsubstantiated claims of humanitarian law violations to justify the continuation of the bombing campaign and may thereby have undermined more careful reporting on abuses. NATO's use of insufficiently substantiated allegations provided Serbian officials with an opportunity to denounce all rape reports as mere propaganda. (Vandenberg 2000, chap. 6)

This is perhaps the clearest and most direct relation between "biopolitics" and IR in the Kosovo case, even if seen only as justification in and of allied action. Of course there is a line between propagandistic use or abuse of systematic rape as an instrument of war, and legally proven cases of it, but in the Kosovo war that may be wisdom in retrospect. Vandenberg's report itself proves that the many claims of rape allegations are substantiated, and the officials in Belgrade who denied that rape was taking place in Kosovo were plainly lying. This may seem like legal hairsplitting, which is useful in court, but in the course of decisionmaking in conditions of actual warfighting, requested evidence is either not available or reduces the importance of rape as an argument to intervene, or both. So, even in the unclear situation of actual warfare, there was enough reason to believe that Serbian forces of different feathers would again, like in Bosnia-Herzegovina, use rape as a systematic weapon of war.

■ Conclusion

An evolutionary or biopolitical approach to the war in Kosovo leads to insights that are absent in traditional IR perspectives, mostly because they are used as unchecked premises. The male character of warfare not only shows up in the actual fighting and highest political decisionmaking—which wasn't worked out in the Kosovo case—but also appears in the use of rape as a biological weapon of war. Taking into account human evolutionary history makes it easier to understand not only why male cooperation in war conditions is a dynamic force of conflict itself and of evolution in general, but also how modern propaganda of either side in the conflict has effectively exploited the deep-structured ingroup/outgroup mechanism. These insights may contribute to the realization that the analysis of large-scale social conflicts—such as expressed in intrastate and international violence—should begin with reflections on evolutionary history, or "human nature" for short.

The mass rape of women has always been a "normal" accompaniment to war. During most of human history, the opportunity to engage in wholesale rape was not just among the rewards of successful war but also, from the soldier's point of view, one of the cardinal objectives for which he fought. Mass rape as an instrument of ethnic cleansing in the former Yugoslavia may look like a novel invention, but in fact it is only one variant of the ingroup/outgroup antagonism, here conceived as an attempt to exterminate another ethnic group. Jennifer Turpin's explanation combines proximate and ultimate mechanisms behind the evolutionary "ratio" of differential reproductive success:

> The idea that genocide could be accomplished through mass rape of women of the enemy ethnic group derives from a patriarchal definition of ethnicity. The child is thought to inherit the ethnicity of her or his father, implying, for example, that if a Serb soldier rapes a Muslim woman and she becomes pregnant, her child would be a Serb. And because women are viewed as symbols of the family, and the family as the basis of society, the humiliation for women giving birth to the enemy's children symbolizes the destruction of the community. (1999: 803; compare Nikolic-Ristanovic 2000)

Human evolutionary prehistory and documented history have been, and continue to be, shaped not only by the means of production, but also, and perhaps all the more certainly, by the means of *re*production and the means of destruction. This is not a claim in favor of biological reductionism, determinism, or natural fallacy of any kind, but a better founded analysis that sees conflict and cooperation in international relations as *evolutionarily rooted behavioral options* that can be understood in a scientific way (e.g., Falger 2001a). The main implication for practical policy is that this behavior-analytic biopolitical dimension should be taken into account when analyzing the opponent's behavior. The male warriors/decisionmakers might also see themselves reflected in a mirror with a very deep perspective. For the victims of war rape in former Yugoslavia, an evolutionary approach provides no consolation, because it has no ethical implications for perpetrators or victims. That, by the way, may be one of the main reasons why "biopolitics" has not gained any popularity in political science, IR included. Another reason, undoubtedly, is that necessarily reductionist evolutionary explanation does not fit easily with detailed historical cases of the day, such as the situations in Africa, Iraq, or North Korea, that cry out for "solutions." An evolutionary approach is, paradoxically, not very *sexy* for mass media consumption, and requires a substantial familiarity with at least parts of a discipline—biology—that usually has no place in a social science curriculum. For the scientifically interested student of human behavior, however, it may be irresistible once one learns more about Darwin's dangerous idea (Dennett 1995).

■ Notes

The first part of this chapter is based on van der Dennen 2002.

1. The concept of "evolution" is frequently used in the nonbiologically oriented social sciences and, with a few exceptions, means nothing more than "development" or change, irrespective of how this change is caused.

2. In some nonstate societies the homicide rates are orders of magnitude higher than the ones in modern societies—even taking into account the statistics from two world wars (Davie 1929; Bigelow 1969; van der Dennen 1995; Keeley 1996; Pinker 2002).

3. Even an innovative study like Joshua Goldstein's *War and Gender* (2001) doesn't escape the traditional one-sidedness of nonevolutionary social science.

4. One aspect of the wars in the former Yugoslavia is their high asymmetry: the Serbs knew they could not gain a victory over the combined NATO forces, but they had the capacity to delay their enemies' victory substantially. Abusing the Kosovar Albanian population was one of the most noticeable elements of this strategy (de Wijk 2000, chap. 5).

5. This is an *explanatory* remark, not a moral or justificatory statement. Even if these behavioral repertoires belong to "human nature," they are neither good nor wrong as such.

6. In two reported cases the officer in charge used his position to exert some influence for the better: the case of the fourteen-year-old girl who wasn't raped because another woman was "available," and the case of the abused pregnant woman who was brought to a hospital afterward by the officer in charge (where the Serbian doctor refused to treat her).

chapter 10

English School
Approaches

Jennifer Sterling-Folker
The English School

As its name suggests, the English School originated in the British study of IR. Yet many of its present practitioners are not of that nationality, and the perspective is sometimes referred to as the "classical" or "international society" approach instead (Dunne 1998: 4). It developed out of what was called the British Committee on the Theory of International Politics, which was funded by the Rockefeller Foundation to be the parallel to an American Committee with a similar mission.[1] The British committee consisted of a group of IR scholars and policymakers who first met in January 1959, and as its membership expanded to include later generations of scholars, it held regular meetings until the early 1980s. Its organizers were Herbert Butterfield and Martin Wight, and some of the other original members who were to prove influential in the development of the English School were Hedley Bull, Adam Watson, and Michael Howard.[2] The committee represented, as Tim Dunne has observed, "the first self-conscious attempt to organize a community of scholars working in Britain for the purpose of generating a deeper understanding of the 'big questions' in International Relations" (1998: 89).

Although the English School did not initially develop a large following in the US discipline, some of its members were involved in the theoretical debate over methodology that roiled the discipline in the 1960s. This debate is often referred to as the "second great debate" in the discipline, and it reflected a fundamental dichotomy that exists to this day regarding how to study the subject matter of IR.[3] On one side were the behavioralists, who argued that the subject matter of IR should be studied scientifically, so that it would be limited only to phenomena that could be empirically observed and measured. They advocated the adoption of methods such as "attitude surveys, content analysis, simulation and gaming, statistical correlations, model building, and the use of computer-driven quantitative analysis as a basis for achieving precision in measurement and analysis" (Dougherty and Pfaltzgraff 1997: 33).[4] On the other side were the traditionalists, among whom Bull was representative; in his essay (1969) about the classical approach he argued that "the most important questions in international relations were not amenable to empirical verification" and that concepts such as "the state, international society, diplomatic community and so on were all knowable even if they were not observable" (Dunne 1998: 9).

While the debate was cast as a methodological disagreement by its participants, it clearly involved epistemological and ontological differences that foreshadowed the contemporary split between IR positivists and post-positivists. English School scholars, along with other traditionalists on both sides of the Atlantic, lost the battle to behavioralists in the US discipline, although the impact of behavioralism was never as totalizing as its critics feared it would be. But one unfortunate effect, as Miles Kahler notes, is that "the apparent defeat of the traditional or classical approach in this second great debate imposed losses even on the empirical program that the victorious scientists would pursue. International relations was severed from political philosophy, diplomatic history, and international law" (1997: 31). Fortunately these were subjects that English School scholars continued to explore, and the perspective continued to develop parallel to, but not in partnership with, subsequent theoretical perspectives and variants in the US discipline. Today the English School has adherents from around the globe, and an ISA section devoted to it was established in 2002.

The English School is often categorized as either a modified version of realism or a variant of liberal IR theorizing,[5] yet both of these characterizations are inaccurate. To be sure, realism was the perspective's starting point, and the committee was heavily influenced by the work of realist E. H. Carr. Hence the role of power in IR, and of balance of power in particular, is a central concern of the perspective. But many of the committee's originating members were dissatisfied with the ethical position that a subscription to realism seemed to suggest. The concern with ethical questions, and a concomitant interest in international diplomacy and law, was derived from classical realism, and it was precisely what was discarded by the scientifically oriented US neorealism (Jackson 1996: 212–213). These subjects were also discarded by many US liberal IR scholars. Despite a common interest in regimes as facilitators of international cooperation, for example, there are clear analytical differences between the English School and liberal IR variants such as neoliberal institutionalism. The result is that the English School attempts to combine elements of realism and liberalism under the same analytical umbrella.

In its focus on international law, the English School draws heavily on the philosophical work of Hugo Grotius, who had argued in the seventeenth century that when states accept international laws as binding, the establishment of an international legal order could effectively neutralize the impact of anarchy. The Grotian tradition, which English School scholars sometimes refer to instead as "rationalism," is juxtaposed to a Hobbesian tradition, which approximates realism and characterizes IR as a zero-sum context in which power is essential and war endemic. It is also juxtaposed to a Kantian tradition, which approximates liberalism and characterizes IR as a transnational social context that has the potential to evolve into a community based on common interests. Alternatively, the Grotian tradition characterizes IR as an "international society" in which states are bound, out of a combination of expediency and morality, by the rules and institutions they create (see Bull 1977: 13; and Bull and Watson 1984: 1). The Grotian tradition combines elements of the other two traditions, but differs in recognizing the critical tension between them, since in any given international situation, what may be minimally necessary to uphold a given legal order on the basis of self-interest might conflict with its moral demands for legal justice.

The concept of an "international society" is central to the English School perspective, which argues that the existence of such a society does not contradict the assumption that IR occurs in an anarchic environment. Rather there is an "anarchical society" (Bull 1977) of sovereign states that arises out of engineered balances of power, established rules based on customary behavior and enlightened self-interest, and a shared subscription to a particular set of universal norms. According to the English School, the creation of an international society allows its members to obtain three basic goals: "some limits on use of force, some provision for sanctity of contracts, and some arrangement for the assignment of property goods" (Buzan 1993: 334). Yet commonly held values and norms play as important a role in the creation and maintenance of international societies as do self-interests and power.

It is the combination of shared values and common self-interests that distinguishes the concept of international society, which is self-conscious and self-regulating, from that of an international system, which merely involves interacting parts (Buzan 1993: 331). There can be ordered relations in a system, but they are quite minimal, involving interactions such as diplomatic exchanges and negotiated treaties. An international society, on the other hand, is several ordering steps beyond this, involving shared understandings, common rules or procedures for interaction and conduct, and some sort of codification of these understandings and rules. It is possible to have international systems without international societies, and in fact the presence of international societies has been the historical exception rather than rule. Some examples of periods and regions that have been identified as international societies are the classical Greek city-states, the Chinese warring states, and the ancient state system of India.

Contemporary international society is founded on the principle of nation-state sovereignty, which constitutes a common understanding that nation-states have an obligation to respect the territorial integrity of other nation-states and refrain from interfering in their internal affairs. This understanding has given rise to long-standing behaviors, normative under-standings, and rules of conduct that have been codified in international law. The centrality of sovereign states to the formation of an international socie-ty is an important clue for distinguishing it from an international system. So too is the presence of self-conscious balance-of-power politics, which English School scholars argue are as essential as international norms and laws for the order and maintenance of an international society.

Given the general parameters of the perspective, a number of central questions drive English School scholarship. How, for example, do interna-tional societies come into being, and at what point can they be distin-guished from the international systems within which they are embedded? Have they always existed, and how is it possible to identify them historical-ly? Do international societies need to first develop out of regional subsys-tems, and must states always be the constitutive units of international soci-eties? To answer these questions, English School scholars have adopted a methodology involving the "historical sociology" of state systems, which traces the evolution of international society norms and behaviors. "In order to understand the institution of sovereignty, for example, an English School approach would advocate a historical sociology of the term and the mean-ings given to it by state leaders at particular historical junctures" (Dunne 1998: 186). In this way, the diplomatic and political practices that devolve from these different cultural and historical meanings may be traced and revealed. The approach is "interpretive" to the extent that it involves histor-ical and philosophical reflection, so that international society "remains bet-ter developed as a historical than as a theoretical concept" (Buzan 1993: 329). It is also "realist" to the extent that, as Dunne (1998: 119–120) notes, there is an implicit assumption that the lessons of history may be applied to contemporary IR.

There are divisions within the English School, however, and one important division involves the minimal foundations upon which interna-tional societies develop. Are societies created out of conscious self-interest, or do they evolve naturally on the basis of a preexisting common identity? In the former situation, which was expounded upon by Bull, international societies are consciously and contractually constructed. They develop out of functional interests that states hold in common, such as a desire to reduce interstate violence or protect property rights, and they do not require any preexisting cultural similarity. Alternatively in the latter situation, argued by Wight, international societies develop out of common experiences and identities, and shared social practices in culture, religion, and language serve as a necessary foundation for shared goals. Obviously these two foundations are not mutually exclusive, and it may be possible for an international society to start from a functional basis and then develop a common identity among its participants. It is also possible that international societies consist of concentric circles in which the core shares a common identity while more peripheral states participate for functional reasons alone (Buzan 1993: 345, 349–350). But an analytical tension between these two foundations remains, and it has interesting implications for how to analyze modern international society.

The tension informs debates between two variants within the English School known as the pluralists and the solidarists.[6] English School pluralists argue that states are interested in peaceful coexistence and will only agree to the minimum requirements for maintaining international order, such as the mutual respect of each other's sovereignty, nonintervention, and abiding by established codes of diplomacy. Beyond these principles, however, states will not act in concert to enforce larger moral principles, and encouraging them to do so can actually destabilize international order. English School solidarists, on the other hand, argue that there is at least the potential for the mutual respect and enforcement of international law and universal ethics based on shared values and norms. Given this potential, elements of solidarity should be encouraged "by drawing attention to them whenever they are left out of legal and political judgements, and by leaving a margin for the use of reason and morality in the interpretation of existing rules of law" (Knudsen 2002: 23). These solidarist concerns are quite clear in Chapter 10.2, in which Tonny Knudsen examines whether NATO's intervention in Kosovo had a legal basis and, if it did not, what this implies for international society and order.

English School pluralism and solidarism are not simply analytical alternatives; they represent alternative moral accounts of the nature of international society and what binds it together. They also suggest alternative policy prescriptions for maintaining the contemporary global order, since the solidarist's insistence on common responsibilities for universal justice is a potential source of conflict and instability from the pluralist point of view.[7] Thus the English School perspective is not simply about whether states *should* conform to international law or how to account for instances when they do not. It is instead about the tension that arises between the need for order and the desire for justice. While there have been attempts to bridge the pluralist-solidarist divide within the English School perspective (for example, Vincent 1986), these positions are not easily reconcilable. Instead they represent a basic philosophical problem that is also suggested by, but not fully delineated in, debates among realists, liberals, and constructivists over what produces cooperation (see, for example, Starr 1995).

The English School also differs from these other theoretical perspectives in that it takes seriously not only our ability to socially construct alternative orders, but also our moral responsibility to do so. The work of early scholars of the English School was influenced by Carr's observation that since people are generally willing to accept a given reality, ideas must have rhetorical and political power that can be mobilized to create new normatively informed social orders (Buzan 1993: 329–330). Thus the English School argues that "the international society tradition can offer critical openings into theorizing a universal moral order" (Dunne 1998: 189), and it is overtly committed to putting these philosophical observations into moral practice. Although the universal moral order envisioned by English School scholars is typically liberal in content, their desire to radically rethink and recast the subject matter of IR places the English School perspective closer to the poststructuralist end of the epistemological spectrum.

The English School does not simply deconstruct, however; rather it seeks to sustain and develop an international society in which the tension between order and justice will not destroy the consensus upon which the society rests. Hence the pluralist-solidarist divide within the perspective also represents a difference over *how* to socially construct the future world order, since "the very act of perceiving international relations in societal terms will itself condition behavior by opening new understandings of what is possible and what is desirable" (Buzan 1993: 330). In this way, the English School combines elements of almost all other IR theoretical perspectives, and at the same time it has maintained a Grotian tradition, involving law, morality, and international order, that was almost entirely lost to the US IR discipline.

■ **Further Reading**

Although he was not a member of the British Committee or an English School scholar, the work of E. H. Carr (1939) had an enormous impact on the perspective's development. The scholar most often identified as the "father" of the English School perspective is Martin Wight, yet the member who has been most influential within the discipline is Hedley Bull, whose book *The Anarchical Society* (1977) is frequently cited. Bull was a student of Wight's and played a lead role in having Wight's work (1991, 1978, 1977) published posthumously. Another member of the original British Committee whose work has been influential is Adam Watson, especially his book *The Evolution of International Society* (1992).

The original founder of the British Committee, Herbert Butterfield, is best known for a volume of early committee papers he and Wight edited, titled *Diplomatic Investigations* (1966). A subsequent edited volume by Bull and Watson, *The Expansion of International Society* (1984), represents the end of the collaboration among original committee members, but not of the English School itself. Tim Dunne's *Inventing International Society* (1998) provides an overview of the school's development and includes chapters devoted to each of its early practitioners.

By the mid-1970s, a second generation of English School scholars had emerged, and included Michael Donelan (1990, 1978), Murray Forsyth (1978), and James Mayall (1982). The work of one of Bull's students, R. J. Vincent (1974, 1986), was particularly influential on the post–Cold War generation of English School scholars. English School works that focus on the Grotius tradition, international law, and war include Best 1994, Bull, Kingsbury, and Roberts 1990, Cutler 1991, Howard 1991, and Howard 1983. Examples that focus on international society throughout history and the origins of the present international society include Buzan and Little 2000, Gong 1984, Suganami 1989, and Zhang 1998.

English School works that focus on ethics, intervention, human rights, and international law include Dunne and Wheeler 1999, James 1986, James 1973, Jackson Preece 1998, Keal 1992, Knudsen 2002, Knudsen 1996, Makinda 1997, Rengger 1999, and Wright 1996. Other seminal works in the English School include Brown 1995, Epp 1998, Fawn and Larkin 1996, Jackson 1999a, Jackson 1999b, Jackson 1995, Jackson 1990, Manning 1962, Miller and Vincent 1990, Navari 1991, and Roberson 2002. Scholars such as Andrew Linklater and Iver Neumann might also be cited as English School participants, although their work has been listed in the overview chapters on postmodernism and critical theory, and constructivism, respectively.

There are a number of works about the relationship between the English School, other IR theories, and the US discipline of IR, including Buzan 2001, Buzan 1993, Der Derian 1988, Dunne 2001, Dunne 1995, Evans and Wilson 1992, Holsti 1997, Hurrell 1993, Jackson 1996, Jørgensen and Knudsen 2006, Little 1995, and Wæver 2002. James Der Derian's volume (1995a), cited in the overview chapter on postmodernism and critical theory, purposely pairs English School essays with articles from positivist and postpositivist perspectives in the discipline. Barry Buzan has also posted a comprehensive bibliography of English School sources on the Web (http://www.ukc.ac.uk/politics/englishschool), which was useful in compiling this list of sources.

■ Notes

1. The American Committee consisted of prominent realists, such as Reinhold Niebuhr, Hans Morgenthau, Arnold Wolfers, Friedrich Nitze, Richard Fox, William

Thompson, and Kenneth Waltz, but Tim Dunne (1998: 90) notes that it was less successful due to divisions between the theorists and the policymakers in the group.

2. Other members of the committee included Desmond Williams, Donald Mackinnon, Geoffrey Hudson, and William Armstrong, most of whom were not scholars of IR (Dunne 1998: xiii). Dunne 1998, chap. 5, provides details on the committee's formation, membership, and inner workings.

3. See Chapter 6.1, endnote 4, in this volume for a description of the other debates.

4. James Dougherty and Robert Pfaltzgraff further note that precision was necessary for "what was hoped would be a cumulative theory linking various islands of theory in a grand or general theory of IR based on interlinked propositions" (1997: 33). The debate between the behavioralists and traditionalists played out in the pages of *World Politics* and *International Studies Quarterly*, and some of the most seminal pieces, including Bull's essay, were later published in an edited volume by Klaus Knorr and James Rosenau 1969. Dunne (1998, chap. 6) provides an interesting discussion of this debate from the traditionalist and non-American perspective.

5. For example, Paul Viotti and Mark Kauppi (1999: 63–64) include a discussion of the English School in their chapter on realism, while Mark Zacher and Richard Matthews (1995: 133–134) discuss it as an institutional strand of liberal theorizing.

6. The terms were introduced by Bull (1966, 1977), and Knudsen notes that they are "a reflection of a much older controversy between the legal traditions of positivism and naturalism over the nature of international society and the proper foundation of international law" (2002: 21). Pluralists are grounded in legal positivism, while solidarists are grounded in cosmopolitan ethics.

7. Dunne (1998: 11) notes that the two variants provide alternative answers to a variety of normative questions in the discipline, including the use of force and conduct of war, justification for intervention, distribution of global resources, and the content of human rights. Knudsen (2002: 24–25) provides a useful discussion and chart of their differences.

Tonny Brems Knudsen

The English School: Sovereignty and International Law

At first sight, the 1998 rebellion of the Albanians of Kosovo and the ensuing patterns of civil war, atrocious conduct, mass expulsion, and international intervention may seem to be just another example of the tragic violent conflicts and the troublesome collective attempts to manage them that plagued the international community after the end of the Cold War. Seen in this light, the Kosovo conflict can be studied as one of several post–Cold War examples of civil war, humanitarian intervention, and collective action based on central international institutions as the UN, NATO, the EU, and the OSCE. In an English School perspective, this gives rise to questions concerning the relationship between sovereignty and human rights, the practices of (humanitarian) intervention, the sometimes conflicting imperatives of international order and international justice, and the managerial and legitimizing roles of international organizations.

However, a closer look reveals that this was not just a "normal" intervention of the 1990s, but one that raised new practical and theoretical questions concerning the legitimacy of humanitarian intervention, the nature of sovereign statehood, the scope of the responsibility of the international community toward individuals and nations at risk, and the pros and cons of a policy that holds on to the rules of the UN Charter and international law. It also raises questions regarding the proper way to deal with the new challenge of post-conflict administration and reconstruction of war-torn societies and contested territories. On these latter questions, Kosovo is not only to be studied as a possible precedent for new practices in the fields of intervention, collective management, and peacebuilding. To the English School, it is also a case that questions some of the norms, rules, institutions, and practices that were thought to be fundamental to the international order. And it is a case that has forced the agent, observer, and student of IR to consider whether the time might be ripe for a revival of ideas and institutions that, at least in some quarters, were seen as discredited, such as international trusteeship, the prosecution of war criminals at international courts of justice, and international society's far-reaching and fundamental responsibility for global order and justice. However, to the English School such ideas and institutional developments should be evaluated not only on the basis of their immediate and practical value, but also in terms of their likely long-term impact on international society and especially the global bases of order and justice.

More precisely, a study of the Kosovo case informed by the English School and its international society approach would, among other things, attempt to answer the following main questions. First, where do the events that took place in Kosovo and the former Yugoslavia in 1998–1999 leave the right of humanitarian intervention, particularly in relation to principles of state sovereignty, nonintervention, and the general prohibition against the use of force? Second, what do the civil war, the atrocities, and the intervention tell us about the principles and politics of international legitimacy at the beginning of the twenty-first century? Third, how far do the responsibility and authority of the international community go with respect to the reconstruction of war-torn societies like Kosovo? More specifically, should the Kosovo conflict (and the situations in Afghanistan and Iraq) lead us to reflect on the possible practical and moral limits of the attempt by the Western world to promote its core values of human rights and democracy throughout the world? This does not cover the entire analytical agenda of the English School, but hopefully the following analyses will give the reader an impression of how this perspective would approach questions that are only touched upon in passing (such as great power cooperation and rivalry, intervention across cultural boundaries, and nationalism and national self-determination). First, however, a brief look at some of the relevant ideas and tools of the English School.

■ Theory of International Society

For the English School, "international society" is not simply another name for what the realist tradition refers to as "international anarchy," that is, a system of states characterized by competition, conflict, and power politics.[1] On the contrary, what is meant by the term "international society" is a social order in which states as well as peoples, individuals, international organizations, and a number of other actors are engaged in habitual and regularized interaction based on shared interests and values, shared norms and rules, and shared institutions and practices.[2] An international *society* is, in other words, much more than an international *system,* since the latter can be conceived of simply as a group of interacting states, meaning a state of affairs in which two or more states have sufficient contact with each other to cause them to behave as parts of a whole (Bull 1977: 9–16).

According to the English School, modern international society is not a fiction, but a reality that can be identified, evaluated, and discussed in terms of several dimensions. First, it is an idea that exists inside the minds of state leaders, diplomats, NGO representatives, journalists, and ordinary citizens throughout the world, and that is shared by them and often appealed to in national and international dialogues at all levels. Second, the idea of international society has a normative expression in shared rules, norms, and standards of morality, and in the related language of social, orderly, and just interaction. Third, it has an institutional manifestation in fundamental practices or arrangements like sovereignty, diplomacy, international law, the balance of power, great power management, and intervention, as well as in international governmental and nongovernmental organizations like the UN and Amnesty International. Finally, it has a physical expression in embassies, in documents of international law, and in the buildings and machinery of international organizations, just to mention a few examples (Manning 1962; James 1973; Bull 1977; Watson 1982).

The main focus of the English School is on the institutionalized practices and shared expectations of international society. At a general level the combined effects of such shared practices and expectations amount to a universal structure of international order and elements of justice. Changes in the most fundamental shared expectations and practices are therefore also potentially changes of relevance to international order and justice. At a more specific level, the institutional insights of the English School provide for analyses of continuity and change as well as accounts of specific behavior, since states and other actors are inclined, but not forced, to act on the basis of existing practices and to justify their actions with reference to existing shared values, norms, and rules. The strong side of the pluralistic approach of the English School is that it captures the interplay between power and norms and the game of international politics as it is played out day-by-day on the basis of diplomatic practices, international rules, and institutional arrangements. It also captures central dilemmas like order versus justice, power versus morality, and national versus international (or global) concerns (James 1973; Bull 1977; Jackson 2000; Buzan 2004). Moreover, it offers insight into dynamics such as the orientations of insiders and outsiders (Wight 1977; Watson 1992; Buzan 1993; Wæver 1996a), the quest for national self-determination and recognition (Mayall 1990; Fawn and Mayall 1996), changes in sovereignty and international legitimacy (Wight 1977; James 1986; Sørensen 1999; Jackson 2000),[3] and the possible transformation of international society to a kind of world society (Bull 1977; Suganami 1989; Buzan 1993; Linklater 1998).[4]

How can state sovereignty be reconciled with human rights in cases like the atrocities and ensuing intervention in Kosovo in 1998–1999? How can human rights be enforced and how important is UN Security Council authorization in such circumstances? How can one settle the legitimacy of an act like NATO's attack on Yugoslavia in 1999 on the grounds of humanity? Who has a right of self-determination and how should it be effectuated? Should the international community take responsibility for war-torn societies like Bosnia, Kosovo, and East Timor? What means of global governance do we have and how can they be improved? The English School does not necessarily have a conclusive answer to all these questions, but it does have the tools for a fruitful discussion and analysis. Some of these tools include the holistic conception of international society, the institutional account of continuity and change, the contrast of order and justice in international politics, the distinction between so-called pluralist and solidarist principles of international conduct,[5] and the theory of situational ethics and legitimacy, which will be further introduced and activated as the chapter unfolds.[6]

■ Legitimacy, Legality, and the Importance of International Organization

According to the English School, the international reception and destiny of a given policy (for instance, the Western promotion of a right of humanitarian intervention in the 1990s or the US promotion of a doctrine of preemptive warfare after September 11, 2001) or a specific step (for instance, the air campaign against Yugoslavia in 1999 or the war against Iraq in 2003) will depend not only on power, position, and national interests, but also, and perhaps even most of all, on the extent to which the given policy or step is in accordance with, or compatible with, already established shared expectations, values, rules, and institutions. Furthermore, it is an English School ground rule that any event or development in international relations must be analyzed, discussed, and understood with a view to the specific context and the historical background (Jackson 2000).

As for the air campaign against Yugoslavia launched by NATO on March 24, 1999, it must be evaluated against the immediate background of thirteen months of civil war and persecution in the province (although of shifting intensity) involving massacres, the burning of villages, looting, killing of livestock, and displacement and expulsion of more than 400,000 people, the great majority being civilian Kosovar Albanians.[7] The wider background included an almost universal common understanding that the international community had reacted too late and too weakly against the atrocious civil war in Bosnia in 1992–1995. Another important factor was the generally good and cooperative climate between the great powers following the end of the Cold War, including a common understanding that the use of force should be based on collective action and legitimization at the UN and directed toward the defense of international peace and fundamental humanitarian standards. Given the context and the background, it was therefore not surprising that to the international community, the Kosovo crisis became a question of whether, when, and how to launch a humanitarian intervention just as it was clear that such a step was expected to be grounded in the collective framework of the UN system.

Although order and stability played a role as well, NATO's own justification at the outset of the air campaign against Yugoslavia was almost exclusively humanitarian:

> We act to protect thousands of innocent people in Kosovo from a mounting military offensive. . . . This is not war in the traditional sense. It is an attack by tanks and artillery on a largely defenseless people, whose leaders already have agreed to peace. . . . Our mission is clear: . . . To deter an even bloodier offensive against innocent civilians in Kosovo and, if necessary, to seriously damage the Serbian military's capacity to harm the people of Kosovo. In short, if President Milosevic will not make peace, we will limit his ability to make war. (Clinton 1999c)[8]

The view that the situation in Kosovo should first and foremost be regarded as a case of humanitarian crisis, atrocious behavior, and forceful displacement of refugees was not just NATO's. It was also the dominating view in the UN Security Council and the UN in general, as evident from the following statement by UN Secretary-General Kofi Annan in June 1998, when he commented on a NATO air exercise designed to make an impression on President Slobodan Milosevic:

> I think if we use diplomacy and force that threatens, we should be able to succeed. . . . All of you, who have been following the last few months in Kosovo must begin to wonder whether another Bosnia looms on the horizon. . . . Already the shelling, the ethnic cleansings, the indiscriminate attacks on civilians in the name of security are taking place. . . . All our professions of regret, all our expressions of determination to never again permit another Bosnia, all our hopes for a peaceful future for the Balkans will be cruelly mocked if we allow Kosovo to become another killing field. It is in our hands now.[9]

However, since the Western leaders never managed to obtain a UN Security Council authorization to use all necessary means to bring an end to the atrocities and mass displacement of civilians, the legality and legitimacy of the intervention can be questioned, as it was by Russia, China, and India in the Security Council and by some observers in the West.[10]

According to the legal system laid down in Article 2(4,7) of the UN Charter, the use of force is illegal unless it takes place in self-defense against an armed attack (Article 51) or in defense of international peace and security when explicitly authorized by the UN Security Council (Articles 39–42). The UN Security Council could have defined the mass violations of international humanitarian law and the humanitarian crisis in Kosovo as a threat to international peace and security and then authorized the use of force for humanitarian reasons without breaking with the practice it had developed in the 1990s (as evident from the UN-authorized humanitarian interventions in Somalia, Bosnia, and Rwanda) on the basis of an extended interpretation of the UN Charter.[11] The fact that it did not do so had nothing to do with the scale of the abuses (they were systematic and excessive) or a lack of diplomatic initiatives (they were numerous, but fruitless). The reason was Russia's persistent policy of preventing the authorization of the use of force in the UN Security Council, something that can only be explained by Russia's special relationship with Yugoslavia. This relationship can be compared with the constructive attitude of Russia in a number of cases where the UN had authorized the use of force for humanitarian purposes, including Somalia, Rwanda, and to some extent even Bosnia, where Belgrade had been the target of international intervention as well. UN Security Council Resolution 1199 of September 23, 1998, demanded that the Yugoslav authorities should "cease all action by the security forces affecting the civilian population and order the withdrawal of security units used for civilian repression." Following its passage, the Russian delegate, who had supported the resolution on behalf of Russia and admitted that the Kosovar Albanian refugees were "fraught with grave humanitarian consequences," was happy to note:

> No use of force and no sanctions are being imposed by the Council at the present stage. The basic provisions of the draft resolution correspond to the fundamental stance taken by the Russian Federation which favours settlement of the conflict in Kosovo exclusively through peaceful and political means on the basis of granting broad autonomy to Kosovo, with strict respect for the territorial integrity of the Federal Republic of Yugoslavia. (S/PV.3930 1998: 2–3)[12]

It was, in other words, a mixed situation in that there were moral and legal grounds (under international humanitarian law) for a humanitarian intervention in Kosovo on the one hand, while on the other hand the ultimate requirement for the legality of such military operations, namely a UN Security Council authorization, was not fulfilled when NATO resorted to force in March 1999. To the English School this puts the questions of the legality and the legitimacy of the intervention at the center of the academic inquiry. Whereas legality is a question to be settled by reference to the relevant principles and documents of international law (including the UN Charter, international humanitarian law, the resolutions of the UN Security Council, and customary law), the question of legitimacy must also be settled by reference to moral and political standards and not least by reference to international public opinion.

In a narrow legal interpretation, the resort to force by NATO was illegal, since it was not a case of self-defense and since the UN Security Council had not authorized the use of force. Furthermore, all other things being equal, the sovereign rights of states, here Yugoslavia, still command much respect and legitimacy among agents and observers of international politics. It can also be argued that force was not really the last option, and that diplomacy combined with a continued presence of OSCE observers on the ground should have been given one more chance following the breakdown of the Rambouillet negotiations.

On the other hand a number of circumstances can be argued to add to the legitimacy and possibly also the legality of the resort to force. First, the West tried time and again to unite the UN Security Council behind political and military pressure for humanitarian purposes, but Russian obstruction made the threat and use of force under the auspices of the UN impossible. Consequently, the ultimate recourse to force outside the UN framework cannot be condemned on the grounds that NATO wanted to bypass the UN and keep Russia out. To the extent that one agrees that NATO tried fully and wholeheartedly to act within the institutional and legal framework of international society, this adds to the legitimacy and arguably also the legality of the intervention.

Second, in his reports to the UN Security Council and elsewhere, UN Secretary-General Kofi Annan repeatedly condemned the assaults on civilians in Kosovo and expressed the opinion that the UN Security Council should resort to the threat and, if necessary, use of force to bring an end to the atrocities and prevent a humanitarian disaster. Annan even indicated that a UN-authorized humanitarian intervention might have been justified in June 1998, as evident from the statement cited above. Although the mandate was never given, and although the position of the UN secretary-general has no direct and immediate legal force, his endorsement of the principle of humanitarian intervention in this specific case (as indicated also in statements after NATO's resort to force) adds to the legitimacy of the acts of NATO. It also lends credence to its legality, if one shares the view of some international lawyers that general public opinion, not least as expressed by persons of special international authority, counts as a secondary source for the interpretation of international law.

Third, diplomatic means and a gradual escalation to the threat of force were tried several times before the NATO campaign was launched. In June 1998 this pressure resulted in a Russian-Yugoslav memorandum of understanding, in October it provided for the deployment of OSCE observers, and in February and March 1999 it produced the two rounds of negotiations in France. But the assaults on the Kosovar Albanian population did not stop. It should be taken into account that the excessive use of force by the Yugoslav army, militia, and police was to some extent deliberately provoked by the assaults of the KLA. However, there is no doubt that the international community and NATO gave diplomacy a reasonable chance to work before the resort to force, as clearly required by international law (note, for instance, the system in Articles 39–42 of the UN Charter). That all other means must be exhausted is also a generally recognized moral and political requirement.

Fourth, before and after the decision to resort to force without the UN, a lot was done to keep Russia on board. These efforts included the attempt to establish a common ground in the UN Security Council, which led to the adoption of three resolutions, the use of the great power Contact Group as the key forum of negotiation and mediation that produced the Rambouillet political accord among other things, and the invitations to Russia to participate in a ground operation along with NATO and other countries, for instance in February and April 1999 ("Kosovo Mediators" 1999). Seen from an English School perspective, this is important for the discussion of legitimacy, since it indicates that there was an attempt to hold on to a truly collective approach (and in a nondictatorial way) guided by the framework of the UN Charter and the political wisdom of collective and concerted great power action. However, the final judgment of the NATO decision to bypass the UN Security Council and thus to ignore the opposition of Russia and China depends on whether the prospects of reaching a possible future agreement on Kosovo and avoiding further atrocities without intervention were so good that the international community would have been justified in giving diplomacy more time.

Fifth, it should be taken into account that when NATO finally did resort to force despite the absence of a mandate, the great majority of the UN Security Council refused to accept a draft resolution from Russia according to which the Council should have declared that it was "deeply concerned that NATO used military force against the Federal Republic of Yugoslavia without the authorization by the Council," and that this was "a flagrant violation of the United Nations Charter" (UNSC/6659 1999: 1). The draft resolution was defeated in a historic vote of twelve against three, China and Namibia being the only members to support Russia. Although this does not amount to a legally valid defense of the resort to force, it does add substantially to its general legitimacy.

Sixth, the fact that UN Security Council Resolution 1244 put the military security on a proper UN mandate (providing for KFOR) and the political responsibility for reconstruction under UN administration (providing for UNMIK) can be said to add to the legitimacy of the outside intervention as a whole, given that it was a testimony of the declared will of NATO to return to the UN and the framework of international law as quickly as possible. However, the initial attempt by the West to prevent a substantial Russian role in postwar Kosovo could be seen as a degrading factor.

In sum, the case for humanitarian interference and intervention was strong, it was underlined by the UN secretary-general on several occasions, and it was pursued by the West under the auspices of the UN over a period of thirteen months before the threat of force was carried out. In the end, the philosophy of the Western great powers was that in order to bring an end to the atrocities and the steady displacement of Kosovar Albanians, President Milosevic had to be faced with the choice between a political settlement that deprived him of the de facto control over the province, at least for a period, and military punishment.

Consequently, it may be argued that whereas the greatest problem in terms of legality was the absence of a UN authorization of the use of force, the greatest problem in terms of the general legitimacy of the intervention was the fact that NATO attempted to conduct a humanitarian intervention from the air without interfering between the Serbian forces and their victims on the ground (Roberts 1999). Although protecting the victims from the perpetrators is the essence of the idea of humanitarian intervention, NATO did not even plan for such an interposition of forces, and for weeks it explicitly ruled out the option despite the crimes that were committed against the Kosovar Albanian population during the air campaign.

The methods and potential of an English School analysis of questions of legality might be further illustrated by means of a comparison with the war against Iraq in 2003. In both cases, a valid and explicit UN authorization of the resort to force was missing. However, in the case of Iraq the humanitarian grounds for the use of force were significantly weaker insofar as there were no ongoing massacres or assaults on parts of the population. Torture was committed in the Iraqi jails and the Marsh Arabs of southern Iraq were treated badly, but the worst of Saddam Hussein's crimes against humanity took place in the late 1980s and the early 1990s. It was too late to undo these crimes against humanity in 2003, and the inevitable costs of war and intervention have to be weighed against the evil that the resort to force is supposed to bring to an end.[13] This is a hard test to pass for the war against Iraq. Clearly the already established right of humanitarian intervention against genocide and massive crimes against humanity does not allow for the resort to force in cases like Iraq 2003 (in contrast to the situation in Iraq in the late 1980s and in 1991). Furthermore, the United States and its allies did not take the case against Iraq to the UN Security Council as a predominantly humanitarian case. It was argued to be a case of Iraqi noncompliance and of Iraqi weapons of mass destruction demanding preemptive action, a case that was not strong enough and evident enough to provide for the use of force in March 2003 according to the majority of the members of the UN Security Council. Finally, and presumably as a consequence of these circumstances, UN Secretary-General Kofi Annan did not indicate his support of the resort to force against Iraq as he did in the case of Kosovo. On the contrary, he dismissed it, although in diplomatic terms.

Although the war against Iraq cannot be defended on the grounds of international law, or the argument that this was the last option to protect international peace and security and a population facing slaughter, it might still be defended. What is left is the moral argument that the war was justified in order to overthrow a brutal dictator for the sake of his population. This means that in the end, the legitimacy of the war against Iraq will depend on the ability of the coalition and the international community to build a better and more humane society in Iraq. Thus, in an English School perspective it is not surprising that the war against Iraq was met with considerably more international criticism and greater skepticism than the intervention in Kosovo. However, in both cases the academic challenge is to pay attention to all the relevant sources of international legitimacy and to balance them against each other.[14]

■ The Importance of the UN

As a part of the agenda concerning legitimacy and legality, Kosovo also posed the question as to what role the UN can play with respect to the defense of peace, security, and the minimum standards of humanity when the organization is paralyzed by disagreement between the great powers. The lesson that can be learned and possibly transferred to other cases of great power disagreement in the UN Security Council is that the UN should not be seen as a competitor to the great powers in questions regarding international order, peace, and security. The UN is first of all an institutional framework in which the great powers and other states have especially good opportunities to agree on and legitimize diplomatic and military steps concerning such central tasks as the maintenance of peace, the prevention of massacres, and the fight against terror, and in which there is a particularly strong expertise in the techniques of peacekeeping and reconstruction of war-torn societies. In other words, the UN is a resource that states can, should, and—as a matter of legal principle when we are talking about the use of force—are obliged to draw on. At the same time, the UN cannot act independently of the support of its member states, in particular the great powers.

Seen in this light, the UN is capable of what leading powers make it capable of, plus the extra value of the diplomatic, legal, political, and operative machinery that—with respect to coalition building, international legitimacy, and conflict management—makes the UN more than the sum of its members and supporters. Judging from Kosovo and Iraq, this institutional platform is not just one the great powers decide to use or bypass at the outset of an international conflict. It is a standing institutional platform for the possible legitimization of diplomatic and military activities and for the possible implementation of political projects like the societal reconstruction in Kosovo, in which the UN played a leading and (depending on the standard of judgment) relatively successful role, and possibly also Iraq depending on whether political consensus can be reached.

The evidence also shows that although the UN cannot, and in some cases should not, undertake military interventions like the ones in Kosovo and Iraq, the world organization may be indispensable when it comes to consensus building, international legitimization, and postconflict peace-building. What unites all quarters of the English School is the view that in the current international order, neither the great powers nor international society can do without the UN, which is at the center of the international legal order and which has become an essential forum for collective management of international conflict and the maintenance of the great power concert. In the terms of the English School, the UN has acquired the status and importance of what may be called a semifundamental international institution.[15]

■ International Trusteeship: Governance and Responsibility in International Society

With the adoption of UN Security Council Resolution 1244 on June 10, 1999, NATO's humanitarian intervention in Kosovo gave way to the establishment of UNMIK and KFOR, which provided the military backup for the UN and its many partners in the ongoing attempt to reconstruct the province (Independent International Commission on Kosovo 2000, pt. 1). The creation of this multiorganizational administration of Kosovo led by the UN is an arrangement that amounts to "an international trusteeship in everything but name" (Jackson 2000: 307).

To the English School this development, which has been paralleled by the establishment of other arrangements (for instance in Bosnia and East Timor) on a scale comparable to the international protectorates and trustee-ships of the first and middle parts of the twentieth century, immediately raises some fundamental political, legal, and normative questions. How far does the responsibility of the international community toward minorities, nations, and peoples go? Under what conditions and for how long may the sovereign rights of a state be suspended? Who should take responsibility for the territory and people in question and how can such a decision be taken? These are questions of statehood, national self-determination, international responsibility, and international governance.

Seen from the international society perspective of the English School, the enforced transferal of authority from a sovereign state (here the former Yugoslavia, which has now been succeeded by the state union of Serbia and Montenegro) to an international organization representing the international community and local centers of government is problematic in several respects. First, what happens to the international faith in the principle of mutual recognition and respect of state sovereignty if the path taken by the international community in dealing with the problems of Kosovo becomes standard practice? Second, can orderly affairs be maintained in the world if a number of states may have reason to fear that their borders and sovereign powers are not respected? Third, can an international trusteeship arrangement, be it formal or informal as in Kosovo, lead to independence for the concerned territory and people despite the attempt of the parent state (here the successor state union of Serbia and Montenegro) to hold on to its sovereignty over the territory in question?

On the other hand, if the international community cannot and should not turn its back on peoples who are exposed to acts of genocide, massacres, mass expulsion, and other crimes against humanity, what are its responsibilities after the atrocities have been brought to an end by means of military intervention? Surely an international coalition cannot leave the people in question behind with a destructed country, refugee problems, and a hostile and murderous climate, nor can it hand the people and the territory back to the government that, directly or indirectly, was responsible for the humanitarian disaster.

The promotion of the well-being and development of the inhabitants of the mandated territories was certainly the main justification of the mandate system established under the League of Nations after World War I, and preparation for self-government or independence became one of the stipulated goals of the postwar UN trusteeship system provided for in Chapter XII and XIII in the UN Charter (Lyon 1993: 99–100; Murray 1957; Brügel 1967). The UN trusteeship system is an obvious starting point for discussion, despite the fact that Kosovo is governed by an interim administration under the auspices of the UN Security Council and the UN secretary-general as provided for in Resolution 1244, instead of being a formal trusteeship under Chapters XII and XIII. However, the UN trusteeship system was intended for (1) former mandates of the League of Nations, (2) territories detached from enemy states in World War II, and (3) colonial territories placed under the trusteeship system by states responsible for their administration (Lyon 1993: 100–105).

In other words, the system was, in reality, intended for territories with an unclear or problematic status as of 1945, and for colonies or similar territories that the sovereign state at some point would be prepared to send on the road toward self-rule and independence. Trusteeships were not to be established against the will of the relevant sovereign state, and territories that progressed to independence were not supposed to fall under outside administration again. Moreover, the system itself became redundant with the wave of decolonization in the 1960s and 1970s, and with the adoption of the Declaration of the Granting of Independence to Colonial Countries and Peoples in the UN General Assembly in 1960, which stressed that backwardness could never be an excuse for the rejection of independence.

From a legal and institutional point of view, then, it is easy to see that international administration of a territory and its population is problematic when we talk about a political unit that is already an established state or a part of such a state. The formal UN trusteeship system is officially suspended, but even if it were functioning, Kosovo could not have fallen under it without a highly creative interpretation, at least not without the explicit and unenforced consent of Belgrade. Moreover, if an imposed trusteeship arrangement—which is a suspension of sovereignty—is followed by independence for a part of the territory of a sovereign state, it becomes legally and institutionally controversial, to say the least. In the case of Kosovo, the imposition of a de facto trusteeship arrangement was already in itself a recognition of minority rights and a right to self-rule as also stated directly in Resolution 1244. If minority protection and self-rule are followed by independence, we are talking about the termination of the sovereign rights of the parent state as a consequence of a process of humanitarian intervention and international administration. Trusteeship becomes a midway station to independence.

For these reasons, it is a very delicate question whether a trusteeship arrangement not wanted by the original holder of sovereign power over the territory in question can give way to independent statehood. On the other hand, there is still such a thing as a right of national self-determination that might be invoked in favor of the independence of Kosovo, and there is still a duty not to turn against one's own population in an atrocious way as the Yugoslav authorities did against their Albanian population in 1998–1999. There is also a historical and political logic of international trusteeship in which the goal of outside administration must be to prepare the people in question for self-rule or independence. If orderly and civilized conditions of governance were a fact at the outset, a kind of international administration could hardly have become a subject at all. These are the kinds of fundamental questions and dilemmas that the English School is inclined to address and answer on the basis of legal principles, political prudence, and practical implications.

Notwithstanding the great variation in the degree and success of the international response, cases of failure in the state-based international order, such as Bosnia, Kosovo, East Timor, Afghanistan, Iraq, and a number of instances in Africa, suggest that the reemerging international trusteeship institution is a valuable and indispensable option in contemporary international society. Its relationship with other fundamental institutions like sovereignty on the one hand (associated with the English School pluralist architecture of international society) and humanitarian intervention and national self-determination on the other (associated with the

English School solidarist architecture of international society) must be resolved by means of legal adjustment, political reasoning, and practical experience.[16]

In other words, the questions concerning the trusteeship of Kosovo and what comes after—in reality a question of what degree of self-determination it will lead to—cannot be answered in any definitive way solely on the basis of a theoretical and historical insight into the requirements of international order. It is clear, however, that the requirements of international order should play a central role in a theoretical judgment of the situation. It is also highly likely that these requirements will be important to the international community, including its central organizations and the great powers, when trying to answer the question of Kosovo's future status. At the same time, however, the lessons learned in Kosovo (and other central cases like East Timor) with respect to international intervention, international administration, and future status will influence the general views and norms regarding sovereignty, international governance, and self-determination. In other words, the current period might turn out to be a transformative one in which the institution of international trusteeship is reinstalled as a central practice or institution in international society and in which the right of national self-determination is reinterpreted in a less strict manner with respect to the possibility of obtaining independence against the will of the parent state.

■ Kosovo and the Study of International Society: Further Implications

Seen from an English School perspective, Kosovo shows that there is such a thing as an international society with moral and political norms (about humanitarianism, responsibility, accountability, etc.), legal rules (about intervention, the use of force, the treatment of individuals, etc.), fundamental institutions (such as diplomacy and great power management), diplomatic endeavors (Rambouillet, the Group of Eight, the Contact Group), and institutional practices (the UN system, humanitarian intervention, international trusteeship, etc.).

It also shows that international rules, institutions, and practices may be challenged, negotiated, and reformulated, sometimes leading to new shared understandings and new practices. In the case of Kosovo, new norms and rules of humanitarian intervention were introduced and so were new practices of international management of war-torn societies. At the same time, the status of the UN as the sole legitimate authorizing body with respect to the use of force was challenged, only to be, in some respects, reconfirmed as indicated by Resolution 1244 and the international debate after the intervention. This was repeated in the more recent case of Iraq, but this time the challenge to the UN, international law, and international cooperation was much more dramatic and costly, but so were, arguably, the lessons paid.

■ Notes

1. For the classical realist view on international politics, see Carr 1939 and Morgenthau and Thompson 1985. For the neorealist view, see Waltz 1979 and Mearsheimer 1990.

2. It should be noted that the primacy ascribed to the state vis-à-vis other actors in international politics varies from writer to writer and from text to text. See, for instance, Manning 1962, Wight 1966, Bull 1977, Jackson 2000, Wheeler 2000, and Buzan 2004.

3. See also *Political Studies* 47 (1999), which is a special issue on sovereignty conducted mainly from an English School perspective.

4. Another interesting line of work is the comparison of historical states systems and the study of world history: Wight 1977, Watson 1992, Wæver 1996a, Buzan and Little 2000.

5. The pluralist conception of international society holds that states can only be expected to agree on the minimum requirements of international order. These would include mutual respect of sovereignty, nonintervention, and the norms and principles of diplomacy; agreement that collective enforcement of common principles is likely to be the exception to the rule; and agreement that there are many different ideas of "the good society" and "the good life" in the world. In contrast, the solidarist conception of international society is based on the assumption of solidarity or potential solidarity among states with respect to the enforcement of international rules, including also the rights and duties of the individual. Consequently, this perspective on international society believes in the existence of common values, in the potential of international organization, and in the responsibility of international society toward individuals, minorities, and peoples at risk. See Bull 1966, Kingsbury and Roberts 1990, Vincent 1990, Wheeler 2000: 21–52, Jackson 2000, and Knudsen 2005.

6. For a more extensive introduction to the English School, see Knudsen 2002 and Jackson and Sørensen 1999: 140–174. For a detailed appreciation of a number of the key writers of the English School, see Dunne 1998. On the school and its potential, see also Buzan 2001 and the associated website, http://www.ukc.ac.uk/politics/englishschool, as well Wæver 1998a.

7. The atrocities and forced displacements were well described by the United Nations High Commissioner for Refugees (UNHCR), by the OSCE (see Hayden 1999), and in the reports by UN Secretary-General Kofi Annan to the UN Security Council in 1998 and 1999.

8. In his speech, Bill Clinton also argued that in addition to the moral imperative, the United States had an interest in preventing the spread of war in the region.

9. Statement by UN Secretary-General Kofi Annan at a news conference in Rome following a joint appearance with NATO Secretary-General Javier Solana before the Italian Senate on June 15, 1998 ("Annan and Solana Hail Action" 1998; "NATO Jets Fly" 1998).

10. See UNSC/6657 1999, and UNSC/6659 1999.

11. On post–Cold War humanitarian intervention, see Knudsen 2005, and Knudsen 1996.

12. In contrast, the British delegate tried to maximize the implicit threat contained in the resolution: "Nothing can justify scorched earth tactics and forcible cre-

ation of hundreds of thousands of refugees . . . the international community's patience is exhausted" (S/PV.3930 1998: 4).

13. This is an example of what Robert Jackson (2000) calls "situational ethics."

14. For further discussion and analysis of the war against Iraq including also a comparison with the intervention in Kosovo, see Knudsen 2004.

15. For an analysis of various levels and examples of the institutional bases of international society, see Buzan 2004.

16. On pluralism and solidarism, see endnote 5 above. Generally, the cautious and skeptical approach toward the trusteeship institution is associated with the pluralist conception of international society, whereas the more enthusiastic approach is associated with the solidarist one. See Jackson 2000.

chapter 11

Applying International Relations Theory

Jennifer Sterling-Folker

This last chapter offers some practical suggestions on how to apply IR theory. As noted in the introductory chapter, applying theory is not exactly easy. It requires a willingness to engage in creative mental play, while simultaneously searching for puzzles and patterns to particular events and larger topics. The theories themselves may also pose problems for application. There are multiple and at times contradictory propositions, hypotheses, and insights that can be culled from the major texts of each theoretical perspective you encounter. Understanding the implications of theoretical perspectives for a particular event or topic can be unclear and ambiguous. And few IR scholars practice applying alternative theoretical perspectives in any systematic fashion. This chapter provides some minimal advice on how to undertake such an application. It does so by walking you through an exercise designed to practice seeing empirical topics with theoretically tinted lenses.

The immediate goal of the exercise is to apply two of the theoretical approaches from the book to an empirical IR topic of your choice. Since this exercise is not meant to be a research paper (although it could easily be turned into one), the first thing you should do is choose a topic about which you already know something or have written about in the past. A current event would do, as would a historical IR event with relatively manageable boundaries. Although considering topics such as globalization or terrorism from alternative theoretical perspectives does give you some understanding of them, such topics are also very diffuse and broad. Hence they will not allow you to develop more in-depth analytical applications and to really understand the theories that you are attempting to apply. A more specific issue or event within the context of such broad topics (e.g., the implications of intellectual property rights agreements or the repercussions of September 11, 2001) would be more appropriate and, in the long run, more useful.

Once you have chosen a topic, reformulate it as a question or puzzle that is amenable to theoretical application. That is, do not approach the topic merely as an empirical event, since that involves description and not theoretical analysis. Instead, ask yourself what makes the topic interesting and what makes it puzzling. This may be the least-intuitive step in the process of an application, but one easy way to accomplish it is to compare your chosen topic to similar events or situations and look for differences between them. In other words, ask yourself, why did this event turn out this way when similar events turned out differently? All of the chapters in this volume have had a puzzle about difference that drives their analyses, and those puzzles usually have an implicit comparison in mind. Why, for example, did NATO or the Clinton administration intervene in Kosovo (when it didn't intervene in other comparatively violent situations such as Rwanda or East Timor)? Why did Yugoslavia fall apart (when other nation-states in Eastern Europe held together after the Cold War)? Why did the major powers adopt the rhetoric they did in order to justify intervention (when they could have chosen different justifications or did not live up to them)? Such questions are looking for what is different about the topic, event, or situation in comparison to similar topics, events, or situations. It is those differences that can give you an analytical wedge into the empirical topic.

An alternative method for developing your topic into a puzzle question is to consider what a particular theoretical perspective would anticipate about the event or issue and then examine the topic for evidence that the theoretical expectations were fulfilled. In other words, if structural realism anticipates balancing, did the participants in the event balance one another? Or if world system theory anticipates the exploitation of peripheral states by core states, is there evidence that such exploitation occurred in the event? Comparing theoretical expectations to empirical evidence is a standard positivist procedure for developing theoretical topics in the discipline, because it essentially involves "testing" analytical perspectives against either the empirical evidence or an alternative theoretical perspective. However, this method for developing topics requires that you be well acquainted with the implications of each theoretical perspective. It might be better if you do not initially focus on proving that one explanation is better than another, since the idea here is simply to see if you can figure out how an analyst from a chosen perspective would think and write about an empirical topic of your choice.

Once you have formulated an appropriate puzzle question, review all of the theories represented in this book, and then briefly puzzle out what each theorist might have to say about the event you have chosen to write about. As a way to help organize your thoughts, write a few sentences or a short paragraph on how you think the theorist would characterize or describe your topic and how they would answer your question. This is the step where creative thinking and mental play become most important. In order to understand theory, you must keep an open mind, be willing to play with alternative ideas and concepts, and get into the mind-set of alternative theorists. This latter point is essential, since it is only by thinking like a particular type of theorist that you can determine how they would view an empirical topic or event, what variables or factors they would highlight, and why they would come to the conclusions they do.

Given this, try to get inside the heads of each of the theorists in this volume and think as they do, then look back at your question and figure out how you think they would answer it. What would they focus on? How would they reconceptualize it? What sorts of variables and factors would they highlight and what would they ignore? What level of analysis would they work with? What type of methodology would they adopt? What kind of evidence would they amass? What sorts of conclusions would they reach? The answers to these questions provide clues as to how to emulate the theoretical application in your own analysis. They will also allow you to begin noticing analytical differences and similarities between theoretical perspectives.

It is important to keep in mind, however, that there are alternative ways to apply the same theoretical perspective. Although this book has attempted to illustrate variety both across and within theoretical perspectives, there are multiple implications of and hence ways to apply every theory. For example, Jeffrey Taliaferro's neoclassical realist application (Chapter 2.3) focused on the psychology of Clinton administration decisionmakers, yet an alternative and equally neoclassical realist analysis could focus on the role of bureaucratic politics instead. In his neoliberal institutionalist application (Chapter 3.2), Sean Kay chose to focus his analysis on NATO's role, but another neoliberal analyst might instead choose to focus on the EU's ability to coordinate a common European response to rebuilding Kosovo. Rosemary Shinko's postmodern application (Chapter 6.2) focused on sovereignty and violence, while an alternative postmodern application could focus on the rhetorical creation of "self" and "other" categories in human rights. Stephen Quackenbush and Frank Zagare (Chapter 4.2) chose to analyze NATO intervention as an example of deterrence; another game theorist might focus on modeling collective action problems within NATO. And while Vincent Falger and Johan van der Dennen focused on war and rape in their biopolitical application (Chapter 9.2), another biopolitical application might have focused on the perceptions and emotions of decisionmakers.

In this context, a brief word about applying postmodernism specifically might be in order, since its potential analytical and empirical focus is probably the most open-ended of all the theories under review. There are two basic postmodern methods that could be utilized in an application. The first is to produce a genealogy, which traces out the lineage of a concept or idea within the issue or event you are analyzing. The second is to deconstruct the event or issue, which "involves demystifying a text, taking it apart to reveal its internal, arbitrary hierarchies and its presuppositions," and hence to "undo, reverse, displace, and re-situate the hierarchies" of polar opposites (P. Rosenau 1990: 87). In both cases you should look for what has been marginalized or taken for granted, and focus your attention on it in order to highlight the oppositional and mutually exclusive arrangement of ideas and concepts in your event or topic. Look, for example, at the values or ideas espoused by powerful actors and the justifications they provide for their actions. What do they assume, leave unstated, or repress? And how and when do justification and action contradict one another? That moment of inconsistency should be your subject of analysis, and it should be traced or pulled apart to reveal further inconsistencies and hence to displace the ideological system that made the justification possible.

Although postmodern applications can be infinitely varied, there are multiple ways to apply almost all theoretical perspectives. Hence you will need to think creatively about and be sensitive to analytical variance. It might initially be easiest to apply the theory to your topic in the same manner utilized by the authors in this book, by focusing on sovereignty in your postmodern application or deterrence in your game theory application, for example. But keep in mind that there are alternative ways to apply these theories. If you read the texts of seminal authors in each theoretical perspective, you will quickly discover alternative theoretical propositions and possible implications. You will also encounter an alternative problem with theory application, which is how to accommodate analytical variance while at the same time remaining consistent with the general parameters of a theory or approach. In other words, while structural and neoclassical realism disagree over levels of analysis, they still share realist assumptions about anarchy and power. Similarly, the two versions of constructivism represented in this volume focus on identity construction or relational rhetoric, yet they share an analytical commitment to concepts such as intersubjective meaning and signaling. Determining just how far an analytical variant can go before it is no longer consistent with the general assumptions of a theory is frequently the subject of debate among IR scholars.

In any case, when you are done briefly considering what each theoretical perspective might have to say about your empirical event or topic, choose two (and only two) of the theories to apply and compare in a relatively short paper (seven to ten pages). The point of such a paper is to lay out what an analysis from each theoretical perspective would look like and also to consider what sorts of insights you might gain from one theory in comparison to another. Pick two that either you feel most comfortable with or you find most challenging and interesting. Map out in greater detail how you think your event, topic, and question would be interpreted by a theorist of each perspective. Reread the relevant chapters to gain some sense of what to look for and discuss in an empirical application of each theory. What would an analysis of the topic look like with each of the theoretical perspectives you have chosen? How do you think the analyst would go about answering your question? What would the answer to your question look like from each perspective? Of what is your topic or question an instance of according to each perspective?

When you turn to writing this paper, structure it so that you introduce the topic and question, and then provide a road map of what you will do in the paper. Briefly describe the first theoretical perspective, explore how it would apply to the topic or answer your question, then briefly describe the second theoretical perspective, and explore how it would apply to the topic or answer your question. Finally, compare and contrast the two theoretical applications and consider what each perspective allows you to see in and about the event that you otherwise would not. In doing so, you will have made sense both of IR itself and of IR theories.

Appendix:
A Brief Overview of Kosovo

From the fourteenth to the seventeenth century the Ottoman Turks ruled over the region that is today Bulgaria, Romania, and the former Yugoslavia. This is crucial for understanding the role that the province of Kosovo played in both the development and the demise of Yugoslavia as a unified nation-state. The Serbs, who were the dominant ethnic group in the former Yugoslavia, observe June 28 as St. Vitus's Day, the day they were defeated by Turkish invaders in 1389, thus ushering in 500 years of Turkish domination over the region. The defeat occurred on the plain of Kosovo Polje, close to Kosovo's capital, Pristina, and one of the centerpieces to Serbian nationalist identity has been the hope that the "occupiers" of Kosovo would someday be expelled so that the province could be returned to its rightful Serbian population. That population may have been ethnically and politically Serbian in the 1300s, but by the late Middle Ages the population was predominantly Albanian.[1] In addition, as Stevan Pavlowitch notes, "the battle of Kosovo in 1389 was fought not between a Serbian and a Turkish army, but between two feudal leagues of no clear ethnic loyalty" (2002: 227). Yet the myth of the Serbian defeat in Kosovo, as well as the longing to reclaim the province for Serbs alone, has been one of the more prominent ideas uniting Serbs as a distinct nation since the nineteenth century. So sacred did Kosovo become to Serbian identity politics that it is commonly referred to by Serbs as "our Jerusalem" and is cited as the very birthplace of Serbian culture (Zenko 2001: 2). It is no accident, in this context, that June 28 was also the day that a Serbian nationalist assassinated Archduke Ferdinand of Austria in Sarajevo in 1914, thus triggering the events that led to World War I.

That assassination reflected a wave of ethnic nationalism that had swept through the Balkans around the turn of the twentieth century and that initiated rapid turnovers in the region's political boundaries and alliances.[2] The Serbian desire to reclaim the territory of Kosovo for Serbs and the Albanian desire for independence led not only to direct fighting between the two groups during this period but also to counterincidents of ethnic cleansing in the province during both world wars.[3] Yugoslavia, whose name means "Land of the Southern Slavs," was recognized as a unified nation-state after World War I, although initially it was called "The Kingdom of Serbs, Croats, and Slovenes," thus indicating it was a mix of distinct ethnic nationalist groups from the start.[4] The Serbs dominated within the Yugoslavian government and maintained a firm political and economic grip on the region of Kosovo, which generated considerable resentment not only within Kosovo's ethnic Albanian population but among Yugoslavian Croats as well.

When the Axis powers invaded Yugoslavia in 1941, the various ethnic nationalisms that composed Yugoslavia were divided over whether the Axis was a conquering or liberating force. This produced a series of overlapping civil wars, genocidal atrocities, and alternative efforts at liberation from Axis occupation. Josip Broz, nicknamed Marshal Tito and commonly referred to in the West as Joseph Tito, was the leader of communist guerrilla partisans who attempted to unify various political and ethnic factions in a fight against the Axis powers in order to liberate Yugoslavia. Tito had a difficult time recruiting Kosovar Albanians, however, since in relative comparison to the Serbs and communism, the Italians, Germans, and Albanians were considered the lesser of evils and even provided the Kosovar Albanians with the opportunity to ethnically cleanse the province of Serbs (Judah 2000: 27–28). To get their cooperation, Tito promised them what had long been a dream of the Kosovar Albanian population: Kosovo could secede from Yugoslavia and join with Albania after the war. But when the creation of the Federal People's Republic of Yugoslavia was declared in 1945, Tito imposed martial law on the province and formally annexed it to Serbia. Although there were small percentages of Serbians living in compact communities near the province's northern and eastern border with Serbia proper, in fact 90 percent of Kosovo's 1.9 million population were ethnic Albanian. Yet for the next twenty years the province of Kosovo would be run by Serbian secret police, who would violently repress the Albanian population and any hint of separatism within it. For many Albanians this period was a "reign of terror," and estimates of Albanian emigration from the province during this period are as high as 250,000 (Silber and Little 1997: 36).

Although ethnic nationalist desires were routinely repressed under Tito's regime for the sake of communist "brotherhood and unity," each of Yugoslavia's six republics—Croatia, Bosnia-Herzegovina, Macedonia, Montenegro, Serbia, and Slovenia—had nominal equality and representation within the federal government.[5] This meant that each republic and province had its own president, parliament, prime minister, and communist party. Although Tito retained firm control over the federal government and the Yugoslav People's Army, his government's unwieldy structure tended to reinforce, in both a material and an ideational sense, a relative autonomy among its constituent units. Changes to the Yugoslavian constitution in 1974 granted relative autonomy to the provinces of Kosovo and Vojvodina, which meant that Kosovo's ethnic Albanian population was able to enjoy relatively greater freedom from Serbian influence in the conduct of the province's political, economic, and social affairs.

Yugoslavia's republics and provinces might have managed to coexist in this unwieldy federal system were it not for the impact of events in the global economy during the 1970s. After World War II, Yugoslavia had briefly aligned itself with the Soviet Union, but Tito's insistence on decisionmaking independence had led to a public falling out between them by 1948. Although it remained a communist regime, Yugoslavia's open defiance of Soviet influence made it the darling of the Western world. It was showered with aid and hefty loans from the United States, Western Europe, and global capitalist financial institutions during the early decades of the Cold War, and its coastline became a favorite vacation spot among Western European tourists. One of the short-term results of this ongoing interaction with the West was that Yugoslavia's standard of living was quite high in comparison with the rest of Eastern Europe, but by the 1970s its economy was strained by its ever-increasing debt burden due to the oil crises of that decade. The result was uneven development across the country's republics, with Kosovo being one of the poorer regions, and this sowed the seed for ethnic discontent.[6]

Yugoslavia's economic problems were obvious by the time Tito died in 1980, but the country did not immediately descend into xenophobic disarray. In fact, in 1984 the Winter Olympics were held in Sarajevo, the capital of Bosnia-Herzegovina. But the first political test of the post-Tito federal government came a year after his death and it occurred in Kosovo. Kosovar Albanians staged protests in spring 1981 demanding that Kosovo be granted republic status. A state of emergency was declared, the Yugoslav People's Army and federal police crushed the protests, and trials and purges followed. Thus Kosovo "was the first point of conflict and the first disaffected community against whom the army was deployed" after Tito's death (Silber and Little 1997: 27). The 1981 protests proved to be significant for reigniting Serbian nationalism, and Serbs began to complain of the discrimination they faced in the very homeland of Serbian civilization.[7] Such sentiments were given written expression in the influential *Memorandum of the Serbian Academy of Sciences and Arts*, which was published in September 1986 and documented the perceived grievances of the Serbs. It caused an immediate sensation in what had by then become fertile nationalist ground in Serbia. Serbian rallies in both Kosovo and Serbia proper became more and more feverish in demanding the arrest and expulsion of ethnic Albanian leaders from the federal and provincial governments.

In April 1987, a relatively unknown communist party official, Slobodan Milosevic, was sent to Pristina in order to impose calm. In addressing the Serbian Kosovar crowd, Milosevic did the exact opposite. "No one should dare to beat you," he announced to a cheering crowd, in reference to the Kosovar Albanian police who were trying to contain them, and it was the phrase that made his political career. By the time he returned to the Serbian capital of Belgrade, he was being hailed by the Serbian media as a national hero. Milosevic used this newfound popularity to manipulate political events in Serbia so that within months he was in control of the government. In early 1989, Milosevic ended Kosovo's autonomous status and moved quickly to gain control over all aspects of the province's political, economic, and social life. To establish incentives for Serbs to relocate to Kosovo, Milosevic purged ethnic Albanians in almost all public and professional occupations, including civil service, managerial positions, police and security forces, doctors and medical staffs, and teachers. Security forces were to be composed only of Serbs, and local school curriculums were to have a Serbian content and to be taught in Serbian by Serbian teachers. This essentially created a two-tiered society with Serbs in all positions of authority and leadership ruling over 90 percent of the population that was ethnically Albanian. Serbian security forces monitored and harassed the population in general, and ongoing human rights violations were the order of the day.[8] It was, as some observers noted, the equivalent of a European apartheid system (Bellamy 2001: 116; Independent International Commission on Kosovo 2000: 49).

The reaction to this two-tier system among the Albanian population was one of passive resistance. A group of Kosovar Albanians formed a political party called the Democratic League of Kosovo (LDK) in December 1989, and it dominated Albanian political life in the province until 1998. In 1992 the LDK held underground elections and Ibrahim Rugova was elected president of what essentially became a parallel Albanian state functioning alongside or under the official Serb-dominated state in Kosovo. The shadow government had a democratically elected president and parliament, and its main responsibility was to develop and oversee parallel educational and health care systems for Kosovar Albanians. It paid for these systems with voluntary taxes on the Kosovar Albanian population and money collected from the Albanian diaspora.[9] In this way the LDK sought to avoid direct conflict with the Serbian government, because it believed that by proving to the West that Albanians could run their own affairs without resort to armed insurrection, they would be supported in their bid for independence from Serbia once the war in Bosnia-Herzegovina was over.[10]

The 1995 Dayton Accords, which officially ended that war, had a decisive effect on the future of Kosovo as a result. Not only did the accords fail to reward the nonviolent strategy of the LDK, but in Bosnia-Herzegovina they essentially rewarded the Bosnian Serbs with their own self-governing republic whose borders were largely determined by their zealous ethnic cleansing during the war. Increasing dissatisfaction with the strategy of passive resistance, and a growing conviction that only violence would attract support from the West, led to the creation of the Kosovo Liberation Army (KLA) in early 1996. The KLA consisted of small bands of Kosovar Albanians who initially embarked on isolated attacks of police outposts and assassinations of Serbian Kosovar leaders.[11] Although it was not well organized, known, or supported by most Kosovar Albanians at the time, the KLA found a ready source of weapons during summer 1997, when the government of Albania collapsed due to several huge pyramid investment schemes. Criminal gangs filled the political vacuum there, looted the weapons facilities of the Albanian army, and sold much of the booty across the border to the KLA (Glenny 1999: 654; Judah 2000: 126–129). The KLA escalated its attacks against Serbian targets as a result, as well as its public declarations of open rebellion to Serbian rule. In early 1998, Milosevic responded by launching a series of violent raids in which Serbian police, paramilitary units, and helicopter gunships swept through the Drenica valley region west of Pristina, killing KLA members and civilians alike and sending hundreds into the forest to escape reprisals. Frustrated Albanians began to swell the ranks of the KLA, financial support for their efforts poured in from the Albanian diaspora, and throughout 1998 the KLA and the Serbs engaged one another in a violent tit-for-tat relationship.

In their attempt to avoid a replay of the war in Bosnia-Herzegovina, the Clinton administration dispatched Richard Holbrooke to Serbia in May 1998 to put pressure on Milosevic and Rugova to end the violence. During the summer the North Atlantic Treaty Organization (NATO) also staged an air exercise in Albania called Operation Determined Falcon with the publicly stated intention of demonstrating its willingness to intervene in Kosovo if the Serbs did not halt their violent activity there.[12] But the major powers were divided among themselves over the proper course of action, and although both the United States and NATO continued to issue toughly worded statements throughout the summer, they did not directly intervene in the conflict. Fighting between Serbian forces and the KLA intensified so that by mid-September 1998 the number of displaced Albanians was roughly 300,000 (Perlez 1998c). The turning point in the conflict occurred in mid-January, when fighting broke out around the village of Racak and the

Serbs executed forty-five civilians who were clearly not KLA fighters. Although the causality numbers were relatively insignificant in comparison to the scale of prior atrocities both in Kosovo and during the war in Bosnia-Herzegovina, the Western powers unanimously condemned Milosevic for the massacre and demanded he return to the negotiating table. A peace conference was held in Rambouillet, France, in early February 1999 and to which representatives from Serbia and both the LDK and the KLA attended.[13] The Kosovar Albanians wanted independence from Serbia, but neither the United States nor any of the other NATO powers would support them and warned instead that if they didn't sign the Rambouillet Agreement and stop fighting, the international community would abandon them. Alternatively the West guaranteed them a NATO peacekeeping mission, which would provide a modicum of autonomy and protection from Serbia. The Albanian delegation signed the agreement in mid-March, but by then the Serbian delegation had balked. The idea of a peacekeeping mission within Serbian borders proved too much for Milosevic, and he refused to sign without further concessions that the United States and NATO argued were impossible.

In a last meeting with Milosevic on March 22, Holbrooke issued a final ultimatum: "You understand what will happen when I leave here today if you don't change your position, if you don't agree to negotiate and accept Rambouillet as the basis of the negotiations?" he asked (quoted in Judah 2000: 227). "Yes," replied Milosevic, "you will bomb us." Yet even then he refused to concede, and on March 24, NATO planes began to bomb Serbian military targets in Kosovo.[14] It was the first time in the alliance's history that it had launched an attack on a sovereign European nation-state. The NATO bombing campaign would continue for seventy-eight days, and as the spring progressed the target list would expand to include bridges, oil refineries and depots, power plants, railroads, and communication facilities throughout Serbia and Montenegro, the two remaining republics that constituted the "rump Yugoslavia." According to William Arkin, NATO would fly "a total of 38,004 sorties of which 10,484 involved strikes on 'strategic' and 'tactical' targets while another 3,100 were suppression of anti-defense missions" (2001: 21). The number of civilians who died as a result of the NATO bombings is somewhere between 500 and 2,000, while the number of casualties is estimated to be 6,000 (Judah 2000: 264).

In apparent retaliation for the NATO attacks, the Serbian military began to ethnically cleanse Kosovo of its entire population of Albanians. The numbers and time frame for this refugee crisis are staggering. Within a week of the initial NATO bombings, 300,000 refugees had been forced across the borders of Kosovo, with accounts of forced expulsion, killings, rapes, torture, looting, and burning at the hands of the Serbian military and police. The refugees were pushed into either Albania, which was already Europe's poorest country, or Macedonia, which was itself at odds with Greece over ethnic issues,[15] or even Montenegro, where the Montenegrin president had increasingly become a political rival to Milosevic in the rump Yugoslavia. As Misha Glenny observes, it was "as though over a quarter of a million people had been dumped on a region the size of Tuscany" overnight (1999: 658). The ethnic cleansing continued throughout the spring, even as NATO expanded its target list, and by June there were approximately 850,000 people who had either been deported or fled Kosovo (Judah 2000: 250). This figure did not include the hundreds of thousands more who were displaced within Kosovo itself, nor did it count those who had refused to leave and were summarily executed.[16]

While the UN High Commissioner for Refugees (UNHCR), along with NATO and a variety of nongovernmental organizations, dealt with the refugee crisis throughout spring 1999, NATO planes continued to bomb Serbian targets and NATO leaders increasingly began to talk of the need for a ground invasion if Milosevic did not capitulate. By early June, Milosevic had had enough.[17] He agreed to withdraw Serbian forces from Kosovo, and the ethnic Albanian population was allowed to return under protection of the NATO peacekeeping mission called Kosovo Force (KFOR), which entered the province on June 12, 1999. While KFOR troops looked on, the Albanian population immediately ethnically cleansed much of the province of the Serbian population who had remained.[18]

Yet the immediate political settlement in Kosovo satisfied almost no one. KFOR was accompanied by the UN Interim Administration Mission in Kosovo (UNMIK), which was supposed to provide "an interim administration for Kosovo under which the people of Kosovo can enjoy substantial autonomy within the Federal Republic of Yugoslavia" (Judah 2000: 333). In other words, the Kosovar Albanians had not gained their formal independence from Serbia, nor did the Serbs have direct control over the province. Instead, Kosovo was designated an autonomous province that required an occupying force to protect its population against the sovereign nation-state that had formal jurisdiction over it. While it was true that the political, economic, and social life of Kosovar Albanians was no longer threatened or dominated by Serbian interests, the international community's solution for Kosovo was not the independent nation-state for which the KLA had fought. And the strange nature of UNMIK's mission was aptly captured by the International Independent Commission on Kosovo's characterization of it as "nation-building for a non-nation" (Judah 2000: 106).

As for Serbia, Milosevic was deposed as president of Yugoslavia in October 2000, after his attempt to rig elections instead generated mass protests in the hundreds of thousands. He was arrested in April 2001 and turned over to authorities in The Hague to be tried by the International

Criminal Tribunal for the former Yugoslavia (ICTY) for crimes against humanity and war crimes committed during the course of the Kosovo conflict. It was the first time that a serving head of state was accused of what are considered the most serious crimes under international law. In 2003 the name "Yugoslavia" passed from the history books, as the rump Yugoslavia voted to officially rename itself the Republic of Serbia and the Republic of Montenegro, with each republic intending to eventually go its separate way.

■ Notes

1. The Albanian population is principally Muslim, but with some Roman Catholics, and in the Albanian language the province of Kosovo is referred to as "Kosova" or "Kosovë." The Serbian population is mostly Christians of the Serbian Orthodox Church, with many of the greatest monuments of this church located in Kosovo, and in the Serbian language the province of Kosovo is referred to as "Kosovo-Metahija." Pavkovic 2001 provides a concise discussion of these alternative names and their significance in the history and politics of the province, while Zehfuss 2002 deconstructs the political implications of choosing among these alternatives from a postmodern perspective.

2. Histories of this period in the Balkans are provided in Djordjevic and Fischer-Galati 1981, Jelavich 1983, Larrabee 1990–1991, Lendvai 1969, Pavkovic 2000, and Sugar and Lederer 1969.

3. According to Claire Walling (2001: 48–49), the term "ethnic cleansing" means forced population transfer and involves activities meant to generate terror and compel flight. It is different from genocide, which seeks to annihilate an entire group and its way of life. Given these definitions, ethnic cleansing is the appropriate term for the type of activity engaged in by Serbs and Albanians and directed toward each other. Judah (2000: 16–21) points out that who was being ethnically cleansed usually depended on who had won on the battlefield in any particular year. In 1912, for example, the Serbs scored various victories against the Albanians and attempted to ethnically cleanse them from the province of Kosovo. By 1915 the tide of battle had turned, and the Albanians ethnically cleansed the province of Serbs. When the Serbs reoccupied the province in 1918, they retaliated in kind against the Albanians.

4. Brankovic 1995, Doder 1979, Dyker and Vejvoda 1996, Judah 1997, Lampe 1996, Pavkovic 2000, Pavlowitch 2002, Seton-Watson 1967, and Wachtel 1998, chap. 2, provide overviews of this period in Yugoslavian history and extended discussions of the competing nationalisms during it.

5. For information about Yugoslavian politics, political structures, and decentralization under Tito, see Bokovoy, Irvine, and Lilly 1997, Allcock, Milivojevic, and Hopton 1999, Cohen 1989, Lampe 1996, Lydall 1989, Meier 1995, Malcolm 1998, Pavkovic 2000, Rusinow 1977, Shoup 1968, Wilson 1979, and Zaninovich 1968.

6. While ethnic nationalism played a key role in Yugoslavia's disintegration, it was entwined with economic factors and differences between the republics. F. Stephen Larrabee (1990–1991: 67) notes that by late 1989 the country's annual inflation rate had risen to 1,500 percent, unemployment was at 20 percent, and the country's hard currency debt was over $20 billion. Slovenia and Croatia were two of the wealthier republics and both sought to control more of their own income,

rather than see it channeled through Belgrade to support the poorer regions of the country. For economic conditions within the former Yugoslavia, see Allcock 2000, Bookman 1990, Dallago and Uvalic 1998, Dyker 1990, Lampe 1996, chaps. 8–11, Magaš 1993, Ramet and Adamovich 1995, Ramet 2002, Rogel 1998, Sell 2002, Udovicki and Ridgeway 2000, Vickers 1998, and Woodward 1995, chaps. 2–3. For sources on Kosovo's economy, see Mertus 1999a: 22–28, Prifti 1984, and Pashko 1998.

7. Julie Mertus provides a fascinating account, based on media reports, oral histories, and personal narratives, of the unfolding relationship between Kosovo's Albanians and Serbs during the 1980s, in which particular atrocities were dwelt upon and "manipulated by a carefully orchestrated, fear-mongering media campaign" (1999a: 13). See also Malcolm 1998: 337–340, and Mayall 1996.

8. Alex Bellamy (2001) documents overall conditions in the province during this period, while numerous reports were published by human rights organizations that meticulously documented the abuse suffered by the Kosovar Albanian population at the hands of Serbian authorities. See, for example, Amnesty International's *Yugoslavia: Ethnic Albanians—Victims of Torture and Ill-Treatment by Police* (1992) and *Yugoslavia: Ethnic Albanians—Trial by Truncheon* (1994); and Helsinki Watch's *Human Rights Abuses in Kosovo 1990–1992* (1992), *Open Wounds: Human Rights Abuses in Kosovo* (1994), and *Yugoslavia (Serbia and Montenegro): Persecution Persists: Human Rights Violations in Kosovo* (1996).

9. The Independent International Commission on Kosovo (2000: 46–47) provides information on this system of taxes, how collected funds were allocated, and the development of an informal economy among Kosovar Albanians.

10. Howard Clark (2000) provides a detailed account of how this belief affected Albanian political strategies throughout this period. Yet as the Independent International Commission on Kosovo (2000: 55–61) documents, the international community did not see Kosovo as a priority in the 1990s and continued to label it an internal Yugoslavian problem.

11. The name and acronym are translated from the Albanian Ushtria Çlirimtare e Kosovës (UÇK). Judah (2000, chap. 4) provides an account of the KLA and its origins, which had links to the Kacaks, Albanian rebels who had fought in World War II against the Serbs and were still active in some parts of Kosovo as village militia. On the Kacaks, see also Malcolm 1998, chap. 14; and on the KLA in general, see Chris Hedges's journalistic account (1999) of his early interactions with it. The KLA formed in 1993 and its creators were primarily the activists who were sent to jail in the purges following the 1981 demonstrations. On the other hand, some of the LDK leaders were the former communist Albanians who were responsible for purging the 1981 protesters. In many ways, then, the KLA was a competing political unit to the LDK. Judah notes that Rugova spent a great deal of time claiming the KLA didn't really exist and was just a plot on the part of the Serbs to incriminate innocent Albanians.

12. The operation consisted of more than eighty fighter planes and helicopters simulating bombing and strafing runs over northern Macedonia and Albania, about fifteen miles from the Serbian border. See Clark 2001: 118–120, Dinmore 1998, and Chapter 3.2 in this volume for more information on the operation.

13. For details of the Rambouillet conference, see Independent International Commission on Kosovo 2000: 151–158, Judah 2000, chap. 7, Weller 1999a, and Weller 1999b.

14. Why Milosevic did not concede to NATO at that point has been the subject of considerable discussion and disagreement among scholars and is also the focus

of this volume's game theory application (Chapter 4.2). For example, see Daalder and O'Hanlon 2000b: 94–96, Posen 2000: 51–52, 66–67, and the list of possible explanations provided in Judah 2000: 228–232.

15. Larrabee (1990–1991: 74–77) provides a concise overview of these tensions.

16. According to Tony Kushner and Katharine Knox (1999: xxviii), NATO estimated that by April 7, 1.1 million ethnic Albanians had been internally displaced or forced out of Kosovo. The Independent International Commission on Kosovo (2000: 2) estimated that between March and June 1999, approximately 863,000 civilians were refugees outside Kosovo, while 590,000 were internally displaced.

17. Judah (2000: 272–285) provides an extended discussion of the factors that may have influenced Milosevic in reaching this decision.

18. As Sergei Medvedev and Peter van Ham comment, "Against the background of an expeditious return of over 800,000 Kosovar refugees—which should be rightly considered a major success of KFOR and UNMIK—the province has been cleansed of 230,000 Kosovo Serbs, Roma and other minorities (a UN estimate)" (2002: 12). For an analysis of the immediate postwar situation in Kosovo under KFOR and UNMIK, see Independent International Commission on Kosovo 2000, chap. 4, Booth 2001, pt. 4, and O'Neill 2002.

References

Abbott, K. W., and D. Snidal (1998) "Why States Act Through Formal International Organizations." *Journal of Conflict Resolution* 42(1): 3–32.

Abdela, L. (2000) "Kosovo: Missed Opportunities: Lessons for the Future." On file with Julie Mertus. February.

Abu-Lughod, J. (1989) *Before European Hegemony: The World System, A.D. 1250–1350.* New York: Oxford University Press.

Achcar, G. (2000) "Rasputin Plays at Chess: How the West Blundered into the Cold War." In T. Ali (ed.), *Masters of the Universe: NATO's Balkan Crusade.* London: Verso.

Achen, C. H. (1987) "A Darwinian View of Deterrence." In J. Kugler and F. C. Zagare (eds.), *Exploring the Stability of Deterrence.* Boulder: Lynne Rienner.

Adamovic, S. (2002) "Domestic Politics and International Economic Relations: The Case of FR Yugoslavia." Paper presented at the annual meeting of the International Studies Association, New Orleans, March 24–27.

––––– (2003) "Economic Sanctions and Economic Revival." Paper presented at the annual meeting of the International Studies Association, Portland, February 25–March 1.

Adamovich, L. S. (2002) "Fiction vs. Facts: National Political Ambitions and International Realities." Paper presented at the annual meeting of the International Studies Association, New Orleans, March 24–27.

Adams, K. R. (2000) "State Survival and State Death: International and Technological Contexts." Ph.D. diss., University of California, Berkeley, 2000. *Dissertation Abstracts International* 62(01): 318 (UMI no. AAT 3001740).

––––– (2002) "Conquering Myths: Testing Realist, Liberal, and Constructivist Arguments About State Vulnerability to Conquest." Paper presented at the annual meeting of the American Political Science Association, Boston.

––––– (2003) "States We Pretend Exist and States We Ignore." Paper presented at the annual meeting of the American Political Science Association, Philadelphia, August.

––––– (2003–2004) "Attack and Conquer? International Anarchy and the Offense-Defense-Deterrence Balance." *International Security* 28(3): 45–83.

Adler, E. (1997) "Seizing the Middle Ground: Constructivism in World Politics." *European Journal of International Relations* 3: 319–363.

Adler, E., and M. Barnett (eds.) (1998) *Security Communities.* Cambridge: Cambridge University Press.

Adler, E., and B. Crawford (eds.) (1991) *Progress in Post-War International Relations.* New York: Columbia University Press.

Albright, M. K. (1998) Press briefing with Italian foreign minister Lamberto Dini. Office of the Assistant Secretary for Public Affairs, U.S. Department of State,

March 7. Available online at http://secretary.state.gov/www/statements/
1998/980307.html.

—— (1999) Special briefing by Secretary of State Madeleine K. Albright. Federal
News Service, March 25. Available online at http://www.lexisnexis.com.

Alexander, M. J., and C. T. Mohanty (1997) *Feminist Genealogies, Colonial
Legacies, Democratic Futures.* New York: Routledge.

Alexander, R. D. (1979) *Darwinism and Human Affairs.* Seattle: University of
Washington Press.

Ali, T. (ed.) (2000) *Masters of the Universe: NATO's Balkan Crusade.* London:
Verso.

Alker, H. R. (ed.) (1996) *Rediscoveries and Reformations: Humanistic
Methodologies for International Studies.* New York: Cambridge University
Press.

Alker, H. R., and T. Biersteker (1984) "The Dialectics of World Order: Notes for a
Future Archeologist of International *Savoir Faire.*" *International Studies
Quarterly* 28(2) (June): 121–142.

Allcock, J. B. (2000) *Explaining Yugoslavia.* New York: Columbia University Press.

Allcock, J. B., M. Milivojevic, and J. J. Hopton (eds.) (1999) *Conflict in the Former
Yugoslavia: An Encyclopedia.* Santa Barbara: ABC-Clio.

Allison, G. (1971) *Essence of Decision: Explaining the Cuban Missile Crisis.*
Boston: Little, Brown.

Almond, G. A., and G. B. Powell Jr. (1996) *Comparative Politics Today.* 6th ed.
New York: HarperCollins.

Amin, S. (1974) *Accumulation on a World Scale: A Critique of the Theory of
Underdevelopment.* New York: Monthly Review Press.

—— (1977) *Imperialism and Unequal Development.* New York: Monthly Review
Press.

Amnesty International (1992) *Yugoslavia: Ethnic Albanians—Victims of Torture
and Ill-Treatment by Police.* New York: Amnesty International.

—— (1994) *Yugoslavia: Ethnic Albanians—Trial by Truncheon.* New York:
Amnesty International.

—— (1998) *Kosovo: The Evidence.* London: Amnesty International.

Andermahr, S., T. Lovell, and C. Wolkowitz (1997) *A Concise Glossary of Feminist
Theory.* New York: Arnold.

Anderson, B. (1991) *Imagined Communities: Reflections on the Origin and Spread
of Nationalism.* London: Verso Books.

Annan, K. (1999) "Two Concepts of Sovereignty." *The Economist,* September 18.

"Annan and Solana Hail Action" (1998) *International Herald Tribune,* June 16.

Archibugi, D. (2000) "Cosmopolitical Democracy." *New Left Review* 4: 34–40.

Arkin, W. (2000) "Smart Bombs, Dumb Targeting?" *Bulletin of the Atomic
Scientists* 56(3) (May–June): 46–53.

—— (2001) "Operation Allied Force: The Most Precise Application of Air Power
in History." In A. J. Bacevich and E. A. Cohen (eds.), *War Over Kosovo:
Politics and Strategy in a Global Age.* New York: Columbia University Press.

Arrighi, G. (1994) *The Long Twentieth Century: Money, Power, and the Origins of
Our Times.* London: Verso.

Arrighi, G., and W. L. Goldfrank (eds.) (2000a) "Festschrift for Immanuel
Wallerstein: Part I." *Journal of World Systems Research* 6(2) (Summer).
Special issue.

—— (2000b) "Festschrift for Immanuel Wallerstein: Part II." *Journal of World
Systems Research* 6(3) (Fall). Special issue.

Arrighi, G., and B. J. Silver (1999) *Chaos and Governance in the Modern World System*. Minneapolis: University of Minnesota Press.

Art, R. J. (1980) "To What Ends Military Power?" *International Security* 4(4): 3–35.

—— (1996) "Why Western Europe Needs the United States and NATO." *Political Science Quarterly* 111(1): 1–36.

—— (1998–1999) "Geopolitics Updated: The Strategy of Selective Engagement." *International Security* 23(3): 79–113.

"As Prelude to Cease-Fire, Outside Observers Comb Kosovo for Truth" (1998) *Christian Science Monitor,* July 13.

Ashley, R. (1984) "The Poverty of Neorealism." *International Organization* 38(2): 225–286.

—— (1987) "The Geopolitics of Geopolitical Space: Toward a Critical Social Theory of International Politics." *Alternatives* 12(4) (October): 403–434.

—— (1988) "Untying the Sovereign State: A Double Reading of the Anarchy Problematique." *Millennium: Journal of International Studies* 17(2): 227–262.

—— (1996) "The Achievements of Post-Structuralism." In S. Smith, K. Booth, and M. Zalewski (eds.), *International Theory: Positivism and Beyond*. Cambridge: Cambridge University Press.

Ashley, R., and R. B. J. Walker (1990a) "Reading Dissidence/Writing the Discipline: Crisis and the Question of Sovereignty in International Studies." *International Studies Quarterly* 34(3) (September): 367–416. Special issue.

—— (1990b) "Speaking the Language of Exile: Dissidence in International Studies." *International Studies Quarterly* 34(3) (September): 259–268. Special issue.

Auerswald, P. E., and D. P. Auerswald (eds.) (2000) *The Kosovo Conflict: A Diplomatic History Through Documents*. Cambridge, England: Kluwer Law International.

Axelrod, R. (1981) "The Emergence of Cooperation Among Egoists." *American Political Science Review* 75 (June): 306–318.

—— (1984) *The Evolution of Cooperation*. New York: Basic Books.

Axelrod, R., and R. O. Keohane (1986) "Achieving Cooperation Under Anarchy: Strategies and Institutions." In K. Oye (ed.), *Cooperation Under Anarchy*. Princeton: Princeton University Press.

Ba, A., and M. J. Hoffmann (2003) "Making and Remaking the World for IR 101: A Resource for Teaching Social Constructivism in Introductory Classes." *International Studies Perspective* 49(1): 15–33.

Bacevich, A. J. (2001) "Neglected Trinity: Kosovo and the Crisis in U.S. Civil-Military Relations." In A. J. Bacevich and E. A. Cohen (eds.), *War over Kosovo: Politics and Strategy in a Global Age*. New York: Columbia University Press.

Bacevich, A. J., and E. A. Cohen (2001a) "Introduction: Strange Little War." In A. J. Bacevich and E. A. Cohen (eds.), *War over Kosovo: Politics and Strategy in a Global Age*. New York: Columbia University Press.

—— (eds.) (2001b) *War over Kosovo: Politics and Strategy in a Global Age*. New York: Columbia University Press.

Baer, D., and D. L. McEachron (1982) "A Review of Selected Sociobiological Principles: Application to Hominid Evolution I: The Development of Group Social Structure." *Journal of Social and Biological Structures* 5: 69–90.

Baghat, G. (2002) "Pipeline Diplomacy: The Geopolitics of the Caspian Sea Region." *International Studies Perspectives* 3(3): 310–327.

Baldwin, D. A. (1979) "Power Analysis and World Politics: New Trends Versus Old Tendencies." *World Politics* 31(2) (January): 161–194.

Baletic, Z., and B. Marendic (1992) "The Policy and System of Regional Development." In R. Lang et al. (eds.), *Essays on the Political Economy of Yugoslavia*. Zagreb: Informator.

Banerjee, N. (2002) "US Remains Dependent on Oil from Mideast but Is Diversifying." *New York Times*, October 22.

Baran, P. (1967) *The Political Economy of Growth*. New York: Monthly Review Press.

Baranovsky, V. (2000) "Russia: Reassessing National Interests." In A. Schnabel and R. Thakur (eds.), *Kosovo and the Challenge of Humanitarian Intervention: Selective Indignation, Collective Action, and International Citizenship*. New York: United Nations University Press.

Barash, D. P. (1977) *Sociobiology and Behavior*. New York: Elsevier.

Barkin, J. S. (2003) "Realist Constructivism." *International Studies Review* 5(3) (September): 325–342.

Barnes, H. (1999) "No Other Honorable Way." *Socialist Campaign Group News (SCGN)* 142. Available online at http://www.poptel.org.uk/scgn/articles/9904/page8.html.

Barratt Brown, M. (1993) "The War in Yugoslavia and the Debt Burden: A Comment." *Capital and Class* 50: 147–160.

Barringer, F. (2003) "UN Renews U.S. Peacekeepers' Exemption from Prosecution." *New York Times*, June 13.

Bartelson, J. (1995) *A Genealogy of Sovereignty*. Cambridge: Cambridge University Press.

Bartlett, K. T. (1999) "Cracking Foundations as Feminist Method." *American University Journal of Gender, Social Policy, and the Law* 8: 31–50.

Bates, R. H., A. Greif, M. Levi, J.-L. Rosenthal, and B. R. Weingast (1998) *Analytic Narratives*. Princeton: Princeton University Press.

——— (2000) "The Analytic Narrative Project." *American Political Science Review* 94: 696–702.

Baylis, J., and S. Smith (2001) *The Globalization of World Politics*. 2nd ed. Oxford: Oxford University Press.

Baynes, K. (1994) "Communicative Ethics, the Public Sphere, and Communication Media." *Critical Studies in Mass Communication* 11: 315–326.

BBC News (1999a) "Germany Faces Kosovo Criticism." May 5.

——— (1999b) "Italian PM's Balancing Act." May 1.

——— (1999c) "Refugee Wave Hits Italy." May 30.

Beams, N. (1999) "IMF 'Shock Therapy' and the Recolonisation of the Balkans." Available online at http://www.wsws.org/articles/1999/apr1999/imf-a17.shtml.

Beckman, P. R., and F. D'Amico (eds.) (1994) *Women, Gender, and World Politics: Perspectives, Policies, and Prospects*. Westport: Bergin and Garvey.

Beer, F. A., and R. Hariman (eds.) (1996) *Post-Realism: The Rhetorical Turn in International Relations*. East Lansing: Michigan State University Press.

Behler, E. (1996) "Nietzsche in the Twentieth Century." In B. Magnus and K. Higgins (eds.), *The Cambridge Companion to Nietzsche*. Cambridge: Cambridge University Press.

Behnke, A. (2002) "'vvv.nato.int': Virtuousness, Virtuality, and Virtuosity in NATO's Representation of the Kosovo Campaign." In S. Medvedev and P. van Ham (eds.), *Mapping European Security After Kosovo*. Manchester: Manchester University Press.

Bell, C. (2000) "Force, Diplomacy, and Norms." In A. Schnabel and R. Thakur (eds.), *Kosovo and the Challenge of Humanitarian Intervention*. New York: United Nations University Press.

Bellamy, A. J. (2001) "Human Wrongs in Kosovo: 1974–99." In K. Booth (ed.), *The Kosovo Tragedy: The Human Rights Dimension*. London: Frank Cass.

—— (ed.) (2005) *International Society and Its Critics*. New York: Oxford University Press.

Bendana, A. (1996) *Power Lines: US Domination in the New Global Order*. New York: Olive Branch Press.

Berger, P. L., and T. Luckmann (1966) *The Social Construction of Reality: A Treatise in the Sociology of Knowledge*. New York: Doubleday.

Berkin, C. R., and C. M. Lovett (eds.) (1980) *Women, War, and Revolution*. New York: Holmes and Meier.

Best, G. (1994) *War and Law Since 1945*. New York: Oxford University Press.

Betts, R. K. (1987) *Nuclear Blackmail and Nuclear Balance*. Washington, D.C.: Brookings Institution.

—— (2001) "Compromised Command: Inside NATO's First War." *Foreign Affairs* 80(4): 126–132.

Bhaskar, R. (1979) *The Possibility of Naturalism*. Atlantic Highlands, N.J.: Humanities Press.

Biersteker, T. J. (1989) "Critical Reflections on Post-Positivism in International Relations." *International Studies Quarterly* 33(3): 235–254.

Biersteker, T. J., and C. Weber (eds.) (1996) *State Sovereignty as Social Construct*. Cambridge: Cambridge University Press.

Bigelow, R. (1969) *The Dawn Warriors: Man's Evolution Towards Peace*. Boston: Little, Brown.

Blackburn, R. (2000) "Kosovo: The War of NATO Expansion." In T. Ali (ed.), *Masters of the Universe: NATO's Balkan Crusade*. London: Verso.

Blair, T. (1999a) "Broadcast to the Nation." March 26. Available online at http://www.fco.gov.uk/news/newstext.asp?2177.

—— (1999b) "Interview with Patrick Wintour of *The Observer*." May 16. Available online at http://www.fco.gov.uk/news/newstext.asp?2423.

—— (1999c) "Speech to the Economic Club of Chicago." April 22. Available online at http://www.fco.gov.uk/news/speechtext.asp?2316.

—— (1999d) "Statement in the House of Commons." March 23. Available online at http://www.fco.gov.uk/news/newstext.asp?2149.

Block, F. (1977) *The Origins of International Economic Disorder*. Berkeley: University of California Press.

Bobrow, D. B., and M. A. Boyer (1997) "Maintaining System Stability: Contributions to International Peacekeeping Operations." *Journal of Conflict Resolution* 41(6): 723–748.

—— (2005) *Defensive Internationalism: Providing Global Public Goods in an Uncertain World*. Ann Arbor: University of Michigan Press.

Bohman, J. (1996) *Public Deliberation: Pluralism, Complexity, and Democracy*. Cambridge: MIT Press.

Bokovoy, M. K., J. A. Irvine, and C. S. Lilly (eds.) (1997) *State-Society Relations in Yugoslavia, 1945–1992*. London: Macmillan.

Bookman, M. Z. (1990) "The Economic Basis of Regional Autarchy in Yugoslavia." *Soviet Studies* 42(1) (January): 93–109.

—— (2002) "Yugoslav Successor States in the New World Order: The Persistence of Regional Inequalities." Paper presented at the annual meeting of the International Studies Association, New Orleans, March 25.

Boot, M. (2003) *The Savage Wars of Peace: Small Wars and the Rise of American Power.* New York: Basic Books.

Booth, K. (ed.) (2001) *The Kosovo Tragedy: The Human Rights Dimension.* London: Frank Cass.

Booth, K., and S. Smith (eds.) (1995) *International Relations Theory Today.* University Park: Pennsylvania State University Press.

Boswell, T., and I. Wallerstein (eds.) (1989) *Revolution in the World System.* Westport: Greenwood.

Botev, N. (1994) "Where East Meets West: Ethnic Intermarriage in the Former Yugoslavia, 1962–1989." *American Sociological Review* 59(3): 461–480.

Boulding, K. (1962) *Conflict and Defense: A General Theory.* New York: Harper and Row.

Boyce, J. K., and M. Pastor Jr. (1998) "Aid for Peace." *World Policy Journal* 15(2): 42–49.

Boyer, M. A. (1993) *International Cooperation and Public Goods: Opportunities for the Western Alliance.* Baltimore: Johns Hopkins University Press.

Bozo, A. (2001) "Kosovar Refugees in Albania: The Emergency Response." In M. Waller, K. Drezov, and B. Gökay (eds.), *Kosovo: The Politics of Delusion.* London: Frank Cass.

Brams, S. (1965) *Rational Politics: Decision, Games, and Strategy.* Washington, D.C.: Congressional Quarterly Press.

——— (1985) *Superpower Games: Applying Game Theory to Superpower Conflict.* Boulder: Lynne Rienner.

Brams, S., and M. Kilgour (1988) *Game Theory and National Security.* New York: Basil Blackwell.

Brankovic, S. (1995) *Serbia at War with Itself: Political Choice in Serbia, 1990–1994.* Belgrade: Sociological Society of Serbia.

Braudel, F. (1979) *The Perspective of the World: Civilization and Capitalism, 15th–18th Century.* New York: Harper and Row.

Brauner, W. (2000). "The German Perspective II: Germany's Europeanized Role in the Development of ESDP." In H. W. Maull, S. Harnisch, and W. Brauner (eds.), *Germany's Participation in the Military Intervention in Kosovo.* Trier: Universität Trier.

Breton, A., et al. (eds.) (1995) *Nationalism and Rationality.* Cambridge: Cambridge University Press.

Brock-Utne, B. (1985) *Educating for Peace: A Feminist Perspective.* New York: Pergamon Press.

Brodie, B. (ed.) (1946) *The Absolute Weapon.* New York: Harcourt and Brace.

Bronner, S. (1994) *Critical Theory and Its Theorists.* Oxford: Blackwell.

Brooks, S. G. (1997) "Dueling Realisms." *International Organization* 51 (Summer): 445–478.

Brooks, S. G., and W. C. Wohlforth (2000–2001) "Power, Globalization, and the End of the Cold War: Reevaluating the Landmark Case for Ideas." *International Security* 25(3): 5–53.

——— (2002) "American Primacy in Perspective." *Foreign Affairs* 81: 20–33.

Brown, C. (1992) *International Relations Theory: New Normative Approaches.* New York: Harvester Wheatsheaf.

——— (1995) "International Theory and International Society: The Viability of the Middle Way." *Review of International Studies* 21(2): 183–196.

——— (1999) "Universal Human Rights: A Critique." In T. Dunne and N. J. Wheeler (eds.), *Human Rights in Global Politics.* New York: Cambridge University Press.

—— (2000) "(Moral) Agency and International Society: Reflections on Norms, the UN, Southampton FC, the Gulf War, and the Kosovo Campaign." Paper presented at the annual meeting of the International Studies Association, Los Angeles, March. Available online at http://wwwc.cc.columbia.edu/sec/dlc/ciao/isa/brc01.

—— (2001) "Fog in the Channel: Continental International Relations Theory Isolated (or an Essay on the Paradoxes of Diversity and Parochialism in IR Theory." In R. M. A. Crawford and D. S. L. Jarvis (eds.), *International Relations: Still an American Social Science? Toward Diversity in International Thought*. Albany: State University of New York Press.

Brown, M. E., O. R. Coté Jr., S. M. Lynn-Jones, and S. E. Miller (eds.) (2000) *Rational Choice and Security Studies*. Cambridge: MIT Press.

Brown, M. E., et al. (eds.) (1995) *The Perils of Anarchy: Contemporary Realism and International Security*. Cambridge: MIT Press.

Brügel, J. W. (1967) "The UN Trusteeship System, 1945–1960." In M. Waters (ed.), *The United Nations: International Organization and Administration*. New York: Macmillan.

Buckley, W. J. (ed.) (2000) *Kosovo: Contending Voices on Balkan Interventions*. Grand Rapids, Mich.: William B. Eerdmans.

Bueno de Mesquita, B. (1981) *The War Trap*. New Haven: Yale University Press.

—— (1998) "The End of the Cold War: Predicting an Emergent Property." *Journal of Conflict Resolution* 42: 131–155.

Bueno de Mesquita, B., and D. Lalman (1992) *War and Reason: Domestic and International Imperatives*. New Haven: Yale University Press.

Bull, H. (1966) "The Grotian Conception of International Society." In H. Butterfield and M. Wight (eds.), *Diplomatic Investigations: Essays in the Theory of International Politics*. London: Allen and Unwin.

—— (1969) "International Theory: The Case for a Classical Approach." In K. Knorr and J. N. Rosenau (eds.), *Contending Approaches to International Politics*. Princeton: Princeton University Press.

—— (1977) *The Anarchical Society: A Study of Order in World Politics*. London: Macmillan.

Bull, H., B. Kingsbury, and A. Roberts (eds.) (1990) *Hugo Grotius and International Relations*. Oxford: Clarendon Press.

Bull, H., and A. Watson (eds.) (1984) *The Expansion of International Society*. Oxford: Clarendon Press.

Burch, K., and R. Denemark (eds.) (1997) *Constituting International Political Economy*. Boulder: Lynne Rienner.

Burchill, S., et al. (2001) *Theories of International Relations*. 2nd ed. New York: Palgrave Macmillan.

Burg, S. L., and M. L. Berbaum (1989) "Community, Integration, and Stability in Multinational Yugoslavia." *American Political Science Review* 83(2): 535–554.

Butterfield, H., and M. Wight (eds.) (1966) *Diplomatic Investigations: Essays in the Theory of International Politics*. London: Allen and Unwin.

Buzan, B. (1993) "From International System to International Society: Structural Realism and Regime Theory Meet the English School." *International Organization* 47(3) (Summer): 327–352.

—— (1995) "The Level of Analysis Problem in International Relations Reconsidered." In K. Booth and S. Smith (eds.), *International Relations Theory Today*. University Park: Pennsylvania State University Press.

—— (1996) "The Timeless Wisdom of Realism?" In S. Smith, K. Booth, and M.

Zalewski (eds.), *International Theory: Positivism and Beyond*. Cambridge: Cambridge University Press.

—— (2001) "The English School: An Underexploited Resource in IR." *Review of International Studies* 27(3): 471–488. In connection with this article, see also http://www.ukc.ac.uk/politics/englishschool.

—— (2004) *From International Society to World Society? English School Theory and the Social Structure of Globalization*. Cambridge: Cambridge University Press.

Buzan, B., C. Jones, and R. Little (1993) *The Logic of Anarchy: Neorealism to Structural Realism*. New York: Columbia University Press.

Buzan, B., and R. Little (2000) *International Systems in World History: Remaking the Study of International Relations*. Oxford: Oxford University Press.

Byman, D. L., and K. M. Pollack (2001) "Let Us Now Praise Great Men: Bringing the Statesman Back In." *International Security* 25(4): 107–146.

Byman, D. L., and M. C. Waxman (2000) "Kosovo and the Great Air Power Debate." *International Security* 24(4): 5–38.

—— (2002) *The Dynamics of Coercion: American Foreign Policy and the Limits of Military Might*. Cambridge: Cambridge University Press.

Byman, D., M. Waxman, and E. Larson (1999) *Air Power as a Coercive Instrument*. MR-1061-AF. Santa Monica: Rand.

Cafruny, A. (1990) "A Gramscian Concept of Declining Hegemony: Stages of US Power and the Evolution of International Economic Relations." In D. Rapkin (ed.), *World Leadership and Hegemony*. Boulder: Lynne Rienner.

—— (1998) "The European Union and the War in Former Yugoslavia: The Failure of Collective Diplomacy." In A. Cafruny and P. Peters (eds.), *The Union and the World: The Political Economy of a Common Foreign Policy*. The Hague: Kluwer Law.

—— (2003) "The Geopolitics of US Hegemony in Europe." In A. Cafruny and M. Ryner (eds.), *A Ruined Fortress? Neoliberal Hegemony and Transformation in Europe*. Lanham: Rowman and Littlefield.

Cahill, L. S. (1980) "Toward a Christian Theory of Human Rights." *Journal of Religious Ethics* 9: 284. [Quoted in Elshtain, J. B. (1999–2000) "The Dignity of the Human Person and the Idea of Human Rights." *Journal of Law and Religion* 14(1): 53–65.]

Callinicos, A. (1985) "Postmodernism, Post-Structuralism, Post-Marxism?" *Theory, Culture, and Society* 23.

Campbell, D. (1992) *Writing Security: United States Foreign Policy and the Politics of Identity*. Minneapolis: University of Minnesota Press.

—— (1993) *Politics Without Principle: Sovereignty, Ethics, and the Narratives of the Gulf War*. Boulder: Lynne Rienner.

Caplan, R. (1998) "International Diplomacy and the Crisis in Kosovo." *International Affairs* 74(4): 745–762.

Caporaso, J. A. (ed.) (1978) "Dependence and Dependency in the Global System." *International Organization* 32(1). Special issue.

Caprioli, M. (2003) "Feminist Phallacies or Scientific Certainties? Examining Feminist Criticisms of Feminist Empiricists and of 'Mainstream' IR." Paper presented at the annual meeting of the International Studies Association, Portland, February 26–March 1.

Cardoso, F. H., and E. Faletto (1979) *Dependency and Development in Latin America*. Berkeley: University of California Press.

Carlsnaes, W. (1992) "The Agency-Structure Problem in Foreign Policy Analysis." *International Studies Quarterly* 36 (September): 245–270.

Carlson, L. J. (2000) "Game Theory: International Trade, Conflict, and Cooperation." In R. Palan (ed.), *Global Political Economy: Contemporary Theories*. London: Routledge.

Carpenter, C. (2003) "'Women and Children First': Gender, Norms, and Humanitarian Evacuations in the Balkans, 1991–1995." *International Organization* 57(4) (Fall): 661–694.

Carpenter, R. C. (2002) "Gender Theory in World Politics: Contributions of a Nonfeminist Standpoint?" *International Studies Review* 4(3): 153–165.

Carr, E. H. (1939) *The Twenty Years' Crisis: 1919–39*. New York: Harper and Row.

Cha, V. D. (2000) "Abandonment, Entrapment, and Neoclassical Realism in East Asia." *International Studies Quarterly* 44(2): 261–291.

—— (2002) "Hawk Engagement and Preventive Defense on the Korean Peninsula." *International Security* 27(1): 40–78.

Chagnon, N. A. (1990) "Reproductive and Somatic Conflicts of Interest in the Genesis of Violence and Warfare Among Tribesmen." In J. Haas (ed.), *The Anthropology of War*. Cambridge: Cambridge University Press.

Chan, S. (1997) "In Search of Democratic Peace: Problems and Promise." *Mershon International Studies Review* 41: 59–91.

Chandler, D. (2000) "International Justice." *New Left Review* 6: 55–66.

—— (2002) "New Labour, New Imperialism: Time for a Real Debate." *Eclipse*, June 15. Available online at www.eclipsereview.org/issue9/realdebate.html.

Charlesworth, H. (1999a) "Feminist Methods in International Law." *American Journal of International Law* 93(2) (April): 379–394.

—— (1999b) "The Method Is the Message." *American Journal of International Law* 93: 379–397.

Charlesworth, H., and C. Chinkin (2000) *The Boundaries of International Law: A Feminist Analysis*. Manchester: Manchester University Press.

Charlesworth, H., C. Chinkin, and S. Wright (1991) "Feminist Approaches to International Law." *American Journal of International Law* 85(4): 613–645.

Charney, J. (1999) "Anticipatory Humanitarian Intervention in Kosovo." *American Journal of International Law* 93(4) (October): 834–841.

Charter of the United Nations. Available online at http://www.un.org/aboutun/charter/index.html.

Chase-Dunn, C. (1981) "Interstate System and Capitalist World-Economy: One Logic or Two?" *International Studies Quarterly* 25 (March): 19–42.

—— (ed.) (1982) *Socialist States in the World-System*. Beverly Hills: Sage.

—— (1989) *Global Formation: Structures of the World Economy*. Oxford: Blackwell.

—— (ed.) (1995) *The Historical Evolution of the International Political Economy*. Aldershot: Edward Elgar.

Chase-Dunn, C., and P. Grimes (1995) "World System Analysis." *Annual Review of Sociology* 21: 387–417.

Chase-Dunn, C., and T. D. Hall (eds.) (1991) *Core-Periphery Relations in Pre-Capitalist Worlds*. Boulder: Westview.

—— (eds.) (1997) *Rise and Demise: Comparing World-Systems*. Boulder: Westview.

Checkel, J. T. (1998) "The Constructivist Turn in International Relations Theory." *World Politics* 50 (January): 324–348.

—— (2001) "Why Comply? Social Learning and European Identity Change." *International Organization* 55(3): 553–588.

Chinkin, C. (1999) "Kosovo: A 'Good' or 'Bad' War?" *American Journal of International Law* 93(4) (October): 841–847.

Chirac, J. (1999) "Speech in Honor of the Prefectoral Corps." March 26. Available online at http://www.ambafrance-us.org/news/statmnts/1999/conflict1.asp.

Chirot, D., and T. D. Hall (1982) "World System Theory." *Annual Review of Sociology* 8: 81–106.

Chomsky, N. (1999a) "The Current Bombings: Behind the Rhetorics." Available online at http://www.zmag.org/chomsky/articles/9903-current_bombings.htm.

—— (1999b) *The New Military Humanism: Lessons from Kosovo*. Monroe, Maine: Common Courage Press.

—— (2000a) "The Kosovo Peace Accord." In T. Ali (ed.), *Masters of the Universe: NATO's Balkan Crusade*. London: Verso.

—— (2000b) *A New Generation Draws the Line: Kosovo, East Timor, and the Standards of the West*. New York: Verso.

Chossudovsky, M. (1997) *The Globalisation of Poverty*. London: Zed Books.

Christensen, T. J. (1996) *Useful Adversaries: Grand Strategy, Domestic Mobilization, and Sino-American Conflict, 1947–1958*. Princeton: Princeton University Press.

Christensen, T. J., and J. Snyder (1990) "Chain Gangs and Passed Bucks: Alliance Patterns in Multipolarity." *International Organization* 44(2) (Spring): 137–168.

Christoff, P., and C. Reus-Smit (2000) "Kosova and the Left." Available online at http://www.polisci.umn.edu/courses/spring2000/3873/a-4-article.html.

Christopher, W. (1993) "New Steps Toward Conflict Resolution in the Former Yugoslavia." Washington, D.C.: US Department of State, February 10.

Cioffi-Revilla, C. (1996) "Origins and Evolution of War and Politics." *International Studies Quarterly* 40: 1–22.

Claiborne, W. (1993) "Dole Decries U.S. Bosnia Policy." *Washington Post*, August 17.

Clark, H. (2000) *Civil Resistance in Kosovo*. London: Pluto Press.

Clark, W. K. (2001) *Waging Modern War: Bosnia, Kosovo, and the Future of Combat*. New York: PublicAffairs.

Clausewitz, C. Von (1976) *On War*. Eds. M. Howard and P. Paret. Princeton: Princeton University Press.

Clinton, W. J. (1998) "Remarks by the President and UN Secretary-General Kofi Annan in Photo Opportunity." White House, Office of the Press Secretary, March 11. Available online at http://clinton6.nara.gov/1998/03/1998-03-11-remarks-by-the-president-and-sg-annan-in-photo-op.html.

—— (1999a) "Address to the Nation." June 10. Available online at http://www.pbs.org/newshour/bb/europe/jan-june99/clinton_6-10.html.

—— (1999b) "Remarks by the President and Secretary General Solana." White House, Office of the Press Secretary, April 22. Available online at http://clinton4.nara.gov/wh/new/html/19990422.4175.html.

—— (1999c) "Statement by the President to the Nation on Kosovo." White House, Office of the Press Secretary, March 24. Available online at http://clinton6.nara.gov/1999/03/1999-03-24-president-remarks-to-the-nation.html.

Clymer, A. (1992) "Bush and Clinton Open Fire on the Foreign Policy Front." *New York Times*, August 2.

Cockburn, C. (2001) "The Gendered Dynamics of Armed Conflict and Political Violence." In C. Moser and F. Clark (eds.), *Victims, Perpetrators, or Actors? Armed Conflict and Political Violence*. London: Zed Books.

Cockrell, M. (2000) "The Secret World of Tony Blair." *New Statesman* 13(592): 13.

Cohen, B. J. (1973) *The Question of Imperialism: The Political Economy of Dominance and Dependence*. New York: Basic Books.

Cohen, E. A. (2001) "Kosovo and the New American Way of War." In A. J. Bacevich and E. A. Cohen (eds.), *War over Kosovo: Politics and Strategy in a Global Age*. New York: Columbia University Press.

Cohen, L. J. (1989) *The Socialist Pyramid: Elites and Power in Yugoslavia*. Oakville, Ontario: Mosaic Press.

—— (1995) *Broken Bonds: Yugoslavia's Disintegration and Balkan Politics in Transition*. Boulder: Westview.

Cohen, R. (1998) "NATO Opens Way to Start Bombing in Serb Province." *New York Times,* October 13.

Coll, A. R. (2001) "Kosovo and the Moral Burdens of Power." In A. J. Bacevich and E. A. Cohen (eds.), *War over Kosovo: Politics and Strategy in a Global Age*. New York: Columbia University Press.

Connolly, W. E. (1989) "Identity and Difference in World Politics." In J. Der Derian and M. J. Shapiro (eds.), *International/Intertextual Relations: Postmodern Readings of World Politics*. New York: Lexington Books.

—— (1991) *Identity/Difference: Democratic Negotiations of Political Paradox*. Ithaca: Cornell University Press.

Conybeare, A. C. (1984) "Public Goods, Prisoners' Dilemmas, and the International Political Economy." *International Studies Quarterly* 28(1) (March): 5–22.

Cooke, M., and A. Wollacott (eds.) (1993) *Gendering War Talk*. Princeton: Princeton University Press.

Cooper, R. N. (1968) *The Economics of Interdependence: Economic Policy in the Atlantic Community*. New York: McGraw-Hill.

Copeland, D. C. (1996) "Neorealism and the Myth of Bipolar Stability: Toward a New Dynamic Realist Theory of Major War." *Security Studies* 5 (Spring): 29–89.

—— (2000) "The Constructivist Challenge to Structural Realism: A Review Essay." *International Security* 25 (Fall): 187–212.

Cornes, R., and T. Sandler (1984) "Easy Riders, Joint Production, and Public Goods." *Economic Journal* 94: 580–598.

Corning, C. R. (1983) *The Synergism Hypothesis. A Theory of Progressive Evolution*. New York: McGraw-Hill.

Corning, P. (1971) "The Biological Basis of Behavior and Some Implications for Political Science." *World Politics* 23 (April): 339–340.

Corrin, C. (2000) "Gender Audit of Reconstruction Programmes in South Eastern Europe." Urgent Action Fund and Women's Commission for Refugee Women and Children, June. Available online at http://www.bndlg.de/~wplarre/gender-audit-of-reconstruction-programmes—ccgaudit.htm.

—— (2001) "Post-Conflict Reconstruction and Gender Analysis in Kosova." *International Feminist Journal of Politics* 3(1) (April): 78–98.

Cottam, M. L. (1986) *Foreign Policy Decision-Making: The Influence of Cognition*. Boulder: Westview.

Cox, R. W. (1981) "Social Forces, States, and World Orders: Beyond International Relations Theory." *Millennium: Journal of International Studies* 10(2): 126–155.

—— (1983) "Gramsci, Hegemony, and International Relations: An Essay in Method." *Millennium: Journal of International Studies* 12(2): 162–175.

—— (1987) *Production, Power, and World Order: Social Forces in the Making of History*. New York: Columbia University Press.

—— (ed.) (1997) *The New Realism: Perspectives on Multilateralism and World Order*. London: Macmillan.

Cox, R. W., with T. J. Sinclair (1996) *Approaches to World Order*. Cambridge: Cambridge University Press.

Crawford, B. (1996) "Explaining Defection from International Cooperation: Germany's Unilateral Recognition of Croatia." *World Politics* 48(4): 482–521.

—— (1998) "Explaining Cultural Conflict in the Ex-Yugoslavia: Institutional Weakness, Economic Crisis, and Identity Politics." In B. Crawford and R. D. Lipschutz, (eds.), *The Myth of "Ethnic Conflict": Politics, Economics, and "Cultural" Violence*. University of California International and Area Studies Digital Collection, Research Series no. 98. Available online at http://repositories.cdlib.org/uciaspubs/research/98.

Crawford, N. C (2000) "The Passion of World Politics: Propositions on Emotion and Emotional Relationships." *International Security* 24 (Spring): 116–156.

—— (2002) *Argument and Change in World Politics: Ethics, Decolonization, and Humanitarian Intervention*. Cambridge: Cambridge University Press.

—— (2003) "Just War Theory and the U.S. Counterterror War." *Perspectives on Politics* 1(1): 5–25.

Crawford, R. M. A. (2000) *Idealism and Realism in International Relations: Beyond the Discipline*. London: Routledge.

Crawford, R. M. A., and D. S. L. Jarvis (eds.) (2000) *International Relations: Still an American Social Science? Toward Diversity in International Thought*. Albany: State University of New York Press.

Crawford, T. J. (2000–2001) "Pivotal Deterrence and the Kosovo War: Why the Holbrooke Agreement Failed." *Political Science Quarterly* 116(4): 499–523.

Cross-National Time-Series Data Archive (2001) Binghamton, N.Y. Available online at http://www.databanks.sitehosting.net/www/main.htm.

Curtis, G. E. (ed.) (1990) *Yugoslavia: A Country Study*. Washington, D.C.: Library of Congress.

Cutler, C. A. (1991) "The 'Grotian Tradition' in International Relations." *Review of International Studies* 17(1): 41–65.

Daalder, I. H. (1996) "Fear and Loathing in the Former Yugoslavia." In M. E. Brown (ed.), *The International Dimensions of Internal Conflict*. Cambridge: MIT Press.

—— (1999) *Getting to Dayton: The Making of America's Bosnia Policy*. Washington, D.C.: Brookings Institution.

Daalder, I. H., and M. E. O'Hanlon (2000a) "The United States in the Balkans: There to Stay." *Washington Quarterly* 23(4): 57–170.

—— (2000b) *Winning Ugly: NATO's War to Save Kosovo*. Washington, D.C.: Brookings Institution.

Daley, S. (2001) "NATO Quickly Gives the US All the Help That It Asked." *New York Times*, October 5.

Dallago, B., and M. Uvalic (1998) "The Distributive Consequences of Nationalism: The Case of Former Yugoslavia." *Europe-Asia Studies* 50(1): 71–90.

Damrosch, L. (2000) "The Inevitability of Selective Response? Principles to Guide Urgent International Action." In A. Schnabel and R. Thakur (eds.), *Kosovo and the Challenge of Humanitarian Intervention*. New York: United Nations University Press.

Danaher, K. (2002) *10 Reasons to Abolish the IMF and the World Bank*. New York: Seven Stories Press.

Darwin, C. R. (1871) *The Descent of Man, and Selection in Relation to Sex*. London: John Murray.

Davie, M. R. (1929) *The Evolution of War: A Study of Its Role in Early Societies*. New Haven: Yale University Press.

de Wijk, R. (2000) *Pyrrhus in Kosovo, or How the West Could Not Win the War and Even Nearly Lost It* [in Dutch]. Amsterdam: Mets and Schilt.

de Wilde, J. (1991) *Saved from Oblivion: Interdependence Theory in the First Half of the Twentieth Century.* Aldershot: Dartmouth.

DeCamp, W. T. (2000) "The Big Picture: A Moral Analysis of Allied Force in Kosovo." *Marine Corps Gazette,* February.

Deibert, R. J. (1997) *Parchment, Printing, and Hypermedia: Communication in World Order Transformation.* New York: Columbia University Press.

Delaisi, F. (1925) *Political Myths and Economic Realities.* New York: Viking.

Delanty, G. (1997) *Social Science: Beyond Constructivism and Realism.* Minneapolis: University of Minnesota Press.

Dempsey, J. (2003) "Frustration for Diplomats as Choice of Envoy Blocked." *Financial Times,* July 4.

Denemark, R. A. (1999) "World System History: From Traditional International Politics to the Study of Global Relations." *International Studies Review* 1(2): 43–76.

Denitch, B. (1994). *Ethnic Nationalism: The Tragic Death of Yugoslavia.* Minneapolis: University of Minnesota Press.

Dennett, D. C. (1995) *Darwin's Dangerous Idea. Evolution and the Meanings of Life.* New York: Simon and Schuster.

Dennis, M., et al. (1999) "NATO's Game of Chicken." *Newsweek,* July 28.

Der Derian, J. (1987) *On Diplomacy: A Genealogy of Western Estrangement.* Oxford: Blackwell.

——— (1988) "Introducing Philosophical Traditions in International Relations." *Millennium: Journal of International Studies* 17: 189–193.

——— (1989) "The Boundaries of Knowledge and Power in International Relations." In J. Der Derian and M. J. Shapiro (eds.), *International/Intertextual Relations: Postmodern Readings of World Politics.* New York: Lexington Books.

——— (1992) *Antidiplomacy: Spies, Terror, Speed, and War.* Oxford: Blackwell.

——— (ed.) (1995a) *International Theory: Critical Investigations.* New York: New York University Press.

——— (1995b) "A Reinterpretation of Realism: Genealogy, Semiology, Dromology." In J. Der Derian (ed.), *International Theory: Critical Investigations.* New York: New York University Press.

——— (1997) "Post-Theory: The Eternal Return of Ethics in International Relations." In M. W. Doyle and G. J. Ikenberry (eds.), *New Thinking in International Relations Theory.* Boulder: Westview.

Der Derian, J., and M. J. Shapiro (eds.) (1989) *International/Intertextual Relations: Postmodern Readings of World Politics.* New York: Lexington Books.

Desch, M. C. (1998) "Culture Clash: Assessing the Importance of Ideas in Security Studies." *International Security* 23(1): 141–170.

——— (2003) "It Is Kind to Be Cruel: The Humanity of American Realism." *Review of International Studies* 29: 415–426.

Dessler, D. (1989) "What's at Stake in the Agent-Structure Debate?" *International Organization* 43 (Summer): 441–473.

——— (1999) "Constructivism Within a Positivist Social Science." *Review of International Studies* 25: 123–137.

Deudney, D. (1993) "Dividing Realism: Structural Realism Versus Security Materialism on Nuclear Security and Proliferation." *Security Studies* 2 (Spring–Summer): 7–36.

—— (1996) "Ground Identity: Nature, Place, and Space in Nationalism." In Y. Lapid and F. Kratochwil (eds.), *The Return of Culture and Identity in IR Theory*. Boulder: Lynne Rienner.

—— (2000) "ReGrounding Realism: Anarchy, Security, and Changing Material Contexts." *Security Studies* 10(1) (Autumn): 1–45.

Deutsch, K. W., and J. D. Singer (1964) "Multipolar Power Systems and International Stability." *World Politics* 16(3) (April): 390–406.

Deutsch, K. W., et al. (1957) *Political Community and the North Atlantic Area*. Princeton: Princeton University Press.

Devetak, R. (2001) "Critical Theory." In S. Burchill, R. Devetak, A. Linklater, M. Paterson, C. Reus-Smit, and J. True (eds.), *Theories of International Relations*. New York: Palgrave.

"Dialogue" (1998) *International Studies Quarterly* 42(1): 193–210.

DiCicco, J., and J. S. Levy (1999) "Power Shifts and Problem Shifts: The Evolution of the Power Transition Research Program." *Journal of Conflict Resolution* 42: 675–704.

Dinmore, G. (1998) "NATO's Display of Force Fails to Halt Kosovo Attacks." *Financial Times*, June 16.

Divale, W. T. (1973) *Warfare in Primitive Societies: A Bibliography*. Santa Barbara: Clio Press.

Dixit, A., and S. Skeath (1999) *Games of Strategy*. New York: Norton.

Djilas, A. (1991) *The Contested Country: Yugoslav Unity and Communist Revolution*. Cambridge: Harvard University Press.

Djordjevic, D., and S. Fischer-Galati (1981) *The Balkan Revolutionary Tradition*. New York: Columbia University Press.

Djukic, S. (2001) *Milosevic and Markovic: A Lust for Power*. Montreal: McGill-Queen's University Press.

Dobnik, V. (1999) "Americans Off to Join Kosovo Army." Associated Press, April 13. Available online at http://h-net.msu.edu/minerva.

Doder, D. (1979) *The Yugoslavs*. London: Allen and Unwin.

Domhoff, W. (1970) *The Higher Circles: The Governing Class in America*. New York: Vintage.

Donelan, M. (ed.) (1978) *The Reason of States*. London: Allen and Unwin.

—— (1990) *Elements of International Political Theory*. Oxford: Clarendon Press.

Donfried, K. (2000) *German Foreign Policy: Kosovo*. Washington, D.C.: Congressional Research Service.

Donnelly, J. (1986) "International Human Rights: A Regimes Analysis." *International Organization* 40(3) (Summer): 599–642.

—— (1999) "The Social Construction of International Human Rights." In T. Dunne and N. J. Wheeler (eds.), *Human Rights in Global Politics*. Cambridge: Cambridge University Press.

Doty, R. L. (1996) *Imperial Encounters*. Minneapolis: University of Minnesota Press.

—— (1998) "Sovereignty and the Nation: Constructing the Boundaries of National Identity." In T. Biersteker and C. Weber (eds.), *State Sovereignty as Social Construct*. Cambridge: Cambridge University Press.

Dougherty, J. E., and R. L. Pfaltzgraff Jr. (1997) *Contending Theories of International Relations: A Comprehensive Survey*. 4th ed. New York: Addison-Wesley Longman.

Downs, G. W., and D. M. Rocke (1990) *Tacit Bargaining, Arms Races, and Arms Control*. Ann Arbor: University of Michigan Press.

Doyle, M. W. (1986) "Liberalism and World Politics." *American Political Science Review* 80: 1151–1169.

—— (1997) *Ways of War and Peace.* New York: W. W. Norton.

Doyle, M. W., and G. J. Ikenberry (1997a) "Introduction: The End of the Cold War, the Classical Tradition, and International Change." In M. W. Doyle and G. J. Ikenberry (eds.), *New Thinking in International Relations Theory.* Boulder: Westview.

—— (eds.) (1997b) *New Thinking in International Relations Theory.* Boulder: Westview.

Dragnich, A. N. (1989) "The Rise and Fall of Yugoslavia: The Omen of the Upsurge of Serbian Nationalism." *East European Quarterly* 23(2): 183–198.

Druckman, D. (1994) "Nationalism, Patriotism, and Group Loyalty: A Social Psychological Perspective." *Mershon International Studies Review* 38 (April): 43–68.

Duffield, J. (1996) "The North Atlantic Treaty Organization and Alliance Theory." In N. Woods (ed.), *Explaining International Relations Since 1945.* Oxford: Oxford University Press.

Duffy, D. M. (2000) "Social Identity and Its Influence on Women's Roles in East-Central Europe." *International Feminist Journal of Politics* 2(2) (Summer): 214–243.

Duke, S., H. G. Ehrhart, and M. Karadi (2000) "The Major European Allies: France, Germany, and the United Kingdom." In A. Schnabel and R. Thakur (eds.), *Kosovo and the Challenge of Humanitarian Intervention: Selective Indignation, Collective Action, and International Citizenship.* New York: United Nations University Press.

Dunne, T. (1995) "The Social Construction of International Society." *European Journal of International Relations* 1(3) (September): 367–390.

—— (1998) *Inventing International Society: A History of the English School.* London: Macmillan.

—— (2001) "Sociological Investigations: Instrumental Legitimist and Coercive Interpretations of International Society." *Millennium: Journal of International Studies* 30(1): 67–91.

Dunne, T., and N. J. Wheeler (eds.) (1999) *Human Rights in Global Politics.* Cambridge: Cambridge University Press.

Durham, W. H. (1976) "Resource Competition and Human Aggression—Part 1: A Review of Primitive War." *Quarterly Review of Biology* 51: 385–415.

Durkheim, E. (1965) *The Elementary Forms of the Religious Life.* New York: Free Press.

Durst, D. C. (2000) "The Place of the Political in Derrida and Foucault" [review of the book *Derrida and the Political*]. *Political Theory* 28: 675–689.

Dyker, D. A. (1990) *Yugoslavia: Socialism, Development, and Debt.* London: Routledge.

Dyker, D., and I. Vejvoda (eds.) (1996) *Yugoslavia and After: A Study in Fragmentation, Despair, and Rebirth.* New York: Longman.

Eckstein, H. (1975) "Case Study and Theory in Political Science." In F. I. Greenstein and N. W. Polsby (eds.), *Handbook of Political Science,* vol. 7, *Strategies of Inquiry.* Reading, Mass.: Addison-Wesley.

Edkins, J. (1999) *Poststructuralism in International Relations.* Boulder: Lynne Rienner.

Efrid, B., P. Galbraith, J. Kugler, and M. Abdollahian (2000) "Negotiating Peace in Kosovo." *International Interactions* 26: 153–178.

Elam, D., and R. Wiegman (1995) *Feminism Beside Itself.* London: Routledge.

el-Bushra, J. (2000) "Transforming Conflict: Some Thoughts on a Gendered Understanding of Conflict Processes." In R. Jacobson, S. Jacobs, and J. Marchbank (eds.), *States of Conflict: Gender, Conflict, and Resistance.* New York: Zed Books.

Ellis, J. O. (1999) "A View from the Top." Briefing slides. On file with Sean Kay.

Ellsberg, D. (1959) "The Theory and Practice of Blackmail." Lecture at the Lowell Institute, Boston, March 10. [Reprinted in O. R. Young (ed.), *Bargaining: Formal Theories of Negotiation.* Urbana: University of Illinois Press, 1975.]

Elman, C. (1996a) "Cause, Effect, and Consistency: A Response to Kenneth Waltz." *Security Studies* 6(1): 58–61.

——— (1996b) "Horses for Courses: Why Not Neorealist Theories of Foreign Policy?" *Security Studies* 6(1): 7–53.

Elshtain, J. B. (1981) *Public Man, Private Woman: Women in Social and Political Thought.* Princeton: Princeton University Press.

——— (1992) "Sovereignty, Identity, Sacrifice." In V. S. Peterson (ed.), *Gendered States: Feminist (Re)Visions of International Relations Theory.* Boulder: Lynne Rienner.

——— (1994) *Women and War.* 2nd ed. Chicago: University of Chicago Press.

——— (1995) "Feminist Themes and International Relations." In J. Der Derian (ed.), *International Theory: Critical Investigations.* New York: New York University Press.

——— (1997) "Feminist Inquiry and International Relations." In M. W. Doyle and G. J. Ikenberry (eds.), *New Thinking in International Relations Theory.* Boulder: Westview.

Elster, J. (2000) "Rational Choice History: A Case of Excessive Ambition." *American Political Science Review* 94: 685–695.

Emirbayer, M. (1997) "Manifesto for a Relational Sociology." *American Journal of Sociology* 103(2): 281–317.

Enloe, C. (1990) *Bananas, Beaches, and Bases: Making Feminist Sense of International Politics.* Berkeley: University of California Press.

——— (1993) *The Morning After: Sexual Politics at the End of the Cold War.* Berkeley: University of California Press.

——— (1996) "Margins, Silences, and Bottom Rungs: How to Overcome the Underestimation of Power in the Study of International Relations." In S. Smith, K. Booth, and M. Zalewski (eds.), *International Theory: Positivism and Beyond.* Cambridge: Cambridge University Press.

——— (2000) *Maneuvers: The Politics of Militarizing Women's Lives.* Berkeley: University of California Press.

Epp, R. (1998) "The English School on the Frontiers of International Society: A Hermeneutic Recollection." *Review of International Studies* 24(5): 47–63.

Epstein, J. M. (1992) "On the Mathematical Biology of Arms Races, Wars, and Revolutions." In L. Nadel and D. Stein (eds.), *1992 Lectures in Complex Systems.* Reading, Mass.: Addison-Wesley.

——— (1994) *Nonlinear Dynamics, Mathematical Biology, and Social Science.* Reading, Mass.: Addison-Wesley.

Epstein, J. M., and R. Axtell (1996) *Growing Artificial Societies: Social Science from the Bottom Up.* Washington, D.C.: Brookings Institution.

Erlanger, S. (1998) "NATO May Act Against Serbs in Two Weeks." *New York Times,* October 2.

———— (1999a) "Kosovo Killings Harden Resistance and Jolt West." *New York Times,* January 25.

———— (1999b) "NATO Was Closer to a Ground War Than Is Widely Realized." *New York Times,* November 7.

European Council (1999) Statement on Kosovo. March. Available online at http://europa.eu.int/council/off/conclu/mar99_en.htm.

Evans, G., and M. Sahnoun (2002) "The Responsibility to Protect." *Foreign Affairs* 81(6): 99–115.

Evans, P. B. (1979) *Dependent Development: The Alliance of Multinational, State, and Local Capital in Brazil.* Princeton: Princeton University Press.

Evans, T., and P. Wilson (1992) "Regime Theory and the English School of International Relations: A Comparison." *Millennium* 21(3): 329–352.

"Exchange on the Third Debate" (1989) *International Studies Quarterly* 33(3): 235–280.

Falger, V. S. E. (1994) "Biopolitics and the Study of International Relations: Implications, Results, and Perspectives." *Research in Biopolitics* 2: 115–134.

———— (1997) "Human Nature in Modern International Relations—Part I: Theoretical Backgrounds." *Research in Biopolitics* 5: 155–175.

———— (2001a) "Evolution in International Relations? From Social Darwinism to Evolutionary Theory in the Study of International Politics." In A. Somit and S. A. Peterson (eds.), *Neo-Darwinism and the Social and Behavioral Sciences.* Stamford: JAI Press.

———— (2001b) "Evolution in International Relations? From Social Darwinism to Evolutionary Theory in the Study of International Relations." In S. A. Peterson and A. Somit (eds.), *Evolutionary Approaches in the Behavioral Sciences: Toward a Better Understanding of Human Nature.* Amsterdam: Elsevier.

———— (2001c) "Evolutionary World Politics Enriched: The Biological Foundations of International Relations." In W. R. Thompson (ed.), *Evolutionary Interpretations of World Politics.* New York: Routledge.

Falk, R. (1988) *Revolutionaries and Functionaries: The Dual Face of Terrorism.* New York: Dutton.

———— (1999) "Kosovo, World Order, and the Future of International Law." *American Journal of International Law* 93: 847–857.

———— (2003) "What Future for the UN Charter System of War Prevention?" Transnational Foundation for Peace and Future Research, June 23, 2003. Available online at http://www.transnational.org/forum/meet/2003/falk_uncharter.html.

Fawn, R., and J. Larkin (eds.) (1996) *International Society After the Cold War: Anarchy and Order Reconsidered.* London: Macmillan.

Fawn, R., and J. Mayall (1996) "Recognition, Self-Determination, and Secession in Post–Cold War International Society." In R. Fawn and J. Larkins (eds.), *International Society After the Cold War: Anarchy and Order Reconsidered.* London: Macmillan.

Fearon, J. D. (1995) "Rationalist Explanations for War." *International Organization* 49(3) (Summer): 379–414.

Ferguson, Y. H., and R. W. Mansbach (1988) *The Elusive Quest: Theory and International Politics.* Columbia: University of South Carolina Press.

———— (1991) "Between Celebration and Despair: Constructive Suggestions for Future International Theory." *International Studies Quarterly* 35(4) (December): 363–496.

———— (1996) *Polities: Authority, Identities, and Change*. Columbia: University of South Carolina Press.

Fetzer, J. H. (ed.) (1985) *Sociobiology and Epistemology*. Boston: D. Reidel.

Fierke, K. (2000) "Logics of Force and Dialogue: The Iraq/UNSCOM Crisis as Social Interaction." *European Journal of International Relations* 6(3): 335–371.

Finn, P. (2002). "NATO Plans to Trim Balkan Force." *Washington Post,* May 11.

Finnemore, M. (1996) *National Interests in International Society*. Ithaca: Cornell University Press.

Finnemore, M., and K. Sikkink (1998) "International Norm Dynamics and Political Change." *International Organization* 52: 887–918.

Flakierski, H. (1989) *The Economic System and Income Distribution in Yugoslavia*. Armonk, N.Y.: M. E. Sharpe.

Fletcher, P. (2000) "Yugoslav Army, Protesters, Mark Women's Day." Reuters, March 8. Available online at http://h-net.msu.edu/minerva.

Forsyth, M. (1978) "The Classical Theory of International Relations." *Political Studies* 26: 411–416.

Foucault, M. (1972a) *The Archaeology of Knowledge*. New York: Pantheon Books.

———— (1972b) *Power/Knowledge*. New York: Pantheon Books.

———— (1978) *The History of Sexuality*. Vol. 1. New York: Vintage.

———— (1984) "What Is Enlightenment?" In P. Rainbow (ed.), *The Foucault Reader*. New York: Pantheon Books.

———— (1995) *Discipline & Punish*. New York: Vintage Books.

Frank, A. G. (1969) *Capitalism and Development in Latin America: Historical Studies of Chile and Brazil*. Rev. ed. New York: Monthly Review Press.

———— (1970) *Latin America: Underdevelopment or Revolution*. New York: Monthly Review Press.

———— (1991) "A Plea for World System History." *Journal of World History* 2 (Winter).

———— (1998) *ReOrient: Global Economy in the Asian Age*. Berkeley: University of California Press.

———— (1999a) "NATO Against the Law and Yugoslavia." Available online at http://csf.colorado.edu/agfrank/nato_kosovo/msg00002.html.

———— (1999b) "NATO Bombs." Available online at http://csf.colorado. edu/agfrank/nato_kosovo/msg00000.html.

———— (1999c) "NATO Violations of International Law." Available online at http://csf.colorado.edu/agfrank/nato_kosovo/msg00003.html.

———— (1999d) "NATO's Kosovo Political Bomb." Available online at http://csf.colorado.edu/agfrank/kosovo_bomb.html.

Frank, A. G., and B. Gills (eds.) (1993) *The World System: Five Hundred Years or Five Thousand?* London: Routledge.

Frankel, B. (ed.) (1996) *Realism: Restatements and Renewals*. London: Frank Cass.

Frederking, B. (2003) "Constructing Post–Cold War Collective Security." *American Political Science Review* 97(3) (August): 363–378.

Freeman, C. (ed.) (1983) *Long Waves in the World Economy*. London: Frances Pinter.

Freud, S. (1961) *Civilization and Its Discontents*. New York: W. W. Norton.

Freyberg-Inan, A. (2003) *What Moves Man: The Realist Theory of International Relations and Its Judgement of Human Nature*. Albany: State University of New York Press.

Fried, M. H. (1967) *The Evolution of Political Society: An Essay in Political Anthropology.* New York: Random House.

Friedberg, A. L. (1988) *The Weary Titan: Britain and the Experience of Relative Decline.* Princeton: Princeton University Press.

Friedman, G., and H. Starr (1997) *Agency, Structure, and International Politics: From Ontology to Empirical Inquiry.* London: Routledge.

"Frontiers of Knowledge: The State of the Art in World Affairs" (1998) *Foreign Policy* (Spring). Special issue.

Fudenberg, D., and J. Tirole (1991) *Game Theory.* Cambridge: MIT Press.

Fukuyama, F. (1989) "The End of History?" *National Interest* 16 (Summer): 3–18.

―― (1997) *Evolutionary Biology.* Sunderland, Mass.: Sinauer.

―― (1998) "Women and the Evolution of World Politics." *Foreign Affairs* 77(5): 24–40.

Fulwood, S. (1992) "Clinton Steps Up His Support for Military Action in Bosnia." *Los Angeles Times,* August 6.

Gagnon, V. P. (1994–1995) "Ethnic Nationalism and International Conflict: The Case of Serbia." *International Security* 19(3): 130–166.

Gall, C. (1999) "Russians Fly Into Kosovo After Impasse Is Resolved." *New York Times,* July 7.

Galtung, J. (1969) "Violence, Peace, and Peace Research." *Journal of Peace Research* 6(3): 167–191.

―― (1971) "A Structural Theory of Imperialism." *Journal of Peace Research* 8(2): 81–98.

Gat, A. (2000) "The Human Motivational Complex: Evolutionary Theory and the Causes of Hunter-Gatherer Fighting—Part 1: Primary Somatic and Reproductive Causes; Part 2: Proximate, Subordinate, and Derivative Causes." *Anthropology Quarterly* 73: 20–34; 74–88.

"Gender and International Relations" (2003) *International Studies Review* 5(2) (June). Special issue.

"Gendering the International" (1998) *Millennium* 27(3) (Winter). Special issue.

George, J. (1988) "The Study of International Relations and the Positivists/Empiricist Theory of Knowledge: Implications for the Australian Discipline." In R. Higgott (ed.), *New Directions in International Relations.* Canberra: Australian National University Press.

―― (1989) "International Relations and the Search for Thinking Space: Another View of the Third Debate." *International Studies Quarterly* 33(3) (September): 269–280.

―― (1994) *Discourses of Global Politics: A Critical (Re)Introduction to International Relations.* Boulder: Lynne Rienner.

George, J., and D. Campbell (1990) "Patterns of Dissent and the Celebration of Difference: Critical Social Theory and International Relations." *International Studies Quarterly* 34(3) (September): 269–294.

Germain, R., and M. Kenny (1998) "Engaging Gramsci: International Relations Theory and the New Gramscians." *Review of International Studies* 24: 3–21.

"Germany Comes Out of Its Post-War Shell" (1999) *The Economist,* July 10. Available online at http://www.lexisnexis.com.

Geuss, R. (2001) "Nietzsche and Genealogy." In J. Richardson and B. Leiter (eds.), *Nietzsche.* Oxford: Oxford University Press.

Geva, N., and A. Mintz (eds.) (1997) *Decision Making on War and Peace: The Cognitive-Rational Debate.* Boulder: Lynne Rienner.

References

Gibbons, R. (1992) *Game Theory for Applied Economists*. Princeton: Princeton University Press.

Gibbs, D. N. (2002) "Western Intervention and the Breakup of the Yugoslav Federation: A Revisionist Analysis." Paper presented at the annual meeting of the International Studies Association, New Orleans, March 24–27. [Published in Serbo-Croatian translation in *Sociological Review* (Belgrade) 35 (2001).]

Giddens, A. (1979) *Central Problems in Social Theory*. Berkeley: University of California Press.

—— (1984) *The Constitution of Society*. Berkeley: University of California Press.

Gill, S. (1988) *The Global Economy: Perspectives, Problems, and Policies*. New York: Harvester.

—— (1990a) *American Hegemony and the Trilateral Commission*. Cambridge: Cambridge University Press.

—— (1990b) "The Emerging Hegemony of Transnational Capital: Trilateralism and Global Order." In D. Rapkin (ed.), *World Leadership and Hegemony*. Boulder: Lynne Rienner.

—— (ed.) (1993) *Gramsci, Historical Materialism, and International Relations*. Cambridge: Cambridge University Press.

—— (1995) "Globalization, Market Civilization, and Disciplinary Neoliberalism." *Millennium: Journal of International Studies* 24: 399–424.

—— (1998) "New Constitutionalism, Democratization and Global Political Economy." *Pacifica Review* 10(1): 23–38.

Gilligan, C. (1982) *In a Different Voice: Psychological Theory and Women's Development*. Cambridge: Harvard University Press.

Gilpin, R. (1975) *US Power and Multinational Corporations*. New York: Basic Books.

—— (1981) *War and Change in World Politics*. Cambridge: Cambridge University Press.

—— (1987) *The Political Economy of International Relations*. Princeton: Princeton University Press.

Glaser, C. L. (1997) "The Security Dilemma Revisited." *World Politics* 50(1): 171–201.

—— (2003) "The Necessary and Natural Evolution of Structural Realism." In J. A. Vasquez and C. Elman (eds.), *Realism and the Balancing of Power: A New Debate*. Upper Saddle River, N.J.: Prentice Hall.

Glennon, M. (2001) *Limits of Law, Prerogatives of Power: Interventionism After Kosovo*. New York: Palgrave.

Glenny, M. (1999) *The Balkans 1804–1999: Nationalism, War, and the Great Powers*. New York: Viking Penguin Books.

Gligorov, V. (1999) "The Kosovo Crisis and the Balkans: Background, Consequences, Costs, and Prospects." Vienna Institute for International Economic Studies, WIIS Current Analyses and Country Profiles. Available online at http://wiiwsv.wsr.ac.at/wiiwpubl/ca13.pdf.

Gligorov, V., and N. Sundstrom (1999) "The Costs of the Kosovo Crisis." Vienna Institute for International Economic Studies, WIIS Current Analyses and Country Profiles. Available online at http://wiiwsv.wsr.ac.at/wiiwpubl/ca12.pdf.

Goff, P. M., and K. C. Dunn (eds.) (2004) *Identity and Global Politics: Theoretical and Empirical Elaborations*. New York: Palgrave Macmillan.

Gokay, B. (2002) "The Most Dangerous Game in the World: Oil, War, and US Global Hegemony." *Alexander's Oil and Gas Connections* 7 (24). Available online at http://www.gasandoil.com/gok.

Goldgeier, J. M., and M. McFaul (1992) "A Tale of Two Worlds: Core and Periphery in the Post–Cold War Era." *International Organization* 46(2) (Spring): 467–491.

Goldstein, J. S. (1987) "The Emperor's New Genes: Sociobiology and War." *International Studies Quarterly* 31 (March): 33–44.

—— (1988) *Long Cycles: Prosperity and War in the Modern Age.* New Haven: Yale University Press.

—— (1991) "The Possibility of Cycles in International Relations." *International Studies Quarterly* 35(4) (December): 455–480.

—— (2001) *War and Gender: How Gender Shapes the War System and Vice Versa.* Cambridge: Cambridge University Press.

Goldstein, J., and R. O. Keohane (eds.) (1993) *Ideas and Foreign Policy: Beliefs, Institutions, and Political Change.* Ithaca: Cornell University Press.

Gompert, D. (1996) "The United Nations and Yugoslavia's Wars." In R. Ullman (ed.), *The World and Yugoslavia's Wars.* New York: Council on Foreign Relations Press.

Gong, G. W. (1984) *The Standard of Civilization in International Society.* Oxford: Clarendon Press.

Goodall, J. (1986) *The Chimpanzees of Gombe: Patterns of Behavior.* Cambridge: Harvard University Press.

Goodby, James (1996) "Can Collective Security Work?" In C. A. Crocker and F. O. Hampson with P. Aall (eds.), *Managing Global Chaos: Sources of and Responses to International Conflict.* Washington, D.C.: US Institute of Peace Press.

Gordon, Michael (2002) "US Asks NATO Nations to Offer Forces for Iraq Campaign." *New York Times,* December 5.

Gow, J. (1997) *Triumph of the Lack of Will: International Diplomacy and the Yugoslav War.* New York: Columbia University Press.

Gowan, P. (2000) "The Euro-Atlantic Origins of NATO's Attack on Yugoslavia." In T. Ali (ed.), *Masters of the Universe: NATO's Balkan Crusade.* London: Verso.

—— (2001) "Neoliberal Cosmopolitanism." *New Left Review* 11 (September–October): 79–94.

Graham, B. (1999) "Joint Chiefs Doubted Air Strategy." *Washington Post,* April 5. Available online at http://www.lexisnexis.com.

Grandits, M., et al. (1999) "Rape Is a War Crime: How to Support the Survivors. Lessons from Bosnia, Strategies for Kosovo." Vienna: Online Conference Report International Centre for Migration Policy Development. Available at www.icmpd.org.

Grant, R., and K. Newland (eds.) (1991) *Gender and International Relations.* Bloomington: Indiana University Press.

Green, D. M. (2002) "Constructivist Comparative Politics: Foundations and Framework." In D. M. Green (ed.), *Constructivism and Comparative Politics.* Armonk, N.Y.: M. E. Sharpe.

Green, D. P., and I. Shapiro (1994) *Pathologies of Rational Choice Theory: A Critique of Applications in Political Science.* New Haven: Yale University Press.

Gregaroy, M. S., et al. (eds.) (1978) *Sociobiology and Human Nature: An Interdisciplinary Critique and Defense.* San Francisco: Jossey-Bass.

Gregory, D. U. (1989) Foreword to J. Der Derian and M. J. Shapiro (eds.), *International/Intertextual Relations: Postmodern Readings of World Politics.* New York: Lexington Books.

Grewal, I., and C. Kaplan (eds.) (1994) *Scattered Hegemonies*. Minneapolis: University of Minnesota Press.

Grieco, J. M. (1990) *Cooperation Among Nations: Europe, America, and Non-Tariff Barriers to Trade*. Ithaca: Cornell University Press.

Griffiths, M., and T. O'Callaghan (2001) "The End of International Relations?" In R. M. A. Crawford and D. S. L. Jarvis (eds.), *International Relations: Still an American Social Science? Toward Diversity in International Thought*. Albany: State University of New York Press.

Groom, A., and P. Taylor (2000) "The United Nations System and the Kosovo Crisis." In A. Schnabel and R. Thakur (eds.), *Kosovo and the Challenge of Humanitarian Intervention*. New York: United Nations University Press.

Groom, A. J. R., and M. Light (eds.) (1994) *Contemporary International Relations: A Guide to Theory*. London: Pinter.

Haas, E. B. (1958) *The Uniting of Europe: Political, Social, and Economic Forces, 1950–1957*. London: Stevens.

—— (1964) *Beyond the Nation-State: Functionalism and International Organization*. Stanford: Stanford University Press.

—— (1990) *When Knowledge Is Power: Three Models of Change in International Organization*. Berkeley: University of California Press.

Haas, P. (1997) *Knowledge, Power, and International Policy Coordination*. Columbia: University of South Carolina Press.

Haas, R. N. (1999) "What to Do with American Primacy." *Foreign Affairs* 78(5): 37–49.

Habermas, J. (1996) *Between Facts and Norms: Contributions to a Discourse Theory of Law and Democracy*. Cambridge: MIT Press.

—— (2000) "Bestiality and Humanity: A War on the Border Between Law and Morality." In W. F. Buckley (ed.), *Kosovo: Contending Voices on Balkan Interventions*. Grand Rapids, Mich.: William B. Eerdmans.

—— (2002) "Letter to America." *The Nation*, December 16.

Haftendorn, H., R. O. Keohane, and C. A. Wallander (eds.) (1999) *Imperfect Unions: Security Institutions over Time and Space*. Oxford: Oxford University Press.

Hagen, W. W. (1999) "The Balkans' Lethal Nationalisms." *Foreign Affairs* 78(4): 52–64.

Halebsky, S., and R. L. Harris (1995) *Capital, Power, and Inequality in Latin America*. Boulder: Westview.

Hall, R. (1998) *National Collective Identity*. New York: Columbia University Press.

Halliday, F. (2002) "The Pertinence of Imperialism." In M. Rupert and H. Smith (eds.), *Historical Materialism and Globalization*. London: Routledge.

Hamburg, D. A., and J. E. Holl (1999) "Preventing Deadly Conflict: From Global Housekeeping to Neighborhood Watch." In I. Kaul, I. Grunberg, and M. A. Stern (eds.), *Global Public Goods: International Cooperation in the 21st Century*. New York: Oxford University Press.

Haraway, D. (1989) *Primate Visions: Gender, Race, and Nature in the World of Modern Science*. New York: Routledge.

Hardin, R. (1995) *One for All: The Logic of Group Conflict*. Princeton: Princeton University Press.

Harding, S. (1986) *The Science Question in Feminism*. Ithaca: Cornell University Press.

—— (1991) *Whose Science? Whose Knowledge?* Ithaca: Cornell University Press.

Harris, J. F. (1999) "Clinton, Aides Vague on Plans for Troops." *Washington Post,* April 6. Available online at http://www.lexisnexis.com.

Harris, M. (1975) *Culture, Man, and Nature.* New York: Thomas Crowell.

Harrod, J. (1987) *Power, Production, and the Unprotected Worker.* New York: Columbia University Press.

Hart, P., E. Stern, and B. Sundelius (eds.) (1997) *Beyond Groupthink: Political Group Dynamics and Foreign Policy Making.* Ann Arbor: University of Michigan Press.

Hartsock, N. (1983) *Money, Sex, and Power: Toward a Feminist Historical Materialism.* Boston: Northeastern University Press.

Hartzell, C. A. (1999) "Explaining the Stability of Negotiated Settlements to Intrastate Wars." *Journal of Conflict Resolution* 43: 3–22.

Harvey, F. P. (2000) "Primordialism, Evolutionary Theory, and Ethnic Violence in the Balkans: Opportunities and Constraints for Theory and Policy." *Canadian Journal of Political Science* 33(1): 37–65.

Hasenclever, A., P. Mayer, and V. Rittberger (1997) *Theories of International Regimes.* Cambridge: Cambridge University Press.

Havel, V. (1999) "Kosovo and the End of the Nation-State." *New York Review of Books* 46(10) (June). Available online at http://www.nybooks.com/articles.

Hayden, R. M. (1996) "Imagined Communities and Real Victims: Self-Determination and Ethnic Cleansing in Yugoslavia." *American Ethnologist* 23(4): 783–801.

Hayden, W. (1999) "The Kosovo Conflict and Forced Migration: The Strategic Use of Displacement and the Obstacles to International Protection," *Journal of Humanitarian Assistance.* Available online at http://www-jha.sps.cam.ac.uk/b/b597.htm.

Hedges, C. (1999) "Kosovo's Next Masters?" *Foreign Affairs* 78(3) (May–June): 24–42.

Held, D. (1980) *Introduction to Critical Theory: Horkheimer to Habermas.* Berkeley: University of California Press.

——— (1996) "The Decline of the Nation State." In G. Eley and R. G. Suny (eds.), *Becoming National: A Reader.* New York: Oxford University Press.

——— (2001) "Violence, Law, and Justice in a Global Age." Available online at http://www.ssrc.org/sept11/essays/held.htm.

Hellmann, G. (ed.) (2003) "Are Dialogue and Synthesis Possible in International Relations?" *International Studies Review* 5(1) (March): 123–153.

Helsinki Watch (1992) *Human Rights Abuses in Kosovo, 1990–1992.* New York: Human Rights Watch/Helsinki Watch.

——— (1994) *Open Wounds: Human Rights Abuses in Kosovo.* New York: Human Rights Watch/Helsinki Watch.

——— (1996) *Yugoslavia (Serbia and Montenegro): Persecution Persists—Human Rights Violations in Kosovo.* New York: Human Rights Watch/Helsinki Watch.

Hempel, C. G. (1965) *Aspects of Scientific Explanation and Other Essays in the Philosophy of Science.* New York: Collier-Macmillan.

Henkin, L. (1999) "Editorial Comments: NATO's Kosovo Intervention." *American Journal of International Law* 93(4) (October): 824–862.

Henwood, D. (1993) "Impeccable Logic: Trade, Development, and Free Markets in the Clinton Era." *NACLA Report on the Americas* 26(5): 56–73.

Hermann, M. G., and C. Kegley Jr. (1995) "Rethinking Democracy and International Peace: Perspectives from Political Psychology." *International Studies Quarterly* 39(4) (December): 511–535.

Hermann, R., and M. Fischerkeller (1995) "Beyond the Enemy Image and Spiral Model: Cognitive-Strategic Research After the Cold War." *International Organization* 49(3) (Summer): 415–450.

Herz, J. H. (1950) "Idealist Internationalism and the Security Dilemma." *World Politics* 5(2) (January): 157–180.

——— (1976) *The Nation-State and the Crisis of World Politics*. New York: David McKay.

Higham, M. T., M. N. Mercurio, and S. W. Ghezzi (eds.) (1996) *The ACCESS Issue Packet on Bosnia-Herzegovina*. Washington, D.C.: ACCESS.

Hinde, R. A. (1993) "Aggression and War: Individuals, Groups, and States." In P. E. Tetlock et al. (eds.), *Behavior, Society, and International Conflict*. New York: Oxford University Press.

Hinsley, F. H. (1966) *Sovereignty*. New York: Basic Books.

Hirschmann, N. (1992) *Rethinking Obligation: A Feminist Method for Political Theory*. Ithaca: Cornell University Press.

Hodge, C. C. (2001) "Woodrow Wilson in Our Time: NATO's Goals in Kosovo." *Parameters* 31(1): 125–135.

Hodson, R., D. Sekulic, and G. Massey (1994) "National Tolerance in the Former Yugoslavia." *American Journal of Sociology* 99(6): 1534–1558.

Hoffman, M. (1987) "Critical Theory and the Inter-Paradigm Debate." *Millennium: Journal of International Studies* 16(2): 231–249.

——— (1991) "Restructuring, Reconstruction, Reinscription, Rearticulation: Four Voices in Critical International Relations Theory." *Millennium: Journal of International Studies* 20(2): 169–185.

Hoffmann, M., and A. Ba (2005) *Contending Perspectives on Global Governance: Coherence, Contestation, and World Order*. London: Routledge.

Holbrooke, R. (1995) "America: A European Power." *Foreign Affairs* 74(2) (March–April): 38–51.

Hollinger, R. (1994) *Post-Modernism and the Social Sciences*. Thousand Oaks, Calif.: Sage.

Hollis, M., and S. Smith (1990) *Explaining and Understanding International Relations*. Oxford: Clarendon Press.

——— (1994) "Two Stories About Structure and Agency." *Review of International Studies* 20 (July): 241–251.

Hollist, W. L., and J. N. Rosenau (1981) *World System Structure: Continuity and Change*. Beverly Hills: Sage.

Holsti, K. (1985) *The Divided Discipline: Harmony and Diversity in International Theory*. Boston: Allen and Unwin.

——— (1989) "Mirror, Mirror on the Wall, Which Are the Fairest Theories of All?" *International Studies Quarterly* 33(3): 255–261.

——— (1997) "America Meets the 'English School': State Interests in International Society." *International Studies Quarterly* 41(2) (November): 275–280.

Holub, R. (1992) *Antonio Gramsci: Beyond Marxism and Postmodernism*. London: Routledge.

Holzner, M. (2003) "Kosovo: A Protectorate's Economy." Vienna Institute for International Economic Studies, WIIW Monthly Report no. 1. Available online at http://www.wiiw.ac.at/balkan/files/kosovo%20wiiw%20monthly%20 report%202003-1.pdf.

Honig, J. W., and N. Both (1996) *Srebrenica: Record of a Warcrime*. London: Penguin.

Hooghe, L., and G. Marks (1997) "Contending Models of Governance in the

European Union." In A. Cafruny and C. Lankowski (eds.), *Europe's Ambiguous Unity: Conflict and Consensus in the Post-Maastricht Era.* Boulder: Lynne Rienner.

―― (1999) "Birth of a Polity: The Struggle over European Integration." In H. Kitshelt, P. Lange, G. Marks, and J. Stephens (eds.), *Continuity and Change in Contemporary Capitalism.* Cambridge: Cambridge University Press.

Hopf, T. (1998) "The Promise of Constructivism in International Relations Theory." *International Security* 23 (Summer): 171–200.

―― (2002) *Social Construction of International Politics: Identities & Foreign Policies, Moscow, 1955 and 1999.* Ithaca: Cornell University Press.

Hopkins, T. K., and I. Wallerstein (eds.) (1980) *Processes of the World System.* Beverly Hills: Sage.

―― (1996) *The Age of Transition: Trajectory of the World-System, 1945–2025.* London: Zed Books.

Hopkins, T. K., et al. (1982) *World-System Analysis: Theory and Methodology.* Beverly Hills: Sage.

Hopple, G. W., and L. Falkowski (1982) *Biopolitics, Political Psychology, and International Politics.* New York: St. Martin's.

Hosmer, S. (2000) *The Conflict over Kosovo: Why Milosevic Decided to Settle When He Did.* MR-1351-AF. Santa Monica: Rand.

Howard, M. (1983) *The Causes of War and Other Essays.* Cambridge: Harvard University Press.

―― (1991) *The Lessons of History.* New Haven: Yale University Press.

Howard, N. (1971) *Paradoxes of Rationality: Theory of Metagames and Political Behavior.* Cambridge: MIT Press.

Hug, S. (2003) "Endogenous Preferences and Delegation in the European Union." *Comparative Political Studies* 36(1–2) (February–March): 41–74.

Hunter, R. (2000) "An Expanded Alliance vis-à-vis the European Union." Paper presented at the conference "NATO & Europe in the 21st Century: New Roles for a Changing Partnership," Woodrow Wilson International Center for Scholars, Washington, D.C., April 19. Available online at http://wwics.si.edu/ees.

Hurrell, A. (1993) "International Society and the Study of Regimes: A Reflective Approach." In V. Rittberger (ed.), *Regime Theory and International Relations.* Oxford: Clarendon Press.

Hurwitz, R. (1989) "Strategic and Social Fictions in the Prisoner's Dilemma." In J. Der Derian and M. J. Shapiro (eds.), *International/Intertextual Relations: Postmodern Readings of World Politics.* New York: Lexington Books.

Hyde-Price, A. (2000) *Germany and European Order: Enlarging NATO and the European Union.* Manchester: Manchester University Press.

Ibrahim, Y. M. (1998) "UN Measure Skirts Outright Threat of Force Against Milosevic." *New York Times,* October 25.

Ignatieff, M. (2003) "America's Empire Is Empire Lite." *New York Times Magazine,* January 10. Available online at http://www.nytimes.com/2003/01/05/magazine/05empire.html.

Ikenberry, G. J. (2000) "The Costs of Victory: American Power and the Use of Force in the Contemporary Order." In A. Schnabel and R. Thakur (eds.), *Kosovo and the Challenge of Humanitarian Intervention: Selective Indignation, Collective Action, International Citizenship.* New York: United Nations University Press.

"Images and Narratives in World Politics" (2001) *Millennium: Journal of International Studies* 30(3). Special issue.

IMF (International Monetary Fund) (2002a) "Yugoslavia, Federal Republic of: Financial Position in the Fund, as of December 31, 2002." Available online at http://www.imf.org/external/np/tre/tad/exfin2.cfm? memberkey1=1072.

—— (2002b) "Yugoslavia, Federal Republic of: Transactions with the Fund from January 01, 1984 to December 31, 2002." Available online at http://www.imf.org/external/np/tre/tad/extrans1.cfm?memberkey1=1072&end-date=2002%2d12%2d31&finposition_flag=yes.

—— (2003a) "Serbia and Montenegro: Financial Position in the Fund, as of June 30, 2003." Available online at http://www.imf.org/external/np/tre/tad/exfin2.cfm?memberkey1=1072&date1key=2003-06-30.

—— (2003b) "Serbia and Montenegro: Transactions with the Fund from January 01, 1984 to June 30, 2003." Available online at http://www.imf.org/external/np/tre/tad/extrans1.cfm?memberkey1=1072&enddate=2003%2d06%2d30&fin position_flag=yes.

Inayatullah, N., and D. L. Blaney (2003) *International Relations and the Problem of Difference*. London: Routledge.

Independent International Commission on Kosovo (2000) *The Kosovo Report: Conflict, International Response, Lessons Learned*. New York: Oxford University Press.

International Crisis Group (2002) *UNMIK's Kosovo Albatross: Tackling Division in Mitrovica*. Balkans Report no. 131. Available online at http://www.crisisweb.org/projects/showreport.cfm?reportid=672.

International Institute for Strategic Studies (1998) *The Military Balance, 1998/99*. Oxford: Oxford University Press.

"Interview with Hubert Védrine" (1999) *LeMonde*, June 11.

"Interview with the German Foreign Minister Joscha Fischer" (1998) *Die Zeit*, November 12. Available online at http://www.zeit.de/archiv/index.

Isaac, J. C. (2002) "Hannah Arendt and the Limits of Exposure, or Why Noam Chomsky Is Wrong About the Meaning of Kosovo." *Social Research* 69: 505–537.

Isaacson, W. F. (1999) "Madeleine's War." *Time Magazine*, May 17. [Also in *Time Canada*, May 17.]

Jackson Preece, J. (1998) *National Minorities and the European Nation-State System*. Oxford: Clarendon Press.

Jackson, P. T. (2003) "Defending the West: Occidentalism and the Formation of NATO." *Journal of Political Philosophy* 11(3): 223–252.

Jackson, P. T., and D. H. Nexon (1999) "Relations Before States: Substance, Process, and the Study of World Politics." *European Journal of International Relations* 5(3): 291–332.

—— (2002) "Globalization, the Comparative Method, and Comparing Constructions." In D. M. Green (ed.), *Constructivism and Comparative Politics*. Armonk, N.Y.: M. E. Sharpe.

Jackson, R. (1990) *Quasi-States, Sovereignty, International Relations, and the Third World*. Cambridge: Cambridge University Press.

—— (1995) "The Political Theory of International Society." In K. Booth and S. Smith (eds.), *International Relations Theory Today*. Cambridge, England: Polity.

—— (1996) "Is There a Classical International Theory?" In S. Smith, K. Booth, and M. Zalewski (eds.), *International Theory: Positivism and Beyond*. Cambridge: Cambridge University Press.

—— (ed.) (1999a) *Sovereignty at the Millennium: Getting Beyond Westphalia*. Oxford: Blackwell.

—— (1999b) "Sovereignty in World Politics: A Glance at the Conceptual and Historical Landscape." *Political Studies* 47: 431–456.

—— (2000) *The Global Covenant: Human Conduct in a World of States.* Oxford: Oxford University Press.

Jackson, R., and G. Sørensen (1999) *An Introduction to International Relations.* Oxford: Oxford University Press.

Jackson, R. H., and M. W. Zacher (1996) "The Territorial Covenant: International Society and the Legitimization of Boundaries." Paper presented at the annual meeting of the American Political Science Association, San Francisco.

Jacobs, S., R. Jacobson, and J. Marchbank (2000) "Introduction: States of Conflict." In S. Jacobs, R. Jacobson, and J. Marchbank (eds.), *States of Conflict: Gender, Conflict and Resistance.* New York: Zed Books.

James, A. (ed.) (1973) *The Bases of International Order: Essays in the Honor of C. A. W. Manning.* London: Oxford University Press.

—— (1986) *Sovereign Statehood: The Basis of International Society.* London: Allen and Unwin.

—— (1999) "The Practice of Sovereign Statehood in Contemporary International Society." *Political Studies* 47: 423–430.

Janis, I. L. (1972) *Victims of Groupthink.* Boston: Houghton Mifflin.

Jayaraman, R., and R. Kanbur (1999) "International Public Goods and the Case for Foreign Aid." In I. Kaul, I. Grunberg, and M. A. Stern (eds.), *Global Public Goods: International Cooperation in the 21st Century.* New York: Oxford University Press.

Jelavich, B. (1983) *History of the Balkans.* Cambridge: Cambridge University Press.

Jelavich, C., and B. Jelavich (1977) *The Establishment of the Balkan National States, 1804–1920.* Seattle: University of Washington Press.

Jentleson, Bruce W. (1997) "Who, What, Why, and How: Debates over Post Cold War Military Intervention." In R. J. Lieber (ed.), *Eagle Adrift: American Foreign Policy at the End of the Century.* New York: Longman.

Jervis, R. (1976) *Perception and Misperception in International Politics.* Princeton: Princeton University Press.

—— (1978) "Cooperation Under the Security Dilemma." *World Politics* 30: 167–214.

—— (1983) "Security Regimes." In S. D. Krasner (ed.), *International Regimes.* Ithaca: Cornell University Press.

—— (1989) *The Meaning of the Nuclear Revolution.* Ithaca: Cornell University Press.

—— (1991) "Domino Beliefs and Strategic Behavior." In R. Jervis and J. Snyder (eds.), *Dominoes and Bandwagons: Strategic Beliefs and Great Power Competition in the Eurasian Rimland.* New York: Oxford University Press.

—— (1991–1992) "The Future of World Politics: Will It Resemble the Past?" *International Security* 16: 39–73.

—— (1994) "Political Implications of Loss Aversion." In B. Farnham (ed.), *Avoiding Losses/Taking Risks: Prospect Theory and International Conflict.* Ann Arbor: University of Michigan Press.

—— (1996) *System Effects: Complexity in Political and Social Life.* Princeton: Princeton University Press.

—— (1998) "Realism in the Study of World Politics." *International Organization* 52(4) (Autumn): 971–991.

—— (1999) "Realism, Neoliberalism, and Cooperation: Understanding the Debate." *International Security* 24 (Summer): 42–63.

Jervis, R., R. N. Lebow, and J. G. Stein (eds.) (1985) *Psychology and Deterrence.* Baltimore: Johns Hopkins University Press.

Johnston, A. I. (1995) *Cultural Realism: Strategic Culture and Grand Strategy in Chinese History.* Princeton: Princeton University Press.

Jones, D. M., S. A. Bremer, and J. D. Singer (1996) "Militarized Interstate Disputes, 1816–1992: Rationale, Coding Rules, and Empirical Patterns." *Conflict Management and Peace Science* 15: 163–213.

Jørgensen, K., and T. Knudsen (2006) *European Approaches to International Relations.* London: Routledge.

Judah, T. (1997) *The Serbs: History, Myth, and the Destruction of Yugoslavia.* London: Yale University Press.

———— (2000) *Kosovo: War and Revenge.* New Haven: Yale University Press.

Kahler, M. (1997) "Inventing International Relations: International Relations Theory After 1945." In M. W. Doyle and G. J. Ikenberry (eds.), *New Thinking in International Relations Theory.* Boulder: Westview.

———— (1998) "Rationality in International Relations." *International Organization* 54(4) (Autumn): 919–941.

Kahneman, D., and A. Tversky (2000a) "Advances in Prospect Theory: Cumulative Representation of Uncertainty." In D. Kahneman and A. Tversky (eds.), *Choice, Values, and Frames.* New York: Cambridge University Press.

———— (2000b) "Prospect Theory: An Analysis of Decision Under Risk." In D. Kahneman and A. Tversky (eds.), *Choice, Values, and Frames.* New York: Cambridge University Press.

Karayianni, M. S. (2001) "Caspian Oil Seeks Safe Transit Route." *Alexander's Gas and Oil Connections* 6(24) (October 20). Available online at http://www.gasandoil.com.

Kardam, N. (1991) *Bringing Women In: Women's Issues in International Development Programs.* Boulder: Lynne Rienner.

Kardelj, E. (1960) *Razvoj Slovenackog Nacionalnog Pitanja* [Development of the Slovenian National Question]. Belgrade: Kultura.

Karl, M. (1995) *Women and Empowerment: Participation and Decision Making.* London: Zed Books.

Katzenstein, P. J. (ed.) (1996) *The Culture of National Security: Norms and Identity in World Politics.* New York: Columbia University Press.

Katzenstein, P. J., R. O. Keohane, and S. D. Krasner (1998) "*International Organization* and the Study of World Politics." *International Organization* 52(4) (Autumn): 645–685.

Kaufmann, C. (1996) "Possible and Impossible Solutions to Ethnic Civil Wars." *International Security* 20(4): 136–175.

Kaul, I., P. Conceição, K. le Goulven, and R. U. Mendoza (eds.) (2003) *Providing Global Public Goods: Managing Globalization.* New York: Oxford University Press.

Kaul, I., I. Grunberg, and M. A. Stern (eds.) (1999) *Global Public Goods.* New York: Oxford University Press.

Kay, S. I. (1998) *NATO and the Future of European Security.* Lanham: Rowman and Littlefield.

———— (1999) "From Operation Alba to Allied Force: Institutional Implications of Balkan Interventions." *Mediterranean Quarterly* 10(4) (Fall): 72–89.

———— (2000) "After Kosovo: NATO's Credibility Gap." *Security Dialogue* 31 (March): 71–84.

Keal, P. (ed.) (1992) *Ethics and Foreign Policy.* St. Leonards, NSW, Australia: Allen.

Keck, M., and K. Sikkink (1998) *Activists Beyond Borders: Advocacy Networks in International Politics*. Ithaca: Cornell University Press.

Keeley, L. H. (1996) *War Before Civilization: The Myth of the Peaceful Savage*. New York: Oxford University Press.

Kellner, D. (1989) *Critical Theory, Marxism, and Modernity*. Baltimore: Johns Hopkins University Press.

Kelly, L. (2000) "War Against Women: Sexual Violence, Sexual Politics, and the Militarized State." In S. Jacobs, R. Jacobson, and J. Marchbank (eds.), *States of Conflict: Gender, Conflict, and Resistance*. New York: Zed Books.

Kennedy, P. (1987) *The Rise and Fall of the Great Powers: Economic Change and Military Conflict from 1500 to 2000*. New York: Random House.

Keohane, R. O. (1984) *After Hegemony: Cooperation and Discord in the World Political Economy*. Princeton: Princeton University Press.

—— (1988) "International Institutions: Two Approaches." *International Studies Quarterly* 32 (December): 379–396.

—— (1989) *International Institutions and State Power: Essays in International Relations Theory*. Boulder: Westview.

—— (1990) "International Liberalism Reconsidered." In J. Dunn (ed.), *The Economic Limits to Modern Politics*. Cambridge: Cambridge University Press.

—— (1998) "International Institutions: Can Interdependence Work?" *Foreign Policy* (Spring): 82–96.

—— (2002). *Power and Governance in a Partially Globalized World*. New York: Routledge.

Keohane, R. O., and L. Martin (1995) "The Promise of Institutional Theory." *International Security* 20 (Summer): 39–51.

Keohane, R. O., and J. S. Nye (eds.) (1971) *Transnational Relations and World Politics*. Cambridge: Harvard University Press.

—— (1975) "International Interdependence and Integration." In F. I. Greenstein and N. W. Polsby (eds.), *Handbook of Political Science*, vol. 8. Reading, Mass.: Addison-Wesley.

—— (1977) *Power and Interdependence: World Politics in Transition*. Glenview, Ill.: Scott, Foresman.

—— (1998) "Power and Interdependence in the Information Age." *Foreign Affairs* 77 (September–October): 81–94.

Keohane, R. O., J. S. Nye, and S. Hoffmann (eds.) (1993) *After the Cold War: International Institutions and State Strategies in Europe, 1989–1991*. Cambridge: Harvard University Press.

KFOR (Kosovo Force) (2002) "Statement to the Press: KFOR Restructuring." KFOR Press Release no. 15-05, May 13. Available online at http://www.nato.int/kfor/press/pr/pr/2002/05/15-05.htm.

Khanna, J., T. Sandler, and H. Shimizu (1998) "Sharing the Financial Burden for U.N. and NATO Peacekeeping, 1976–1996." *Journal of Conflict Resolution* 42(2): 176–195.

—— (1999) "The Demand for UN Peacekeeping, 1975–1996." *Kyklos* 52(fasc. 3): 345–368.

Kingsbury, B., and A. Roberts (1990) "Introduction: Grotian Thought in International Relations." In H. Bull, B. Kingsbury, and A. Roberts (eds.), *Hugo Grotius and International Relations*. Oxford: Clarendon Press.

Kinsella, H. (2003) "For a Careful Reading: The Conservatism of Gender Constructivism." *International Studies Quarterly* 5(2) (June): 294–297.

Kissinger, H. A. (1964) *A World Restored*. New York: Grosset and Dunlap.

Klein, B. (1994) *Strategic Studies and World Order.* Cambridge: Cambridge University Press.

Kleinknecht, A., E. Mandel, and I. Wallerstein (1992) *New Findings in Long-Wave Research.* New York: St. Martin's.

Klotz, A. (1995) *Norms in International Relations: The Struggle Against Apartheid.* Ithaca: Cornell University Press.

Knop, K. (1993) "Re/Statements: Feminism and State Sovereignty in International Law." *Transnational Law and Contemporary Problems* 3(2) (Fall): 293–344.

Knorr, K., and J. N. Rosenau (eds.) (1969) *Contending Approaches to International Politics.* Princeton: Princeton University Press.

Knudsen, T. B. (1996) "Humanitarian Intervention Revisited: Post–Cold War Responses to Classical Problems." *International Peacekeeping* 3(4) (Winter): 146–165.

—— (2002) "The English School of International Relations and the International Society Approach." In K. Imbusch and K. Segbers (eds.), *International Relations Online.* Berlin: Free University of Berlin. Available at http://www.ir-online.org.

—— (2004) "Denmark and the War Against Iraq: Losing Sight of Internationalism?" In P. Carlsen and H. Mouritzen (eds.), *Danish Foreign Policy Yearbook 2004.* Copenhagen: Danish Institute for International Studies.

—— (2005) *Humanitarian Intervention: Contemporary Manifestations of an Explosive Doctrine.* New International Relations Series. London: Routledge.

Kondratieff, N. (1984) *The Long Wage Cycle.* Trans. G. Daniels. New York: Richardson and Snyder.

Koremenos, B., C. Lipson, and D. Snidal (eds.) (2001) "The Rational Design of International Institutions." *International Organization* 55(4) (Autumn). Special issue.

"Kosovo Mediators Aim to Persuade Ethnic Albanians First" (1999) *Washington Post,* February 22.

Kostakos, G. (2000) "The Southern Flank: Italy, Greece, Turkey." In A. Schnabel and R. Thakur (eds.), *Kosovo and the Challenge of Humanitarian Intervention: Selective Indignation, Collective Action, and International Citizenship.* New York: United Nations University Press.

Kostovicova, D. (1997) *Parallel Worlds: Response of Kosovo Albanians to the Loss of Autonomy in Serbia, 1989–1996.* Keele, England: Keele European Research Centre.

Kowert, P. (1998) "Agent Versus Structure in the Construction of National Identity." In V. Kubalkova, N. Onuf, and P. Kowert (eds.), *International Relations in a Constructed World.* Armonk, N.Y.: M. E. Sharpe.

Krasner, S. D. (ed.) (1983) *International Regimes.* Ithaca: Cornell University Press.

—— (1999) *Sovereignty: Organized Hypocrisy.* Princeton: Princeton University Press.

Kratochwil, F. (1989) *Rules, Norms, and Decisions.* Cambridge: Cambridge University Press.

Kratochwil, F., and J. G. Ruggie (1986) "International Organization: A State of the Art on an Art of State." *International Organization* 40 (Autumn): 753–776.

Kubalkova, V., N. Onuf, and P. Kowert (eds.) (1998) *International Relations in a Constructed World.* Armonk, N.Y.: M. E. Sharpe.

Kugler, J., and D. Lemke (2000) "The Power Transition Research Program: Assessing Theoretical and Empirical Progress." In M. I. Midlarsky (ed.), *Handbook of War Studies,* vol. 2. Ann Arbor: University of Michigan Press.

Kugler, J., and F. C. Zagare (eds.) (1987) *Exploring the Stability of Deterrence.* Denver: University of Denver, School of International Studies.

Kumar, K. (ed.) (2001) W*omen and Civil War: Impact, Organizations, and Actions.* Boulder: Lynne Rienner.

Kupchan, C. A. (1994) "The Case for Collective Security." In G. W. Downs (ed.), *Collective Security After the Cold War.* Ann Arbor: University of Michigan Press.

Kurth, J. (2001) "First War of the Global Era: Kosovo and US Grand Strategy." In A. J. Bacevich and E. A. Cohen (eds.), *War over Kosovo: Politics and Strategy in a Global Age.* New York: Columbia University Press.

Kushner, T., and K. Knox (1999) *Refugees in an Age of Genocide: Global, National, and Local Perspectives During the Twentieth Century.* London: Frank Cass.

Kvinna Till Kvinna. (2001) "Getting It Right? A Gender Approach to UNMIK Administration in Kosovo." Available online at http://www.iktk.se/english/index.html.

Kydd, A. (1997) "Game Theory and the Spiral Model." *World Politics* 49(3) (April): 371–400.

——— (2000) "Trust, Reassurance, and Cooperation." *International Organization* 54(2) (Spring): 325–357.

Lacher, H. (2002) "Making Sense of the International System: The Promises and Pitfalls of Contemporary Marxist Theories of International Relations." In M. Rupert and H. Smith (eds.), *Historical Materialism and Globalization.* London: Routledge.

Lafontaine, O. (2000) "May Day Speech at Saarbrucken." In T. Ali (ed.), *Masters of the Universe: NATO's Balkan Crusade.* London: Verso.

Lake, A. (1993) "From Containment to Enlargement: Remarks of Anthony Lake." Johns Hopkins University, School of International Studies, September 21. Available online at http://www.fas.org/usa/1993.

Lalman, D., J. Oppenheimer, and P. Swistak (1993) "Formal Rational Choice Theory: A Cumulative Science of Politics." In A. Finifter (ed.), *Political Science: The State of the Discipline.* Washington, D.C.: American Political Science Association.

Lambeth, B. S. (2001) *NATO's Air War for Kosovo: A Strategic and Operational Assessment.* Santa Monica: Rand.

Lampe, J. R. (1996) *Yugoslavia as History: Twice There Was a Country.* Cambridge: Cambridge University Press.

LaPalombara, J. (2001) "Italy's Hobbled Search for a Better Place in the Sun." *International Spectator* 36(1): 93–98.

Lapid, Y. (1989) "The Third Debate: On the Prospects of International Theory in a Post-Positivist Era." *International Studies Quarterly* 33(3) (September): 235–254.

——— (2003) "Through Dialogue to Engaged Pluralism: The Unfinished Business of the Third Debate." *International Studies Review* 5(1) (March): 128–131.

Lapid, Y., and F. Kratochwil (eds.) (1996) *The Return of Culture and Identity in IR Theory.* Boulder: Lynne Rienner.

Larrabee, F. S. (1990–1991) "Long Memories and Short Fuses: Change and Instability in the Balkans." *International Security* 15(3) (Winter): 58–91.

Larson, D. W. (1985) *Origins of Containment: A Psychological Explanation.* Princeton: Princeton University Press.

Layne, C. (1993) "The Unipolar Illusion: Why Great Powers Will Rise." *International Security* 17(4): 5–51.

—— (2000a) "Miscalculations and Blunders Lead to War." In T. G. Carpenter (ed.), *NATO's Empty Victory: A Postmortem on the Balkan War.* Washington, D.C.: Cato Institute.

—— (2000b) "US Hegemony and the Perpetuation of NATO." *Journal of Strategic Studies* 23(3): 59–91.

Layne, C., and B. Schwarz (1999) "For the Record." *National Interest* 57(9) (Fall). Available online at http://www.lexisnexis.com.

Lebor, A. (2002) *Milosevic*. London: Bloomsbury.

Lebow, R. N. (1981) *Between Peace and War: The Nature of International Crisis.* Baltimore: Johns Hopkins University Press.

Lee, M. (1983) "Kosovo Between Yugoslavia and Albania." *New Left Review* 140: 62–91.

Leffler, M. P. (1993) *A Preponderance of Power: National Security, the Truman Administration, and the Cold War.* Stanford: Stanford University Press.

Lendvai, P. (1969) *Eagles in the Cobwebs: Nationalism and Communism in the Balkans.* New York: Doubleday.

Lenski, G., and J. Lenski (1970) *Human Societies: An Introduction to Macrosociology.* New York: McGraw-Hill.

Leonard, S. T. (1990) *Critical Theory in Political Practice.* Princeton: Princeton University Press.

Lepgold, Joseph (1998) "NATO's Post–Cold War Collective Action Problem." *International Security* 23(1): 78–106.

Levy, J. F. (1983) "Misperception and the Causes of War." *World Politics* 36(1) (October): 76–99.

—— (1994a) "An Introduction to Prospect Theory." In B. Farnham (ed.), *Avoiding Losses/Taking Risks: Prospect Theory in International Conflict.* Ann Arbor: University of Michigan Press.

—— (1994b) "Prospect Theory and International Relations: Theoretical Applications and Analytical Problems." In B. Farnham (ed.), *Avoiding Losses/Taking Risks: Prospect Theory in International Conflict.* Ann Arbor: University of Michigan Press.

—— (1997) "Prospect Theory, Rational Choice, and International Relations." *International Studies Quarterly* 41(1): 87–112.

—— (1998) "The Causes of War and the Conditions of Peace." *Annual Review of Political Science* 1: 139–166.

—— (2000) "Loss Aversion, Framing Effects, and International Conflict: Perspectives from Prospect Theory." In M. I. Midlarsky (ed.), *Handbook of War Studies,* vol. 2. Ann Arbor: University of Michigan Press.

Libal, M. (1997) *Limits of Persuasion: Germany and the Yugoslav Crisis, 1991–1992.* New York: Praeger.

Lieven, A. (2001) "Hubris and Nemesis: Kosovo and the Pattern of Western Military Ascendancy and Defeat." In A. L. Bacevich and E. A. Cohen (eds.), *War over Kosovo: Politics and Strategy in a Global Age.* New York: Columbia University Press.

Lindblom, C. A. (1977) *Politics and Markets.* New York: Basic Books.

Linklater, A. (1990) *Beyond Realism and Marxism: Critical Theory and International Relations.* New York: St. Martin's.

—— (1992) "The Question of the Next Stage in International Relations Theory: A Critical-Theoretical Point of View." *Millennium: Journal of International Studies* 21(1): 77–98.

——— (1996) "The Achievements of Critical Theory." In S. Smith, K. Booth, and M. Zalewski (eds.), *International Theory: Positivism and Beyond.* New York: Cambridge University Press.

——— (1998) *The Transformation of Political Community: Ethical Foundations of the Post-Westphalian Era.* Cambridge, England: Polity.

Little, R. (1995) "Neorealism and the English School: A Methodological, Ontological, and Theoretical Reassessment." *European Journal of International Relations* 1(1): 9–34.

——— (1996) "The Growing Relevance of Pluralism?" In S. Smith, K. Booth, and M. Zalewski (eds.), *International Theory: Positivism and Beyond.* Cambridge: Cambridge University Press.

Locher, B., and E. Prügl (2001) "Feminism and Constructivism: Worlds Apart or Sharing the Middle Ground?" *International Studies Quarterly* 45(1) (March): 111–130.

Locke, J. (1980) *Second Treatise of Government.* Indianapolis: Hackett.

——— (1988) *Two Treatises of Government.* Ed. P. Laslett. Cambridge: Cambridge University Press.

Lorber, J. (1998) *Gender Inequality: Feminist Theories and Politics.* Los Angeles: Roxbury.

Lorenz, K. (1967) *On Aggression.* Trans. M. K. Wilson. New York: Bantam.

Low, B. S. (1993) "An Evolutionary Perspective on War." In W. Zimmerman and H. K. Jacobson (eds.), *Behavior, Culture, and Conflict in World Politics.* Ann Arbor: University of Michigan Press.

——— (2000) *Why Sex Matters: A Darwinian Look at Human Behavior.* Princeton: Princeton University Press.

Luban, D. (2002) "Intervention and Civilization: Some Unhappy Lessons of the Kosovo War." In P. De Greiff and C. Cronin (eds.), *Global Justice and Transnational Politics: Essays on the Moral and Political Challenges of Globalization.* Cambridge: MIT Press.

Luke, T. (1993) "Discourses of Disintegration, Texts of Transformation: Re-Reading Realism in the New World Order." *Alternatives* 18: 229–258.

——— (1998) "The (Un)Wise (Ab)Use of Nature: Environmentalism as Globalized Consumerism." *Alternatives* 23(2): 175–212.

Lydall, H. (1989) *Yugoslavia in Crisis.* Oxford: Clarendon Press.

Lynch, M. (1999) *State Interests and Public Spheres: The International Politics of Jordan's Identity.* New York: Columbia University Press.

——— (2000) "The Dialogue of Civilizations and International Public Spheres." *Millennium* 29: 307–330.

Lyon, P. (1993) "The Rise and Fall and Possible Revival of International Trusteeship." *Journal of Commonwealth and Comparative Studies* 31(1): 96–110.

MacDonald, S., P. Holden, and S. Ardener (eds.) (1988) *Images of Women in Peace and War: Cross-Cultural and Historical Perspectives.* Madison, Wis.: University of Wisconsin Press.

Magaš, B. (1993) *The Destruction of Yugoslavia: Tracking the Breakup, 1980–1992.* London: Verso.

Magdoff, H. (1969) *The Age of Imperialism.* New York: Monthly Review Press.

Makinda, S. (1997) "International Law and Security: Exploring a Symbiotic Relationship." *Australian Journal of International Law* 51(3): 325–338.

Malcolm, N. (1998) *Kosovo: A Short History.* London: Macmillan.

Mandelbaum, M. (1999) "A Perfect Failure: NATO's War Against Yugoslavia." *Foreign Affairs* 78(5): 2–8.

Manning, C. A. W. (1962) *The Nature of International Society.* London: London School of Economics.

Manson, J. H., and R. W. Wrangham (1991) "Intergroup Aggression in Chimpanzees and Humans." *Current Anthropology* 32: 369–377.

Maoz, Z., and B. Russett (1993) "Normative and Structural Causes of Democratic Peace, 1946–86." *American Political Science Review* 87: 624–638.

Markey, D. (1999) "Prestige and the Origins of War: Returning to Realism's Roots." *Security Studies* 8(4): 126–173.

Marr, A. (1999) "War Is Hell: But Not Being Ready to Go to War Is Undignified and Embarrassing." *The Guardian* (Manchester), April 25.

Marsh, J. L. (2002) *Unjust Legality: A Critique of Habermas's Philosophy of Law.* New York: Rowman and Littlefield.

Martin, L. L. (1992) *Coercive Cooperation: Explaining Multilateral Economic Sanctions.* Princeton: Princeton University Press.

Martin, L. L., and B. Simmons (1998) "Theories and Empirical Studies of International Institutions." *International Organization* 52(4): 729–758.

Mastanduno, M. (1997) "Preserving the Unipolar Moment: Realist Theories and US Grand Strategy After the Cold War." *International Security* 21 (Spring): 49–88.

Masters, R. (1983) "The Biological Nature of the State." *World Politics* 35 (January): 161–193.

Mattern, J. B. (2001) "The Power Politics of Identity." *European Journal of International Relations* 7(3): 349–397.

Matustik, M. B. (2002) *Jurgen Habermas: A Philosophical-Political Profile.* New York: Rowman and Littlefield.

Maull, Hanns W. (1999) "Germany and the Use of Force: Still a Civilian Power?" Presentation originally prepared for the workshop "Force, Order, and Global Governance," Brookings Institution, Washington, D.C., July 1–2.

Mayall, J. (ed.) (1982) *The Community of States: A Study in International Political Theory.* London: George Allen and Unwin.

―――― (1990) *Nationalism and International Society.* Cambridge: Cambridge University Press.

―――― (ed.) (1996) *The New Interventionism, 1991–1994: United Nations Experience in Cambodia, Former Yugoslavia, and Somalia.* Cambridge: Cambridge University Press.

―――― (2000) "The Concept of Humanitarian Intervention Revisited." In A. Schnabel and R. Thakur (eds.), *Kosovo and the Challenge of Humanitarian Intervention.* New York: United Nations University Press.

McCalla, R. (1996) "NATO's Persistence After the Cold War." *International Organization* 50(3): 445–475.

McEachron, D. L., and D. Baer (1982) "A Review of Selected Sociobiological Principles—Application to Hominid Evolution II: The Effects of Intergroup Conflict." *Journal of Social and Biological Structures* 5: 121–139.

McGrath, B. (2003) "Blackballed by Bush." *New Yorker,* July 28.

McManus, D. (1999) "Debate Turns to Finger Pointing on Kosovo." *Los Angeles Times,* April 11.

Mead, G. H. (1934) *Mind, Self, and Society.* Chicago: University of Chicago Press.

Mearsheimer, J. J. (1990) "Back to the Future: Instability in Europe After the Cold War." *International Security* 15(1) (Summer): 5–56.

―――― (1994–1995) "The False Promise of International Institutions." *International Security* 19(3): 5–49.

―――― (2001) *The Tragedy of Great Power Politics.* New York: W. W. Norton.

Medvedev, S., and P. van Ham (eds.) (2002) "Preface: Kosovo and the Outlines of Europe's New Order." In P. van Ham and S. Medvedev (eds.), *Mapping European Security After Kosovo*. Manchester: Manchester University Press.

Meier, V. (1995) *Yugoslavia: A History of Its Demise*. New York: Routledge.

Melotti, U. (1990) "War and Peace in Primitive Human Societies." In J. M. G. van der Dennen and V. S. E. Falger (eds.), *Sociobiology and Conflict: Evolutionary Perspectives on Competition, Cooperation, Violence, and Warfare*. London: Chapman and Hall.

Mercer, J. (1995) "Anarchy and Identity." *International Organization* 49(2): 229–252.

—— (1996) *Reputation and International Politics*. Ithaca: Cornell University Press.

—— (1999) "Emotion Adds Life." Paper presented at the annual meeting of the International Studies Association, Washington, D.C., February 18–21.

Mertus, J. (1999a) *Kosovo: How Myths and Truths Started a War*. Berkeley: University of California Press.

—— (1999b) "Women in Kosovo: Contested Terrains." In S. P. Ramet (ed.), *Gender in the Western Balkans: Women and Society in Yugoslavia and the Yugoslav Successor States*. University Park: Pennsylvania State University Press.

—— (2000a) "Considering Nonstate Actors in the New Millennium: Toward Expanded Participation in Norm Generation and Norm Application." *New York University Review of International Law and Policy* 23: 537–560.

—— (2000b) *War's Offensive on Women: The Humanitarian Challenge in Bosnia, Kosovo, and Afghanistan*. Bloomfield, Conn.: Kumarian Press.

—— (2001) "Legitimizing the Use of Force in Kosovo." *Ethics and International Affairs* 15(1): 133–152.

—— (2004) "Shouting from the Bottom of the Well." *International Journal of Feminist Politics* 6(1): 110–128.

Meyer, P. (1981) *Evolution und Gewalt: Ansätze zu einer biosoziologischen Synthese*. Hamburg: Parey Verlag.

Mies, M. (1986) *Patriarchy and Accumulation on a World Scale: Women in the International Division of Labour*. London: Zed Press.

Miliband, R. (1969) *The State in Capitalist Society: An Analysis of the Western System of Power*. New York: Basic Books.

Miller, J. D. B., and R. J. Vincent (eds.) (1990) *Order and Violence: Hedley Bull and International Relations*. Oxford: Oxford University Press.

Milliken, J. (2002) *The Social Construction of the Korean War: Conflict and Its Possibilities*. Manchester: Manchester University Press.

Milner, H. (1991) "The Assumption of Anarchy in International Relations Theory: A Critique." *Review of International Studies* 17: 67–85.

Ministère de la Défense (France) (2000) *The UN, Europe, and Crisis Management*. Report of the Directorate for Strategic Affairs. Paris, October 20.

Ministère des Affaires Étrangères (France) (1999) *France's Role in the Kosovo Crisis*. Background paper. Paris, August 18.

Mitrany, D. (1943) *A Working Peace System: An Argument for the Functional Development of International Organization*. London: Royal Institute of International Affairs.

Mittelman, J. H. (ed.) (1997) *Globalization: Critical Reflections*. International Political Economy Yearbook, vol. 9. Boulder: Lynne Rienner.

Mladjenovic, L., and D. M. Hughes (1999) *Feminist Resistance to War and Violence in Serbia.* New York: Frontline Feminisms Garland Press.

Modelski, G. (1978) "The Long Cycle of Global Politics and the Nation-State." *Comparative Studies in Society and History* 20(2) (April): 214–235.

—— (ed.) (1987a) *Exploring Long Cycles.* Boulder: Lynne Rienner.

—— (ed.) (1987b) *Long Cycles in World Politics.* Seattle: University of Washington Press.

—— (1996) "Evolutionary Paradigm for Global Politics." *International Studies Quarterly* 40: 321–342.

Modelski, G., and W. R. Thompson (1988) *Seapower in Global Politics, 1493–1993.* Seattle: University of Washington Press.

—— (1996) *Leading Sectors and World Powers: The Coevolution of Global Politics and Economics.* Columbia: University of South Carolina Press.

—— (1999) "The Long and the Short of Global Politics in the Twenty-First Century: An Evolutionary Approach." *International Studies Review* 1(2): 109–140.

Moghadam, V. (1993) *Identity Politics: Cultural Reassertions and Feminisms in International Perspectives.* Boulder: Westview.

Mohanty, C. (1988) "Under Western Eyes: Feminist Scholarship and Colonial Discourses." *Feminist Review* 30 (Autumn): 61–88.

—— (1991) *Third World Women and the Politics of Feminism.* Bloomington: University of Indiana Press.

Monbiot, G. (2001) "A Discreet Deal in the Pipeline." *The Guardian,* February 15. Available online at http://www.guardian.co.uk/archive/article/0,4273,4136440,00.html.

Morgan, P. M. (1986) *Theories and Approaches to International Politics.* New Brunswick, N.J.: Transaction Books.

Morgenthau, H. J. (1946) *Scientific Man vs. Power Politics.* Chicago: University of Chicago Press.

—— (1965) *Politics Among Nations: The Struggle for Power and Peace,* 3rd ed. New York: Alfred A. Knopf.

Morgenthau, H. J., and K. W. Thompson (1985) *Politics Among Nations: The Struggle for Power and Peace,* 6th ed. New York: Alfred Knopf.

Morrow, J. D. (1994) *Game Theory for Political Scientists.* Princeton: Princeton University Press.

—— (1997) "A Rational Choice Approach to International Conflict." In N. Geva and A. Mintz (eds.), *Decisionmaking on War and Peace: The Cognitive-Rational Debate.* Boulder: Lynne Rienner.

Morse, E. S. (1976) *Modernization and the Transformation of International Relations.* New York: Free Press.

Mueller, J. (1989) *Retreat from Doomsday: The Obsolescence of Major War.* New York: Basic Books.

Murdoch, J. C., and T. Sandler (1982) "A Theoretical and Empirical Analysis of NATO." *Journal of Conflict Resolution* 26: 237–263.

Murphy, C. N. (1990) "Freezing the North-South Bloc(k) After the East-West Thaw." *Socialist Review* 20(3) (July–September): 25–46.

—— (1994) *International Organization and Industrial Change.* New York: Oxford University Press.

—— (1998) "Understanding IR: Understanding Gramsci." *Review of International Studies* 24: 417–425.

Murphy, C. N., and R. Tooze (eds.) (1991) *The New International Political Economy.* Boulder: Lynne Rienner.

Murphy, S. D. (ed.) (1999) "Contemporary Practice: Legal Regulation of the Use of Force." *American Journal of International Law* 93(3) (July): 630.

——— (2000) "Contemporary Practice of the United States Relating to International Law: *Ex Gratia* Payment for Bombing of Chinese Embassy in Belgrade." *American Journal of International Law* 94 (January): 127 131.

Murray, J. N., Jr. (1957) *The United Nations Trusteeship System*. Urbana: University of Illinois Press.

Myerson, R. (1991) *Game Theory: Analysis of Conflict*. Cambridge: Harvard University Press.

Nadelmann, E. (1990) "Global Prohibition Regimes: The Evolution of Norms in International Society." *International Organization* 44(4): 479–526.

Nairn, T. (1998) "Reflections on Nationalist Disasters." *New Left Review* 230(1) (July–August): 145–152.

Nakarada, R. (2000) "The Uncertain Reach of Critical Theory." In P. Wapner and L. E. J. Ruiz (eds.), *Principled World Politics*. New York: Rowman and Littlefield.

Nalebuff, B. (1986) "Brinkmanship and Nuclear Deterrence: The Neutrality of Escalation." *Conflict Management and Peace Science* 9: 19–30.

"NATO Forces Spur Prostitution Boom" (2000) Agence France-Presse, January 5. Available online at http://h-net.msu.edu/minerva.

"NATO Jets Fly to Warn Serbs, but Attacks on Albanians Go On" (1998) *Baltimore Sun,* June 16.

Naumann, K. (1999) Statement by Klaus Naumann to hearings before the Senate Committee on the Armed Services, "Lessons Learned from the Military Operations Conducted as Part of Operation Allied Force," 106th Cong., 1st sess., November 3.

Navari, C. (ed.) (1991) *The Condition of States*. Buckingham: Open University Press.

Neufeld, M. (1995) *The Restructuring of International Relations Theory*. Cambridge: Cambridge University Press.

Neumann, I. (1999) *Uses of the Other: "The East" in European Identity Formation*. Minneapolis: University of Minnesota Press.

Neumann, I. B., and O. Wæver (eds.) (1997) *The Future of International Relations: Masters in the Making?* London: Routledge.

The New Encyclopaedia Britannica (2002) Chicago: Encyclopaedia Britannica.

Nicholson, M. (1992) *Rationality and the Analysis of International Conflict*. Cambridge: Cambridge University Press.

——— (1996) "The Continued Significance of Positivism." In S. Smith, K. Booth, and M. Zalewski (eds.), *International Theory: Positivism and Beyond*. Cambridge: Cambridge University Press.

Nielson, D. L., and M. J. Tierney (2003) "Delegation to International Organizations: Agency Theory and World Bank Environmental Reform." *International Organization* 57 (Spring): 241–276.

Nietzsche, F. (1967) *On the Genealogy of Morals*. New York: Random House.

Nikolic-Ristanovic, V. (ed.) (2000) *Women, Violence, and War: Wartime Victimization of Refugees in the Balkans*. Budapest: Central European University Press.

North, R. C. (1969) "Research Pluralism and the International Elephant." In K. Knorr and J. N. Rosenau (eds.), *Contending Approaches to International Politics*. Princeton: Princeton University Press.

North Atlantic Treaty. Available online at http://www.nato.int/docu/basictxt/treaty.htm.

Nye, J. S., Jr. (1987) "Nuclear Learning and U.S.-Soviet Security Regimes." *International Organization* 41: 371–402.

O'Connor, J. (1973) *The Fiscal Crisis of the State*. London: Macmillan.

O'Connor, M. (1998) "Kosovo Rebels Gain Ground Under NATO Threat." *New York Times*, December 4.

Olson, E. (1999) "Report Finds Shared Guilt Inside Kosovo." *New York Times*, April 2.

Olson, M. (1965) *The Logic of Collective Action*. Cambridge: Harvard University Press.

Olson, M., and R. Zeckhauser (1966) "An Economic Theory of Alliances." *Review of Economics and Statistics* 48: 266–279.

Olson, W. C., and A. J. R. Groom (1991) *International Relations Then and Now: Origins and Trends in Interpretation*. London: HarperCollins.

O'Neill, W. G. (2002) *Kosovo: An Unfinished Peace*. Boulder: Lynne Rienner.

Onuf, N. G. (1989) *World of Our Making: Rules and Rule in Social Theory and International Relations*. Columbia: University of South Carolina Press.

—— (1998) "Constructivism: A User's Manual." In V. Kubálková, N. Onuf, and P. Kowert (eds.), *International Relations in a Constructed World*. Armonk, N.Y.: M. E. Sharpe.

Organization of African Unity (2000) *International Panel of Eminent Personalities to Investigate the 1994 Genocide in Rwanda and the Surrounding Events*. Lagos.

Organski, A. F. K. (1968) *World Politics*. 2nd ed. Ann Arbor: University of Michigan Press.

Ottaway, M. (2003) "Promoting Democracy After Conflict: The Difficult Choices." *International Studies Perspectives* 4: 314–322.

Otterbein, K. F. (1999) "Clan and Tribal Conflict." In L. R. Kurtz (ed.), *Encyclopedia of Violence, Peace, and Conflict*, vol. 1. San Diego: Academic Press.

Overbeek, H. W. (ed.) (1993) *Restructuring Hegemony in the Global Political Economy: The Rise of Transnational Neo-Liberalism in the 1980s*. London: Routledge.

Oye, K. A. (ed.) (1986) *Cooperation Under Anarchy*. Princeton: Princeton University Press.

Packenham, R. (1992) *The Dependency Movement: Scholarship and Politics in Development Studies*. Cambridge: Harvard University Press.

Palan, R. P. (ed.) (2000a) *Global Political Economy: Contemporary Theories*. London: Routledge.

—— (2000b) "A World of Their Making: An Evaluation of the Constructivist Critique in International Relations." *Review of International Studies* 26: 575–598.

Palan, R. P., and B. Gills (eds.) (1994) *Transcending the State-Global Divide: A Neostructuralist Agenda in International Relations*. Boulder: Lynne Rienner.

Parmentier, G. (2000) "Redressing NATO's Imbalances." *Survival* 42(2): 96–112.

Pashko, G. (1998) "Kosovo: Facing Dramatic Economic Decline." In T. Vermemies and E. Kofos (eds.), *Kosovo: Avoiding Another Balkan War*. Athens: ELIAMEP (Helenic Foundation for European and Foreign Policy), University of Athens.

Pasqua, C. (2001) "Which France for Which Europe?" In R. Tiersky (ed.), *Euroskepticism*. Lanham: Rowman and Littlefield.

Pateman, C. (1970) *Participation and Democratic Theory*. Cambridge: Cambridge University Press.

———— (1988) *The Sexual Contract.* Stanford: Stanford University Press.

Patten, C. (2000) "Speech to the Parliament of the Former Yugoslav Republic of Macedonia." March 7. Available online at http://europa.eu.int/comm/external_relations/news/patten/speech_00_73.htm.

Pavkovic, A. (1997) *The Fragmentation of Yugoslavia: Nationalism in a Multinational State.* London: Macmillan.

———— (2000) *The Fragmentation of Yugoslavia: Nationalism and War in the Balkans.* 2nd ed. New York: St. Martin's.

———— (2001) "Kosovo/Kosova: A Land of Conflicting Myths." In M. Waller, K. Drezov, and B. Gökay (eds.), *Kosovo: The Politics of Delusion.* London: Frank Cass.

Pavlowitch, S. K. (2002) *Serbia: The History of an Idea.* New York: New York University Press.

Payne, R. A. (2001) "Persuasion, Frames, and Norm Construction." *European Journal of International Relations* 7 (March): 37–61.

Payne, R. A., and N. H. Samhat (2004) *Democratizing Global Politics: Discourse Norms, International Regimes, and Political Community.* Albany: State University of New York Press.

PBS (2000) *Frontline: War in Europe.* February 2. Available online at http://www.pbs.org/wgbh/pages/frontline/shows/kosovo/interviews.

"Peace Agreement" (1999) Available online at http://jurist.law.pitt.edu/peace.htm#plan.

Peet, R. (ed.) (2003) *Unholy Trinity: The IMF, World Bank, and the World Trade Organization.* London: Zed Books.

Perlez, J. (1998a) "Defying Warnings, Serbs Press Attacks on Kosovo Albanians." *New York Times,* September 24.

———— (1998b) "Holbrooke Meets Milosevic on Pullback." *New York Times,* October 6.

———— (1998c) "Milosevic Accepts Kosovo Monitors, Averting Attack." *New York Times,* October 14.

———— (1998d) "NATO Stance Is Said to Hurt Both Alliance and Kosovo." *New York Times,* September 21.

———— (1998e) "New Massacres by Serb Forces in Kosovo Villages." *New York Times,* September 30.

Pesakovic, G. (2001) "Pauperization of a Nation: Effects of Economic Sanctions upon Health, Education, Social Welfare, and Income Distribution in Yugoslavia." Paper presented at the annual meeting of the International Studies Association, Chicago, February 24.

———— (2002) "Promoting or Hampering Transition Processes in Yugoslavia: The Role of International Institutions." Paper presented at the annual meeting of the International Studies Association, New Orleans, March 24–27.

———— (2003) "International Financial Institutions and Economic Revival of Yugoslavia." Paper presented at the annual meeting of the International Studies Association, Portland, February 25–March 1.

Peters, J. E., et al. (2001) *European Contributions to Operation Allied Force: Implications for Transatlantic Cooperation.* MR-1391-AF. Santa Monica: Rand.

Petersen, R. D. (2002) *Understanding Ethnic Violence: Fear, Hatred, and Resentment in Twentieth-Century Eastern Europe.* Cambridge: Cambridge University Press.

Peterson, V. S. (ed.) (1992a) *Gendered States: Feminist (Re)Visions of International Relations Theory.* Boulder: Lynne Rienner.

—— (1992b) "Transgressing Boundaries: Theories of Knowledge, Gender, and International Relations." *Millennium* 21 (Summer): 183–206.

—— (2000) "Rereading Public and Private: The Dichotomy Is Not One." *SAIS Review* 20(2) (Summer–Fall): 11–28.

Peterson, V. S., and A. S. Runyan (1999) *Global Gender Issues*. 2nd ed. Boulder: Westview.

Pettman, J. J. (1996) *Worlding Women: A Feminist International Relations*. London: Routledge.

—— (2001) "Transcending National Identity: The Global Political Economy of Gender and Class." In R. M. A. Crawford and D. S. L. Jarvis (eds.), *International Relations: Still an American Social Science? Toward Diversity in International Thought*. Albany: State University of New York Press.

"Philosophical Traditions in International Relations" (1988) *Millennium* 17(2). Special issue.

Pinker, S. (2002) *The Blank Slate: The Modern Denial of Human Nature*. New York: Viking.

Pipa, A. (1989) "The Political Situation of the Albanians in Yugoslavia, with Particular Attention to the Kosovo Problem: A Critical Approach." *East European Quarterly* 23(2): 159–181.

Pitt, R. (1978) "Warfare and Hominid Brain Evolution." *Journal of Theoretical Biology* 72: 551–575.

Pollack, M. A. (1997) "Delegation, Agency, and Agenda Setting in the European Community." *International Organization* 51(1) (Winter): 99–134.

Posen, B. R. (1993) "The Security Dilemma and Ethnic Conflict." *Survival* 35(1): 27–57.

—— (1984). *The Sources of Military Doctrine: France, Britain, and Germany Between the World Wars*. Ithaca: Cornell University Press.

—— (2000) "The War for Kosovo: Serbia's Political-Military Strategy." *International Security* 24(4) (Spring): 39–84.

Poulantzas, N. (1975) *Classes in Contemporary Capitalism*. London: New Left Books.

Poundstone, W. (1992) *Prisoner's Dilemma*. New York: Doubleday.

Powell, R. (1990) *Nuclear Deterrence Theory: The Search for Credibility*. New York: Cambridge University Press.

—— (1991) "Absolute and Relative Gains in International Relations Theory." *American Political Science Review* 85(4) (December): 1303–1320.

—— (1994) "Anarchy in International Relations Theory: The Neorealist-Neoliberal Debate." *International Organization* 48: 313–344.

Prebisch, R. (1963) *Toward a Dynamic Development Policy for Latin America*. New York: United Nations.

Price, R., and C. Reus-Smit (1998) "Dangerous Liaisons? Critical International Theory and Constructivism." *European Journal of International Relations* 4: 259–294.

Price, R. M., and N. Tannenwald (1996) "Norms and Deterrence: The Nuclear and Chemical Weapons Taboos." In P. J. Katzenstein (ed.), *The Culture of National Security: Norms and Identity in World Politics*. New York: Columbia University Press.

Priest, D. (1999) "A Decisive Battle That Never Was." *Washington Post,* September 19. Available online at http://www.lexisnexis.com.

Prifti, P. (1984) "Kosovo's Economy: Problems and Prospects." In A. Pipa and S. Repishti (eds.), *Studies on Kosova*. New York: Columbia University Press.

Qirezi, A. (2002) "Kosovo: UN Facing Backlash." Balkan Crisis Report no. 361. Institute for War and Peace Reporting, August 23. Available online at http://www.iwpr.net/index.pl?archive/bcr2/bcr2_20020823_1_eng.txt.

Quackenbush, S. L. (2003) "General Deterrence and International Conflict: Bridging the Formal/Quantitative Divide." Ph.D. diss., State University of New York–Buffalo.

———— (2004) "The Rationality of Rational Choice Theory." *International Interactions* 30: 87–107.

Raffer, K. (1993) "International Financial Institutions and Accountability: The Need for Drastic Change." Available online at http://www-personal.umich.edu/~russoj/debt/raffer93.html. [Reproduced from S. Mansoob Murshed and K. Raffer (eds.) (1993), *Trade Transfers and Development: Problems and Prospects for the Twenty-First Century.* Cheltenham, England: Edward Elgar.]

"Rambouillet Agreement" (1999) *Interim Agreement for Peace and Self-Government in Kosovo.* Available online at http://jurist.law.pitt.edu/ramb.htm.

Ramet, S. P. (1996) *Balkan Babel: The Disintegration of Yugoslavia from the Death of Tito to Ethnic War.* 2nd ed. Boulder: Westview.

———— (2002) *Balkan Babel: The Disintegration of Yugoslavia from the Death of Tito to the Fall of Milosevic.* Boulder: Westview.

Ramet, S. P., and L. S. Adamovich (eds.) (1995) *Beyond Yugoslavia: Politics, Economics, and Culture in a Shattered Community.* Boulder: Westview.

Randall, V. (1987) *Women and Politics: An International Perspective.* 2nd ed. Chicago: University of Chicago Press.

Rapoport, A. (1960) *Rights, Games, Debates.* Ann Arbor: University of Michigan Press.

Rapoport, A., and A. Chammah (1965) *Prisoner's Dilemma: A Study in Conflict and Cooperation.* Ann Arbor: University of Michigan Press.

Rasler, K. A. (1989) *War and State Making: The Shaping of the Global Powers.* Boston: Unwin Hyman.

Rasler, K. A., and W. R. Thompson (1994) *The Great Powers and Global Struggle: 1490–1990.* Lexington: University of Kentucky Press.

Rasmusen, E. (1994) *Games and Information: An Introduction to Game Theory.* 2nd ed. New York: Basil Blackwell.

Raven, C. (1999) "Why It's OK to Be a War Wussy: The Heavy Heart of the Matter." *The Guardian* (Manchester), April 27.

Ray, J. L. (1989) "The Abolition of Slavery and the End of International War." *International Organization* 43 (Summer): 406–439.

———— (1995) *Democracy and International Conflict: An Evaluation of the Democratic Peace Proposition.* Columbia: University of South Carolina Press.

"Realist Constructivism" (2004) *International Studies Review* 6(3) (September). Symposium.

"Rebuilding Kosovo and Stabilizing Southeast Europe: EU Plays Major Role" (1999) EU press release, November 19. Available online at http://www.eurunion.org/news/press/1999/1999074.htm.

Reinicke, W. (1996) "Can International Financial Institutions Prevent Internal Violence? The Sources of Ethno-National Conflict in Transitional Societies." In A. Chayes and A. H. Chayes (eds.), *Preventing Conflict in the Post-Communist World: Mobilizing International and Regional Organizations.* Washington, D.C.: Brookings Institution.

Rengger, N. (1999) *Beyond International Relations Theory? International Relations, Political Theory, and the Problem of Order.* London: Routledge.

Report to the President on Foreign Economic Policies (1950) Washington, D.C.: US Government Printing Office.

Reus-Smit, C. (1999) *The Moral Purpose of the State: Culture, Social Identity, and Institutional Rationality in International Relations.* Princeton: Princeton University Press.

Reynolds, V., V. S. E. Falger, and I. Vine (eds.) (1987) *The Sociobiology of Ethnocentrism: Evolutionary Dimensions of Xenophobia, Discrimination, Racism, and Nationalism.* London: Croom Helm.

Rhodes, E. (1989) *Power and Madness: The Logic of Nuclear Coercion.* New York: Columbia University Press.

Richardson, J. L. (2001a) *Contending Liberalisms in World Politics: Ideology and Power.* Boulder: Lynne Rienner.

——— (2001b) "International Relations and Cognate Disciplines: From Economics to Historical Sociology." In. R. M. A. Crawford and D. S. L. Jarvis (eds.), *International Relations: Still an American Social Science? Toward Diversity in International Thought.* Albany: State University of New York Press.

Rieff, D. (1995) *Slaughterhouse: Bosnia and the Failure of the West.* New York: Simon and Schuster.

——— (1999) "A New Age of Liberal Imperialism?" *World Policy Journal* 16(2): 1–10.

Riker, W. H. (1962) *The Theory of Political Coalitions.* New Haven: Yale University Press.

Ringmar, E. (1996) *Identity, Interest, and Action.* Cambridge: Cambridge University Press.

Risse, T. (2000) "Let's Argue! Communicative Action in World Politics." *International Organization* 54 (Winter): 1–39.

Risse, T., S. C. Ropp, and K. Sikkink (eds.) (1999) *The Power of Human Rights: International Norms and Domestic Change.* New York: Cambridge University Press.

Risse-Kappen, T. (1995a) *Bringing Transnational Relations Back In: Non-State Actors, Domestic Structures, and International Institutions.* New York: Cambridge University Press.

——— (1995b) *Cooperation Among Democracies: The European Influence on U.S. Foreign Policy.* Princeton: Princeton University Press.

Rittberger, V. (ed.) (1993) *Regime Theory and International Relations.* Oxford: Oxford University Press.

Roberson, B. A. (ed.) (2002) *International Society and the Development of International Relations.* London: Continuum.

Roberts, A. (1999) "NATO's 'Humanitarian War' over Kosovo." *Survival* 41(3): 102–123.

Robinson, W. (2002) "Capitalist Globalization and the Transnationalization of the State." In M. Rupert and H. Smith (eds.), *Historical Materialism and Globalization.* London: Routledge.

Rogel, C. (1998) *The Breakup of Yugoslavia and the War in Bosnia.* Westport: Greenwood Press.

Rohde, D. (1997) *Endgame: The Betrayal and Fall of Srebrenica—Europe's Worst Massacre Since World War II.* New York: Farrar, Strauss, and Giroux.

Romany, R. (1994) "State Responsibility Goes Private: A Feminist Critique of the Public/Private Distinction in International Human Rights Law." In R. J. Cook (ed.), *Human Rights of Women: National and International Perspectives.* Philadelphia: University of Pennsylvania Press.

Ron, J. (2001) "Kosovo in Retrospect." *International Studies Review* 3(3) (Fall): 103–115.

Rose, G. (1998) "Neoclassical Realism and Theories of Foreign Policy." *World Politics* 51 (October): 144–172.

Rose, W. (2000) "The Security Dilemma and Ethnic Conflict: Some New Hypotheses." *Security Studies* 9(4): 1–54.

Rosecrance, R. (1986) *The Rise of the Trading State: Commerce and Conquest in the Modern World.* New York: Basic Books.

Rosenau, J. N. (1976) "Capabilities and Control in an Interdependent World." *International Security* (Fall): 32–49.

——— (1980) *The Study of Global Interdependence: Essays on the Transnationalization of World Affairs.* London: Frances Pinter.

——— (1990) *Turbulence in World Politics: A Theory of Change and Continuity.* Princeton: Princeton University Press.

——— (1999) "Thinking Theory Thoroughly." In P. R. Viotti and M. V. Kauppi (eds.), *International Relations Theory: Realism, Pluralism, Globalism, and Beyond.* 3rd ed. Boston: Allyn and Bacon.

Rosenau, J. N., and M. Durfee (2000) *Thinking Theory Thoroughly: Coherent Approaches to an Incoherent World.* Boulder: Westview.

Rosenau, P. (1990) "Once Again into the Fray: International Relations Confronts the Humanities." *Millennium: Journal of International Studies* 19: 83–110.

——— (1992) *Post-modernism and the Social Sciences: Insights, Inroads, and Intrusions.* Princeton: Princeton University Press.

Rosenberg, J. (1994) *The Empire of Civil Society: A Critique of the Realist Theory of International Relations.* London: Verso.

Rostow, W. W. (1962) *The Process of Economic Growth.* 2nd ed. New York: W. W. Norton.

Rothstein, R. L. (1991) *The Evolution of Theory in International Relations.* Columbia: University of South Carolina Press.

Rousseau, J. J. (1968) *The Social Contract.* New York: Penguin Books.

Rubin, J. (2000) "A Very Personal War, Part II." *Financial Times,* October 6.

Rubin, P. (2002) *Darwinian Politics: The Evolutionary Origin of Freedom.* New Brunswick, N.J.: Rutgers University Press.

Ruddick, S. (1989) *Maternal Thinking: Towards a Politics of Peace.* London: Women's Press.

Rudolph, Christopher (2003) "Security and the Political Economy of International Migration." *American Political Science Review* 97(4): 603–620.

Ruggie, J. G. (1983) "International Regimes, Transactions, and Change: Embedded Liberalism in the Postwar Economic Order." In S. Krasner (ed.), *International Regimes.* Ithaca: Cornell University Press.

——— (1998) *Constructing the World Polity: Essays on International Institutionalization.* New York: Routledge.

Rummel, R. J. (1979) *Understanding Conflict and War.* 5 vols. Beverly Hills: Sage.

Rupert, M. (1995) *Producing Hegemony: The Politics of Mass Production and American Global Power.* Cambridge: Cambridge University Press.

——— (1998) "Re-engaging Gramsci: A Response to Germain and Kenny." *Review of International Studies* 24: 427–434.

Rupert, M., and H. Smith (2002) *Historical Materialism and Globalization: Essays on Continuity and Change.* London: Routledge.

Rusinow, D. (1977) *The Yugoslav Experiment, 1948–1974.* London: Hurst.

Russett, B. M. (1993) *Grasping the Democratic Peace: Principles for a Post–Cold War World.* Princeton: Princeton University Press.

Ryner, M. (2003) "Disciplinary Neoliberalism and the Social Market in German Restructuring: Implications for the EU." In A. Cafruny and M. Ryner (eds.), *A Ruined Fortress? Neoliberal Hegemony and Transformation in Europe.* Lanham: Rowman and Littlefield.

Rynning, S., and P. M. Gallois (2001) *Changing Military Doctrine: Presidents and Military Power in Fifth Republic France.* New York: Praeger.

Sahlins, M. D., and E. R. Service (eds.) (1960) *Evolution and Culture.* Ann Arbor: University of Michigan Press.

Said, E. (1999) "Treason of the Intellectuals." *Al-Ahram Weekly,* June 24. Available online at http://www.ahram.org.eg/weekly/1999/435/op1.htm.

Sanderson, S. K. (2001) *The Evolution of Human Sociality: A Darwinian Conflict Perspective.* Lanham: Rowman and Littlefield.

Sandler, T. (1977) "The Impurity of Defense: An Application to the Economics of Alliances." *Kyklos* 30: 443–460.

—— (1992) *Collective Action: Theory and Applications.* Ann Arbor: University of Michigan Press.

—— (1997) *Global Challenges: An Approach to Environmental, Political, and Economic Problems.* Cambridge: Cambridge University Press.

Sandler, T., and J. F. Forbes (1980) "Burden-Sharing, Strategy and Design of NATO." *Economic Inquiry* 18: 425–444.

Schaeffer, R. K., and I. Wallerstein (eds.) (1989) *War in the World System.* Westport: Greenwood.

Schelling, T. C. (1960) *The Strategy of Conflict.* Cambridge: Harvard University Press.

—— (1966) *Arms and Influence.* New Haven: Yale University Press.

Schimmelfennig, F. (1998–1999) "NATO Enlargement: A Constructivist Explanation." *Security Studies* 8(2–3): 198–234.

Schmemann, S. (2002a) "U.S. Peacekeepers Given Year's Immunity from New Court." *New York Times,* July 13.

—— (2002b) "US Vetoes Bosnia Mission, Then Allows 3-Day Reprieve." *New York Times,* July 1.

Schmidt, B. C. (1998) *The Political Discourse of Anarchy: A Disciplinary History of International Relations.* Albany: State University of New York Press.

Schneider, E. (1986) "The Dialectics of Rights and Politics: Perspectives from the Women's Movement." *New York University Law Review* 61: 589–652.

Schroeder, G. (1999) "Regierungserklärung zur Aktuellen Lage im Kosovo." Available online at http://www.bundesregierung.de/nachrichten.

Schwartz-Shea, P., and D. Burrington (1990) "Free Riding, Alternative Organization and Cultural Feminism: The Case of Seneca Women's Peace Camp." *Women and Politics* 10(3): 1–37.

Schwarz, H.-P. (1966) *Vom Reich zur Bundesrepublik: Deutschland im Widerstreit der außenpolitischen Konzeptionen in der Jahren der Besatzungsherrschaft, 1945 bis 1949.* Berlin: Hermann Luchterhand Verlag.

Schweller, R. L. (1998) *Deadly Imbalances: Tripolarity and Hitler's Strategy of World Conquest.* New York: Columbia University Press.

—— (1999) "Realism and the Present Great Power System: Growth and Positional Conflict over Scarce Resources." In E. B. Kapstein and M. Mastanduno (eds.), *Unipolar Politics: Realism and State Strategies After the Cold War.* New York: Columbia University Press.

Schweller, R. L., and D. Priess (1997) "A Tale of Two Realisms: Expanding the Institutions Debate." *Mershon International Studies Review* 41(1): 1–32.

Sciolino, E., and E. Bronner (1999) "How a President Distracted by Scandal, Entered the Balkan War." *New York Times,* April 18.

Scott, J. (1991) "Gender: A Useful Category of Historical Analysis." In A. Rao (ed.), *Women's Studies International: Nairobi and Beyond.* New York: Feminist Press.

Searl, J. R. (1995) *The Construction of Social Reality.* New York: Free Press.

Seifert, R. (1994) "War and Rape: A Preliminary Analysis." In A. Stiglmayer (ed.), *Mass Rape. The War Against Women in Bosnia-Herzegovina.* Lincoln: University of Nebraska Press.

Sekelj, L. (1992). *Yugoslavia: The Process of Disintegration.* Boulder: Atlantic.

Sekulic, D., G. Massey, and R. Hodson (1994) "Who Were the Yugoslavs? Failed Sources of a Common Identity in the Former Yugoslavia." *American Sociological Review* 59(1): 83–97.

Sell, L. (2002) *Slobodan Milosevic and the Destruction of Yugoslavia.* Durham, N.C.: Duke University Press.

Selten, R. (1975) "A Re-examination of the Perfectness Concept for Equilibrium Points in Extensive Games." *International Journal of Game Theory* 4: 25–55.

Senese, P. D., and S. L. Quackenbush (2003) "Sowing the Seeds of Conflict: The Effect of Dispute Settlements on Durations of Peace." *Journal of Politics* 65: 696–717.

Seton-Watson, H. (1967) *Eastern Europe Between the Wars, 1918–1941.* New York: Harper Torchbooks.

Shalom, S. (1999) "Reflections on NATO and Kosovo." *New Politics* 7(2). Available online at http://www.zmag.org/crisescurevts/shalomnp.htm.

Shannon, T. R. (1989) *An Introduction to the World-System Perspective.* Boulder: Westview.

Shapiro, M. J. (1987) *The Politics of Representation: Writing Practices in Biography, Photography, and Policy Analysis.* Madison: University of Wisconsin Press.

——— (1989) "Textualizing Global Politics." In J. Der Derian and M. J. Shapiro (eds.), *International/Intertextual Relations: Postmodern Readings of World Politics.* New York: Lexington Books.

Shapiro, M. J., and H. R. Alker (1996) *Challenging Boundaries: Global Flows, Territorial Identities.* Minneapolis: University of Minnesota Press.

Shattuck, John (2003) *Freedom on Fire: Human Rights Wars and America's Response.* Cambridge: Harvard University Press.

Shaw, R. P., and Y. Wong (1987) "Ethnic Mobilization and the Seeds of Warfare: An Evolutionary Perspective." *International Studies Quarterly* 31 (March): 5–32.

——— (1989) *Genetic Seeds of Warfare: Evolution, Nationalism, and Patriotism.* Boston: Unwin Hyman.

Shnabel, A., and R. Thakur (eds.) (2000) *Kosovo and the Challenge of International Intervention: Selective Indignation, Collective Action, and International Citizenship.* New York: United Nations University Press.

Shotter, J. (1993) *Cultural Politics of Everyday Life.* Toronto: University of Toronto Press.

Shoup, P. (1968) *Communism and the Yugoslav National Question.* New York: Columbia University Press.

Silber, L., and A. Little (1997) *Yugoslavia: Death of a Nation.* New York: Penguin Books.

Silverberg, J., and J. P. Gray (eds.) (1992) *Introduction to Aggression and Peacefulness in Humans and Other Primates.* New York: Oxford University Press.

Simons, J. (1995) *Foucault and the Political.* New York: Routledge.

Simpson, D. (2003a) "Nostalgia for Old Name Lingers in Uneasy Union." *New York Times,* March 9.

——— (2003b) "Yugoslavia Is Again Reinvented, in Name and Structure." *New York Times,* February 5.

Sinclair, T. J. (1994) "Passing Judgement: Credit Rating Processes as Regulatory Mechanisms of Governance in the Emerging World Order." *Review of International Political Economy* 1(1) (Spring): 133–159.

——— (1999) "Synchronic Global Governance and the International Political Economy of the Commonplace." In M. Hewson and T. J. Sinclair (eds.), *Approaches to Global Governance Theory.* Albany: State University of New York Press.

Singer, J. D. (1969) "The Level-of-Analysis Problem in International Relations." In J. N. Rosenau (ed.), *International Politics and Foreign Policy: A Reader in Research and Theory.* New York: Free Press.

Singer, J. D., and M. Small (1999) *Correlates of War National Material Capabilities Data, 1816–1993.* Available online at http://www.umich.edu/%7ecowproj/dataset.html#intrastatewar.

Sjolander, C. T., and W. S. Cox (eds.) (1994) *Beyond Positivism: Critical Reflections on International Relations.* Boulder: Lynne Rienner.

Slaughter, A.-M., and S. R. Ratner (1999) "The Method Is the Message." *American Journal of International Law* 93: 410–424.

Smith, A. (1995) "Alliance Formation and War." *International Studies Quarterly* 39(4) (December): 405–426.

——— (1998) "Deterring Enemies and Reassuring Friends: Extended Deterrence and Alliance Formation." *International Interaction* 24(4): 315–343.

——— (1999) "Testing Theories of Strategic Choice: The Example of Crisis Escalation." *American Journal of Political Science* 43(4): 1254–1283.

Smith, J. (1999) "This Time, Walker Wasn't Speechless: Memory of El Salvador Spurred Criticism of Serbs." *Washington Post,* January 23.

Smith, J., J. Collins, T. Hopkins, and H. Muhammad (eds.) (1988) *Racisim, Sexism, and the World-System.* New York: Greenwood Press.

Smith, J., and I. Wallerstein (1992) *Creating and Transforming Households.* Cambridge: Cambridge University Press.

Smith, P. (1993) "Feminist Jurisprudence and the Nature of Law." In P. Smith (ed.), *Feminist Jurisprudence.* New York: Oxford University Press.

Smith, S. (1996) "Positivism and Beyond." In S. Smith, K. Booth, M. Zalewski (eds.), *International Theory: Positivism and Beyond.* Cambridge: Cambridge University Press.

——— (2002) "The United States and the Discipline of International Relations: Hegemonic Country, Hegemonic Discipline." *International Studies Review* 4(2) (Summer): 67–85.

Smith, S., K. Booth, and M. Zalewski (1996) *International Theory: Positivism and Beyond.* Cambridge: Cambridge University Press.

Smoke, R. (1987) *National Security and the Nuclear Dilemma.* Reading, Mass.: Addison-Wesley.

Snidal, D. (1985) "Coordination Versus Prisoners' Dilemma: Implications for International Cooperation and Regimes." *American Political Science Review* 79 (December): 923–942.

—— (1986) "The Game Theory of International Politics." In K. A. Oye (ed.), *Cooperation Under Anarchy*. Princeton: Princeton University Press.

—— (1991) "Relative Gains and the Pattern of International Cooperation." *American Political Science Review* 85 (September): 701–726.

Snyder, G. H., and P. Diesing (1977) *Conflict Among Nations: Bargaining, Decision-Making, and System Structure in International Crises*. Princeton: Princeton University Press.

Snyder, J. (1991) *Myths of Empire: Domestic Politics and International Ambition*. Ithaca: Cornell University Press.

Snyder, J., and R. Jervis (1999) "Civil War and the Security Dilemma." In B. F. Walter and J. Snyder (eds.). *Civil Wars, Insecurity, and Intervention*. New York: Columbia University Press.

Solana, J. (1999) Press statement, March 23. Available online at http://www.lib.umich.edu/govdocs/text/nato323.txt.

Somit, A., and S. A. Peterson (1998) "Review Article: Biopolitics After Three Decades—A Balance Sheet." *British Journal of Political Science* 28: 559–571.

—— (1999) "Rational Choice and Biopolitics: A (Darwinian) Tale of Two Theories." *PS: Political Science and Politics* 32 (March): 39–44.

—— (eds.) (2001) *Neo-Darwinism and the Social and Behavioral Sciences*. Stamford: JAI Press.

Sørensen, G. (1999) "Sovereignty: Change and Continuity in a Fundamental Institution." *Political Studies* 47: 590–604.

Spirtas, M. (1996) "A House Divided: Tragedy and Evil in Realist Theory." In B. Frankel (ed.), *Realism: Restatements and Renewals*. London: Frank Cass.

Spruyt, H. (1994) *The Sovereign State and Its Competitors: An Analysis of Systems Change*. Princeton: Princeton University Press.

S/PV.3930 (1998) "UN Security Council Meeting, New York." UN Security Council, September 23.

Starr, H. (1995) "International Law and International Order." In C. W. Kegley Jr. (ed.), *Controversies in International Relations Theory: Realism and the Neoliberal Challenge*. New York: St. Martin's.

Stearns, J. (1998) *Gender and International Relations*. New Brunswick, N.J.: Rutgers University Press.

Sterling-Folker, J. (1997) "Realist Environment, Liberal Variables, and Domestic-Level Variables." *International Studies Quarterly* 41(1): 1–25.

—— (1998) "Between a Rock and a Hard Place: 'Assertive Multilateralism' in Post–Cold War US Foreign Policy-Making." In J. M. Scott (ed.), *After the End: Making U.S. Foreign Policy in the Post–Cold War World*. Durham, N.C.: Duke University Press.

—— (2000) "Competing Paradigms or Birds of a Feather? Constructivism and Neoliberal Institutionalism Compared." *International Studies Quarterly* 44 (March): 97–119.

—— (2001a) "Evolutionary Tendencies in Realist and Liberal IR Theory." In W. R. Thompson (ed.), *Evolutionary Interpretations of World Politics*. New York: Routledge.

—— (2001b) "Realism and the Constructivist Challenge: Rejecting, Reconstructing, or Rereading." *International Studies Review* 3 (Fall): 73–97.

—— (2002) *Theories of International Cooperation and the Primacy of Anarchy: Explaining U.S. International Monetary Policy-Making After Bretton Woods*. Albany: State University of New York Press.

Stern, E. (1991) "Evolution and the Lessons of Adjustment Lending." In V. Thomas, A. Chibber, M. Dailami, and J. De Melo (eds.), *Restructuring Economies in*

Distress: Policy Reform and the World Bank. New York: Oxford University Press.

Stiehm, Judith (1989) *Arms and the Enlisted Woman.* Philadelphia: Temple University Press.

Stienstra, D. (1994) *Women's Movements and International Organization.* New York: St. Martin's.

Stigler, A. L. (2002–2003) "A Clear Victory for Air Power: NATO's Empty Threat to Invade Kosovo." *International Security* 27(3): 124–157.

Stiglmayer, A. (1994) "The Rapes in Bosnia-Herzegovina." In A. Stiglmayer (ed.), *Mass Rape: The War Against Women in Bosnia-Herzegovina.* Lincoln: University of Nebraska Press.

Stojanovic, S. (1997) *The Fall of Yugoslavia: Why Communism Failed.* Amherst, N.Y.: Prometheus Books.

Stremlau, J., and F. R. Sagasti (1998) *Preventing Deadly Conflict: Does the World Bank Have a Role?* New York: Carnegie Commission on Preventing Deadly Conflict.

Suganami, H. (1989) *The Domestic Analogy and World Order Proposals.* Cambridge: Cambridge University Press.

Sugar, P. F., and I. J. Lederer (eds.) (1969) *Nationalism in Eastern Europe.* Seattle: University of Washington Press.

Sumner, W. G. (1906) *Folkways: A Study of the Sociological Importance of Usages, Manners, Customs, Mores, and Morals.* Boston: Ginn.

Sylvester, C. (1991–1992) "Feminist Theory and Gender Studies in International Relations." *International Studies Notes* 16–17(3/1) (Fall–Winter): 32–38.

—— (1994) *Feminist Theory and International Relations in a Postmodern Era.* Cambridge: Cambridge University Press.

—— (1996) "The Contributions of Feminist Theory to International Relations." In S. Smith, K. Booth, and M. Zalewski (eds.), *International Theory: Positivism and Beyond.* Cambridge: Cambridge University Press.

Symons, D. (1979) *The Evolution of Human Sexuality.* Oxford: Oxford University Press.

Taliaferro, J. W. (2000–2001) "Security-Seeking Under Anarchy: Defensive Realism Revisited." *International Security* 25(3) (Winter): 128–161.

—— (2001) "Realism, Power Shifts, and Major War." *Security Studies* 10(4): 145–178.

—— (2004) *Balancing Risks: Great Power Intervention in the Periphery.* Ithaca: Cornell University Press.

Taylor, M. (1987) *The Possibility of Cooperation: Studies in Rationality and Social Change.* Cambridge: Cambridge University Press.

Taylor, S. (2002) "The Most Dangerous Place on Earth." *Ottawa Citizen,* June 22.

Telhami, S. (2002) "Kenneth Waltz, Neorealism, and Foreign Policy." *Security Studies* 11(3): 158–170.

Tetreault, M. A. (ed.) (1994) *Women and Revolution in Africa, Asia, and the New World.* Columbia: University of South Carolina Press.

Thakur, R. C. (1982) "Tacit Deception Revisited: The Geneva Conference of 1954." *International Studies Quarterly* 26: 127–140.

Thatcher, M., and A. S. Sweet (2003) *The Politics of Delegation.* London: Frank Cass.

Thayer, B. (2000) "Bringing in Darwin: Evolutionary Theory, Realism, and International Politics." *International Security* 25 (Fall): 124–151.

Thienpont, K., and R. Cliquet (eds.) (1999) *In-Group/Out-Group Behaviour in Modern Societies: An Evolutionary Perspective.* Brussels: NIDI CBGS.

Thompson, K. W. (1996) *Schools of Thought in International Relations.* Baton Rouge: Louisiana State University Press.

Thompson, W. R. (ed.) (1983) *World System Analysis: Competing Perspectives.* Beverly Hills: Sage.

—— (1988) *On Global War: Historical-Structural Approaches to World Politics.* Columbia: University of South Carolina Press.

—— (ed.) (2001) *Evolutionary Interpretations of World Politics.* New York: Routledge.

Thompson, W. R., C. Chase-Dunn, and J. Sokolovsky (1983) "An Exchange on the Interstate System and the Capitalist World-Economy." *International Studies Quarterly* 27(3) (September): 341–374.

Thucydides (1954) *The Peloponnesian War.* London: Penguin Classics.

—— (1993) *History of the Peloponnesian War.* Trans. R. Crawley. Ed. W. R. Connor. London: Everyman.

Tickner, J. A. (1992) *Gender in International Relations: Feminist Perspectives on Achieving Global Security.* New York: Columbia University Press.

—— (1995) "Hans Morgenthau's Principles of Political Realism." In J. Der Derian (ed.), *International Theory: Critical Investigations.* New York: New York University Press.

—— (1996) "International Relations: Post-Positivisit and Feminist Perspectives." In R. E. Goodin and H.-D. Klingemann (eds.), *A New Handbook of Political Science.* Oxford: Oxford University Press.

—— (1997) "You Just Don't Understand: Troubled Engagements Between Feminists and IR Theorists." *International Studies Quarterly* 41(4) (December): 611–632.

—— (2001) *Gendering World Politics: Feminist Approaches in the Post–Cold War Era.* New York: Columbia University Press.

Tiger, L. (1972) *Men in Groups.* London: Panther.

Tilly, C. (1998) "International Communities, Secure or Otherwise." In E. Adler and M. Barnett (eds.), *Security Communities.* Cambridge: Cambridge University Press.

Toktas, S. (2002) "Nationalism, Militarism, and Gender Politics: Women in the Military." *Minerva: Quarterly Report on Women in the Military* 20(2) (Summer): 29–44.

Tonelson, A. (2000) "NATO Burden Sharing: Promises, Promises." *Journal of Strategic Studies* 23(3): 29–58.

Tong, R. P. (1998) *Feminist Thought: A More Comprehensive Introduction.* Boulder: Westview.

Tooby, J., and L. Cosmides (1988) "The Evolution of War and Its Cognitive Foundations." *Proceedings of the Institute for Evolutionary Studies* 88: 1–15.

Tooze, R. (1990) "Understanding the Global Political Economy: Applying Gramsci." *Millennium: Journal of International Studies* 19(2): 273–280.

Trivers, R. L. (1985) *Social Evolution.* Menlo Park, N.J.: Benjamin/Cummings.

Trofimov, Y. (2003) "US Army Camp in Kosovo Attracts Local Workers." *Wall Street Journal,* January 3.

Turney-High, H. H. (1949) *Primitive War: Its Practice and Concepts.* Columbia: University of South Carolina Press.

Turpin, J. (1999) "Women and War." In L. R. Kurtz (ed.), *Encyclopedia of Violence, Peace, and Conflict,* vol. 3. San Diego: Academic Press.

Turpin, J., and L. A. Lorentzen (eds.) (1996) *The Gendered World Order.* New York: Routledge.

Tversky, A., and D. Kahneman (eds.) (2000a) *Choices, Values, and Frames.* New York: Cambridge University Press.

—— (2000b) "Rational Choice and the Framing of Decisions." In A. Tversky and D. Kahneman (eds.), *Choices, Values, and Frames.* New York: Cambridge University Press.

Udovicki, J., and J. Ridgeway (eds.) (2000) *Burn This House: The Making and Unmaking of Yugoslavia.* Rev. ed. Durham, N.C.: Duke University Press.

United Nations (1998) *Srebrenica Report: Report of the Secretary-General Pursuant to the General Assembly Resolution 53/55.*

UNSC/6657 (1999) "NATO Action Against Serbian Military Targets Prompts Divergent Views as Security Council Holds Urgent Meeting on Situation in Kosovo." UN Security Council press release. New York: United Nations, March 24.

UNSC/6659 (1999) "Security Council Rejects Demand for Cessation of the Use of Force Against Federal Republic of Yugoslavia." UN Security Council press release. New York: United Nations, March 26.

US Department of State (1998) "Observer Mission Documents Mass Killings of Civilians; NATO Challenges Milosevic by Approving Airstrikes; Belgrade Averts Strikes by Removing 4000 Serbian Police" *Foreign Policy Bulletin* 6: 32.

—— (1999a) *KFOR Deployment.* Fact sheet. Washington, D.C.: Office of the Special Adviser to the President and the Secretary of State for Kosovo and Dayton Implementation, July 26. Available online at http://www.state.gov/www/regions/eur/kosovo/fs_990726_kfor_deploy.html.

—— (1999b) "Turkey Country Report on Human Rights Practices for 1998." Washington, D.C., February 26.

US Institute of Peace (2002) *Taking Stock and Looking Forward: Intervention in the Balkans and Beyond.* Washington, D.C.: Balkans Working Group.

van Apeldoorn, B. (2002) *Transnational Capitalism and the Struggle over European Integration.* London: Routledge.

van der Dennen, J. M. G. (1995) *The Origin of War: The Evolution of a Male-Coalitional Reproductive Strategy.* Groningen: Origin Press.

—— (2002) "(Evolutionary) Theories of Warfare in Preindustrial (Foraging) Societies." *Neuroendocrimological Letters* supp. 4(23): 55–65. Special issue.

van der Pijl, K. (1984) *The Making of an Atlantic Ruling Class.* London: Verso.

—— (1998) *Transnational Classes and International Relations.* London: Routledge.

—— (2001) "From Gorbachev to Kosovo: Atlantic Rivalries and the Re-incorporation of Eastern Europe." *Review of International Political Economy* 8(2): 275–310.

van Evera, S. (1999) *Causes of War: Power and the Roots of Conflict.* Ithaca: Cornell University Press.

van Ham, P. (2002) "Simulating European Security: Kosovo and the Balkanisation-Integration Nexus." In P. van Ham and S. Medvedev (eds.), *Mapping European Security After Kosovo.* Manchester: Manchester University Press.

Vandenberg, M. E. (2000) "Federal Republic of Yugoslavia. Kosovo: Rape as a Weapon of 'Ethnic Cleansing.'" *Human Rights Watch Report.* Available online at www.hrw.org/reports/2000/fry.

Vanhanen, T. (1999) *Ethnic Conflicts Explained by Ethnic Nepotism.* Stamford: JAI Press.

Vasquez, J. A. (2002) "The Kosovo War: Causes and Justification." *International History Review* 24: 103–112.

Vedrine, H. M. (1999) Interview, March 25. Available online at http://www. ambafrance-us.org/news/statmnts/1999/conflict1.asp.

Vertzberger, Y. (1990) *The World in Their Minds: Information Processing, Cognition, and Perception in Foreign Policy Decision Making.* Stanford: Stanford Univeristy Press.

Vickers, M. (1998) *Between Serb and Albanian: A History of Kosovo.* New York: Columbia University Press.

—————— (2001) "Revolution Deferred: Kosovo and the Transformation of War." In A. J. Bacevich and E. A. Cohen (eds.), *War over Kosovo: Politics and Strategy in a Global Age.* New York: Columbia University Press.

Vincent, R. J. (1974) *Nonintervention and International Order.* Princeton: Princeton University Press.

—————— (1986) *Human Rights and International Relations.* New York: Cambridge University Press.

—————— (1990) "Grotius, Human Rights, and Intervention." In H. Bull, B. Kingsbury, and A. Roberts (eds.), *Hugo Grotius and International Relations.* Oxford: Clarendon Press.

Viotti, P. R., and M. V. Kauppi (1999) *International Relations Theory: Realism, Pluralism, Globalism, and Beyond.* 3rd ed. Boston: Allyn and Bacon.

Vljevic, N. V. (2002) "Nationalism, Social Movement Theory, and the Grass Roots Movement of Kosovo Serbs, 1985–1988." *Europe-Asia Studies* 54(5): 771–790.

Vreeland, J. R. (2003) *The IMF and Economic Development.* Cambridge: Cambridge University Press.

Wachtel, A. (1997) "Postmodernism as Nightmare: Milorad Pavic's Literary Demolition of Yugoslavia." *Slavic and East European Journal* 41(4) (Winter): 627–644.

—————— (1998) *Making a Nation, Breaking a Nation: Literature and Cultural Politics in Yugoslavia.* Stanford: Stanford University Press.

Walker, R. B. J. (1987) "Realism, Change, and International Political Theory." *International Studies Quarterly* 31: 65–86.

—————— (1988a) "Genealogy, Geopolitics, and Political Community: R. K. Ashley and the Critical Social Theory of International Politics." *Alternatives* 13: 84–88.

—————— (1988b) *One World, Many Worlds: Struggles for a Just World Peace.* Boulder: Lynne Rienner.

—————— (1993) *Inside/Outside: International Relations as Political Theory.* Cambridge: Cambridge University Press.

Walker, R. B. J., and S. H. Mendlovitz (eds.) (1990) *Contending Sovereignties: Redefining Political Community.* Boulder: Lynne Rienner.

Wallander, C. (2000) "Institutional Assets and Adaptability: NATO After the Cold War." *International Organization* 54(4) (Autumn): 705–735.

Wallander, C., and R. O. Keohane (1999) "Risk, Threat, and Security Institutions." In H. Haftendorn, R. O. Keohane, and C. A. Wallander (eds.), *Imperfect Unions: Security Institutions over Time and Space.* Oxford: Oxford University Press.

Wallerstein, I. (1974) *The Modern World System.* Vol. 1, *Capitalist Agriculture and the Origins of the European World-Economy in the Sixteenth Century.* New York: Academic Press.

———— (1979) *The Capitalist World-Economy.* Cambridge: Cambridge University Press.

———— (1980) *The Modern World System.* Vol. 2, *Mercantilism and the Consolidation of the European World-Economy, 1600–1750.* New York: Academic Press.

———— (1991) *Geopolitics and Geoculture: Essays on the Changing World System.* Cambridge: Cambridge University Press.

———— (1999a) "Bombs Away!" Available online at http://www.ess.uwe.ac.uk/kosovo/kosovo-controversies13.html.

———— (1999b) "The Clinton-Milosevic Chess Match." Commentary no. 19. Fernand Braudel Center, Binghamton University, July 1. Available online at http://fbc.binghamton.edu/19en.htm.

———— (2004) *World-Systems Analysis: An Introduction.* Durham, N.C.: Duke University Press.

Walling, C. B. (2001) "The History and Politics of Ethnic Cleansing." In K. Booth (ed.), *The Kosovo Tragedy: The Human Rights Dimension.* London: Frank Cass.

Walt, S. M. (1987) *The Origins of Alliances.* Ithaca: Cornell University Press.

———— (2002) "The Enduring Relevance of the Realist Tradition." In I. Katznelson and H. V. Milner (eds.), *Political Science: The State of the Discipline.* New York: W. W. Norton.

Waltz, K. N. (1959) *Man, the State, and War: A Theoretical Analysis.* New York: Columbia University Press.

———— (1960) "International Conflict: Three Levels of Analysis." *World Politics* 12 (April): 453–461.

———— (1964) "The Stability of a Bipolar World." *Daedalus* 93 (Summer): 881–909.

———— (1979) *Theory of International Politics.* New York: McGraw-Hill.

———— (1986) "Reflections on *Theory of International Politics:* Response to My Critics." In R. O. Keohane (ed.), *Neorealism and Its Critics.* New York: Columbia University Press.

———— (1996) "International Politics Is Not Foreign Policy." *Security Studies* 6(1): 54–57.

———— (2000) "Structural Realism After the Cold War." *International Security* 25(1): 5–41.

———— (2002) "Structural Realism After the Cold War." In G. J. Ikenberry (ed.), *America Unrivaled: The Future of the Balance-of-Power.* Ithaca: Cornell University Press.

Wanniski, J. (1999) "Memo to A. M. (Abe) Rosenthal." *New York Times,* April 15. Available online at www.polyconomics.com/searchbase/04-15-99.html.

Wareham, R., and D. Quick (2001) "Problems or Partners? Working with Women to Rebuild the Balkans." *Forced Migration Review* 11 (October): 16–17. Oxford: Refugee Studies Centre. Available online at http://www.fmreview.org/fmr-pdfs/fmr11/fmr11full.pdf.

Watson, A. (1982) *Diplomacy: The Dialogue Between States.* London: Methuen.

———— (1992) *The Evolution of International Society: A Comparative Historical Analysis.* London: Routledge.

Wæver, O. (1996a) "Europe's Three Empires: A Watsonian Interpretation of Post-Wall European Security." In R. Fawn and J. Larkins (eds.), *International*

Society After the Cold War: Anarchy and Order Reconsidered. London: Macmillan.

—— (1996b) "The Rise and Fall of the Inter-Paradigm Debate." In S. Smith, K. Booth, and M. Zalewski (eds.), *International Theory: Positivism and Beyond*. Cambridge: Cambridge University Press.

—— (1997) "Figures of International Thought: Introducing Persons Instead of Paradigms." In I. B. Neumann and O. Wæver (eds.), *The Future of International Relations: Masters in the Making?* London: Routledge.

—— (1998a) "Four Meanings of International Society: A Trans-Atlantic Dialogue." In B. A. Roberson (ed.), *International Society and the Development of International Relations Theory*. London: Pinter.

—— (1998b) "The Sociology of a Not So International Discipline: American and European Developments in International Relations." *International Organization* 52: 687–728.

—— (2002) "Four Meanings of International Society: A Trans-Atlantic Dialogue." In B. A. Roberson (ed.), *International Society and the Development of International Relations*. London: Continuum.

Weber, C. (1994) "Good Girls, Little Girls, and Bad Girls: Male Paranoia in Robert Keohane's Critique of Feminist International Relations." *Millennium* 23(2) (Summer): 337–349.

—— (1995) *Simulating Sovereignty Intervention: The State and Symbolic Exchange*. Cambridge: Cambridge University Press.

—— (2001) *International Relations Theory: A Critical Introduction*. London: Routledge.

Weber, M. (1949) "'Objectivity' in Social Science and Social Policy." In E. A. Shils and H. A. Finch (eds.), *The Methodology of the Social Sciences*. New York: Free Press.

—— (1968) *Economy and Society: An Outline of Interpretive Sociology*. Vol. 1. New York: Bedminister Press.

—— (1949) *The Methodology of the Social Sciences*. Glencoe, Ill.: Free Press.

Weber, S. (1992) "Does NATO Have a Future?" In B. Crawford (ed.), *The Future of European Security*. Berkeley: Center for German and European Studies.

Weldes, J. (1999) *Constructing National Interests: The United States and the Cuban Missile Crisis*. Minneapolis: University of Minnesota Press.

—— (ed.) (2003) *To Seek Out New Worlds: Exploring Links Between Science Fiction and World Politics*. London: Palgrave Macmillan.

Weller, M. (1999a) *The Crisis in Kosovo, 1989–1999: From the Dissolution of Yugoslavia to Rambouillet and the Outbreak of Hostilities*. Vol. 1. Cambridge: Cambridge University Press.

—— (1999b) "The Rambouillet Conference on Kosovo." *International Affairs* 75(2): 211–251.

Wendt, A. (1987) "The Agent-Structure Problem in International Relations Theory." *International Organization* 41 (Summer): 335–370.

—— (1992) "Anarchy Is What States Make of It: The Social Construction of Power Politics." *International Organization* 46 (Spring): 391–425.

—— (1994) "Collective Identity Formation and the International State." *American Political Science Review* 88(20) (June): 384–396.

—— (1999) *Social Theory of International Politics*. Cambridge: Cambridge University Press.

West, L. (ed.) (1987) *Feminist Nationalism*. New York: Routledge.

Wheeler, N. J. (2000) *Saving Strangers: Humanitarian Intervention in International Society*. Oxford: Oxford University Press.

White, E., and J. Losco (eds.) (1986) *Biology and Bureaucracy: Public Administration and Public Policy from the Perspective of Genetic and Neurobiological Theory*. Lanham: University Press of America.

Whitman, J. (2001) "The Kosovo Refugee Crisis: NATO's Humanitarianism Versus Human Rights." In K. Booth (ed.), *The Kosovo Tragedy: The Human Rights Dimension*. London: Frank Cass.

Whitney, C. R. (1998) "Britain Joins France's Call for European Force." *New York Times*, December 5.

Whitney, C. R., and E. Schmidt (1999) "NATO Had Signs Its Strategy Would Fail in Kosovo." *New York Times*, April 1.

Whitworth, S. (1994) *Feminism and International Relations: Towards a Political Economy of Gender in Interstate and Non-Governmental Institutions*. New York: St. Martin's.

Wiegele, T. C. (1979) *Biopolitics: Search for a More Human Political Science*. Boulder: Westview.

——— (ed.) (1982) *Biology and the Social Sciences: An Emerging Revolution*. Boulder: Westview.

Wiegele, T. C., et al. (1985) *Leaders Under Stress: A Psychological Analysis of International Crisis*. Durham, N.C.: Duke University Press.

Wiggershaus, R. (1994) *The Frankfurt School*. Cambridge, England: Polity.

Wight, C. (1999) "They Shoot Dead Horses Don't They? Locating Agency in the Agent-Structure Problematique." *European Journal of International Relations* 3(3): 365–392.

Wight, M. (1966) "Western Values in International Relations." In H. Butterfield and M. Wight (eds.), *Diplomatic Investigations: Essays in the Theory of International Politics*. London: Allen and Unwin.

——— (1977) *Systems of States*. Ed. H. Bull. Leicester: Leicester University Press.

——— (1978) *Power Politics*. 2nd ed. Ed. H. Bull. London: Penguin.

——— (1991) *International Theory: The Three Traditions*. Eds. B. Porter and G. Wight. Leicester: Leicester University Press/Royal Institute of International Affairs.

Wilmer, F. (2002) *The Social Construction of Man, the State, and War: Identity, Conflict, and Violence in the Former Yugoslavia*. New York: Routledge.

Wilson, D. (1979) *Tito's Yugoslavia*. Cambridge: Cambridge University Press.

Wilson, E. O. (1975) *Sociobiology: The New Synthesis*. Cambridge: Harvard University Press.

——— (1978) *On Human Nature*. Cambridge: Harvard University Press.

Wohlforth, W. C. (1993) *The Elusive Balance: Power and Perceptions During the Cold War*. Ithaca: Cornell University Press.

——— (1999) "The Stability of a Unipolar World." *International Security* 21(1): 1–36.

——— (2002) "U.S. Strategies in a Unipolar World." In G. J. Ikenberry (ed.), *America Unrivaled: The Future of the Balance-of-Power*. Ithaca: Cornell University Press.

Wolfers, A. ([1952] 1962) "National Security as an Ambiguous Symbol." In A. Wolfers, *Discord and Collaboration*. Baltimore: Johns Hopkins University Press.

"Women in IR" (1988) *Millennium* 17(3) (Winter). Special issue.

Wood, E. (2002) "Global Capital, National States." In M. Rupert and H. Smith (eds.), *Historical Materialism and Globalization*. London: Routledge.

Woodward, S. L. (1995) *Balkan Tragedy: Chaos and Dissolution After the Cold War.* Washington, D.C.: Brookings Institution.

World Bank (1991) *Industrial Restructuring Study: Overview and Strategy of Reconstructing.* Washington, D.C.

────── (2001) *Global Development Finance: Building Coalitions for Effective Development Finance.* Washington, D.C.

────── (2002a) "Kosovo Brief." September 2002. Available online at http://lnweb18.worldbank.org/eca/eca.nsf/countries/yugoslavia/f86765438208 927185256c3000710ce9?opendocument.

────── (2002b) "Serbia and Montenegro Country Brief." September 1, 2002. Available online at http://lnweb18.worldbank.org/eca/eca.nsf/countries/ yugoslavia/a2aa7ce96ec98ff285256c24005408bd?opendocument.

────── (2002c) "Yugoslavia, Fed. Rep. at a Glance." September 23, 2002. Available online at http://www.worldbank.org/data/countrydata/aag/yug_aag.pdf.

Wrangham, R. W. (1999) "Evolution of Coalitionary Killing." *Yearbook of Physical Anthropology* 42: 1–30.

Wrangham, R. W., and D. Peterson (1996) *Demonic Males: Apes and the Origins of Human Violence.* Boston: Houghton Mifflin.

Wright, M. (ed.) (1996) *Morality and International Relations.* Aldershot: Avebury.

Wright, Q. (1942) *A Study of War.* Chicago: University of Chicago Press.

Wyn Jones, R. (1999) *Security, Strategy, and Critical Theory.* Boulder: Lynne Rienner.

────── (ed.) (2001) *Critical Theory and World Politics.* Boulder: Lynne Rienner.

Yee, A. (1996) "The Causal Effects of Ideas on Policies." *International Organization* 50(1): 69–108.

Yost, D. S. (2000) "The NATO Capabilities Gap and the European Union." *Survival* 42(4): 97–218.

Young, I. M. (1990) "Polity and Group Difference: A Critique of the Ideal of Universal Citizenship." In C. Sunstein (ed.), *Feminism and Political Theory.* Chicago: University of Chicago Press.

Young, O. (1989) *International Cooperation: Building Resources for Natural Resources and the Environment.* Ithaca: Cornell University Press.

Zacher, M. W. (1992) "The Decaying Pillars of the Westphalian Temple: Implications for International Order and Governance." In J. N. Rosenau and E. Czempiel (eds.), *Governance Without Government: Order and Change in World Politics.* Cambridge: Cambridge University Press.

────── (2001) "The Territorial Integrity Norm: International Boundaries and the Use of Force." *International Organization* 55(2): 215–250.

Zacher, M. W., and R. A. Matthews (1995) "Liberal International Theory: Common Threads, Divergent Strands." In C. W. Kegley Jr. (ed.), *Controversies in International Relations Theory: Realism and the Neoliberal Challenge.* New York: St. Martin's.

Zacher, M. W., with B. A. Sutton (1996) *Governing Global Networks: International Regimes for Transportation and Communication.* Cambridge: Cambridge University Press.

Zagare, F. C. (1979) "The Geneva Conference of 1954: A Case of Tacit Deception." *International Studies Quarterly* 23: 390–411.

────── (1982) "Competing Game-Theoretic Explanations: The Geneva Conference of 1954." *International Studies Quarterly* 26: 141–147.

────── (1984) *Game Theory: Concepts and Applications.* Beverly Hills: Sage.

————— (1990) "Rationality and Deterrence." *World Politics* 42(2) (January): 238–260.

————— (1996) "Classical Deterrence Theory: A Critical Assessment." *International Interactions* 21: 365–387.

Zagare, F. C., and D. M. Kilgour (2000) *Perfect Deterrence.* Cambridge: Cambridge University Press.

Zakaria, F. (1998) *From Wealth to Power: The Unusual Origins of America's World Role.* Princeton: Princeton University Press.

Zalewski, M. (1995) "Well, What Is the Feminist Perspective on Bosnia?" *International Affairs.* 71(2) (April): 339–356.

————— (1996) "'All These Theories Yet the Bodies Keep Piling Up': Theory, Theorists, Theorising." In S. Smith, K. Booth, and M. Zalewski (eds.), *International Theory: Positivism and Beyond.* Cambridge: Cambridge University Press.

————— (2003) "'Women's Troubles' Again in IR." *International Studies Review* 5(2) (June): 291–294.

Zalewski, M., and J. Parpart (eds.) (1998) *The "Man" Question in International Relations.* Boulder: Westview.

Zaninovich, M. G. (1968) *The Development of Socialist Yugoslavia.* Baltimore: Johns Hopkins University Press.

Zehfuss, M. (2002) "Kosovo and the Politics of Representation." In P. V. Ham and S. Medvedev (eds.), *Mapping European Security After Kosovo.* Manchester: Manchester University Press.

Zelikow, P., and C. Rice (1995) *Germany United and Europe Transformed: A Study in Statecraft.* Cambridge: Harvard University Press.

Zenko, M. (2001) *Coercive Diplomacy Before the War in Kosovo: America's Approach in 1998.* Pew Case Studies in International Affairs no. 252. Washington, D.C.: Institute for the Study of Diplomacy, School of Foreign Service, Georgetown University.

Zhang, Y. (1998) *China in International Society Since 1949.* Basingstoke: Macmillan.

Zimmerman, W. (1996) *Origins of a Catastrophe: Yugoslavia and Its Destroyers.* New York: Basic Books.

Zizek, S. (1999) "Against the Double Blackmail." Unpublished essay. Available online at http://www.soc.qc.edu/ssc/zizek.html.

Zolo, D. (2002) *Invoking Humanity: War, Law, and Global Order.* New York: Continuum.

The Contributors

Karen Ruth Adams is assistant professor of political science at the University of Montana. Her research focuses on the causes and conduct of international conflict and the domestic, international, and technological sources of national security and insecurity.

Mark A. Boyer is professor of political science at the University of Connecticut. His most recent book is *Defensive Internationalism* (coauthored with Davis B. Bobrow).

Michael J. Butler is assistant professor of political science and faculty member in the Security Studies Program at East Carolina University. His research focuses primarily on military intervention and international crisis.

Alan W. Cafruny is Henry Platt Bristol Professor of International Affairs at Hamilton College. His research focuses on international political economy and European politics. He is author of *A Ruined Fortress? Neoliberal Hegemony and Transformation in Europe* (with Magnus Ryner).

Francine D'Amico is assistant professor of political science in the Maxwell School of Citizenship and Public Affairs at Syracuse University. She is coeditor of *Gender Camouflage: Women and the US Military* and *Women, Gender, and World Politics: Perspectives, Policies, and Prospects*.

Vincent S. E. Falger is senior lecturer in the Department of International Relations, University of Utrecht, the Netherlands. His research interests include group formation (ingroup/outgroup, ethnocentrism, state formation), sex/gender differences in international politics, prehistory of international politics, and theory formation in IR.

Annette Freyberg-Inan is assistant professor for world and European politics at the University of Amsterdam. Her research interests include "first image" in IR theory, the evolution of the EU, and Romanian politics. She is author of *What Moves Man: The Realist Theory of International Relations and Its Judgment of Human Nature.*

Matthew J. Hoffmann is assistant professor in the Department of Political Science and International Relations at the University of Delaware. His research interests include IR theory, global governance, and complexity theory. He is author of *A Global Response.*

Patrick Thaddeus Jackson is assistant professor of international relations in the School of International Service at the American University in Washington, D.C. He is author of *Stopping Asia at the Elbe: Postwar German Reconstruction and the Invention of "Western Civilization."*

Sean Kay is associate professor of politics and government and chair of the International Studies Program at Ohio Wesleyan University. His books include *NATO and the Future of European Security* and the coedited volume *NATO After 50 Years.*

Tonny Brems Knudsen is associate professor of political science at the University of Aarhus, Denmark. He is author of *Humanitarian Intervention: Contemporary Manifestations of an Explosive Doctrine.*

Marc Lynch is associate professor of political science at Williams College. His research focuses on international public spheres and the potential for communicative action in world politics. He is author of *State Interests and Public Spheres* and *Iraq and the New Arab Public.*

Julie Mertus is associate professor and codirector of the master's program "Ethics, Peace, and Global Affairs" at American University. She is author of *Bait and Switch: Human Rights and American Foreign Policy* and *Kosovo: How Myths and Truths Started a War.*

Stephen L. Quackenbush is assistant professor of political science at the University of Missouri. His research focuses on formal and quantitative evaluations of international security and deterrence.

Rosemary E. Shinko is lecturer in political science at the University of Connecticut and coordinator of Source for Active Learning at the Stamford campus. Her research interests include political theory, international politics, and feminism.

Jennifer Sterling-Folker is associate professor of political science at the University of Connecticut. She is author of *Theories of International Cooperation and the Primacy of Anarchy.*

Jeffrey W. Taliaferro is associate professor of political science at Tufts University. He is author of *Balancing Risks: Great Power Intervention in the Periphery.*

Johan M. G. van der Dennen is senior researcher in political science in the Department of Legal Theory, University of Groningen. He is author of *The Origin of War: The Evolution of a Male-Coalitional Reproductive Strategy* and editor of *The Evolution of War* (with Peter Corning).

Frank C. Zagare is professor and chair in the Department of Political Science, University at Buffalo, SUNY. He is coauthor of *Perfect Deterrence,* author of *The Dynamics of Deterrence,* and editor of *Modeling International Conflict.*

Index

Achen, Christopher, 103
Adams, Karen, 16, 18–36
Adenauer, Konrad, 150
Adler, Emanuel, 116, 118, 122(n2)
Adorno, Theodor, 158
Afghanistan, 51
Africa, 277
After Hegemony (Keohane), 60
Agent-structure problem, 117, 140–144, 153(n5)
Agnostic politics, 169
Air war strategy: and acceleration of ethnic cleansing, 48, 68, 108–109, 193, 222, 296, 338; air war as "clean" war, 26, 29, 295–296; air war as credible but not capable threat, 108–109, 112; beliefs about effectiveness of air power, 67; Chinese embassy bombing, 68–69; ineffectiveness of, 47–48, 65, 71, 193–194, 222; and legitimacy of NATO actions, 319; statistics, 83, 338; warnings about ineffectiveness ignored, 48. *See also* Collateral damage
Albania: government collapse, 337; history of, 21; NATO air exercise in, 90(n5), 337; and refugees, 339; and rise of the KLA, 337
Albanians: and competing ideas of identity in Yugoslavia, 123–137; dissatisfaction with current conditions, 238; and history of Yugoslavia, 20–23, 129–130, 333–340; levels of ethnic and religious intolerance in Kosovo (1989), 233; as Muslims, 138(n7), 340(n1); secessionist movement, 23, 104, 174, 227, 233, 274, 334; Serb propaganda against Albanian

women, 298; and sovereignty, 174; war's failure to protect, 38, 48, 68, 108, 109, 193–194, 222, 296, 338. *See also* Ethnic cleansing; Ethnic tensions; Kosovo Liberation Army; Operation Horseshoe; Refugee crisis
Albright, Madeline: and Bosnia, 224(n4); escalating ultimatums to Milosevic, 45; expectation of a short war, 109; ground war advocacy, 49; and insufficiency of economic sanctions, 79; and nested community arguments, 148; rationale for conflict, 46; reaction to Milosevic's indictment, 152
Allison, Graham, 98
The Anarchical Society (Bull), 308
Anarchy: and constructivism, 116; and English School, 305; international anarchy as permissive cause of war, 18–19, 24; and lack of long-term solution to conflict, 32; and lack of Security Council authorization for war, 25, 35(n15); and neoliberalism, 63; and peacekeeping in Kosovo, 30–31; and postmodernism, 161; and realism, 14, 18–19, 24, 25, 27–32
Anderson, Benedict, 125
Annan, Kofi: on consensus, 185; and "humanity" vs. sovereignty, 152, 173; and Iraq war, 319; and legality/legitimacy of NATO intervention, 187, 315, 317; pressured on choice of peacekeeping administrators, 31
Apache helicopters, 27
Arkin, William, 26
Ashley, Richard, 165
Attributional error theory, 385

About the Book

What does it mean to adopt a realist, or a world system, or a feminist approach to international relations? Does the plethora of "isms"—liberalism and constructivism and postmodernism, to name just a few—have any relevance to the real world of global politics and policymaking? *Making Sense of International Relations Theory* addresses these questions by illustrating theories in action.

With the case of Kosovo as a common point of reference, each contributor presents a particular framework for interpreting world affairs. This structure offers students tangible examples of the use of varying theories, while illuminating the explanatory differences among them. Incorporating extensive introductory sections, the book is uniquely designed to explore alternative ways of understanding current events—to assist students in making sense of, as well as with, IR theory.

Jennifer Sterling-Folker is associate professor of political science at the University of Connecticut. She is author of *Theories of International Cooperation and the Primacy of Anarchy: Explaining U.S. International Monetary Policymaking After Bretton Woods.*